Black Action Films

Black Action Films

*Plots, Critiques, Casts and Credits
for 235 Theatrical and
Made-for-Television Releases*

James Robert Parish
George H. Hill

FOREWORD BY
RICHARD ROUNDTREE

McFarland & Company, Inc., Publishers
Jefferson, North Carolina, and London

British Library Cataloguing-in-Publication data available

Library of Congress Cataloguing-in-Publication Data

Parish, James Robert.
Black action films.

1. Afro-Americans in motion picutres — Handbooks, manuals, etc.
2. Adventure films — Handbooks, manuals, etc.
I. Hill, George A.
II. Title.
PN1995.9.N4P37   1989   791.43′6520396073   89-42871

ISBN 0-89950-456-6 (lib. bdg. : 50# alk. paper)

Printed in the United States of America

McFarland & Company, Inc., Publishers
Box 611, Jefferson, North Carolina 28640

Acknowledgments

Academy of Motion Picture Arts & Science Library
W. Frank Bell
Beverly Hills Public Library
Beverly Bare Buehrer
John Cocchi
Howard Davis
Jon Davison
George Dean
Sharon R. Fox
Alex Gildzen
Pierre Guinle
Georgette, Paulette, Marynda, George Michael Hill V
Kim Holston
Dr. Roland Jefferson
Steve and Jane Klain
Doug McClelland
Alvin H. Marill
Lee Mattson
Jim Meyer
Peter Miglierini
Eric Monte
Michael R. Pitts
Margie Schultz
Vincent Terrace
Kevin Thomas (*Los Angeles Times*)
UCLA Film Archives Study Center (Ed Carter)
UCLA Theater Arts Library
Unicorn Video
USC Cinema Library
Wayne Valero
Bret Wood

Editorial Consultant: T. Allan Taylor

Table of Contents

Foreword

A book on black action films is long overdue. Forty years of portrayals on the silver screen speaks for itself. When I was asked to write this foreword by co-author Dr. George Hill, my classmate at Southern Illinois University, I chose to do so because the world needs a book which chronicles black cinema history. Who were the stars? What were the films? Which of these had all black casts?

Why should these films be remembered? The answer is obvious. Blacks are and have always been a part of America, yet institutional racism has smothered many of our accomplishments, including our achievements in Hollywood. White authors have excluded us from most film history books. When we are included it is usually only a few paragraphs. Rare exceptions to this rule are Sidney Poitier, Richard Pryor, Eddie Murphy, and possibly Louis Gossett, Jr.

As a young man I saw film crews in New York shooting *Cotton Comes to Harlem,* which starred Godfrey Cambridge and Raymond St. Jacques. It was a magic time. It made me realize blacks could be in major motion pictures, and my desire to participate in the medium was enhanced. Part of my dream was fulfilled when I starred in the three *Shaft* films. *Shaft* is still the only black cast feature to have three installments and three soundtrack albums. The American public would appreciate and pay to see more dramas involving black life in America.

Those were my first three films. Since that time I have appeared in more than 30 films and have had my own television program, but the road has been a rocky one, as it is for most blacks in Hollywood. Yet we continue to persevere and hone our craft. We continue to seek excellence regardless of the barriers.

I commend the authors of this book for putting black film history in print. This book serves as a unique educational tool for researchers, scholars, students, and film buffs the world over who desire to explore the world of action films from an ebony perspective. For black Hollywood: it is a tribute to your magnificence; it is a statement of your succeeding against all odds, just as black Americans have done for 400 years. It can serve as the impetus and hope for another 40 years of black motion picture magic.

RICHARD ROUNDTREE

Preface

"You've been coffized, blacurized, superflied! You've been macked, hammered, slaughtered, and shafted!" So stated the advertisement for the satirical comedy film *Five on the Black Hand Side* (1973) directed by Oscar Williams who had himself contributed to several black action feature films. We met Cleopatra Jones, Mr. Mean, Claudine, Truck Turner, Tenafly, Sheba Baby, and Action Jackson. Remember? If not, this book contains a spectrum of information on the phenomenon known as black action pictures.

The long-puzzling question has been why this lucrative genre pretty much disappeared from the American marketplace. Four reasons are commonly stated in the press: 1) there were no *big* grosses; 2) TV did not buy such product for telecasting; 3) Europe was not interested in distributing such product; 4) the diminishing ghetto audience had become quickly sophisticated and now hungered for better product. Let us examine the reality of these "causes."

Several of these black action pictures—such as *Sweet Sweetback's Baadasssss Song* (1971), *Shaft* (1971) and *Super Fly* (1972)—were big moneymakers in their day, especially considering their low budgets. (Today Eddie Murphy's big-budget offshoot films are tremendous box-office bonanzas.) Frequently these features were produced for $150,000 or less and grossed in domestic film rentals ten to twenty times their negative cost. A great many of these pictures were just as profitable as the mainstream product being turned out at the time. So the low-box-office theory for the demise of the genre does not hold true.

Network television has always been slow at reflecting what is happening in the world, and in the 1970s it was not prepared (or willing) to expose the so-called typical white audience to the grim realities of ghetto life. It was considered too strong a subject. Even today, with the far more permissive moral code for programs telecast, very few of the vintage black action pictures discussed in this book are aired. Instead, when the black experience was eventually depicted on mainstream television, it would be in broad (and very successful) situation comedies such as "The Jeffersons," "Good Times," "Diff'rent Strokes," and "The Cosby Show." At the other end of the spectrum were the rare dramatic programs such as "Roots," "The Autobiography of Miss Jane Pittman," and "Sister, Sister," which ennobled the black individual. There seemed to be no midground for displaying the grimness of blacks coping in a white man's world, even when the presentation did not rely on gunplay and bloodshed but instead focused on dramatic and very human characterizations (e.g. *Brothers; Cornbread, Earl and Me; Together Brother; Trick Baby*). In short, it was a case of racism at work.

xi

European audiences have always embraced and befriended black artists such as Josephine Baker and Tina Turner. Michael Jackson's 1988 tour of the Continent was phenomenally successful. Additionally, Europe has traditionally taken in numerous black expatriates, including James Baldwin and Eldridge Cleaver, and it was in France that Melvin Van Peebles was able to make his *The Story of a Three Day Pass.*

It seems nothing more than an unsubstantiated myth that the black community per se rejected the black action films as being spurious, repetitive, and filled with anti-social behavior. At their most flagrant, these black action films, peopled with hoods, pimps, and easy-living folks, are no different from the formula Charles Bronson, Sylvester Stallone, and Chuck Norris action features which continually get made and remade today. Yes, there were *some* segments of the black intelligentsia who decried that black action films depicted only the amoral, fast-acting strata of the ghetto and gave too little or no heed to law-abiding, family-oriented, and humane values. But voices in the wind rarely prevent people—the filmgoing, videocassette-watching masses—from viewing what they really want to see, when it is made available to them.

Moreover, there was a great deal about these black action films that appealed to the black community at that time. For one thing there was the opportunity to finally see on the big screen black players in major film releases playing major roles in stories revolving around them, with the white person as the (subordinate) adversary. It was cathartic, not repulsive, even taking into account the cardboard heroes and heroines such as Foxy Brown, John Shaft, Friday Foster, the Mack, or the Candy Tangerine Man.

In addition, there was the terrific music so associated with the genre. Generally these motion pictures were rich in black musical talent, with the likes of J.J. Johnson, Solomon Burke, Barry White, Curtis Mayfield, and Isaac Hayes. Hayes created the lively and hugely popular score to *Shaft,* which won an Academy Award and a Grammy. A rash of great songs came from these black pictures, songs that were heartily endorsed by the black (and white) community. Remember Curtis Mayfield's "Fred Is Dead" and "Super Fly" from *Super Fly;* Bobby Womack and J.J. Johnson's title cut from *Across 110th Street;* James Brown's "Down and Out in New York City" from *Black Caesar;* Roy Ayers's "Coffy Is the Color" from *Coffy;* the Staples' title cut from *Let's Do It Again;* DeBarge's "Rhythm of the Night" from *The Last Dragon;* and Chaka Khan's "Krush Groove," "Shiela E," and "Holly Rock" from *Krush Groove.* Consequently the entire creative black community became involved in the making of films, not just the actors.

The black action film phenomenon faded, not because it had worn itself out and was no longer viable, but because it pushed too far against the boundaries of racial discrimination. If *Blacula, Cleopatra Jones, Nigger Charley, Melinda,* and *Shaft* had gone as far as they could go in one creative direction, they could have taken another and come up with new offshoots, just as the white cinema has done and redone for decades. Instead, the establishment film industry closed up ranks in the mid-1970s and the major studios, with rare exceptions, stopped producing the black film featuring black talent, in front of or behind the camera. Today it will produce the occasional *A Soldier's Story* or a vehicle built around a successful comedy star such as Eddie Murphy, Whoopi Goldberg, or Richard Pryor; or it will allow the black performer to have a constricted lead role in which his blackness is never made an issue, or indeed even mentioned (such as Billy Dee Williams in *Nighthawks* or Danny Glover in *Lethal Weapon*). But the rareness of a black filmmaker such as Jamaa Fanaka *(Penitentiary 1–3)* or Spike Lee *(She's Gotta Have It; School Daze)* succeeding is too clear.

The recent revolution in video technology has brought us the cinema of the seventies, sixties and before. For forty-nine cents to three dollars, I can sit in my living room and see those whom I have idealized since my youth. Those who are my contemporaries on the silver screen and the small screen. Scores of black films and TV programs are available at neighborhood video rental stores (although many suburban outlets remain racially discriminatory in what they showcase on their shelves for their non-black customers.) It was but a few years ago that I told my daughter about *Shaft* and *Super Fly*. At that time we examined photographs in books. Now she can see why *Shaft* was a "bad mother." How *Sheba, Baby* is as "cool" as *Cleopatra Jones*. More importantly, why the black community reveres Malcolm X, praises Adam Clayton Powell, laughs at Amos 'n' Andy, and loves Billie Holiday, Dizzie Gillespie and Martin Luther King. She can see and hear them with her own eyes and ears.

Today, with the release of so many more black action films, not only can my children view the cinema of my youth, but I can see the films of my parents' generation such as *Cabin in the Sky, Stormy Weather,* and *Bronze Buckaroo*. This new video accessibility makes black history, including the unique black action films, alive and able to be placed into proper perspective.

GEORGE A. HILL, PH.D., APR

Introduction

This is a comprehensive and detailed compilation of four decades of black action-adventure films. Although this genre phenomenon peaked in the marketplace in the early 1970s, it had its origins in 1950s and 1960s mainstream American-made feature films which dared to include black performers interacting with whites — especially Sidney Poitier in a succession of landmark screen roles. The genre transmuted in the 1980s into the action-comedies of Eddie Murphy, Whoopi Goldberg, and Richard Pryor, which still play to some degree on the fact that the star is black. Yet another new and overlapping trend in today's Hollywood permits such Oscar-winning stars as Louis Gossett, Jr., to base their box-office appeal on their talent, not their color.

Most reference books examining the history of the black film experience in the United States have shunted aside these zesty black action features (a.k.a. "blaxploitation" films). Yet over the decades these products have been extremely popular and profitable. They represent a contemporary mixture of insight, reflection, and reaction to the effects of the 1960s Civil Rights movement in the United States as focused on the crusading work of Dr. Martin Luther King, Jr. These motion pictures typically feature raw action, sex, and massive violence accomplished in flavorful style. They created a rash of vivid genre stars, including Pam Grier, Fred Williamson, Vonetta McGee, Jim Brown, Richard Roundtree, and Ron O'Neal and spawned an assortment of disturbing movie role models (Shaft, Cleopatra Jones, Super Fly, Hammer, Coffy, Willie Dynamite). These were dynamic screen characters who grabbed what they wanted *any* way they could and enjoyed material pleasures along the gory path to survival, and often to the top of the heap.

Many of the pioneering black action motion pictures of the late 1960s and very early 1970s were independent productions, crudely and rudely made to express harsh feelings on the subjects of integration and racism. Often they had low-keyed but lucrative release only in urban centers with heavy concentrations of likely filmgoers. Soon mainstream Hollywood realized how profitable this type of film could be — shot quickly, with a low budget (often on the streets of Watts) and little care for costly or time-consuming aesthetics. Once the major motion picture studios took an interest in this film category, America as a whole became very aware of the genre. These blood-and-guts pictures, tinged with social conscience, were given multi-media promotion to draw in all types of audiences. By 1971 or 1972, the craze had swept the nation. When filmmakers exhausted themselves and the public by rehashing the same storylines of life on the wild side in the ghetto, they expanded the genre by splicing it onto the western, the horror, the science fiction, and other established types of films.

1

Movies such as *The Asphalt Jungle* (1950) were remade (as *Cool Breeze,* 1972) with black casts and reflecting black sentiments and lifestyles.

Like most fads which oversaturated the marketplace, the black action film peaked from overexposure and by the mid-1970s was on a downswing. By the early 1980s it had become almost invisible, a result of a strange mixture of backlash and integration in the American social structure. (In late 1988 Keenen Ivory Wayans directed *I'm Gonna Git You Sucka,* a spoof of the blaxploitation film. Featured in the cast were such genre regulars as Jim Brown, Bernie Casey and Antonio Fargas. Composers Isaac Hayes — also cast in the film — and Curtis Mayfield each wrote themes to be played in the low-budget comedy.)

Due to their frequent R (and near X) ratings, many of these violent and sex-filled pictures were never shown on television, or if so, only in a severely edited form. However, the videocassette revolution has changed that, and each month sees more of these features — in their complete forms — being made available for home viewing.

It is through the emergence of such videocassettes, the kindness of archives (such as UCLA Film Archives Study Center), and the helpfulness of private collectors that researching this volume has been possible. Many of the motion pictures detailed herein were never documented in established sources, or if so, in only abbreviated format.

We have sought to present the full spectrum of features which fall within the range of black action films: from the pathfinding Sidney Poitier features of the 1950s and 1960s, to the low-budget independent social statement films of the 1960s, to the major studio releases of the 1970s and onward. The offshoot made-for-television feature films that reflect the genre have also been detailed. In our choice of photographs our aim has been to present a wide variety of the black players who populated this intriguing species of film.

The authors would be grateful for readers' comments; please write c/o the publishers.

JAMES ROBERT PARISH   GEORGE H. HILL

The Films

1. Aaron Loves Angela (Columbia, 1975). Color, 99 minutes.

Executive producer Morton J. Mitosky; *producer* Robert J. Anderson; *co-producer* Diana Young; *director* Gordon Parks, Jr.; *screenplay* Gerald Sanford; *music* Jose Feliciano; *songs* Jose Feliciano and Janna Merlyn Feliciano; *assistant director* Kurt Baker; *stunt co-ordinator* Alex Stevens; *sound* G. Lee Bost, Keith Stafford; *camera* Richard Kratina; *editor* William E. Anderson.

Cast: Kevin Hooks (Aaron James); Irene Cara (Angela); Moses Gunn (Ike James); Robert Hooks (Beau); Ernestine Jackson (Cleo); Leon Pinkney (Willie); Walt Frazier (Himself); *and:* Frank Aldrich, Norman Evans, Jose Feliciano, William Graeff, Jr., Charles McGregor, Louis Quinones, Alex Stevens, Wanda Velez.

There was certainly nothing original in the artistic concept of adapting Shakespeare's *Romeo and Juliet* into a modern idiom; *West Side Story,* both as a Broadway musical (1957) and an Oscar-winning motion picture (1961), had accomplished all that with its sensational mixture of poignant drama and rich music. But Gordon Parks, Jr., was a creative force with a bankable track record in the film industry. Parks, the son of noted black filmmaker-photographer Gordon Parks, Sr., had already directed the 1972 black action bonanza *Super Fly* (q.v.), which had grossed $18,900,000 for Warner Bros. in domestic film rentals on a production cost of $149,000. It was little wonder, then, that Columbia Pictures was eager to produce Parks's fourth motion picture, *Aaron Loves Angela.*

At its core, *Aaron Loves Angela* is a tender love story of sixteen-year-old black Aaron James (Kevin Hooks) and fourteen-year-old Puerto Rican Angela (Irene Cara), both living in the New York ghettos. Rising above their ethnic differences, they are drawn together by their common alienation from the adult world. Angela has spent too much of her life traipsing around the country with her restless mother, and she longs for her detached father, a trumpeter in Los Angeles. Aaron's disillusioned dad Ike (Moses Gunn) is an ex-professional football player who operates a modest neighborhood diner and devotes too much of his time getting drunk and being abusive in order to forget his dancer wife who ran off to Paris years ago.

(It is Ike who wants his innocent son to rise out of the ghetto through professional basketball, and he drives his boy to practice shots constantly on the playing court. His guiding motto for Aaron negotiating that big league contract one day is, "It's not whether you win or lose; it's how many points you score that counts." In one moment, Ike can be mean drunk and beat up his son; in the next he is pathetically contrite: "I didn't mean any of it boy. I just got

3

to have someone to hurt sometimes and you're all I got." There is a wonderful sequence where Ike, who brags about his celebrity contacts in the sports world, insists on taking Aaron to meet sports great Walt Frazier. The security guards will not let Ike and Aaron in to see Frazier, which makes Ike embarrassed and aggressive, while Aaron in a moment of great understanding insists it doesn't matter if they see Frazier. Later Frazier strolls out, and Ike initiates a conversation with the star.)

The film's main text is the growing bond between the two young people as they sneak off from their families and neighborhoods to spend time together, sharing their dreams, hurt, and budding love. Aaron gladly forsakes his basketball practice and willingly lies to his dad and pals about where he disappears to, intent on consummating his love for Angela. He is full of braggadocio, thinking he can talk his way out of any situation (yet he hardly ever does). He has all the prejudices of his black neighborhood, referring to Angela's fellow Puerto Ricans as "you people." She has her own set of stereotyped beliefs about blacks (she has a wonderful moment doing an impression of a religious elderly black woman). But their love rises above all this, as they rendezvous in abandoned tenement buildings, run along the beach, visit a deserted amusement park where they ride the merry-go-round, and Aaron chalks his affection for Angela in graffiti. Such is the courtship of these two sensitive youths who live in a hell of poverty and indifference.

A sub-theme of this film, and one which the studio doubtlessly wished had been emphasized more to please action filmgoers — even in the then-diminishing black exploitation marketplace — is the cruel world of pimps, drug pushers, and hoodlums. Downstairs from Aaron and Ike's tattered apartment is Cleo (Ernestine Jackson), a good-natured prostitute involved with hedonistic drug dealer Beau (Robert Hooks — the real-life father of Kevin). It is greedy Beau who attempts to hold out cash due to white mobsters (led by Charles McGregor), which leads to Cleo being beaten up, and the murder of another person. After Aaron finds Beau's suitcase full of syndicate money and the mob learns he has the loot, he and Angela are on the run. The chase ends at Grant's Tomb with Aaron throwing the money to the crowd, and the young lovers escaping the hoods.

Because *Aaron Loves Angela* is unsuccessful in its attempt to blend two genres together, it failed to find its commercial market. As Richard Eder *(New York Times)* assessed, "It comes to a lot of stickiness, a little violence and fun, lovely shots of young people running through the open rubble sites of upper Manhattan." *Variety* noted that ". . . he seems caught at cross-purposes, trying to make two films at once, a routine meller of street action, and a more human exploration of feelings."

This motion picture marked the screen debut of (off-) Broadway stage performer Irene Cara who would gain her greatest popularity to date for the film *Fame* (1980) and for co-composing and singing the Oscar-winning song "Flashdance — What a Feeling!" from *Flashdance* (1983). She would later appear in black actioners (e.g. *Certain Fury,* q.v.) and black musical/street films (e.g. *Busted Up,* q.v.). Kevin Hooks went on to co-star in the teleseries "The White Shadow" (1978–81) and "He's the Mayor" (1986), but motion picture success eluded him. For Gordon Parks, Jr., *Aaron Loves Angela* would be the final motion picture. He died in 1979 at age 44 in a plane crash in Nairobi, Kenya.

2. Abby (American International, 1974). Color, 89 minutes.

Presenter Samuel Z. Arkoff; *producers* William Girdler, Mike Henry, Gordon C. Layne; *director* Girdler; *story* Girdler, Layne; *screenplay* Layne; *production designer* J. Patrick Kelly III; *makeup* Joe Kenney; *music* Robert O. Ragland; *songs* Carol Speed; *assistant director* Hugh Smith; *technical adviser* Garry Cruise; *sound* John Asman, Chuck Haillau; *sound effects* Edit International; *special effects* Gene Griggs, Sam Price; *camera* William Asman; *editors* Corky Ehlers, Henry Asman.

Cast: William Marshall (Bishop Garnet Williams); Carol Speed (Abby Williams); Terry Carter (Reverend Emmett Williams); Austin Stoker (Cass Potter); Juanita Moore (Mama Potter); Charles Kissinger (Dr. Hennings); Elliott Moffitt (Russell); Nathan Cook (Taft Hassan); Bob Holt (Voice of the Demon); Nancy Lee Owens (Mrs. Wiggins); *and:* Billy Bradford, Casey Brown, Don Henderson, Joann Holcomb, Robin James, Bill Wilson, John Miller, Joan Ray.

If the mainstream *The Exorcist* (1973) could gross $89,000,000 in domestic film rentals on a $10,000,000 cost, American International Pictures intended to grab its fair share of that box-office gold with its black "variation" of the same tale. In fact, at one point the studio considered titling the new version *The Blackorcist.*

Black Bishop Garnet Williams (William Marshall) leads an archaeological expedition to Nigeria, where he uncovers a strange wooden box, a relic from the primitive worship of the evil Eshu, the god of sexuality. When the carved chest is opened, a mysterious, violent whirlwind is unleashed. Meanwhile, back in Louisville, Kentucky, Williams' son, Reverend Emmett Williams (Terry Carter), has just moved into a new parish with his pleasant young bride, Abby (Carol Speed). There is an unexplainable ethereal disturbance in their house, and the next day Abby is overwhelmed by an unexplainable presence. Brooding forces are at work: she cuts herself severely when she becomes entranced with the sight of chicken blood; later, during Emmett's debut sermon, she experiences a seizure. The fits recur, and Abby becomes more frenzied and sexually ravenous. The wanton Abby, having caused the death by heart attack of church organist Mrs. Wiggins (Nancy Lee Owens), is hospitalized. Her distraught husband begs his father to come to the rescue. By the time the Bishop arrives, Abby has forcibly removed herself from the hospital, and in a tantrum of wide-eyed and foaming violence, she shrieks to her aghast husband and father-in-law—in foul-mouthed language—her right to do whatever she pleases. She escapes, and her distraught husband goes in pursuit, abetted by Abby's policeman brother Cass (Austin Stoker). The Bishop is convinced now Abby is possessed by the spirit of Eshu, and when he finds her at a local nightclub he performs the necessary exorcism. After a battle of wills, the evil presence is fully exorcised.

"More silly than shocking even if it seems to take itself seriously," was the

Advertisement for *Abby* (1974).

verdict of A.H. Weiler *(New York Times),* while *Variety* chided the low-budget effort because it "...hovers close to parody in its cartoonish approach to character and plot...." However, even if the cheaply assembled feature boasted crummy sets, low-calibre special effects (including the unfrightening demon's voice), and too much hokum in the transformation of the heroine from churchgoer to rampaging hooker (complete with purple lips, a slight mustache and a vocabulary of four-letter words), *Abby* had a certain grotesque appeal to undemanding moviegoers. It grossed $2,600,000 in domestic film rentals!

Stentorian-voiced, experienced actor William Marshall appeared uncomfortable in the improbable lead assignment, chasing diminutive Carol Speed in and out of the creaky plot. Marshall should have been used to such genre nonsense, for he had already starred in the blaxploitation horror feature *Blacula* (1972) and its sequel, *Scream, Blacula Scream* (1973), qq.v.

3. Across 110th Street (United Artists, 1972). Color, 102 minutes.

Executive producers Anthony Quinn, Barry Shear; *producers* Ralph Serpe, Fouad Said; *associate producer* Richard Senta; *director* Shear; *based on the novel by* Wally Ferris; *screenplay* Luther Davis; *art director* Perry Watkins; *set decorator* Ray Murphy; *costume designer* Joe Freetwell; *makeup* Enrico Cortese; *music* J.J. Johnson; *songs* Johnson and Bobby Womack; *music editor* John Caper, Jr.; *assistant director* John E. Quill; *post production supervisor* Robert Stambler; *stunt co-ordinators* Eddie Smith, Calvin Brown; *special effects* Joe Lombardi Enterprises; *camera* Jack Priestley; *editor* Bryan Brandt.

Cast: Anthony Quinn (Captain Frank Mattelli); Yaphet Kotto (Detective Lieutenant William A. Pope); Anthony Franciosa (Nick D'Salvio); Paul Benjamin (Jim Harris); Ed Bernard (Joe Logart); Richard Ward (Doc Johnson); Norma Donaldson (Gloria Roberts); Antonio Fargas (Henry Jackson); Gilbert Lewis (Shevvy); Marlene Warfield (Mrs. Jackson); Tim O'Connor (Lieutenant Jack Hartnett); Nat Polen (Lieutenant Reilly); Charles McGregor (Chink); Frank Mascetta (Don Gennaro); Joe Attles (Mr. Jessup); Betty Haynes (Mrs. Jessup); *and:* Frank Adu, Frank Aldrich, Frank Arno, Tina Beyer, Gerry Black, Samuel Blue, Jr., Alex Brown, Norman Bush, Antony Cannon, Joe Canutt, Maria Carey, Antony Charnota, Dick Crockett, Keith Davis, George DiCenzo, Joe Dismas, Brendan Fay, Joe Fields, Clebert Ford, Bernetta Fowler, Andrea Lynn Frierson, George Garro, Joseph George, Steve Graves, Paul Harris, Dallas Edward Hayes, Jimmy Hayeson, Hilda Haynes, Gloria Hendry, Betty Howard, Pete Hock, Robert Jackson, Phil Kennedy, Nick La Padula, Al Leberfield, Ken Lynch, Ric Mancini, Charlene Mathies, Norman Matlock, Stephen Mendillo, Robert Sacchi, Janet Sarno, Thurman Scott, Eddie Smith, George Strus, Adam Wade, Marvin Walters, Arnold Williams, Mel Winkler, Burt Young.

The title tune from this aggressively violent film, set in the brutal turf of New York City, speaks of pushers and junkies "across 110th Street." This production further shaped the mold for black gangster movies of the 1970s, in which the uptown black ghetto — both the good and bad elements — aligns itself against the downtown Italian mobsters.

Three black men, Jim Harris (Paul Benjamin), Henry Jackson (Antonio Fargas), and Joe Logart (Ed Bernard), disguise themselves as policemen and rob a Harlem numbers bank of $300,000. In the process five syndicate members and two real policemen are killed. Both the New York City police and the Mafia respond instantly. Tough, aging police veteran Captain Frank Mattelli (Anthony Quinn) is resentful that much younger Lieutenant William A. Pope (Yaphet Kotto), a cultured black detective with two years of college, is made the spearhead in this major case. It is not their racial differences that primarily aggravates Mattelli about Pope; it is that he of the old guard is being pushed out by the new regime. (On the other hand, Pope has his own chip on his shoulder about dealing with Captain Mattelli: "You think because I'm black I'll blow the whistle on you. I want it [your job] on my terms. When are you going to start looking at me on my terms?") Moreover, Mattelli is of the old school who accepts beating up defendants and bribe taking as a way of life; virtuous but equally tough Pope abhors such tactics. Meanwhile Mafia ganglord Don Gennaro (Frank Mascetta) dispatches his fearful, bullying son-in-law Nick D'Salvio (Anthony Franciosa) to both find the money and regain control over the Harlem hoodlums. The black syndicate is headed by Doc Johnson (Richard Ward) and his henchman Shevvy (Gilbert Lewis). They taunt D'Salvio and promise only minimal assistance and laugh at Mattelli who has been on Johnson's payroll for years.

The robbers go their separate ways. Harris leaves his girl, Gloria Roberts (Norma Donaldson), and retreats to a slum apartment hideout. Logart returns to his dry cleaning plant job, and addict Jackson is back on the streets hunting

Marlene Warfield, Yaphet Kotto, and Anthony Quinn in *Across 110th Street* **(1972).**

heroin. Jackson is soon caught by D'Salvio's goons, who castrate and murder him. Under torture Logart reveals Harris' name to D'Salvio; then he is dropped from the top of a building to the street below. The downtowners track Gloria as she takes medicine to epileptic Harris. She is murdered, but Harris manages to kill them. He retreats with the $300,000 to the roof of the tenement, where he is gunned down by Pope. And Mattelli is shot by Shevvy, he having outlived his usefulness to the mob.

Beyond its cagey mixture of slickly paced, gory activity and pulsating music by J.J. Johnson (a frequent contributor to the genre), *Across 110th Street* makes sure viewers do not forget that it is very much a part of the burgeoning black action cycle. Much is made of the structural battle of Harlem versus Little Italy, with both sides equally stereotyped and bigoted and racial slurs tossed about frequently by both sides. (One of the more telling comments in the film is made by Jim Harris to his girlfriend, Gloria: "You gotta get your mind out of that white woman's dream.") Then there are the two pivotal lead performances. Anthony Quinn is the corrupt fifty-five-year-old cop who hates himself as much as he does the system and the crooks on the street. In counterpoint is Yaphet Kotto as the educated black career policeman who looks beyond a man's skin color to judge his merit and is resentful when another black tries to trade on his race ("Don't give me any of the brother crap!"). Both the old timer and the newcomer learn to respect and accept qualities in each other, and by the end of the story, Kotto's character is doing his best to protect his case partner.

Judith Crist (*New York* magazine) appreciated that in *Across 110th Street,*

"You'll find no tougher, more brutal and, sad to realize, truer portrait of the way things are between cops and robbers — organized crime variety." On the other hand, Roger Greenspun *(New York Times)* was not impressed because the film ". . . manages at once to be unfair to blacks, vicious towards whites, and insulting to anyone who feels that race relations might consist of something better than improvised genocide." *Variety* reported, ". . . it is a virtual blood bath. Those portions of it which aren't bloody violent are filled in by the squalid location sites in New York's Harlem or equally unappealing ghetto areas leaving no relief from depression and oppression." *Soul* magazine would later dismiss this film with, "If ever they were to give a prize to the most horrendously violent, senselessly brutal, rampantly stereotyped so-called Black movie ever made, then *Across 110th Street* would win hands down. It is unabashedly exploitive, shamelessly sex riddled and, in terms of plot, trite to the point of boredom."

Across 110th Street, co-produced by star Anthony Quinn, grossed $12,979,475 in domestic film rentals, on a production cost of just $1,300,000.

4. Action Jackson (Lorimar, 1988). Color, 95 minutes.

Producer Joel Silver; *associate producer* Steve Perry; *director* Craig R. Baxley; *screenplay* Robert Reneau; *art director* Virginia Randolph; *set decorator* Phil M. Leonard; *makeup* Scott M. Ddoo; *costume designer* Marilyn Vance-Straker; *music* Herbie Hancock, with Michael Kamen; *assistant director* Benjamin Rosenberg; *stunt co-ordinator* Joseph Brown; *sound* Jim Webb; *sound effects* Stephen Flick, Richard Shoor; *camera* Matthew F. Leonetti; *editor* Mark Helfich.

Cast: Carl Weathers (Jericho "Action" Jackson); Craig T. Nelson (Peter Dellaplane); Vanity (Sydney Ash); Sharon Stone (Patrice Dellaplane); Thomas F. Wilson (Officer Kornblau); Bill Duke (Captain Armbruster); Robert Dany (Tony Meretti); Roger Aaron Brown (Officer Lack); Stan Foster (Albert); Mary Ellen Trainor (Secretary); Ed O'Ross (Stringer); Bob Minor (Gamole); David Glen Eisley (Torn); *and:* Bill Duke, Armelia McQueen, Chino "Fats" Williams, Nicholas Worth.

In the late 1980s there were few major black film stars beyond Eddie Murphy, Bill Cosby, Whoopi Goldberg, Richard Pryor, and Louis Gossett, Jr.; even fewer were the black action pictures. *Action Jackson* was a slick bid to update the likes of Jim Brown's *Slaughter* (1972) and Fred Williamson's *Hammer* (1972) (qq.v.) to the high tech proficiencies of contemporary filmmaking.

Starring in the custom-made vehicle was ex–Oakland Raider football star and graduate of San Diego State College (with a B.A. in drama) Carl Weathers. He had come into the entertainment industry in the declining days of the black exploitation film cycle, playing a heavy in Pam Grier's *Coffy* (1974) and Fred Williamson–Grier's *Bucktown* (1975) (qq.v.). However, it was the role of Apollo Creed, Sylvester Stallone's nemesis-turned-compatriot in the first four *Rocky* features (1976, 1979, 1982, 1985) (qq.v.), that built Weathers' popularity with moviegoers. In the box-office success *Predator* (1987) as Arnold Schwarzenegger's equally athletic and physically resourceful pal he proved

again that he was no slouch in the action type of film. *Predator* producer Joel Silver then hired 6'2" Weathers for the slambang *Action Jackson,* geared to be the successor to Clint Eastwood's "Dirty Harry" character.

Lieutenant Jericho "Action" Jackson (Carl Weathers), a graduate of Harvard Law School, was demoted to Detective Sergeant and lost his gun permit on the Detroit police force when in arresting Sean, the sexual deviant son of auto magnate Peter Dellaplane (Craig T. Nelson), he got overly rough with the punk and tore off his arm. Because of his disgrace, Jackson's wife left him. Now it is Jackson who is investigating the gory assassinations of several Auto Alliance executives, all of them done in by a ruthless hit squad controlled by sinister Dellaplane. Along the bumpy route Jackson encounters Sydney Ash (Vanity) a heroin-addicted, gorgeous club singer "owned" by Dellaplane. She would like muscular Jackson to bed her, but first he wants to solve the case and for her to rid herself of her drug habit. It develops that Dellaplane intends to murder the union head so he can take over and control a power block that will be influential in United States politics. However, in the final showdown, Jackson and Dellaplane have a hand-to-hand scuffle, karate style, and when the unscrupulous executive plays too dirty, the cop shoots him dead. Jackson is rewarded with being reinstated to Lieutenant, and he and Sydney, who is already kicking her drug habit, pursue their romance.

Logic has never been a criteria of such macho cinema excursions into mayhem. But the title character here strains every shred of credulity. For a graduate of an Ivy League law school, Action Jackson does dumb things. He is an easy target for a pickpocket who steals his I.D. badge; thinks a person can break a drug habit in the blink of an eye; and that the best way to reach the second-story bedroom of the villain's mansion is to drive a car up the staircase. There is plenty of tough talk ("There wasn't enough of him left to spread on a pizza") and lots of exploding cars, yachts, and bodies. For distraction there is the frequently disrobed Vanity, blonde and curvaceous Sharon Stone (as the abused, soon-disposed-of spouse of Dellaplane), and of course star Weathers who can outrun a taxi, do backflips over a car, withstand beatings, and remove his shirt.

As expected, the film was critically roasted. "...[Former second-unit] director Craig R. Baxley just misses on the knockabout elan needed to put this action free-for-all over..." *(Los Angeles Reader).* "The action may be fast, but the dialogue consistently substitutes ugliness for cleverness." (Michael Dare, *Los Angeles Weekly).* "It's a generic action movie with more guns than brains, more car crashes than coherence and more opportunism than originality." (Michael Wilmington, *Los Angeles Times*). On the flip side, Deborah J. Kunk *(Los Angeles Herald-Examiner)* acknowledged, "For the genre, this film impresses in a few areas, though. It's better written than it has to be.... Second, *Action Jackson* can boast more solid black character actors in small roles than you're likely to see in three dozen typical Hollywood movies."

Weathers, who starred in the cop telefeature *Braker* (1985) and the short-lived police TV series "Fortune Dane" (1986) — for which he was in control as

Carl Weathers and Vanity in a publicity pose for *Action Jackson* (1988).

the executive producer—made *Action Jackson* as part of a financial deal with his own Stormy Weathers production company. As he explained to John Voland of the *Los Angeles Times* in 1988, "I struggled a pretty long time at the beginning of it, trying to figure out what role I might have in the entertainment industry.... It would've been easy to put it in cruise control and let everyone else take care of everything.... [However] I'm a little bit of a control freak. I've got to have my *hands* in the pie." As for making "art" rather than commercial ventures, he admitted to Voland, "...what I have to do, [is] please folks who buy tickets.... For the time being, cars flipping in the air and assault rifles going off are what does it.... You have to give the people what they want." Regarding the benefits of being a known entity and having his own production company, "It means having a bit of power to say no, to initiate the things I'd like to get done. And it means juggling about 12,000 concerns at once."

Action Jackson grossed a respectable $19,606,142 in its first seven weeks at the box-office. When it was released on videocassette a hasty three months later, it became a hot item, proving, as Sylvester Stallone, Chuck Norris, and Arnold Schwarzenegger know, that there is a definite market for this type of knockabout film.

5. Adios Amigo (Atlas, 1975). Color, 87 minutes.

Executive producer Lee Winkler; *producer/director/screenplay* Fred Williamson; *music/music conductor* Luici De Jesus; *camera* Tony Palmieri; *editors* Gene Ruggiero, Eva Ruggiero.

Cast: Fred Williamson (Big Ben); Richard Pryor (Sam Spade); Thalmus Rasulala (Noah Abraham Lincoln Brown); *and:* James Brown, Heidi Dobbs, Suhalia Farhat, Mike Henry, Victoria Jee, Lynne Jackson, Joy Lober, Robert Phillips, Liz Treadwell.

"*Adios Amigo* ... is worthy of note not for what it accomplishes ... but for what it avoids, namely the blaxploitation formula. Williamson, perhaps recoiling from the outcry by members of the black community against standard black mellers, has fashioned a light-hearted comedy-western with no strong violence, no sex and little black vs. white hatred" *(Variety)*.

Whatever the validity of *Variety's* evaluation, multi-faceted filmmaker Fred Williamson had another distinct goal in mind when he conceived *Adios Amigo:* "I'd thought that *Blazing Saddles* was a silly film. I wanted to make a comedy western without the extremes of showing Gucci saddlebags and other anachronisms, a down-and-dirty, dusty western whose comedy came about from the presence of Richard Pryor." Ironically, Pryor had contributed to the screenplay of Mel Brooks's *Blazing Saddles* (1974) and, at one point, was scheduled to play the black sheriff. However, the coveted role of Bart went to Cleavon Little, which was a bitter disappointment to Pryor. And at the time he agreed to make *Adios Amigo* he was at a brief lull in his rising film career, which caused the comedian to want to work, no matter what the project, especially when the role was offered by Williamson, with whom he had been friends for several years.

When unfriendly whites chase Big Ben (Fred Williamson) from his land, he retaliates by shooting up the white leader's house, and he is arrested.

Enroute to prison, he is freed when con man–thief Sam Spade (Richard Pryor) robs the group. "I is the robber, you is the rob-ee," says slick, buoyant Sam. Thereafter the two team up, with Sam constantly getting them into one scrape after another and always making Big Ben the foil for his backfiring capers. Ben chides his manipulative "friend": "I wish you'd stop callin' me Amigo because every time you do, it causes trouble for me." Still later the two end up on a chain gang at a mine and Ben steams, "Don't be my friend any more. I don't find it too healthy." Along the way Ben must deal with a knife-thrower, escaping from the chain gang, combatting a giant hulk of a man, and eluding the pursuing posse. At the illogical finale, Ben and Sam discover their saddlebag full of money has only counterfeit bills. They ride off into the sunset.

Episodic, with its crudely conceived sequences strung together only by the pulsating title theme song (sung by the Infernal Blues Machine), and scenes ending in freeze frames, *Adios Amigo* is a very unslick Western. In *Richard Pryor: Black and Blue* (1984), an unauthorized biography by Jeff Rovin, the author quotes Fred Williamson's description of how the film was made: "I only had a twelve-page script. Going into this film, I was counting heavily on him [Richard Pryor] to improvise; I wanted to give him an idea, a concept, then just turn the light on him and let him do whatever he wanted.... [Instead] we'd be on location or on the set and he'd keep turning to me and saying, 'What do you want me to do, what should I say?' I'd look at him and answer, 'Hey, this is your scene....'" There was another problem with Pryor, according to the producer-director-star: "Richard also couldn't ride a horse.... We had this pinto for him, and that kind of horse is a little extra-frisky.... We spent half our shooting schedule [nine days] chasing Richard Pryor on that damn animal."

Nevertheless, the film boasts several congenial comedic moments by jive-talking Pryor, especially as he imitates a shuffling water boy on the chain gang or when he is working out a new scam to outwit everyone in sight. In addition, it has an assortment of undraped females, and, most of all, it is a far cry from the more professional but overly violent and angry *The Legend of Nigger Charley* (1972) and *The Soul of Nigger Charley* (1973) (qq.v.), both of which starred Fred Williamson.

Adios Amigo, made by Williamson for his Chicago-based Po' Boy Productions for Atlas Films release, earned $110,000 in its first two weeks of release in Chicago and went on to make a profit in its limited distribution, added to by its years-later (1988) videocassette release. However, the film caused a riff between the two co-stars when Williamson learned Pryor had told the press of this Western, "Tell them [the public] I'm sorry. Tell them I needed the money."

6. The Arena (New World, 1973). Color, 85 minutes.

Executive producer Roger Corman; *producer* Mark Damon; *director* Steve Carver; *screenplay* John Corrington, Joyce Hooper Corrington; *production designer* Mimmo Scavia; *wardrobe* Renato Morroni; *makeup* Emilio Trani, Antonio Mura; *music* Francesco De Masi; *stunt co-ordinator* Granfraco Pasquetto; *assistant director* Romano Scandariato; *sound* Francesco Proppioni;

sound effects Alvaro Gramigna; *special effects* Sergio Chiusi; *camera* Aristide Massacessi; *editor* Jann Carver.

Cast: Pam Grier (Mamawi); Margaret Markov (Bodicia); Lucretia Love (Deidre); *and:* Salvatore Baccaro, Sara Bay, Peter Cester, Mary Count, Ivan Gasper, Jho Jhenkins, Vic Karis, Sid Lawrence, Marie Louise, Ann Melita, Paul Muller, Christopher Oakes, Dick Palmer, Pietro Torrisi, Daniel Vargas, Anthony Vernon.

"Black Slave versus White Slave.... See Wild Women Fight to the Death!" So claimed the teasing advertising campaign for this very offbeat, almost campy, variation on the black/sexploitation theme filmed in wide screen and color in Italy. Many of the subordinate roles, played by Italians, were re-dubbed for its R-rated American release.

In 44 B.C. the Roman Empire holds a fierce control over the countryside. Among the prisoners of the Empire brought in chains to the port of Brundisium for sale as slaves are blonde Bodicia (Margaret Markov), a Druid High Princess from Britanny, voluptuous black Mamawi (Pam Grier) of Nubia, and wily Deidre (Lucretia Love). They are sold to a local coliseum owner, who intends using them to fulfill the nightly whims of his flock of gladiators. ("You mean we have to satisfy their animal heat?" asks one young innocent, before the first of many orgies commences.) Soon it is decided as a joke to have the women fight in the arena, and they undergo the necessary gladiator training. What starts as a gimmick to amuse the crowd becomes deadly serious as the arena owner realizes his female slaves must fight one another to the death to please the jaded crowd. Mamawi is forced to kill her distaff adversaries, which leads her to instigate a revolt against her master, who is dispatched by the aroused crowd, along with his effeminate, nasty assistant. Mamawi and Bodicia are among the few survivors who escape through the cavern maze to freedom.

"*The Arena* . . . is one of the more perverse side effects of women's lib. It would be just another routinely gory Italian spear-and-sandal spectacular, the kind Steve Reeves hasn't made for a decade, except that its gladiators are female.... Miss Grier is spirited and game, as usual" (Kevin Thomas, *Los Angeles Times*). "It's primitive entertainment but it does have a certain raw appeal.... Pam Grier rapidly becoming the Maria Montez of the 1970s, is a very beautiful woman (from certain angles she resembles Ava Gardner) who seems to be able to act" (Richard Cuskelly, *Los Angeles Herald-Examiner*).

The Arena was filmed quickly and on the cheap ($75,000) in Italy by American Film Institute graduate Steve Carver (who had been assistant director on Dalton Trumbo's *Johnny Got His Gun* [1971] and would direct Chuck Norris' *An Eye for an Eye* [1981] and *Lone Wolf McQuade* [1983]). The film is a mini-spectacle rip-off of Kirk Douglas's *Spartacus* (1960) and owes most of its enjoyment to the statuesque presence of Pam Grier. She struts like an Amazon through the trashy story with poise, performing her share of exotic dancing, disrobing, ersatz lovemaking with the gladiators, and athletics in the arena with a trident. Thanks to Grier, in particular, *The Arena* is a miniature exercise in fantasy fulfillment. The star even has her moments of black-is-beautiful proselytizing, as when she chides her black gladiator lover, "The

Romans have taught you to live like an animal. Have they also told you to forget your past?" Compared to Grier, blonde Margaret Markov (who also co-starred with Grier in *Black Mama, White Mama,* 1972, q.v.) is pallid indeed.

In the summer of 1988, *The Arena* was released for the videocassette market under the more exploitive title *Naked Warriors.* The publicity material for cassette store distributors read, "The competitive spirit of the [1988 Korean] summer Olympics will put your customers in the perfect mood for this Olympian-theme release."

7. The Avenging Godfather (Communications International, Inc., 1979). Color, 93 minutes.

Executive producer Burt Steiger; *producers* Rudy Ray Moore, Theodore Toney; *associate producers* Jules Bihari, Cliff Roquemore; *director* J. Robert Wagoner; *story* Toney, Moore; *screenplay* Wagoner, Roquemore; *production designer* Jerry Lunch; *art director* Robert A. Luens; *makeup* Donna Smith; *wardrobe* Kimberly Sizemore; *music arranger/music conductor* Ernie Fields, Jr.; *songs* Greg Middleton and Fields, Jr.; Bob Boobs, Toney, George Sterling III and Fields, Jr.; Steve Sullivan; Moore; *fight sequence co-ordinators* Howard Jackson, Cliff Stewart; *sound* Brian Frank; *special effects* Luens; *camera* Arledge Armenaki; *editor* Garner M.J. Morris.

Cast: Rudy Ray Moore (Tucker Moore); Carol Speed (Noel); Jimmy Lynch (Sweetmeat); Lady Reed (Mrs. Edwards); James H. Hawthorne (Stinger Ray); Frank Fink (Lieutenant Frank Hayes); Julius J. Carry III (Bucky); Leroy Daniels (Disco M.C.); Melvin Smith (Disc Jockey); Ronny Harris, Satin Gonzales, Antar Mubarek, Marshall Williams (Hitmen); Debbie Fisher (Mrs. Kilroy); Dolores Parr (Tucker's Girl); Clarice Wilson, Robin Keith (Angels Against Dust); Sophia Bibbs, Ron Bass (Disco Skate Dancers); Yetta Colber (Miss Wonderful of Philadelphia); Pat Washington (Miss Wonderful of Chicago); Howard Jackson (Special Karate Fighter); Doc Watson (District Councilman); Pucci Jhones (Angel of Death); Fred Strother, Lonnie Malcolm, Cleveland Posey, Sonny Smalley (Squad).

This film proves to be a poorly executed amalgam of disco music/gangster melodrama/fantasy exploitation. Ex-fighter and nightclub–party album comic Rudy Ray Moore stars as Tucker Moore, a cop, whose basketball player nephew, Bucky (Julius J. Carry III), becomes dope-addicted and nearly dies. Tucker decides to go after the pushers, but himself becomes involved in the world of drugs. The thin plot allows for much sermonizing against drugs, drug-induced dream sequences, lots of musical sequences at a disco club, and the by-then *de rigeur* lovemaking sequences by not-so-young Moore. This film was definitely not a step upwards for Moore, the star of *Dolemite* (1975) and *Human Tornado/Dolemite II* (1976) (q.v.).

8. The Bad Bunch (Dimension, 1976). Color, 82 minutes.

Executive producers Mardi Rustam, Robert Brown; *producer* Alvin L. Fast; *associate producers* Mohammed Rustam, Sheldon Lee; *director* Greydon Clark; *story/screenplay* Clark, Fast; *music* Ed Cobb, Delvey Linden Oldham,

Emory Gordy, Jr., Dennis St. John; *song* Lee; *camera* Louis Horwath; *second unit camera* Michael Mileham; *editor* Earl Watson, Jr.

Cast: Greydon Clark (Jim); Tom Johnigarn (Makimba [Tom]); Aldo Ray (Lieutenant Stams); Jock Mahoney (Sergeant Berry); Bambi Allen (Bobbi); Jacquelin Cole (Nancy Dorian); Pamela Corbett (Tina); Fred Scott (Mr. Washington); Carl Craig (Willie); Hugh Warden (Hooker's Customer); William Bonner (Fats Colackain); Robert Munk (Clay Washington); Barbara Perry (Jim's Mother); Frank White (Jim's Father); Laurence Bame (Al Webster); Mardi Rustam (Nancy's Father); Evelyn Frank (Nancy's Mother); Bob Frank (Mr. Adams); Dawn Sherwood (Ms. Kelly); Sheldon Lee (Young Man at Pool); Marvyn Brody (Older Man at Pool); *and:* the people of Watts.

Jim (Greydon Clark) survives his military tour of duty in war-torn Vietnam, but his black soldier pal, Clay Washington (Robert Munk), doesn't. When Jim returns to Los Angeles he comes to Watts to tell Mr. Washington (Fred Scott) that his son died bravely in combat and to deliver a letter that Clay had written before dying. The still-grieving old man is appreciative that his son's white pal has made the gesture, but the dead soldier's angry younger brother, Tom (Tom Johnigarn), is suspicious of this honky and joins his neighborhood gang pals in harassing the persistent Jim. (He snarls at Jim, "Tom is my slave name. Makimba is my [real] name.") This causes scuffles between Jim and the very hostile blacks, all of which are monitored by two strongly anti-black cops, Lieutenant Stams (Aldo Ray) and Sergeant Berry (Jock Mahoney). The cops become suspicious of Jim's friendship with Mr. Washington, who later dies. Thrown into the mix are Jim's hippie girlfriend, Nancy Dorian (Jacquelin Cole), whom he marries eventually at a very establishment wedding; a sluttish gal named Bobbi (Bambi Allen), to allow for onscreen sexual coupling between her and Jim; several impassioned speeches about the injustices of whites against blacks; and the killing of aggressive, bloated Stams by the violent blacks.

What might have been a forceful and then topical study of a Vietnam War veteran returning home is marred by amateurish scripting, acting and direction, with too much emphasis on softcore pornographic scenes. Additional negative points are the cliche-filled handling of white mobsters (who really have little to do with the narrative) in an extended swimming pool party sequence filled with nudity, and abysmal performances by once-professional screen players Ray and Mahoney. The best performers in this would-be gritty urban action drama are the people of Watts, shown going about their daily business.

9. Badge of the Assassin (CBS-TV, 11/2/85). Color, 100 minutes.

Executive producers Daniel H. Blatt, Robert Singer; *co-executive producer* Robert K. Tannenbaum; *associate producer* Pixie Lamppu; *director* Mel Damski; *based on the book by* Tannenbaum, Philip Rosenberg; *teleplay* Lawrence Roman; *production designer* Allen Jones; *music* Tom Scott; *camera* John Lindley, Joao Fernandes; *supervising editor* Elio Zarmati; *editor* Andrew L. Cohen.

Cast: James Woods (Robert K. Tannenbaum); Yaphet Kotto (Cliff Fenton); Alex Rocco (Bill Butler); David Harris (Lester Day); Steven Keats

(Skelton); Larry Riley (Herman Bell); Pam Grier (Alexandra "Alie" Horn); Rae Dawn Chong (Christine Horn); Richard Bradford (J.J. Delsa); Kene Holliday (Albert Washington); Toni Kalem (Diane Piagentini); Tamu Blackwell (Gloria Lapp); Richard Brooks (Tony Bottom); Akosua Busia (Ruth); Lewis Arquette (First Foreman); Alan Blumenfeld (Charlie); Ernie Lively (U.S. Marshal); Ray Girardin (Agent King); David Wohl (Ken Kelin); Kelly Minter (Rachel Torres); Lew Palter (Judge Greenfield); Noble Willingham (Airport Guard); Paul Perri (Joseph Piagentini); Henry G. Sanders (Second Foreman); Michael Sandoval (Francisco Torres); Drew Snyder (Inspector McCoy); Judy Brown, Daniel H. Blatt (Reporters); Kim Delgado (Waverly Jones); John Brandon (Clerk); Terry Brannon (Mississippi Officer); Reginald Bruce (Road Gang Guy); Tomas Gorosteita (Gabriel Torres); Sheila Johns (Linda McGill); Glenn Michael Jones (San Francisco Officer); Tom Kindle (New Orleans Officer); Paul McCauley (Mississippi Judge); Fred Leneer (Sergeant Kowalski); Robert B. Pope (Ulysses Tatum); Charlie Stavola (Judge Aloysius Melia); Dierk Torsek (Defense Attorney); Charles Walker (Court Clerk).

Filmed in New York and Los Angeles, this teleplay is based on the true story of black cop killers in New York City and the 1979 best-selling book. The focus is on the restrictions of the American judicial system as Assistant District Attorney Robert K. Tannenbaum (James Woods) relentlessly pursues members of the Black Liberation Army and attempts to prove the guilt of three assassins in the 1971 deaths of two policemen. Helping him on this difficult case is self-assured, powerful police detective Cliff Fenton (Yaphet Kotto) and another bureau investigator, Bill Butler (Alex Rocco). The trail leads from the Bronx, to Harlem, to San Francisco, to New Orleans, and to Mississippi in the course of the two-year-long investigation. Tannenbaum and Fenton must deal with finding a missing revolver, and the wavering testimony of scared witnesses (including Tamu Blackwell and Akosua Busia). Among the participants in the case are radical defense attorney Skelton (Steven Keats); Albert Washington (Kene Holliday), one of the three killers; and Lester Day (David Harris), who knows where the crucial gun is buried.

"Well-made, professional and convincing; loaded with important message, it still doesn't command dramatic interest," decided *Daily Variety* of this telefilm. "The teleplay," analyzed the trade paper, "is methodical to the point of distraction." With most of the focus on James Woods and his typical nervous-energy performance, former black action star Pam Grier as Alexandra "Alie" Horn had too little to do in the proceedings.

10. Best Defense (Paramount, 1984). Color, 94 minutes.

Producer Gloria Katz; *director* Willar Huyck; *based on the novel* "Easy and Hard Ways Out" *by* Robert Grossbach; *screenplay* Katz, Huyck; *production designer* Peter Jamison; *art directors* Robert W. Welch III, Ariel Roshko; *set decorators* R. Chris Westlund, Giora Porter; *costumes* Kristi Zea, Gordon Brockway, Jennifer Parsons; *music* Patrick Williams; *supervising music editor* Richard Stone; *assistant directors* Jerry C.G. Grandey, Jerald B. Sobul, Catherine Wanek; *stunt co-ordinator* Everett Creach; *military adviser* Jaci

Eshel; *special effects* Richard E. Johnson, John R. Elliott; *sound* Jerry Jost, Robin Gregory; *supervising sound editor* Frank Warner; *camera* Don Peterman; *editor* Sidney Wolinsky, Michael A. Stevenson.

Cast: Dudley Moore (Wylie Cooper); Eddie Murphy (Lieutenant Landry); Kate Capshaw (Laura Cooper); George Dzundza (Loparino); Helen Shaver (Claire Lewis); Mark Arnott (Brank); Peter Michael Goetz (Frank Joyner); Tom Noonan (Holtzman); David Rashce (Jeff the Spy); Paul Comi (Chief Agent); Darryl Henriques (Colonel Zayas); Joel Polis (Agent); John A. Zee (Colonel McGunn); Matthew Laurance (Ali); Christopher Mahar (Sayyd); Larry Goldman (Rupp); Stoney Richards (Mugger); Tyler Tyhurst (American Captain); Eduardo Ricard (Garcia Vega); William Marquez (Padilla); Deborah Fallender (Toni); Raye Birk (Sonny); Ellen Crawford (Sonya); Gene Dynarski (Gil); John Hostetter (Quirk); David Paymer (Kurly); Dennis Redfield (Specs); Jerry Hyman (Colonel Kleinman); Hugo L. Stanger (Blevin); Tracey Ross (Arab Girl); Michael Scalera (Morgan); Rob Wininger (Lieutenant Chapin); Gary Bayer (Lubell); Ronald Salley (Transportation Captain); Paul Eiding (Tourist); Stephen Bradley (Deputy Director); Sanford Jensen, Gerald Jann (Engineers); Jennifer Wallace (Waitress); Renny Temple (Coffee Machine Mover); Ziporah Tzabari (Ancient Kuwaiti Woman); Gabi Amrani (Old Villager); Rozsika Halmos (Seamstress); Diane Carter (Technician); Jake Dengel (Doorman); Billy Ray Sharkey (Radio Man); Burton Collins (Cameraman); Bill Geisslinger (Walkie-talkie Agent); Itzhak Neeman (Refugee); Jim Jansen (Lieutenant); Javier Grajeda (Freddie Gomez); Patricia Pivaar (Newscaster); Julie Ellis (Waitress); Yulis Ruval (French Singer); Pamela Stonebrook (Singer); Elizabeth Kubota (Japanese Singer).

This film is surely one of the more bizarre efforts by Hollywood to cash in on the box-office appeal of two extremely diverse comedians; Britisher Dudley Moore and American Eddie Murphy. Moore, best known onscreen for his pratfalls and drunk routines, was struggling to find a commercial success to equal his earlier *10* (1979) and *Arthur* (1981). Smart-mouthed, rambunctious Murphy had scored heavily in Paramount's *48 Hours* (1982) and *Trading Places* (1983) and had recently signed a five-picture pact with the studio. A sign of how confused a project *Best Defense* was: the two comics share *no* scenes in this mishmash. In fact, Murphy is listed as a "strategic guest star," and his appearance is relatively brief; obviously tacked onto the movie as a desperation measure to save the floundering project, which could not decide if it was a satire on industrial and political espionage or a slapstick comedy-adventure about warfare.

In 1984 Kuwait, the United States Army is demonstrating its new XM-10 supertank for local government leaders. The tank crew is commanded by womanizing Lieutenant Landry (Eddie Murphy), and he and his men are at a loss for what to do—beyond cursing and doing double takes—when the tank runs amok due to mechanical problems.

The scene shifts back to 1982 Seal Beach, California, where unsuccessful electronics engineer Wylie Cooper (Dudley Moore) is struggling to keep himself employed and to save his marriage with Laura (Kate Capshaw). At the moment, if lazy Cooper does not solve the problem of a faulty gyro design, he will be unemployed. A fortuitous encounter at a bar with a man named Holtzman (Tom Noonan) saves the day. The latter insists he is fleeing an assassin, and soon he is found dead. Meanwhile he had tucked into Cooper's attache case a blueprint which answers the gyro design problem. Cooper's company and position are saved, but he must cope with Jeff (David Rasche), the killer spy who is now on Cooper's trail. This leads hapless Cooper into working with the FBI to trap the murderer-smuggler. Back at the defense plant he finally convinces his superiors to correct the gyro problem in the tank.

Jumping forward again to 1984 Kuwait, Landry and his men are caught behind enemy lines when Iraq opens warfare. The tank is used to rescue stranded troops and is attacked by enemy planes. Because of Wylie's design adjustments, Landry and his men survive the skirmish.

"Everything about this lame and boring comedy seems to be an afterthought. Moore's scenes were filmed in Hollywood; Murphy's scenes were shot in Israel.... Not only do these parallel movies [i.e. the two stories] seem years apart in style, content and even color processing, but they seem to have been filmed two years apart as well. You get two bad movies for the price of one" (Rex Reed, *New York Post*).

Once the word-of-mouth was out about this jumbled concoction, not even Eddie Murphy's ingratiating, if foul-mouthed, comedy bits could save the picture. On an estimated negative cost of $18,000,000 *Best Defense* earned only $10,500,000 in domestic film rentals.

11. Beverly Hills Cop (Paramount, 1984). Color, 105 minutes.

Producers Don Simpson, Jerry Bruckheimer; *director* Martin Brest; *story* Daniel Petrie, Jr., Danilo Bach; *screenplay* Petrie; *production designer* Angelo Graham; *art director* James J. Murakami; *set decorators* Jeff Haley, John M. Dwyer; *costumes,* Tom Bronson; *music* Harold Faltermeyer; *special effects* Kenneth D. Pepiot; *camera* Bruce Surtees; *editors* Billy Weber, Arthur Coburn.

Cast: Eddie Murphy (Axel Foley); Judge Reinhold (Detective Billy Rosewood); John Ashton (Sergeant John Taggart); Lisa Eilbacher (Jenny Summers); Ronny Cox (Lieutenant Andrew Bogomil); Steven Berkoff (Victor Maitland); James Russo (Mikey Tandino); Jonathan Banks (Zack); Stephen Elliott (Chief Hubbard); Gilbert R. Hill (Inspector Todd); Art Kimbro (Detective Foster); Joel Bailey (Detective McCabe); Bronson Pinchot (Serge); Paul Reiser (Jeffrey); Michael Champion (Casey); Frank Pesce (Cigarette Buyer); Gene Borkan (Truck Driver); Michael Gregory (Hotel Manager); Alice Cadogan (Hotel Clerk); Philip Levien (Donny); Karen Mayo-Chandler (Maitland Receptionist); Gerald Berns, William Wallace (Beverly Hills Cops); Israel Jurarbe (Room Service Waiter); Randy Gallion (Bell Hop); Damon Wayans (Banana Man); Chuck Adamson, Chip Heller (Crate Openers); Rick Overton (Bonded Warehouse Night Superintendent); Rex Ryon (Bonded Warehouse Security Guard); Michael Pniewski, Douglas Warhit (Bonded Warehouse Clerks); Paul Drake, Tom Everett (Holdup Men); Sally Kishbaugh (Waitress); Barry Shade (Valet); Jack Heller (Maitre d')' Michael Harrington (Arresting Officer); David Wells (Dispatcher); Scott Murphy (Detective Owenby); John Achorn, Darwyn

Carson, Anthony De Fonte, Dennis Madden, John Pettis, Mick Shields, Carl Weintraub (Detroit Cops); Mark E. Corry (Pool Player); Thomas J. Hageboeck (Maitland Bodyguard).

(See summary under *Beverly Hills Cop II*).

12. Beverly Hills Cop II (Paramount, 1987). Color, 103 minutes.

Executive producers Robert D. Wachs, Richard Tienken; *producers* Don Simpson, Jerry Bruckheimer; *director* Tony Scott; *based on characters created by* Danilo Bach, Daniel Petrie, Jr.; *story* Eddie Murphy, Wachs; *production designer* Ken Davis; *art director* James J. Murakami; *set decorator* John Anderson; *illustrator* Sherman Labby; *costume supervisors* James W. Tyson, Bobbie Read; *music* Harold Faltermeyer; *music editor* Bob Badami; *music consultant* Kathy Nelson; *song* Faltermeyer, Keith Forsey, and Bob Seger; *assistant directors* Peter Bogart, Hope Goodwin, Michael Amundson; *title designer* Dan Curry; *computer consultants* Steve Grummett, Roger Sweetzer; *police technical adviser* T.J. Hageboeck; *stunt co-ordinators* Gary McLarty, Alan Oliney; *special effects co-ordinator* Tom Ryba; *assistant special effects* Dave Blitstein, Tom Tokunaga, Johnny Borgese; *laser special effects* Laser Media, Inc.; *sound* William B. Kaplan; *sound re-recording* Donald O. Mitchell, Rick Klein, Kevin O'Connell; *sound effects* John Paul Fasal; *supervising sound editors* Cecilia Hall, George Watters II; *sound editors* Marshall Winn, Barbara McBane, Frank Howard, Kimberly Harris, Victor Grodecki, Julia Evershade, Marty Nicholson; *camera* Jeffrey L. Kimball; *editors* Billy Weber, Chris Lebenzon, Michael Tronick.

Cast: Eddie Murphy (Axel Foley); Judge Reinhold (Billy Rosewood); Jurgen Prochnow (Maxwell Dent); Ronny Cox (Lieutenant Andrew Bogomil); John Ashton (John Taggart); Brigitte Nielsen (Karla Fry); Allen Garfield (Harold Lutz); Dean Stockwell (Charles "Chip" Cain); Paul Reiser (Jeffrey Friedman); Gilbert R. Hill (Inspector Todd); Paul Guilfoyle (Nikos Thomopolis); Robert Ridgley (Mayor Egan); Brian O'Connor (Biddle); Alice Adair (Jan Bogomil); Eugene Butler (May); Glenn Withrow (Willie); Stephen Liska (Chauffeur); Gilbert Gottfried (Sidney Bernstein); Tom Bower (Russ Fielding); Valerie Wildman (Gun Club Receptionist); Hugh M. Hefner (Himself); Carrie Leigh (Herself); Frank J. Pesce (Carlotta); Vic Manni (Rap Singing Guard); Sheri Levinsky (Waitress); Ray Murphy, Sr. (Uncle Ray); Todd Susman (Foreman); Chris Rock (Parking Valet); Susan Lentini (Receptionist at Hefner's); Anthony D'Andrea (Granby); Robert Pastorelli (Vinnie); Kopi Sotiropulos (Barkeep); Richard Tienken (Mr. Anderson); Teal Roberts, Peggy Sands (Strippers); Larry Carroll (TV Reporter); Carlos Cervantes (Mendoza); Michael DeMarlo (Doorman at Adriano's); Dana Gladstone (Francesco); Richmond Harrison (Construction Worker); Darryl Henriques (Maitre d' at 385); John Hostetter (Stiles); Tom "Tiny" Lister, Jr. (Orvis); Ed Pansullo (Ailey); Rudy Ramos (Ignacio); Ritch Shydner (Guard at Hefner's); John Lisbon Wood (Bobby Morgan); Carl Bringas, Joe Duquette, Michael Hehr, Sam Sako (Bodyguards); Michael F. Kelly (Guard at Gate); William Lamar, Christopher R. Adams, Danny Nero, Devin Barlett (Thugs); Dayna O'Brien (Girl at Club); Eugene Mounts (Policeman); Everètt Sherman, Jr. (Man at Street Corner);

Catrin Cole (Vinnie's Girl); Rebecca Ferratti, Kymberly Herrin, Venice Kong, Luann Lee, Kymberley Paige, Ola Ray, Alana Soares (*Playboy* Playmates); Marlenne Kingland, Anne Lammot, Sarah Quick, Pamela Santini, Natalie Smith, Leilani Soares, Monet Swann, Kari Whitman (*Playboy* Models).

Many of the millions of viewers who saw *Beverly Hills Cop* (1984) expressed the thought, "The role of Axel Foley was made for Eddie Murphy." Actually the film had been conceived of initially as a project for Sylvester Stallone. But it was Murphy as the street-wise Detroit cop caught in the lush underworld of palm-lined Beverly Hills that made the action feature so hugely successful. It also did a great deal financially and career-wise for Murphy, whose Eddie Murphy Productions made this project in association with Paramount Pictures.

Detective Axel Foley (Eddie Murphy) of the Detroit police force likes to get the job done, but in his own way, no matter the cost or whatever the unconventional procedures. He is the bane of his harassed black superior officer, Inspector Todd (Gilbert R. Hill), who yells at him, "I'm tired of taking the heat for you. One more time and you're out on the street." This applies when boyhood pal and ex-convict Mikey Tandido (James Russo) turns up at Foley's apartment and is soon killed by two thugs. Foley is convinced the homicide revolves around the stolen deutsche mark bearer bonds Tandido told Foley he had stolen in Los Angeles, but Todd orders Foley to keep out of the case. Determined to solve the death of his pal, Foley goes on leave and drives to Los Angeles in his "crappy blue Chevy Nova." He checks into the expensive Beverly Palms Hotels. His next stop is the Hollis-Benton Art Gallery in Beverly Hills, run by Jenny Summers (Lisa Eilbacher), a childhood friend of both Foley and Tandido, the latter of whom she employed at the shop. The trail leads to the gallery's ominous owner, Victor Maitland (Steven Berkoff), whom Foley quickly surmises has some connection to his friend's killing. When the annoyed Maitland has him carted out to the street, the fussy Beverly Hills police come on the scene. Newcomer detective Billy Rosewood (Judge Reinhold) and the older, equally by-the-books Sergeant John Taggart (John Ashton) are assigned to tail Foley. The latter is amazed by the vast contrast in tactics and ambiance between Detroit and Beverly Hills law enforcement. Clues lead to Maitland's warehouse, where Foley, accompanied by Jenny, finds that Maitland and his men are trafficking in stolen bonds and drugs. Never far behind physically but always five steps behind mentally, Rosewood and Taggart are temporarily replaced as Foley's shadow by two other cops, also under the stringent command of Lieutenant Andrew Bogomil (Ronny Cox). Later Foley persuades Rosewood to come with him to Maitland's warehouse, where Foley is captured but rescued by Rosewood. Then joined by Taggart they head to Maitland's mansion where Jenny is held captive. In the melee, Maitland and his men are killed. Bogomil, who has had a change of heart about Foley's unorthodox procedures, lies to his superior, Chief Hubbard (Stephen Elliott), to explain his men's singular but successful strategy.

Just as much as *Beverly Hills Cop* is a satisfactory police action adventure, it is a study of black people, one in particular, dealing in white-controlled America. There are references to racial prejudices and stereotypes throughout the film, but unlike the blatantly violent and vicious black action pictures of the 1970s, here the tone is mock serious or downright outrageously comic. Nevertheless the jibes are just as relevant and effective. At one point the angered Inspector Todd informs his nemesis Foley, "I just didn't walk into this town [Detroit] from a cottonfield." When Foley arrives in lush Beverly Hills and decides to do things right, he fast-talks the registration clerk at the exclusive Beverly Palms Hotels into giving him a room, despite his lack of a reservation. "Don't you think I know what's goin' on here ... no nigger allowed. ..." Afraid he will cause a further scene, the hotel not only gives him immediate accommodations, but provides him with a luxuriant suite for the lesser price of a regular room (all of which is later paid for by the grateful Beverly Hills police department). Still later, when one of the Beverly Hills police assigned to Foley proves righteous and stuffy, Foley attempts to give him a practical lesson in jive talk, but the uppity man will not buy it.

On another level, *Beverly Hills Cop* is about diverse lifestyles. What could be more different than inner city Detroit and upscale (sub)urban Beverly Hills? In a wonderful montage, ex–slum boy Foley tours the new environs, absorbing the mind-boggling material splendors it presents: extravagant mansions, luxurious overpriced automobiles, and gorgeous, available women everywhere — all offered against a glittery backdrop of palm-lined vistas.

Throughout the film, which boasts a best-selling soundtrack score, Eddie Murphy's Foley is always "on." His favorite words are "trust me," and he runs the gamut of hip-talk comedy, all punctuated with raunchy toughness and grinning double takes. He takes on all comers, from the officious, punctilious Beverly Hills police (who grow to like his street charm and his successful police methods) to the arrogantly aristocratic crime lord Victor Maitland. Along the way there are some bizarre encounters as he trades quips with the posh art gallery's effete general assistant (Bronson Pinchot) or punctures the pomposity of the maitre d' (Jack Heller) at the exclusive Harrow Club. One of the strange sidelights of the film is that woman-loving Foley is given no romantic interlude in the picture, not even with his childhood friend Jenny, who is his cohort throughout a goodly portion of the story. (There are some who insist this happened because the filmmakers did not want to risk an interracial onscreen romance.)

Most critics were enthralled with *Beverly Hills Cop.* "Dirtier and hotter than Harry, Eddie Murphy is also the funniest screen cop since the Keystones.... Even when the plot misfires, Murphy comes out shooting from the funny bone—and it's bull's eyes all the way" (*People* magazine). Rex Reed *(New York Post)* endorsed, "*Beverly Hills Cop* fit the cool, fresh-mouthed, jiveass hipness of Murphy's screen persona like a crash helmet."

With an estimated negative cost of $14,000,000, *Beverly Hills Cop* grossed $108,000,000 in domestic film rentals. With such a huge profit, there was no doubt that a sequel was in the offing. The only question was when. (After *Beverly Hills Cop,* Murphy was offered several other pictures which he rejected, including a few later made with Whoopi Goldberg in the "Murphy" role.) Three years later, when his schedule permitted, Eddie Murphy starred in *Beverly Hills Cop II.*

Chris Rock *(left)* **and Eddie Murphy in** *Beverly Hills Cop II* **(1987).**

At the end of *Beverly Hills Cop,* Axel Foley had been escorted out of town by his now-buddies Billy Rosewood and John Taggart, and in the friendliest sort of way asked not to return. But when his now-good-friend police captain Bogomil (Ronny Cox), who is investigating the rash of "Alphabet Crimes" in Beverly Hills, is gravely wounded, Foley concocts an elaborate ploy to disappear for a few days from duty and flies to Los Angeles to offer his assistance. He teams with his pals Rosewood (Judge Reinhold) and Taggart (John Ashton), who have been demoted recently by the antagonistic new deputy police chief Harold Lutz (Allen Garfield).

The path leads to the Beverly Hills Shooting Club, where Charles "Chip" Cain (Dean Stockwell) is in charge, on behalf of owner Maxwell Dent (Jurgen Prochnow). Dent's assistant is six-foot-tall Karla Fry (Brigitte Nielsen), who was in charge of the heist at Adriano's Jewelry Store in Beverly Hills. Fearful that Foley *et al.* are on to his criminal schemes, Dent orders the Detroit policeman killed, but the attempt is foiled. After discovering that stripclub owner Nikos Thomopolis (Paul Guilfoyle) is tied to Dent and his international gun smuggling operations, the trio returns to the Shooting Club, where they figure out the next "Alphabet Crime" will be at the City Deposit Bank. Foley and Rosewood impede the crime in progress and follow the gang to the Playboy mansion where Foley locates snide Dent among Hugh Hefner's guests and accuses Dent of gun-running. The next target of Dent's men is his own Empyrean Race Track, which he plans to rob to gain the insurance. In the robbery Karla kills Cain, to get him out of the way and thrust the blame for the robbery on him. Chief Lutz falls for the bait and announces the case is solved, but Foley, Rosewood, and Taggart know differently and, in a final showdown over heavy odds, they corral the surviving members of Dent's gang. Lutz is fired by the mayor for insolence and incompetence, and after a reunion with the recuperating Bogomil, Foley returns to Detroit to deal with Inspector Todd (Gil Hill).

It is a Hollywood maxim that no sequel can or does equal its predecessor, and *Beverly Hills Cop II* is no exception. "The convoluted writing credits give a good indication of the scissors-and-paste story-line of *Beverly Hills Cop II,* which relies on an unlikely series of coincidences where it is not a straight retread of the first installment.... The Foley character has also undergone a disappointing transformation in a conservative direction.... Foley no longer represents the social threat of the street-wise black guy; even as an undercover cop he has become upwardly mobile, sporting a $2,000 suit and a red Ferrari" (Adam Barker, British *Monthly Film Bulletin*). Roger Ebert in his *Movie Home Companion 1988* (1987) was equally unimpressed. "It's filled wall-to-wall with the kind of routine action and violence that Hollywood extrudes by the yard and shrink wraps to order. But it makes no particular effort to be funny, and actually seems to take its ridiculous crime plot seriously—as if we cared.... What I don't like is the unstated assumption, in *Cop II,* that he [Murphy] is funny by definition, and that anybody who gets in his way is a fool.... Because he's the star, of course, no one else in the plot is allowed to lay a glove on him."

As indicated, many of the scenes play like reruns of the first *Beverly Hills Cop:* Foley's conning of Inspector Todd, his conflicts with the stodgier, more prejudiced members of the Beverly Hills law enforcement department, etc. (When Chief Lutz screams to Foley, "I want you out of this department," the nonplussed out-of-towner quips, "Is this a black thing?") There are moments to be savored, though, such as the gambit where Foley, caught by Lutz leafing through police files, pretends to be Johnny Wishbone, a crazy psychic from St. Croix. Less effective, but still amusing, is the protracted sequence where Foley convinces a construction crew renovating a Beverly Hills home on Hillcrest Drive that they are doing the job wrong: "There are supposed to be *no* right angles," shouts an irate Foley. (Once the crew leaves in shock, he moves into the temporarily vacant white manse.) Another new twist to the sequel is the "humanizing" of the policemen. We learn that Taggart's wife has left him (she later returns), that Rosewood in his private life is an off-the-wall guy, and that Bogomil has an attractive, very nice daughter (Alice Adair).

Made on an estimated negative cost of $20,000,000, *Beverly Hills Cop II* grossed $80,900,000 in domestic film rentals. Even with the reduced profits, rumors insist a *Beverly Hills Cop III* could happen.

13. The Big Bird Cage (New World, 1972). Color, 93 minutes.

Producer Jane Schaffer; *director/screenplay* Jack Hill; *art director* Ben Otico; *set decorator* Marshall Henry; *makeup* Ray Solomon; *music* William A. Castleman, William Loose; *production supervisor* Carl B. Raymond; *assistant director* Paul MacLang; *camera* Philip Sacdalan; *editors* James Mitchell, Jere Huggins.

Cast: Pam Grier (Blossom); Anita Ford (Terry Rich); Candice Roman (Carla); Teda Bracci (Bull Jones); Carol Speed (Mickie); Karen McKevic (Karen); Sid Haig (Django); Marissa Delgado (Rina); Vic Diaz (Roccio); Andy Centenera (Warden Zappa); Rizza Fabria (Lin Tsiang); Wendy Green (Gerdie); Subas Herrero (Moreno).

"Women so hot with desire they melt the chains that enslave them!" insisted the advertising campaign for this sexploitation feature. Geared as a calculated followup to the successful *The Big Doll House* (q.v.), *The Big Bird Cage* is less satisfying in all departments except for the set piece of the title.

Blossom (Pam Grier) sings at a tropical nightclub in the Philippines, which boasts a sign at the front door, "Check firearms here." After performing one evening she and her comrades rob the premises to support their revolution cause, with Blossom wielding a machine gun beside her boyfriend Django (Sid Haig). (Obviously, Blossom is a no-nonsense type. At one point a fellow revolutionary says, "If only we had more women like her. What a revolution we could have." But this budding counterpart to Rambo has her feminine side as she and Django later engage in a mudfight frolic.) Some of Blossom's female co-conspirators are caught by the police and sent to a government jungle work camp outside of Manila controlled by the sadistic Warden Zappa (Andy Centenera), the type of crude man who kicks dogs and snarls at his prisoners, "No fornication of any kind with anyone ever." He advises the women that to escape is futile because the guard dogs "...know who you are and they will always be able to find you no matter what or how far you run." Among the inmates are Bull Jones (Teda Bracci), a Bette Midler act/lookalike; Terry Rich (Anita Ford), a luscious actress imprisoned because of flagrant indiscretions with politicians; and Mickie (Carol Speed), a diminutive black girl. And there is Roccio (Vic Diaz), the pudgy gay prison guard. At the compound those girls who do not meet their work quotas in the fields or who are caught lying or stealing are put to work in the Big Bird Cage. This is a forbiddingly tall sugar mill made of bamboo. "You don't ever come out for anything," warns one frightened prisoner. In fact it is a custom for prisoners to take discovered informers and toss them from the heights.

Blossom and Django infiltrate the prison and incite a bloody riot that turns into a holocaust. They burn down the compound and escape down the rapids, with the prison guards in quick pursuit. A few of the girls survive to make it to safety and (literally) sail off into the sunset.

Shot economically (and primitively) in the Philippines, *The Big Bird Cage* sounds far more lurid and enticing than it actually is. There are moments when the film takes a jovial turn, as when one female inmate says to another, "Anyone know a new dirty joke?" And in case the viewer can forget for a moment that this is a softcore pornography outing, the erstwhile hero says of the escaping women prisoners, "You're lookin' good, girls. You're lookin' good!"

Variety's Addison Verrill noted, "The women's prison epic is about as hardy a cinema chestnut as one can find these days, but it's a perfect showcase for the nudity, sex, violence, raw language and comic relief necessary in this type of exploitation programmer. All the ingredients are here, and pic should rate high in the urban saturation and suburban drive-in blood-and-bosoms markets. . . . Happily audiences for this type of feature couldn't care less about histrionics as long as blouses are kept unbuttoned."

14. The Big Bust-Out (New World, 1973). Color, 75 minutes.

Producer/director Richard Jackson; *screenplay* Sergio Garrone; *music* Burt Rexon, Elsi Mancuso; *wardrobe* Patti Kidwell; *assistant director* Serge Pettrich; *sound* Joseph Slemmer; *camera* Robert Galeassi; *editors* Cesare Bianchini, Barbara Pokras.

With: Vonetta McGee, Monica Taylor, Linda Fox, Karen Carter, Gordon Mitchell, Christin Thorn, Tony Kendall, William Berger, Mara Krup, George Dolph, Rebecca Mead, Miller Drake.

An Italian-made entry starring rising black star(let) Vonetta McGee as one of a disparate group of prisoners (of varying nationalities and assorted criminal offenses) incarcerated in a high security prison somewhere in Italy. Seven of these assorted females become co-conspirators against the sadistic cellblock matrons. They make their escape to the home of an ex-boyfriend of one of them, with a nun (!) in tow. He betrays them and sells them into white slavery. They soon escape from their new captors, but this is only the start of a long perilous journey. Before the bloody finale, several of the inmates and the nun have died.

Filled with the obligatory scenes of nudity, lesbianism, men brutalizing the "weaker" sex, and amateurish performances, this dubbed-for-American release entry did little to elevate the career of anyone involved.

15. The Big Doll House (New World, 1971). Color, 93 minutes.

Executive producers Eddie Romero, John Ashley; *producer* Jane Schaffer; *director* Jack Hill; *screenplay* Don Spencer; *production designer* Ben Otico; *set decorator* Bobby Bautista; *makeup* Antonio Artiesda; *wardrobe* Felisa Salcedo; *music* Hall Daniels; *assistant director* Maria S. Abelardo; *special effects* Teofilo C. Hilario; *camera* Freddie Conde; *supervising editor* Millie Paul; *editor* Cliff Fenneman.

Cast: Judy Brown (Collier); Roberta Collins (Alcott); Pam Grier (Grear); Brooke Mills (Harrad); Pat Woodell (Bodine); Sid Haig (Harry); Christiane Schmidtmer (Miss Dietrich); Kathryn Loder (Lucian); Jerry Franks (Fred); Jack Davis (Dr. Phillips); Gina Stuart (Ferina); Letty Mirasol (Leyte); Shirley De Las Alas (Guard); *and:* Siony Cordona, Myrna De Vera, Kathy McDaniels.

Warden of the raggedy prison in this Philippines-lensed sexploitation picture is the well-bred Miss Dietrich (Christiane Schmidtmer), who is allied with the sinister Colonel Mendoza, head of the secret police. Among her assistants is the newcomer Dr. Phillips (Jack Davis) who has the mistaken notion of wanting to treat the prisoners more humanely, even if it means less torturing, exploiting, and humiliating of the girls. The inmates include Harrad (Brooke Mills), a junkie who killed her baby, and Bodine (Pat Woodell), a political prisoner. Grear (Pam Grier) is a hustler whose "john" worked for the government, and she happened to overhear things she should not have. As a result she has a thirty-year sentence.

Tough-as-nails Grear refers to herself as the "old man," and she forces the others to respect her. (The only one she really fears is even tougher Lucian [Kathryn Loder], the sadistic prison guard.) Red-headed Collier (Judy Brown) is Grear's love interest (though Grear certainly does not believe in the etiquette of courtship — when Collier gets out of line, possessive Grear barks, "Get your ass back here or I'll cave it in!") Grear has no use for the opposite sex. As she informs horny Harry (Sid Haig), one of the drivers who visits the prison frequently with deliveries, "You're rotten, Harry . . . You know why? 'Cause you're a man. All men are filthy. All they ever want to do is to get at you. . . . But no more . . . I'm not goin' to let a man's filthy hands touch me again!" As it develops, Grear is the warden's stool pigeon, but she is not above pilfering through the administrator's private office.

It is Harry and Fred (Jerry Franks) who help some of the girls escape. Along the way, Harrad kills Grear the informer and is herself later killer by the pursuing guards.

All the requisite ingredients of a proper sexploitation picture are encased in *The Big Doll House*. At the least excuse, the women prisoners are stripped naked; they take frequent showers; they engage in mud wrestling, scampering in the slimy ooze; they are often tortured (one of them is tied to a rack and a cobra lowered onto her — a scene full of phallic and Freudian implications). Much is done to insure that as many as possible sexual fantasies are fulfilled in the course of the film. At one point the women appear vulnerable, which leads to their being subjected to bondage and sadism, with recurring shots of half-naked prisoners being flogged. The film touts the chauvinistic conceit that all women are sexually starved and eager to be raped. Sid informs Fred, "They are so horny . . . sometimes at night you can hear them honking." There is lesbian and heterosexual coupling. And to be sure no one's fancies are ignored, the other side of the coin is shown: the brutally rugged female prison guards, cooly sadistic prisoner-keeper Miss Dietrich, and of course, the street-wise, statuesque Grear, who can hold her own against any odds. These odds include females who can match the men in any contest of mental or physical will and control. One later scene during the prison riot and escape has some of the women raping a male guard.

The Big Doll House was the real start of Pam Grier's film career. The Air Force brat cousin of ex-football-player-turned-actor Rosey Grier, she had been spotted in a Colorado beauty contest and invited to Hollywood where, after an abortive romance with basketball star Kareem Abdul-Jabbar, she sought a modeling and acting career. She had a brief cameo in Russ Meyer's *Beyond the Valley of the Dolls* (1970). When nothing further materialized, she took a post as a switchboard operator at American International Pictures, which led to her being cast in *The Big Doll House*. With her jaunty presence and her striking physique, 5'8" Grier was the perfect person to handle action and sexploitation roles, especially when it was discovered black players in blaxploitation films were hot box-office. Unlike other black actresses who came and went after a picture or two, Grier was an innately talented actress who could, and did, jump from one screen role to another, always bringing authority, allure, and a subtle, vulnerable friendliness to her characterizations.

The success of *The Big Doll House* — it grossed $5,000,000 in domestic film rentals! — led to Grier performing in several other Philippines-shot exploitive low budget features. (Because the pictures were shot on the cheap, there was nothing glamorous about being on location outside of Manila. For example, instead of the typical "honeywagon" or comfort station on the outdoor set, Pam Grier would be given a shovel and pointed in the direction of a nearby bush.) *The Big Bird Cage* (q.v.), *Black Mama, White Mama* (1972) (q.v.), *Twilight People* (1972) (q.v.), and *Women in Cages* (1972), the latter directed by Cirio Santiago and co-starring Judy Brown, were among the Philippines films.

16. The Big Score (Almi, 1983). Color, 85 minutes.

Executive producer Harry Hurwitz; *producers* Michael S. Landes, Albert Schwartz; *associate producer* Irving Schwartz; *director* Fred Williamson; *screenplay* Gail Morgan Hickman; *music* Jay Chattaway; *songs* Clyde Otis and Ana Iza Otis; Clyde Otis and Herman Kelly; Anthony B. Stephens; Peter Chapman; Charles Stepney; *wardrobe supervisor* H. Delton Williams; *stunt co-ordinator* John Sherrod; *assistant director* Marvin G. Towns, Jr.; *sound* Ray Cymossinki; *camera* Joao Fernandes; *editor* Dan Loewenthal.

Cast: Fred Williamson (Frank Hooks); John Saxon (Pete Davis); Richard Roundtree (Gordon); Ed Lauter (Chief Parks); Nancy Wilson (Angie Hooks); D'Urville Martin (Easy); Michael Dante (Goldie Jackson); Bruce Glover (Koslo); Joe Spinell (Mayfield); Frank Pesce (J.C.); Tony King (Jumbo Allen); James Spinks (Cheech Jones); Karl Theodore (Huge); Ron Dean (Kowalski); Jerome Landfield (Chief of Detectives); Chelcie Ross (Hoffa); Stack Pierce (New); Katherine Wallach (Prostitute); Ernest Perry, Jr. (Allen); Greg Noonan (Martin); Wilbert Bradley (Old Man); Phillip East (Al); Jenifer Hunt (Woman); Frank Viviqua (Maitre d'); Jenifer Curtis (Woman in Limbo); Camilla Long (Fat Girl); David Whittaker, Jack Wallace, Joe Krowka (Cops); Gerard Pedrini (Butler); Lee McClain (Bud).

Rugged, violent, but honest Chicago narcotics cop Frank Hooks (Fred Williamson) has become embittered fighting the system. He is hot after the town's big drug ring, and during a bloody narcotics bust he engineers, $1,000,000 of Mafia money disappears. Both the police (who toss him off the force) and the mob are after Hooks, convinced he must have the cache. Among those involved in the caper are Angie Hooks (Nancy Wilson), a club singer who hates the cynical changes in her man; Pete Davis (John Saxon) and Gordon (Richard Roundtree), two of Hooks's police pals, with Davis being killed on the case; Koslo (Bruce Glover) the sinister ganglord; Parks (Ed Lauter), Hooks's unamused superior on the force; Cheech Jones (James Spinks) as a hefty and hearty drug runner who ends up castrated and dead; and Easy (D'Urville Martin), an ex-convict narcotics user with an illegal arsenal of guns and dynamite available for Hooks's personal crusade.

The Big Score benefits from superior cinematography (by Joao Fernandes, who under his pseudonym of "Harry Flecks" did the lensing of such pornographic films as *Deep Throat* and *Devil in Miss Jones*. There is a good pounding score which accentuates the assorted chases and mayhem. Considering the tight budgets and inferior calibre of many of Fred Williamson's 1980s action films that he packaged personally (for his Po' Boy Productions), this one boasts a superior cast, especially Nancy Wilson in her film debut. She is rather convincing as his estranged wife who finds time to sing numbers at the club when she is not fortifying Hooks's pessimistic outlook on life. The interaction between the two is pleasantly reminiscent of the Sidney Poitier–Barbara McNair (also a vocalist) tandem in *They Call Me Mister Tibbs!* (1970) and *The Organization* (1971) (qq.v.).

The film's dialogue is rough and dirty, even if it is the expected tough, mean talk. (Reportedly Fred Williamson acquired several Gail Morgan Hickman scripts from Clint Eastwood that she had written as potential installments in Eastwood's "Dirty Harry" movie series and which he sold when he thought he had finished with his Harry Callahan adventures, which he obviously has not.) A blonde sexpot has a snappy interchange with the incorruptible Hooks:

"Say baby. Lookin' for some action?"

"I don't think they got a needle big enough to kill the shit you got."

"Well, you can kiss my ass."

So much for courtship.

Compared to several of Williamson's post–Hollywood stardom films which received spotty theatrical distribution, *The Big Score* did not go unnoticed by the critics. "The gritty South Side of Chicago, photographed by Joao Fernandes, works well as an ugly backdrop for the film. Williamson is more of a star presence than an actor. As a director, his work lacks distinction. *The Big Score* is rated R for a bloodbath of relentless violence and for its language" (Linda Gross, *Los Angeles Times*). Archer Winsten *(New York Post)* recorded, "Fred Williamson, known as 'The Hammer' when he was spreading terror and injury in the National Football League, again draws on his yen for mayhem in *The Big Score....*"

The Big Score's release on videocassette led Doug Brod (*Video Review* magazine) to enthuse, "...a gritty, though unexpectedly dumb cops-vs.-evildruglord flick. B stalwarts John Saxon and Richard Roundtree lend admirable support as his [Williamson's] buddies."

17. The Black Angels (Merrick International, 1970). Color, 89 minutes.
Producer Leo Rivers; *director/screenplay* Lawrence Merrick; *music* Lou Peralta; *camera* Merrick; *editor* Clancy Syrko.
Cast: King John III (Johnny Reb); Des Roberts (Chainer); Linda Jackson (Jackie); James Whitwirth (Big Jim); James Young-El (Jimmy); Clancy Syrko (Lieutenant Harper); Beverly Gardner (Wallflower); John Donovan (Frenchy); Gene Stowell (Fixer); Miller Pettit (One-Eye); Frank Donato (Clyde); The Choppers Gang (Themselves); Channon Scott (Jawbone); Robert Johnson (Knifer); Sumner Spector (Daddy).

The Wild One (1954) with Marlon Brando and *The Wild Angels* (1966) with Peter Fonda and Bruce Dern set the stage for a series of Hollywood motorcycle pictures, including the very superior *Easy Rider* (1969), starring Peter Fonda, Jack Nicholson and Dennis Hopper. Then along came *The Black*

Angels, an excessively violent chopper film. The ads warned, "God forgives. . . . The Black Angels don't!"

Taking into account the new cycle of black action pictures gaining popularity, filmmaker Lawrence Merrick concocted a scenario which featured a white cycle gang, the Serpents, headed by Chainer (Des Roberts), in mortal combat with a black one, the Chopper (a real-life California clan who played themselves in the film), led by snarling Knifer (Robert Johnson). When the Serpents learn that their newest member Johnny Reb (King John III) is really a black Chopper passing for white, warfare erupts between the two factions. Among the film's trashy songs are "Military Disgust" and "What's Going On." The entertainment trade journal *Boxoffice* magazine reported, ". . . this very topical, very tense study of modern-day American emotional elements emerges as a full-blown, compelling indictment of moral decay."

For the record, this film has no relationship to *The Black Angels* (1985), a hardcore pornographic film starring Candy Staton, Streeta Taylor, and Tash Voux.

18. Black Belt Jones (Warner Bros., 1974). Color, 85 minutes.

Producers Fred Weintraub, Paul Heller; *associate producer* Oscar Williams; *director* Robert Clouse; *story* Alex Rose, Weintraub; *screenplay* Williams; *set decorator* Charles Pierce; *music/music director* Luchi De Jesus; *music theme* Dennis Coffy; *music arrangers* Coffy, Mike Theodore; *fight coordinator* Robert Wall; *sound* Darin Knight; *sound effects* Marvin Kerner; *special effects* Gene Griggs; *camera* Kent Wakeford; *editor* Michael Kahn.

Cast: Jim Kelly (Black Belt Jones); Gloria Hendry (Sidney Byrd); Scatman Crothers (Pop Byrd); Alan Weeks (Toppy); Eric Laneuville (Quincy); Andre Phillipe (Don Steffano); Vincent Barbi (Big Tuna); Nate Esformes (Roberts); Malik Carter (Pinky); Mel Novak (Blue Eyes); Eddie Smith (Oscar); Alex Brown (Plumber); Clarence Barnes (Tango); Earl Brown (Jelly); Esther Sutherland (Lucy); Sid Kaiser (Ellis); Doug Sides (Militant); Jac Emil, Wayne Musgrove, Ray C. Davis, Leroy Wofford, Earl Maynard (Bogarts). [Note: "Bogarts," or sometimes "Bogards," is ethnic talk for a tough dude, derived from the characters played onscreen by Humphrey Bogart.]

Producers Fred Weintraub and Paul Heller hit paydirt with their Bruce Lee karate film, *Enter the Dragon* (1973) (q.v.), which introduced black black-belt champion Jim Kelly to film audiences. When "chop socky" star Lee died in 1973, the movie producers turned to martial arts expert Kelly for their next feature, shrewdly anticipating that mixing two popular screen genres (kung fu and black action) could only mean additonal box-office success. To direct this carbon copy Lee-type adventure, they utilized Robert Clouse, who had helmed *Enter the Dragon.* The screenplay was by associate producer Oscar Williams, the black filmmaker who had come to screen prominence as producer, director and scenarist of *The Final Comedown* (1972) (q.v.).

When drug-and-gambling bigshot Pinky (Malik Carter) cheats Mafia boss Don Steffano (Andre Phillipe), the latter orders henchmen Blue Eyes (Mel

Jim Kelly and Gloria Hendry in *Black Belt Jones* (1974).

Novak) and Big Tuna (Vincent Barbi) to demand retribution from the cheater. Pinky is told his debt will be forgotten *if* he persuades Pop Byrd (Scatman Crothers) to sell his karate school to Don Steffano. The school is situated in the midst of a redevelopment area in Watts that the ganglord is planning to control. Pinky and his hoods lean on Pop, but he refuses to budge and is aided by students Quincy (Eric Laneuville) and Toppy (Alan Weeks), as well as by federal agent and kung fu expert Black Belt Jones (Jim Kelly) whose agency superior is investigating Mafia activities. Pop is killed accidentally by Pinky's men. At the funeral Jones meets Pop's daughter, Sidney (Gloria Hendry), who proves to be expert at kung fu. She later holds off Pinky's men, but thereafter his thugs kidnap Quincy and hold him for ransom. Jones and Sidney counterpunch by storming the Mafia headquarters, aided by a crew of female acrobats. They take $250,000 and use it to ransom Quincy. The climactic showdown occurs at a car wash, with Jones and Sidney emerging the victors.

Artistically this black-power-versus-the-Mafia exercise was no better nor worse than many other such comic book kung fu–dom excursions. Thankfully its fast pacing diverts the viewers from many of the juvenile situations, performances, and frequently stilted dialogue, and the result is entertaining. The *New York Times*'s A.H. Weiler rated it "basically silly" and "obvious as a karate chop." As for the performances, Verinia Glaessner (British *Monthly Film Bulletin*) decided, "Jim Kelly plays Jones as a carbon copy of Bruce Lee (even reproducing Lee's characteristic facial mannerisms and stances in the fight sequences), but Gloria Hendry is a capable and charismatic Sidney, and Eric Laneuville as Quincy gives a notably unhyped performance which is a joy to watch amid the array of black stereotypes decorating the fringes of the action."

Here stiff and stoic Kelly proved himself bankable at the box-office, an ideal role model for black youth more used to identifying with the screen shenanigans of black gangsters, pimps, and the like. But just as it was the popularity of the genres that made Kelly a fad movie success, so it was the downslide of these genres that would end his screen tenure in less than a decade.

19. Black Caesar (American International, 1973). Color, 94 minutes.

Executive producer Peter Sabiston; *producer* Larry Cohen; *co-producer* Janelle Cohen; *associate producer* James P. Dixon; *director/screenplay* Larry Cohen; *art director* Larry Lurin; *music* James Brown, Fred Wesley; *music supervisor* Barry De Vorzon; *song* Bodie Chandler and De Vorzon; *technical adviser* Paul Stader; *camera* Fenton Hamilton; *Harlem sequence camera* James Signorelli; *editor* George Folsey, Jr.

Cast: Fred Williamson (Tommy Gibbs); Phillip Roye (Joe Washington); Gloria Hendry (Helen); Julius W. Harris (Mr. Gibbs); Val Avery (Sal Cardoza); Minnie Gentry (Mama Gibbs); Art Lund (John McKinney); D'Urville Martin (Reverend Rufus); William Wellman, Jr. (Alfred Coleman); James Dixon (Bryant); Myrna Hansen (Virginia Coleman); Don Pedro Colley (Crawdaddy); Patrick McAllister (Grossfield); Cecil Alonzo (Motor); Allen Balley (Sport); Omer Jeffrey (Tommy Gibbs as a Boy); Michael Jeffrey (Joe Washington as a Boy); Francisco De Garcia (Taxi Driver); Larry Lurin (Carlos).

British Release Title: *The Godfather of Harlem.*

Society in general, and Americans in particular, have always been intrigued by success stories, especially those about self-made individuals who attain material splendor. *Black Caesar* is such a celluloid saga, tracing the rise of Tommy Gibbs, a power-hungry black mobster who admits, "I'm trying to break into the business at the top."

In a Harlem tenement, corrupt white cop John McKinney (Art Lund) is making his "collections." When young shoeshine boy Tommy Gibbs (Omer Jeffrey) gets in his way accidentally, he slams him in the leg, leaving the black youth with a permanent physical and mental scar. The scene jumps to October 23, 1965, and continues the chronicle of game-legged Tommy Gibbs (Fred Williamson), now an adult. He cooly kills a gangster leader in full daylight and then goes downtown to Little Italy to visit Sal Cardoza (Val Avery), the New York City Mafia boss, demanding recognition after years of being abused and used by the Organization. "Don't I qualify?" he asks. "I spent eight years in some of your finest institutions." In exchange for agreeing to being the Family's trigger man, he is given full power over 127th and Edgecomb Avenue. To insure his position and life, he kills the downtown gang's bookkeeper and appropriates the tell-all ledgers which cover all transactions back to 1955. Next, prosperous Mafia attorney Alfred Coleman (William Wellman, Jr.) is annexed by Gibbs as an employee, and the fast-rising Gibbs shows his power and contempt by throwing Coleman and his voluptuous wife Virginia (Myrna Hansen) out of their fancy high rise apartment and taking it for himself. Later Cardoza is supplanted by Gibbs as crime lord. When Gibbs learns that the Mafia faction in California is fighting his attempt at total control, he arrives on the scene with his henchmen and they machine-gun-massacre the Cardoza brothers poolside. Meanwhile, Gibbs discovers that his girlfriend, Helen (Gloria Hendry), who had come to the West Coast to become a singer, has fallen in love with Gibbs's best friend, Joe Washington (Phillip Roye), and married him. Disillusioned but driven, Gibbs continues his lonely quest for power, intending to gain control over all the big cities, shaping his power from each and every ghetto. All these years rising police officer McKinney has watched angrily the rise of Gibbs and now joins forces with Coleman. They trick Helen into regaining the ledgers, and then they have Gibbs shot in the street. The badly wounded Gibbs asks Washington to help recover the ledgers. McKinney murders Coleman and Washington, intending to put the blame on Gibbs. In the final confrontation, Gibbs kills McKinney and weaves his way back to the ghetto to die in his old home.

To flesh out the tapestry of the Tommy Gibbs story, there is a wide array of supporting characters. There is the bogus Reverend Rufus (D'Urville Martin), a good-natured scam artist and a long-time friend of Gibbs. (Fast-talking Rufus, who would have made an excellent television evangelist, is fond of saying, "Never fear brother, I'm always here to save the souls and heal the ills and cash the checks.") Mama Gibbs (Minnie Gentry) was long ago deserted by her man and had to survive the Depression and the Harlem tenement life is best she (and little Tommy) could. Gibbs's father (Julius W. Harris), a cosmetic salesman, shows up in New York, and becomes the continuity in his son's slam-bang life, especially after Mama Gibbs dies. And balancing the picture are

Helen (Gloria Hendry) and Joe Washington (Phillip Roye), long-time friends of Gibbs who are aghast at his track record of mayhem but always remember the goodness that once guided him.

Black Caesar is filled with real (and sometimes commercially calculated) anger at the generations-old mistreatment of blacks by whites. It is the governing motif that turns good-natured young Tommy Gibbs into the hardened criminal. All his young life he has been put upon by "the Man," whether it be wealthy white people for whom his mother has always sweated, corrupt officials like Joe McKinney, law enforcement agencies which put him in prison, or the Mafia which exploited uptown Harlem and him. It is suggested, even demanded, that this reason (rationalization?) explains and purifies all of Gibbs's criminal activities. As an adult hoodlum his dream in general is to take charge of the Harlem underworld turf so he can help his people. (In his heinous rise to power this is forgotten.) His goal in particular is to make life easier for his mother. (Ironically, when he has the funds to give her anything she desires, she admits she is happy being a domestic and that she wants to remain a servant, especially if her emancipation would have to come from the ill-gotten gains of his wrongdoings.) It is not long after he achieves some of his success before Gibbs focuses all his ambition and action on pleasing himself. When he confiscates the Colemans' expensive upper East Side Manhattan apartment, the catharsis is apparent. As he evicts the stunned Colemans, he spits out to the white couple, "I grew up wearing your things, mister . . . everything you wore out, got dirty or you outgrew. I even ate your leftovers." Alone in the apartment, he angrily tosses some of the couple's prize possessions over the balcony.

The crux of Gibbs's fury at the "corrupt" white world is Joe McKinney. It was the grafting, bigoted cop who told Tommy Gibbs the innocent boy, "I'll cut your black balls off" [if you get in my way] and who left Gibbs with a permanent limp leg. As Gibbs grabs more and more control over the years he keeps his eye on McKinney but does not eliminate the now-promoted police politician. "I want him nice and fat before I kill him," Gibbs gloats. When the inevitable showdown occurs it is a tough confrontation. Gibbs is surprised by a gun-wielding McKinney and made to shine the policeman's shoes. The impact on Gibbs is tremendous, and soon he grabs the shoeshine box and wields it at his opponent. In the fight for control, Gibbs is the victor. He slaps black shoe polish over the cowering cop's face and punches him relentlessly, hysterically demanding he sing "Mammy" like Al Jolson would have. Then he kills his longtime enemy.

When one realizes that Sammy Davis, Jr., was the original choice to star in *Black Caesar,* it is a blessing that Fred Williamson played the role instead. It is perhaps the ex-footballer's most sensitive performance to date (and certainly the role that did the most for his screen career). With his powerful frame, good looks, and cultured demeanor (a bit at odds with his characterization) he gives the focal part conviction, not only in the menacing gangster fisticuffs and gunplay that punctuates the story at every turn, but in the more intimate one-on-one encounters. There are wonderfully touching sequences between Williamson's Tommy Gibbs and Julius W. Harris as the long-absent father.

When the two visit their deserted old tenement home in Harlem, the interchange is fully convincing. Gibbs Sr. explains that he was just a kid when he met Tommy's mother and that he wasn't ready for the responsibility of family life. After the horrors of the Depression he had joined the army in World War II and, as one thing after another just happened, he never came back. Williamson's character in this segment changes subtly from anger to hurt and to gradual understanding. Later, after Mama Gibbs dies, father and son meet at the cemetery. Gibbs Jr. attempts to make amends with his father, who, bewildered by his son's power and evil deeds, gently declines to be a part of the boy's sinister life.

For some, *Black Caesar* is merely a crafty updating of *Little Caesar* (1931) and many subsequent gangster yarns, including *The Godfather* (1972) jazzed up to contemporary standards. But producer-director-screenwriter Larry Cohen makes *Black Caesar* a full-bodied entity of its own. Granted the low budget is evident in the tacky sets and production values, but when the film focuses on the streets of Harlem it breathes with real life. One of the motion picture's and the decade's more memorable cinema moments is the long section filmed in midtown Manhattan as Tommy Gibbs is gunned down in front of the elegant Tiffany's store. As *Variety* applauded, "Remarkable photography, particularly in those sequences in which Williamson, seriously wounded, staggers through the packed street of N.Y. in an effort to escape a police assassin.... Cohen stages these sequences, obviously unrehearsed, so adroitly that he gets sock reaction from the crowds." *Video Review* magazine would decide, "*Black Caesar* is violent, well-acted and full of Cohen's trademark quirkiness."

(Larry Cohen's credits include *It's Alive* [1976], *The Private Files of J. Edgar Hoover* [1977], *It Lives Again* [1980]. In 1972 he had directed the small-budgeted *Bone,* which featured black actor Yaphet Kotto in an arty tale of suburban domestic friction. The other actors, including Joyce Van Patten and Andrew Duggan, were all white. According to Cohen, "American International called me up and said, 'Listen, we want to make some pictures with black casts and you know how to direct those black actors.' One black actor in my first film and 'you know how to direct those black actors!'")

Besides the raw visual action, there is a pulsating soundtrack by the "Godfather of Soul" James Brown, punctuated by the song "Down and Out in New York City" by Bodie Chandler and Barry De Vorzon.

Mainstream critics were cautious in their praise of the film ("evolves more as exploitation than as clear, convincing exposition of man's inhumanity to man," said A.H. Weiler, *New York Times*) but the public endorsed the film at the box-office. It grossed a hefty $2,000,000 in domestic film rentals and would spawn a sequel, *Hell Up in Harlem* (1974) (q.v.).

20. Black Chariot (Goodwin, 1971). Color, 90 minutes.

Producer/director/screenplay Robert L. Goodwin.

With: Bernie Casey, Barbara O. Jones, Richard Elkins, Paulene Myers, Gene Dynarski, Mike Warren, Dennis Pryor.

In the summer of 1970 Robert L. Goodwin, a black TV scriptwriter, decided to film a project about which he felt intensely. To raise the necessary financing, he sent a dozen youths, including three of his own, into the black community streets of Los Angeles to gain the needed cash. His original budget was $125,000, but he had to settle for a disappointing $44,000, which caused him to shoot the interiors (at Carthay Studios) on videotape and the exteriors (on Central Avenue) in 35 mm. Touted as the first *all*-black motion picture, which it was not, the film premiered at Santa Monica Civil Auditorium on July 2, 1971, at $10 a seat. The reviewers were not appreciative. "Produces responses like boredom, anger, resentment, and disrespect for the lack of talent displayed and passed off..." (Douglas Jones, *The Hollywood Reporter*). "Storyline is so confused and jumbled as to be unintelligible" *(Variety)*. "Displays tremendous feeling but no sense of pace or style or, in some instances, even characterization. Yet the sheer dint of his conviction makes the film at last come alive in its final and most significant moments" (Kevin Thomas, *Los Angeles Times*). The film soon disappeared from view.

Bernie Casey plays a cynical drifter/loner who joins a Black Panther–type organization when he is seduced by one of the group's leaders (Barbara O. Jones). Just as his commitment to the militant group becomes sincere, members of the pack are killed by a black cop after being betrayed by one of their number. Jones demands that the traitor die, but Casey insists that such retribution is only mimicking how white people would handle the matter. For once, he is thinking first instead of acting out his responses.

Among the other players in *Black Chariot* are Richard Elkins as the cool organization leader; Paulene Myers as Casey's devoutly religious mother; and Gene Dynarski as the liberal white doctor held prisoner while Casey is treated for a gun wound.

Ex-professional football player (with the Los Angeles Rams and San Francisco 49ers) Bernie Casey began his film and television career in the late 1960s, and had already appeared in the feature film ...*Tick*...*Tick*...*Tick* (1970) (q.v.).

21. Black Cobra (Almi, 1986). Color, 87 minutes.

Executive producer Pino Burrichi; *producer* Luciano Appignani; *director* Stelvio Massi; *screenplay* Danilo Massi; *set designer* Franco Cuppini; *makeup* Pino Ferrante; *music* Paolo Rustichelli; *assistant director* Massi; *camera* Stefano Catalano; *editor* Alessandro Lucidi.

Cast: Fred Williamson (Police Detective Robert); Adlo Menegolino (Politician); Sabina Gaddi (Nurse); Laura Lancia (Girl); Ronald Russo (Alan); Rita Bartolini (Model); Luciana Cirenei (Neighbor); Riccardo Mioni, Claudio Zicchet, Angelo Ragusa, Pietro Sarubi, Umberto Moschini, Giovanni Cianfriglia (Stunts); *and:* Eva Grimaldi, Vassili Karis, Karl Landgren, Maurice Poli, Sabrina Siani.

One of Fred Williamson's Italian-produced action features churned out with even less care than most of his B-grade movies of this period. Even Sylvester Stallone's crummy *Cobra* (1986), from which *Black Cobra* "borrowed" its title and "theme," is more enjoyable than this dubbed offering, which made its United States film bow on videocassette in 1988.

Once again Williamson is a cigar-smoking tough, this time a New York

City police detective named Robert. He is rough (he carries a .45 automatic and is not afraid of a shootout alone against many criminal scumbags), but he has his tender side (he has a cat at home), and he most certainly has an urbane eye for women, including a comely fashion photographer named Alyce, who is in peril. Masked crooks, with a penchant for motorcycle riding, are terrorizing the Big Apple, and it is Robert who tackles them almost singlehandedly. The climactic, elongated gun battle is pointless and disappointing.

22. The Black Eliminator (Movietime, 1978). Color, 90 minutes.

Executive producers Oscar L. Nichols, Dick Randell; *producer* Harry Hope; *director* Al Adamson; *story/screenplay* Hope; *art director* Eddie Garetti; *music/music conductor* Chuck Ransdell; *songs:* Chuck and Judith Ransdell, Jack Gross; *assistant director* Michael Dockman; *camera* Barry Craver; *editor* Dan Seeger.

Cast: Jim Kelly (Police Lieutenant John Ash); Aldo Ray (Mr. Verdy); Harold Sakato (Santavacino); Terry Moore (Marie [Joan Mason]); *and:* George Lazenby, Myron Bruce Lee, Patch Mackenzie, Bob Minor, April Sommers.

Take Jim Kelly (*Black Belt Jones* [q.v.]), Terry Moore *(Mighty Joe Young),* George Lazenby (the James Bond of *On Her Majesty's Secret Service*), Harold Sakato ("Odd Job" in *Goldfinger*) and Aldo Ray *(Battle Cry).* Put them together in one film and what have you got? A covey of actors fallen on hard times being non-directed by Al Adamson in a mishmash. It's allegedly about a martial arts expert police lieutenant (Kelly) out to stop a madman known as "the Pig" and his maniacal bloodthirsty bodyguard (Harold Sakato) from gaining control of a freeze bomb that will instantly kill anything in its range.

As is typical with so many of Adamson's productions, this is a paste-together of many film genres with sequences shot at different times and obviously no overall continuity. Like the rest of Adamson's oeuvre, it would be recycled several times under assorted titles, including *Death Dimension.*

23. Black Eye (Warner Bros., 1974). Color, 98 minutes.

Executive producer Jack Reeves; *producer* Pat Rooney; *associate producer* Larry Noble; *director* Jack Arnold; *based on the novel* "Murder on the Wild Side" *by* Jeff Jacks; *screenplay* Mark Haggard, Jim Martin; *art directors* Charles Pierce, John Rozman; *music* Mort Garson; *sound* Bud Alper, Gene Ashbrook, Andrew Gilmore; *camera* Ralph Woolsey; *editor* Gene Ruggiero.

Cast: Fred Williamson (Shep Stone); Rosemary Forsyth (Miss Francis); Teresa Graves (Cynthia); Floy Dean (Diane Davis); Richard Anderson (Raymond Dole); Cyril Delevanti (Talbot); Richard X. Slattery (Bill Bowen); Larry Mann (Reverend Avery); Bret Morrison (Max Majors); Susan Arnold (Amy Dole); Frank Stell (Chess); Nancy Fisher (Vera Brownmiller); Teddy Wilson (Lindy); Gene Elman (Lou Siegal); Wayne Sutherland (Worm); Jim Malinda (Pusher); Joanne Bruno (Moms); Belinda Balaski (Mary); Edmund Penny (Marcus Rollo); *and:* Marie Cheatham, Bob Minor, John Moskoff, Nick Ramus, Clyde Ventura.

Jim Kelly in *The Black Eliminator* (1978).

"What could have been an almost savage commentary, juxtaposing the traditional private eye to a modern California backgroud of Jesus freaks, pornographic film makers, the narcotics trade and transitional sexual styles, stutters over the script and its performances" (Lawrence Van Gilder, *New York Times*).

Because he killed a drug dealer (responsible for his sister's death from a dope overdose), police lieutenant Shep Stone (Fred Williamson) is suspended from the force. He is now a private investigator in a California beach community. After discovering the corpse of prostitute Vera Brownmiller (Nancy Fisher) in his apartment house, he is attacked with a fancy cane by her murderer, Chess (Frank Stell). Afterwards, he is assigned to undercover work on the case by Lieutenant Bill Bowen (Richard X. Slattery). A lead to pornographic filmmaker Max Majors (Bret Morrison) is a dead end, but then he meets Raymond Dole (Richard Anderson) who wants him to find his daughter Amy (Susan Arnold). Stone traces her to a dissident born-again group led by the dishonest Reverend Avery (Larry Mann). The path takes him to Chess and to the finding of an important clue: the elaborate cane which he finds once held drugs. Two hoodlums take the stick from Stone, but later Max Majors and his

Fred Williamson and Teresa Graves in *Black Eye* (1974).

henchmen insist he still has it. The chase leads to a seaside service of Avery's flock, where Dole shoots Avery and nearly kills Amy before Stone intervenes. It develops that Amy is not actually Dole's daughter, but was a pusher who stole drugs from the tell-tale cane to help Avery's cause.

"By the halfway mark, the film's somewhat naive format has worn thin, with each new example of white decadence ushered on-stage like a variety number, while the obligatory fight, sub–Peckinpah car chases and truly awful slow-motion love scene all have a quite perfunctory air about them" (Gareth Jones, British *Monthly Film Bulletin*). Archie Ivy (*Soul* magazine) added, "At least Fred Williamson is becoming a decent actor; he gets enough work."

Fred Williamson's Shep Stone is no relation to Richard Roundtree's *Shaft* (1971) (q.v.). "Don't use that super-spade bullshit with me," says Stone, a very low-keyed fellow, who is closer to the Sam Spade–Philip Marlowe school of detection. Stone is living in a topsy-turvy world of fast-changing values, and if he is to survive he must somehow make sense of them. Directed by Jack Arnold (appreciated for such science fiction entries as *The Creature from the Black Lagoon,* [1954], and *The Incredible Shrinking Man* [1957]), *Black Eye* is a handsomely executed black action film with quite unusual leading ladies. Stone's black girlfriend Cynthia (Teresa Graves) is bisexual, and when she is not with Stone she is cavorting with white fashion designer Miss Francis (Rosemary Forsyth). This would be one of several mainstream films to examine the world of sleazy pornographic movies, but here the "hero" is not surprised but amused by the goings-on at Max Majors's soundstages.

24. Black Fist (Worldwide, 1977). Color, 94 minutes.

Executive produer Charles L. Hamilton; *producers* William Larrabure, William D. Sklar, Richard Kaye; *director* Timothy Galfas; *screenplay* Tim Kelly; *music* Warren Sams; *camera* unknown; *editor* Andrew Maisner.

Cast: Richard Lawson (Leroy Fist); Dabney Coleman (Heinekin); Robert Burr (Mr. Logan); *and:* Morris Buchanan, Carolyn Calcote, Ron Carson, Annazette Chase, Al Checco, Eddie Crawford, Stephanie Faulkner, Denise Gordy, H.B. Haggerty, Richard Kaye, John Wesley Rodgers, Ed Rue, Joseph Ruskin, Philip Michael Thomas.

According to screenwriter Tim Kelly in a 1986 article for *Los Angeles Reader, Black Fist* was engineered as part two of a trilogy. The first entry was produced in 1974 as *Bogard,* which is Harlem vernacular for a tough guy and derives from the type of rough screen characters played by Humphrey Bogart. The ads for the original release of *Bogard* read, "*Bogard.* Bet him to win . . . the meanest, baddest street fighter in town. Check it out!" In its first six days of regional release in March 1975, *Bogard* grossed $204,906 in six states.

The storyline of both *Bogard* and *Black Fist* focused on the rough-and-tumble street boxers who used no rules to flatten their opponents, and on whom spectators bet very heavily. There was a good deal of violence in the narrative as well as an interracial sex scene. That was cut when *Black Fist* had distribution in 1974 and 1975. The film had additional releasing in 1976 under the new title *The Black Street Fighter,* with some of the footage reassembled and new material added, largely from *Black Fist.* A good deal of the outdoor action was filmed in the area around West Hollywood's Sunset and Crescent Heights boulevards.

Black Fist (with the working title *Bogard II*) cropped up in 1976 and 1977, and it used not only footage shown already in *The Black Street Fighter* but materials and storyline order planned for Part III *(Bogard III).* However, the third part of the trilogy never happened. The black exploitation cycle had been waning for some time by now, and, more to the point, C.O.R.E. (Congress of Racial Equality) came down heavily on the first two films, the first one in particular. There were several points of contention because:

1) the filmmakers had used no creditable (onscreen) blacks on their crews
2) the movies were detrimental to the full human race
3) the films could misguide young viewers of any race
4) the films stir up racial intolerance
5) the films utilized too many derogatory remarks and cliches
6) the sexual scenes were "racially motivated"
7) black manhood was insulted in several scenes

Black Fist is the more coherent of the two films. Its now existing scenario format revolves around Leroy Fist (Richard Lawson), a strapping black man who is lured into joining the street fighter stable of promoter Mr. Logan (Robert Burr), an arrogant white guy who tells his latest moneymaker, "You fight mean, you win mean." Fist takes on all comers, including hulking white Moose, and is a winner. He and his girlfriend (Annazette Chase) start to enjoy the fruits of his combative life. But everything soon turns sour. "All I wanted in life was not to have to kiss white's ass," says Fist in a moment of drunken candor to a pal. But then he must deal with corrupt, bigoted Mr. Logan (who in turn is responsible to the big man, Mr. Ingo), who informs Fist, "You're nothing but a nigger living in someone else's world." By now the battle lines are drawn in and out of the street ring, with Fist and his black friends pitted against Logan and his obnoxious grafting policeman pal Heinekin (Dabney Coleman).

It is vicious, sleazy Heinekin who becomes Fist's chief opponent. The shady cop who collects kickbacks from anyone anyhow admits freely, "Some of us never pay the piper because some of us are the piper." He fears nothing, not even his enemy Fist when the latter tells him, "There's a black lion walking in your jungle."

In the jumbled chronicle, Fist purchases a nightclub, and later his pregnant wife and his brother-in-law are blown up in a car explosion planted by Logan. Then the final vendetta is set into motion as opposing forces wipe one another out: shooting, incinerating, pummeling their enemies to death. Soon Logan is killed, and Fist takes manipulative Heinekin for a one-way ride, hanging him up on a hook in a warehouse meat cooler room and leaving him to freeze to death. Then he trots to Ingo's plush Pacific Coast Highway house and shoots him.

Richard Lawson brings a convincing physical presence to his role, but the confused scenario makes it very tough to believe in his characterization, let alone in more natural players like Philip Michael Thomas. Most such genre films as this have the white criminal element played by amateurish or sleazy performers. Dabney Coleman, ever the professional as he would be in such TV series as "Mary Hartman, Mary Hartman" (1976–78), "Buffalo Bill" (1983–84) and "Slap Maxwell" (1987–88), brings gusto to his assignment. At one point when Heinekin is being his weasel self, a black moll slaps him and calls him "white trash." An amused Heinekin retorts, "They don't say white trash anymore."

Buried within the exploitable and indulgent elements of *The Black Street Fighter* and *Black Fist* is the thesis that for many blacks the only way out of ghetto hell is through sports; and even then there is a high price to pay, especially when their careers and fortunes are controlled by sinister white forces.

25. The Black Gestapo (Bryanston, 1975). Color, 88 minutes.

Executive producer Ronald K. Goldman; *producer* Wes Bishop; *director* Lee Frost; *screenplay* Frost, Bishop; *art director* Richard Schuyler; *set decorator* Conrad H. Ballard; *stunt co-ordinator* Paul Huckies; *assistant director* Mariann Proctor; *sound* George E. Carey; *camera* Derek Scott; *editor* Jounnu Terbush.

Cast: Rod Perry (General Ahmed); Charles P. Robinson (Colonel Kojah); Phil Hoover (Vito); Ed Cross (Delmay); Angela Brent (Marsha); Wes Bishop (Ernest); Lee Frost (Vincent); Dona Desmond (White Whore); Charles Howerton (Joe); Rai Tasco (Dr. Lisk); David Bryant (Pusher).

This example is surely one of the more crass, preposterous, and disturbing films of its vintage.

"Martin Luther King had a dream and it was blasted into eternity with him. I offer you reality. You've got to stand tall and demand your right. Nobody's going to give you a damn thing." So speaks Colonel Kojah (Charles P. Robinson), aide to General Ahmed (Rod Perry). Ahmed, an ex–Vietnam general, campaigned unsuccessfully for years for a grant from Los Angeles to operate a black organization (a people's army) devoted to solving the problems of the black ghetto. Ahmed had been against Kojah's militant idea to form a security force, fearful that the man's violent nature will ignite a battle between blacks and whites. Finally, discouraged by the failure of his own dream, he gives into the subordinate's scheme. What follows is a blood bath as the 1970s black gestapo (garbed in black military uniforms and red berets) start a reign of terror. (One of the film's more bizarre moments is to witness the Neo-Black Fascists during goose-stepping drill practice on tennis courts.) Finally the soul brothers of Watts fight back.

The presentation is cheap, trashy, and violent, and most of the acting — including that by the filmmakers in small roles as white gangland hood preying on the blacks — is embarrassingly inept. But Ron Perry as the General lends authority to his role, and the juxtaposed shots of Hitler's army on the march versus the new Los Angeles militia make their point. As in many of these low-budget efforts, there is a great deal of macho sexism as females (black and white) disrobe and become willing or unwilling playtoys for the men. There are moments of shocking, psychotic violence (a man castrated in the bathrub, a hood fired in a car crash), and surprising moments of much-needed comic relief. A black numbers racket underling is hit upon for $650 by a superior. He responds, "I'm sayin' that I'm tapped, broke, short of funds, hard up, impoverished, stripped, beat.... Besides, I don't have $650 to spare for shit like you."

26. The Black Godfather (Cinemation, 1974). Color, 97 minutes.

Producer/director/screenplay John Evans; *art director* Erik Nelson; *music/songs* Martin Yarbrough; *music arranger* Phil Moore; *special effects* Dick Parker; *camera* Jack Steely; *editor* Jim Christopher.

Cast: Rod Perry (J.J. [J. Johnson]); Damu King (Diablo); Don Chastain (Tony); Diane Sommerfield (Yvonne Williamson); Jimmy Witherspoon (Big Nate Williamson); Duncan McLeod (Lieutenant Joe Sterling); Tony Burton (Sonny Spider Brown); Anny Green (Honey); John Alderman (Cockroach); Betsy Finley (Junkie); Ken Bell (Eddie); Cinque Attucks (Winston); Tom Scott (Newscaster); Ricardo Brown (Danny); Kathryn Jackson (Mrs. Willa Mae Brown); Charles Lamkin (Danny's Father); Herb Jefferson, Jr. (Tommy); Ernie Banks (Cabbage); Randy Williams (Nick); *and:* Jim Arnett, Philip Clark, David Fields, Jack Oliver, Henry Sanders, Ken Spring.

"A good example of the type of black action movie that killed off the black movie market. Black audiences had just *had* it with this kind of slovenly, poorly scripted and directed mess" (Donald Bogle, *Blacks in American Film and Television,* 1988).

J.J. (Rod Perry) is a black soul brother gone bad, but he is resilient and seems invincible against the punks, hoods, and cops, whether black or white. He understands the system: "It has always been here and always be." And he reasons, "Money buys dignity. Poverty is a crime. Nobody asks you where you got your dollars; they ask you do you have it." His criminal activities lead him to elder black ghetto boss Big Nate Williamson (Jimmy Witherspoon), but J.J. wants to be modern and aggressive. He intends to fight the white Mafia contingent led by Tony (Don Chastain). His goal is to rid the black part of town from these infiltrators and to clean the streets of dope pushers. (Other types of reprehensible crime are okay in his book.) To further his aims his men masquerade as minions of Diablo (Damu King), who leads a black Guardian Angels type organization in Watts, and they attack and confuse all their enemies. In a clever ploy (used frequently in such films), J.J. enlists the aid of black domestics who work in influential white people's homes, and this handy spy network provides him with the means of crushing Tony. He learns that Burton's associate, a judge, is flying back with a shipment of heroin. J.J. and his henchmen attack the plane when it lands and kill the judge. The drugs are blown up with the plane, but this fact is unknown to Tony, who kills Big Nate and kidnaps his daughter Yvonne (Diane Sommerfield) — wanting his drug shipment back. In the showdown, self-sufficient Yvonne, a definite chip off the old block, eliminates Tony with a meat cleaver.

The romance sequences provide ample occasions for obligatory nudity, the nightclub scenes allow for good and bad soul music, and to give the violent chronicle its cloak of righteousness, the blacks spout such phrases as "Down with the Man," and, "Power to the people," in the midst of a never-ending chorus of, "Right on, brother."

"The movie drags," insisted Nora Sayre of the *New York Times,* "because so much of the action requires the characters to take messages to and from one another. The performers aren't too bad, but the karate is negligible." *Variety* weighed, "Rod Perry plays the title role, usually in convincing style, and Don Chastain is the chess-playing Mafia leader. He's rough enough but character hasn't been developed logically for type of role he portrays.... Jimmy Witherspoon as an elder black leader and Damu King give good accounts of themselves."

With its (derivative) action going full steam, *The Black Godfather* grossed $1,300,000 in domestic film rentals. Black filmmaker John Evans would also produce, direct and script the much-less-seen *Blackjack* (1978) which featured many of the cast from *The Black Godfather,* including Tony Burton, Diane Sommerfield, and Damu King.

27. Black Gunn (Columbia, 1972). Color, 94 minutes.

Producers John Heyman, Norman Priggen; *associate producers* Franklin Coen, Eric H. Senat; *director* Robert Hartford-Davis *based on an idea by* Hartford-Davis *and a screenplay by* Robert Shearer; *new screenplay* Franklin Coen; *art director* Jack DeShields; *set decorator* Cheryl Kearney; *music/music director* Tony Osborne; *sound* [Howard] Bud Alper; *sound re-recording* Peter Leonard, Gerry Humphreys; *special effects* Joe Lombardi, Paul Lombardi; *camera* Richard H. Kline; *editors* David De Wilde, Pat Somerset.

Cast: Jim Brown (Gunn); Martin Landau (Capelli); Brenda Sykes (Judith); Luciana Paluzzi (Toni); Vida Blue (Sam Green); Stephen McNally

(Laurento); Keefe Brasselle (Winman); Timothy Brown (Larry); William Campbell (Rico); Bernie Casey (Seth); Gary Conway (Adams); Chuck Daniel (Mel); Tommy Davis (Webb); Rick Ferrell (Jimpy); Bruce Glover (Ray Kriley); Toni Holt (Betty); Herbert Jefferson, Jr. (Scott Gunn); Jay Montgomery (Junkie); Mark Tapscott (Cassidy); Gene Washington (Elmo); Jim Watkins (Lieutenant Hopper); Jonas Wolfe (Val); Tony Young (Dell); Sandra Giles (Prostitute); Kate Woodville (Louella); Gyl Roland (Celeste); Lavelle Roby (Jane); Jeanne Bell (Lisa); Tony Giorgio (Ben); Frank Bello (Robbo); Arell Blanton (Television Director); Manuel DePina (Bowling Alley Manager); Deacon Jones (Himself).

"Most black gangster pix currently glutting the market are cheaply produced, either because this genre has a limited playoff or because filmmakers share one major-company president's view that the audiences don't care about possible 'cheating on the budget.' For whichever reason this ... production looks even tackier than most of its contemporary counterparts."

Gunn (Jim Brown) is the owner of a black nightclub in Los Angeles. His brother Scott (Herbert Jefferson, Jr.) belongs to BAG (Black Action Group), made up of Vietnam veterans. To finance their guerrilla raids, they rob a gambling shop owned by the Mafia. Black police Lieutenant Hopper (Jim Watkins) is sure the robbery was executed by BAG, while the Organization's leader, Capelli (Martin Landau), sends underling Ray Kriley (Bruce Glover) to Gunn's club to retrieve the vital ledger books acquired during the robbery. When Gunn refuses to help the mob, Scott turns up dead the next day and Gunn embarks on a vendetta. The trail leads to a civic fund-raising party hostessed by wealthy dabbler Toni (Luciana Paluzzi), where her boyfriend Winman (Keefe Brasselle) admits that Capelli is tied to Scott Gunn's death. Assisted by BAG and Hopper, Gunn corrals Capelli and his goons at a waterfront warehouse. Although he is wounded, he kills Capelli.

"*Black Gunn* contains most of the usual ingredients; an invincible hero (woodenly played by Jim Brown), a strong emphasis on violent action, a *Shaft*-style music score and a veneer of social consciousness. But despite several self-conscious references to Black Power and 'taking it to the man,' Gunn is in no sense a radical hero, significantly using the police group for personal revenge and nearly getting them wiped out in the process" (John Raisbeck, British *Monthly Film Bulletin*).

This project was originally conceived by its British backers for an English setting. The resultant film is filled with screen players having a lark (Martin Landau), those on their way down (Gary Conway, Keefe Brasselle of *The Eddie Cantor Story*), and a few on their way up (black performers Bernie Casey and Jeanne Bell). For the record, any resemblance between their derivative feature film and the stylish Blake Edwards TV series (1958–61) or even Edwards' abortive feature *Gunn* (1967), both of which starred an urbane Craig Stevens, is less than minimal.

28. The Black Klansman (US Films, 1966). 88 minutes.

Executive producer Joe Solomon; *producer/director* Ted V. Mikels; *screenplay* John T. Wilson, Arthur A. Names; *art director* Wally Moon;

wardrobe Vana Carroll; *music* Jaime Mendoza-Nava; *assistant director*
Names; *sound* Austin McKinney; *camera* Robert Caramico; *editor* Mikels.

Cast: Richard Gilden (Jerry Ellsworth [John Ashley]); Rima Kutner (An-
drea); Harry Lovejoy (William Rook); Max Julien (Raymond Estes); Jackie
Deslonde (Farley); Jimmy Mack (Lonnie); Maureen Gaffney (Carole Ann
Rook); William McLennan (Wallace); Gino De Augustino (Sawyer); Tex Arm-
strong (Jenkins); Byrd Holland (Mayor Buckley); Whitman Mayo (Alex);
Francis Williams (Ellis Madison); Ray Dennis (Sloane); William Collins
(Deputy); Anita Hurrel (Mrs. Ellsworth); Gary Kent (Watkins); Kirk Kirsey
(Delbert); Jimmy Robinson (Barnaby).

A.K.A. *I Crossed the Color Line.* British release title: *Brutes* (with 6
minutes trimmed from the running time).

In Turnerville, Alabama, the Knights of White Supremacy, a self-
contained branch of the Ku Klux Klan, burn a church in the black part of town
in retaliation for a black youth named Delbert (Kirk Kirsey) daring to enter and
to sit at the counter of a coffee shop in the white part of town. A six-year-old
girl is killed in the fire, and soon Delbert is found shot to death. When Jerry
Ellsworth (Richard Gilden), a pale-skinned black musician in Los Angeles,
learns of his daughter's murder, he returns home intending revenge. He poses
as a white building contractor named John Ashley and asks Klan leader
William Rook (Harry Lovejoy) to let him join the group. Also new in town are
Ellsworth's white mistress Andrea (Rima Kutner), along with her black friend
Lonnie (Jimmy Mack), and Raymond Estes (Max Julien), a black militant
drawn to Turnerville by Farley, Delbert's brother. Estes tells his black audience
in Turnerville, "You're all a bunch of cowardly Uncle Toms. . . . Follow me for
forty-eight hours and you'll not have to follow again. I work for two things.
Money and self respect in that order." Estes shoots a white man to make his
stand clear, while Ellsworth, dating Rook's daughter Carole Ann (Maureen
Gaffney) to find out who killed his child, is indoctrinated into the Klan. When
photographs of Andrea and Lonnie bedding together (contrived by the sheriff)
are circulated, Andrea, Lonnie, and Estes are captured by the Klan, who intend
to lynch them. Ellsworth learns it was Hook who threw the fire bomb and
draws a gun on the man. Estes and his helper are hanged during Rooks' escape
attempt, but Jerry shoots the culprit. The white mayor (Byrd Holland) promises to help the blacks of Turnerville, and Ellsworth sends Andrea away,
deciding, "My place is here. I think I can help. I don't know how. I'm just going
to have to find a way."

With all the Civil Rights agitation in the South in the mid-1960s, the topic
of *The Black Klansman* was timely. (The film concludes with a quotation by
the late President John F. Kennedy: "If an American because his skin is dark
cannot eat lunch in a restaurant open to the public, if he cannot send his
children to the best public school available, if, in short he cannot enjoy the full
and free life which all of us want, then who among us would be content to have
the color of his skin changed and stand in his place.") The subject in reverse
had already been done in the film *Black Like Me* (1964) starring James Whitmore, based on a best-selling book about a white man who darkens his skin
chemically to "pass" as a black. The problem with *The Black Klansman* is its

execution, which ranges from bad to worse. The cinematography is grainy, the acting puerile except by screen newcomer Max Julien, and many of the KKK scenes play like a bad serial.

> ELLSWORTH: (To the exalted cyclops, Rooks): You're not fit to be alive....
> (Then, yanking off his hair cover): I'm not even a white man. I'm a negro!
> ROOK: You're a nigger ... a real nigger. You got into my clan.... You dated my Carol Anne....

To round out the tawdriness of the piece, there is repeated softcore pornography, 1960s style, to "spice up" the proceedings. Ted V. Mikels would go on to direct that most awful film, *The Astro-Zombies* (1968) starring John Carradine.

29. Black Lolita (Parliament, 1975). Color, 85 minutes.

Executive producer Parker Johnson; *producer/director* Stephen Gibson; *screenplay* Gibson, Mike Brown; *music supervisor* Steve Dexter; *sound* Bruce Scott; *camera* Gibson.

Cast: Yolanda Love (Lolita); Ed Cheatwood (Cleon); Joey Ginza (Buddah); Susan Ayres (Shirley); Zenobia Wittacre (Pearl); Larry Ellis (Tinker).

Promoted as the first black action picture to be filmed in 3-D, the ads for *Black Lolita* enthused, "Foxier than Foxy Brown. Deadlier than Cleopatra Jones. She's a one-woman blast of T.N.T."

Beautiful Lolita (Yolanda Love) is an up-and-coming vocalist who has worked her way up from poor beginnings. When she learns her aunt and uncle are being intimidated by hoodlum Buddah (Joey Ginza) and his men, she returns home seeking revenge. She sizes up the extent of Buddah's chokehold on the community and persuades her friends to help even the score. Tinker (Larry Ellis) is a master of disguises and a technical expert; Pearl (Zenobia Wittacre) and Shirley (Susan Ayres) are street-wise tarts with connections; and another friend is a karate expert/strategist. Together they rip Buddah off in a variety of escapades. Shirley and Pearl infiltrate his gang so Lolita can always be one jump ahead. She and her team hit and run at will. Eventually Buddah figures out the traitors in the group and there is a showdown at a closed amusement park, with a final, wild shootout on the merry-go-round.

The film starred Yolanda Love of Miss Black Galaxy fame and was promoted also under the alternate title *Bad Lolita* for distributors who were tired of the rash of black action pictures glutting the marketplace.

30. Black Mama, White Mama (American International, 1973). Color, 87 minutes.

Executive producer David J. Cohen; *producers* John Ashley, Eddie Romero; *director* Romero; *story* Joseph Vila, Jonathan Demme; *screenplay* H.R. Christian; *art director* Roberta Formosa; *music/music director* Harry Betts; *assistant director* Maria Abelardo; *sound* Gabriel Castellano; *camera* Jousto Paulino; *editor* Asagni V. Pastor.

Cast: Pam Grier (Lee Daniels); Margaret Markov (Karen Brent); Sid Haig (Ruben); Lynn Borden (Warden Densmore); Zaldy Zshomack (Ernesto); Laurie Burton (Logan); Eddie Garcia (Captain Alfredo Cruz); Alona Alegre (Juana); Dino Fernando (Rocco); Vic Diaz (Vic Cheng); Wendy Green (Ronda); Lotis M. Key (Jeanette); Alfonso Carvajal (Galindo); Bruno Punzalah (Truck Driver); Ricardo Herrero (Luis); Jess Ramos (Alfredo).

British release title: *Hot, Hard and Mean.*

Ever since Hollywood shackled Sidney Poitier and Tony Curtis together in *The Defiant Ones* (1958) (q.v.), to tremendous artistic and financial results, filmmakers had the notion of replaying the situation. The time was right in the early 1970s, with screenwriters giving the original concept a twist by having the co-leads be women—attractive females, one black, one white—on the lam from the law.

Among the new arrivals at a women's prison in a Latin American island republic are cynical black prostitute Lee Daniels (Pam Grier), convicted on a trumped-up charge, and idealistic white guerilla fighter Karen Brent (Margaret Markov) from the United States. Both these shapely females draw the immediate interest of lesbian Warden Densmore (Lynn Borden), with Karen giving in to Densmore's advances, thinking it will benefit her escape plans. Pugnacious, resentful Lee starts a fight with Karen, and the two women end up chained together and being transferred to another prison compound. En route, Karen's revolutionary group ambushes the bus, and during the skirmish Lee and Karen escape. As always, they are at cross purposes: Lee wants to recoup a suitcase of money stolen from her pimp-spouse Vic Cheng (Vic Diaz), while Karen insists she must rejoin the revolutionaries to lead them to an arsenal cache. Using stolen nuns' garb for disguises, the two flee from the police. The latter is led by the humane Captain Alfredo Cruz (Eddie Garcia). Simultaneously Cheng and the guerrillas, led by Ernesto (Zaldy Zshomack), search for the women. Cruz relies on raunchy gangster Ruben (Sid Haig) to track the girls. Ruben and his men employ guard dogs to find the two escapees, but their animals are stolen by the guerrillas, who continue the pursuit. In the gunplay between Ruben's men and the revolutionaries, Ernesto's outfit is victorious. He meets the fleeing women, who now tolerate, and even like, each other, and he promises Lee he will get her to her destination. However, Cheng is waiting at the harbor where her boat is ready. Lee escapes while the guerrillas combat Cheng's men in a gun battle. Meanwhile, Karen dies in a bomb blast. When Cruz arrives the survivors scatter. The well-meaning police captain muses that he will be rewarded with a promotion for his "good" work.

Yet another of the several prison pictures starring Pam Grier, filmed in the Philippines with minimum budget and a sparse shooting schedule. In all these outings Pam Grier is an intriguing mixture of pugnacity and femininity, with a heavy dose of world-weary cynicism. As the emerging star of the black exploitation phenomenon she was definitely a unique role model, far different from any contemporary star(let) being manufactured by Hollywood.

Contrasting blonde Margaret Markov had already appeared in *The Hot Box* (1972), yet another prison yarn set in Latin America; it was co-scripted and produced by Jonathan Demme, who co-conceived the story idea for *Black*

Mama, White Mama. Grier and Markov would star together in *The Arena* (1974), (q.v.), this time sharing space in gladiatorial arenas of ancient Rome.

If the action market for whom this sex-and-sadism picture was geared was undemanding, *Variety* was more discerning and judged, "Performances range from bad to mediocre with one exception, that of Garcia which rises above the material by studious underplaying." The film grossed an impressive $1,000,000 in domestic film rentals.

31. Black Samson (Warner Bros., 1974). Color, 87 minutes.

Producer Daniel B. Cady; *director* Charles Bail; *story* Cady; *screenplay* Warren Hamilton, Jr.; *art director* Ed Cosby; *makeup* Tino Zacchia; *wardrobe* Peg Hopkins; *music* Allen Toussaint; *assistant director/stunt coordinator* Eddie Donno; *sound* Clark Will; *sound effects* Pat Somerset, Bob Biggart; *special effects* Roger George, Greg Auer, Howard Jensen; *camera* Henning Schellerup; *editor* Duane Hartzell.

Cast: Rockne Tarkington (Samson); William Smith (Johnny Nappa); Connie Strickland (Tina); Carol Speed (Leslie); Michael Payne (Arthur Haven); Joe Tornatore (Harry); Titos Vandis (Joseph Nappa); Napoleon Whiting (Old Henry); John Alderman (Michael Briggs).

The advertising copy endorsed, "Every Brother's Friend. Every Mother's Enemy," but the critics were not fooled. "In the guise of presenting a story of courage against odds, it is in truth, an ugly and brutal film, reveling in cruelty and the bloody abuse of women" (Lawrence Van Gelder, *New York Times*); "...reduces whites to corrupt sadistic scum and makes the black hero and heroine plaster-of-paris paragons of virtues" (Linda Gross, *Los Angeles Times*).

Soft-spoken, genteel Samson (Rockne Tarkington) owns a nightclub in south central Los Angeles called Samson's. He has a pet lion (a club mascot) and a faithful girlfriend names Leslie (Carol Speed). He also has a social conscience and patrols or prowls the streets of his neighborhood carrying a cane for protection. Meanwhile seedy white mobster Johnny Nappa (William Smith) wants to extend his criminal activities (especially drug pushing) to the streets around Samson's club. When Samson will not cooperate with Nappa the latter orders his blonde girlfriend Tina (Connie Strickland) to get hired at Samson's establishment as a nude dancer to feed him strategic information. When Nappa kidnaps Leslie to force Samson's hand, the latter arrives at the hood's warehouse for the combative showdown in which Samson employs the Japanese art of kindo fighting. The people of Samson's neighborhood join in to subdue the mobsters.

Herein enterprising producer and story conceiver Daniel B. Cady mixes piety (the Biblical-like bearded Samson mouths such quaint lines as "My people down there" and "Don't cry my streets") with graphic and titillating visuals (Nappa slashing at Leslie's breasts; the topless club dancers) in the hope of keeping audiences engrossed and film censors at bay. More engaging than this inconsistent Biblical Mr. Clean is Arthur Haven (Michael Payne) as the mortician/gangster with a penchant for cocaine. And not to be overlooked is intense, dignified and petite Leslie (played by the underrated actress Carol Speed,

Top: **Zaldy Zshomack, Pam Grier, and Margaret Markov in** *Black Mama, White Mama* **(1973).** *Bottom:* **Rockne Tarkington, Carol Speed, and player in** *Black Samson* **(1974).**

who appeared in such genre pieces as *The Big Bird Cage* and *The Mack* [qq.v.]). One wonders why the police are never around when they are needed and why the presence of Old Henry (Napoleon Whiting) for stereotyped ethnic comic relief is really needed.

This production was filmed in the summer of 1973 in Los Angeles and acquired by Warner Bros. in December 1973. At that time the original title of *Black Samson, White Delilah* was shortened to the final release tag.

32. Black Samurai (B.J.L.J. International, 1977). Color, 84 minutes.

Executive producer Laurence Joachim; *producer* Barbara Holden; *associate producer* John Bud Cardos; *director* Al Adamson; *based on the novel by* Marc Olden; *additional story idea* Marco Joachim; *screenplay* B. Radick; *makeup* Melanie Levitt; *music editor* Jim Landis; *Jim Kelly's fight scenes staged by* Kelly; *additional fight sequences staged by* Jace Khan; *camera* Louis Horvath; *editor* Landis.

Cast: Jim Kelly (Robert Sand); Bill Roy (Janicot); Roberto Contreras (Victor Chavez); Marilyn Joi (Synne); Essie Lin Chia (Toki Konuma); Biff Yeager (Pines); Charles Grant (Bones); Jace Khan (Jace); Erurn Fuller (Bodyguard); Peter Dane (Farnsworth); Felix Sella (Rheinhardt); Cowboy Lang (Himself); Little Tokyo (Himself); Jerry Marin (Shotgun Spiro); Alfonzo Walters, Charles Walter Johnson (Leopard Men); Jesus Thillit, Cliff Bowen (Martial Arts Fighters); Gina Adamson (Voodoo Dancer); Alvin Boudreaux, Charles Crawford, Ray Davis, George Griffin, Cliff Lawson, Fernando Lujan, Jerry Mitchell (Stunts).

Robert Sand (Jim Kelly) is a top government agent for D.R.A.G.O.N. who leads the good life; nice digs, plays tennis, and drives a blue Ferrari. His girlfriend Toki Konuma (Essie Lin Chia), the daughter of the Minister of the Samurai Code, is kidnapped by the Warlock, who heads a cult of voodoo worshippers who engage in ritualistic murders. He uses his victims to further his dope trafficking and prostitution trade. Sand goes on the offensive to rescue Toki and to put an end to the Warlock and his followers. The final showdown has him combating rattlesnakes and throwing exploding powder.

This film is an unsatisfactory concoction of James Bondian spy thriller, Bruce Lee karate fest, and Dr. Fu Manchu mysticism-horror. The lead character is decked out with a cannon-equipped sports car, a strap-on jet flying pack (sound familiar?), and the ability to use karate and kung fu. Among his nemeses are Rheinhardt (Felix Sella), a midget henchman of the Warlock, and Victor Chavez (Roberto Contreras), and Argentinian cohort of the dastardly crimelord.

If only the agile, muscular, good-looking Jim Kelly had learned to relax on screen, his cinema career might have lasted. But he was stiff and expressionless, and too insistent about always playing a (non-dimension) squeaking clean good guy.

The poorly executed film, when not concentrating on having the hero mouth hip ethnic talk ("Man . . . your credibility has reached an all-time low"), does have moments of snappy dialogue:

VILLAINESS: I like to think of you as the white knight come to the rescue.
KELLY: Never the black knight.

But that is just what martial arts champion Jim Kelly was right for — a black
good-guy hero role model.

Originally *Black Samurai,* based on the strong-selling novel by Marc
Olden, was scheduled for production in late 1975 with actor D'Urville Martin
directing and Jeanne Bell (the black model then dating actor Richard Burton)
co-starring. In the spring of 1976 Al Adamson began production with the announced intention of having Ron Van Clief (four-time 8th Degree black belt
champ) starring, and with a screenplay by Ray Wells.

33. Black Shampoo (Dimension, 1976). Color, 83 minutes.

Producer Alvin L. Fast; *director* Greydon Clark; *screenplay* Fast, Clark;
makeup Tino Zacchia; *music* Gerald Lee; *songs* Lee; Ronald Batiste; *sound*
Bob Dietz; *sound editor* Earl Watson, Jr.; *camera* Dean Cundey, Michael J.
Mileham; *editor* Watson, Jr.

Cast: John Daniels (Jonathan Knight); Tanya Boyd (Brenda St. John);
Joe Ortiz (Mr. Wilson); Skip Lowe (Artie); Gary Allen (Richard); Jack Mehoff
(Maddox); Bruce Kerley (Jackson); Diana St. Clair (Mrs. Simpson); Salvator
Benissimo (Chauffeur); Annie Gaybis (Mrs. Phillips); Fred Scott (Freddie);
Marl Pero (Peg); Kelly Beau (Meg); Ruby Williams (Ruby); Helen Farber
(Manicurist); Edith Wheeler (New Receptionist).

Having paralleled, borrowed, or ripped off nearly every other exploitable
genre or trend-setting film, the seemingly insatiable black exploitation film
movement gobbled up Warren Beatty's *Shampoo* (1975) with this low-case carbon copy.

Mr. Jonathan's ritzy hairdressing salon is so popular because the female
customers hope that rich Jonathan Knight (John Daniels) will do more than
blow-dry their hair. While musucular Knight is making one of his famous
house calls, thugs appear at the shop to force Brenda St. John (Tanya Boyd),
the new receptionist, to return to her last employer, the crooked Mr. Wilson
(Joe Ortiz). She refuses, and Artie (Skip Lowe) is injured protecting her. Later
the ruffians return to destroy the salon. Feeling guilty that she is indirectly
responsible, Brenda makes love to Knight and the next day returns to Wilson.
Knight attempts to woo her back, but she will not leave. A confused, sulking
Knight goes off to his mountain cabin to relax. Brenda arrives and confides that
she has stolen incriminating ledgers from Wilson. Wilson's goons torture Artie
into revealing his boss's whereabouts and the henchmen arrive, running over
Knight's caretaker Freddie (Fred Scott) in the process. Before being captured,
Knight eliminates two of the hoodlums with a chainsaw. Wilson and his surviv-
ing muscle man beat up Knight and Brenda. Freddie reappears and kills the
thug with a hatchet. Knight shoves a broken pool cue into Wilson's stomach.
The battle is over.

As can be expected, this movie is rampant with softcore sex scenes (Mr.
Jonathan making it with a mother and her two daughters is the kinkiest). In-
nuendoes fly faster than the fists: "If he won't do me, nobody will," announces

one horny customer. "You've got what you want. But your hair looks like shit," observes the superstud hairdresser to his worker-lover Brenda after a tumble in bed. And if the usual black stereotypes are mostly avoided, the ones dealing with another minority, gays, are not. There is the gnome-like white Artie and the flittery black Richard (Gary Allen). The gory mayhem is repulsive, but because the acting is of such a low calibre, the credibility is nonexistent anyway. As for John Daniels, who looks like a black Lou Ferrigno, he was to show himself far more polished and at ease in the same year's *The Candy Tangerine Man* (q.v.), playing a high-living pimp.

There is one technically effective moment when the pictures on the wall turn into live action.

Released by Dimension Pictures, which distributed a lion's share of the independently made genre offerings, *Black Shampoo* won no critical plaudits. "There is so much gratuitous sex and violence in *Black Shampoo* there really isn't room for anything else, least of all story" (*Variety*). "Contrary to the film's title, the fact that the two leading players are black is irrevelant; so, as it transpires, is the hair salon setting since the plot is eventually abandoned in favour of a more hackneyed chase.... Script and performances are strictly make-and-mend; the direction, which contrives several flashily irrelevant optical effects, and finally sacrifices all for a blood bath involving a fashionable chain-saw, is audacious" (David McGillivray, British *Monthly Film Bulletin*).

34. The Black Six (Cinemation, 1974). Color, 91 minutes.

Producer Matt Cimber; *associate producer* Rafer Johnson; *director* Cimber; *screenplay* George Theakos; *music* David Moscoe; *associate director* Jef Richard; *sound* Richard Dameon; *special effects* Michael Blowitz, Harry Woolman; *camera/editor* William Swenning.

Cast: Gene Washington (Bubba Daniels); Carl Eller (Junior Bro); Lem Barney (French); Mercury Morris (Boakie); Willie Lanier (Tommy); "Mean" Joe Greene (Kevin); Rosalind Miles (Ceal); John Isenbarger (Moose King); Ben Davidson (Thor); Maury Wills (Coach Edwards); Robert Howard (Eddie Daniels); Cynthia Daly (Jenny King); Mikel Angel (Snake); Garnett Higgins (Mrs. Perkins); Bill King (Postman); Doug Carroll (Jeff); Marilyn MacArthur (Flora); Hannah Dean (Mrs. Daniels); Lydia Dean (Sissy); Jef Richard (Strawhat); Andy Livingston (Bartender); Dick Gordon (Young Man in Bar); Fred Scott (Old Man in Bar); Ron Le Brane (Copperhead); John Tarver (Pool Hall Man).

"Six Times Tougher Than *Shaft!* Six Times Rougher Than *Super Fly!*" It was an inspired concept by Matt Cimber to team six black pro football players for this action film. They are: Gene Washington (San Francisco 49ers), Willie Lanier (Kansas City Chiefs), Lem Barney (Detroit Lions), "Mean" Joe Greene (Pittsburgh Steelers), Mercury Morris (Miami Dolphins), and Carl Eller (Minnesota Vikings). But alas, good intentions and nonprofessional actors (trying to be cool with such lines as "that's a bad piece of road, man") do not make a good film. "Gene Washington and his fellow athletes have considerable charm, which comes through despite the arthritic development. Even so, charm will never be a substitute for acting" (Nora Sayre, *New York Times*).

One night black Eddie Daniels (Robert Howard) and his white girlfriend Jenny King (Cynthia Daly) are out on the football field talking. Her brother Moose (John Isenbarger), a crazy redneck biker, and his chain-swinging gang, arrive on the scene and murder Eddie. Bubba (Gene Washington), Eddie's resigned brother, a newly returned Vietnam veteran, wants to live in peace (after five years of combat action) and hits the high road on motorcycle with five of his buddies: Junior Bro (Carl Eller), French (Lem Barney), Boakie (Mercury Morris), Tommy (Willie Lanier), and Kevin ("Mean" Joe Greene). They find manual labor, get paid, and move on. Eventually they return home and Bubba finds that his girl has become a prostitute to survive in the ghetto. This and his mother's constant prodding awakes his need to avenge his brother's death. He learns from Jenny that her brother and his pals were responsible for Eddie's death. He and his pals then engage Moose and *his* pals—as well as Thor (Ben Davidson) and other biker gangs—in a final confrontation using clubs, knives, dynamite, and fists to settle the score.

Just as *Welcome Home, Soldier Boy* (1971), and *Gordon's War* (1973) (q.v.), among others, had dealt with the plight of Vietnam War veterans adjusting to civilian life, so does *The Black Six*—but with as heavy an emphasis on the black minority problem as on the biker action. The social consciousness aspect is highlighted by the advertising tagline, "When you hurt my brother, I feel the pain. And when I feel the pain, I'll do something about it!"

At one point Bubba complains, "I'm tired of fighting. No one cares. No ones gives you nothing. I had my war. I didn't come back here to change it for another one. I'm not out to change the world and I don't want it to change me. I just want to be left alone." Which is why he and his buddies drop out: "We've got the open road, country air, the wind, and most of all no hassles."

But Bubba wakes up, realizing that, "Seems like wherever I'm at, somebody's asking me to go." He decides, "I'm living in a dream world. The new breed of Uncle Tom. A man who runs from trouble, just runs to it."

In the film's most touching moment, Bubba awakens to his roots:

MRS. DANIELS: You be comin' home Bubba?
BUBBA: Mamma, I never left home.

The Black Six concludes with a warning message, very reminiscent of the one employed at the finale of *Sweet Sweetback's Baadasssss Song* (1971) (q.v.): "Honky.... Look out. Hassle a brother and the Black Six will return!"

35. Black Starlet (Omni, 1974). Color, 90 minutes.

Executive producer Ken Rogers; *producer* Daniel B. Cady; *director* Chris Muinger; *screenplay* Howard Ostroff; *wardrobe supervisor* Emmett Cash; *music* Dee Ervin, Joe Hinton; *assistant director* Duane Hartzell; *sound* Kirk Francis; *camera* Henning Schellerup; *editors* Warren Hamilton, Jr., Don Walters.

Cast: Juanita Brown (Clara/Carla); Eric Mason (Briscoe); Damu King (Scully); Rockne Tarkington (Ben Caulder); Diane Holden (Joyce); Noah Keen

(Phil); Peter Dane (Les); Al Lewis (Sam Sharp); Crane Jackson (Bar Owner); Nicholas Worth (Motorcycle Cop); Rai Tasco (Black Director); Jack Donner (Fake Director); Kip King (Commercial Director); James Broadhead (Lewis); Joe Billins (Mel); Marlene Selsman (Connie); Gary Battaglia (Tony); James Paul Vitale (Weird Cameraman); Emanuel Thomas (Photographer); Marland Proctor (Steve the Writer); *and:* Bob Sukosky.

A person's esteem and soul can just as easily be destroyed by words and situations as by brutal force. Here the action does not revolve on the street turf with white mobsters against exploited black citizens, but on the Hollywood system with its casting couches, segregation, competition, and the pressure to succeed and stay on top (not just in bed). As this film's advertising slogans read, "They set a high price for stardom.... She had what it took to be a star, plus talent."

Clara (Juanita Brown) lives in Gary, Indiana, with her main man, Scully (Damu King). He insists their tawdry life together is all there is; she has dreams of something more. She takes her $700 in savings and leaves town. En route to the West Coast and a chance in movies a cop arrests her for hustling (which she wasn't). Later, an apparently honest white man, Tony (Gary Battaglia), gives her a ride, but steals her money. She reaches Hollywood in the dilapidated truck of an old black couple. Tinseltown leaves her agog. She wisely rejects an offer to be a topless waitress and instead takes a job at Sam Sharp's (Al Lewis) dry cleaning shop as a steam presser. Her co-worker is twenty-five-year-old Joyce (Diane Holden), an ex-actress who has been through it all. She invites Clara to share an apartment. At a wild Hollywood party Clara meets a would-be producer who offers her a role *if* she will come home with him; she does and then discovers he is a fraud. Later Briscoe (Eric Mason), an insensitive, self-impressed associate of Joyce's, offers to place Clara in an acting job. At his office, she meets financial counselor Ben Caulder (Rockne Tarkington). Now in the film industry, Clara changes her name to Carla. Before long, Briscoe is demanding she sleep with him (she does) and service assorted business contacts (she does). She becomes colder and bitchier as she rises up the Hollywood ladder. Then comes her hit film, and at her plush Beverly Hills home she gives a celebration party and is obnoxious to everyone. One of her guests is aspiring writer Steve (Marland Proctor); she tells him that if he will sleep with her, she will help his budding career. In the morning it dawns on her what she has become. Suddenly everything Ben has been telling her all these months makes sense. Back at the studio she becomes her human self again.

Not exactly of the calibre of *The Goddess* (1958) or *Inside Daisy Clover* (1965), *Black Starlet* does have its own message to tell, and in the midst of the cliches there is a street honesty along with its upbeat finale.

Produced by Daniel B. Cady, who had made *Black Samson* (1974) (q.v.), which also starred Rockne Tarkington, the film was distributed by the Atlanta-based Omni Pictures, which released several of the 1970s black-themed motion pictures. Shot in Hollywood in March 1974, the film had a special invitation preview on December 6, 1974, at the Los Angeles Breakfast Club to benefit the building fund for the Kedren Community Mental Health Center. Appealing Juanita Brown had been in *Willie Dynamite* (1973) (q.v.), Jonathan Demme's prison picture *Caged Heat* (1974), and Pam Grier's *Foxy Brown* (1974) (q.v.).

36. The Black Street Fighter (New Line, 1975). Color, 87 minutes.

Executive producer Peter S. Traynor; *producer* William D. Sklar; *director* Timothy Galfas; *story* Tim Kelly; *screenplay* Kelly, Melvyn Frohman; *music* Ed Townsend.

With: Richard Lawson, Annazette Chase, Robert Burr, Joseph Ruskin. *See **Black Fist.***

37. Blackboard Jungle (Metro-Goldwyn-Mayer, 1955). 101 minutes.

Producer Pandro S. Berman; *director* Richard Brooks; *based on the novel by* Evan Hunter; *screenplay* Brooks; *art directors* Cedric Gibbons, Randall Duell; *music adaptor* Charles Wolcott; *assistant director* Joel Freeman; *camera* Russell Harland; *editor* Ferris Webster.

Cast: Glenn Ford (Richard Dadier); Anne Francis (Anne Dadier); Louis Calhern (Jim Murdock); Margaret Hayes (Lois Hammond); John Hoyt (Mr. Warneke); Richard Kiley (Joshua Edwards); Emile Meyer (Mr. Halloran); Basil Ruysdael (Professor A.R. Kraal); Warner Anderson (Dr. Bradley); Sidney Poitier (Gregory Miller); Vic Morrow (Artie West); Dan Terranova (Belazi); Rafael Campos (Peter V. Morales); Paul Mazursky (Emmanuel Stoker); Horace McMahon (Detective); Jamie Farr (Jameel Farah); Danny Dennis (DeLica); Chris Randall (Levy); Hoshi Tomita (Tomita); Gerald Phillips (Carter); David Alpert (Lou Savoldi); Dorothy Neumann (Miss Panucci); Henny Backus (Miss Brady); Paul Hoffman (Mr. Lefkowitz); Robert Foulk (George Katy); *and:* Richard Deacon, John Erman, Tom McKee.

To today's viewers jaded by far more gruesome realities both onscreen and in real life, *Blackboard Jungle* seems very tame material indeed. But in its day it was considered a sharp condemnation of the ongoing battle between juvenile delinquents and harassed, underpaid school faculty. Based on Evan Hunter's best-selling novel, it boosted the careers of several of its many fine actors (including Sidney Poitier) and was Oscar-nominated for Best Screenplay and Cinematography. Its oft-repeated rock and roll theme song, "Rock Around the Clock" (performed by Bill Haley and his Comets), became a major jukebox classic.

Young Navy veteran Richard Dadier (Glenn Ford) is tackling his first teaching assignment at an all-male vocational school in a large metropolitan city. To his truculent hoodlum teenaged students he is "Daddy O" and "Teach," and he finds that his most difficult daily assignment in this inner city high school is to survive the ongoing nightmare. Disgusted by his students' savage behavior, he is equally disgusted at his inability to raise their intellectual curiosity. Among the faculty are idealistic jazz record–collecting Joshua Edwards (Richard Kiley), who attempts to warn Dadier of the problems he faces; shapely English instructor Lois Hammond (Margaret Hayes), who spells out several after-school assignments she would enjoying sharing with Dadier; older, acerbic teacher Jim Murdock (Louis Calhern), who is waiting for retirement; and Principal Warneke (John Hoyt), who likens himself to a prison warden sitting on a hotbed of trouble. When Dadier prevents knife-using Artie West (Vic Morrow) from raping Lois, he earns the hatred of the gang leader and his followers. Later Dadier's pregnant wife, Anne (Anne Francis), receives obscene telephone calls at home and anonymous letters suggesting her husband and Lois are coupling. Dadier has a breakthrough when he and recalcitrant, complex black student Gregory Miller (Sidney Poitier) reach a point of mutual respect. Dadier sees promise in this brooding, rebellious student who needs more encouragement, not stifling. In a confrontation with West, Dadier takes away his switchblade and humiliates him in front of his gang. The only one to step to the teacher's defense is West himself.

Bosley Crowther *(New York Times)* lauded *The Blackboard Jungle* for being "vivid and hair-raising" and "hard and penetrating as a nail." This breakthrough youth rebellion picture contributed to the much later blaxploitation film craze, for it: 1) helped to establish Sidney Poitier as a major black star and thus make black stars and films bankable in white Hollywood; 2) showed there was a market for presenting the seamier side of everyday life; 3) proved that animosity at life's injustices (social and moral) could be acceptable motion picture themes; and 4) demonstrated that there could be black anti-heroes (such as Poitier's Gregory Miller) who would rightly or wrongly stand up to the white system, demanding attention and respect.

The Blackboard Jungle grossed $5,459,000 in domestic film rentals.

38. Blackenstein (Exclusive International, 1973). 93 minutes.

Executive producer Ted Tetrick; *producer* Frank R. Salertri; *director* William A. Levy; *screenplay* Salertri; *music* Cardella De Milo, Lou Frohman; *assistant director* Paul Keslin, Don Goldman; *makeup* Gordon Freed; *special electronic effects* Ken Strickfadden; *camera* Robert Caramico; *editor* Bill Levey.

Cast: John Hart (Dr. Stein); Ivory Stone (Winifred Walker); Joe De Sue (Eddie Turner); Andrea King (Eleanor); Nick Bolin (Bruno Strager); Karin Lind (Hospital Supervisor); Liz Renay, Jerry Soucie (Couple in Bed); Beverly Haggerty, Daniel Faure (Couple in Car); Andy "E" (Club Comedian); Robert L. Hurd, Marva Farmer (Couple in Alley); Don Brodie (Police Lieutenant); Dale Bach (Girl in Dune Buggy); *and:* James Cousar, Roosevelt Jackson.

A.K.A. *Black Frankenstein.*

Since American International had done so well with adapting the Dracula legend to the blaxploitation phenomenon in *Blacula* (1972) (q.v.), it was an assumption that a spin-off of Mary Shelley's *Frankenstein* might do equally as well. The low-budget filmmakers even hired noted special effects wizard Kenneth Strickfadden (who had created the electronic gadgetry for the Boris Karloff classic motion picture *Frankenstein,* 1931). But he could not create miracles from this pathetic mess.

Black soldier Eddie Turner (Joe De Sue) has had his limbs blown off by a land mine in Vietnam. He is now hospitalized back in the United States. His girlfriend, Winifred Walker (Ivory Stone), is the Ph.D. assistant to Nobel Prize winner in physics Dr. Stein (John Hart). Together they are working on experiments that may lead to breakthroughs in the field of genetic engineering, which would mean that new limbs could be constructed for Turner. Belligerent, disillusioned Turner finally agrees to submit to experiments, but the doctor's black assistant, who loves Winifred, interferes and causes the operation to run

amok. The results are disastrous: Turner turns into a man̄
who is impervious to fists, bullets, or anything else his victim
at him. Dr. Stein is killed and his lab destroyed by his
Finally it is vicious Doberman pinscher dogs who do in th

Everything is abysmally handled in this bottom-of-the-
There is little logic to the presentation. The potentially intr
Vietnam War theme gets short shrift. There are the seeming ̄ ̄ ̄ ̄ ̄ ̄ (a la
Blacula and *Abby* [qq.v.]) nightclub scenes for the monster to parade through;
there are naive teenagers parked in the hills and being terrorized by the
monster; and at every turn a nubile young lady is having her blouse (partially)
ripped off. Sadly, on hand are ex–movie serial star John Hart (as the daring
experimentor) and former Warner Bros. contract lead Andrea King (as a
middle-aged woman going through a youth transplant operation and killed by
the creature). Liz Renay would go on to star in the psycho ward fantasy
Desperate Living (1977), directed by Baltimore filmmaker John "Pink Fla-
mingoes" Waters.

39. Blacula (American International, 1972). Color, 93 minutes.

Executive producer Samuel Z. Arkoff; *producer* Joseph T. Narr; *director*
William Crain; *screenplay* Joan Torres, Raymond Koenig; *art director* Walter
Herndon; *costumes* Ermon Sessions, Sandy Stewart; *makeup* Fred Phillips;
music/music director Gene Page; *songs* Wally Holmes; *special effects* Roger
George; *stunt co-ordinator* George Fisher; *sound* Charles Knight; *camera* John
Stevens; *editor* Allan Jacobs.

Cast: William Marshall (Mamuwalde [Blacula]); Vonetta McGee (Tina/
Luva); Denise Nicholas (Michelle); Thalmus Rasulala (Dr. Gordon Thomas);
Gordon Pinsent (Lieutenant Peters); Charles Macauley (Count Dracula);
Emily Yancy (Nancy); Lane Taylor, Sr. (Swenson); Ted Harris (Bobby); Rick
Metzler (Billy); Hitu Cumbuka (Skillet); Logan Field (Barnes); Ketty Lester
(Juanita); Elisha Cook, Jr. (Sam); Eric Brotherson (Real Estate Agent).

In 1790 Transylvania, African Prince Mamuwalde (William Marshall) and
his wife Luva (Vonetta McGee) visit Castle Dracula hoping to persuade the
Count (Charles Macauley) to help them ban the slave trade. Instead the
perverse Count, who lusts after Luva, locks her in a mausoleum, and after subjecting Mamuwalde to vampirism, places a curse on the Prince: "[You will be]
doomed to a living hell . . . a hunger . . . wild animal gnawing hunger! You will
starve for an eternity. . . . You shall be Blacula, a living fiend doomed to never
know that sweet blood which will become your only desire."

The scene shifts to present-day Los Angeles, where two gay antique
dealers who have brought the centuries-old coffin to California become the
vampire's first victims. After the death of a black cab driver, Juanita (Ketty
Lester), Dr. Gordon Thomas (Thalmus Rasulala) is convinced a vampire is
loose on the West Coast. Meanwhile Blacula has found Tina (Vonetta McGee),
whom he believes to be the reincarnation of his lost love. At first she is frightened
by his sudden appearance, but she responds to the subtle approach of the man
who calls himself Mamuwalde. He turns her into a vampire. Later Tina's pal
Thomas and his assistant Michelle (Denise Nicholas) know something is foul

William Marshall and Vonetta McGee in _Blacula_ (1972).

and wrong when Mamuwalde's likeness does not show up in recently taken photographs. After the vampire claims additional victims, they finally convince Police Lieutenant Peter (Gordon Pinsent) and his men to attack Blacula at his lair in an electrical factory. The encounter causes several casualties. Tina is staked through the heart, and Blacula walks out onto the roof into the sunlight where he dissolves into a pile of bones and dust.

"Anyone who goes to a vampire movie expecting sense is in serious trouble," Roger Greenspun _(New York Times)_ insisted correctly when reviewing _Blacula_. This film was the first and the best of the black horror film cycle that would engulf Hollywood for a brief period in the mid-1970s. (Other entries would include _Blackenstein_ [1972], _Ganja and Hess_ [1973], _Abby_ [1974], _Sugar Hill_ [1974], and _Dr. Black, Mr. Hyde_ [1976] [qq.v.].) Had he been alive, Bela Lugosi of the 1931 motion picture _Dracula_ would certainly have approved. Not only does the production boast a stylishly urbane William Marshall in the lead role, but it benefits from the dual role of Vonetta McGee, whom Greenspun of the _New York Times_ labeled "just possibly the most beautiful woman currently acting in movies." Moreover there is a lightness — almost campiness — to the presentation, which makes for added fun. Decked out in his cape and bizarre clothing, Marshall is a sight to behold even to contemporary black

brothers decked out in the hip finery of the day. "That is a
admits a jive-talking soul brother. At a later point at the dis
of the modern-day vampire, "That man isn't some nut from
That's the real thing." And not even Mamuwalde always take
After disappearing from sight, he reappears suddenly at th
surprise of a startled patron. "I say, are you looking for m
ingly. Setting the tone for the entire film are the animated opening credits by
the talented Sandy Dvore. Similarly, Julian Myers, in his liner notes for the
Blacula soundtrack album, cannot be taken too seriously when he makes
statements such as, "[Composer Gene] Page and his fellow musicians used a
world of sounds, the full world of sounds for the sounds of *Blacula*....
Dracula's legendary trappings and appetites had to be translated to engage the
ear. Page did it by using old instruments in new ways, new instruments in new
ways and sometimes non-instruments to produce effects." Some of the musical
interludes on the soundtrack have their own wry titles: "Heavy Changes," "Run,
Tina, Run!", "Good to the Last Drop," and "Finding Love, Losing Love."

There were some who looked for (and missed finding) deeper meanings in
Blacula: "...a black Dracula let loose in contemporary America might effectively have provided a focus for the guilt and neurosis of the dominant white
culture. But apart from a rather feeble prologue in which Mamuwalde fleetingly
appears as a representative of the emerging black nations, the film con-
spicuously fails to pick upon any of its theme's more interesting possibilities —
cinematic or philosophical" (David Pirie, British *Monthly Film Bulletin*).

Blacula grossed a healthy $1,200,000 in domestic film rentals and
prompted a sequel, *Scream, Blacula, Scream* (q.v.), also with Shakespearian
actor William Marshall in the lead assignment.

40. Blue Collar (Universal, 1978). Color, 110 minutes.

Executive producer Robin French; *producer* Don Guest; *associate pro-
ducer* David Nichols; *director* Paul Schrader; *based on materials by* Sidney A.
Glass; *screenplay* Paul Schrader, Leonard Schrader; *production designer*
Lawrence G. Paull; *set decorator* Peggy Cummings; *costumes* Ron Dawson,
Alice Rush; *makeup* Donl Morse; *music/music director/music arranger* Jack
Nitzche; *special music arrangements* Ry Cooder; *song* Nitzche, Cooder, Paul
Schrader; *assistant directors* Rusty Meek, Dan Franklin, George Marshall;
stunt co-ordinator Glenn Wilder; *sound* Willie Burton, Marvin Lewis, Winfred
Tennison; *sound effects* Neiman-Tillar Associates; *camera* Bobby Byrne;
editor Tom Rolf.

Cast: Richard Pryor (Zeke Brown); Harvey Keitel (Jerry Bartowski);
Yaphet Kotto (Smokey); Ed Begley, Jr. (Bobby Joe); Harry Bellaver (Eddie
Johnson); George Memoli (Jenkins); Lucy Saroyan (Arleen Bartowski); Lane
Smith (Clarence Hill); Cliff De Young (John Burrows); Borah Silver (Dogshit
Miller); Chip Fields (Caroline Brown); Harry Northrup (Hank); Leonard
Gaines (IRS Man); Milton Selzer (Sumabitch); Sammy Warren (Barney);
Jimmy Martinez (Charlie T. Hernandez); Jerry Dahlman (Superintendent);
Denny Arnold (Unshaven Thug); Rock Riddle (Blonde Thug); Stacey Baldwin
(Debby Bartowski); Steve Butts (Bob Bartowski); Stephen P. Dunn (Flannigan);

Left–right: **Yaphet Kotto, Harvey Keitel and Richard Pryor in** *Blue Collar* **(1978).**

Speedy Brown (Slim); Davone Florence (Frazier Brown); Eddie Singleton (Ali Brown); Rya Singleton (Aretha Brown); Vermetta Royster (Neighbor); Jaime Carreire (Little Joe); Victoria McFarland (Doris); Gloria Delaney, Rosa Flores, Crystal McCarey, Debra Fay Walker (Party Girls); Gino Ardito, Sean Fallon Walsh (Detectives); Vincent Lucchesi (Newspaper Reporter); Jerry Snider, Colby Chester (TV Reporters); Donl Morse, William Pert, Tracey Walter (Union Members); Almeria Quinn (Union Secretary); Lee McDonald (Security Guard); Rodney Lee Walker (Boy in Dime Store).

By the late 1970s, (low budget) black action pictures of the rough-and-tumble sort were becoming a Hollywood rarity. If minority anger and frustration were to be a film's focal theme, it was now dressed in high moral tones and arty presentation. Such was *Blue Collar,* the first feature to be directed by acclaimed screenwriter Pual Schrader (*The Yakuza* [1975], *Taxi Driver* [1976], *Rolling Thunder* [1977]) and released as a prestige item by Universal Pictures.

Three friends, buddies at and away from the job, work on the assembly line in a Detroit car factory. They are: black Zeke Brown (Richard Pryor), who is married with three children, in debt to the Internal Revenue Service for creative tax reporting, and uncontrollably rude and often angry; black Smokey (Yaphet Kotto), a hulking, unmarried ex-convict who has illusions of living a fantasy Playboy bachelor's life; and white Jerry Bartowski (Harvey Keitel), married, in debt and juggling two jobs to survive like Zeke. Initially as a joke to get even with their oppressive foreman Dogshit Miller (Borah Silver), the trio decide to rob the union funds. Zeke rationalizes to the group that their shop steward (Lane Smith) does little to protect their well-being. Their foray nets only $600, which is less than the crime costs them, for Smokey owes pal Charlie T. Hernandez (Jimmy Martinez) $1,000 for his consultation on the robbery. The three are amazed when the local union president (Harry Bellaver) tells the press the stolen amount is around $10,000 (thereafter the sum is raised to $20,000 for insurance claims). Only later do the trio comprehend that a stolen notebook from the safe reveals illegal loans made by the union. Devout union man Jerry wants to expose the organization officials, but Smokey suggests blackmail. Meanwhile Hernandez earns his freedom from a separate illegal transaction by telling federal agents about the union shenanigans. Jerry is almost beaten up by union thugs, and Smokey is killed accidentally-on-purpose in the paint shop. Zeke replaces his dead friend as shop steward and tries to justify his action to an angered Jerry. After an attempt is made on his life, Jerry asks investigating F.B.I. agent John Burrows (Cliff De Young) to provide protection. Jerry, with an F.B.I. escort, picks up his gear at the factory, while Zeke and his co-workers condemn him as a rat.

"[*Blue Collar*] is a film about which you are likely to have very mixed feelings. It is a sort of poor man's *On the Waterfront,* a movie that simply — often primitively — describes corruption. . . . Is *Blue Collar* an action film or a meditation upon the American Dream? I suspect it wants to be both though it's not very serious at being either" (Vincent Canby, *New York Times*). Pauline Kael (*New Yorker* magazine) decided, "Schrader's jukebox Marxism carries the kind of cyncial charge that encourage people in the audience to yell 'Right on!'. . . . He has imposed his personal depression on characters who, in dramatic terms, haven't earned it. The picture seems dogged and methodical, though it is graced with a beautiful performance by Kotto . . . and an unusual one by Pryor, who plays a turncoat with menacing, calculating little eyes." On the other hand, Roger Ebert (*Movie Home Companion 1988,* 1987) in reassessing the film years later, was far more appreciative: "Schrader goes for a nice, raunchy humor in the scenes involving the three guys. . . . We understand their friendship, too, because it defies one of the things the movie passionately charges: That unions and management tacitly collaborate on trying to set the rich against the poor, the black against the white. . . . *Blue Collar* is a stunning debut, taking chances and winning at them."

The expensively (for its kind) produced feature film made in May and June of 1977 and released in February 1978 was considered a box-office failure, even though it eventually grossed approximately $4,000,000 in domestic film rentals. Filmgoers went to *Blue Collar* expecting a typical rowdy and raunchy

ɪ Richard Pryor and were surprised, and perhaps disap-
ɪmatic showcase he had chosen instead. Many viewers felt the
ip of the two blacks and one white was too artificial for the
picture was attempting to tell. Others were annoyed by the
ɪmbiguities and by the pastiche of politics and dramatic bits.
scripter-director would relate later that because the three stars
wᴇɪ~ to promote their individual careers, they were very suspicious
of one other on the set and extremely protective of their own moments to shine.
Pryor was especially concerned. "I don't want to be used to bring in the black
audience and then to have them devastated. I don't think I could stand the re-
jection." Even though the movie would be a commercial failure, it would
bolster the comedian's Hollywood standing, and he would admit later, "I carry
no negative shit about that movie."

41. Body and Soul (Cannon, 1981). Color, 122 minutes.

Producers Menaham Golan, Yoram Globus; *associate producer* Cliff
Roquemore; *director* George Bowers; *based on the original screenplay by*
Abraham Polonsky; *screenplay* Leon Isaac Kennedy; *art director* Bob Ziem-
bicki; *set decorator* Cricket Rowland; *costumes* Celia; *makeup* Jerry
Muchweiler, Tom Shouse; *music* Webster Lewis; *music supervisor* Rex
Cevereaux; *orchestrator* Greg Poree; *songs* Webster Lewis and Zoom, Lewis;
choreography Hope Clarke; *fight choreography* Bob Minor; *assitant director*
Sati Jamal; *sound* Andrew Babbish, Robb Newell; *supervising sound editor*
David B. Cohn; *camera* James Forrest; *editors* Sam Pollard, Skip Schoolnick.

Cast: Leon Isaac Kennedy (Leon Johnson); Jayne Kennedy (Julie
Winters); Perry Lang (Charles Golphin); Nikki Swassy (Kelly Johnson);
Michael Grazzo (Frankie); Kim Hamilton (Mrs. Johnson); Muhammad Ali
(Himself); Peter Lawford (Big Man); Danny Wells, Johnny Brown (Sports An-
nouncers); Azizi Johari (Pussy); Rosanne Katon (Melody); Chris Wallace (Dr.
Bachman); Robbie Epps (Iceman); J.B. Williamson (St. Louis Assassin); Al
Danavo (Mad Man Santiago); Mel Welles (Joe Gillardi); Deforrest Covan (Cut
Man); Al Garcia (Mad Man's Manager); Jimmy Lennon (Ring Announcer);
Mike Garfield (Fight Official); Howard Zazove, Cheryle Tyre Smith, James
Carter, John Isaacs (Reporters); Eddie Mustafos (Himself); Lonnie Bennett,
Al Chavez, John Liechy, Andy Price, Lonnie Epps, Leonard Bailey, John
Sherrod (Boxers); Rita Minor, Regina Clayton, Noel Chacon, Janice Lester,
Edgy Lee, Deborah Willis Lacey (Pretty Laces); Ola Ray, Ingrid Greer, Laurie
Senit (Hookers); Mark Isaacs (Boy in Car); Lyle Baker (Bodyguard); Miguel
Delgado Dancers (Latin Dancers); Hasel Girtman (Nurse); Cheryle "Charlie"
Kynard, Darlene Horer, Arlene Alexander, Haruko Leolington (Card Girls).

Robert Rosson's *Body and Soul* (1947), a searing drama of corruption,
greed, and despair in the fight game, has long been valued as a landmark classic
film in general and one in particular by which any boxing movie would be
judged. In 1981, Leon Isaac Kennedy, the muscular, dynamic black star of
Penitentiary (1979) (q.v.), audaciously and loosely remade the original *Body
and Soul,* serving as scenarist, co-producer, and leading man (in the part made
so memorable by John Garfield). This hokey film was obviously Kennedy's

answer to Sylvester Stallone's *Rocky,* the boxer movie series (q.v.). It was also an opportunity to provide a variety of black performers with acting assignments, including Kennedy's then-wife, the extremely beautiful model, actress, and TV commentator and game show hostess Jayne Kennedy. (Kennedy had already helped finance *Big Time* [1977] with Smokey Robinson and Christopher Joy. The Andrew Georgias–directed film starred Joy, Jayne Kennedy, and Roger E. Mosley. That same year Kennedy and his wife Jayne co-starred in *Death Force* with James Iglehardt.)

Adept amateur boxer Leon Johnson (Leon Isaac Kennedy) learns his young sister, Kelly (Nikki Swassy), is suffering from deadly sickle cell anemia. Although his mother (Kim Hamilton) wants him to become a doctor, Johnson decides to become a professional boxer so he will have the funds to pay for his sister's expensive treatment. With white trainer Frankie (Michael Gazzo) and manager Charles Golphin (Perry Lang), Johnson chalks up victories in the ring. Meanwhile he falls in love with sportscaster Julie Winters (Jayne Kennedy), who chides him for his commercialism in the ring (i.e. he wears a red heart on his boxing shorts and is tagged "The Lover"). His successes attract the interest of crooked promoter "the Big Man" (Peter Lawford), who intends replacing Golphin with himself. Before long the high-rolling Big Man turns Golphin into a drug addict and has Johnson involved with an assortment of women, which causes Julie to leave him. Only after the Big Man, needing quick cash and having a new contender in his stable, orders Johnson to fake a loss in a welterweight championship fight does the boxer realize what he has become. He confesses everything to Julie, and when he learns she has bet all her money on his success, he gains new strength. At the ringside for the big fight are Julie, his mother, Kelly, and a rehabilitated Golphin. Leon wins the bout against Mad Man Santiago (Al Denavo), despite the latter's dirty tactics.

Set in Chicago and with script ploys borrowed from William Holden's *Golden Boy* (1939) and John Garfield's *Humoresque* (1947), the new *Body and Soul* is tremendously self-indulgent and cliched. Its saving grace is the magnetic presence of Leon Isaac Kennedy, especially in the ring sequences. There is a self-conscious cameo by Muhammed Ali and a terrible performance by an aging, hollow Peter Lawford, and the film is filled with nonsensical maudlin interludes at every turn. "The main problems in *Body and Soul* come from the triteness of the screenplay. Still, it's a story that people can cheer for" (Linda Gross, *Los Angeles Times*). ". . . [D]oesn't have a great deal to recommend it to lovers of either the manly sport or bedside encounters of the sexy kind" (Archer Winsten, *New York Post*). "Outrage for solemn outrage . . . this 'remake' is even more outrageous than the parody of 30s boxing cliches in [Stanley] Donen's *Movie Movie*. In a concoction of disgustingly calculated sentimentality, every conceivable platitude is given a turn . . . Leon Isaac Kennedy and Jayne Kennedy give performances worthy of better things"(Tom Milne, British *Monthly Film Bulletin*). ". . . [A]t least it's one of the few reasonably entertaining movies to be directed toward black audiences lately."

When *Body and Soul* opened in Chicago in October 1981 *Variety* stated, "It remains an open quesiton whether the black action film market, which poured on the grosses for a number of low budget items in the late 1960s and early 1970s, still exists. This remake ... won't shed much light on the issue since it looms as a limp b.o. draw no matter what the patron coloration or film genre." The trade paper proved correct.

42. Book of Numbers (Avco Embassy, 1973). Color, 81 minutes.

Producer Raymond St. Jacques; *associate producers* Joe Dennis, Mike Fields; *director* St. Jacques; *based on the novel by* Robert Deane Pharr; *screenplay* Larry Spiegel; *art director* Bob Shepherd; *music/music arranger* Al Schuckman; *assistant director* Drake Walker; *sound* Greg Valtierra; *camera* Gayne Rescher; *editor* Irv Rosenblum.

Cast: Raymond St. Jacques (Blueboy Harris); Freda Payne (Kelly Simms); Philip [Michael] Thomas (Dave Greene); Hope Clark (Pigmeat Goins); Willie Washington, Jr. (Makepeace Johnson); Doug Finell (Eggy); Sterling St. Jacques (Kid Flick); C.L. Williams (Blip); D'Urville Martin (Billy Bowlegs); Jerry Leon (Joe Gaines); Gilbert Greene (Luis Antoine); Frank DeSal (Carlos); Ternie Mae Williams (Sister Clara Goode); Pauline Herndon, Ethel Marie Crawford (Sisters); Mimi Lee Dodd (Bus Station Prostitute); Charles F. Elyston (Mr. Booker); Queen Esther Gent (Mrs. Booker); Irma Hall (Georgia Brown); Chiquita Jackson (Didi); Katie Peters (Honey); Pat Peterson (Becky); Ray McDonald, Charles Lewis (Goons); Reginald Dorsey (June Bug).

In many ways deep-voiced Raymond St. Jacques has long been more versatile and certainly equally as talented as the far more popular Sidney Poitier. Like Poitier, St. Jacques was at the forefront of the token blacks in Hollywood films in the late 1960s; he appeared in such entries as *The Pawnbroker* (1965), *Mister Buddwing* (1966), *The Comedians* (1967), *The Green Berets* (1968), and *Madigan* (1968), and played the recurring character "Solomon King" in the TV Western series "Rawhide" (1965–68). When the blaxploitation craze swept Holywood, he was readily cast in a variety of films showcasing his multiple talents, including *If He Hollers, Let Him Go* (1968), *Uptight* (1968), *Cotton Comes to Harlem* (1970), *Come Back Charleston Blue* (1972), *Cool Breeze* (1972), and *The Final Comedown* (1972) (qq.v.).

For his screen directing debut, St. Jacques chose to film Robert Deane Pharr's novel, a period story of two slick urban waiters, Blueboy Harris (St. Jacques) and Dave Greene (Philip [Michael] Thomas), who establish a numbers game in the small town of El Dorado, Arkansas, in the 1930s. They soon earn the enmity of the local criminals. Furious white crime lord Antoine (Gilbert Greene) sends his enforcers, including psychotic Carlos (Frank de Sal), to set things right. By the finale, paternalistic, low-keyed Blueboy Harris is dead, while handsome, exuberant Greene has found a sense of purpose to life as well as a wonderful girlfriend.

Among those peppering the episodic storyline in this *Bonnie and Clyde*–type comedy-drama are Joe Gaines (Jerry Leon), who fronts for Antoine's criminal activities; Kelly Simms (Freda Payne), who is Greene's love interest); the pungent Pigment (Hope Clarke); and best of all Billy Bowlegs (D'Urville Martin), a very comedic numbers racket runner.

"An uncommonly well-balanced movie, intelligently directed, very cleverly edited ... with an air of real enjoyment in what it is about," decided Roger

Top, left–right: **Leon Isaac Kennedy, Muhammad Ali, and Jayne Kennedy in** *Body and Soul* **(1981).** *Bottom, left–right:* **Hope Clarke, D'Urville Martin, player, Philip Michael Thomas, and Freda Payne in** *Book of Numbers* **(1973).**

Greenspun *(New York Times).* He added, "Its spirit comes mainly from its music—background music, blues and spirituals, dance tunes—rather than from the requirements of melodramatic plotting."

It was *Variety* who best summed up the film's commercial potential: "The film's ambitions are modest but largely realized. This is not a black extravaganza ... but a relatively simple, uncompromising, candid evocation of a corner of an era. The distinction [from the typical blaxploitation feature] is likely to inhibit some b.o. action, except in the market for which it was exclusively made.... The modest budget shows in some of the artistic rough edges...."

Book of Numbers, an Avco Embassy release of a Brut Company presentation, was filmed in sections of Dallas, Texas.

43. **Boss Nigger** (Dimension, 1974). Color, 92 minutes.

Executive producers Lee Winkler, Don Call, Dwight Call; *producers* Fred Williamson, Jack Arnold; *associate producer* Myrl A. Schreibman; *director* Arnold; *screenplay* Williamson; *set decorator* Robert E. Reed; *music/song* Leon Moore, Tom Nixon; *orchestrator* Mike Terry; *sound* Ted Gomillion; *special effects* Jack De Brun, Norval Crutcher, Howard A. Anderson Co.; *camera* Bob Caramico; *editors* Gene Ruggiero, Eva Ruggiero.

Cast: Fred Williamson (Boss Nigger); D'Urville Martin (Amos); R.G. Armstrong (Mayor); William Smith (Jed Clayton); Carmen Hayworth (Clara Mae); Barbara Leigh (Miss Pruitt); Don "Red" Barry (Doc); Ben Zeller (Pete the Blacksmith); Carmen Zapata (Marguerita); Bruce Gordon (Storekeeper); Sonny Robbins (Bad Foot); Don Hayes (Park); Paul Conlzan (Todd); Mark Brito (Pancho); Joe Alfasa (Pedro); Lou Brito (Pedro's Wife); Kip Allen (Clerk); Jonathan Banks (Drunk); Sonny Cooper (Wash Lady); Phil Mead (Mayor's Man); Harry Luck (Uppity Man); Elizabeth Saxon (Uppity Wife); Paul Barby (Walter); Luke Jones (Dan); Don Hawn (Paul); V. Phipps-Wilson (Bubbles); Mike Eiland, Judson Kane, Joe Kurtzo, Otis Lewellen, Dickson Newberry, George Oja, Leo Petrie, Hardy Phelps, Wayne Waterhouse (Outlaws).

British release title: *The Black Bounty Killer.*

In the 1870s black bounty hunters Boss (Fred Williamson) and Amos (D'Urville Martin) kill several bank robbers, including one recently appointed sheriff of San Miguel. Boss and Amos decide to collect the reward. En route they save black Clara Mae (Carmen Hayworth), whose father has been shot by gunmen. Boss appoints himself the sheriff of San Miguel, much to the consternation of the white mayor (R.G. Armstrong) and local bad man Jed Clayton (William Smith). Clayton's outlaws dynamite the jail, almost eliminating Amos, and killing Pancho (Mark Brito), the son of Amos's Mexican woman, Marguerita (Carmen Zapata). Later Boss and Clara Mae are captured by Clayton's men, but they are rescued by sidekick Amos. In a skirmish back in town, Clara Mae is murdered, while Boss, Amos and the townfolk hold off the gang. Boss kills Jed but is himself badly wounded. He leaves town in a wagon driven by Amos.

Filled with Western genre perennials (Don "Red" Barry, R.G. Armstrong, and Bruce Gordon), *Boss Nigger* is too episodic in its continuity and too often shows it was lensed quickly on the cheap. But the unpretentious film has many virtues. "Most black Westerns either ignore race or make it the fundamental point of the movie. *Boss Nigger* somehow manages to do both quite successfully.... It's fun because it's no 'big-deal'" (Vincent Canby, *New York Times*). "*Boss Nigger* is proof of the enduring strengths of the Western movie. It's a passel of cliches, but that's exactly what makes it tolerable" (Jerry Oster, *New York Daily News*). In *The Film Encyclopedia: The Western* (1983), Phil Hardy

points up, "An interesting transitional black Western, this bridges the gap between Williamson's violent Nigger Charley films (*Legend of,* 1972, and *Soul of,*
1973) and the gentle comedy of *Adios Amigo* (1975). . . . The action is as much
comic as violent."

In its own way, *Boss Nigger* makes a strong statement about blacks versus
whites for equality, but employs satirical comedy for its effective language
rather than uncontrolled violent diatribes. There is the prim, bigoted Boston
schoolteacher, Miss Pruitt (Barbara Leigh), who prattles on about her family's
jolly black servants, but who later yearns for the handsome, virile Boss. (When
Boss is wounded, she screams out, "Oh my God. Bring him in and put him in
my bed!") It is Boss who confounds the none-too-bright Clayton gang by
pretending to be a stereotyped servile black; and it is Boss the self-appointed
sheriff who pokes fun at the pompous mayor in front of the entire town by talking down to him: "Dis here da mayor." When the storekeeper, who is as bigoted
against Mexicans as he is against blacks, refuses to serve Clara Mae and
Marguerita, Boss fines him for racial discrimination! One of the movie's most
amusing moments is provided by the ever-effervescent Amos, who has more lives
than a cat. When the jail is blown up and Amos is found alive in his bed covered
with debris, he wipes away the dirt and remarks, "My daddy always told me that
bed would be the death of me." And in the confusingly solemn finale, a mortally
wounded Boss tells Amos, "Don't let me die in a white man's town."

Co-producer and director Jack Arnold and co-producer, screenwriter and
star Williamson had teamed previously on *Black Eye* (1974) (q.v.), a detective
thriller.

44. **Bronx Warriors** (United Film Distribution, 1983).
Color, 84 minutes.

Producer Fabrizio De Angelis; *director* Enzo G. Castellari; *story* Dardana
Sachetti; *screenplay* Sachetti, Elisa Livia Brighanti; *production designer*
Massimo Lentini; *set decorator* D'Angelo; *costumes* Lentini; *makeup* Maurizio
Trani; *music* Walter Rizzati; *special effects* Antonio Corridori, Walter Bat-
tistelli, Pasquino Benassati, Pasquale Sarao; *camera* Sergio Salvati; *editor*
Gianfranco Amicucci.

Cast: Vic Morrow (Hammer); Christopher Connolly (Hot Dog); Fred
Williamson (The Ogre); Mark Gregory (Trash); Stefani Girolami (Anne); John
Sinclair (Ice); *and:* Betty Dessy, George Eastman, Enio Girolami [Enzo G.
Castellari], Rocco Lerro, Angelo Ragusa, Massimo Vanni.

A.K.A.: *The New Barbarians; 1990: The Bronx Warriors.*

This Italian-made science fiction fantasy film was made as *I Guerrieri del
Bronx* and shot in the Bronx and Italy. It borrows very heavily from the far
more stylish and successful *The Warriors* (1979) and *Escape from New York*
(1981). As with several other Enzo G. Castellari productions of this period, this
deals with a nihilistic wasteland and the savage, macabre survivors who inhabit
it. It is one of a series of such films Fred Williamson appeared in, usually as
a (token) guest star, in the 1980s.

In 1990 the ravaged Bronx is labeled No Man's Land and controlled by the
Ogre (Fred Williamson) and his assorted youth gangs. When Anne (Stefani

1age heiress to the controlling interest in the sinsister
tion, runs away to the Bronx, she is hunted by paid killer
mber Hammer (Vic Morrow) and rescued from the roller-
Trash (Mark Gregory), leader of the Riders. Anne is later
mbies, and Trash, who now loves her, asks Ogre to help
nt skirmishes filled with mutilations of all sorts, Anne and
......their deaths, Trash kills Hammer with a grappling hook.
"The direction of Enzo G. Castellari is stylized, slowly paced and so strangely
staged that in spite of all the violence there is very little sense of action. Performances are generally poor. Actors such as Williamson stand out because of
their star presence. . . . The atrocious screenplay . . . is often obscene and occasionally unintentionally funny" (Linda Gross, *Los Ageles Times*).

45. The Brother from Another Planet (Cinecon International, 1984). Color, 108 minutes.

Producers Peggy Rajski, Maggie Ranzi; *director/screenplay* John Sayles;
production designer Nora Chavooshian; *art director* Steve Lineweavers;
makeup Tim D'Arcy; *special makeup* Ralph Cordero; *costume designer* Karen
Perry; *music* Mason Daring; *songs* Daring and Sayles; Frank London, Daring,
and Efrain Salgeado; *stunt consultant* Edgar Mourino; *sound* Eric Taylor,
Michael Golub; *sound editor* Carol Dysinger; *sound effects* Natalie Lardner;
camera Ernest R. Dickerson; *editor* Sayles.

Cast: Joe Morton (The Brother); Tom Wright (Sam Prescott); Caroline
Aaron (Randy Sue Carter); Herbert Newsome (Little Earl); Dee Dee
Bridgewater (Malverne Davis); Darryl Edwards (Fly); Leonard Jackson
(Smokey); Bill Cobbs (Walter); Steve James (Odell); Edward Baran (Mr.
Vance); John Sayles, David Strathair (Men in Black); Maggie Renzi (Noreen);
Olga Merediz (Noreen's Client); Minnie Gentry (Mrs. Brown); Red Woods
(Bernice); Reggie Rock Bythewood (Rickey); Alvin Alexis (Willis); Rosetta Le
Noire (Mama); Michael Albert Mantel (Mr. Lowe); Jaime Tirelli (Hector);
Lance Curtis (Ace); Chip Mitchell (Ed); David Babcock (Phil); Sidney Sheriff,
Jr. (Virgil); Carl Gordon (Mr. Price); Fisher Stevens (Card Trickster); Randy
Frazier (Bouncer); Copper Cunningham (Black Hooker); Marisa Smith (White
Hooker); Ishmae Houston-Jones (Dancer); Kim Staunton (Teacher); Dwania
Kyles (Waitress); Leon W. Grant, Anthony Thomas (Basketball Players);
Andre Robinson, Jr. (Pusher); Josh Mostel (Casio Vendor); Deborah Taylor
(Vance's Receptionist); John Griesemer (White Cop).

One of the genres little exploited in the heyday of the blaxploitation film
was science fiction. The independently made and released *The Brother from
Another Planet* is a mid-1980s social statement allegory garbed in sci-fi trappings and with a good sense of humor. It was a rightful entry in the 1984
Cannes Film Festival. As David Denby (*New York* magazine) reported, "The
glory of *Brother* is its talk. At a time when most filmmakers are indifferent to
blacks, [Jonathan] Sayles has restored to Harlem some of its voice."

The Brother, a tall, mute extraterrestrial in black human form, crash-
lands his spaceship at Ellis Island, New York. He has come in search of adventure and freedom. He heads for Harlem where the regulars at O'Dell's Bar,

including Fly (Darryl Edwards), Smokey (Leonard Jackson), and Walter (Bill Cobbs), are amused by the strange newcomer's inability to communicate, not knowing that he is telepathic and can read minds. Social worker Sam Prescott (Tom Wright) has him board with Randy Sue Carter (Caroline Aaron), her philandering black husband and her youngster Earl (Herbert Newsome). With his capacity to fix broken machinery "magically" and to heal human ailments as well, the alien (with Prescott's help) finds a job at a video arcade. Outer space bounty hunters (John Sayles, David Strathairn) arrive in pursuit of the Brother and trace him from O'Dell's to Randy Sue's. Meanwhile the compassionate Brother partakes of everyday Harlem life from being mugged to basketball playing, from getting high to falling in love. His love interest is energetic club jazz singer Malverne Davis (Dee Dee Bridgewater), who confides to the peculiarly three-toed brother after their coupling, "You were great. . . . But you gonna have to do somethin' about those toenails." There is a wonderful subway scene in which the Brother is treated to card gymnastics and other street tricks by a hip con artist. This strange Brother with the peculiar three-toed feet wants nothing more than to better understand the baffling people and experiences he encounters. To avenge the death of a young junkie the Brother tracks the ladder of dope connections to the exploitive downtowner Mr. Vance (Edward Baran) of Advance Communications and kills him. When the bounty hunters finally confront the Brother, his Harlem brothers come to his rescue and the aliens self-destruct. The Brother happily resumes his city life.

In *The Brother from Another Planet* the science fiction special effects are old-fashioned and tacky, giving it at times a home-movie quality. And the film might have benefitted as much from the central figure talking as his being mute. Nevertheless, this overlong and sometimes meandering movie makes its own touching and penetrating commentary on contemporary life both in and out of the black ghetto. Reactions to and about blacks are treated from the point of view of bigoted tourists from Indiana, immigrant shopkeepers, and assorted strata of the Harlem denizens. Throughout, the Brother is amazed and surprised (not angered or violent as would be the case in such films of the 1970s) at how being black makes a difference in the society in which he has landed. As Roger Ebert acknowledges in his *Movie Home Companion 1988* (1987), "There is . . . a curious way in which the film functions as more subtle social satire than might seem possible in a low-budget good-natured comedy."

Based on an estimated cost of $300,000, *Brother from Another Planet* grossed $5,000,000 in domestic film rentals.

46. Brother John (Columbia, 1971). Color, 94 minutes.

Producer Joel Glickman; *director* James Goldstone; *screenplay* Ernest Kinoy; *art director* Al Brenner; *set decorator* Audrey Blasdel; *costumes* Guy Ventrille; *makeup* Al Fleming; *music* Quincy Jones; *song* Jones and Ernie Sheldon; *assistant directors* Tom Schmidt, Charles Washburn; *special effects* Geza Gaspar; *sound* William Randall; *camera* Gerald Perry, Finnerman; *editor* Edward A. Biery.

Cast: Sidney Poitier (John Kane); Will Geer (Doc Henry L. Thomas); Bradford Dillman (Lloyd Thomas); Beverly Todd (Louisa MacGill); Ramon

Foreground, left–right: **Lincoln Kilpatrick, Sidney Poitier and Beverly Todd in** *Brother John* **(1971).**

Bieri (Sheriff Orly Ball); Warren J. Kemmerling (George); Lincoln Kilpatrick (Charley Gray); P. Jay Sidney (Reverend Macgill); Richard Ward (Frank); Paul Winfield (Henry Birkhardt); Zara Cully (Miss Nettie); Michael Bell (Cleve); Howard Rice (Jimmy); Darlene Rice (Marsha); Harry Davis (Turnkey); Lynn Hamilton (Sister Sarah); Gene Tyburn (Calvin); E.A. Nicholson (Perry); Bill Crane (Bill Jones); Richard Bay (Lab Deputy); John Hancock (Henry's Friend); Lynne Arden (Nurse); William Houze (Motel Owner); Maye Henderson, Lois Smith (Neighbors).

If filmgoers, especially black, chose to regard Sidney Poitier as the great black hope of establishment filmmaking, *Brother John,* the first of his films produced by his own (E & R) production company, took it all a step further by casting the superstar as a mystical human come to right wrongs in a southern town full of racial intolerance and strife. Unfortunately the prettified version of vicious bigotry and the softened retaliation by its victims depicted in this film vitiates any punch the major studio release might have had. In short, it needed to get down and get dirty. The production was roundly trounced by critics for the star-producer's indulgences. "[Poitier] ends up with a sort of rickety soapbox of melodrama, trapped by a script that expresses things smugly when it bothers to articulate social problems at all and trapped inside a role that encourages a lot of inscrutable, self-righteous pose-striking" (Gary Arnold, *Washington Post*). Richard Schickel (*Life* magazine) agreed, "Mr. Poitier's acquiescence in the process of his own canonization continues to mystify me. He's really too good an actor and too valuable a figure to be abused in this fashion."

Ailing black Sister Sarah (Lynn Hamilton) is admitted to the hospital for further testing by Dr. Henry L. Thomas (Will Geer) and dies during the night. The next morning her brother, John Kane (Sidney Poitier), appears suddenly in the sleepy southern town for the funeral, repeating a pattern that occurred after the death of his mother and father. Sheriff Orly Ball (Ramon Bieri) and District Attorney Lloyd Thomas (Bradford Dillman), the doctor's son, suspect Kane of being a high-level agitator from the north sent to stir up the black workers striking at the local Hill-Donaldson lumber factory. The sheriff and district attorney discover Kane's passport has visa stamps from many off-limits foreign countries and learn he is a fluent linguist. Meanwhile Kane and black schoolteacher Louisa MacGill (Beverly Todd) begin an affair. Kane is under constant observation, and when overaggressive policeman George (Warren J. Kemmerling) confronts him, Kane uses karate to outmaneuver him, just as he does later with three pugnacious black youths. Kane's intention to leave town is hampered by the police, who arrest him on a trumped-up charge. Matters are not helped when his prophecy that strike leader Charles Gray (Lincoln Kilpatrick) would die comes mysteriously true. It is Dr. Thomas who manages to free Kane so he can leave town. The elder physician is sure Kane is an alien envoy.

"Fortunately, the silly mystical mystery around the plot of *Brother John* revolves is not suggested until the end of the film. . . . Nothing in Goldstone's warm and unpatronising treatment of his characters provides any foundation for Brother John's vision of a human race racked by greed, hatred and ambition." (Herschel Weingrod, British *Monthly Film Bulletin*).

Only because of Sidney Poitier's tremendous following and the distribution clout of Columbia Pictures did *Brother John* squeak through financially at the box-office.

47. Brotherhood of Death (Downtown, 1976). Color, 85 minutes.

Producers Richard Barker, Bill Berry; *director* Berry; *story* Ronald K. Goldman; *screenplay* Berry; *song* Susan Minsky and Mark Schimmel; *sound* David Fraker; *camera* Fritz Roland; *editor* Berry.

Cast: Michael Hodge (Ace); Ron David (Leroy Winniford); Rick Ellis (Harold Turner, the Grand Cyclops); Brian Domorie (Mick); Ed Heath (Preacher); Mike Bass (Captain Quinn); Brian Clark (Sheriff); Kandy Hooker (Louise Freeman); Henry Peirkey (Boyfriend); Mark Robinson (Dope Dealing Soldier); Jon Rutledge (Registration Clerk); Vacountess E. Payne (Rose); Jon Feather (Army Instructor); Holly Haretberg (Winniford's Girlfriend); Wally Lamont (Gas Station Attendant); Barbara Cherry (Raymond's Girlfriend); Erich Holand (Soldier on Guard Duty); Mike Nash, Don Schmidt, Kip Nash, Greg Kelly, Richard York, Dick David, Chris Benson (Klansmen); *and:* Haskell Anderson, Frank Grant, Roy Jefferson, Larry Jones, Mike Thomas, Lee Tori.

As *Gordon's War* (1973) and the far lesser *The Black Six* (1974) (qq.v.) had demonstrated earlier, a wartime tour of duty in Vietnam could be useful to black citizens put upon on the homefront. Unfortunately this thesis is given such shoddy production values in *Brotherhood of Death* that much of the potential impact of the film falls flat. One of the picture's best moment is handled by Captain Quinn (Mike Bass), the veteran Vietnam officer who indoctrinates his southern black charges into the realities of combat duty. "This is a sick-ass war, troops, and the enemy's imagination is unlimited." He then gives them a full guide to aggressive survival. If only the movie could have kept this intensity and pacing.

Unfortunately the story deteriorates as the black U.S. military veterans return to Kincaid County in the Deep South and discover nothing has improved in their racially intolerant hometown. When the United Klan of America burns a black church, the brotherhood led by the black ex-soldiers fights back. To help their cause they establish a network of black domestics to learn what is happening among the white folk, and they also marshall their brothers into registering for the vote so they will have legitimate power at a future time.

48. Brothers (Warner Bros., 1977). Color, 104 minutes.

Executive producer Lee Savin; *in association with* Robert H. Greenberg, Herb Forgash; *producers* Edward Lewis, Mildred Lewis; *in charge of production* Sidney Galanty; *director* Arthur Barron; *screenplay* Edward Lewis, Mildred Lewis; *art director* Vince Creseman; *wardrobe* Gerry Pumaia; *music* Taj Mahal; *assistant director* Michael Blum; *sound editor* John Post; *camera* John Morrill; *editor* William Dornisch.

Cast: Bernie Casey (David Thomas); Vonetta McGee (Paula Jones); Ron O'Neal (Walter Nance); Rennie Roker (Lewis); Stu Gilliam (Robinson); John Lehne (Chief Guard McGee); Owen Pace (Joshua Thomas); Joseph Havener (Warden Leon); Martin St. Judge (Williams); Ricardo Brown (Morton); Susan Barrister (Tina); John Zaremba (Judge #2); Alonzo Bridges (Guard); Al Turner (Henry Taylor); Samantha Harper (Joan Kline); Richard Collen (Davis Brother); Richard Peck (Davis Brother); Mercedes Alberti (Woman Guard); Thomas Bellen (Guard); John Shay (Judge #1); Robert Cortes (Stuart); Janet Dey (F.B.I. Agent); Oliver Fletcher (Lacy); Sidney Galanity (Balaban); Trace Hunt (Mrs. Williams); Connie Morgan (Mrs. Thomas); Len Jewell (Mr. Thomas); Joan Lewis (Student); Bruce Simon (F.B.I. Man); Alphonso Williams (Bill); Dick Yarmy (District Attorney Wayne); David Shaw (Newscaster).

"He was a nobody; a black man in a white man's prison. She was a somebody; a notorious, beautiful, radical black professor. Their love story shocked the nation. This film is that story. And it happened."

In the late 1960s and early 1970s the highly publicized romance between intellectual black activist college professor Angela Davis and black militant convict George Jackson struck a national chord. Their courtship was conducted while he was in San Quentin prison for bank robbery. Later she would be tried but acquitted for helping to plan Jackson's breakout attempt during which his younger brother Jonathan and a judge died at the Marin County Courthouse. Jackson himself would later be killed in prison.

The uncompromising, hot-blooded narrative traces the sorrowful events leading to David Thomas (Bernie Casey) being arrested in Los Angeles as an accessory to armed robbery at a gas station. He is sentenced to one year to life, the duration depending on his behavior in prison. Once incarcerated he experiences the horrendous mistreatment of blacks in general (and him in particular) by the white guards and inmates of Lincoln City Prison. One of the few helpful influences behind bars is his cellmate, Walter Nance (Ron O'Neal), an intellectual who convinces Thomas of the need for education. ("You've been doin' time instead of usin' time," Nance explains, and urges him to read Malcom X and others to find out "who's been kickin' your ass.") The awakened Thomas participates in preparing the underground prison newspaper for the black brothers. Subsequently Nance is beaten to death by one of the sadistic white guards. Then Thomas's brother (Owen Pace) dies attempting to free him during his courtroom trial (for the murder of a guard he did not commit). Thomas becomes involved in a breakout attempt of his own and is killed. Through it all is the presence of the Paula Jones/Angela Davis (Vonetta McGee) character, who takes a growing interest in Thomas' plight and falls in love with him. Their doomed, unrequited romance, one only of words and feelings, is carried on at arms' length in the visitors' room of the prison, always under guard surveillance.

While critics acknowledged attractive Vonetta McGee's subtle performance as the film's dynamic heroine, it was Bernie Casey in the impassioned pivotal lead role who rightly received the bulk of plaudits. "[He] contributes a taut, thoughtful characterization of a man educated into organizing his fellow black inmates toward a seeming, ultimate victory" (A.H. Weiler, *New York Times*). Archer Winsten *(New York Post)* complimented Casey for demonstrating ". . . strength and dignity, and he is not asked by director Arthur Barron to indulge in theatrical excesses." Not to be overlooked was Ron O'Neal's all too brief role as the long-oppressed cellmate. *Newsweek* magazine reported, "Black movies, like O'Neal, have developed a whole new sobriety since the days of *Super Fly*."

What bothered many reviewers was that the facts of the case, which has many real-life ambiguities, received such a lopsided, slanted treatment in the film. "Anger is the strident keynote," observed Weiler of the *New York Times* about the film's biased script. *Variety* concurred, "With all of its good ingredients, it's a shame that a quality effort like this — stripped of all the usual exploitation elements that even many blacks have complained of — still falls back on 'Get Whitey' as its only lasting message." For Charles Michener (*Newsweek* magazine) this ". . . thorough, thoughtful film biography might have raised some troubling questions about the thin line separating radical tactics from common criminality, and it might have examined the conditions that made Jackson's brand of politics so compelling during the turbulent climate of the late 1960s. . . . *Brothers* robs Jackson of all the idiosyncrasies that helped make him a hero." Connie Johnson (*Soul* magazine) decided that ". . . *Brothers* is definitely a must-see for people who hunger for thought-provoking, sensitive, and uncompromising portrayals of Black experience," but she acknowledged it is "heavy-handed and depressing at times."

With filming of the jail scenes at the North Dakota State Penitentiary, *Brothers* captured all too well the horrors and raw reality of prison and its adverse effects on inmates of any race.

49. Buck and the Preacher (Columbia, 1972). Color, 102 minutes.
   Producer Joel Glickman; *associate producer* Herb Wallerstein; *director* Sidney Poitier; *story* Ernest Kinoy, Drake Walker; *screenplay* Kinoy; *production designer* Sydney Z. Litwack; *set decorator* Ernesto Carrasco; *costumes* Guy Berhille; *music* Benny Carter; *songs* Sonny Terry and Brownie McGee; *assistant directors* Sheldon Schrager, Jesus Marin; *sound* Tom Overton; *special effects* Leon Ortega; *camera* Alex Phillips, Jr.; *editor* Pembroke J. Herring.
   Cast: Sidney Poitier (Buck); Harry Belafonte (Preacher [Reverend Willis Oakes Rutherford]); Ruby Dee (Ruth); Cameron Mitchell (Deshay); Denny Miller (Floyd); Nita Talbot (Mme. Esther); John Kelly (Sheriff); Tony Brubaker (Headman); Bobby Johnson (Man Who Is Shot); James McEachin (Kingston); Clarence Muse (Cudjo); Lynn Hamilton (Sarah); Doug Johnson (Sam); Errol John (Joshua); Ken Maynard (Little Henry); Fred Waugh (Mizoo); Bill Shannon (Tom); Phil Adams (Frank); Walter Scott (Earl); John Howard (George); Enrique Lucero (Indian Chief); Julie Robinson (Sinsie); Jose Carlo Ruiz (Brave); Jerry Gatlin (Deputy); Ivan Scott (Express Agent); John Kennedy (Bank Teller).
   Buck and the Preacher, the first feature film both co-produced and directed by star Sidney Poitier, is dedicated to "...those whose graves are as unmarked as their place in history." This sets the stage for the underlying message of "brotherhood" in this black Western, which, unlike so many of the genre that followed, tells its slam-bang tale *not* with blatant militarism but using a vibrantly paced comic Westen motif. At heart *Buck and the Preacher* is pure family entertainment. Vincent Canby noted in his *New York Times* review, "If they do nothing else, these new Soul Westerns may serve to desegregate our myths, which have always been out of the jurisdiction of the Supreme Court."
   Former Union Army cavalryman Buck (Sidney Poitier) serves as guide for wagon trains of blacks migrating westward seeking freedom in the new land. This exodus upsets the Louisiana farmers, who want cheap labor kept in the South. They hire bounty hunter Deshay (Cameron Mitchell) and his men to bring back the latest batch of ex-slaves. After destroying one wagon train led by Buck, Deshay focuses on Buck as his enemy and offers a $500 reward for information leading to his capture. This bounty intrigues the Preacher (Harry Belafonte), a charlatan (of the fictitious High and Low Orders of the Holiness Persuasion Church) who uses his disguise to woo charity from unwary victims. (In case any prey is reluctant to surrender his valuables, the Preacher carries a persuasive pistol in his Bible.) The scoundrelly Preacher catches up with Buck as he is convincing the Indians to permit his convoy of former slaves safe passage through their territory. Soon thereafter Deshay and his night riders set upon the St. Anne Parish wagon train, burning the supplies, killing some of the travelers including Little Toby (Dennis Hines), and stealing the pioneers' savings. When the travelers keep on going, the Preacher is impressed enough to join them. Buck and the Preacher track Deshay and most of his men to the bordello of Madam Esther (Nita Talbot) in Copper Springs and kill them, only to discover the culprits have frittered away the black people's money. Buck, the Preacher and Buck's lady love, Ruth (Ruby Dee in one of her too-few screen

Top, seated left–right at table: **Stu Gilliam, Martin St. Judge and Bernie Casey in** *Brothers* **(1977).** *Bottom, left–right:* **Harry Belafonte, Ruby Dee and Sidney Poitier in** *Buck and the Preacher* **(1971).**

assignments), retaliate by robbing the local bank and then rejoin their wagon train. The Indians agree to help them against the law, but they refuse to sell Buck the firearms he wants, claiming to need the weapons and ammunition themselves to combat the white man. Nevertheless, when Deshay's henchman Floyd (Denny Miller) and his posse attack the wagon train, the Indians perform a last-minute rescue. With the renegade attackers defeated, the wagon train continues its journey westward to the green valleys of Colorado.

Buck and the Preacher was a reunion for Sidney Poitier and co-producer/co-star Harry Belafonte, who had been part of the American Negro Theater in the mid-1940s. The film had begun production in February 1971 in Durango, Mexico, with Joseph Sargent directing. Five days later, Poitier assumed the role of director. "It was at the insistence of Belafonte, with my concurrence," Poitier would explain to an *Ebony* magazine interviewer. "I thought that Sargent was not giving us what we wanted and it was certainly too late to ask Columbia to wait and send us another director."

Arthur Knight (*Saturday Review* magazine) labeled *Buck and the Preacher* "... a kind of 'Wagon Train' in blackface," while Kevin Thomas (*Los Angeles Times*) thought the film "... even takes on the comic aspects of *Butch Cassidy and the Sundance Kid.*" Colin L. Westerbeck, Jr. (*Commonweal* magazine), observed, "Yet I don't want to give the impression that Buck and his unscrupulous sidekick, the Preacher, are just Roy Rogers and Gabby Hayes in blackface. There is also an undertone in the film, whispered benignly, 'Up against the wall, m-f, this is a stick-up.'" And it was *Variety* which highlighted, "Poitier also directed, which may explain his occasional air of not really being involved in the acting [and] it is Belafonte who dominates the film."

Perhaps the most heartfelt review was by Maurice Peterson, writing in the black magazine *Essence*: "I usually dislike westerns because they are the hardest for me to 'color in' especially when the cowboys are slaughtering red men. In *Buck and the Preacher,* however, I was watching western heroes with whom I could identify completely for the first time. There on the screen were the courageous Black men and women I'd kept quiet and secret in the back of my mind all my life—people who had a real place in history. The emotional reaction was explosive!" And Peterson adds, "...judging from the howling cheers, thunderous applause, and even the tears that were in some eyes, I know that the rest of the Black audience felt as gratified as I did."

Buck and the Preacher grossed a solid $3,100,000 in domestic film rentals. Sidney Poitier and Harry Belafonte would reunite next on screen in a contemporary action comedy, *Uptown Saturday Night* (1974) (q.v.).

50. **Bucktown** (American International, 1975). Color, 94 minutes.

Executive producer Ric R. Roman; *producer* Bernard Schwartz; *associate producer* Philip Hazelton; *director* Arthur Marks; *art directors* George Costello, John Carter; *makeup* Gordon Freed; *wardrobe* Casey Spencer; *music* Johnny Pate; *song* Luther Rabb; *stunt co-ordinator* Eric Cord; *assistant director* Bert Gold; *sound* Glen Mabson; *sound effects* Marvin Lerner; *camera* Robert Virchall; *editor* George Folsey, Jr.

Cast: Fred Williamson (Duke Johnson); Pam Grier (Aretha); Thalmus Rasulala (Roy); Tony King (T.J.); Bernie Hamilton (Harley); Art Lund (Chief Patterson); Tierre Turner (Steve); Morgan Upton (Sam); Carl Weathers (Hambone); Jim Bohan (Clete); Robert Burton (Merle); Gene Simms (Josh); Bruce Watson (Bag Man).

In one of his revealing interviews in 1975, Fred Williamson remarked, "I'm not interested in social, uplifting movies. I'm not involved in elevating anybody's social standards through the movie industry." *Bucktown* certainly proves his point. "AIP's blaxploitation mill grinds out films that are merely flimsy excuses for prolonged violent confrontations between protagonists, usually black and white. This Fred Williamson topliner veers slightly from the formula only in the fact that blacks beat up as much on other blacks as they do whites" *(Variety)*. The trade paper was quite correct, but this picture adds several dimensions to the already familiar genre context.

The city of Buchanan (somewhere in the South) has deservedly earned its reputation as a freewheeling town of gambling joints, whorehouses, and crooked police. It is a metropolis where, according to one citizen, "The dice keep rolling, the 'ho's keep 'ho'ing, and the cash keeps flowing" (hence the name Bucktown). Home to this vice-ridden city comes Duke Johnson to bury his brother, Ben, who was pummeled to death by the local police for failing to pay the monthly graft. (Pummeling is a favorite sport of white police chief Patterson [Art Lund], who at one point in the movie is seen beating up a black suspect. "You sure do enjoy your work," observes a cop. "You sure got that right," admits the gleeful Patterson.) Duke's arrival allows the filmmakers to emphasize the town's corruption with exchanges such as the following between Duke and a cab driver:

CABBIE: Do you believe in God?
JOHNSON: Yeah. Sure. Why not?
CABBIE: Then you're in the wrong place.

But Johnson is a fearless big city dude, as the viewer learns early on. Even the sinister police chief Patterson eyes the sharp black man warily, saying, "You're not much for manners," already fearful of the powerful newcomer. Johnson is the kind of man — unlike most in Bucktown — who won't stand for any nonsense, even from the white authorities. "You can eat the crap they dish out, but not this baby," he tells his brother's girlfriend, Aretha (Pam Grier).

Former football star Harley (Bernie Hamilton) convinces Johnson to reopen Ben's lucrative gambling salon, the Club Alabam. Two policemen try to intimidate him, but Johnson disposes of them, impressing Aretha. Later that night, Chief Patterson and his men attack Johnson's house to scare him into leaving town. Instead he decides to stay. He telephones his old street pal Roy (Thalmus Rasulala) to bring some muscle to town. Roy arrives quickly with an assortment of burly black hoods, including Hambone (Carl Weathers). In short order, the newest gangsters in town dispatch many of the local police and generally kick ass. With the acquiescence of the town's black mayor, Johnson and Roy replace those they have killed with their own men, and begin swindling the citizens themselves. Meanwhile, Johnson has fallen in love with Aretha. Although Johnson insists he does not care about his share of the graft, Roy saves it for him. Because Roy's goons resent Johnson's influence over Roy, they secretly beat up Harley, hoping it will split the two leaders. When Johnson accuses Roy of betrayal, the latter orders his men to silence Johnson. The henchmen threaten to burn the Club Alabam. Johnson, with a street-smart boy named Steve in tow, steals a tank from the local military installation and crashes into the town jail to rescue Aretha and Harley. The hoods are all killed

in the ensuing gunplay, leaving Johnson and Roy to fight it out without guns—
the loser will leave Bucktown. Soon the bloody fisticuffs that start in the city
hall move outside, and Roy is knocked unconscious. Duke and Aretha walk
away. The closing theme song insists that life in Bucktown is improving.

Bucktown examines several major idioms of the blaxploitation genre.
There are the corrupt, conniving white law "enforcers" headed by Chief Patterson. He and his men are sadistic and viciously bigoted. "Get your black ass out
of town," says one of their number to a victim. Another confides to a fellow
officer, "Hell, what's one more dead nigger more or less." *Bucktown* also shows
that some of the black citizenry are equally corrupt. As Aretha lectures
Johnson, "Let me tell you something about people, big shot. Whether they're
white, black, green or purple, when they smell a few dollars they all act alike."
And the storyline of this film proves her point.

If the general tenor of many films of the genre is to have the black heroes
stand up to the Man, *Bucktown* points out that being super cool and indifferent
to crime, squalor, and inhumanity is equally desirable. As Roy sees it, "Respect
comes from knowin' how it is in the street. What you have to do to get by and
doin' it. Doin' well ... damn well. That's what it's all about." All the lead
characters of this motion picture believe this tenet: Tough-as-nails Johnson
thinks nothing of killing a man and allows, "You're damn right I play it safe.
I'm tired of leading the charge." Little Steve admits, "I'm just trying to grow
up fast in a fast town." Easy-virtued Aretha has seen it all and rolls with the
punches. She suggests why she has become blase to the venality around her
when she asks, "Do you think you have a monopoly on hard times?" Roy used
to be a good guy and is now as bad as they come. According to this ultimate
cynic, "You show me anybody who cares about anyone and I'll show you a
fool. It all revolves around the big 'G'—the big green." Even downtrodden
Harley's best dream is a twisted hope for the rebirth of the sleazy saloon which
robs his brothers and sisters of their money and gives them false peace of mind
through liquor and drugs. "I ain't nothing but an old football player, Duke.
Maybe drink too much every now and then. But if you open that club it would
sure make me feel like somebody."

All in all, the *New York Times'* Vincent Canby labeled *Bucktown* "silly
and vicious." As for the lead performers, *Variety* commented that "Williamson
is a genuine actor of promise who doesn't help his career in such vehicles." The
United Catholic Conference gave the "vicious, mindless" movie a "condemned" rating, adding that it was "...produced as usual by whites, a little
paradox that brings to mind the Communist maxim about the greedy capitalist
eager to sell the rope that will be used to hang him."

Of Grier's performance as the life-weary, luscious Aretha who has seen
too much and isn't sure if Johnson is really her Great Black Hope, *Variety* said
that she "looks stunning as ever, but *Bucktown* mires her in a role that could
set back femme lib at least a decade." Grier appears exceedingly passive in her
reactive role, in itself a strong change of pace from her last several movie
assignments. She goes through her paces, alternately snarling at and playing
up to and with Johnson, but her acting mind seems elsewhere, even when tussling in bed with her superstud protector-turned-lover.

Bucktown was shot on location in Platte City and Kansas City, Missouri. Screen newcomer Carl Weathers also appeared the same year with Pam Grier in *Friday Foster* (q.v.). *Bucktown* was a reunion for Fred Williamson and Art Lund, who had earlier squared off in *Black Caesar* (1972) (q.v.). In 1988 *Bucktown* was freshly reissued on videocassette, leading *Video Review* magazine to note, "Fred Williamson and the fabulously monickered Thalmus Rasulala butt heads when they both want to clean up a corrupt town in this angry, suspect 'message' movie."

51. Burglar (Warner Bros., 1987). Color, 102 minutes.

Producers Kevin McCormick, Michael Hirsh; *director* Hugh Wilson; *based on books by* Lawrence Block; *screenplay* Joseph Loeb III, Matthew Weisman, Wilson; *production designer* Todd Hallowell; *art director* Michael Corenblith; *set decorator* Daniel Loren May; *costumes* Susan Becker; *music* Sylvester Levay; *camera* William A. Fraker; *editors* Fredric Steinkamp, William Steinkamp.

Cast: Whoopi Goldberg (Bernice Rhodenbarr); Bob Goldthwait (Carl Hefler); G.W. Bailey (Ray Kirschman); Lesley Ann Warren (Dr. Cynthia Sheldrake); James Handy (Carson Verrill); Anne DeSalvo (Detective Todras); John Goodman (Detective Nyswander); Elizabeth Ruscio (Frankie); Vyto Ruginis (Graybow); Larry Mintz (Knobby); *and:* Raye Birk, Scott Lincoln.

If *Jumpin' Jack Flash* (1986) (q.v.) was a creative setback for very talented Whoopi Goldberg, *Burglar* was a bigger artistic step downward. It was the type of new wave black action-comedy film that could have been (and was) written for Eddie Murphy and instead ended up with another fine comedian being wasted in the environs. As *TV Guide* magazine acknowledged when the lackluster film appeared on television less than a year after its theatrical release, "*Burglar* is a run-of-the-mill whodunit made barely redeemable by the presence of Whoopi Goldberg. . . ."

Bernice Rhodenbarr (Whoopi Goldberg) has recently been released from prison and works in a San Francisco bookshop. Being a habitual cat burglar, she cannot resist robbing the wealthy. A dishonest retired policeman, Ray Kirschman (G.W. Bailey), warns her that unless she pays him a bribe of $20,000-plus, he will alert the police to her current activities. A fence touts Bernice to Dr. Cynthia Sheldrake (Lesley Ann Warren), a neurotic dentist who wants the thief to steal back jewelry taken from her by her estranged spouse. Bernice attempts the caper, but in midstream the husband returns, and while she is hiding in the closet, he is stabbed to death with a dental instrument. Sheldrake is arrested for the crime. However, the police suspect Bernice may be the real culprit, and they tear up her raggedy apartment looking for evidence. Because her mentally unbalanced friend and poodle groomer Carl Hefler (Bob Goldthwait) wants Bernice to go straight, he agrees to help her prove her innocence. The trail leads to the Maytime bar, where she learns Sheldrake's late husband associated with violent Graybow (Vyto Ruginis), a truly bizarre artist. When Graybow proves a seemingly dead-end trial, the next clue leads to the bald-headed Knobby (Larry Mintz), in whose apartment she finds $100,000 in counterfeit bills. This sheds new light on the case and leads to her uncovering the counterfeit plates in Graybow's place. Just as things are making sense, both of these men are killed. Sheldrake is released from jail and Bernice appears at her apartment for a confrontation. The jigsaw puzzle falls into place, leading to Sheldrake's homosexual lawyer, Carson Verrill (James Handy). The finale occurs in a deserted wooded area with boxing champ (!) Bernice slugging it out with the bulky Verrill.

If any sequence in this artistic jumble — filled with violence, gutter talk, and pointless slapstick chases — is enjoyable, it is the opening segment. Bernice is disguised as a shuffling elderly domestic, trudging into a large suburban home. While the owner is out jogging, she expertly robs the premises of money, jewelry, and (from a wall safe) rare stamps. As she makes her getaway, the owner and his chauffeur encounter her, and in a snap of a script page, Bernice becomes a screaming buffoon, insisting hysterically she saw the burglars fleeing through the hedges. While they chase "thataway" after the phantom crooks, she makes her timely exit. If only the film had ended there.

Burglar was directed and co-scripted by Hugh Wilson, who created the highly regarded teleseries "Frank's Place" the same year. Wilson also helmed *Police Academy* (1984), which featured *Burglar* co-stars G.W. Bailey and Bob Goldthwait. Although the movie was dismissed by most critics as claptrap, *People* magazine reasoned, "Whoopi Goldberg and Bob Goldthwait between them have enough charisma to float a battleship, so they keep this comedy mystery bobbing along." *Burglar* grossed an amazing, but still disappointing, $16,337,355 in its first eight weeks of U.S. theatrical distribution before disappearing into pay-TV and videocassette limbo.

52. The Bus Is Coming (William Thompson International, 1971). Color, 109 minutes.

Producer Horace Jackson; *associate producer* Thurston G. Frazier; *director* Wendell James Franklin; *screenplay* Jackson, Robert H. Raff, Mike Rhodes; *art directors* Haags/Jacobsen; *music* Tom McIntosh; *production coordinator* Herbert H. Dow; *assistant directors* Ruben Watt, Ralph Sariego; *sound* Nancy Shaffer; *sound effects editors* Sidney Lubow, Jack Lowry, Richard Raderman; *camera* Rhodes; *editor* Donald R. Rode.

Cast: Mike Simms (Billy Mitchell); Stephanie Raulkner (Tanya); Burl Bullock (Michael); Tony Sweeting (Dobie); Jack Stillman (John); Sandra Reed (Miss Nickerson); Bob Brubaker (Chief Jackson); Morgan Jones (Tim Naylor); Dick Ryal (Corie Smith); Juan Russell (Little Horace); Cinnamon Jones (Black Teacher); Connie Milton (White Teacher); Garland Minor, Sherri Ann Shorter, Richard Paxton, Coleen "Pae" Rush, Phillip E. Pulling, Tara Kelly, Stanley Patrick, Hil Basen, Ann Mack, Lonnie Bradford (Militants); *and:* Eddie Kendrix.

Black Vietnam War veteran Billy Mitchell (Mike Simms) returns home to the black community of Watts in Los Angeles, only to find his older brother, Joe, has been murdered for no good reason by a racist white policeman. The police, led by Chief Jackson (Bob Brubaker) and his two sinister bigoted cops Jim Naylor (Morgan Jones) and Corie Smith (Dick Ryal) fear that clean-cut Mitchell will become a troublemaker. Meanwhile, Michael (Burl Bullock), as

Top, left–right: **Raye Birk, Whoopi Goldberg, and Scott Lincoln in** *Burglar* **(1987).**
Bottom: **Burl Bullock** *(left)* **and Tony Sweeting in** *The Bus Is Coming* **(1971).**

the head of the militant Black Fists, wants to unite his people and thinks making a martyr of Mitchell's dead brother can be the needed catalyst. Before long Mitchell is pushed into the action to join together with the brothers and sisters; the methods turn from peaceful to violent as he and the others cope with the menacing law enforcers (with whom there is a shootout). The film ends with a saying from Isaiah 40:31: "But they that wait upon the Lord shall renew their strength."

"Story line, which approaches its premise honestly," reported *Variety,* "makes no particular effort to excoriate the police as a whole but rather the actions of two individual officers in straightforward narrative.... Technical credits are well executed, particularly Mike Rhodes' color photography."

Told in leisurely fashion, there is a riveting inevitability to the story's outcome. The film's title is metaphoric, referring to the bus of hope coming to relieve the downtrodden black citizens. Throughout the film a blind, black harmonica player sits at the bus stop waiting. Constantly a little boy asks him, "Is the bus coming? Is the bus coming?" "It will," is his regular reply. At the finale, the youngster spots a public bus moving down the main throughfare of the slums, and he runs jubilantly to find the elderly man at the bus stop. Together they proudly and happily board the bus.

The Bus Is Coming was filmed on the Los Angeles streets of Watts with the cooperation of the municipal government.

53. Busted Up (Shapiro, 1986). Color, 90 minutes.

Executive producer Laurence Nesis; *producers* Damian Lee, David Mitchell; *associate producer* Curt Peterson; *director* Conrad E. Palmisano; *screenplay* Lee; *art director* Stephen Surjik; *set decorator* William Fleming; *costumes* Nancy Kaye; *makeup* Kathleen Graham; *music* Charles Barnett; *songs:* Gordon Groddy, Carlotta Kee, Irene Cara, Donna Summers, Michael Omartian; *fight co-ordinator* Tony Morelli; *stunt co-ordinator* Ted Hanlan; *assistant director* Roman Buchon; *sound* Nolan Roberts; *special effects props* Peter Ferri; *camera* Ludvik Bogner; *editor* Gary Zubeck.

Cast: Paul Coufolos (Earl Bird); Irene Cara (Simone); Stan Shaw (Angie); Tony Rosato (Irving Drayton); Frank Pellegrino (Nick Sevins); Gordon Judges (Tony Tenera); Nika Kaufhold (Sara); Mike D'Aguilar (Granite Foster); George Buza (Captain Hook); John Dee (Daddy Ray); Nick Nichols (Mr. Greene); John Ritchie (Phil); Rick Orman (Teddy); Garfield Andrews (Bobby); Al Bernardo (Al); Lawrence King-Phillips (Kenny); David Mitchell (Greg Bird); Sonja Lee (Darlene); Tony Morelli (Jackson); Lousi Di Bianco (Frankie); Marshall Perlmuter (Superintendent); Zack Nesis (Spence); Raymond Marlowe (Jake); Dan Dunlop (Man in Restaurant); Teddy McWharters (Johnny); Pat Patterson (Neil); Dennis Strong (Fight Promoter); Damian Lee, John Lapadula, Helder Goncalves (Gangsters); Gordon Masten (Justice of the Peace); Reg Dreger (Jail Cop); Conrad E. Palmisano (Monty); Frank Ruffo, Errol Slue, Robert Welsh (Fight Referees); Richard Todd, Jerome Tiberghien, John Scott, Paul MacCullum (Drayton's Thugs); Kevin Godding, Dennis Salovic (Corsican Brothers); Wendy Lands (Drayton's Date); Janet Good (Fat Rosie); Goerge Hevenor (Croupier); Annie McCauley (Cigarette Girl); William

Paris, Ken Stern (Prison Inmates); Kim Carjuso, Joanne Garfinkle (Girls in Restaurant); Daryl Sarkisian (Guy in Restaurant); John Dario (Man in Gym).

In the later 1980s the influence of music videos, martial arts, and mixed ethnic ghetto life were combined for a rash of action-musical features geared to young moviegoers. The thread of these films' plots hinged often on the slight moral message of fairness to minorities. Usually the colorful street gangs in these entries are more interested in fast romance, hot music, and a good (relatively harmless) street melee, than in any serious gunplay or heavy moralizing against the Man.

Earl Bird (Paul Coufolos), a good-natured fighter, and his pal Angie (Stan Shaw) own a neighborhood gym. Their youth center is located in the heart of the slum neighborhood that crooked Irving Drayton (Tony Rosato) and his mob want to develop for big dollars. The fact that many poor tenement dwellers have nowhere else to live does not concern Drayton. When pressuring Earl Bird and Angie doesn't work, he comes up with an appealing scheme. Earl Bird and his squad are to be pitted against Drayton's meanest contenders. If Earl Bird's team loses, Drayton gets to buy the club and the neighborhood.

What gives this too predictable motion picture a twist from the *Rocky*-type film is that Earl Bird is not the usual boxer using conventional rules, but a professional street fighter — a round ring boxer like those of *The Black Street Fighter* (1976) and *Black Fist* (1977) (qq.v.). Then there is the picture's saving grace, Irene Cara of *Fame* (1980). She is the feisty club vocalist who six years before left her husband and baby girl to pursue a singing career which never materialized in the big leagues. She's now home to reclaim her child and, unknown to her (but known to the audience), Earl Bird. An accomplished actress, Cara's Simone has several telling moments when she explains to her bewildered spouse how hurt she was that he never once tried to stop her when she left town to foster her show business career. She admits she never made a success of her efforts, but at least, she wails with pride, she tried. Then, of course, she sings several songs, including "She Works Hard for the Money" and "I Can't Help Feeling Empty" (which she composed) and "Busted Up" (which she co-composed with Gordon Groddy). In many quiet ways Irene Cara has proven to be the most versatile young black film actress of the 1980s.

The independently produced *Busted Up* was filmed on location in Canada. It also featured the much-overlooked Stan Shaw, who made several blaxploitation films in the 1970s: *Truck Turner* (1974), *Darktown Strutters* (1975), and *T.N.T. Jackson* (1975) (qq.v.), as well as appearing in such non-genre entries as *Rocky* (1976) and *The Boys in Company C* (1978). His sensitive, responsive performance is a joy to see, especially in contrast to the wooden "acting" of Paul Coufolos. *Busted Up* had very slight distribution before joining the ranks of videocassette releases.

54. Bustin' Loose (United Artists, 1981). Color, 94 minutes.

Executive producer William Greaves; *producers* Richard Pryor, Michael S. Glick; *director* Oz Scott; *story* Pryor; *adaptor* Lonne Elder III; *screenplay* Roger L. Simon; *art directors* Charles R. Davis, John Corso; *set decorators* John M. Dwyer, Marc Meyer; *costume designers* Bill Whitten, Stephen Loomis;

makeup Ron Snyder, Charles House, Tony Lloyd, Michael Blake; *music/ music conductor* Mark Davis; *songs* Roberta Flack; *music editor* Robert Mayer; *assistant directors* Clifford C. Coleman, Maximiliano Bing, Hope Goodwin, John Syrjamaki; *stunt co-ordinators* George Sawaya, Richard Washington; *sound* Jim Alexander; *sound effects editors* John Stacy, Glenn Hoskinson; *special effects* Melbourne Arnold; *camera* Dennis Dalzell; *editor* David Holden.

Cast: Richard Pryor (Joe Braxton); Cicely Tyson (Vivian Perry); Alphonso Alexander (Martin); Kia Cooper (Samantha); Edwin De Leon (Ernesto); Jimmy Hughes (Harold); Edwin Kinter (Anthony); Tami Luchow (Linda); Angel Ramirez (Julio); Janet Wong (Annie); Robert Christian (Donald); George Coe (Dr. Wilson T. Schuyler); Peggy McCay (Gladys Schuyler); Luke Andreas (Loader); Earl Billings (Man at Parole Office); Michael A. Esler (Cop); Paul Gardner (Anchorman); Ben Gerard (Man); Gary Coetzman (Store Manager); Joe Jacobs (Watchman); Paul Mooney (Marvin); Lee Noblitt (Farmer); Inez Pedroza (Herself); Morgan Roberts (Uncle Humphrey); Rick Saways, Vern Taylor (Patrolmen); Gloria Jewel Waggener (Aunt Beedee); Shila Turna (Girl in Card Game); Jonelle White (Sales Clerk); Jewell Williams (Thiss Thomas); Sunny Woods (Linette).

Bustin' Loose is an odd film in many ways. Even with Richard Pryor starring as a unscrupulous small-time crook, it is a far cry from the tumultuous action pictures like *The Mack* (1973), *Uptown Saturday Night* (1974), or *Greased Lightning* (1976) (qq.v.) that superstar comic Pryor had populated in the 1970s. It is a congenial low-key family comedy that one might have expected to boast of Sidney Poitier as a more likely star. But this was the 1980s, and the angry message films of the 1970s were a worn-out device in Hollywood. *Bustin' Loose* teams flippant, high-living Richard Pryor with conservative Emmy Award–winning *(The Autobiography of Miss Jane Pittman)* and Oscar-nominated *(Sounder)* Cicely Tyson, acknowledged to be the top contemporary black dramatic actress. Pryor, wanting to stretch his acting style and reach new audiences, had personally selected Cicely Tyson as his co-star.

Bustin' Loose, under the working title *Family Dreams,* had begun shooting on location in Ellensburgh, Washington, in the winter of 1979–80. Universal was not thrilled with the results and planned a delayed fall 1980 release for it. Meanwhile Pryor made three more films, including *Stir Crazy* (1980) (q.v.). Then, on the night of June 9, 1980, the drug-prone Pryor accidentally set himself ablaze and only by a miracle survived the severe burns to his body. After an amazingly swift recovery and after *Stir Crazy* proved a box-office bonanza, a newly enthused Universal ordered additional takes and retakes on *Bustin' Loose* as well as adding several Roberta Flack songs to the proceedings.

Bungling burglar Joe Braxton (Richard Pryor) narrowly misses being returned to jail by employing hysterical chicanery in the courtroom. But his Philadelphia parole officer, Donald Kinsey (Robert Christian), has plans for him. He tells the footloose Braxton he must fix and drive a fifteen-year-old bus to Redmond, Washington, outside of Seattle . . . or else! His passengers include the idealistic but no-nonsense Vivian Perry (Cicely Tyson) and eight

Cicely Tyson, Richard Pryor, and a busload of child actors in *Bustin' Loose* (1981).

children from the Claremont School for emotionally disturbed and special children. The school has been closed for lack of funding, and rather than see the youths transferred to a ghetto school, she is going to somehow transplant them to her family's small farm across the country. As they start their journey, Braxton must contend with a nightmare of road mishaps, a determined schoolteacher leader, and, worst of all, the combativeness of these contentious youths. They include water-pistol-carrying Ernesto (Edwin De Leon), pyromaniac Anthony (Edwin Kinter), blind Harold (James Hughes), street-tough Martin (Alphonso Alexander), sexually precocious Linda (Tami Luchow), and silent Annie (Janet Wong). The trek across America is fraught with disasters caused by nature, the old bus, the disturbed children, and an assortment of unpleasant people (including Ku Klux Klansmen). Meanwhile, the jealous Kinsey catches up with the bus and is convinced Braxton and Vivian are having an affair. He pursues the group to Washington with a stop-off in jail himself. The bus reaches Washington, and the children, most of whom have solved at least some of their emotional problems, quickly adapt to farm life. But there is a $15,000 mortgage loan overdue. "We're not losers," Braxton insists. He happens onto a pyramid financing scam in town and cons the con artists. After escaping the angered crooks when Vivian tosses the ill-gotten money out of the truck window, they return to the farm to find the children have charmed the local banker and his wife into offering financial support. Kinsey appears on the scene, but seeing that Braxton and Vivian are truly in love, he tells his charge to remain with the teacher.

"Check out this mediocre patch job, if only to see how Richrd Pryor transforms it into bracing entertainment.... Veteran theatrical director Oz

Scott lets things turn to sentimental goo near the end, but before that Pryor (who has to share the blame, since the story idea was his) has cajoled mirth out of everything from white guilt to the Ku Klux Klan" (*People* magazine). Richard Schickel (*Time* magazine) was critical of the project: "Considering his box office strength, one would think that Pryor could command the creation of vehicles to match his gift. Or perhaps he likes being the best thing about a picture. . . ." Equally critical was Vincent Canby (*New York Times*): "Only the incomparable Richard Pryor could make a comedy as determinedly, aggressively sentimental as *Bustin' Loose*. . . . [It is his] somewhat obsequious attempt to capture the family audience, though I suspect there are plenty of family audiences who prefer him at his more obscene. This movie is a cheerfully hackneyed, B-picture vehicle. . . ."

The R-rated (mostly for Richard Pryor's colorful language) *Bustin' Loose* grossed a respectable $15,417,626 in domestic film rentals. It led to a derivative and far-different-postured teleseries version which debuted in syndication in the fall of 1987 for a season's run. This family-oriented sitcom starred Jimmie Walker as Sonny and Vonetta McGee as Mimi.

[*Note:* There are very noticeable physical differences on screen between the pre- and post-accident Richard Pryor, and the star was the first to admit that the accident had caused him to do a lot of reevaluating of his much-reported lifestyle.]

55. The Cable Car Murder (CBS-TV, 11/19/71). Color, 78 minutes.

Producer E. Jack Neuman; *associate producer* Lloyd Richard; *director* Jerry Thorpe; *teleplay* Herman Miller; *art director* Bill Malley; *music* Jerry Goldsmith; *camera* Fred J. Koenekamp; *editors* Alex Beaton, John W. Holmes.

Cast: Robert Hooks (Inspector Lou Van Alsdale); Jeremy Slate (Sergeant Pat Cassidy); Robert Wagner (Howard McBride); Carol Lynley (Kathy Cooper); Simon Oakland (Captain E.J. Goodlad); Jose Ferrer (Dr. Charles Bedford); John Randolph (Frederick D. Cooper); Don Pedro Colley (Fred Trench); Joyce Jameson (Lulu); Wesley Lau (Inspector Poole); James McEachin (Don Cope); Lawrence Cook (Harold Britten); H.B. Haggerty (J.P. Moose); Ta-Tanisha (Rainie Lewis); Milton Stewart (Ernie Deeds); Mario Van Peebles (Rafael); Fred Carson (Victor Shoddy); Marian Collier (Surgical Nurse); Ta-Ronce Allen (Lilly); Jarrod Wong (Ben).

"Ultimately film blurs around the edges but earnest quality of performances generally sustain" *(Daily Variety)*.

Three black youths, including Rafael (Mario Van Peebles), create a disturbance on a San Francisco cable car to distract from the murder of a white man. The victim is the son of wealthy urbanite Frederick D. Cooper (John Randolph), whose other son died mysteriously and recently at sea. According to the surviving offspring, Kathy Cooper (Carol Lynley), the latter was on heroin. Black Inspector Lou Van Alsdale (Robert Hooks) and white Sergeant Pat Cassidy (Jeremy Slate) are assigned to the case by tough and impatient Captain E.J. Goodlad (Simon Oakland). The complex murder trail leads to the Coopers' posturing physician, Dr. Charles Bedford (Jose Ferrer); to seemingly good-natured Howard McBride (Robert Wagner), who knew the deceased; to a helpful desk clerk tipster, Lulu (Joyce Jameson); to frustrated do-gooder Rainie Lewis (Ta-Tanisha), who is killed; and, most menacingly of all, to Fred Trench (Don Pedro Colley), the head of the black underworld. The latter warns Van Alsdale, "You take chances, brother."

At this juncture in Hollywood, black leading men were gaining increased popularity, but the television medium was not ready for any down-and-dirty on-camera shenanigans from a pivotal black focal character. Thus the safer way to take advantage of the more pungent blaxploitation craze in theatrical films was to have the TV counterpart be a clean-cut, intelligent citizen on the right side of the law. Robert Hooks had starred previously as Detective Jeff Ward in the teleseries "N.Y.P.D." (1967–69). *The Cable Car Murder* was the pilot for a projected series to have featured Hooks, Oakland, and Slate, which never materialized. This production was later expanded to a ninety-six-minute version and released under the title *Cross Current*. Nearly two decades later Mario Van Peebles, the son of trendsetting Melvin Van Peebles *(Sweet Sweetback's Baadasssss Song,* 1971), would become a TV star with his "Sonny Spoon" teleseries for NBC in 1988.

56. The Candy Tangerine Man (Moonstone, 1975). Color, 88 minutes.

Producer/director Matt Cimber; *screenplay* George Theakos; *sets* Cloudberry-Thunderstone; *makeup* Gale Peterson; *wardrobe* Caroline Davis; *music* Smoke; *assistant director* Jef Richard; *production supervisor* Bethel G. Buckalew; *production co-ordinator* Norma Rosenberg; *stunt co-ordinator* Bill Drake; *sound* Dick Damon, Don Courad; *sound editor* Colin Waddy; *special effects* Harry Woolman; *camera* Ken Gibb; *editor* Bud Wainer.

Cast: John Daniels (Black Baron/Ron); *with:* Tracy King, Tom Hankerson, Marva Farmer, Buck Flower, Richard Kennedy, George Pelster, Mike Angel, Talia Cochrane, Eli Haines, Pat Wright, Teng Lan Linn, Carolyn Shelby, Zeonolia Whita, Barbara Burbon, Robin Murphy, Kim Joseph, Edye Ramsey, Doug Haverty, Joann Brudo, Bobbie Jean Williams, Gene Rutherford, Jef Richard, Bill Drake, Jim Sims and "the actual hookers and blades of the Sunset Strip in Hollywood."

If the raw and energetic *The Mack* (1973) (q.v.), is a gilt-edged study of the swift rise and fall of an aggressive black pimp, *The Candy Tangerine Man* is a resourceful distillation of the same subject. "Matt Cimber directs with energy and confidence," enthused the *Los Angeles Times.* "Henry Woolman's sound effects are eye-boggling."

Respectable businessman Ron (John Daniels) lives in an upscale Los Angeles suburban neighborhood with his attractive wife (Tracy King) and two kids, Robbie and Doris. Unbeknownst to his family or neighbors, he is also a high-living Sunset Boulevard pimp driving a yellow and red Rolls Royce and known as the Black Baron. He operates his stable of nubile women out of a Hollywood Boulevard massage parlor run by his partner and sometime lover (Marva Farmer). He is tough on the new girls recruited for his business, but he is tougher yet on his rivals in the street, especially the grasping Mafia contingent, whom he overcomes eventually in bloody battle. When one of his girls

John Daniels in *The Candy Tangerine Man* (1975).

escapes with a suitcase full of his money, the Black Baron pursues her and retrieves it. But the cumulative effect of his experiences has sobered him, and he decides to retire from the arena before his two contrasting lives collide disastrously. He tells his unsuspecting wife at the end, "Everyone knows a pimp. Why I even knew one myself once upon a time."

There is much that is crude and amateurish in this low-budget production, but it has a sly sense of humor which dresses up the tawdry tale nicely. The Black Baron is quite a sight in his multi-colored Rolls Royce driving along in his white suit and white hat. As one of his prostitutes describes him, "You look like some kind of ice cream cone with licorice between your legs." Early on in the film, there is a scene of two white vice cops, bigoted sleazebags, discovering the hard way that a suspected prostitute is really a man in drag. Later these same police officers are chasing the Candy Tangerine Man down a winding canyon road, but they are outmaneuvered and their damaged car hangs perilously over a cliffside. The wimpering men beg their adversary to help. He says magnanimously, "I'm goin to let you go," and, true to his word, pushes their car—with them trapped inside—over the cliff, where it explodes. At another juncture, the Baron explains his (double entendre) philosophy to one of his girls, "Look mama, you got to eat them before they eat you ... get it together."

The film also is filled with graphic violence. One of the prostitutes has her breasts cut off on-camera, Baron shoves an opponent's hand down a garbage disposal, etc., etc.

The Candy Tangerine Man, directed by filmmaker Matt Cimber (who helmed *The Black Six* [1974] [q.v.]) grossed $1,000,000 in domestic film rentals.

The following year star John Daniels would appear as the lothario hairdresser in *Black Shampoo* [q.v.].

57. Carter's Army (ABC-TV, 1/17/70). Color, 78 minutes.

Producers Danny Thomas, Aaron Spelling; *associate producer* Shelley Hull; *director* George McCowan; *teleplay* Spelling, David H. Kidd; *art director* Paul Sylos; *music* Fred Steiner; *camera* Arch R. Dalzell; *editor* George W. Brooks.

Cast: Stephen Boyd (Captain Beau Carter); Robert Hooks (Lieutenant Edward Wallace); Susan Oliver (Anna); Rosey Grier (Big Jim); Moses Gunn (Doc); Richard Pryor (Jonathan Crunk); Glynn Turman (George Brightman); Billy Dee Williams (Lewis); Paul Stewart (General Clark); Bobby Johnson (Robinson); Napoleon Whiting (Fuzzy).

This telefeature about World War II combat soldiers might easily have been lost in the shuffle of a TV season. However, *Carter's Army* had a plot gimmick. It focuses on a redneck army captain named Beau Carter (Stephen Boyd), who finds himself the commanding officer of an inexperienced, all-black rear-line service detachment. They are ordered to stand fast against the Germans at an important dam. In retrospect, the cast can be appreciated as an all-star amalgam from the black acting community, including Rosey Grier, Moses Gunn, Robert Hooks, Richard Pryor, Glynn Turman, Billy Dee Williams, and Napoleon Whiting. It caused a mild brouhaha because in the course of the storyline a white woman (Susan Oliver as the German Anna) is kissed (innocently) on the cheek by the black Lieutenant (Robert Hooks). Reportedly this was the first interracial kiss on dramatic TV.

The action for *Carter's Army* is set on the road to Berlin in July 1944 as Captain Carter learns to value men for their courage, not their skin color. Some of the command die in the skirmish with the enemy, others, like Jonathan Crunk (Richard Pryor), prove themselves courageous and, albeit wounded, survive. A telling scene at the finale finds Carter, Wallace, and Crunk trudging along a road, glad to be alive and full of respect for one another. A truckload of white soldiers passes by and makes disparaging remarks about Wallace and Crunk, tossing them a shovel to go dig a latrine. The regenerated Carter looks on in disgust at this bigotry, helps the injured Crunk into a jeep, and he and Wallace set off down the road, two equal comrades in arms.

58. Certain Fury (New World, 1985). Color, 87 minutes.

Executive producer Lawrence Vanger; *producer* Gilbert Adler; *director* Stephen Gyllenhaal; *story consultant* Nancy Audley; *screenplay* Michael Jacobs; *production designer* Beala Neel; *set decorators* Marti Wright, John Chilton; *costumes* Lynda Kemp; *music* Bill Payne, Russell Kunkel, George Massenburg; *songs* Drew Arnott and Darryl Kromm, Irene Cara and Tony Prendatt; *stunt co-ordinators* Conrad E. Palmisano, Jack Rupp; *animal co-ordinator* Debbie Coe; *sound* Ralph Parker; *supervising sound designer* David Lewis Yewdall; *sound effects editors* Dick LeGrand, R.J. Palmer, Chuck Smith; *special effects co-ordinator* Thomas Fisher; *special effects* Dave Kelsey; *camera* Kees Van Oostrum; *editor* Todd Ramsay.

Cast: Tatum O'Neal (Scarlet McGinnis); Irene Cara (Tracy Freeman); Nicholas Campbell (Sniffer); George Murdock (Lieutenant Speier); Moses Gunn (Dr. Freeman); Peter Fonda (Rodney); Rodney Gage (Superman); Jonathon Pallon (Barker); David Longworth (Streetdog); Dawnlea Tait (Crystal); Alana Shields (Laura Gibbs); Sharon Schaffer (Gisela); Gene Hartline (Ignatius); Peter Anderson (Dealer); Catherine Mead (Matron Guard); Dean Regan (Public Defender); Ted Stidder (Judge); Shirley Barclay (Clerk); Joe Goland (Bailiff); Bill Murdock (Graydon); Stuart Kent (Guard); Frank Turner (Dimitri); Paul Batten (Chase); Bruce McLeod (Sergeant); Tammy Kusian (Bride); Gilbert Adler (Groom); T.J. Jimmy McLean, Angie Tavahan (Junkies); Harry Kalinski (Rabbi Guest); Bill Buck, Gary Chalk, Daryl Hayes (Policemen); *and:* Bruce Barbour, Bill Ferguson, Alex Green, Sandra Hall, Gene Hartline, Jacqui Janzen, George Josef, Ken Kersinger, Tom McBeath, J.J. Makaro, Tony Morelli, Debby Lynn Ross, Jacob Rupp, Sharon Schaffer, John Scott, Frank Serio, Bill Stewart, Howard Storey, William Taylor, Stephen Thorne, Dale Wilson.

With two Academy Award–winners in one picture (O'Neal won Best Supporting Actress for *Paper Moon* [1973]; Cara won for co-writing the theme song to *Fame* [1980]) one would have expected much more from *Certain Fury,* a blatant action exercise with great possibilities wasted. It is structured as an intriguing variation on *The Defiant Ones* (1958) (q.v.), with a switch (the black girl is wealthy, cultured, and semi-innocent; the white teenager is street-tough from a poor environment and hardened to everything). But as Nigel Floyd (British *Monthly Film Bulletin*) notes, what emerges is "an exploitation picture in which the potentially interesting racial and class tensions between the two female fugitives are subordinated to a fast-moving plot." *Variety* concurred: "Director Stephen Gyllenhaal and lenser Kees Van Oostrum handle the action well enough, but sacrifice none of it to linger very long over character development. It's pretty plain the girls had to struggle for what they got."

Among the women prisoners brought into court are repeated offender Scarlet McGinnis (Tatum O'Neal), a street-rough, illiterate hooker who killed a kinky client in self-defense; and Tracy Freeman (Irene Cara), a bewildered upper-middle-class girl who was arrested with her boyfriend in a stolen Jaguar. During the chaos when two of the other defendants grab policemen's guns and turn the courtroom into a bloodbath, Scarlet and Tracy escape into a rat-infested sewage tunnel. A pursuing policeman is killed when he lights a match and causes a gas explosion. Life-scarred Scarlet convinces frightened Tracy that if they surrender now they will certainly be charged with killing a cop. The two girls dislike and distrust one another: Scarlet slams out, "For a nigger, you're stupider than you look." Tracy shoots back, "You illiterate white trash whore." And so it goes. Nevertheless, they realize they need each other to survive. Tracy follows Scarlet to drug pusher–pornographer Sniffer's (Nicholas Campbell) apartment. After forcing Scarlet to leave at knifepoint, Sniffer attempts to rape Tracy in the shower, and she beats him unconscious with a towel rail. Meanwhile Scarlet runs to well-heeled criminal Rodney (Peter Fonda) for help. No sooner does she leave his yacht headquarters than he phones the police, making an agreement with police Lieutenant Speiers

Irene Cara *(left)* **and Tatum O'Neal in** *Certain Fury* **(1985).**

(George Murdock) to turn the girls over if the law will release his hoodlum pals. Scarlet returns to Sniffer's to find Tracy holding Sniffer at bay with his gun. They steal his drug cache and depart before Rodney's thugs arrive. Sniffer later finds Tracy and shoots her full of drugs, but before he can rape her, Scarlet returns. Rodney's men catch up with the girls and set the building they are in on fire. The girls escape while Sniffer dies in the blaze. Tracy and Scarlet are led to believe the police think they died in the fire, but this is a trick. They find themselves trapped by the law and Tracy surrenders. However, Scarlet attempts to flee and is shot. Tracy rushes to Scarlet's aid — for by now their attitude toward each other is changed:

> Tracy: We should stick together.
> Scarlet: Even if it kills us.
> Tracy: Even if it doesn't.

Certain Fury is definitely a bizarre odyssey through a perverse wonderland of bums, pimps, prostitutes, drug addicts and dealers, pornographers, and murderers. Whatever the initial transgressions of the two "heroines," thereafter they are the *Les Misérables*-like victims of circumstances with a desperate desire to survive. Burned-out Scarlet relies on the wrong people, and Tracy is caught in a nightmarish world initially beyond her comprehension. Ironically, those that could help Tracy remain ineffectually on the sidelines: her bewildered physician father (Moses Gunn), who has ignored his maturing daughter in his grief at the death of his wife eight months earlier, and the conclusion-jumping, insensitive Lieutenant Speiers (George Murdock).

59. Chained Heat (Jensen Farley, 1983). Color, 95 minutes.

Executive producers Ernst Von Theumer, Lou Paciocco; *producer* Billy Fine; *associate producer* Gerhard Scheurich; *director* Paul Nicholas; *screenplay* Vincent Mongoi, Nicholas; *art director* Bob Ziembicki; *wardrobe* Jacqueline Kinnaway, Susie De Santo; *music/music conductor* Joseph Conlon; *music editor* Dino Moriana; *music consultants* Bob Reno, Stephen Metz; *creative consultant* Aaron Butler; *assistant director* Nancy King; *sound* Anna De Lanzo; *supervising sound editor* Richard Raderman; *special effects* Doug White; *camera* MacAhlber; *editor* Nino di Marco.

Cast: Linda Blair (Carol); John Vernon (Warden Bachman); Sybil Danning (Ericka); Tamara Dobson (Dutchess); Stella Stevens (Captain Taylor); Sharon Hughes (Val); Henry Silva (Lester); Jennifer Ashley (Grinder); Edy Williams (Paula); Susan Meschner (Genderson); Diana Rose (Dr. Pascal); Christina Cardan (Miss King); Ann Dane (Harriet); Kelly Lawrence (Carmel); Charles Messenger, Jeff Goodman (Guards); Martha Gallub (Miller); Gloria Fioramonti (PCP Girl); Leala Chrystie (Chana); Aaron Butler (Willy); Nicole Geus, Donna Rizzitello, Annie Davidson, Sharon Hoffman, Chrissie Quinn, Katherine Vernon (Cellmates); *and:* Greta Blackburn, Michael Callan, Sharon Hughes, Kandal Kaldwell, Jody Medford, Louisa Moritz, Nita Talbot.

Chained Heat is the steamy follow-up to the previous year's *The Concrete Jungle,* and its conglomeration of disparate screen types is equaled only by its assorted onscreen perversities. If Pam Grier was the black queen of prison hell in such 1970s opuses as *The Big Doll House* (1971) and *The Big Bird Cage* (1972) (qq.v.), then Tamara Dobson certainly deserves recognition for her *Chained Heat* appearance. It was the reemergence of this statuesque black model and actress who had made such an impact in the *Cleopatra Jones* movie series (q.v.). She then returned to the world of modeling. By the time of this women-in-chains exercise, she was a bit peaked, which added dimension to her character.

Back in the 1930s and 1940s prison flicks focused "merely" on inmates serving out their wearisome time, dealing with brutalities from the law enforcers and the systems, and the more hardened types making their breaks to hopeful freedom. Such later films as Jim Brown's *Riot* (1969) (q.v.) and Bernie Casey's *Brothers* (1977) (q.v.) being part of the blaxploitation cycle, fastened on racial strife within the big house. This theme figures heavily in *Chained Heat.* At one point, righteous, tough black cellblock queen Duchess challenges, "Those girls out there are people, not just numbers.... I sure as hell can take care of my black sisters." Later she threatens white rival leader Ericka, "If it comes over into our lap, we'll come and take you out."

Moreover, being a sexploitation feature at heart, *Chained Heat* revels in the assorted unique situations afforded by toughened female prisoners behind bars. Hetero- and homosexual coupling, bondage, torture, and as much nudity and vicious laguage as possible always lurk one scene ahead in these celluloid cellblock yarns.

New inmate Carol (Linda Blair) arrives at the overcrowded women's correctional facility. Her transition from student-gone-wrong to seasoned prison inmate is a nightmare she barely survives. Corrupt prison warden Bachman

(John Vernon), when not trafficking in drugs, plans robberies and heads a prostitution ring (he whisks prisoners in and out of the facility to do the assorted
crimes, always with perfect alibis for their whereabouts). Libido-driven
Bachman revels in orgiastic couplings with his "girls" and videotapes his
athletic hot tub action in his office as well. Butch Captain Taylor (Stella
Stevens) is the warden's chief henchman, along with Lester the drug dealer
(Henry Silva). Imposing, 6'2" tall Dutchess (Tamara Dobson) leads the black
faction among the prisoners; her opposite number among the white women inmates is blonde Ericka (Sybil Danning), whose followers insist, "We don't want
any black pu--y in here." They both strive to dominate the action within the
big walls, and they are not above kicking, punching, knifing, and strangling
their opponents.

The warden meets a violent end when Captain Taylor drowns him in his
hot tub; and, since the videotape camera is running the whole time, Captain
Taylor is eventually undone as well.

Made in West Germany in December of 1982 and released independently
in 1983, *Chained Heat* in no way matched its predecessor in the box-office race.
The Concrete Jungle, distributed by major league Metro-Goldwyn-Mayer, had
grossed $3,223,700 in domestic film rentals. Later in 1983 *Chained Heat* was
released on videocassette by Vestron. It led *Video Review* magazine in a
retrospective article in August 1988 to judge the film as ". . . what could be the
most entertaining babes-behind-bars flick ever made. . . ." Tamara Dobson and
Stella Stevens had appeared together onscreen previously in *Cleopatra Jones
and the Casino of Gold* (1975) (q.v.).

60. Charley One Eye (Paramount, 1972). Color, 96 minutes.

Presenter David Paradine; *producer* James Swann; *director* Don Chaffey;
screenplay Keith Leonard; *music* John Cameron; *assistant director* Nick
Granby; *sound* Roy Charman; *camera* Kenneth Talbot; *editor* Mike Campbell.

Cast: Richard Roundtree (The Black Man); Roy Thinnes (The Indian);
Nigel Davenport (Bounty Hunter); Jill Pearson (Officer's Wife); Aldo Sam-
breill (Mexican Driver); Luis Aller (Mexican Youth); Rafael Albaicin (Mexican
Leader); Alex Davion (Tony); Johnny Sekka (Bob); Madeline Hinde
(Penelope); Patrick Mower (Richard); Imogen Hassall (Chris); Edward Wood-
ward (Holstrom); William Mervyn (Honeydew); David Lodge (Colonel).

Charley One-Eye was the first film produced by TV celebrity David Frost's
British production firm. It was geared as a dramatic allegory set in Western sur-
roundings. It starred Richard Roundtree, then in the midst of his *Shaft* film
series successes. His co-star was Roy Thinnes, best known for playing lead
character David Vincent on "The Invaders" sci-fi teleseries (1967–68). The
Western was shot in Almeria, Spain.

The Black Man (Richard Roundtree) is a Union Army deserter who heads
to Mexico after killing his commanding officer. Along the way he meets the Indian (Roy Thinnes), an outcast from his tribe because of mixed blood and his
lame leg. The Black Man has fits of anger and outrage and frequently is abusive
of his newfound confederate. The latter remains stoic to his partner's brutality.
The sadistic Bounty Hunter (Nigel Davenport) on the Black Man's trail traces

them to a deserted Mexican church. Eventually the Black Man's killing of two Mexicans leads to his being stoned to death.

With its low-keyed scenario, *Charley One Eye* could not compete with the likes of such "soul Westerns" as *The Legend of Nigger Charley* (1972) and *The Soul of Nigger Charley* (1973) (q.v.). As *Variety* summarized, "...may be well made but holds little popular interest ... script [is] too often inclined to be static."

61. Cleopatra Jones (Warner Bros., 1973). Color, 89 minutes.

Producer William Tennant; *co-producer* Max Julien; *director* Jack Starrett; *story* Julien; *screenplay* Julien, Sheldon Keller; *art director* Peter Wooley; *set decorator* Cheryal Kearney; *music/music director* J.J. Johnson; *additional music* Carl Brandt, Brad Shapiro, Joe Simon; *title theme* Simon; *assistant director* Julien; *stunt co-ordinator* Ernest Robinson; *hapkido karate master* Bong Soo Han; *sound* Bud Alper; *camera* David Walsh; *editor* Allan Jacobs.

Cast: Tamara Dobson (Cleopatra Jones); Bernie Casey (Reuben Masters); Shelley Winters (Mommy); Brenda Sykes (Tiffany); Antonio Fargas (Doodlebug); Bill McKinney (Officer Purdy); Dan Frazer (Detective Lou Crawford); Stafford Morgan (Sergeant Kert); Mike Warren (Andy); Albert Popwell (Matthew Johnson); Caro Kenyatta (Melvin Johnson); Esther Rolle (Mrs. Johnson); Paul Koslo, Joseph A. Tornatore (Mommy's Hoods); Hedley Mattingly (Chauffeur); George Reynolds, Theodore Wilson (Doodlebug's Hoods); Christopher Joy (Snake); Keith Hamilton (Maxwell Woodman); Angela Gibbs (Annie); John Garwood (Lieutenant Thompkins); John Alderman (Mommy's Assistant.)

"Cleopatra Jones." What images that character's name conjurs up! A sleek, beautiful six-foot-two black mama who is equally at home with couturier clothing, martial arts, and fast retorts. As the ultimate black fantasy heroine, not only is she cool, hip, and unbeatable, but she works tirelessly and fearlessly on the side of law and order (as a narcotics agent for an altruistic branch of the United States Central Intelligence Agency). Maybe only ex–Baltimorian Tamara Dobson, a fashion model turned actress (having already appeared in television commercials and in Burt Reynolds's 1977 *Fuzz*) could have played the pop art role so satisfactorily, just as maybe only Max Julien—the man who gave us the super pimp *The Mack* (1973) (q.v.)—could have dreamed up such an alluring, satisfying superheroine. (He had actually conceived the part for his then-girlfriend Vonetta McGee.)

And who in filmdom could be a worthy opponent to tough, velvety-voiced Dobson? Why, Oscar-winning Shelley Winters as stocky, shrill, sadistic Mommy, the lesbian queen of the Los Angeles underworld. Mommy's favorite possessions are her girlfriends and her aquarium. She has little use for her male underlings, who reaffirm constantly just how stupid men are. It is her procession of sultry, very feminine ladyfriends who provide solace. "You're the only one around here who understands Mommy," she confides to each new girl. Leather-clad Mommy is one mean babe when her underworld turf is threatened. One of her black criminal associates call this vulgar broad "super honky," and when she gets mad she lashes out physically at her boys. "I'm tired of being a

Shelley Winters *(left)* **and Tamara Dobson in** *Cleopatra Jones* **(1973).**

pussycat," she shrieks. Noting with relish that her arch foe is a woman, she announces to her dumbstruck men, "Cleopatra Jones is sticking her nose in my business. Well, the honeymoon is over." (That announcement is filled with amazing levels of double meanings.) This is Winters's most oversized and outrageous screen performance, and that is saying a great deal indeed.

Central Intelligence Agency agent Cleopatra Jones (Tamara Dobson) oversees the destruction of a huge field of opium poppies in Turkey. As she tells as associate, "That's right baby. Thirty million dollars of shit that ain't goin' in some kid's vein." She may be jubilant but someone on the other side of the world isn't. "That god damn black bitch!" shrieks gangster chieftain Mommy (Shelley Winters). "How dare she mess around with my poppies. My god, everyone in Turkey must be flying!" There's not much Mommy's henchmen can do to calm her — although one of her alluring female helpmates tries. "I want her black ass back heeeere!!" Mommy tells her killer brood. Mommy arranges for crooked policeman Purdy (Bill McKinney) to storm the B & S, a halfway house for recovering ex-drug addicts run by Cleopatra's boyfriend, Reuben Masters (Bernie Casey). This brings fur-cloaked Cleopatra back to town immediately. Her pal Detective Lou Crawford (Dan Frazer) explains that someone unknown at police headquarters gave permission for the raid. Her goal is to ferret out the corrupt cops and to destroy the underworld organization paying for their services. She promises Reuben it will take her only 72 hours to accomplish her goal.

One of Cleopatra's best contacts is Tiffany (Brenda Sykes), the moll of Mommy's best dope pusher, Doodlebug (Antonio Fargas). Tiffany is ready to help clean up the drug trade until her honest brother puts pressure on her, and

Doodlebug is assassinated for trying to freelance drugs on his own. The seemingly helpful Sergeant Kert (Stafford Morgan) turns out to be in Mommy's pay and was the one who maneuvered the raid on the B & S house. He helps Mommy capture Tiffany and, in turn, the pursuing Cleopatra. The prisoners are taken to an auto junk yard, where the arch criminal intends to destroy them in the car-mashing machinery. Nevertheless, they escape and, in the final confrontation, Mommy is killed and her gang subdued by Cleopatra and her karate-wielding friends.

"My jurisdiction extends from Ankara, Turkey, to Watts Tower" claims the self-sufficient, sexy Cleopatra Jones to an intimidated white law enforcer. And to back up her words, she is ready to deal out karate chops at a moment's notice. Action is never more than a step away when she enters a room which she sometimes does unconventionally: "Why don't you come through the door like a normal woman?" asks one aghast criminal as she splinters the entranceway planking. She drives a customized black corvette with license plates reading "Cleo." Her favorite work outfit includes slacks, boots, and exotic turbans. As bad dude Doodlebug admiringly admits, "That broad is ten miles of bad roads." And indeed she is, as she tools along on her souped-up motorcycle packing a menacing machine gun. She snarls to one slimy creature, "Your head and your body is going to need separate maintenance."

Cleopatra Jones is an engaging fantasy study of super-women tussling in a world where men are passive (Reuben), disloyal (Doodlebug), or corrupt (Sergeant Kirk, Officer Purdy) and bigoted. The tried-and-true theme of cleaning the drug pushers out of the black ghetto is marched out, as is a tour of all levels of the inner city: from righteous Reuben to the well-meaning Mrs. Johnson (Esther Rolle), who runs a numbers outlet at her restaurant. There is a (near-obligatory for this genre) visit to a swinging neighborhood night spot, a club that puts "more dips in your hips, more cut in your strut, more glide in your stride," and even a number sung by a Supremes-like vocal group. Obviously *Cleopatra Jones* is successfully put together as the distaff answer to *Shaft* (1971), *Slaughter* (1972) or *Hammer* (1972) (qq.v.). Despite all the slam-bang action and tough people, everything is geared to the light touch, and the film received a PG rating.

"This thrilling and sometimes funny movie will have you on the edge of your seat, jabbing your neighbor in the ribs, and yelling, 'Right on, Cleo! Do it, mama!' *Cleopatra Jones* is definitely not to be missed" (Janette C. Tolbert, *Encore* magazine). "Tamara Dobson makes a smart feature film starring debut," approved *Variety,* who agreed the film "...provides a regular flow of rough-and-tumble, utilizing some rare-to-film L.A. location areas, thereby adding more freshness to the 89-minute film."

Cleopatra Jones grossed a noteworthy $3,250,000 in domestic film rentals, and its soundtrack album by J.J. Johnson (with songwriter Joe Simon singing "Theme from Cleopatra Jones" and Millie Jackson vocalizing "Love Doctor" and "It Hurts So Good") sold well over 500,000 copies. The bulk of the stunts for the film were provided by Ernest Robinson and the Black Stuntmen's Association. The success of the picture led to *Cleopatra Jones and the Casino of Gold* (1975) (q.v.).

62. Cleopatra Jones and the Casino of Gold (Warner Bros., 1975). Color, 94 minutes.

Producer William Tennant; *director* Chuck Bail; *based on characters created by* Max Julien; *screenplay* Tennant; *art director* Johnson Tsao; *music* Dominic Frontierre; *assistant directors* Bobby Canavarro, William Chaung Kin; *stunt co-ordinator* Eddy Donno; *Chinese fighting instructors* Tang Chia, Yuen Shian Yan; *sound* Cyril Swern; *sound effects* Billie Owens, Arthur Pullen, Bill Rivol; *special effects* Nobby Clark, Milt Rice; *camera* Alan Hume; *editor* Willy Kemplen.

Cast: Tamara Dobson (Cleopatra Jones); Stella Stevens (Bianca Jovan [The Dragon Lady]); Tanny (Mi Ling); Norman Fell (Stanley Nagel); Albert Popwell (Matthew Johnson); Caro Kenyatta (Melvin Johnson); Chan Sen (Soo); Christopher Hunt (Mendez); Lin Chen Chi (Madalyna); Liu Loke Hua (Tony); Eddy Donno (Morgan); Bobby Canavarro (Lin Ma Chen); Mui Kwok Sing (Benny); John Cheng (David); Tony Lee (Lao Di); Rich King (Mr. Han); Gigo Tevzadze (Chew Lun); Lok Sing (Mike); Paul Chen (Man in Walled City); Victor Kahn (Man in Hallway).

At the end of *Cleopatra Jones* (q.v.), Cleopatra (Tamara Dobson) is asked, "How long this time, baby [before you come home to stay]?" "Till it's finished," she solemnly replies. And so in *Cleopatra Jones and the Casino of Gold* the intrepid, world-traveling heroine arrives in Hong Kong after two other government agents—black friends from the Los Angeles ghetto, Matthew (Albert Popwell) and Melvin Johnson (Caro Kenyatta)—are captured by the sinister gang leader Bianca Jovan, better known as the Dragon Lady (Stella Stevens). Loner Cleopatra rejects help from the Hong Kong police, but agrees to team with private eye Mi Ling (Tanny) and her group of rough motorcyclists. As Cleopatra and Mi Ling search for clues regarding the Johnson boys, the Dragon Lady does her best to accommodate her prisoners, wanting to woo them to her cause. The trail leads Cleopatra and Mi Ling to Macao and the Dragon Lady's casino. Soon several of the Dragon Lady's drug trade subordinates are killed for making too many mistakes, and Cleopatra and Mi Ling raid the casino, overcoming the criminal leader's goon squad. Cleopatra and the Dragon Lady have a fight to the finish in which the villainess dies in a pool of water. Now that the Johnson boys are rescued and the drug trafficking stopped, Cleopatra leaves Hong Kong. She learns that Mi Ling and her helpers are actually members of the Hong Kong undercover police force.

With such a zesty predecessor that explored all levels of her one-dimensional superheroine character so efficiently, there is *not* much that a sequel can do to follow upon *Cleopatra Jones.* We know so much about high-kicking Cleopatra Jones's talents and virtues that to hear them recited again is redundant. (Cleopatra admits chastely to a confederate, "I never claimed to be God, only close to him." Regarding her self-sufficiency, she explains that it's better to work alone ". . . than with some partner who's going to screw up and get me knocked off, man. It's healthier!" In a more vulnerable moment, Jones confesses there is a softer side to her, "Off the job I'm a real pussycat." But she is quick to assure a horny male hot on her trail, "Don't race your motor baby, it's not leaving the garage.") Her outfits are more outrageous, her makeup more severe (she resembles a giant Eartha Kitt), but her character seems at a loss. In the original film Cleopatra is in her true element bringing law and order to the streets of her black community in Los Angeles, but in *Cleopatra Jones and the Casino of Gold* she is a stranger in a strange land. She must rely on her female partner, Mi Ling, and her tactical squad to help out. And the film, seemingly aware that the blaxploitation fad was nearly over, devotes almost as much screen time to the Oriental co-lead and her minions as to the title figure. Moreover, after the strident but unforgettable Mommy (of Shelley Winters), the Dragon Lady (with Stella Stevens as a very butch criminal leader) is a pale successor who quickly fades from mind.

"Miss Dobson is a large, beautiful overwhelming presence whose real sexuality is denied by her movie role and by costumes that seem to have been designed for a female impersonator," complained Vincent Canby *(New York Times)*. "With little to do but pose in bizarre outfits in between shoot-outs and bouts of martial arts action, the title character is effectively reduced to a joke," insisted Verina Glaessner (British *Monthly Film Bulletin*). Moreover, added Glaessner in the *Bulletin,* "The film is cut together quite incoherently . . . [and] is only remarkable for the unintentional humour of the particularly inept, over-dubbed rhubarbing."

Cleopatra Jones and the Casino of Gold was an American–Hong Kong co-production made in conjunction with Run Run Shaw and failed to make much of a mark at the box-office. It ended the series and diminished the potential of towering Tamara Dobson in Hollywood. She would appear in a supporting role in *Norman . . . Is That You?* (1976) starring Redd Foxx and Pearl Bailey and then return to the world of fashion and television (spokes)modeling, reemerging for the prison exploitation yard *Chained Heat* (1983) (q.v.) reteamed with Stella Stevens, and for a forgettable role in the telefeature *The Amazons* (1984).

63. Cocaine and Blue Eyes (NBC-TV, 1/2/83). Color, 100 minutes.

Executive producer O.J. Simpson; *producer* Dan Mark; *director* E.W. Swackhamer; *based on the novel by* Fred Zackel; *teleplay* Kendall J. Blair; *art directors* Ross Bellah, William L. Campbell; *set decorators* Audrey Basdell Goddard, Jim Duffy; *costume designers* Grady Hunt, Christina Smith; *music* Morton Stevens; *music editor* Erma Levin; *assistant director* Mack Bing; *sound* Richard Rague; *sound editor* Joseph Melody; *camera* Richard C. Glouner; *editor* George B. Hively.

Cast: O.J. Simpson (Michael Brennen); Cliff Gorman (Rikki Anatole); Candy Clark (Ruthann Gideon); Eugene Roche (Sergeant Khoury); Maureen Anderman (Lillian Anatole); Cindy Pickett (Catherine); Tracy Reed (Chris Brennan); Leonardo Cimino (Orestes Anatole); Van Nessa L. Clarke (Maid); Keye Luke (Tana Ng); Irene Ferris (Blue Eyes [Dani Anatole]); John Spencer (Joey Crawford); Evan Ki (Davy Huey); Ted LePlat (Alex Simons); Belita Moreno (Waitress); Dick Balduzzi (Barkeep); Stepehen Toblowsky (TV Clerk); Haunani Minn (Receptionist); Bumper Robinson (Brennen's Son); Micah Morton (Brennen's Daughter); Jessica Biscardi (Mexican Nurse); Nigel Butland (Arnold); Stephen Burks (Doc); Beach Dickerson (Bartender); Marc Silver (Morgue Clerk); Sam Vicenzio (Hotel Clerk).

"Weak, by-the-numbers murder story never creates a stir" *(Daily Variety)* was the verdict on this too-predictable detective yard telefeature. It was the pilot produced by and starring O.J. Simpson for an unsold television series. It would have revived the plot premise of a black detective such as television's earlier short-lived series "Shaft" (1973) and "Tenafly" (1973) (qq.v.).

Michael Brennen (O.J. Simpson) is a San Francisco private eye who becomes embroiled in a drug-smuggling scam while hunting for the girlfriend, named Blue Eyes (Irene Ferris), of a dead client. The trail leads him to a politically prominent family in the fish cannery business headed by patriarch Oreste Anatole (Leonardo Cimino) and his double-dealing son Rikki (Cliff Gorman). It turns out that the venerable Tana Ng (Keye Luke) is a drug-dealing partner of Rikki and that the latter was planning to leave his wife (Maureen Anderman) to run off to Mexico with his relative (the missing Blue Eyes).

This ineptly conceived detective caper is rife with cliches. There is lots of hackneyed Mickey Spillane private eye narration ("They say hindsight is 20-20..."); lots of hard-boiled chatter ("I don't like my place being broken into. I don't like being threatened and I don't like being considered a fool") and lots of "useful" shop lingo ("when you take a man down with a gun, you stick it in his ear"). There are in-jokes about O.J. Simpson's character onscreen not knowing anything about football or the San Francisco 49ers. (Clean-cut, handsome O(rentahl) J(ames) Simpson had played professional football for the Buffalo Bills and the San Francisco 49ers. He became a television network sportscaster in 1969 and began appearing in dramatic assignments on teleseries and in such feature films as *The Towering Inferno* [1974]. He produced and starred in the telefeatures *Goldie and the Boxer* [1979] and *Goldie and the Boxer Go to Hollywood* [1981] and became a frequently seen product spokesman on television and in print ads.) And there is plenty of bigoted talk to continually remind the audience that this lead character is someone different, a black detective. "You're the original Sam Spade," scoffs a hitchhiker-turned-client. *Daily Variety* saw this racist patter as "...tasteless smartalecky references to blacks by many of the white characters, presumably to establish character; it's the short-hand method of development." The one pleasant ingredient of this misfire is pert Tracy Reed as the detective's ex-wife and the devoted young mother of their two children.

64. Coffy (American International, 1973). Color, 91 minutes.

Executive producer Salvatore Billiteri; *producer* Robert A. Papazian; *director/screenplay* Jack Hill; *art director* Perry Ferguson; *set decorator* Charles Pierce; *wardrobe supervisor* James George; *makeup* Ray Brooks; *music/music director* Roy Ayers; *songs* Ayers and Carl Clay, Ayers and Roselle Weaver; *music arrangers* Ayers, Harry Whitaker; *music editor* Ving Hershon; *stunt co-ordinator* Bob Minor; *sound* Don Johnson; *sound effects* Gene Corso; *special effects* Jack DeBron; *camera* Paul Lohmann; *editor* Charles McClelland.

Cast: Pam Grier (Coffy); Booker Bradshaw (Howard Brunswick); Robert DoQui (King George); William Elliott (Carter Brown); Allan Arbus (Arturo Vitroni); Sid Haig (Omar); Barry Cahill (McHenry); Morris Buchanan (Sugar

Man); Lee de Broux (Nick); Bob Minor (Studs); John Perak (Aleva); Ruben Moreno (Ramos); Carol Lawson (Priscilla); Linda Haynes (Meg); Lisa Farringer (Jeri); Mivako Cumbuka (Grover); Ray Young (Jake); Wally Strauss (Doctor); Gail Davis (Bricke Redd); Lyman Ward (Orderly); Bobby Johnson (Floyd); Nat Jones (Stoned Boy); Bibi Louis (Helen); Walter Blakel (Director).

"She's the *Godmother* of them all. . . . The baddest One-Chick Hit-Squad that ever hit town!"

Usually such film advertising is fanciful hyperbole, but in the case of *Coffy* it is true . . . and then some!

Nurse Coffy (Pam Grier) has other things on her mind besides tending the ill. At the apartment of Sugar-Man (Morris Buchanan) she seduces the small-time pusher and then blows his face off with a rifle. Before compelling his stooge to overdose, she explains this is her revenge for his causing her eleven-year-old sister, LuBelle, to become a hopeless, mindless addict. The next day her childhood pal Carter Brown (William Elliott), an honest young policeman, is beaten senseless when he threatens to expose his partner, McHenry (Barry Cahill), for corruption. He suffers extensive brain damage. With information Carter had given her, Coffy makes Priscilla (Carol Lawson), who used to be the prized hooker in the stable of King George (Robert DoQui), help her join the underworld leader's team posing as a Jamaican call girl. One of her stunts (substituting sugar for heroin in a drug deal) brings her to the attention of Arturo Vitroni (Allan Arbus), the local Mafia chief. She turns Vitroni against King George, and the latter is brutally killed. Meanwhile her romance with conniving politician Howard Brunswick (Booker Bradshaw) takes a sour turn when he sacrifices Coffy's safety for his own life. She escapes from Vitroni's henchmen and kills them. She then murders Vitroni. At Brunswick's beach house she eliminates her double-dealing lover.

At the end of this amazingly violent and vicious screen thriller, Pam Grier's Coffy says, "I don't know how I did it. It seems like I'm in a dream." But this 91 minutes of gore, mayhem, and raw sexuality is more like a stinging nightmare. And as producing film company American International knew, its contract star Pam Grier was perhaps the only one in Hollywood who could carry off the demanding assignment. This lead character is intriguing, even baffling. She is one moment righteous and pure, the next a lady with her own brand of heated bedside manner. She survives forced drug overdoses, beatings, and double-crossings at every turn. If attaining her goals requires fornicating with a scumball, she shrugs her shoulders and carries on. She may love her drugged-up sister and adore her pulverized honest cop friend Carter, but she is vulnerable enough to fall for the phony charms of chameleon-like politico Brunswick. If she doesn't have a shotgun handy, she is resourceful enough to do in a thug with sharp needles. Her conscience is evidently nonexistent for the end justifies any means.

"Despite a good deal of lip service against the evils of drugs and the like, there's a maximum of footage devoted to exposing Miss Grier," cited A.H. Weiler *(New York Times)*. Disrobing onscreen had long been an integral part of the action roles handed to shapely Grier. Her bigger-than-life characters always have freewheeling attitudes towards sex, and this makes her a definite "role model" of the 1970s women's lib movement. Her Coffy is an emancipated lady who doesn't need to rely on a man for comfort, security, or safety. Because this is an action film of a definite genre, she inhabits an (all-too-familiar) vice-ridden world of pimps, prostitutes, and drug lords where lives are not worth much and torturing victims to death seems to be an admired art. Once again it is the black underworld versus the Mafia, with both factions equally corrupt, sadistic, and bigoted, while the victor is a black avenging miss who, at heart, is fighting for a good cause despite her extreme anti-human tactics.

"What distinguishes this . . . effort from the run of the black sexploitation mill is its all-embracing grimness. Its moral blackness, in fact. Coffy is shown to inhabit a world where exploitation, both sexual and political, is simply the norm. . . . [I]t quite casually reveals the one person in a position to give voice to the radical policies the [drug] situation demands, and to implement them, to be totally corrupt himself" (Verina Glaessner, British *Monthly Film Bulletin*).

Coffy, made at an estimated cost of $500,000, would gross well over $2,000,000 in domestic film rentals. But already the black intellectual community was complaining about such commercially crass productions. Maurice Peterson editiorialized in *Essence* magazine, "By now, trash has begotten so much more trash that, more than ever before, the thinking brother and sister have to be selective about movie-going." In reference to the "coarse brand of sex and violence" in *Coffy,* Peterson wrote, "But movies can offer something a little more subtle and a lot more elegant than this shoot-'em-up pulp."

65. Come Back Charleston Blue (Warner Bros., 1972).
Color, 100 minutes.

Producer Samuel Goldwyn, Jr; *associate producer* Al Fann; *director* Mark Warren; *based on the novel* "The Heat's On" *by* Chester Himes; *screenplay* Bontche Schweig [Ernest Kinoy], Peggy Elliott; *production designer* Robert Gundlach; *art director* Perry Watkins; *set decorator* George De Titta; *costumes* Anna Hill Johnstone; *music/music conductor* Donny Hathaway; *music supervisor* Quincy Jones; *songs* Jones and Al Cleveland, Earl DeRouen and Edward Howard; *assistant director* Terence A. Donnelly; *second unit director* Max Kleven; *sound* James J. Sabata, Richard Vorisek; *camera* Dick Kratina; *editors* Gerald Greenburg, George Bowers.

Cast: Godfrey Cambridge (Gravedigger Jones); Raymond St. Jacques (Coffin Ed Johnson); Peter De Anda (Joe); Jonelle Allen (Carol); Maxwell Glanville (Caspar); Minnie Gentry (Her Majesty); Dick Sabol (Jarena); Leonardo Cimino (Frank Mago); Percy Rodriguez (Bryce); Tony Brealond (Drag Queen); Tim Pelt (Earl J.); Darryl Knibb (Douglas); Marcia McBroom (Girl Barber); Adam Wade (Benjy); Joseph Ray (Bubba); Theodore Wilson (Cemetery Guard); Dorothi Fox (Streetwalker).

". . . [A] convoluted plot and dialogue that is often too 'in' for the uninitiated serve to make only some parts of *Charleston* better than the whole frenetic business" (A.H. Weiler, *New York Times*). What had been spontaneous and joyous in the predecessor *Cotton Comes to Harlem* (1970) (q.v.) now seemed derivative, stilted, and flat.

Left–right: **Peter De Anda, Raymond St. Jacques, unidentified legs, and Godfrey Cambridge in** *Come Back Charleston Blue* **(1972).**

Police detectives Gravedigger Jones (Godfrey Cambridge) and Coffin Ed Johnson (Raymond St. Jacques), the former sensible and sensitive, the latter hot-headed and brittle, find themselves again at the mercy of Bryce (Percy Rodriguez), their humorless black police commander at Manhattan's 27th precinct. At a Harlem social function a kitchen man is found dead on a freezer meat hook, and a folding blue steel razor blade for shaving is nearby. This clue leads Johnson and Jones to Her Majesty (Minnie Gentry), an old-time psychic with a penchant for the numbers game. She tells them her gangster boyfriend Charleston Blue used to import such elegant razor blades from E.P. Douglas & Co., in Charleston, South Carolina, for his special line of enforcement work. He had left a dozen such items with her when he went to do battle with mobster Dutch Schultz back in 1932. She is convinced the now-legendary Charleston Blue has returned to town, for the blades have vanished! When the next ghetto murder occurs (a junkie is found hanged on a net on a basketball court), the clues start to fall into place. It develops that Vietnam War veteran Joe (Peter De Anda), now a photographer, intends not only to woo beautiful debutante Carol (Jonelle Allen) but to supplant her aging Uncle Caspar (Maxwell Glanville) as king of the Harlem drug trade. If this means tussling with the Mafia's downtown chief, Mago (Leonardo Cimino), he is willing. Before the caper is solved and concluded, Johnson and Jones have lost their firearms permits, Johnson has been reputedly blown to bits in an explosion, Casper has been murdered, and Carol has learned the true nature of her devious, murderous boyfriend. And Her Majesty wreaks her own revenge on the murderer for toying with the memory of her beloved Charleston Blue.

Come Back Charleston Blue more closely resembles a Keystone Kops excursion than a translation of detective fiction writer Chester Himes's famed offbeat detection duo to the screen. Since first-time feature director Mark Warren had previously helmed the "Rowan and Martin's Laugh-In" comedy series on television, that is understandable. With its ragtime music score, its frenetic episodic sequences, and its prettified view of Harlem life, this expensively mounted entry is a far cry from the typical gritty blaxploitation spin-off. Roger Ebert *(Chicago Sun-Times)* enthused, "The movie has been photographed lovingly on location in Harlem, and shows this as a place of beauty and ugliness, pride and corruption, community-building and drug pushing, all side by side. Sometimes this makes the movie seem a little schizo." And, Ebert adds, the film "...doesn't feel a necessity to present us with still another black superman." There were those who were less impressed, including the trade paper *Variety*: "Besides the low-key gore and sex (which is not necessarily a liability) the film also lacks punch. The gags and the set-ups are fine; they just don't quite add up to solid laughs or excitement."

Come Back Charleston Blue grossed a relatively modest $2,250,000 in domestic film rentals and ended this detective series on film.

66. Cool Breeze (Metro-Goldwyn-Mayer, 1972). Color, 101 minutes.

Producer Gene Corman; *director* Barry Pollack; *based on the novel* "The Asphalt Jungle" *by* W.R. Burnett; *screenplay* Pollack; *art director* Jack Fusk; *music* Solomon Burke; *music co-ordinator* Jerry Styner; *orchestrator* Jerry Page; *assistant director* Arne Schmidt; *sound* Jeff Wexler; *camera* Andy David; *editor* Morton Tubor.

Cast: Thalmus Rasulala (Sidney Lord Jones); Judy Pace (Obalese Eaton); Jim Watkins (Travis Battle); Lincoln Kilpatrick (Lieutenant Brian Knowles); Sam Laws (Stretch Finian); Margaret Avery (Lark); Wally Taylor (John Battle); Raymond St. Jacques (Bill Mercer); Rudy Challenger (Roy Harris); Royce Wallace (Emma Mercer); Pamela [Pam] Grier (Mona); Paula Kelly (Mrs. Harris); Stewart Bradley (Captain Lloyd Harmon); Edmund Cambridge (Bus Driver); Stack Pierce (Tinker); Biff Elliot (Lieutenant Carl Magers); John Lupton (Lieutenant Holster).

Having done so well financially with *Shaft* (1971) (q.v.) and while preparing sequels to it, Metro-Goldwyn-Mayer looked around its story department for additional material to exploit in the black action vein. It decided to remake the classic suspense thriller *The Asphalt Jungle* (1950), which had been so astutely directed by John Huston. In addition, it had starred Sterling Hayden and had done much to advance the career of screen newcomer Marilyn Monroe. The film had already been remade as the Alan Ladd western *The Badlanders* (1958), and as the international adventure tale *Cairo* (1962) with George Sanders and Audie Murphy. Now this story of avaricious double crosses and violent death was reconstructed for a nearly all black cast and to reflect their brand of hopes, problems, and way of life.

Sidney Lord Jones (Thalmus Rasulala) has just been paroled from San Quentin prison and is under the surveillance of white Captain Lloyd Harmon (Stewart Bradley) of the Los Angeles police force. Jones suggests to bookie

Stretch Finian (Sam Laws) that they pull off a $3,000,000 diamond heist with the proceeds used to establish a black people's bank. Respectable, well-to-do Bill Mercer (Raymond St. Jacques) agrees to supply $50,000 to finance the operation and to later fence the diamonds in exchange for a percentage of the new bank. Rounding out the robbery squad are Roy Harris (Rudy Challenger) as the minister and occasional safecracker; Vietnam War hero Travis Battle (Jim Watkins) as the muscle; and Battle's half-brother John (Wally Taylor) as the getaway driver. The robbery is executed successfully, but fate and the men's greed work against them. Mercer plans to make off with the diamonds himself, and after his henchman Tinker (Stack Pierce) is killed, Jones demands that Mercer deal with the insurance company to get a settlement. Finian is arrested by black policeman Lieutenant Brian Knowles (Lincoln Kilpatrick) who is being squeezed by Harmon to produce some action in the case. Overwhelmed, Mercer maneuvers the police into killing him. Roy, who was wounded in the robbery, dies, and John Battle is caught. Sidney heads for Chicago after almost being arrested. Travis and his girlfriend, Obalese Eaton (Judy Pace), depart for Texas.

Filled with all the appropriate set pieces of the new black film genre (i.e. a disgruntled returning Vietnam war veteran mistreated by white Americans; black wrongdoers with a good ulterior motive, in this case establishing the bank; the token black police officer harassed in a white precinct), this new edition of *The Asphalt Jungle* is not up to the original, which had a far sharper depiction of venality and a riveting fatalistic tone. "For an action movie it is curiously short on action ... and long on characters...." observed Roger Greenspun *(New York Times)*. "What remains is therefore much less than *The Asphalt Jungle;* a neat, competent thriller, strikingly acted and making good use of its Los Angeles locations, but never really matching even *Shaft* in pace, enterprise and excitement" (Tom Milne, British *Monthly Film Bulletin*).

Besides resourceful performances by the always-reliable Thalmus Rasulala and Raymond St. Jacques, not to be overlooked in this crime caper are its four central female characters. They are Obalese (Judy Pace) who tries to soften her tough man Travis; Mrs. Harris (Paula Kelly) as the spouse of the moonlight preacher; Emma (Royce Wallace), the nagging, wheelchair-bound wife of Mercer; and Lark (Margaret Avery), Mercer's slithery mistress. The last-named part had been the one to launch Marilyn Monroe's screen career into high gear.

The music score for *Cool Breeze* is by soul singer Solomon Burke, who already had fourteen million-seller records to his credits. This was his first film score and, for the soundtrack, eight of Burke's children perform the music with him.

67. The Cool World (Cinema 5, 1963). 125 minutes.

Producer Frederick Wiseman; *director* Shirley Clarke; *based on the novel by* Warren Miller *and the play by* Miller and Robert Rossen; *screenplay* Clarke; *set decorator* Roger Furman; *music/music director* Mal Waldron; *assistant director* Alex Gotein; *sound* Richard Vorisek, David Jones; *camera* Baird Bryant; *additional camera* Leroy McLucas; *editor* Clarke.

Cast: Hampton Clanton [Rony Clanton] (Richard "Duke" Custis); Yolanda Rodriguez (Lu-Anne); Bostic Felton (Rod); Gary Bolling (Littleman); Carl Lee (Priest); Gloria Foster (Mrs. Custis); Georgia Burke (Grandma); Charles Richardson (Beep Bop); Bruce Edwards (Warrior); Teddy McCain (Saint); Ronald Perry (Savage); Lloyd Edwards (Foxy); Ken Sutherland (Big Jeff); Billy Taylor (Mission); Jay Brooks (Littleman's Father); Clarence William III (Blood); Claude Cave (Hardy); Marilyn Cox (Miss Dewpoint); Jerome Raphel (Mr. Shapiro); Joe Oliver (Angel); J.C. Lee (Coolie); John Marriott (Hurst); Bert Donaldson (45); Joseph Dennis (Douglas Thurston); Maurice Sneed (Rocky); William Ford (Ace); Alfred Callymore (China); Ted Butler (Mrs. Osborne); Pheta Canegata (Pheta); Nettie Avery (Big Daddy); Riley Mac (Mac); Sandra McPherson (Coney Island Girl); Wilbur Green (Priest's Buddy); Val Bisoglio, Vic Romano (Gangsters); William Canegata, Dean Cohen, Peter De Anda, Alan Mercer (Cops); George W. Goodman (Newscaster); Richard Ward (Street Speaker); Esther Bodie, Irma Williams (Ladies); *and:* Evadney Canegata, Milton Williams.

Shirley Clarke, the famed cinema verite director of *The Connection* (1960) and *Portrait of Jason* (1967) — the latter a study of a black hustler — turned her attention to another sensitive subject in *The Cool World,* based on a 1959 novel by Warren Miller and the 1960 Broadway play by Miller and Robert Rossen. Made several years after the far more expensive and successful *The Blackboard Jungle* (1955) (q.v.) and long before the black street life picture became fashionably commercial, *The Cool World* is a remarkably controlled, unexploitive motion picture on its own. It is the desperate odyssey of the fifteen-year-old "hero," Duke, who seeks to achieve manhood by gaining power. And, to him, power is owning a gun and becoming a leader of his street gang. *The Cool World* was an official United States entry in the 1963 Venice Film Festival and is worthy of being known more than just as a footnote in film history. It also contains a Mal Waldron music score with a jazz group featuring Dizzy Gillespie. Location filming was done entirely on the streets of Harlem.

"*The Cool World* is as shocking as the truth; it is the truth!" (James Farmer, National Director, Congress of Racial Equality). "A loud, long, powerful cry of outrage!" (Judith Christ, *New York Herald-Tribune*). *Variety* judged it ". . . a telling look at Harlem and probably one of the least patronizing films ever made on Negro life in New York.... A counterpoint jazz background is an asset as is the well textured lensing, cogent editing and the natural thesping by a mainly non-pro cast." More critical was Bosley Crowther *(New York Times):* "Miss Clarke's omnivorous camera tends to wander at times, to go racing after some aspect of Harlem atmosphere.... This gives to the film a hectic, nervous and disjointed quality that may be significant of the looseness and vagrancy of the characters, but it makes for much disconcertion. This is not a tight and direct film."

Duke Custis (Hampton Clanton) is a black teenager living in the raw world of the Harlem ghetto with his world-weary mother and grandmother. His environment is as narrow as that of any prisoner. He looks up to Priest (Carl Lee), who has made something of his life in their circumscribed world — he has become a full-time hood. (But even Priest is at the mercy of the white man: the

Mafiosi from downtown.) Duke is a member of the Royal Pythons gang and wants to buy a gun (from Priest) so he can become its undisputed leader. When the father of pal Little (Gray Bolling) runs off, the Pythons take over the apartment and establish LuAnne (Yolanda Rodriguez) as the group whore. Although LuAnne is the girlfriend of Python leader Blood (Clarence Williams III), she and Duke fall in love. After the gang realizes Blood's heroin kick distracts him from being their leader, Duke takes over gang leadership. Later, during a Coney Island adventure, LuAnne, a lost soul in the ghetto who had never even seen the ocean before, disappears. Duke returns to Harlem alone. During a gang fight with the rival Wolves, Duke wounds an opponent with a knife. At the Python headquarters he finds the body of Priest, killed by the downtown mobsters. A shocked Duke rushes home, where he is arrested by the brutalizing law enforcers. He is dragged off to jail as his mother walks down the street with her new boyfriend.

While this ahead-of-its-time study received artistic praise, Pauline Kael in *The New Yorker* magazine suggested, "The film tries to encompass too much: you get the feeling that the director thought she could use everything good that she caught." What sticks in the mind long after the film's plot becomes vague is the young anti-hero's search for meaning to his seemingly hopeless life. With the grimness of his environment, the despair of his downtrodden family, and no role models other than his gang companions, he is drawn into the very mess he (sub)consciously wants to escape, a Kafkaesque nightmare.

Sensitive performer Hampton Clanton would appear later in *The Education of Sonny Carson* (1974) and *Rappin'* (1985) (qq.v.), under the name Rony Clanton.

68. Cooley High (American International, 1975). Color, 107 minutes.

Executive producer Samuel Z. Arkoff; *producer* Steve Krantz; *director* Michael Schultz; *screenplay* Eric Monte; *art director/set decorator* William B. Fosser; *music/music director/music arranger* Freddie Perren; *songs* Perren and Christine Yarrion; *production supervisor* Elliot Schick; *assistant directors* Frank Beetson, Roy Peterson; *stunt co-ordinator* James Kingsley; *sound* Bill Pellak; *sound effects* Edit International; *camera* Paul von Brack; *editor* Christopher Holmes.

Cast: Glynn Turman (Robert "Preach" Morris); Lawrence-Hilton Jacobs (Larry "Cochise" Jackson); Garrett Morris (Mr. Mason); Cynthia David (Brenda); Corin Rogers (Pooter); Maurice Leon Havis (Willie); Joseph Carter Wilson (Tyrone); Sherman Smith (Stone); Norman Gibson (Robert); Maurice Marshall (Damon); Steven Williams (Jimmy Lee); Christine Jones (Sandra); Jackie Taylor (Johnny Mae); Lynn Caridine (Dorothy); Mary Larkins (Preach's Mother); Cherene Snow (Totty); Alicia Williams (Dee); Lily Schine (Cochise's Mother); Mukai Richardson (Beverly); Juanita McConnell (Martha); Sharon Murff (Loretta); Jimmy Whig (Trick); Nathaniel Reed, Frank Beetson (Detectives); Marlene Howton (Girl in Toilet); Colostine Boatwright, Keita L. Keita (Prostitutes); James Kingsley, James George (Police on Pier); Mary Jane Schaefer (Schoolteacher); Brandon Schultz (Tommy).

"*Cooley High* is being pitched as a black *American Graffiti,* and the

description is apt. Furthermore, you don't have to be black to enjoy it em-
mensely" *(Variety)*. "*Cooley High* pulsates with the careless exuberance of
youth and captivates with characterizations and incidents presented"
(Lawrence Van Gelder, *New York Times*). The comedy grossed $2,600,000 in
domestic film rentals, even coming late in the black film cycle as it did. Years
later, when reviewing this feature for a television airdate, Kevin Thomas *(Los
Angeles Times)* would assess, "*[Cooley High]* shows what the black American
can be when creative talents are given an opportunity free of the strong sex-
and-violence requirements of exploitation pictures. A bittersweet, nostalgic
coming-of-age drama inspired by its writer Eric Monte's own experiences."

In 1964 Chicago, Cochise (Lawrence-Hilton Jacobs), crap-shooting, girl-
chasing Preach (Glynn Turman), and Pooter (Corin Rogers) play hookey from
Edwin G. Cooley Vocational High School one Friday. They visit the Lincoln
Park Zoo and then play basketball. Although his heart belongs to the more
sympathetic Sandra (Christine Jones), the bespectacled Preach flirts with snobbish Brenda (Cynthia Davis). Later, after a fight started by Damon (Maurice
Marshall), he and Cochise join Robert (Norman Gibson) and Stone (Sherman
Smith) for a madcap joyride in a stolen car. They barely miss being caught by
the pursuing police. Preach and Brenda, who is impressed by his writing of
poetry, make love, and the next day at school she kisses him in front of Sandra
and their other classmates. Preach and Cochise are arrested for their car stealing. Because his teacher (Garret Morris) tells the sympathetic police that
Preach is really a good student who has won a scholarship, he and Cochise are
let off, but Robert and Stone are prosecuted. On the lam from his angry friends
who think he turned traitor, Preach discovers Cochise has been beaten to
death. He attends Cochise's funeral from afar, privately reads a farewell poem
he composed, and then sets out to.... The epilogue indicates that Preach is
now a Hollywood scriptwriter, Brenda a librarian who is married and has three
children, Pooter a factory worker, and Damon an army sergeant; Robert and
Stone were killed in a 1966 holdup attempt.

As the movie ranges from the comic to the serious in a wide variety of
adolescent experiences, the period flavor is punctuated by use of Motown
Records hits of the 1960s featuring the Supremes, the Temptations, Stevie
Wonder, Martha and the Vandellas, the Marvelettes, Smokey Robinson, *et al.*
It was written by Eric Monte, who created the "Good Times" (1974–79)
teleseries, and directed enthusiastically if not overly slickly by first-time direc-
tor Michael Schultz, who later directed such features as *Car Wash* (1976),
Greased Lightning (1977) (q.v.), *Which Way Is Up?* (1977), *Sgt. Pepper's
Lonely Hearts Club Band* (1981), *Carbon Copy* (1981), and others.

Actor Glynn Turman (Preach) was born in New York City in 1946 and
made his mark early on in television appearing as the teen-aged son of Percy
Rodriguez and Ruby Dee in the prime-time soap opera "Peyton Place." A fre-
quent TV performer, he appeared in a variety of telefeatures, including
Carter's Army (1970) (q.v.), and was featured in such TV comedy series as
"Hail to the Chief" (1985) and "A Different World (1988–   ). Next to *Cooley
High* he is best known for his performance in *J.D.'s Revenge* (1976) (q.v.).

Cooley High grossed $2,600,000 in domestic film rentals.

69. Coonskin (Bryanston, 1975). Color, 82 minutes.

Producer Albert S. Ruddy; *director/screenplay* Ralph Bakshi; *music* Chico Hamilton; *still photographers* Bakshi, Johnnie Vita; *assistant director* Vita; *camera* William A. Fraker; *animation camera* Ted C. Bemiller; *editor* Donald W. Ernst.

Cast: Barry White (Samson/Brother Bear); Charles Grodone (Preacher/ Brother Fox); Scatman Crothers (Pappy/Old Man Bone); Philip [Michael] Thomas (Randy/Brother Rabbit).

A.K.A. *Street Fight.*

Thirteen years before *Who Framed Roger Rabbit?* amazed moviegoers with its fascinating interaction of live action and animated figures, Ralph Bakshi's *Coonskin* did the same thing (granted on a far more primitive level). That was not the only innovative element to this provocative, R-rated cartoon feature which has live action sequences. In an extensive *New York Times* essay, film critic Richard Eder analyzed, ". . . Bakshi's biggest risks are the matter of taste. Because cartoons have no softening human texture, their bite, their bitterness, is unrelieved. . . . It is the whites who are monstrous in *Coonskin*. The blacks are smart, weak, violent, hopeful, crooked, enduring and desperate. They are human: the whites are not. . . . Bakshi's movie is about a segment of black experience as he [a Brooklyn-born white Jew] can grasp it. . . . He is not saying that white people are nightmares in fact; but that they are nightmares for many blacks . . . at a deeper level he given expression to a tentative horror about life itself."

Coonskin opens in the film-framing story of two black convicts down South waiting in the prison yard through the long night for an escape car to appear. Pappy (Scatman Crothers) fills in the time by telling the impatient Randy (Philip [Michael] Thomas) a fable.

The rousing story, a modernizing of Uncle Remus tales, is of a slick rabbit (the voice of Philip [Michael] Thomas), a bewildered bear (the voice of Barry White), and a weak-willed fox (the voice of Charles Grodone) who head north, come to Harlem and take over, vanquishing their enemies which range from the police to the Mafia. And the trio enjoys every bit of their luscious victory. Throughout their richly textured adventure they meet stereotypes of both races (as well as a slick Puerto Rican): from a redneck Southern sheriff to a black garbage picker who can't believe his luck in finding a 100 percent natural cotton red sweater that a white person had stupidly thrown away, to the drag queen sons of the New York Godfather, to the voluptuous and deadly blonde, blue-eyed "Miss America" siren (who lures several black men to their demise) and a tough black stripper.

With the parable ending on a raunchy high note, the tale reverts to full live action. It is daybreak and the prison escape plan goes into its fumbling execution. The rescued convicts ride off to freedom.

"*Coonskin* is by no means avant garde; the story of young men who start essentially the same but turn out differently is as old as mankind; and the contemporary urban plot turns are drawn from the treasury of modern pulp dramaturgy. . . . *Coonskin* seems to be telling it 'the way it was'—in the filmmaker's own earlier life, for example—but in a unique cinematic context" *(Variety).*

Ralph Bakshi had directed previously the raunchy R-rated cartoons *Fritz the Cat* (1971) (q.v.), *Heavy Traffic* (1973), and *The Nine Lives of Fritz the Cat* (1975). Originally Paramount Pictures was to have distributed *Coonskin* (which was made in the summer of 1974) but then C.O.R.E. (Congress of Racial Equality) screened the cartoon film and denounced it as both racist and insulting. "It depicts blacks as slaves, hustlers, and whores." An intimidated Paramount backed out of the project, and independent Bryanston Pictures took over distribution in August 1975, coping with the picket lines and brouhaha in the press that followed its limited openings.

Boasting technical originality and biting earthiness, *Coonskin* tells more about ghetto life than many live action black action features. *Variety* noted, "There is heart in his plots, so superficial putdown is totally absent." Richard Eder *(New York Times)* further pointed out, ". . . Bakshi is making a most serious and difficult kind of artistic commitment in trying to capture black Harlem's human condition by heightening rather than softening its miseries."

70. Cornbread, Earl and Me (American International, 1975).
Color, 94 minutes.

Presenter Samuel Z. Arkoff; *executive producer* Leonard Lamensdorf; *producer* Joe Manduke; *associate producer* Martin Penn; *director* Manduke; *based on the novel* "Hog Butcher" *by* Ronald Fair; *screenplay* Lamensdorf; *art director* David Haber; *costumes* Ann McCarthy; *music* Donald Byrd; *music supervisor* Coleridge-Taylor Perkinson; *assistant director* Tony Brand; *camera* Jules Brenner; *editor* Aaron Stell.

Cast: Moses Gunn (Ben Blackwell); Rosalind Cash (Sarah Robinson); Bernie Casey (Atkins); Madge Sinclair (Leona); Keith Wilkes (Cornbread); Tierre Turner (Earl); Antonio Fargas (One Eye); Vincent Martorano (Golich); Charles Lampkin (Fred Jenkins); Stack Pierce (Sam); Logan Ramsey (Deputy Coroner); Thalmus Rasulala (Charlie); Bill Henderson (Watkins); Sarina C. Grant (Mrs. Parsons); Stefan Gierasch (Sergeant Danaher); Larry Fishburne III (Wilford); the Blackbyrds (Themselves).

In its simplicity and unrelenting grimness, *Cornbread, Earl and Me* is remarkably effective. Filled with all the frustrations of ghetto life, it is very much a message picture, but uniquely tries to be unbiased in its presentation of black peole confronting the white man's system. What mars the overall results is "a certain unevenness in the acting and a slapdash air about the climactic inquest. . ." (Lawrence Van Gelder, *New York Times*).

In two weeks wholesome, hard-studying teenager Cornbread (Keith Wilkes) is scheduled to go to college. His passport out of the ghetto is his ability at sports. "This basketball is going to take us off the street. . . . This is all kinds of food," he says. Then one day Cornbread, whose neighborhood admirers include the younger Earl (Tierre Turner) and Wilford (Larry Fishburne III), is shot down in error by police (one black, one white) who are pursuing an apparent psychopath who nearly killed a woman. Witnessing this tragedy is twelve-year-old Wilford, who is traumatized by the event. Cornbread's strong-willed mother, Leona (Madge Sinclair), is shattered but determined to clear her son's name. She puts well-mannered attorney Ben Blackwell (Moses Gunn) in charge of the case. As the inquest proceeds, with racist Sergeant Danaher (Stefan Gierasch) interfering at every step, focus is on the two policemen in the shooting: the troubled black cop, Atkins (Bernie Casey), and the regretful white lawman, Golich (Vincent Martorano), who actually pulled the trigger. The crucial testimony can only be supplied by young Wilford (the "Me" of the film title). As his mother, Sarah (Rosalind Cash), urges her frightened child, "I want you to be a man right now." Wilford's statement proves the policemen had actually shouted warnings at Cornbread, who was rushing home at top speed (to win a bet on his running ability), but the noise from a passing garbage truck prevented him from hearing the police shout, "Stop." The dead youth's innocence is proven.

"Made with a fine cast and the best of intentions . . . [this picture] turns into a lumbering TV-style courtroom drama reminiscent of the Reginald Rose liberal soap operas of the 1950s. . . . Early segs of the film . . . are an affectionate and moving composite of ghetto life" *(Variety).* "Not only is it one of the precious few PG-rated movies coming out of Hollywood these days, it also contains some of the most moving acting performances you will have seen in a long time" (Walter Burrell, *Essence* magazine). In the tapestry of this drama, several performances stand out: Madge Sinclair as the heartbroken mother of the victim, her tough-as-nails but radiant neighbor Rosalind Cash, who has a lusty, kindhearted man friend (Thalmus Rasulala), Antonio Fargas as the flavorful, one-eyed numbers runner, and Charles Lampkin as the ghetto storekeeper. Most important are the three youths. Cornbread is played honestly and simply by Keith Wilkes, former UCLA All-American and later basketball star of the Golden State Warriors. Earl is played by the excellent young actor Tierre Turner, who also in 1975 appeared in *Bucktown* and *Friday Foster* (qq.v.), and would himself portray a basketball player in the short-lived comedy teleseries "The Waverly Wonders" (1978). And most crucial of all to the storyline of *Cornbread, Earl and Me* is Larry Fishburne III as little Wilford, prankish enough to steal candy bars from the corner grocery store, who must grow up awfully fast when his testimony is needed to solve this case that has so aroused the community.

Cornbread, Earl and Me grossed $2,020,000 in domestic film rentals.

71. Cotton Comes to Harlem (United Artists, 1970). Color, 97 minutes.

Producer Samuel Goldwyn, Jr.; *director* Ossie Davis; *based on the novel by* Chester Himes; *screenplay* Davis, Arnold Perl; *art director* Manny Gerard; *set decorator* Bob Drumbeller; *costumes* Anna Hill Johnstone; *music* Galt MacDermot; *songs* MacDermot and Joseph S. Lewis; MacDermot and Davis; MacDermot and William Dumaresq; MacDermot and Paul Laurence Dunbar; *choreography* Louis Johnson; *assistant director* Domenic D'Antonio; *stunt coordinator/second unit director* Max Kleven; *sound* Newton Avrutis; *camera* Gerald Hirschfield; *second unit camera* Gil Geller; *editors* John Carter, Robert Q. Lovet.

Cast: Raymond St. Jacques (Coffin Ed Johnson); Godfrey Cambridge (Grave Digger Jones); Calvin Lockhart (Reverend Deke O'Malley); Judy Pace (Iris); Redd Foxx (Uncle Bud); John Anderson (Bryce); Emily Yancy (Mabel);

Advertising art for *Cotton Comes to Harlem* (1970).

J.D. Cannon (Calhoun); Mabel Robinson (Billie); Dick Sabol (Jerema); Theodore Wilson (Barry); Eugene Roche (Anderson); Frederick O'Neal (Casper); Vinnette Carrol (Reba); Gene Lindsey (Luddy); Van Kirksey (Early Riser); Cleavon Little (Lo Boy); Helen Martin (Church Sister); Turk Turpin (Dum Dum); Tom Lane (44); Arnold Williams (Hi Jenks); Lou Jacobi (Goodman); Leonardo Cimino (Tom); *and:* Maxwell Glanville, Irwin C. Watson.

Preposterous, zesty, uneven, stereotypical, madcap. These descriptive words all apply equally to *Cotton Comes to Harlem*. This trendsetting mainstream feature film from a major Hollywood studio boasts many firsts. It was the first of expatriate Chester Himes's detective novels, all first published in France in French, to be pictorialized. It was acclaimed actor Ossie Davis's debut as a motion picture director. And it was the first really successful black action film, especially notable because it makes no strong attempt to tell any violent ghetto message about the Man. (It has enough difficulty keeping up with the careening, rollercoasting Himes plotline.)

Stylish Reverend Deke O'Malley (Calvin Lockhart) convinces his Harlem followers to donate $87,000 for his "Back to Africa" boat. Suddenly, armed men arrive and take off with the money. Harlem police officers Gravedigger Jones (Godfrey Cambridge) and Coffin Ed Johnson (Raymond St. Jacques) pursue the van, but it disappears. Jones and Johnson are sure O'Malley was scamming his contributors, but precinct Captain Bryce (John Anderson) is convinced otherwise. O'Malley, who has disappeared from sight, is positive his white partner, Calhoun (J.D. Cannon), double-crossed him, and his partner believes the reverse. Actually the money, hastily concealed in a bale of cotton, had fallen off the getaway truck and was found by elderly junkman Uncle Bud (Redd Foxx). After Uncle Bud vanishes, O'Malley is detained at police headquarters, but when his followers begin rioting, Bryce lets him go. Jones and Johnson promise the agitated crowd the money will be returned. Although the two policemen have been officially taken off the case for their unorthodox theories and methods, they still follow up clues. The trail leads to the Apollo Theatre, where the bale of cotton is now a prop in an exotic dancer's act. By the finale everyone is happy. Uncle Bud has used the original $87,000 in Africa, and the people have their donations back, compliments of the unwilling white Mafiosa chieftain, who was blackmailed into compliance by Jones and Johnson by their suggestions that if he did not do so, black power would take over Harlem mob activities.

Certainly the too-frequent hesitancy of Ossie Davis's directing style is not one of this film's virtues. Nor are the recurring stereotyped characterizations (by Redd Foxx in particular) helpful to an impartial viewing of this comedy thriller. And the plot (as in the book original) has so many unexplained twists and turns, that it is as tough to decipher and rationalize as any Raymond Chandler detective opus. However, there are many pluses. There is unabashed energy supplied as much by the buoyant, racy soundtrack music as by the onscreen shenanigans of the materialistic participants. With such a snappy supporting cast, especially Calvin Lockhart as the cool con artist Reverend and Judy Pace as the slick seductress Iris, the focal point sometimes drifts from the film's striking leads: the constantly quizzical Gravedigger and the perpetually righteous Coffin Ed. The latter is the spokesman for his community's fight against internal black as well as external white corruption.

Because of or in spite of its foul-mouthed language, nudity and ethnic depiction, *Cotton Comes to Harlem,* made on an estimated cost of $2,200,000, eventually grossed $15,375,000 in film rentals. It was impressive enough for producer Samuel Goldwyn, Jr., who had optioned the rest of the Coffin Ed/Gravedigger capers, to make a followup picture, *Come Back Charleston Blue* (1972) (q.v.).

72. **Countdown at Kusini** (Columbia, 1976). Color, 99 minutes.

Producer Ladi Ladebo; *director* Ossie Davis; *story* John Storm Roberts; *screenplay* Davis, Ladebo, Al Freeman, Jr.; *music* Manu Dibango; *assistant directors* Dwight Williams, Joseph Ray Johnson; *sound* Lee Bost; *camera* Andrew Laszlo.

Cast: Ruby Dee (Leah Matanzima); Ossie Davis (Ernest Motapo); Greg Morris (Red Slater); Tom Aldredge (Ben Amed); Michael Ebert (Charles Henderson); Thomas Baptiste (John Okello); Jab Adu (Juma Bakari); Elsie Olusola (Mamouda); Funso Adeolu (Marni [Yola]).

This offbeat and now little-seen feature was produced by Delta Sigma Theta, the largest service organization of black women in the United States. It was filmed completely on location in Nigeria and directed by Ossie Davis, who co-starred with his real-life wife, Ruby Dee.

Left–right: **Ruby Dee, Greg Morris and Ossie Davis in** *Countdown at Kusini* **(1976).**

Set in Lagos, the chief city of Nigeria, the storyline focuses on idealistic patriot Ernest Motapo (Ossie Davis), whose goals for his (unnamed) nation are in conflict with the financial well-being of a huge foreign syndicate. A mercenary (Ben Amed) is hired to assassinate Motapo. Others in the chronicle are Leah Matanzima (Ruby Dee) as his African liaison, Red Slater (Greg Morris) as the visiting jazz pianist who awakens to the country's struggle for freedom, Marni (Funso Adeolu) as Motapo's scheming nephew, and Charles Henderson (Michael Ebert) as the white journalist observing all the interaction.

This well-meaning if somewhat crude production, filled with overzealous, "meaningful" performances, was not what audiences of any race in the mid-1970s expected or wanted from filmfare. It quickly disappeared into television syndication.

73. Crazy Joe (Columbia, 1974). Color, 100 minutes.

Executive producer Nino E. Krisman; *producer* Dino De Laurentiis; *director* Carlo Izzani; *based on the story by* Nicholas Gage; *screenplay* Lewis John Carlino; *art director* Robert Gundlach; *music* Gian Carlo Caramello; *sound* Dennis Maitland; *camera* Aldo Tonti; *editor* Peter Zinner.

Cast: Peter Boyle (Crazy Joe); Paula Prentiss (Anne); Fred Williamson (Willy); Charles Cioffi (Coletti); Rip Torn (Richie); Luther Adler (Falco); Fausto Tozzi (Frank); Franco Lantieri (Nunzio); Eli Wallach (Don Vittorio);

Louis Guss (Magliocco); Carmine Caridi (Jelly); Henry Winkler (Mannie); Gabrielle Torrei (Cheech); Guido Leontini (Angelo); Sam Coppola (Chick); Mario Erpichini (Danny); Adam Wade (J.D.); Timothy Holey (Lou); Ralph Wilcox (Sam); Peter Savage (DeMarco); Herve Villechaize (Samson); Dan Resin, Robert Riesel (FBI Agents); Nella Dina (Mrs. Falco).

In its day many critics dismissed *Crazy Joe* as just another *The Godfather* (1972) ripoff, branding it "a lumpy, violent fictionalized biography" (Vincent Canby, *New York Times*). But in actuality this gangster thriller, a U.S./Italian co-production, was a very sturdy depiction of the life and last days of Joseph "Crazy Joe" Gallo, the flamboyant New York Mafia hood gunned down on April 7, 1972, at a clam house in Little Italy. Peter Boyle provides one of his best performances as the success-seeking gangster who realizes, "I gotta go for broke this time. I don't wanna die in the street."

Crazy Joe (Peter Boyle) and his brother Richie (Rip Torn) lead the faction who want to splinter off from the Mafia family and control their own criminal activities and profit. Before this happens Joe is arrested and spends the next six years in prison. Meanwhile he learns that Don Vittorio (Eli Wallach) has taken control of the turf and that Joe's brother Richie has committed suicide. Joe is a self-improved man when he leaves prison and has many, many powerful black friendships, including that of Willy (Fred Williamson). Don Vittorio pretends to make amends with Joe, but in reality is afraid of a power pact between Joe and his black hood pals. While celebrating his birthday at dinner in lower Manhattan, Joe is machine-gunned to death.

One of the interesting facets of this resourceful film is its depiction of the unification of Harlem and Little Italy mobsters in the joint goal of displacing the big man. With Fred Williamson's Willy allied with Crazy Joe, it seems likely their scheme could have worked. A good deal of the prison segment of *Crazy Joe* is devoted to the racial mistreatment of the black inmates.

Spotted in this intriguing cast of professionals are Henry "Happy Days" Winkler and Herve "Fantasy Island" Villechaize.

74. Cutter (NBC-TV, 1/26/72). Color, 78 minutes.

Executive producer Richard Irving; *producer* Dean Hargrove; *associate producer* Peter Allan Fields; *director* Irving; *teleplay* Hargrove; *art director* William H. Tuntke; *set decorator* William Fosser; *costumes* Bill Jobe; *music* Oliver Nelson; *assistant director* Kenny Williams; *sound* John Bosco; *camera* Jack Priestley; *editor* Frank Morris.

Cast: Peter De Anda (Frank Cutter); Cameron Mitchell (Riggs); Barbara Rush (Linda Henderson); Gabriel Dell (Leone); Janet MacLachlan (Diane Hayden); Robert Webber (Richard Meredith); Marlene Warfield (Susan Macklin); Archie Moore (Ray Brown); Herbert Jefferson, Jr. (Steve Macklin); Anna Navarro (Miss Aguilera); Stepin Fetchit (Shoeshine Man); Karen Carlson (Janice); John Alexander, Jr. (Billy); Arlene Banas (Arlene French); Jim Antonio (Ray); Tom Erhart (Paul Benedict); Ira W. Rogers (Jerome); Tony Mockus (Stanley); Curley Ellison (Don); John W. Huston (Carl); Patrick Mulvihil (Security Guard); Harold C. Johnson (Sergeant Johnson); Spencer Milligan (Harris).

Left–right: **Peter Boyle, player, and Fred Williamson in** *Crazy Joe* **(1973).**

Peter De Anda, who had scored as the duplistic killer in *Come Back Charleston Blue* (1972) (q.v.), starred on the other side of the law in this television pilot about yet another black private eye. (See *Cocaine and Blue Eyes; Shaft; Tenafly.*). This banal detective yarn focuses on the search for a missing black pro football quarterback in and around Chicago. Along the way detective Cutter is helped by swank public relations executive Linda Henderson (Barbara Rush); given a clue by an elderly shoeshiner (Stepin Fetchit); harassed by a black police sergeant (Howard Johnson); confused by aging football coach Riggs (Cameron Mitchell); and nearly undone by pro team owner Richard Meredith (Robert Webber).

"You got a big head, Cutter. You live big, you talk big, and you act big," says one unfriendly soul of detective Frank Cutter. Much is made of the fact that the private eye is a self-made man who rose from the street and whose good deeds and fair-mindedness lead nearly everyone to say "I owe you." He is the type of self-employed man with "no office, just a phone number, it keeps life simple." To benefit from the fashionable racial intolerance angle, there are white hoods who warn the black gumshoe, "Friend, I think you're real lost. You keep showing up in places *you* don't belong." (To which, unafraid, Cutter replies, "I belong anywhere I happen to be!")

Variety rated it "routine" and added, "With its eye clearly on *Shaft,* the pilot evolved in standard fast-paced action fashion — all chase and no content."

75. D.C. Cab (Universal, 1983). Color, 104 minutes.

Executive producers Peter Guber, Jon Peters; *producer* Topper Carew; *co-producer* Cassius Vernon Weathersby; *associate producer* Peter V. Herald;

director Joel Schumacher; *story* Carew, Schumacher; *screenplay* Schumacher; *production designer/set decorator* John J. Lloyd; *art director* Bernie Cutler; *costumes* Roberta Weiner; *music* Giorgio Moroder; *music arrangers* Arthur Barrows, Richie Zito, Kristian Schultze; *music co-ordinators* Gary LeMel, Bob Destocki; *music editor* Richard Stone; *songs* Moroder, Irene Cara, and Pete Bellote; Moroder and Bellotte; Phil Galdston and Peter Thorn; Richard Feldman, Rick Kelly, and Larry John McNally; Gary Busey; Andy Goldmark and Galdston; Ron Finch and Daryl Ross; Allee Willis, Danny Sembello and Dennis Matkosky; *choreography* Jeffrey Hornaday; *assistant directors* Newton D. Arnold, Russ Harling, Ron Kinwald; *second unit directors* M. James Arnett, Alan Oliney; *stunt co-ordinator* Oliney; *sound* Will Yarbrough; *supervising sound editor* Richard Anderson; *camera* Dean Cundey; *second unit camera* Rex Metz; *editor* David Blewitt.

Cast: Adam Baldwin (Albert Hockenberry); Charlie Barnett (Tyrone); Irene Cara (Herself); Anne DeSalvo (Myrna); Max Gail (Harold); Gloria Gifford (Miss Floyd); DeWayne Jessie (Bongo); Bill Maher (Baba); Whitman Mayo (Mr. Rhythm); Mr. T (Samson); Jose Perez (Bravo); Paul Rodriguez (Xavier); David Barbarian (Buzzy); Peter Barbarian (Buddy); Marsha Warfield (Opehlia); Gary Busey (Dell); Bob Zmuda (Cubby); Jim Moody (Arnie); Denise Gordy (Denise); Alfredine P. Brown (Matty); Scott Nemes, Senta Moses (Ambassador's Son and Daughter); Jill Schoelen (Claudette); Diane Bellam (Maudie); John Diehl, Bonnie Keith, J.W. Smith (Kidnappers); Moriah Shannon (Waitress); Newton D. Arnold (FBI Chief); Jacki Clark (Hooker in Samson's Cab); Don Jacob (Ambassador Rayburn); Ann Guilford-Grey (Ambassador's Wife); Timothy Rice (Airport Drunk); Patricia Duff (Elegant Blonde in Bar); Martha Jane Urann (Passenger in Cab); Michael DeSanto, Dale Stephenson (Embassy Security Guards); Timothy Agoglia Carey (Angel of Death); Esther Lee (Oriental Tourist); Scott Perry (FBI Agent); Marti Soyoa (Drive-in Manager); Irvin Matsukiyo (Chinese Waiter); Karen Leigh Hopkins (Camera Woman); Charles J. Baron (Flight Attendant); Carmen J. Gray (Emerald Driver); Kenneth Van Auken (Garfinkel's Doorman); Charles Bouvier, Bob Maroff, J. Christopher Sullivan, Ron Canada (Policemen); Carla Folk (Pregnant Passenger); Walter Wyatt (Truck Driver); Dawan Scott (Venus Club Bouncer); Jaycee Cooper (Reporter).

British release title: *Street Fleet.*

What are the likes of Irene Cara, Gary Busey, Marsha Warfield and a host of other solid performers doing in this dumb comedy? Making money like co-lead Mr. T., that oversized, gaudy ex-star of *Rocky III* (1982) (q.v.), and television's "The A-Team." "*D.C. Cab* is a musical mob scene, a raucous, crowded movie that's fun as long as it stays wildly busy, and a lot less interesting when it wasted time on plot or conversation" (Janet Maslin, *New York Times*). The meandering comedy would gross $6,964,697 in domestic film rentals, which proves a lot of people can be fooled at least some of the time.

Albert Hockenberry (Adam Baldwin) comes to Washington seeking the D.C. Cab Company, a near-broke hack firm run by Harold Oswell (Max Gail), who was an army buddy of Hockenberry's dead father. Hockenberry becomes one of the group's cabbies, which also include do-gooder Samson (Mr. T.), who is fearful of the effect drug dealers are having on the neighborhood kids; a zany young black named Tyrone (Charlie Barnett), the musician Baba (Bill Maher); a sex-hungry macho called Xavier (Paul Rodriguez); and the nerdy but resilient Dell (Gary Busey). Albert later teams with the other drivers to revive the failing company, and he begins dating Claudette (Jill Schoelen). When the two children of Ambassador Rayburn (Don Jacob) are kidnapped right from under the watchful eyes of Tyrone's housekeeper mother (Diana Bellamy), the madcap cabbies come to the rescue. All is saved, and there is a tumultuous parade through the streets of the nation's capital.

Irene Cara is on hand as herself to belt out "The Dream," a song she co-wrote.

76. Darktown Strutters (New World, 1975). Color, 93 minutes.

Producer Gene Corman; *director* William N. Witney; *screenplay* George Armitage; *production designer* Jack Fisk; *art director* Peter Jamison; *set decorator* Fisk; *costumes* Michael Nicola; *assistant director* Frank Beetson; *stunt co-ordinator* Paul Nuckles; *sound* Don Lusby; *camera* Joao Fernandes; *editor* Morton Tubor.

Cast: Trina Parks (Syreena); Edna Richardson (Carmen); Bettye Sweet (Miranda); Shirley Washington (Theda); Roger E. Mosley (Mellow); Christopher Joy (Wired); Stan Shaw (Raunchey); DeWayne Jessie (V.D.); Charles Knapp (Tubbins); Edward Marshall (Emmo); Dick Miller (Hugo); Milt Kogan (Babel); Norman Bartold (Colonel Cross); Gene Simms (Flash); Sam Laws (Philo); Frankie Crocker (Stuff); Della Thomas (Lixie); Ed Bakey (Reverend Tilly); Fuddle Bagley (Casabah); Frances Nealy (Cinderella); Barbara Morrison (Mrs. Parasol); Raymond Allen (Six Bits); Charles Woolf (Fallow); Alvin Childress (Bo); Zara Cully (Lorelai); *and:* the Dramatics, John Gary Williams and the Newcomers, the Minstrels, Okay Miller and Company.

This film is one of those formless, would-be zany comedies that relies on its blacks-versus-whites theme to give it topicality. "The sight gags and raunchy quips are not rib-tickers..." (A.H. Weiler, *New York Times*). *Boxoffice* magazine judged this a film "...for those who prefer their humor so wild that there isn't time to think between assaults on the senses...." Never has one film devoted so much onscreen time to depicting life in the fast lane at the take-out counters of so many different fast-food emporiums!

When Syreena's (Trina Parks) mother, Cinderella (Frances Nealy), is kidnapped, Syreena and her singing group/motorcycle-riding girlfriends—all decked out in space-age helmetry—embark on an odyssey to rescue the lady. (The resigned Syreena sighs as she starts on her latest do-good mission, "Somebody's always missing.") It develops that Cinderella had worked for the Cross Foundation run by the sinister fast-food giant Colonel Cross (Norman Bartold), a Colonel Sanders lookalike. The perverted Colonel is holding Cinderella, among other blacks, prisoner in the dungeon of his mansion. It is his way of getting even with the blacks who despise him because he is profiteering by selling overpriced rib dinners to black customers in his fast-food franchises.

Darktown Strutters, with its nonsensical episodes, is full of pleasant and unpleasant digs at both races but especially at the whites. There is the exploitive Colonel, who prances about his manse in his devilish costume; the pompous and snobbish Mrs. Parasol (Barbara Morrison); the police station with a "nigger alarm"; etc. But the other side of the coin comes in for kidding as well. There is the black Good Humor man who has a freezer chest full of candy bars, drugs, and cough medicines, and Syreena's grandpa who runs a profitable general store which sells merchandise (stolen from them in the first place) to the unsuspecting white folks. And there is Syreena's moralizing, pacifistic mother, who decides after all is said and done that "kicking their asses" is the best way to handle an enemy.

Trina Parks had been in the James Bond adventure *Diamonds Are Forever* (1971) as the karate-using menace, named Thumper, while Roger E. Mosley would gain his greatest fame to date as Tom Selleck's sidekick Theodore Calvin on "Magnum, P.I." (1980–88). Among the occasional songs in *Darktown Strutters* is "What You See Is What You Get," performed by the Dramatics.

77. Deadly Illusion (Cinetel, 1987). Color, 90 minutes.

Executive producers Michael Shapiro, Rodney Sheldon; *producer* Irwin Meyer; *associate producer* Steve Mirkovich; *directors* William Tannen, Larry Cohen; *screenplay* Cohen; *art directors* Mariana Zivkow, Ruth Lounsbury; *music* Patrick Gleeson; *song* Carol Connors and Gleeson; *music editor* Doug Lackey; *assistant directors* Michael Tedross, Chris Gerity; *stunt co-ordinator* Peter Hook; *sound editors* R.J. Palmer, F. Hudson Miller; *sound* Jonathan D. Evans; *sound effects/foley editor* Kelly Tartan; *special effects* Wilfred Caban; *camera* Daniel Pearl; *editors* Mirkovich, Ronald G. Spang.

Cast: Billy Dee Williams (Hamberger); Vanity (Rina); Morgan Fairchild (Jane Malloy/Sharon Burton); John Beck (Alex Burton); Joe Cortese (Paul Lefferts); Michael Wilding, Jr. (Costillian); Dennis Hallahan ("Burton" Imposter); Jenny Cornualle (Gloria Reed); Allison Woodward (Nancy Costillian); Joe Spinell (Crazy Man in Gun Bureau); Harriet Rogers (Mrs. Bains); George Oros (Levante); Charles Malcolm (Assistant District Attorney); Thom Curley (Wexler); Richard Triggs (Toll Booth Attendant); Joe Cirillo (Cop in Gun Bureau); Julie Gordon, Mary Kaplan (Receptionists); Debbie Dickinson (Woman on Phone); Michael Emil (Medical Examiner); Don Torres (Man at Ball Park); John Woehrle, Jim Kane, Jack McLaughlin, John Means (Boardroom Executives); Clint Bowers, David Holbrook, Everett Quinton (Clerks); Nick Smith (Security Guard); Al Cerrillo (Helicopter Pilot); Kathryn Leigh-Davis (*Mademoiselle* Magazine Reporter).

"I thought this Christmas season was going to be, you know, the kind you see in the movies. Me and Rina in front of a warm fire. Instead you know the rest. Here I am driving fifty miles out into the suburbs because some guy offers me $100,000 to kill his wife. I want to meet the woman that's worth $100,000. After all, I did take the down payment."

So begins this off-key detective escapade with unlicensed private eye Hamberger (Billy Dee Williams), who works out of a Manhattan cafeteria, embarking on his newest misadventure. He meets Sharon (Morgan Fairchild), the "wife" of "Burton" (Dennis Hallahan) and they quickly decide to fornicate. When he awakes he is implicated in the woman's murder, but that is only the beginning, and he has less than forty-eight hours to prove his innocence. Soon he discovers nothing makes sense. The woman he thought was Sharon Burton wasn't; nor was the man who hired him her husband—and the real Burton (John Beck) can prove that. The case leads him to a shootout atop a posh Rockefeller Center restaurant (with machine-gunning hit men firing from helicopters!), a fracas in the midst of the Center's mammoth Christmas tree, shootouts at a fashion show and at Shea Stadium. Helping Hamberger survive the marathon of life-defying events is his ever-lovin' Rina (Vanity), a New York cab driver. By the end it is proven that drug-smuggling fashion designer Jane Malloy (Morgan Fairchild) is one bad lady.

From the moment the film's hero says "My names is Hamberger. No jokes, please," the light motif is set. Hamberger is the type of sarcastic ladykilling detective who enjoys zinging smart dialogue as much as he does fornicating. To one woman he announces, "You've got a great body, but that gun is distracting." He also can't resist a good wise crack regarding his profession, even if he's the straight guy in the exchange:

HAMBERGER: I don't like the sight of dead bodies.
CLIENT: Then why do you make so many?

He is a true philosopher of the Mickey Spillane school. "I never did like two-faced women. It's amazing how greed and growing old make people act strange. At least, there are two things I'll never have to worry about." But there are times in *Deadly Illusion* when the parody become self-consciously stilted and tiresome. Narrator Hamberger says of the Jane Malloy character, "Every time I get in trouble there's a woman involved. Why does this one scare me?" Later he admits, "I don't know what is happening. Somebody is setting me up."

When he's in danger, fractious levity is his best weapon. At the Shea baseball Stadium shootout there is one final goon to be subdued. As he shoots the hood, Hamberger remarks, "You're out."

Even though it is downplayed, it is always evident that black gumshoe Hamberger is still operating in a world where blacks are stereotyped and still subject to the whims of whites. For example, during the chic midtown Manhattan fashion show sequence, there is this flippant exchange:

HONKY (to Hamberger): Aren't you Reggie Jackson, the ball player?
HAMBERGER: No. I'm Jesse Jackson, the presidential candidate.
HONKY: Right on!

With its off-center point of view, it is not surprising that filmmaker Larry Cohen (*Black Caesar* [1973], *Hell Up in Harlem* [1974] [qq.v.], others) was involved in the project. (He was replaced midstream by William Tannen.) At every turn, the expected and bizarre are highlighted, from the setpiece (the skyscraper shootout) to such unexpected dialogue as the cop at the Shea Stadium encounter yelling to a dim-witted armed goon, "Over here, asshole." The stooge turns around, and the policeman shoots him dead.

When the R-rated *Deadly Illusion* received a quick saturation release in Decmeber 1987, the ad tag line read, *"Hot Blooded Action ... Cold Blooded Murder."* Vincent Canby *(New York Times)* endorsed, "There's an engaging bravado about *Deadly Illusion;* a brassy suspense-melodrama...." Jami Bernard *(New York Post)* rated it three (out of a possible four) stars. When it was released on videocassette in mid-1988, Doug Brod *(Video Review* magazine) also gave it three stars. "Chalk up another wacked-out winner from the mind of Larry Cohen.... [He] has created a goofy, affectionate update of those wiseacre movie dicks of the '40s and '50s.... It's far from profound or, for that matter, slick, but's diverting enough."

78. Deadly Impact (European International Films, 1984). Color, 90 minutes.

Executive producer Richard Garrett; *producer/director* Larry Ludman; *story* David Parker, Jr.; *screenplay* Parker, Ludman; *art director* Alexander M. Colby; *wardrobe* Jane Sutton; *makeup* Mike Terry; *music* Frank Pentarey; *assistant director* Rocky Larsen; *car stunts* Alan Petit; *sound* Steve Connelly; *special effects* Albert Cooper, Dennis Rothbard, Bill Allen; *camera* Robert D. Forges; *editor* Vincent P. Thomas.

Cast: Fred Williamson (Lou); *and:* Bo Svenson, Marcia Clingan, John Morghen, Vincente Conte, Alan Blondeau, Norma Thyssen, Karen DeWitt, Rik Wallace, Bill Dunun, Genie Thompson, Wanita Brown, Don Champlin, Alan Sylvia, Jeanne Marie, Janet Francis.

This is one of a trio of films to co-star enduring black action star Fred Williamson and Bo Svenson. (The others are *Counterfeit Commandos,* a World War II actioner made in 1977 as *Bastardi Senza Gloria* [Counterfeit Bastards] by Italian director Enzo G. Castellari, and *Delta Force Commando,* shot in Nevada and Wisconsin in early 1987 under producer Pierluigi Ciraci's direction.) *Deadly Impact* is set in Las Vegas as a young couple from Phoenix, Arizona, arrive in town and, using a device tied into a computer, scam the casinos by knowing which slot machines will pay off when. The mob does not like the sudden winners, and the husband is gruesomely eliminated while the wife flees town. This brings a police lieutenant (Bo Svenson) and a swindling helicopter pilot named Lou (Fred Williamson) into the caper. Before the finale the pursuing thugs and the gal-on-the-lam are dead. Svenson, who has shaky morals, demands that he and Lou return the money to the authorities. But in a plot twist, the finale finds the two men back in Las Vegas using the computer device on the slot machines themselves.

Deadly Impact was obviously hastily filmed, with the car chases, gunfire, explosions, and occasional murders substitution for decent scripting or acting by the supporting players. The action film's only virtues are continued demonstrations of athletic prowess by cigar-smoking Williamson and extended on-location shots of the gambling capital, especially the Golden Nugget.

79. Death Journey (Atlas, 1976). Color, 84 minutes.

Producer/director Fred Williamson; *story/screenplay* Abel Jones; *wardrobe* Howard Stanley, Dalton Williams; *music* Anthony Shinault; *music super-*

visor/conductor The Mighty Manchurian; *special effects* Greg Auer; *sound* Thomas Nelson Productions; *post production sound* Marvin Kerner.

Cast: Fred Williamson (Jesse Crowder); Bernard Kuby (Finley); D'Urville Martin (Lockjaw Sampson the Gas Station Attendant); Art Mailer (District Attorney Virgil Reilly); Lou Bedford (Assistant District Attorney); Ed Kovins (Attorney Stern); Jim Campbell (Judge); Sam Coppola (Detective Johnson); Elliot Robins (Detective White); Jean Dancy (Girl at Gas Station); John Hopkins (Witness); Alexis Tramunt (Alice); Geoffrey Land (Ted); Jack Oliver (Don); June Christopher (Girl); Emile Farcus (Karate Instructor); *and:* Heidi Dobbs, Stephanie Faulkner.

Of the several Jesse Crowder private eye capers turned out by director and star Fred Williamson for his independent Po' Boy Productions, *Death Journey* is the most professional and resilient.

In New York a criminal syndicate is being investigated by the District Attorney's office, and a key witness, Finley (Bernard Kuby), is needed in the Big Apple to testify. Los Angeles private investigator Jesse Crowder is hired to bring the man east from California. This mission impossible seems just that, for: 1) he has forty-eight hours to accomplish the job, and 2) several other such witnesses have already been murdered. Finley the accountant is in hiding in the Palm Springs area of California, and it takes all of Crowder's resourcefulness to get him out alive from the mobster hit men on their tail. They eventually take a bus to Kansas City, where they switch to a train, and at Chicago's O'Hare airport fly on to New York. Crowder has done his job.

"That bum ... that ex-cop. Wherever he goes there's always a few bodies left behind. He shoots first and asks questions later. He's like a page out of the old West." The listener agrees, but then adds, "He's the one man who can get the witness here alive."

Crowder is a black-belt champion, has a Rolls Royce as his *second* car, and finds frequent sexual coupling is always a good tonic before starting a new case. The wry, tough, cigar-smoking dude has a bevy of girls (of all colors and sizes) lusting after his body. His fee per case is $25,000 (which on this tough assignment is raised to $50,000 when the bodies begin piling up). As he candidly admits, "I'm Pisces. I do anything for money." At every turn there is a curvaceous woman ready to hit on Crowder — much to the envy of his unprepossessing witness-charge — and one such gal proves to be a hit lady. When he realizes his latest conquest intends to fatally dispose of him, he tosses her off the moving eastbound train, dismissing her with, "Have a happy landing, bitch." In a bathroom stall, at a gas station, in his Manhattan hotel room, everywhere there is a parade of hit men and women eager to eliminate him.

The unpretentious, action-ful, and charming *Death Journey* was filmed economically on location in California in Los Angeles, Palm Springs and Apple Valley with additional shooting in Kansas City, St. Louis, Chicago, and New York City. This 1975-made film deserved to have greater theatrical release than it did. And not to be overlooked was a cameo appearance by frequent Fred Williamson co-star D'Urville Martin as the friendly gas station attendant who receives far more than he bargains for when Jesse Crowder appears on the scene.

80. The Defiant Ones (United Artists, 1958). Color, 97 minutes.

Producer/director Stanley Kramer; *screenplay* Nathan E. Douglas, Harold Jacob Smith; *production designer* Rudolph Sternad; *art director* Fernando Carrere; *music* Ernest Gold; *camera* Sam Leavitt; *editor* Frederic Knudtson.

Cast: Tony Curtis (John "Joker" Jackson); Sidney Poitier (Noah Cullen); Cara Williams (The Woman); Theodore Bikel (Sheriff Max Muller); Charles McGraw (Captain Frank Gibbons); Lon Chaney, Jr. (Big Sam); King Donovan (Solly); Claude Akins (Mac); Lawrence Dobkin (Editor); Whit Bissell (Lou Gans); Carl "Alfalfa" Switzer (Angus); Kevin Coughlin (The Kid); Boyd "Red" Morgan (Joe); Robert Hoy (Wilson); Don Brodie (State Trooper).

See summary under *The Defiant Ones* (ABC-TV, 1/5/86).

81. The Defiant Ones (ABC-TV, 1/5/86). Color, 100 minutes.

Supervising producer David Lowell Rich; *producer* Robert Lovenheim; *co-producers* Robert Urich, Carl Weathers; *director* Rich; *based on the original screenplay by* Harold Jacob Smith, Nathan E. Douglas; *teleplay* James Lee Barrett; *production designer/art director* Beala Neel; *music* Steve Dorff; *camera* Rexford Metz; *editor* Richard Bracken.

Cast: Robert Urich (Johnny "Joker" Johnson); Carl Weathers (Cullen Monroe); Barry Corbin (Floyd Carpenter); Ed Lauter (Sheriff LeRoy); Ritch Brinkley (Lonny); Thalmus Rasulala (Deputy Fred); Charles Bartlett (Jeffcoat); Laurie O'Brien (Pauline); Bill Couch (Fisherman); John Shearin (Sergeant Randall); Ebbie Roe Smith (Deputy Miller); Richard Fullerton, Charles Bazaldus (Guards); Gregg Norberg (Lieutenant); Bob Harris (Driver); Dan Levoff (Deputy); Will Wheaton (Clyde); Monty Cox (Dog Man); William Sanderson (Mason).

Stanley Kramer's 1958 *The Defiant Ones* is a sturdy film classic, more noted for its breakthrough, blunt social message of racial tolerance and for its fine acting than as an action picture. But like so many of Sidney Poitier's films in the 1950s and 1960s, without this entry much of what came later would *not* have been possible.

Southern black man Noah Cullen (Sidney Poitier) is an angry Southerner, frustrated by a lifetime of racism. He is arrested for hitting a white man who had insulted him. Boastful John "Joker" Jackson (Tony Curtis) is a redneck bully. The two are among a truckload of prisoners being driven to a work detail. When the truck crashes into a ditch, Cullen and Jackson, who are chained together at the wrist, escape. They may hate one another violently, but they share a goal: to escape the pursuing sheriff's posse. As they stay one step ahead of their trackers, they pull through one harrowing experience after another, surviving their battles against nature and mankind. At one juncture they are saved from lynching only because a former chain gang member, Big Sam (Lon Chaney, Jr.), frees them. At a farmhouse they meet the lonely, romance-hungry woman (Cara Williams) and her eleven-year-old son (Kevin Coughlin). She provides them with lodging, food, and most importantly a chisel to cut the chain. She seduces Jackson that night and convinces him to take her and her boy with him. Meanwhile she directs Noah to a "short cut" through the swamp.

When Jackson learns what she has done, he goes after his comrade, unmindful of the rifle wound in his shoulder he got when the boy shot him. Jackson and Cullen survive the swamp and reach the railroad tracks. Cullen jumps onto a freight car rumbling by and reaches back to grab Jackson's hand. Jackson is too weak and falls to the ground. Cullen drops off the train to tend his friend. Meanwhile the posse closes in, and Cullen begins singing "Long Gone."

The Defiant Ones was praised both for the fine execution of its laudable concept and for its intrinsic artistic values. Paul V. Beckley *(New York Herald-Tribune)* labeled it "one of the finest dramatic films of our time," and Bosley Crowther *(New York Times)* ranked it as ". . . a remarkably apt dramatic visualization of a social idea. . . . Mr. Poitier stands out as the Negro convict and Mr. Curtis is surprisingly good. Both men are intensely dynamic. Mr. Poitier shows a deep and powerful strain of underlying compassion."

Both Sidney Poitier and Tony Curtis were Oscar-nominated, with Poitier being named Best Actor at the Berlin Film Festival. *The Defiant Ones* was selected as Best Picture of the Year and Stanley Kramer as Best Director by the New York Film Critics.

Nearly thirty years later, actors Robert Urich and Carl Weathers starred in a remake of *The Defiant Ones,* more notable for being a scene-by-scene replay of the original than for any new twists of its own. Because the 1958 original is so well known and regarded (even if today's audiences find it stilted, obvious, and too preachy), it was difficult for this "replay" to gain any recognition beyond its good intentions. Subtle changes were made to make the story more contemporary, such as having that fine black actor Thalmus Rasulala play a deputy! That would have been unthought of in the late 1950s. Throughout the telefeature, stars and co-producers Robert Urich and Carl Weathers seem intensely aware that they are playing "classic" parts, and they are far too stiff in their *déjà vu* characterizations.

82. Detroit 9000 (General, 1973). Color, 108 minutes.

Executive producer Donald Gottlieb, William Silberkleit; *producer* Arthur Marks; *associate producer* Charles Stroud; *director* Arthur Marks; *story* Arthur Marks, Orville Hampton; *screenplay* Hampton; *art director* Robert Gundlach; *makeup* Chuck House, Jerry Daniels; *wardrobe* Ed Marks; *music/music director* Luchi De Jesus; *songs* Holland, Dozier and Holland; *assistant director* Ken Swor; *sound* Bud Alper; *camera* Harry May; *additional camera* Bradford May; *editor* Richard Greer.

Cast: Alex Rocco (Lieutenant Danny Bassett); Hari Rhodes (Detective Sergeant Jesse Williams); Vonetta McGee (Roby Harris); Ella Edwards (Helen); Scatman Crothers (Reverend Markham); Herbert Jefferson, Jr. (Ferdy); Robert Phillips (Inspector Morgan Chalmers); Rudy Challenger (Congressman Aubrey Hale Clayton); Ron McIlwain (Sam Orr); Sally Baker (Ethel); George Skaff (Oscar Beaufort); June Fairchild (Barbara); Detroit Police Commissioner John Nichols (Himself); Inspector Richard Boutin (Himself); Martha Jean Shapiro (Hostess of "Buzz the Fuzz" TV Show); *and:* Bob Charlton, Jerry Dahlman, Don Hayes, Dilart Heyson, Doris Ingraham, Stacey Keach, Sr., Ron Khoury, Hedgemon Lewis, Erik Nelson, Davis Roberts,

Don Shapiro, Jason Summers, Michael Tylo, Whit Vernon, Woody Willis, Ernie Winstanley, Herb Weatherspoon.

"*It's the Murder Capital of the World.* Motortown — where the *honkies* are the *minority race . . . Detroit 9000.* A City Torn Apart."

In the midst of the Honor Our Heroes Ball honoring black congressman Aubrey Hale Clayton (Rudy Challenger), masked bandits steal $400,000 of jewels and valuables donated by the black guests for Clayton's gubernational campaign. Veteran Detroit police detective Lieutenant Danny Bassett (Alex Rocco), whose hospitalized wife requires expensive psychiatric treatment, is assigned to the homicide case, and he is partnered (against his will because he wants the glory for himself) with black detective Sergeant Jesse Williams (Hari Rhodes). It is Williams who discovers that a dead Indian (minus his legs) found in a trunk in the river is tied to the robbery. The clues lead the duo to a madam, Ethel (Sally Baker), and to one of her call girls, Roby Harris (Vonetta McGee), whom Williams knew years ago. The police trace the Indian's previous path to Windsor, Canada, and learn that the dead man had been the intermediary with an unknown fence for the stolen items. Meanwhile Roby alerts Ferdy (Herbert Jefferson, Jr.) about the police being on his trail. Ferdy's murderous confederates later shoot Roby and, as she dies, she informs Williams it was her idea about the holdup since she had heard details of Clayton's campaign while on the job in his hotel room. After the gang is eliminated, Bassett uncovers the whereabouts of Oscar Beaufort (George Skaff), the fence. The latter figures the policeman is out to entrap him and shoots him. Bassett dies on the way to the hospital, and Williams is uncertain whether his partner planned to complete the case or to abscond with the funds himself. Williams is left wondering, "I don't know if he was the worst cop I ever knew or the best."

Considering its role models, this is one of the sturdier black action pictures. It has several interesting characterizations: idealistic but cynical Lieutenant Danny Bassett and his paranoid, hospitalized wife; straight-from-the heart whorehouse madam Ethel; flashy, chiseling pimp Ferdy; Oscar Beaufort, the overly refined and continental fence; wheeler-dealer black congressman Aubrey Hale Clayton; and real-life talk show personality Martha Jean Shapiro.

Between the detailed display of police procedural work and the assorted violent confrontations, there are many pointed statements on the racial issues, all of which give the film a dimension unusual for its breed. The film opens with a black newspaper seller on the street shouting to no one in particular, "Want to know how all the rich muther fuckers got it all together? By shafting the hell out of poor sons-of-bitches like us." The irony is he is referring to the wealthy blacks arriving for a fancy dress ball. When the film's "hero" white Lieutenant Bassett is accused of being prejudiced, he denies it loud and clear (and honestly) over radio: "When an asshole commits a felony," he explains, "I'm goin' to do my damndest to bust him no matter what color asshole he is." On the other hand his institutionalized wife is paranoid about all minority groups from blacks to Polish to everyone. The black members of the robbery team have their racial preference. They insist their Indian co-conspirator was typical of his race when he accidentally shot himself in the leg, which led to his death. ·

("No wonder they always lost [against the cowboys and troopers].") And crafty Ferdy advises number-one lady Roby, "You got to realize not every black man is your brother." The film's biggest irony is that the focal heist was not committed as an anti-black tactic by honkies; instead it was an integrated squad of greedy people out to make some real quick and big bucks.

"For a change in black exploits, the white and blacks come out about even in good and evil ... editing and cutting is jerky and the one flashback, an important part of the denouement, is so abrupt that it takes several moments to realize that a dying girl didn't suddenly get up and start walking down the street" *(Variety)*. The trade paper also noted that this bloody urban action film "...probably will not do the Detroit image any more harm than similar films grinding out of Los Angeles and San Francisco do to their mother towns."

For the record, Detroit police commissioner John Nichols plays himself in the film, and the movie's title number ("9000") refers to "officer in trouble." *Detroit 9000* grossed a positive $1,200,000 in domestic film rentals.

When distributed in England in 1977 under the title *Call Detroit 9000,* nine minutes of the gore and mayhem were deleted from the release print.

83. Dr. Black, Mr. Hyde (Dimension, 1976). Color, 87 minutes.

Executive producer Manfred Bernhard; *producer* Charles Walker; *director* William Crain; *suggested by the novel* "The Strange Case of Dr. Jekyll and Mr. Hyde" *by* Robert Louis Stevenson; *screen idea* Lawrence Woolner; *screenplay* Larry LeBron; *costumes* Emmett Cash; *special makeup* Stan Winston; *makeup* Harry Woolman; *music* Johnny Pate; *camera* Tak Fujimoto; *editor* Jack Horger.

Cast: Bernie Casey (Dr. Henry Pride/Mr. Hyde); Rosalind Cash (Dr. Willie Worth); Marie O'Henry (Linda Monte); Ji-Tu Cumbuka (Lieutenant Jackson); Milt Kogan (Lieutenant O'Connor); Stu Gilliam (Silky).

A.K.A. *The Watts Monster.*

Robert Louis Stevenson's classic 1886 story has been filmed countless times in the United States and abroad, starring such luminaries as John Barrymore (1920), Fredric March (who won an Oscar) (1932), and Spencer Tracy (1941). There have been assorted variations of the theme, including *Dr. Jekyll and Sister Hyde* (1972) and Jerry Lewis's zany interpretation of the split personality in *The Absent-Minded Professor* (1961). William Crain, who had directed the highly successful *Blacula* (1972) (q.v.), turned his attention to this enduring horror tale in a film that did not find release until early 1976.

In Watts, Los Angeles, wealthy Dr. Henry Pride (Bernie Casey) is engaged in experiments that could retard cirrhosis of the liver. He discovers the dangerous side effects include pigmentation changes. At the free clinic where he volunteers his time and is assisted by Dr. Billie Worth (Rosalind Cash), who loves him, he experiments on a patient and notes the bizarre changes. Determined to push on with his work no matter how unethical human experimentation may be, he sets his sights on testing the drug on Linda Monte (Marie O'Henry), a black prostitute who works out of the Moonlight Lounge. It is not long before the driven Pride has tried the drugs on himself and he becomes a (white) rampaging monster, later killing Linda and her pimp, Silky (Stu Gil-

Marie O'Henry and Ji-Tu Cumbuka in *Dr. Black, Mr. Hyde* (1976).

liam. Black Lieutenant Jackson (Ji-Tu Cumbuka) and white Lieutenant O'Connor (Milt Kogan) are on the case, which climaxes in a wild chase at the Watts Tower. There the doctor-monster is trapped atop the structure. Badly wounded by police bullets, he tumbles to his death.

There are many not-so-subtle alterations to the Stevenson horror tale in this film. Upwardly mobile Dr. Pride (note the surname!) is accused by his fellow blacks in Los Angeles of being an Uncle Tom in his ambitions to be assimilated into white society. And, as the viewer learns, it is all a reaction to his impoverished childhood in which his hard-working mother had been a domestic to white people and he and his mother had always been treated second-best. The implications of Pride's color change when he becomes Dr. Hyde are symbolic indeed. And like his celluloid predecessors, the monster in the doctor wants to kill the evil that attracts him (i.e. the prostitutes and pimps). In this rendition the only justification given for his inhumane experiments on humans is that his mother had died in a hospital while doctors stood around doing nothing; he thus intends to push on with his liver regeneration work no matter what. The finale, which is a borrowing from *King Kong* (1932), carries its own message.

Variety noted, "... this black approach to story may be more fun in certain communities.... Casey handles his dual character role effectively, inserting proper menace as the serum turns his skin to an odd white and his features become distorted, eyes strange and opaque." Walter Burrell (*Soul* magazine) judged it "... camp, well-acted, sensitively directed and thoroughly enjoyable."

A few sequences in *Dr. Black, Mr. Hyde* were deleted to change its rating from X to R.

84. The Dynamite Brothers (Cinemation, 1975). Color, 95 minutes.

Executive producer Samuel M. Sherman; *producer* Jim Run; *director* Al Adamson; *screenplay* John D'Armato; *music* Charles Earland; *camera* Michael Stringer; *editor* John Winfield.

Cast: Timothy Brown (Stud Brown); *and:* James Hong, Susan McGiver, Don Oliver, Aldo Ray, Carolyn Ann Speed, Alan Tang.

A.K.A. *Stud Brown.*

Former professional football player Timothy Brown (who had appeared as Spearchucker Jones in the "M*A*S*H" teleseries in 1972) had the lead in this amateurish drivel. "Although ... [it] is American-made the dialogue is so dreadful that the movie sounds as if it were dubbed in Hong Kong" (Linda Gross, *Los Angeles Times).*

Stud Brown (Timothy Brown) is a subdued man on the run, hounded by bad luck and the law. James Hong, a martial arts expert from Hong Kong, arrives in California intent on finding his brother who disappeared as well as the man responsible for his wife's murder. In San Francisco Hong, arrested as an illegal alien, and Brown, being held on a minor narcotics charge, meet in a squad car as a racist, crude cop (Aldo Ray) is taking them to headquarters. With a quick hapkido kick, Hong and Brown are free. They hitch a ride to Los Angeles, where they learn there is a deadly tie between Hong's missing brother and a mob selling heroin in Watts. They lock horns with a syndicate drug supplier (Alan Tang) and along the way meet a sensitive mute girl (Carol Ann Speed).

The exploitive advertisements tag lines read, "Cross him and there's nowhere to hide. He has what every woman wants—he packs the biggest rod in town." The film was made in 1973.

85. Ebony, Ivory and Jade (CBS-TV, 8/3/79). Color, 78 minutes.

Executive producer Ernie Frankel; *producer* Jimmy Sangster; *associate producer* Art Seid; *director* John Llewellyn Moxey; *story* Ann Beckett, D.B. Cooper; *teleplay* Sangster, Annie Scott, Cooper; *art director* Rodger Maus; *music* Earle Hagen; *camera* Arch R. Dalzell; *editor* Seid.

Cast: Bert Convy (Mick Jade); Debbie Allen (Claire Bryant—"Ebony"); Martha Smith (Maggie David—"Ivory"); Donald Moffat (Ian Cabot); Nina Foch (Dr. Adela Teba); Clifford David (Grady); Nicolas Coster (Linderman); Lucille Benson (Mrs. Stone); Ji-Tu Cumbuka (Thurston); Claude Akins (Joe Blair); David Brenner (Himself); Frankie Valli (Himself); Ted Shackelford (Barnes); Bill Lane (Herman); Ray Guth (Conductor); Cletus Young (Plant Cop); Quinn Redeker (Johnson).

A prefabricated telefeature offering that was a pilot to a potential series. "None of the characters' motivations are clear or developed" (Gail Williams, *The Hollywood Reporter).*

Mick Jade (Bert Convy) is a tennis pro turned entertainer turned government agent. He uses two singers, Ebony (Debbie Allen) and Ivory (Martha Smith), as his cover, posing as their manager. The setting is the Middle East, where the girls perform their dance-song act at a local club and Jade is involved with scientist Dr. Adela Teba (Nina Foch), who has developed a red oozing explosive that detonates in 80° temperatures. When the formula and the two performers disappear, Jade comes to the rescue. Later in Las Vegas the trio prevent the Aladdin Casino and Theatre from being blown up.

To many this film was all lumbering lowjinks, relieved only by the ebullient and talented Debbie Allen as the black half of the hip performing team.

86. Edge of the City (Metro-Goldwyn-Mayer, 1957). 85 minutes.

Producer David Susskind; *director* Martin Ritt; *based on the teleplay* "A Man Is Ten Feet Tall" *by* Robert Alan Aurthur; *screenplay* Aurthur; *art director* Richard Sylbert; *costumes* Anna Hill Johnstone; *music* Leonard Rosenman; *camera* Joseph Brun; *editor* Sidney Meyers.

Cast: John Cassavetes (Axel North); Sidney Poitier (Tommy Tyler); Jack Warden (Charlie Malik); Kathleen Maguire (Ellen Wilson); Ruby Dee (Lucy Tyler); Robert Simon (Mr. Nordmann); Ruth White (Mrs. Nordmann); William A. Lee (Davis); Val Avery (Brother); John Kellogg (Detective); David Clarke (Wallace); Estelle Hemsley (Lucy's Mother); Charles Jordan (Old Stevedore); Ralph Bell (Night Boss).

On October 2, 1955, Sidney Poitier and Don Murray co-starred in the teleplay *A Man Is Ten Feet Tall* on "Philco Playhouse." Two years later David Susskind produced a motion picture version of the acclaimed production with Robert Alan Aurthur adapting his own drama. It was retitled *Edge of the City.* Its depiction of bigotry and murder at the loading docks of New York's railroad yards was another pathbreaking step in Hollywood's growth and maturity in dealing with interracial themes set in inner city slums.

Sullen army deserter Axel North (John Cassavetes) is haunted by his A.W.O.L. status and his belief that he was responsible for his brother's death in an accident. When North is hired on at the freightcar loading docks he becomes friendly with co-worker Tommy Tyler (Sidney Poitier), and the latter attempts to draw out the neurotic young man. Their obnoxious boss, Charlie Malik (Jack Warden), has a reputation for being a killer and, besides disliking Tyler, develops a hatred for the deserter, whom he is blackmailing. In a fight between Malik and North, Tyler intervenes and is killed. When Tyler's wife Lucy (Ruby Dee) confronts North and accuses him of betraying his late friend, North gives himself up to the authorities, knowing Malik will now be punished for his crimes.

At the time it was considered quite daring to have a major studio film depict a black individual as the boss of a white man, leading Dorothy Masters *(New York Daily News)* to acclaim in her four-star review, "The superb sensitivity and projection apparent in *Edge of the City* offers a challenge few can hope to equal in a long, long time. . . ." *Time* magazine went a step further in wondering, "The mystery is why so engaging a Negro would waste time on so boringly primitive a white man."

87. The Education of Sonny Carson (Paramount, 1974). Color, 104 minutes.

Producer Irwin Yablans; *associate producer* David Golden; *director* Michael Campus; *based on the book by* Sonny Carson [Mwina Imiri Abubadika]; *screenplay* Fred Hudson; *art director* Manny Gerard; *set decorator* Robert Drumheller; *costumes* Gene Coffin, Gregory Lecakin; *music/music arranger/music conductor* Coleridge-Taylor Perkinson; *songs* Perkinson and Bob Kessler; *assistant director* Stephen Barnett; *stunt co-ordinator* Franklin Scott; *sound* G. Lee Bosi; *camera* Ed Borwin; *editors* Edward Warschilka, Harry Howard.

Cast: Rony Clanton (Sonny Carson); Don Gordon (Detective Pigliani); Joyce Walker (Virginia); Paul Benjamin (Pops); Thomas Hicks (Young Sonny Carson); Mary Alice (Moms); Ram John Holder (Preacher); Jerry Bell (Lil' Boy); Ray Rainbow Johnson (Benny); Derrick Champ Ford (Wolfe); Roger Hill (Lil' John); Chris Forster (Donovan); George Miles (Uncle Cal); Jess Bolero (Cousin Red); B.T. Taylor (Crazy); Roger [D.A.] Davis (Willie); Eleanora Douglas (Sally Jean); Clifton Steere (Psychiatrist); Dennis Keir (Western Union Boy); Linda Hopkins (Lil' Boy's Mother); Mervyn Nelson (Parole Board Chairman); Prince Olafami, Ronnie Cole, Steve Sellers (Supermarket Kids); David Kerman (Judge); Ellerine Hardin (Funeral Singer); Benny Diggs and the New York Community Choir, the Jolly Stompers, the Tomahawks, the Black Spades, Pure Hell, Students of the Morningside High School (Themselves).

Filmed in the slum areas of Brooklyn's Bedford-Stuyvesant, *The Education of Sonny Carson* is that rare contemporary drama, a study of desperation in the black community which relies on cinema verite, honest drama, and human interaction to tell its tragic (yet here inspiring) account. All the more surprising is that it was directed by Michael Campus, who had guided *Super Fly* (1973) (q.v.), that ultra-exploitive, highly commercial black action motion picture.

The thoughtful narrative is an odyssey of young Sonny Carson (Thomas Hicks), a prize-winning school boy who falls too easily into criminal activity (burglary) and finds himself enduring the horrors of jail. The toughened young adult Sonny Carson (Rony Clanton) returns to the streets, where he becomes embroiled in gang rivalries and confrontations, eventually becoming a ganglord. He participates in an assortment of crimes (including robbery) that lead him to prison. For many criminals, a return to the grueling life in the slammer would signal the end of the road. But Carson is determined not to fall prey to the inmates' best friends: drugs, hostilities and violence. The new goals for this black activist (who now calls himself Mwina Imiri Abubadika) include wanting to become a community leader. Among those sharing Sonny Carson's trip into redemption are Virginia (Joyce Walker) as Carson's girlfriend who becomes drug-addicted; Lil' Boy (Jerry Bell), who dies in a gang brawl; the dynamic preacher (Ram John Holder); Sonny's parents, especially Pops (Paul Benjamin); Carson's pals Crazy (B.T. Taylor), Willie (Roger [D.A.] Davis), and Lil' John (Roger Hill); and brutalizing white Detective Pigliani (Don Gordon), who wants things done by the book at any cost.

"Riddled with flaws, inexpressive as art, it shakes off its shortcomings with a primal energy that imbues it with terrifying eloquence" (Lawrence Van Gelder, *New York Times*). *Variety* decided that this unique movie "...should stand up as one of the most outstanding in the genre.... Its action values are raw and raunchy, but they are motivated to such an extreme degree of perfection that they are not shameless ripoff gore. ... If the white American middle-class ever wanted a non-polarized answer to why urban environments have become what they are, this film is it." Walter Burrell (*Soul* magazine) judged it "the really definitive Black film achievement." On another level, Maurice Peterson in *Essence* magazine observed, "The conventional methods of introducing and developing characters are not employed. People drift in and out of the picture without any explanation, giving the characters a reasonless existence, like mythical figures in an allegory." Peterson also noted, "The soundtrack fluidly mixes a melange of inner-city sounds, ranging from the gang's drums and chants to sirens and stoned raps. Of course, this has been attempted in most Black dramas, but never so deliberately or with such insistence on authenticity." Peterson, like many reviewers and viewers, had reservations about the film's unevenness. He decided, "Perhaps Michael Campus, who is white, was not comfortable enough with Black material and Black people to sustain such an ambitious undertaking. ... Uneven movies, nonetheless, are sometimes more rewarding for their good parts than those smooth films which are consistently mediocre."

Lauded as a superior piece of artistic achievement, *The Education of Sonny Carson* never found its rightful place at the box-office. As Hampton Clanton, the star of this film had appeared previously in *The Cool World* (1973) (q.v.).

88. Emma Mae (Pro International, 1976). Color, 100 minutes.

Executive producers William Silberkleit, Peer J. Oppenheimer; *producer* Jamaa Fanaka; *associate producer* Arnie Magidow; *director/screenplay* Fanaka; *art director* Adel Mazen; *costumes* Stephanie A. Bell, Beverly Ventriss, Marva Farmer; *makeup* Dwaine Fobbs; *music* H.B. Barnum; *second unit director/stunt co-ordinator* Alex Brown; *assistant director* Henry Sanders; *sound* Don Sanders; *sound editor* Linda Dove; *camera* Stephen Posey; *editor* Robert Fitzgerald.

Cast: Jerri Hayes (Emma Mae); Ernest Williams II (Jesse Amos); Charles David Brooks III (Zeke Johnson); Eddie Allen (James); Robert Slaughter (Devo); Malik Carter (Big Daddy Johnson); Teri Taylor (Dara Stansell); Leopoldo Mandeville (Clay); Grammy Burdett (Daisy Stansell); Laetitia Burdett (Melik Stansell); Eddy Dyer (Huari Stansell); Synthia James (Ulika); Jewell Williams (Maddie); Hank Smith (Mrs. Davies); Michelle Davison (Shirley); Ruth Delahoussaye (Bea); Garst Reese (Police Captain); Tyrone S.B. Thompson (Businessman Leader); Alex Brown, Eddie Smith (Cops); Charles Elder, John Laud (Plainclothesmen); Dexter King (Fight Spectator); Stephanie A. Bell, Cherryl Moffitt, Sherri Drake (Hun-Ettes).

Resourceful black filmmaker Jamaa Fanaka is best known for his *Penitentiary* trilogy (1979, 1981, 1987) (qq.v.). As a U.C.L.A. graduate he wrote, directed and produced *Welcome Home, Brother Charles* (1975), dealing with a returning black Vietnam War veteran whose outrage at injustices on the home front lead to shocking, perverse results. This film was followed a year later by *Emma Mae,* written to complete his master's thesis at U.C.L.A. film school and using a \$250,000 budget garnered from a grant from the American Film Institute and the U.C.L.A. Black Studies Center.

Emma Mae traces the meteoric transformation of a naive young girl (Jerri Hayes) from Mississippi who comes to Los Angeles to live with Daisy Stansell (Grammy Burdett) and her family. "You gotta start keepin' yourself up now. You're in California," advises Daisy. At a party one night she meets charming but unscrupulous hood Jesse Amos (Ernest Williams II), and her life is never the same afterward. She falls in love with him and transforms herself into a contemporary big-city girl who will do anything for her man. When Jesse and his humorous partner Zeke (Charles David Brooks III) are arrested on a drug bust, Emma Mae is determined not to sit around. She mobilizes his gang into becoming honest workers to earn the money for their friends' legal defense. When jobs at a rundown car wash fall through, Emma Mae gets mad, and she also gets more inventive. She robs a bank to fill up the coffers. To her surprise, after her unique fundraising wins Amos's freedom, she finds him in bed with another woman. In a drag-out brawl, she shows him up to be the creep he is.

There is much that is rough about the performances in *Emma Mae,* and the tight budget shows in the often skimpy production values. But there is a vitality to Jerri Hayes' unpolished but intensely sincere performance. When she warns her unimaginative cohorts to get out of their ruts — "You face time ever day you live and breathe. You're doing time every day and don't know it" — she is quite convincing. She tells a sympathetic but bewildered white man who had tried to help her cause, "I don't understand. They're always talkin' about us young people never doing nothing but use dope and kill each other up in the street. Then when we try to do something the way they say it's supposed to be done they mess with us and try to shove us down.... What is it all about?" The man's thoughtful answer is, "You scare them because you embarrass them." And there is a wonderful moment when an old black man says with disarming simplicity, "Why, if I was anybody at all I'd be dead."

"Fanaka considers *Emma Mae* a tribute to the strength and resiliency of black womanhood ... and that aspect gives the film its warmest qualities.... It's one of the most positive female images in recent American pix. The scene in which she beats up the astonished Williams is a real crowd-pleaser" *(Variety).*

In 1987, when Unicorn Video issued this minor gem on videocassette, it was retitled *Black Sister's Revenge.*

89. Enter the Dragon (Warner Bros., 1973). Color, 98 minutes.

Producers Fred Weintraub, Paul Heller; *associate producer* Raymond Chow; *director* Robert Clouse; *screenplay* Michael Allin; *art director* James Wong Sun; *costume designer* Louis Sheng; *music* Lalo Schifrin; *music editor* Gene Marks; *assistant director* Chaplin Chang; *fight arranger* Bruce Lee; *sound* Zee Shao Lin; *camera* Gilbert Hubba; *second unit camera* Charles Low; *editors* Kurt Hirshler, George Watters.

Cast: Bruce Lee (Lee); John Saxon (Roper); Jim Kelly (Williams); Shih Kien (Han); Bob Wall (Oharra); Ahna Capri (Tania); Angela Mao Ying (Su-Lin); Betty Chung (Mei Ling); Geoffrey Weeks (Braithwaite); Yang Sze (Bolo);

Peter Archer (Parsons); Ho Lee Wan (Old Man); Marlene Clark (Secretary); Allan Kent (Golfer); William Keller, Mickey Caruso (Los Angeles Police); Mike Bissell, Darnell Garcial, Pat Johnson (Hoods).

Of all the kung fu movies of the 1970s, *Enter the Dragon* is perhaps most people's favorite—it grossed $11,500,000 in domestic film rentals. Today, many years after star Bruce Lee's death (1973), it is still a popular videocassette item. It was also one of the first major Hollywood studio feature films to cagily blend another then-popular genre, black action, into its mix. Black Jim Kelly, the 6′1″, 180-pound 1971 International Middleweight Karate Champion from Paris, Kentucky, was given the co-lead. (Kelly started in films with *Melinda* [1972] [q.v.], and his career would reach its zenith the following year in *Black Belt Jones* [q.v.].) The film also featured Bob Wall, 1970 U.S. professional karate champion; Peter Archer, 1971 Commonwealth karate champion; Yang Sze, Sholokan Champion of Southeast Asia; Angela Mao Ying, Black Belt Hapkido Champion of Okinawa. Hollywood leading man John Saxon was a longtime practitioner of the martial arts.

British intelligence agent Braithwaite (Geoffrey Weeks) convinces Lee (Bruce Lee), a martial arts master at the Shaolin Temple, to join the crusade against the drug and prostitution trafficking controlled by Han (Shih Kien), also from the Shaolin Temple. Lee journeys to Han's island on the pretext of participating in Han's triennial martial arts tournament. He is joined by Americans Roper (John Saxon) and Williams (Jim Kelly). Once at the fortress Lee talks with government agent Mei Ling (Betty Chung), who is working undercover at the facility. At the competition Lee kills Oharra (Bob Wall), Han's henchman, who had been responsible previously for the death of Lee's sister. Han kills Williams and then asks Roper to join his group. That night Lee destroys much of Han's underground operation and radios Braithwaite for help. He and Roper fight off Han's guards whil Mei Ling frees the prisoners. In Han's mirrored chamber Lee and Han battle it out, with the latter finally impaled on a spear. Braithwaite's men arrive to subdue the remaining renegades.

While the film's focus is primarily on the athletic prowess of martial arts star Bruce Lee, Jim Kelly's Williams has his share of the limelight as he deals with the Fu Manchu–like Han.

> HAN: Your style is unorthodox.... It is not the art but the combat that you enjoy. We are all ready to win just as we are born only knowing life. It is defeat that you must learn to prepare for.
> WILLIAMS: I don't waste my time on it. When it comes I won't even notice. I'll be too busy look-in' good.

Williams is forever boastful of his prowess with women and is always complaining about the exotic food served by their host. But in his showdown with Han, he is the loser who is tortured, killed, and put on display as a warning to the agog Roper.

Pauline Kael (*New Yorker* magazine) endorsed, "...a kung-fu movie that's a good-natured example of the pleasures of schlock art. There's so much going on that the whole history of movies seems to be recapitulated in scrambled form. It could be billed as the movie with a thousand climaxes . . . and many of the fights that could be merely brutal come across as lightning-fast choreography."

90. Fatal Beauty (Metro-Goldwyn-Mayer/United Artists, 1987). Color, 103 minutes.

Producer Leonard Kroll; *director* Tom Holland; *story* Bill Svanoe; *screenplay* Hilary Henkin, Dean Riesner; *production designer* James William Newport; *set decorator* E.C. Chen; *costume supervisor* Mort Schwartz; *costumes* Aggie Guerard Rodgers; *makeup* Mike Germain, Joe McKinney; *music* Harold Faltermeyer; *music editor* Daniel Allan Carlin; *assistant director* Michael Green; *stunt co-ordinator* Walter Scott; *special effects* Kenneth D. Pepiot; *supervising sound editor* John Riordan; *camera* David M. Walsh; *editor* Don Zimmerman.

Cast: Whoopi Goldberg (Detective Rita Rizzoli); Sam Elliott (Mike Marshak); Ruben Blades (Carl Jimenez); Harris Yulin (Conrad Kroll); John P. Ryan (Lieutenant Kellerman); Jennifer Warren (Cecile Jaeger); Brad Dourif (Leo Nova); Mike Jolly (Earl Skinner); Charles Hallahan (Deputy Getz); David Harris (Raphael); James Le Gros (Zack Jaeger); Neil Barry (Denny Miflin); Mark Pellegrino (Frankenstein); Clayton Landey (Jimmy Silver); Fred Asparagus (Delgadillo); Catherine Blore (Charlene); Michael Champion (Buzz); Steve Akahoshi (Shigeta); Richard Milholland (Charlie); David Dunard (Cowboy Hat); Cheech Marin (Bartender); James Smith (Ritchie); Larry Hankin (Jerry Murphy); Michael DeLorenzo (Falco); Rick Telles (Epifanio); Carlos Cervantes (Basqual); Emilia Ayarza (Candy); Ebbie Roe Smith (Marty); Walter Robles (Clay); M.C. Gainey (Barndollar); Bernie Hern (Mike Weinstein); Prince Highes (Big Bubba); Jim Bentley (Paramedic); Lucia Lexington (Stripper); Jane Chung (Chinese Lady); Ellarye (Chinese Mother); Jonathan Wong (Chinese Son); Tom Spiroff (Cop in Kitchen); William Martin Brennan (Assistant Chef); Boyd "Red" Morgan (Fletch); Cliff Murdock (Len); Belinda Mayne (Traci); Celeste Yarnall (Laura); Sandra Bogan (Teri); Parker Whitman (Coroner's Attendant); Dower Phillips, Josh Pickard (Teenagers).

It seems such a waste that multi-talented Whoopi Goldberg mires herself in the rut of mindless police action pictures à la Eddie Murphy's *Beverly Hills Cop* and *Beverly Hills Cop II* (1984, 1987) (qq.v.). But when one is paid $2,250,000 to perform in a movie. . .

Detective Rita Rizzoli (Whoopi Goldberg) is a dedicated cop with a vengeance. She especially hates dope dealers and maintains a list of all the people she knows who died from drugs, intending to have revenge for them. She also has a penchant for going undercover in disguise (especially as a street hooker complete with blonde wig, spike heels, and sunglasses). When several people overdose from bad drugs (all from envelopes marked "Fatal Beauty"), Rizzoli makes a connection to crimelord Conrad Kroll (Harris Yulin), who lives on a large guarded estate. She outwits Kroll's security force, headed by Mike Marshak (Sam Elliott), and confronts the kingpin only to have his city politician friends ease her off the case (at least temporarily). Meanwhile Kroll orders Marshak to shadow Rizzoli. Along with her partner, Carl Jimenez

(Ruben Blades), Rita investigates a drug distribution center and relies on Marshak to get them out of the rain of bullets. Later Rita and Marshak combat Kroll's henchmen Leo Nova (Brad Dourif) and Earl Skinner (Mike Jolly) in a shopping mall shootout. Marshak is wounded and must go to jail (for a short stay?) with Rita promising to wait for him.

Thankfully *Fatal Beauty* has a few engrossing sequences such as when Rita tearfully explains to Marshak she used to be a druggie years ago and that, because of it, her unsupervised daughter died. Then there is the physical tussle and shouting match between Rita and the upscale, tennis-playing Cecile Jaeger (Jennifer Warren). Also worth mentioning is the bartender, played by Cheech Marin of Cheech and Chong fame.

Kevin Thomas *(Los Angeles Times)* decided, "Rickety, violent star vehicle for Whoopi Goldberg.... Whoopie is fun but the film is so ramshackle and ludicrous that it self-destructs. Sam Elliott has a nothing role as Goldberg's leading man." Originally rated X for its violence, it was recut to obtain an R rating. It grossed a disappointing total of $10,838,082 in its five weeks of national distribution.

91. The Final Comedown (New World, 1972). Color, 84 minutes.

Producer Oscar Williams; *co-producer* Mel Taylor; *director/screenplay* Williams; *music/music conductor* Wade Marcus; *camera* William B. Caplan; *editor* Bick Van Enger, Jr.

Cast: Billy Dee Williams (Johnny Johnson); Raymond St. Jacques (Imir); D'Urville Martin (Billy Joe Ashley); R.G. Armstrong (Mr. Freeman); Celia Kaye (Rene Freeman); Pamela Jones (Luanna); Maidie Norman (Mrs. Johnson); Morris Erby (Mr. Johnson); Billy Durkin (Michael Freeman); Edmund Cambridge (Dr. Smalls).

The Final Comedown is a fiercely grim drama of impassioned hatred and violence. "You may find it relentlessly singleminded in its theme but it is acted and directed with such fire that you aren't likely to be bored" (Frances Herridge, *New York Post*).

Johnny Johnson (Billy Dee Williams) is a college-educated young man who cannot find a decent job in his field (electronical engineering) because he is black. His resentment grows, and his parents — a docile father (Morris Erby) and domestic servant mother (Maidie Norman) — are at a loss for how to deal with him. He is influenced by the militant Imir (Raymond St. Jacques) and soon becomes the impassioned spokesman for his followers. His anger increases, and a confrontation with the white police leads to a bloody alleyway massacre where his friend Billy Joe Ashley (D'Urville Martin) is tear-gassed, his mother is shot to death, and he is badly wounded. In the concluding shootout Johnson and the rest die as do his white followers Rene Freeman (Celia Kaye) and Michael Freeman (Billy Durkin).

Much of the heated narrative is told through flashback, and a good deal of the rhetorical film is strident, forced, and cliched, with the acting scenes mostly amateurish. (Roger Greenspun in the *New York Times* insisted, "Wholly exploitive of both its dramatic form and its social situation.") But there is a unifying power in the film as Johnny Johnson graduates from law-abiding pacifist to ardent activist. "We got to know what we want. It's got to be important," he reasons. Later he acknowledges agonizingly, "The system is destroying us. But we're alone and we want to live so we have to fight and some of us have to die." Still later he tells his girlfriend Luanna (Pamela Jones), "Bitter? Baby, I'm not bitter. I was bitter 350 years ago. I'm violent! Hear me, violent!" The genesis is complete and his fate sealed.

Even in the context of the harshly constructed scenario, Billy Dee Williams, without his later trademark mustache, emerges charismatic with his eye-catching mixture of strength, charm, sincerity, and intensity. Williams (born William D. Williams in 1937 in New York City) began his acting career on stage at age seven and made his film debut in Paul Muni's *The Last Angry Man* (1959). He was in "The Guiding Light" soap opera in the mid-1960s and made his television breakthrough with the co-starring role in the movie-for-television *Brian's Song* (1971). It was while under contract to Motown Records to make motion pictures that he made the very mainstream *Lady Sings the Blues* (1972) and *Mahogany* (1975), both opposite Diana Ross. He starred in several black action features, including *Hit!* (1973) (q.v.) and *The Take* (1974) (q.v.). Later he appeared in the lead as *Scott Joplin* (1977), as the opportunistic Lando Calrissian in *The Empire Strikes Back* (1980) and its sequel *The Return of the Jedi* (1983). He was opposite Sylvester Stallone in the police thriller *Nighthawks* (1981) and with John Cassavetes in the underrated *Marvin and Tige* (1983). He continued making telefeatures such as *Chiefs* (1983), had a recurring guest role opposite Diahann Carroll in "Dynasty," starred with Ken Wahl in a short-lived police action teleseries, "Double Dare" (1985), and has been in a string of recent action pictures including *Fear City* (1985), *Number One With a Bullet* (1987) and *Deadly Illusion* (1987) (q.v.). In *The Final Comedown, Variety* singled out Williams among the many "excellent" performances, praising his "savvy handling of the many emotional levels of militant Johnny Johnson."

Black director Oscar Williams partially financed *The Final Comedown* with a grant from The American Film Institute. This film would be reissued in 1977 under the title *The Blast* with Oscar Williams' name in all the credits changed to pseudonymous Frank Arthur Wilson.

92. Fingers (Brut, 1978). Color, 90 minutes.

Producer George Barrie; *director/screenplay* James Toback; *production designer* Gene Rudolf; *set decorator* Fred Weller; *costumes* Albert Wolsky; *makeup* Irving Buchman; *classical music co-ordinator* James Fields; *assistant directors* Daniel McCauley, Peter Runfolo, Stewart Lyons; *sound* John Fundus; *sound editor* the Ross Effects; *camera* Mike Chapman; *editor* Robert Lawrence.

Cast: Harvey Keitel (Jimmy "Fingers" Angelelli); Tisa Farrow (Carol); Jim Brown (Dreems); Michael V. Gazzo (Ben Angelelli); Marian Seldes (Ruth Angelelli); Carol Francis (Christa); Danny Aiello (Butch); Ed Marinaro (Gino); Georgette Muir (Anita); Dominick Chianese (Arthur Fox); Anthony Sirico (Riccamonza); Tanya Roberts (Julie); Lenny Montana (Luchino); Vasco Vallandares (Luchino's Son); Tom Signorelli (Italian Prisoner); Woodrow Garrian (Conventioneer); James Fields (Pianist); A. Andrew Pastorio (Elderly

Driver); Frank Pesch (Carmine); I.W. Klein (Bail Bondsman); Murray Mosten (Dr. Fry); Emmy Falahi (Young Gangster); Tina Fox (Young Girl); Henry Baker (Leonard); Charles Polk (J.R.); Linda Blia, Francine Gabel, John Clark (Pizza Customers); Sam Coppola (Sam); Pembrose Deans, Arthur French (Black Prisoners); John F. Dempsey (Police Clerk); Joe De Kama (Dr. Schwartz); Josie Johnson, Susan McWilliams, Tia Rance, Aida Random, Leza van Beuren, Largo Woodruff (Dreems' Girls); Zack Norman (Patrolman Levy); Murray Mosten (Dr. Fry); Jane Elder (Esther); Frank Pesce (Raymond).

"Some will love it. Others will be angered by it. Everyone will be stunned by it." So read the "provocative" advertising blurbs for *Fingers.* Mostly the critics ranted about the story's perversities and the amateurishness of scenarist and director James Tomack, who had scripted previously the well-regarded *The Gambler* (1974). ". . . James Toback seems to be playing the literary-adolescent's game of wanting to go crazy so he can watch his own reactions," insisted Pauline Kael (*New Yorker* magazine), adding, "Because he doesn't censor his masculine racial fantasies, his foolishness and his terrible ideas pour out freely." On the other hand, when *Fingers* opened in England in 1980, Tom Milne (British *Monthly Film Bulletin*) championed, "His [Toback's] style here is a cool, classical elegance."

Musician Jimmy Angelelli (Harvey Keitel) is practicing for a Carnegie Hall audition as concert pianist when he observes an attractive girl named Carol (Tisa Farrow), who refuses his advances. Meanwhile his aging gangland father Ben Angelelli (Michael V. Gazzo) forces his ex–hit man son to collect two overdue gambling debts. Jimmy has no probelm with Lucino (Lenny Montana), who owns a pizza shop, but it is a different story with Mafia gangster Riccamonza (Anthony Siroco), whose girl (Tanya Roberts) he rapes as a warning to the debtor. Intrigued by the unresponsive Carol, he follows her and discovers she has a black lover, Dreems (Jim Brown). He fails his pianist audition and must later be bailed out of jail when Riccamonza has his stooges plant incriminating evidence on him. Despondent over a visit to his musician mother (Marian Seldes) in the mental asylum, he persuades Carol to make love with him, after which she rushes off to see Dreems. He follows, and Dreems invites him to a party, where Angelelli later watches as the man makes love to both Carol and another girl. Once more he asks Carol to leave Dreems, and she refuses. When his father is murdered by Riccamonza, Angelelli reciprocates, brutally killing the killer.

With its rampant symbolism and ethnic myth-building and following, *Fingers* is a bizarre excursion into the depraved subcultures of the Big Apple. Although Jim Brown's role is smallish, one of the film's "highlights" is his appearance as the ex-boxer who owns a eatery and has two devoted blonde girlfriends. For Brown, who a decade ago was Hollywood's hottest property and whose career would be periodically revived by fellow black actor-director Fred Williamson, *Fingers* brought a lot of notoriety. "Jim Brown, as the only real sex object in the movie (he's the only character who doesn't wear underwear) has the film's most memorably silly moment in which he smacks two women's heads together because they don't want to kiss each other" (Vincent Canby, *New York Times*). "Jim Brown, as ever a strong screen presence, has a few good scenes as the man whom Farrow cannot leave despite occasional revulsion" *(Variety)*. Most to the mark is Donald Bogle in *Blacks in American Film and Television* (1988): "Decked out in a tight pink shirt and tighter white pants, Brown . . . looks as if he's about to burst at the seams. . . . Brown may be better here than in most of his other films, but he has little . . . to do. . . . The picture freezes Brown. His blatant pimp/stud/buck hero has been pinned down. Cheapened and vulgarized here, Brown is not viewed as anything but, again, a walking phallus. . . ."

93. Firehouse (ABC-TV, 1/2/73). Color, 78 minutes.

Executive producer Dick Berg; *producer* Joe Manduke; *associate producer* John A. Ireland; *director* Alex March; *teleplay* Frank Cucci; *art director* Rodger Maus; *music* Tom Scott; *camera* Alan Stenvold; *editor* John A. Martinelli.

Cast: Richard Roundtree (Shelly Forsythe); Vince Edwards (Spike Ryerson); Andrew Duggan (Captain Jim Parr); Richard Jaeckel (Hank Myers); Sheila Frazier (Michelle Forsythe); Val Avery (Sonny Caputo); Paul LeMat (Bill Daizell); Michael Lerner (Ernie Bush); Mel Scott (Mamu); Howard Curtis (Eddie Doyle); Joshua Shelley (Mr. Warneche the Landlord); Alan Beltram (Spanish Lady); Mwako Cumbuka (Clarence); Ty Henderson (Bobby); De-Wayne Jessie (Oldest Boy); Bobby Johnson (Bartender); Scott Smith (Battalion Chief).

Television executives were still wondering how best to capitalize on Richard Roundtree's big screen popularity from *Shaft* (1971) (q.v.) and its follow-ups when they dreamed up this made-for-television movie inspired by the success of *Report from Engine Co. 82* (1972), a factual book that had become a best-seller.

Captain Jim Parr (Andrew Duggan) is the head honcho of the harmonious Fire Co. 23, which erupts with dissension when a black recruit (Richard Roundtree) joins this urban firefighting unit to replace a fallen buddy. When a rash of arson in the black ghetto explodes, bigotry at the firehouse heats up.

When the modest telefeature, full of stock footage, became a shortlived 13-episode TV series in 1974, Richard Roundtree and Sheila Frazier (as his wife) were among the missing ingredients. Also James Drury replaced Vincent Edwards as (now) Captain Spike Ryerson, with Richard Jaeckel repeating his assignment as Hank Myers.

94. Fist of Fear, Touch of Death (Aquarius Releasing, 1980). Color, 90 minutes.

Producer Terry Levene; *director* Matthew Mallinson; *story* Ron Harvey, Mallinson; *screenplay* Harvey; *music* Keith Mansfield; *stunt co-ordinators* Ron Van Clief, Bill Louis; *sound* Jimmy Kwei; *camera* John Hazard; *editors* Mallinson, Jeffrey Brown.

With: Fred Williamson, Ron Van Clief, Adolph Caesar, Aaron Banks, Bill Louis, Teruyuki Higa, Gail Turner, Richard Barathy, Hollywood Browde, Louis Neglia, Cydra Karlyn, Annette Bronson, Ron Harvey, John Flood; *and:* film clips of Bruce Lee.

arts grind circuit is one of the few remaining exhibition ates promotional flim flammery and *Fist of Fear Touch of* dvantage of audience credulity" *(Variety).*

ed clips from Bruce Lee feature films, the so-called narrative d martial arts championship exhibition at New York's ware Garden. Lee, in the restructured footage, is queried about the tricks of his sport; Ron Van Clief is shown working out in Central park and preparing à la *Rocky* for the big matches; and at the arena Fred Williamson (in nothing more than a guest cameo) appears as a cigar-smoking bigshot somehow connected with the competition in the arena. To round out the 90 minutes, there is plenty of stock footage from the actual tournament held at the Garden a few years prior to this compilation film.

95. 48 Hours (Paramount, 1982). Color, 96 minutes.

Executive producer D. Constantine Conte; *producers* Lawrence Gordon, Joel Silver; *director* Walter Hill; *screenplay* Roger Spottiswoode, Hill, Larry Gross, Steven E. de Souza; *production designer* John Vallone; *set decorator* Richard C. Goddard; *costumes* Marilyn Kay Vance; *music* James Horner; *assistant directors* David Sosna, Deborah A. Love; *camera* Ric Waite; *editors* Freeman Davies, Mark Warner, Billy Weber.

Cast: Nick Nolte (Jack Cates); Eddie Murphy (Reggie Hammond); Annette O'Toole (Elaine); Frank McRae (Haden); James Remar (Albert Ganz); David Patrick Kelly (Luther); Sonny Landham (Billy Bear); Brion James (Kehoe); Kerry Sherman (Rosalie); Jonathan Banks (Algren); James Keane (Vanzant); Tara King (Frizzy); Greta Blackburn (Lisa); Margot Rose (Casey); Denise Crosby (Sally); Olivia M. Brown (Candy); Todd Allen (Young Cop); Bill Dearth (Thin Cop); Ned Dowd (Big Cop); Jim Haynie (Old Cop); Jack Thibeau (Detective); Jon St. Elwood (Plainsclothesman); Clare Nono (Ruth); Sandy Martin (Policewoman); Matt Landers (Bob); Peter Jason (Cowboy Bartender); Bill Cross, Chris Mulkey (Cops); James Marcelino (Parking Attendant); Bennie Dobbins, Walter Scott, W.T. Zacha (Road Gang Guards); Begona Plaza (Indian Hooker); Lloyd Catlett, B.G. Fisher, Reid Cruickshanks (Prison Guards); R.D. Call (Duty Sergeant); Brenda Venus, Gloria E. Gifford (Hookers); John Hauk (Henry); Clint Smith (Leroy); *and:* the Busboys, Luis Contreras, Nick Dimitri, John Dennis Johnston, J. Wesley Huston, Dave Moordigian, Jack Lightsy, Gary Pettinger, Ola Ray, Suzanna M. Regard, Angela Robinson, Bjaye Turner, Rock A. Walker, Marguerita Wallace, Bob Yanez.

"There's nothing quite like the unexpected pleasure of watching a newcomer light up the screen. This is what Eddie Murphy, a 'Saturday Night Live' regular, does in Walter Hill's smart, rambunctious cops-and-crooks comedy *48 Hours*. . . . Murphy, in sharp threads, shows his stuff when he enters a redneck bar with all the bravado of Mae West. Backed only by [Nick] Nolte's badge, Murphy makes short work of the entire dive. (Urban cowboys will never be the same.)" (Kevin Thomas, *Los Angeles Times*.) Equally enthusiastic was David Denby (*New York* magazine): "As the slick con artist Reggie, Murphy has flashing eyes and a fast-breaking smile that let you know how good Reggie feels to be out of prison, on the streets operating, even if it's only for two days.

Murphy is going to be a very big star. The audience is alive to his brazenness, his speed, his intelligence — the self-interest so transparent and yet so fundamentally good-natured that it becomes richly comical."

Albert Ganz (James Remar) escapes from prison, and with his helper, Billy Bear (Sonny Landham), goes to San Francisco. They kidnap Rosalie (Kerry Sherman), the bewildered girlfriend of their one-time associate, Luther (David Patrick Kelly). Detectives Algren (Jonathan Banks) and Vanzant (James Keane) allow their stubborn co-worker Jack Cates (Nick Nolte) to help them corral the felons. Before the fracas is over, Vanzant and Algren are dead, and Cates, who had to surrender his gun to Ganz, is in hot water. Cates maneuvers a 48-hour pass for black Reggie Hammond (Eddie Murphy), another member of the gang with six months left of his sentence to serve. Hammond has his own reasons for hating double-dealing Ganz. Street-smart Hammond helps Cates track down Luther, who refuses to cooperate. Crafty Hammond learns of Billy Bear's whereabouts at a country and western bar but, at the man's apartment, they find trouble but no Billy Bear. It takes a whopping punching fest between Cates and Hammond to set new limits to their strange working relationship. Hammond admits the money Ganz is after is locked in the trunk of Hammond's car at a parking garage. The trail lead to Luther's picking up the money and his rendezvous with Ganz. Bus-driving Luther dies in a wild chase, but the money and Ganz escape. Back at Billy Bear's apartment the law-enforcing partners find the two criminals. Hammond shoots Billy Bear, and Ganz is killed by Cates. As Hammond returns to prison to finish out his short term, Cates promises to keep his money safe.

Early on in this fast-paced feature, spiffy Hammond has his first gander at loutish Cates's wreck of a Cadillac. "This you car, man? Looks like you bought it from one of the brothers." This is the start of the verbal slugfest as the two exchange racial slurs and putdowns. (At one point Cates refers to his "partner" as "a colored loser" and later jibes, "I don't know what you're smiling at, Watermelon." On the other hand, in Hammond's most daring scheme — entering the unfriendly country and western bar — he admits, "I don't like people, I hate rednecks." And then he blurts out outrageously to the tough assemblage, "I'm your worst fuckin' nightmare, man. I'm a nigger with a badge.") And when Reggie Hammond is not defaming the other race, he is (un)consciously playing with black stereotypes, especially as the horny dude who wants badly to make up for lost time. ("The one advantage to the casting of a disconcertingly comic type like Eddie Murphy," decided Andrew Sarris in the *Village Voice,* "is that he can step over the line of phallic bravado to a disinfecting self-parody.") The funniest moment comes in the film when Hammond finishes toying with the customers at the country and western bar, haivng withstood enormous odds in the powerplay. He tells the outfoxed patrons, "There's a new sheriff in town. You all be cool." And no one is as cool as jive-talking Hammond, who admits what he wants most out of his special respite from jail is ". . . some food, good atmosphere, nice people." By the caper's end, each man has had a brief glimpse of the other's disparate world and gotten a new perspective on his own life. The loner Cates admits of Hammond, "He's got more brains than you'll ever know. He's got more guts than any partner ever had."

Nick Nolte and Eddie Murphy in *48 Hours* (1982).

Brooklyn-born (April 3, 1961) Eddie Murphy, the son of a policeman, began his professional career as as stand-up comic at assorted Long Island night spots, moving into Manhattan showcases by the age of seventeen. He joined the lineup of NBC-TV's "Saturday Night Live" in the 1980–1981 season (at $750 per week), and when the executive production management was switched midstream Murphy emerged as one of the show's top featured performers (at $8,700 per episode). As a result of watching Murphy on "Saturday Night Live" director Walter Hill signed Murphy for fast-talking, urbane convict Reggie Hammond.

In summing up the reasons why audiences responded so readily to the comedian in his first feature film, *Variety* analyzed, "...fact that everything about Murphy, from his body language to the look in his eyes, immediately signals that he's a nice guy takes any edge off the picture which would have been provided by a more potentially dangerous sort.... His fundamental likability, on the other hand, makes the picture more palatable from a straight entertainment point of view." The screen debut Murphy enjoyed was far different from the one the black action stars of the late 1960s and early 1970s "enjoyed." Like his screen brothers before, Murphy's character is filled with rage over indignities, a joy in putting one over on the Man, and a need for self-worth and equality. But Murphy's weapons are not violence and polemics, but a far more engaging albeit deadly weapon: smart one-liners.

48 Hours grossed an exceptionally strong $30,328,000 in domestic film rentals.

96. Foxtrap (Snizzlefritz, 1986). Color, 88 minutes.

Executive producers Linda Radova, Marcello Ciraci, Pier Luigi Cirlaci; *producer/director/story* Fred Williamson; *screenplay* Aubry K. Rattan; *set decorator* Eugenio Liverani; *wardrobe* Maria Spigarelli; *music* Patrizio Fariselli; *stunt co-ordinator* Peter Honak; *assistant director* Vivalda Vigorelli; *sound* Clark Will, Olivier Schwob, Giuseppe Testa; *sound effects editors* Paolo Frati, Mario Gracco; *camera John Stephens, Steve Shaw; editor* Giorgio Venturoli.

Cast: Fred Williamson (Thomas Fox); Chris Connelly (John Thomas); Arlene Golonka (Emily); Donna Owen (Susan); Beatrice Palme (Mariana); Cleo Sebastian (Josie); Lela Rochon (Lindy); Jean-Marie Pallaroy (Rico); Daniel Romey (Monique); Maurizio Bonuglia (Marco); Cleo Sebastian (Jose); Kimberley Rae (Secretary); Pete Gonneau (Landlord).

Los Angeles courier-escort-troubleshooter Thomas Fox (whose sports car license plates read *"Da Fox"*) is hired by John Thomas (Chris Connelly) to find his niece Susan (Donna Owen), who has disappeared somewhere in Europe. Fox stops in Cannes (it is film festival time) and the clues lead to chic Marianne (Beatrice Palme) in Rome, who says (besides "Ciao") that Susan is masquerading as Belinda and will be at a party that night hosted by Marco (Maurizio Bonuglia). With the help of Marianne's black, gay male roommate, Susan is rescued and dragged back to Los Angeles. There Fox discovers that Susan is actually part of sinister Thomas's prostitution–drug trafficking deals and had stolen revealing videotapes from Thomas to blackmail clients and to finance her European sojourn.

Foxtrap is an extremely indulgent outing stuffed with lots of meaningless filler of the Thomas Fox character strutting along the streets of Cannes, Rome, or Los Angeles with gaping passersby substituting for crowd extras. With the exception of the raid on Marco's home, during which Marianne and her black male roommate die, there is no pacing to this would-be thriller. *Variety* sniped, "In place of action Williamson applies his budget to frequent costume changes for himself. Another personal touch is the presence of an array of international beauties who, naturally, can't keep their hands off the star."

There is scant character development given to the high-living, swinging bachelor known as Thomas Fox. The cigar-smoking macho man thinks of his girlfriend, Lindy (Lela Rochon), as a playful black doll; insists he is *not* really a private detective; and uncharacteristically for his very chauvinistic character, is quite tolerant of the black gay young man who sacrifices his life to help Fox. If Thomas Fox was meant to be a 1980s black James Bond, the ambitious aim fell far short of its goal.

Made in 1985 for his Po' Boy Productions with Italian backing and production, Foxtrap flashes a title card at the end to alert viewers to "watch for *The Fox and the Cobra* next summer." What emerged was *Black Cobra* (q.v.), which found Fred Williamson not as Thomas Fox, but as a New York police detective named Robert. Evidently the producer-director-scripter realized he had nowhere to go with the Fox characterization.

97. Foxy Brown (American International, 1974). Color, 92 minutes.
Presenter Samuel Z. Arkoff; *producer* Buzz Feitshans; *director/ screenplay* Jack Hill; *art director* Kirk Axtel; *wardrobe supervisor* James George; *set decorator* Charles Pierce; *makeup* John Norin; *music* Willie

Hutch; *assistant director* Frank Beetson; *stunt co-ordinator* Bob Minor; *sound* John Dignan; *special effects* Roy Downey; *camera* Brick Marquand; *editor* Chuck McClelland.

Cast: Pam Grier (Foxy Brown); Antonio Fargas (Link Brown); Peter Brown (Steve Elias); Terry Carter (Michael Anderson [Dalton Ford]); Kathryn Loder (Katherine Wall); Harry Holcombe (Judge Fenton); Sid Haig (Hays); Juanita Brown (Claudia); Sally Ann Stroud (Deb); Bob Minor (Oscar); Tony Giorgio (Eddie); Fred Lerner (Bunyan); Judy Cassmore (Vicki); Jon Cedar (Doctor); Kimberly Hyde (Jennifer); Esther Sutherland (Nurse); Mary Foran (Bartender); Roydon E. Clark (Sly); Don Gazzamici (O'Brien); Gary Wright, Fred Murphy (Cops); Edward Cross (Willard); Larry Kinley, Jr. (Jason); *and:* Jack Bernardi, H.B. Haggerty, Boyd "Red" Morgan.

Made as a follow-up to the highly successful *Coffy* (1973) (q.v.), the formula still worked, with *Foxy Brown,* also directed and scripted by Jack Hill, grossing a hefty $2,460,000 in domestic film rentals. But, noted Verina Glaessner (British *Monthly Film Bulletin*), "Gone is Coffy's essential independence — Foxy Brown is basically just someone's girlfriend — and excised along with the earlier film's all-pervasive pessimism is Coffy's total single-mindedness and her neatly ironic means of revenge...." A.H. Weiler *(New York Times)* reported that Pam Grier, "...the black beauty whose clothes — if not her good intentions — have been torn away in several bargain-basement epics ... is in a rut." And Donald Bogle offers in *Blacks in American Film and Television* (1988), "She infuses this cheap pulp project with her own highly charged, misdirected energy. And it is her perverse straightforwardness, her cockeyed determination to carry through on her do-goodism ... and her supreme single-mindedness as well as her bizarre belief in her material (she actually seems to think these movies mean something) that make her pictures pleasurable to some audiences today."

Saving her brother, Link (Antonio Fargas), from two pursuing hoodlums, Foxy Brown (Pam Grier) learns he is unable to pay back $20,000 in numbers racket funds to the gang. Link uncovers that Foxy's boyfriend, Mike Anderson (Terry Carter), is actually her narcotics agent lover Dalton Ford, who underwent plastic surgery to hide his trail. Link tells the gangsters of the man's whereabouts to pay off his debt. When Anderson is killed, Foxy vows reprisals. She forces her brother to tell her who the gangster leaders are, and she soon infiltrates the compound of Katherine Wall (Kathryn Loder), queen of the dope-prostitution-protection rackets. Katherine's lover-enforcer is Steve Elias (Peter Brown). Using the alias of Misty Cotton, Foxy becomes a call girl and, with Claudia (Juanita Brown), arrives at the hotel suite of Judge Fenton (Harry Holcombe) to insure that he will acquit one of the gang's big dealers the next day in court. Instead the rebellious hookers maneuver the situation to embarrass the judge publicly. Katherine's henchmen are ordered to beat, rape, and torture Foxy and then send her to the "ranch" to be force-fed high doses of drugs. She escapes from the ranch, incinerating the drug lab and the two henchmen. In town Oscar (Bob Minor), leader of a black neighborhood anti-drug group, agrees to help Foxy waylay a big heroin shipment. They destroy several members of Katherine's gang (with Foxy piloting a plane and wreaking havoc on the gangsters) and castrate Elias. Foxy gamely delivers Elias's extracted parts to a horrified Katherine and meanwhile mows down the remaining stooges. Foxy and Oscar go off together.

"She's a whole lot of woman," Link says admiringly of his well-endowed sister. And he is correct. She is a resourceful, resilient, randy woman who has a way with gutter language. Foxy Brown can navigate a plane, maneuver a careening car, manipulate a gun or any other handy weapon, and when all else fails, capitalize on her sensational body to stay one step ahead of the creeps that dog her trail. Her topsy-turvy world may revolve around her government agency boyfriend (she thinks nothing of fornicating with him in his unprivate hospital room to jazz his spirits), but when he is mowed down, she is a hellcat on wheels. She knows exactly what she must do: "The only way to handle those smart-ass hoods is with a bullet in the gut." She can be empathetic to a confused prostitute (Juanita Brown). She handles herself equally well against assertive lesbians and the pursuing hoods at a rambunctious gay bar. And even when at the ranch she is tied spread-eagle to the bed (a macho fantasy trip familiar to Pam Grier films), she manages to work herself loose. Not content with disposing of one degenerate with a trusty wire hanger, she sets the other on fire with gasoline and destroys the drug plant as well. Revenge is sweet for the life-threatening Foxy. Her arch foes are the self-consciously cultured Katherine and her menacing right hand man Steve Elias. Elias meets a gruesome, painful end, but Foxy has special retribution planned for the pretentious, sadistic Katherine who caused her lover and her brother's deaths. Not only does she present the aghast foe with a pickle jar containing Elias's best parts, but she refuses to kill off the deposed crime queen. "Death is too easy for you, bitch," she tells Katherine. "I want you to suffer!"

When *Foxy Brown* was released in England in the spring of 1975, eight minutes of sex, gore, and brawling were excised.

98. Friday Foster (American International, 1975). Color, 90 minutes.

Producer/director Arthur Marks; *based on the comic strip and on the story by* Marks; *screenplay* Orville Hampton; *costumes* Izzy Berne; *makeup* Louis Lane, Bob Westmoreland; *music* Luchi De Jesus; *song* Bodie Chandler; *assistant director* Gene De Ruelle; *stunt co-ordinator* Richard Geary; *sound* George Malley; *sound effects* John Post; *camera* Harry May; *editor* Stanley Frazen.

Cast: Pam Grier (Friday Foster); Yaphet Kotto (Colt Hawkins); Godfrey Cambridge (Ford Malotte); Thalmus Rasulala (Blake Tarr); Eartha Kitt (Madame Rena); Jim Backus (Enos Griffith); Scatman Crothers (Reverend Noble Franklin); Ted Lange (Fancy Dexter); Tierre Turner (Cleve Foster); Paul Benjamin (Senator David Lee Hart); Jason Bernard (Charley Foley); Edmund Cambridge (Lieutenant Jake Wayne); Julius W. Harris (Monk Riley); Rosalind Miles (Cloris Boston); Carl Weathers (Yarbro); Tony Brubaker (Chet Freed); Stan Stratton (Shawn North); John Anthony Bailey, Frenchie Guizon (Cops); James Cousar, William Sims (Chauffeurs); William Gill (Minister); Almeria Quinn (Dresser); Alice Jubert (Senator Hart's Secretary); Candy All (Prostitute); Samuel Daris (Dolley); Bebe Drake Hooks (Neighbor); Harold Jones (Buzzy); Charles Stroud (Drunk); Mel Carter (Gate Guard).

Pam Grier in *Friday Foster* **(1975).**

Considering the stereotypical projects that came before, *Friday Foster* was an immense change of pace for Pam Grier. Based on a Chicago Tribune/New York News Syndicate cartoon strip, *Friday Foster* is *Batman*-style pop art. In this production her features, especially her hairdo, are softened, her wardrobe is more sophisticated and subtle, her tactics are almost law-abiding, and most amazing of all her language is of the uptown street not the gutter. In short, her screen character had cleaned up its act.

Glance magazine photographer Friday Foster (Pam Grier) is on the scene when black tycoon Blake Tarr (Thalmus Rasulala) arrives at a New York airport. She is a witness to an assassination attempt on this eccentric billionaire. The following day at Madame Rena's (Eartha Kitt) fashion show, she spots Yarbro (Carl Weathers), one of the would-be assassins. She tells this to boyfriend Colt Hawkins (Yaphet Kotto), a private detective. Backstage Friday is told by dying model friend Cloris Boston (Rosalind Miles) the code words

"Black Widow." Friday assumes this ties into the case because it develops that Cloris's boyfriend, Chet Freed (Tony Brubaker), had been involved in the airport shootout as well. The police later inform Friday that Cloris was involved sexually with several Washington politicians. The trail leads to the nation's capital and Senator David Hart (Paul Benjamin). Surviving a murder attempt, Friday — with Colt one step behind/ahead — is an uninvited guest at a gathering given by religious leader Noble Franklin (Scatman Crothers). There she is introduced to Hart and his aide, Charles Foley (Jason Bernard). Meanwhile Tarr alerts her he is also seeking the "Black Widow." Friday and Hawkins show up at Franklin's country retreat, where he is hosting a major peace conference of black leaders. With the help of the police they round up the racist henchmen of Foley and white bigot Enos Griffith (Jim Backus), who have masterminded the entire scheme.

The tapestry of this cartoonish adventure is filled with singular characters (cast against type with a wide variety of name performers). They are exotic couturiere Madame Rena (Eartha Kitt), who becomes a murder victim; gay Washingtonian dresss designer Ford Malotte (Godfrey Cambridge), who discovers making a phone call can be deadly business; seemingly complacent but violently racist Enos Griffith (Jim "Mr. Magoo" Backus); the determined, athletic hit man Yarbro (Carl Weathers) who meets his match in Friday; Friday's exasperated publisher boss, Monk Riley (Julius W. Harris); unorthodox Reverend Noble Franklin (Scatman Crothers) who enjoys mortal pleasures; jivin' pimp Fancy Dexter (Ted "Love Boat" Lange), who courts Friday with expensive presents; Cleve Foster (Tierre Turner), Friday's enterprising, precocious little brother with his heart set on becoming a black capitalist; and Blake Tarr, the Howard Hughes–like black industrialist with whom, among others, Friday beds down. Not to be overlooked is Friday's muscular, jocular "main man" lover Colt Hawkins (Yaphet Kotto in a nicely paced amiable hero's role) who neatly tosses quips and clues back and forth with zesty, hip Friday. (He coyly reminds her, "It ain't the size of the ship, it's the motion of the ocean" that's important.) He is always full of boyish levity.

"This is one of those movies where everything and everybody looks a little too good — the clothes; the pimps; the hookers; the cars; the streets; the bosoms fleetingly bared; and even the blood, which looks as though it ought to carry a vintage" (Lawrence Van Gelder, *New York Times*). *Variety* was quick to observe that Pam Grier herein "...isn't totally macho and radiates a lot of traditional feminine charms along the way. The film has a certain ambivalence in that Grier is liberated in most ways, but ultimately wants men to control her.... Still one can't blame shoddy plot elements on her, since she so far transcends the silliness of her vehicles."

When the relatively expensively mounted *Friday Foster* failed to generate even $1,000,000 in domestic film rentals, it was the end of the box-office road for Pam Grier at American International Pictures. After five unhappy years with the economy film production company, her reign as queen of blaxploitation features had ended, as had the craze for the once-lucrative genre. Having been exploited by the prime manufacturers of exploitation pictures, she was unceremoniously dumped. Her next screen role would not be until the mainstream action drama *Greased Lightning* (1977) (q.v.), made with her then-boyfriend Richard Pryor for Warner Bros.

99. Fritz the Cat (Cinemation, 1972). Color, 77 minutes.

Producer Steve Krantz; *director* Ralph Bakshi; *based on characters created by* Robert Crumb; *adaptor* Bakshi; *music* Ed Bogas, Ray Shanklin; *music director* Bogas; *animation supervisors* Virgil Ross, Manuel Perez, John Sparey; *sound* Glen Glenn; *special effects* Helen Jordan; *editor* Renn Reynolds.

Voices: Skip Hinnant (Fritz); Rosette Le Noire, John McCurry, Judy Engles.

For those brought up on Walt Disney, Chuck Jones, and Hanna-Barbera cartoons, the gross *Fritz the Cat* is a shocking experience. With something to offend nearly everyone, it was American cinema's first X-rated feature length cartoon, based on the underground comics of Robert Crumb where the libidinous animals fornicate, display oversized ethnic characteristics, and are more bigoted and politically hotheaded than any real-life counterparts. Fritz the Cat is a far cry from his predecessor in cartoonland, Felix the Cat. In this Candide-like odyssey, Fritz is a sex-starved idealist student who journeys through 1970s America mingling with and conflicting with a wide variety of bawdy lifestyles. "Excellent animation and montage shore up a plot which has a few howls, several chuckles and many smiles" *(Variety)*.

The action opens in New York City's Washington Square Park. In this opening sequence there is a heated sociological debate in the park, which synthesizes a great deal of overripe thought on black culture:

> GIRL A: I read everything James Baldwin's written. He has a true sense of the problems of black people.
>
> GIRL B: I worked for Head Start for free last summer. Black kids are so much groovier.
>
> GIRL C: I went to a couple of Black Panther meetings. The time for non-violent revolution is past. I'm taking a course in African studies in school.... I had no idea you people were so civilized. Do you know property values actually go up when a black family move in.... Freud didn't write for black men.... Why does James Earl Jones always have to play a black man.... It's so great black people are wearing their hair natural.

The action quickly switches to an East Village crash pad, where Fritz lures a trio of innocent girls to participate in a bathtub orgy. The cops (pigs here) arrive to investigate pot-smoking and Fritz is once more on the lam. He finds brief sanctuary in an orthodox synagogue, is partly responsible for a huge fire on his campus, and then zips up to Harlem. On the road with his girl, Winston (a fox), in her Volkswagen bug they head westward, later are embroiled with drugged-out Hells Angels motorcyclists and then with a gang of revolutionaries determined to explode a power plant. Fritz is drafted to plant the dynamite and after being injured is next seen in a Los Angeles hospital, where he throws off his bandages and enjoys a gang bang with his female visitors.

In the Harlem segment, *Fritz the Cat* encompasses everything that could be found in a live-action black action feature. He becomes embroiled in a brawl with pool-shooting crows, has sex with an old-fashioned black party gal named Big Bertha on a junk pile, goes on a wild joy ride across the George Washington Bridge, gets high on marijuana at a Harlem speakeasy, and incites a street crowd against two cops which starts a devastating race riot, insisting "we shall overcome!" As one jive-talking black crow who befriends Fritz tells him, "You gotta be up here, man, to find out what's happening."

The unique cartoon's soundtrack includes Billie Holiday singing "Yesterdays," Charles Earling playing "Black Talk" and Bo Diddley vocalizing "Bo Diddley."

Fritz the Cat grossed $4,200,000 in domestic film rentals. The iconoclastic Ralph Bakshi would later be responsible for *Heavy Traffic* (1973), *The Nine Lives of Fritz the Cat* (1975), *Wizards* (1977), *Lord of the Rings* (1978), *American Pop* (1981), *Hey Good Lookin'* (1982), and, in 1987, would have the Saturday morning network cartoon series "Mighty Mouse." His 1975 part-animated, part-live action cartoon feature *Coonskin* (q.v.) would cause an outrage among certain factions of the black community.

100. Ganja and Hess (Kelly-Jordan Enterprises, 1973).
Color, 110 minutes.

Executive producer Quentin Kelly, Jack Jordan; *producer* Chiz Schultz; *associate producer* Joan Shigekawa; *director/screenplay* Bill Gunn; *production designer* Tom John; *costumes* Scott Barrie; *music* Sam Waymond; *assistant director* Anthony Major; *camera* James E. Hinton; *editor* Victor Kanefsky.

Cast: Duane Jones (Dr. Hess Green); Marlene Clark (Ganja); Bill Gunn (George Meda); Sam Waymon (Reverend Luther Williams); Leonard Jackson (Archie); Candece Tarpley (Girl in Bar); Richard Harrow (Dinner Guest); John Hoffmeister (Jack); Betty Barney (Singer); Mabel King (Queen of Myrthia); Betsy Thurman (Poetess); Enrico Fales (Green's Son); Tommy Lane (Pimp); Tara Fields (Woman with Baby).

A.K.A. *Blood Couple; Double Possession.*

"In addition to bringing writing skills to his directorial debut, actor-playwright-novelist-screenwriter Bill Gunn is also a painter. You will appreciate his feel for composition and color in *Ganja and Hess.*... You cannot possibly record the richness of sound, color, rhythm and tension in one sitting. You cannot possibly get all of Duane Jones or Marlene Clark, he of the Olympian detachment, she of the perfectly accessible breasts. You will incur addiction, you will return" (Terry Guerin, *Andy Warhol's Interview* magazine).

Black anthropologist Dr. Hess Green (Duane Jones) is studying the culture of Myrthia, an ancient black civilization which disappeared a millennium before the Egyptians evolved. Strangest of all, Myrthia was a civilization addicted to blood due to a transmittable parasite. Assisting Dr. Green in his museum scholarship is George Meda (Bill Gunn). One night after dinner at Dr. Green's Hudson River mansion, a drunken Meda stabs his superior several times with a Myrthian bone knife taken from his host's collection. A remorseful

Meda shoots himself with a pistol, and Green is left to deal with his blood-thirsty addiction and the newly discovered fact that he cannot die. The next day Meda's widow, Ganja (Marlene Clark), arrives from Denmark and soon falls under Green's spell. It is Dr. Green's friend and chauffeur, Reverend Luther Williams (Sam Waymond), who suggests finally a religious solution to his curse in the shadow of the cross. As for the similarly infected Ganja, she has no immediate plans to leave her earthly mantle.

The fable within *Ganja and Hess* cuts deep. As Phil Hardy perceives in *The Encyclopedia of Horror Movies* (1986), "But here blood becomes more than just a symbol of life; it is an atavistic reminder of the indestructibility of the black race, or a suppressed but not destroyed African heritage. After his infection with the Myrthian virus Jones becomes like a black god, inverting Christian symbols and myths and invoking rich, plentitudinous sensuality that is the very reverse of western puritanism."

It may have been striving for some sort of artistic virtue to be so different from the blood-and-guts of such other black-theme horror movies as *Blacula* (1972) and *Blackenstein* (1972) (qq.v.), but audiences found this offering too intellectual, stylized, and without sufficient visual special effects. Moreover, as *Variety* reported, "The nudity ... is so much an element of the film that one tends to think of it as a sex film with blood. Some very handsome people are given such ridiculous roles that laughter in the wrong place is their due." In 1975 the film was recut, with new music added, and reissued as *Double Possession,* playing up the horror angles more. Bill Gunn was no longer listed as director, an E.H. Novikov listed in his place. The ad campaign promised, "The story of a man and woman possessed by the devil.... The devil wanted their souls.... She wanted their bodies ... and more!"

101. Getting Over (Maverick International, 1976). Color, 100 minutes.

Producer John R. Daniels; *co-producer* Cassius V. Weathersby, Jr.; *associate producers* Joseph A. Hubbard, Jr., Alonzo K. Daniels; *director* Bernie Rollins; *story* John R. Daniels, Rollins; *screenplay* Rollins; *song* Alonzo K. Daniels; *music arranger/music conductor* Johnny Rogers.

Cast: John Daniels (Mike Barnett/Narrator); *and:* The Love Machine — Gwen Brisco, Paulette Gibson, Sandra Sully, Mary Hopkins, Sheila Dean, Renee Gentry, Bernice Given; *and:* Mabel King, David Hubbard, Bryan O'Dell, Buzz Cooper (Guest Stars).

This ego-massaging mild action-picture-cum-musical was created by John Daniels, "the" star of *The Candy Tangerine Man* (1975) and *Black Shampoo* (1976) (qq.v.). It purportedly deals with the corruption, bigotry, and myriad hard knocks of the recording industry. But the scripting is so puerile, the production values so lean, and the energy so low that nothing much comes across.

Black Mike Barnett (John Daniels) has dreams of succeeding in a big way in the music industry, along with a singing group, "the Heavenly Sisters." Meanwhile the bigoted white mobster board chairman of a top music company in Los Angeles suggests that Barnett head Impossible Funky Records. The sole purpose for this subsidiary firm's existence is to prove to the Unfair Discriminatory Law Enforcement Board that the corporation is not biased.

Barnett agrees to being used because he hopes to outmaneuver his employer. His philosophy is, "I guess everybody does what they got to do." Meanwhile Barnett falls in love with a talented singer/dancer (Gwen Brisco) and with the help of two financiers creates a high-energy show group (the Love Machine). His dreams come true.

102. The Glove (Pro International, 1978). Color, 90 minutes.

Producer Julian Roffman; *director* Ross Hagen; *screenplay* Roffman, Hubert Smith; *wardrobe* Rafael Arragola, Janet Keisnick; *art directors* Brenton Swift, Al Locatelli; *makeup* Chris Bruce; *music* Robert O. Ragland; *assistant directors* Thomas Selden, Anthony Lorea, Concetta Rinaldo; *action/fight director* Roffman; *camera* Gary Graver; *additional camera* Michael Mileman; *editor* Bob Fitzgerald.

Cast: John Saxon (Sam Kellough); Roosevelt [Rosey] Grier (Victor Hale); Joanna Cassidy (Sheila Michaels); Joan Blondell (Mrs. Fitzgerald); Jack Carter (Walter Stratton); Keenan Wynn (Bill Schwartz); Aldo Ray (Prison Guard); Michael Pataki (Harry Iverson); Misty Bruce (Lisa); Howard Honig (Lieutenant Kruger); Frances E. Williams (Grandma Hale); Candy Bowen (Hooker); Nicholas Worth (Chuck); Logan Clarke (Young Man); Noel De Souza (Cab Driver); Roger Crawford (Willard); Bob O'Neil (Doctor); Gloria Torres (Nadia); Dean Stern (Joe Arrigo).

A.K.A. *Blood Mad.*

The black action film had almost entirely faded from view, but occasionally its frequent themes of racial intolerance and injustice would be brought forth as the rationale for a twist in plotline. Such was the case with *The Glove,* a poorly directed detective thriller that wasted a very experienced cast.

Black Victor Hale (Roosevelt Grier) had been the victim of sadistic prison guards who experimented with a new torture device ("the glove") on him. Having escaped from jail, the guitar-strumming, usually benevolent Hale goes on a rampage, killing the guards who tormented him. He himself is murdered before he can assist with a tenement rejuvenation project, and the killer is then fatally beaten by the slum dwellers. Sam Kellough (John Saxon) is the burned-out detective eager for the $20,000 reward on Hale, but who later comes to respect the man.

It is sad to see so many good performers in such claptrap. Saxon's ex-cop-turned-bounty-hunter lead throughout appears more addicted to bad similes than good detection work. He's the type of inveterate gambler who announces (on the soundtrace narration), "Real trouble comes in a dirty suit and a wrinkled collar." Later he muses, "I wonder, does anything really last." This offering was far less entertaining than Roosevelt [Rosey] Grier's tacky but entertaining *The Thing with Two Heads* (1972) (q.v.).

103. The Golden Child (Paramount, 1986). Color, 93 minutes.

Executive producers Richard Tienken, Charles R. Meeker; *producers* Edward S. Feldman, Robert D. Wachs; *co-producer* Dennis Feldman; *associate producer* Gordon A. Webb; *director* Michael Richie; *screenplay* Dennis Feldman; *production designer* J. Michael Riva; *art director* Lynda Paradise;

set designer Virginia Randolph; *set decorator* Marvin March; *costumes* Wayne Finkelman; *makeup* Ken Chase; *music* Michael Colombier; *special effects* Industrial Light & Magic; *visual effects supervisor* Ken Ralston; *visual effects coordinator* Pamela Easley; *sound* Jim Alexander; *camera* Donald E. Thorin; *second unit camera* Robert Thomas; *editor* Richard A. Harris.

Cast: Eddie Murphy (Chandler Jarrell); Charles Dance (Sardo Numspa); Charlotte Lewis (Kee Nang); Victor Wong (The Old Man); J.L. Reate (The Golden Child); Randall "Tex" Cobb (Til); James Hong (Dr. Hong); Shakti (Kala); Tau Logo (Yu); Tiger Chung Lee (Khan); Pons Maar (Fu); Peter Kwong (Tommy Tong).

"*The Golden Child* is a golden turkey . . . superstar [Eddie Murphy], while still likeable, is operating here at reduced levels of energy, sass and humor. . . . Michael Ritchie, who used to make films that were about something, directs in a visually busy and cluttered manner. . . . There is no better than Eddie Murphy when he plays the right guy in the wrong place (or vice versa). This movie, however, is so wrong there's no guy right enough to fix it." (*People* magazine). On the other hand, Roger Ebert in his *Movie Home Companion 1988* (1987) found this comedy "entertaining from beginning to end." He added, "It is funnier, more assured and more tailored to Murphy than *Beverly Hills Cop* and it shows a side of his comic persona that I don't think has been much appreciated: his essential underlying sweetness. . . . His famous laugh is not aimed as a weapon at anybody, but is truly amused. He is perfectly suited to survive this cheerfully ridiculous movie, and even lend it a little charm." *The Golden Child,* with an estimated production cost of $25,000,000, grossed "only" $39,700,000 in domestic film rentals.

Dedicated but eccentric social worker Chandler Jarrell (Eddie Murphy) has a larger mission in life: to find missing children. Kee Nang (Charlotte Lewis) flies to Los Angeles to ask Jarrell to take on his biggest case to date: to find the Golden Child (J.L. Reate), a Tibetan holy youth stolen from a Shangri-La temple by the evil Sardo Numspa (Charles Dance), an emissary of the devil, who fears the child will bring peace to earth. Once in Tibet, Jarrell must convince the venerable Holy Man (Victor Wong) that he is fit for the task. Later Jarrell is given a magical sword to help in his holy quest. And before the villain is dispatched finally, Kee Nang has been slain and brought back to life by the Golden Child recently freed from his prison pen.

The Golden Child borrows from the *Indiana Jones* movies, *Camelot,* and a host of martial arts pictures. What emerges is a potpourri of bits and pieces that work occasionally, thanks to Murphy's charm. (Two of the film's better scenes occur when Chandler Jarrell appears on a TV talk show and makes mincemeat of the posturing host. Later, when seeking the child, Jarrell must be guided by a parrot who knows the proper path to be followed, and to Jarrell this makes perfect sense.) Because the star's role in *The Golden Child* is so one-dimensional, more than one reviewer equated the comedian's own persona with his onscreen role, drawing on real-life Murphyisms for his reel image. "What makes *The Golden Child* refreshingly different from other Murphy films is that this hip, know-it-all black man can be surprised and even somewhat disconcerted about things that are not in his ken. . . . The offbeat casting of an

Asian woman with a black man is a welcome change. . . . Had Murphy been
allowed to show a little more vulnerability in his love for [Charlotte] Lewis, as
well as in his quest for the Golden Child, the film might have made an original
contribution to screen comedy and to social criticism." (Carl E. Rollyson, Jr.,
Magill's Cinema Annual, 1987).

Originally Paramount had offered Eddie Murphy a Neil Simon comedy
script to star in, but he rejected it in order to make *The Golden Child.* The John
Barry music score written for this film was replaced before national release with
a very noisy one by Michael Colombier. Having profited from *The Golden
Child* experience, Murphy's next all-out comedy would be the very sweet, low-
keyed *Coming to America* (1988) which grossed $117,382,908 in its first nine (!)
weeks of domestic distribution.

104. Gordon's War (Twentieth Century–Fox, 1973). Color, 90 minutes.

Executive producer Edgar J. Scherick; *producer* Robert L. Schaffel; *direc-
tor* Ossie Davis; *screenplay* Howard Friedlander, Ed Spielman; *art director*
Perry Watkins; *set decorator* Robert Drumheller; *costume designer* Anna Hill
Johnstone; *music* Andy Badale, Al Elias; *music director* Horace Ott; *songs*
Andy Badale, Al Elias; *assistant directors* Dwight Williams, Neil Machlis;
stunt co-ordinator Everett Creach; *technical advisers* Horace Balmer, Joseph
DeCosta; *sound* Al Gramaglia; *sound effects editors* Filmsounds, Inc.; *camera*
Victor J. Kemper; *editor* Eric Albertson.

Cast: Paul Winfield (Gordon Hudson); Carl Lee (Bee Bishop); David
Downing (Otis Russell); Tony King (Roy Green); Gilbert Lewis (Spanish
Harry); Carl Gordon (Luther the Pimp); Nathan C. Heard (Big Pink); Grace
Jones (Mary); Jackie Page (Bedroom Girl); Charles Bergansky (Caucasian
Killer); Adam Wade (Hustler); Nansford Rowe (Dog Salesman); Warren
Taurien (Goose); Ralph Wilcox (Black Hit Man); David Connell (Hotel Pro-
prietor); Rochelle LeNoir (Gordon's Wife); Michael Galloway (Gray-Haired
Executive).

If Ossie Davis's directorial film debut, *Cotton Comes to Harlem* (1970)
(q.v.), was a joyous, irreverent comedy-action yarn, his *Gordon's War* was a
dramatic turn-of-face. "The picture is tough, fast, moves in a straight line with
no sideline fiddling but with pungent humor and vividly jabs the crime
underbelly of Harlem" (Howard Thompson, *New York Times*). "We get the
customary quota of violent action, but without the feeling that this is merely
to see how many people can be knocked-off in an infinite variety of ways. The
film has an underlying sense of despair at the mess that exists. . . . The film
doesn't reach any great heights, but neither is it just another dip into exploitation of the black scene" (William Wolf, *Cue* magazine).

Gordon Hudson (Paul Winfield) returns to Harlem after service as a Green
Beret captain in the Vietnam War to find his wife died of a drug overdose in
his absence. When he learns drug pusher Big Pink (Nathan C. Heard) was
responsible, he breaks the man's legs. The hospitalized Big Pink orders Spanish
Harry (Gilbert Lewis) to have his goons beat up Hudson. Their actions spur Gordon to join forces with three friends, all members of his Vietnam unit: Bee
Bishop (Carl Lee), Roy Green (Tony King), and Otis Russell (David Downing).

warfare against Harlem drug dealers. They methodically
lves as a military unit and drive the pushers and their wares
k community. Next they work on closing down the fleabag
s habituated by addicts. During a meeting of Spanish Harry
n gangland leaders to discuss the drug situation, the commando blows up their cars. Gordon's goal is to eliminate the mysterious
white syndicate boss (who contacts his minions by closed-circuit TV). Meanwhile
the big man contracts hit men to snuff out the Gordon problem. Play-
boy-ish Roy Green is killed in an ambush along with his white whore, and in
revenge, Gordon, Bishop, and Russell murder Spanish Harry's triggermen. Gordon hops on a motorcycle and pursues the fleeing Harry. After a lengthy chase
he catches up with his victim, who is hurled through a plate glass car window
and dies. Gordon meets with the top syndicate boss and kills him right under the
mob's noses.

The film plays like a video manual of "How to Clean up the Drug Problem
in Your Neighborhood — Militant Style." What gives the often slowly paced film
its credibility is Paul Winfield in the key acting assignment. Often the star of
more genteel pictures such as *Sounder* (1972 — for which he was Oscar-
nominated) and *Conrack* (1974), it is brooding Winfield who brings conviction
to the proceedings. And that is not easy, for at one moment he is waxing lyrical
(the flashback sequence in which he and his wife are seen bicycling joyfully
through a sunny Central Park), and at the next he is jumping on an enemy's
propped-up legs and breaking them.

In *Essence* magazine, Maurice Peterson wrote approvingly of Paul
Winfield's characterization. "Traditionally, Shaft and James Bond types over-
emphasize savior-faire and ruthlessnesss to project a superhuman aura. But
Winfield's *Gordon* is earthy, the direct opposite of the cliched action hero. He
isn't a fast talker, has no physical or emotional invulnerability and has no
wonder way with money or women. Gordon comes across as a real person,
enhancing the believability of a basically fanciful story."

With its emphasis on violence in the name of mortality, *Gordon's War*
makes too little of the tremendous problems facing the black quartet's attempt
to adjust to civilian life in the ghetto.

Gordon's War grossed $1,250,000 in domestic film rentals. It remained a
landmark of black action how-to gore along with the same year's *The Spook
Who Sat by the Door* (q.v.).

105. Greased Lightning (Warner Bros., 1977). Color, 96 minutes.

Executive producers Richard Bell, J. Lloyd Grant; *producer* Hannah
Weinstein; *associate producer* James E. Hinton; *director* Michael Schultz;
screenplay Kenneth Vose, Lawrence DuKore, Melvin Van Peebles, Leon
Capetanos; *art director* Jack Senter; *set decorator* James I. Berkeley; *costumes*
Celia Bryant, Henry Salley; *music* Fred Karlin; *stunt co-ordinator* Ted Dun-
can; *designer of race sequences* Neil Castle; *technical adviser* Wendell Scott;
assistant directors Terry Donnelly, Dwight Williams, Preston Holmes; *sound*
Willie Burton, Harland Riggs; *sound effects* Ed Scheid, Billie Owens, Arthur
H. Pullen, Lee Chaney, Jack Dennis, Hank Salerno; *special effects* Candy

Flanagan, Tom Ward; *camera* George Bouilliet; *second unit camera* Richard Glouner; *editors* Bob Wyman, Christopher Holmes, Randy Roberts.

Cast: Richard Pryor (Wendell Scott); Beau Bridges (Hutch); Pam Grier (Mary Jones); Cleavon Little (Peewee); Vincent Gardenia (Sheriff Cotton); Ritchie Havens (Woodrow); Julian Bond (Russell); Earl Hindman (Beau Welles); Minnie Gentry (Mrs. Scott); Lucy Saroyan (Hutch's Wife); Noble Willingham (Billy Joe Brynes); Bruce Atkins, Steve Fifield (Deputies); Bill Cobbs, Georgia Allen (Mary's Parents); Maynard Jackson (Minister); Danny Nelson (Wayne Carter); Cara Dunn (Restaurant Owner); Alvin Huff (Moonshiner); Willie McWhorter (Wendell, Jr.); Frederick Dennis Greene (Slack); Bill Bonnell (Speedway Announcer).

Wendell Scott was the first black championship race car driver. *Greased Lightning* is his story.

Wendell Scott (Richard Pryor) returns home to Danville, Virginia, after military service in World War II and marries Mary Jones (Pam Grier). He buys a taxi cab and intends opening a garage repair shop one day, although his dream is to become a winning racing driver. To supplement his income, Scott drives shipments of moonshine for bootleggers. The excitement of eluding the pursuing police through expert driving is more gratifying to Scott than the money he receives. ("It's not the risk, I like to ride," he insists.) His luck runs out and Sheriff Cotton (Vincent Gardenia) arrests him. However, racing promoter Billy Joe Byrnes (Noble Willingham) steps into the picture. He suggests to the grasping sheriff, "Let's get that boy out of jail and make some money out of his black ass." Byrnes arranges for Scott's release on condition that he participate in a local stock car race. Byrnes is positive the rednecks will flock to see a black man beaten on the track. Scott survives the efforts of white drivers to eliminate him from the race, and when he enters another race, he is disqualified on racial grounds. Eventually Wayne Carter (Danny Nelson) invites him to race at Cluster Springs. By now his moonshine-running friend Peewee (Cleavon Little) has become his manager, and junkyard worker Woodrow (Ritchie Havens) is his brooding mechanic. At the rally Scott comes in fourth, which entitles him to two free meals at a segregated restaurant. With the help of white driver Hutch (Beau Bridges), who soon becomes his mechanic, Scott collects his winning dinner (not without causing a ruckus). Despite the persistent bigotry on the track, Scott continues his career, chalking up more wins. When he is badly injured in a crash, Mary begs the middle-aged man to quit, especially since he has a family. But Scott will not stop. ("I ain't no quitter," he insists.) He enters the Grand National Championship, and despite a faulty wheel that almost destroys him, he wins.

Richard Pryor made *Greased Lightning* because it was ". . . a fun-time kind of movie without any wrath-against-the-world stuff." It was also an opportunity to present a positive black image in this biography of the determined sports player who overcomes bigotry to achieve his dream. This was the first of a new four-picture deal that Pryor made with Warner Bros. which overlapped with his existing Universal Pictures multi-film contract. It was reminiscent in approach and period (1939) to the baseball story *The Bingo Long Traveling All-Stars and Motor Kings* (1976) Pryor had made with Billy Dee Williams and James Earl Jones.

Pam Grier and Richard Pryor in *Greased Lightning* (1977).

Greased Lightning showcases a fresh onscreen Richard Pryor. As Janet Maslin *(New York Times)* acknowledged, "Mr. Pryor has a gift for being almost effortlessly amusing, so much so that movie audiences often burst out laughing at the mere sight of him. The first few minutes of *Greased Lightning* are a little dicey for that reason, until it becomes clear that Mr. Pryor is out to give a coolly sustained dramatic performance, even a rather subtle one. After that, it's smooth sailing all the way." *Variety* approved of the new Pryor, who was ". . . creating and developing a continuing character throughout an entire story. Such versatility is no minor achievement, especially for a performer who previously comes to public notice in the field of comedy. All comics are actors, but the public usually overlooks this fact, thereby leading to performer frustration. Pryor has escaped that traditional curse."

Greased Lightning was made in the summer and early fall of 1976, with location filming in Madison, Georgia. The original director, Melvin Van Peebles, was replaced by Michael Schultz, who had directed *Car Wash* (1976) (q.v.). "I did a fireman's job," says Schultz. "[I] took over somebody else's film and finished it up." The results are a mixed bag with too many sluggish scenes. "Right from the dewey-eyed opening flashback with young Wendell routing a sneering gang of white kids by his derring-do in a bicycle race, it is stamped 'wish fulfillment' as clearly as anything Hollywood ever produced in its palmy Depression days. . . . What chiefly dismays about the film . . . is that both script and direction opt for a welter of cosily antiquated devices: vaselined nostalgia for the period scenes; the passage of time indicated by the sudden addition of a child to the family, and later by the child's appearance grown up; the endless racing footage clumsily spliced into the drama..." (Tom Milne, British *Monthly Film Bulletin*).

The *Greased Lightning* casting is intriguing. Atlanta Mayor Maynard Jackson and black politician Julian Bond appear in cameos. Singer-actor Ritchie Havens appears as an amalgam of Wendell Scott's various real mechanics, and, in a strange twist of fate, Cleavon Little (as the manager) is seen here supporting the star, whom he had replaced as the black sheriff in Mel Brooks's *Blazing Saddles* (1974). Pam Grier, who was then engaged to marry Pryor, has the non-focal role of his ever-patient wife. (Janet Maslin in the *New York Times* assessed, "Pam Grier, as Mr. Scott's preternaturally patient wife, manages at times to make herself seem almost inconspicuous, which constitutes a triumph of willpower over natural assets even more impressive than that [sic] of her co-star.") And sixty-three-year-old Wendell Scott, who had mixed feelings about how the film distorts the presentation of some of the characters, was on hand as technical advisor and after much persuasion was allowed to perform some of the race track stunts. Beau Bridges — whose younger brother Jeff had starred in another racing story, *The Last American Hero* (1973) — appears to great advantage as the hot-headed, initially bigoted redneck driver-mechanic.

The PG-rated *Greased Lightning* opened weeks after Pryor's *Silver Streak* (q.v.). But unlike that commercial bonanza, the sentimental *Greased Lightning* did relatively disappointing box-office business, grossing $7,600,000 in domestic film rentals based on a $3,200,000 estimated production cost. Not only were most such racetrack pictures poison with the public, but moviegoers wanted to see Pryor as the smart-mouthed, outrageous comic they knew from concerts, films, television, and recordings.

106. The Greatest (Columbia, 1977). Color, 114 minutes.

Producer John Marshall; *director* Tom Gries; *based on the book* "The Greatest: My Own Story" *by* Muhammad Ali, Richard Durham, Herbert Muhammad; *screenplay* Ring Lardner, Jr.; *production designer* Bob Smith; *set decorator* Solomon Brewer; *costumes* Eric Seelig, Sandra Stewart; *makeup* William Tuttle, Tom Tuttle; *music* Michael Masser; *songs* Masser and Linda Creed, Masser and Jerry Goffin; *assistant director* Tom Shaw; *special effects* Candy Flanagin; *sound* Bill Randall; *camera* Harry Stradling, Jr.; *editor* Byron Brandt.

Cast: Muhammad Ali (Himself); Ernest Borgnine (Angelo Dundee); Lloyd Haynes (Herbert Muhammad); John Marley (Dr. Pacheco); Robert Duvall (Bill McDonald); David Huddleston (Cruikshank); Ben Johnson (Hollis); James Earl Jones (Malcolm X); Dina Merrill (Velvet Green); Roger E. Mosley (Sonny Liston); Paul Winfield (Lawyer); Annazette Chase (Belinda Ali); Mira Waters (Ruby Sanderson); Philip MacAllister (Young Cassius Clay, Jr.); Arthur Adams (Cassius Clay, Sr.); Dorothy Meyer (Odessa Clay); Lucille Benson (Mrs. Fairle); Theodore R. Wilson (Gardener); Skip Homeier (Major); Sally Gries, Elizabeth Marshall (Sponsor's Wife); Malachi Throne (Payton Jory); Richard Gullage (Commission Doctor); Richard Venture (Colonel); Stack Pierce (Johnson); Ben Medina (Ronnie); Paul Mantee (Carrara); George Garro

(Mr. Curtis); David Clennon (Captain); Ernie Wheelwright (Bossman Jones); George Cooper (Lawyer); James Gammon ("Mr. Harry"); Toni Crabtree (Hooker); Don Dunphy (Commentator); Fernand A. Larrieu, Jr. (Grocer); Nai Bonet (Suzie Gomez); Alberto Marti (Doctor); Ray Holland (Reporter); Rahaman Ali, Howard Bingham, Drew "Bundini" Brown, Harold Conrad, Gene Kilroy, W. Youngblood Muhammad, Pat Patterson, Lloyd Wells (Themselves).

Before he was overshadowed in the early 1980s entertainment and sports worlds by the likes of Mr. T., Muhammad Ali (born Cassius Marcellus Clay) was rated one of America's most vivid personalities. Not only did he work his way up through the highly competitive boxing world of the 1960s with match after successful match, but through television appearances, print interviews, and Greenwich Village coffee shop poetry readings, he proved himself a flavorful, multi-talented personality with a rowdy knack for gaining amazing publicity. When he became a Black Muslim and started crusading strongly for his beliefs, another dimension was added to this unique sports and entertainment figure.

The Greatest, based on his co-authored autobiography, is a surprisingly conventional rendering of his unusual life story utilizing unremarkable production values. "Charming curio of a sort Hollywood doesn't seem to make anymore.... Once you get beyond the embarrassingly simple-minded introduction sequences, *The Greatest* is winning entertainment" (Vincent Canby, *New York Times*). As for the rambunctious star, Canby assessed, "You might call Muhammed Ali a natural actor, but that would be to deny his wit, sensibility, drive, ability, enthusiasms, poise and common sense, all of which are the conscious achievement of an ambitious man who has known exactly what he has wanted for a long time."

The film opens with young Cassius Clay (Philip MacAllister) returning home to Louisville, Kentucky, from Rome, where he has won the light heavyweight gold medal in boxing. Thereafter, ". . .incidents proceed at a pace that obscure a needed perspective in the subject's life; the sequences parade by as though prepared for interrupted TV viewing instead of by a theatrical audience.... Precise location of places and dates has been diffused" *(Variety).* Overcoming discrimination, he establishes his lifetime pursuit of many goals. At the point in the narrative where he turns professional boxer, Muhammed Ali takes over the focal acting assignment.

There follows a chronicle of key events in his life: his growing friendship with Malcolm X (James Earl Jones), his baiting and beating of humorless boxing champion Sonny Liston (Roger E. Mosley), his refusal to serve in the army in Vietnam (claiming exemption as a Black Muslim minister) and his eventual exoneration by the Supreme Court; and his telling victory over Goerge Forman in Zaire. Too many of the milestone bouts are depicted through spliced-in newsreel footage.

Also to be appreciated is the find supporting cast who rise above the material, including Annazette Chase as his second wife, Lucille Benson as a patronizing bigot, Paul Winfield as his attorney during the Army fracas, Ernest Borgnine as his manager, Robert Duval as one of his earliest backers, James

Earl Jones as the inspiring Malcolm X, and especially Roger E. Mosley as his feisty ring opponent, Sonny Liston. The well-regarded director of *The Greatest,* Tom Gries, died during post-production on this sports biography.

Muhammed Ali would later star in the two-part telefilm *Freedom Road* (1979). Based on Howard Fast's 1944 novel and co-starring Kris Kristofferson, Ron O'Neal, and Ossie Davis, it tells the story of an ex-slave elected to the United States Senate.

107. **Halls of Anger** (United Artists, 1970). Color, 100 minutes.

Executive producer Walter Mirisch; *producer* Herbert Hirschman; *director* Paul Bogart; *screenplay* John Shaner, Al Ramrus; *art director* Addison Hehr; *music* Dave Grusin; *song* Grusin and Norman Gimbel; *music editor* Richard Carruth; *assistant directors* Victor Vallejo, Fred Brost, Joe Ellis; *technical adviser* Mike Warren; *sound* Don Rush; *sound editor* Frank Warner; *camera* Burnett Guffey; *editor* Bud Molin.

Cast: Calvin Lockhart (Quincy Davis); Janet MacLachlan (Lorraine Nash); James A. Watson, Jr. (J.T. Watson); Jeff Bridges (Douglas); Rob Reiner (Leaky Couloris); Dewayne Jessie (Lerone Johnson); Patricia Stich (Sherry Vaughn); Roy Jenson (Harry Greco); John McLiam (Lloyd Wilkerson); Edward Asner (Ernie McKay); Lou Frizzell (Phil Stewart); Helen Kleeb (Rita Monahan); Luther Whitsett (Ivan Fowler); Florence St. Peter (Miss Rowland); Maye Henderson (Mrs. Taylor); *and:* Marti Blaine, Barry Brown, Alex Clark, Paris Earl, Randy Fredericks, Gilbert Green, Arline Hamlin, Hilly Hicks, Christopher Joy, Richard Levin, Kim Manners, Davis Roberts, Linda Smith, Linda Thomas, Ta-Tanisha, Gary Tigerman, Cal Wilson.

By court order sixty middle-class white students are bused to the predominantly black inner city Lafayette High School. Rigidly by-the-rules white principal Lloyd Wilkerson (John McLiam) remains unperturbed, since he is far too busy politicking for a school board post, but upscale black vice-principal, English teacher, and former basketball star Quincy Davis (recently transferred from an all-white suburban school) must cope with the crisis. The white newcomers are deeply resented by black militants led by J.T. Watson (James A. Watson, Jr.). The very bigoted Leaky Couloris (Rob Reiner) represents the anti-black student element. Throughout it all Davis remains the beacon of hope. He encourages failing black student Lerone Johnson (De-Wayne Jessie) to read by a rather unique method (he gives him pornographic books for homework). Later he copes with spunky white basketball player Douglas Falk (Jeff Bridges) having been brutally beaten by the blacks during team tryouts, and blonde Sherry Vaughn (Patricia Stich), being stripped and humiliated by black girls in the locker room. Couloris and Johnson square off eventually, with both being expelled and the student body going on strike. Thanks to Davis's negotiations with student leader Watson, the brewing riot is averted. Davis convinces black teacher Lorraine Nash, with whom he is having a romance, and victimized Falk to stay at Lafayette.

Filmed at Los Angeles high schools and on the streets of Watts, *Halls of Anger* took advantage of the then-topical and highly controversial busing situation that was rocking the United States. The film is an updating of the

Left–right: **James A. Watson, Jr., Janet MacLachlan and Calvin Lockhart in** *Halls of Anger* **(1970).**

schoolroom racial tensions of *The Blackboard Jungle* (1955) (q.v.) and *To Sir with Love* (1967). The plot gimmick is to reverse the situation and have the whites be the victimized minority and the blacks be the aggressive majority. Many of the white adults are presented as oafish hardhats. But, wrote Howard Thompson *(New York Times)* of this "occasionally purposeful" melodrama, the "...resolution is predictable a mile away."

Sleek, sophisticated, handsome Calvin Lockhart, then a very promising rising star, shines as the saavy vice-principal, who at one point becomes so discouraged with his impossible mission that he quits his post, reasoning, "They've got their indifference and their hate. What do they need me for?" But an educational tour through the life-teaching streets of Watts changes his mind, especially when he sees the promise of the future (represented by a smiling little black boy playing in the midst of junkyard rubble). Ever-reliable Janet MacLachlan shines as a very human teacher frustrated by her charges and exhilarated by her love for Lockhart.

Halls of Anger was not a money-maker, being judged too grimly realistic by some and too contrived and slanted by others.

108. Hammer (United Artists, 1972). Color, 92 minutes.

Executive producer Philip Hazelton; *producer* Al Adamson; *director* Bruce Clark; *screenplay* Charles Johnson; *art director* Skip Troutman; *music* Solomon Burke; *music director* Jerry Styner; *assistant director* Byron Roberts; *technical adviser;* Ron Henriquez; *stunt co-ordinator* Eric Cord; *sound* George

Alch; *sound effects* Marv Kerner, Jim Nownes; *camera* Bob Steadman; *editor* George Folsey, Jr.

Cast: Fred Williamson (B.J. Hammer); Bernie Hamilton (Davis); Vonetta McGee (Lois); William Smith (Brenner); Charles Lampkin (Big Sid); Elizabeth Harding (Rhoda); Mel Stewart (The Professor); D'Urville Martin (Sonny); Stack Pierce (Roughhouse); Jamal Moore (Henry Jones); Nawana Davis (Mary); John Quade (Riley); Johnny Silver (Tiny); John de Carlos (Bruiser); Perrie Lott (Nagi); Leon Isaac [Kennedy] (Bobby Williams); Phillip Jackson (Landlord); Al Richardson (Black Militant); Tracy Ann King ("The Black Magic Woman" Dancer); George Wilber (Irish Joe Brady); Gene le Bell (Referee); Jimmy Lennon (Ring Announcer).

The world of boxing has more perils outside the ring than in, especially when you are a powerhouse black boxer on the way up the ladder of success.

Hot-tempered black dock worker B.J. Hammer (Fred Williamson) is fired from his job and returns to the boxing ring, one of the few places a black man can show his muscle and earn some sizeable dollars. Black fight promoter Big Sid (Charles Lampkin) offers to sponsor him in the Los Angeles arena. The drug-dealing Sid, who is controlled by white Mafioso, provides him with "the Professor" (Mel Stewart) as his trainer, and Hammer romances the initially resistant Lois (Vonetta McGee), Sid's black secretary, while rejecting seductive Rhoda (Elizabeth Harding), Sid's white mistress. Black law enforcer David (Bernie Hamilton) asks Hammer to help his investigation against Sid and the latter's drug transactions, but Hammer cannot be bothered, even after Sid's demented hit man, Brenner (William Smith), kills a simple-minded underling named Bruiser (John de Carlos). Hammer rises to the top and, now successful, finds himself detached from his former pals, who resent his elevated set of values. Big Sid is told to have Hammer lose the big match against the champion, and the Professor is clobbered for not cooperating. Then the sadistic Brenner and his white cronies kidnap Lois to force Hammer into compliance. While Hammer is pummeling his heavyweight opponent in the ring, Davis locates Lois at the last moment. Hammer wins his match. Sid is killed in the showdown while Hammer and his friends beat up Brenner and his thugs.

If only *Hammer* had been as forceful as the lead character's surname. "Its one potentially interesting aspect is an active and fairly intricate appreciation of lowlife types and stereotypes" (Roger Greenspun, *New York Times*). While applauding the film's depiction of life at all levels in the ghetto, the critics gave more attention to the film's director than to rising genre star Fred Williamson. Bruce Clarke, a New Zealander and U.C.L.A. graduate, had already two exploitation feature pictures to his credit. "It is a measure of his [Clarke's] skill that he manages to use the flashy stylistics of the genre (hand-held fights, bed scene with slow pace and long dissolves, car chase shot mainly on wide-angle, Reggae score) not as weapons against his audience but as devices for involvement. The ring scenes are all outstandingly well handled, and the film's pace is endangered only by a slightly over-long plot." *Hammer* is filled with a full spectrum of avarice and crime, where one act of violence is worth a thousand words. In this blend of chauvinism, mayhem, and skullduggery in the boxing world, women (black or white) do not get a fair shake, especially the loudmouthed hooker (Nawana Davis) at whom the upwardly mobile boxing champ sneers.

In the rash of black action pictures grabbing distribution space, *Hammer* was not a noteworthy winner, earning less than $1,000,000 in domestic film rentals. The movie's title was a reference to Fred Williamson's nickname of "the Hammer" when he played professional football.

For the record, Bobby Williams, the college-studying protege of Big Sid, is played by Leon Isaac, who later became Leon Isaac Kennedy of *Penitentiary* (1979) (q.v.) fame. Beautiful Vonetta McGee, a staple of such films, is at her finest here, as the flinty miss who picks and chooses her men and leads Fred Williamson on a merry race before she succumbs to twinkling eyes, rediscovered goals in life, and bedroom charms.

109. Heat Street (City Light, 1987). Color, 86 minutes.

Executive producer Ronald L. Gilchrist; *producers* Richard Pepin, Joseph Merhi; *associate producer* Michelle Tondo; *director/screenplay* Merhi; *music* John Gonzales; *stunt co-ordinator* Red Horton; *special visual effects* Judy Yosemoto; *sound editor* Christopher B. Fry; *camera* Richard Repin; *editor* Paul G. Volk.

Cast: Del Zamora (Blake); Quincy Adams (Virgil); Wendy McDonald (Sarah); Yvette Davis (Jane); Deborah Gibson (Mary Williams); Tomas Trujillo (Todd); John Gonzales (Sonny); R.J. Walker (Manager); Kitty Leigh (Pregnant Lady); James McNay (Jason); Adrian Drake (Detective); Jason Scott Lee (Asian Gang Leader); Charla Driver (Linda); George Dunn (Pimp); Marcus Johnson, Calvin Meeks, Larry Musgrove, Alex Patton, Aaron Windom (Boxers); Neil Oxenburg, Andrew M. Roemer, David Perrin, Kimberly A. Mentel, Adam Garret, Heather Kay, Angela M. Porcell, James Daniel, Cynthia Marie Miguel, John Adrian Drake, Howard Hesson, Alan Comeaux (Gang Members).

This outing proved to be an overly earnest, poorly mounted, low-budget panorama of street life with white against black, Hispanics against the world, and no one the winner. When black teenager Jane (Yvette Davis) is hit over the head by a marauding motorcycle gang who rape her, the tragedy begins snowballing. Her boxing coach father (Quincy Adams) finds himself involved, not only with black counselor Mary Williams (Deborah Gibson), but also with a white car thief named Blake (Del Zamora), who happened upon Jane's car after the molestation. The two culturally opposite men become friendly, which leads to more heartache and disaster as Jane dies in a boutique store shootout while out shopping with Blake's white girlfriend, and Blake, in turn, is murdered by a punk street gang.

110. Hell Up in Harlem (American International, 1973). Color, 96 minutes.

Executive producer Peter Sabiston; *producer* Larry Cohen; *co-producer* Janelle Cohen; *director/screenplay* Larry Cohen; *production designer* Larry Lurin; *music* Fonce Mizell, Freddie Perrin; *music consultant* Barry De Vorzon; *sound* Alex Vanderkar; *sound effects editor* Marvin Kerner; *camera* Fenton Hamilton; *editors* Peter Honess, Franco Guerri.

Cast: Fred Williamson (Tommy Gibbs); Julius W. Harris (Papa Gibbs); Gloria Hendry (Helen Bradléy); Margaret Avery (Sister Jennifer); D'Urville Martin (Reverend Rufus); Tony King (Zach); Gerald Gordon (Mr. DiAngelo); James Dixon (Irish); Esther Sutherland (The "Cosh"); Charles MacGuire (Rap).

"*Black Godfather Is Back!* . . . and he's takin' over the town . . . and there's gonna be *Hell Up in Harlem*." In Hollywood, anything is possible, especially when there is cash to be generated. At the end of *Black Caesar* (1972) (q.v.), wounded black crimelord Tommy Gibbs (Fred Williamson) drags himself back to Harlem to die. Thanks to director-scriptor Larry Cohen (who prepared the original entry), Tommy Gibbs is now alive and well and living in New York. He's also fit enough to do battle again with everyone.

How did this medically amazing resuscitation occur? At the opening of the sequel Tommy Gibbs is seen mowed down by gunfire on Fifth Avenue but staggering alive through it all. "He's bleeding like a pig," acknowledges one of the white hit men. "You need a cannon to kill those niggers, for cryin' out loud. . . ." Presto, the stage is set for the further exploits of that handsome, mean dude — that black Caesar of the underworld.

And there are other transformations in this follow-up film. Gibbs' ex–cosmetic salesman father, Papa Gibbs (Julius W. Harris), is no longer a peace-abiding senior citizen. He gets a bloody taste of the criminal life and likes it — and how! After almost single-handedly killing two goons who have been working him over, father has a rendezvous with son:

PAPA GIBBS: I killed them. I had to.
TOMMY GIBBS: You done well. *(Smirking)* It must run in the family.
PAPA GIBBS: *(Proudly)* It went down so easy.
TOMMY GIBBS: If Mom could see us now.

And it is not long before fur-trimmed-coat-wearing Papa Gibbs is strutting down the street with a homburg, red jacket and snazzy boots and an easy-lovin' girl on each arm. He has his own entourage of bodyguards and is soon locked in deadly rivalry with his son for control of the Harlem turf.

As in the first edition, *Hell Up in Harlem* focuses on the white Mafioso from Little Italy — this time Mr. DiAngelo (Gerald Gordon) — who disputes Tommy Gibbs's rule of the black part of town. Again Gibbs comes into possession of vital syndicate ledgers (this time a photocopied set) which could rip open the Organization's chokehold on New York City.

Helen (Gloria Hendry), who had left Tommy for his best friend (who was terminated in *Black Caesar*), is back in this installment. It is not long before the pampered lady and her two children are kidnapped by Mr. DiAngelo to bring Tommy into line. Later Helen is murdered. Also returning is the irrepressible Reverend Rufus (D'Urville Martin), the born-again evangelist who had been a pimp up on Lenox Avenue. Less a con artist than before, he is determined to reform their neighborhood. "I'm going to appeal to all the decent black people" — which, to his mind, still includes his boyhood-friend-gonewrong Tommy. In fact, he is later willing to commit murder to save his pal.

And there is Tommy's lieutenant Zach (Tony King), of whom Tommy says, "...your ambition's gonna get you in a lot of trouble." And it does when the overly covetous punk double-crosses his boss. In contrast, attractive sister Jennifer (Margaret Avery) is on Tommy's side, thrilled that through her newfound love "...we have the names of all the men who exploited the black community since we were kids." (A protracted nude love scene demonstrates just how much she loves her stud.)

Obviously the *raison d'être* of *Hell Up in Harlem* is action ... and plenty of it. There are montages of Papa Gibbs and Tommy each on the warpath viciously mowing down their common enemies (the white gangsters) and each other. Machine guns are their favorite weapons, but they are resourceful killers. At Coney Island Tommy pierces a victim with a beach umbrella pole; another target is stabbed with a pen and then has his head encased with a suffocating plastic bag. (Even after all this, sister Jennifer can still say to her man, "You still don't see anything wrong with killing people.")

There is a lengthy, James Bond–like sequence set in the Florida Keys filled with wry humor and killing. As Tommy's black frogmen reach the shoreline and mount their attack on the Mafia's compound, one commando says to another, "Who made up all that bullshit that black people don't know how to swim?" At the big house it develops several of the domestics include not only people in Tommy's pay but Tommy himself. He personally serves the hoods at the house soul food and before killing them remarks, "Just goes to show you don't know who's doing up your socks and underwear."

In the final confrontation with DiAngelo, who had stolen Tommy's son, the black crime leader mockingly tells his enemy, "You're going to be the first white hung by a nigger."

At the conclusion of *Hell Up in Harlem* Tommy is seen holding his young son and saying, "We're gong to start over where nobody knows us and I'm going to love you just like my pa..." They disappear into the night. The stage was set for part three of the series, but it never was produced. As *Variety* decided, "Unless the black market has not yet tired of these blaxploitational exercises, this pic's probable lack of strong b.o. reception should terminate AIP's Caesarian operation." The trade paper went on to brand the direction as "sloppy," the production values as "poor" and "...the action sequences are staged with little geographic or narrative coherence. Performances generally fall flat, although Williamson is naturalistically competent...."

Hell Up in Harlem grossed $1,550,000 in domestic film rentals — $450,000 less than its predecessor. It was a sign of the future.

111. Hickey and Boggs (United Artists, 1972). Color, 111 minutes.

Executive producer Richard L. O'Connor; *producer* Fouad Said; *associate producer* Joel Reisner; *director* Robert Culp; *screenplay* Walter Hill; *costumes* Bill Thiese, Pauline Campbell; *music* Ted Ashford; *song* George Edwards; *assistant director* Edward Teets; *special effects* Joe Lombardi; *sound* George Cantamessa; *camera* Wilmer Butler; *second unit camera* Rex Hosea; *editor* David Berlatsky.

Cast: Bill Cosby (Al Hickey); Robert Culp (Frank Boggs); Rosalind Cash

(Nyona); Sheila Sullivan (Edith Boggs); Isabel Sanford (Nyona's Mother); Ta-Ronce Allen (Nyona's Daughter); Lou Frizzell (Lawyer); Nancy Howard (Apartment Manager's Wife); Bernard Nedell (Used Car Salesman); Carmen (Mary Jane); Louis Moreno (Quemando the Prisoner); Ron Henrique (Quemando the Florist); Cary Sanchez (Mary Jane's Daughter); Jason Culp (Mary Jane's Son); Robert Mandan (Mr. Brill); Michael Moriarty (Ballard); Bernie Schwartz (Bernie); Denise Renfro (Brill's Daughter); Vincent Gardenia (Papadakis); Jack Colvin (Shaw); James Woods (Lieutenant Wyatt); Ed Lauter (Ted); Lester Fletcher (Rice); Gil Stuart (Farrow); Sil Words (Mr. Leroy); Joe Tate (Coroner's Assistant); Jerry Summers (Bidsoe); Dean Smith (Bagman); Bill Hickman (Monte); Keri Shuttleton, Wanda Spell, Winston Spell (Playground Kids).

Bill Cosby was born in Philadelphia in 1937 and first came to national attention in the early 1960s as a club comedian and comedy record performer. He and Robert Culp were teamed with tremendous success in the satiric adventure teleseries "I Spy" (1965–68), the first United States network series to cast black and white co-leads. (Cosby won three Emmy awards during its three-season run.) During the height of the black film grind, Cosby and Culp reunited for a detective caper, with Culp making his directing debut. Audiences expecting the stars to be replaying their popular television series characters were disappointed.

"There's nothing left in this profession, it's not *about* anything," complains burned out-private eye Al Hickey (Bill Cosby). Before long he and his equally down-and-out private investigator partner, Frank Boggs (Robert Culp), are hired at $200 per day to find a missing girl. The trail provided by their effete employer, Rice (Lester Fletcher), leads only to murder and to hassles with the police. Then Rice disappears. The two detectives learn that the vanished girl, Mary Jane (Carmen) — helped by her now-jailed florist husband, Quemando (Ron Henrique) — has $400,000 in stolen bank money tucked away in a suitcase. When she tries to fence the cache, she arouses a lot of people's interest. Among those wanting the case are Mr. Leroy (Sil Words) and his black power faction, as well as Mr. Brill (Robert Mandan), chief of the syndicate which financed the robbery. Now working for the bank, which offers a $25,000 reward, Hickey and Boggs are on hand at an attempt to turn over the money to a buyer at the empty Los Angeles Coliseum. When they are lured into a trap with Brill's hoods by Mary Jane, the frightened detectives want out. But they are brought back into the game when Nyoma (Rosalind Cash), Hickey's estranged wife, is killed by Brill's men. The partners force Quemando, now out of jail, to lead them to Mary Jane at a deserted beach, where she intends to hand over the money to Leroy. There is a violent skirmish between Leroy's black power troops and Brill's hit squad (who arrive by helicopter). When the smoke clears, Hickey and Boggs are the only survivors. Hickey notes, "Nobody came. Nobody came. It's still not about anything." Boggs responds, "Yeah, you told me."

Beyond the (by now too-) familiar black action trappings, *Hickey and Boggs* is a resourceful private eye caper that never received its sufficient due: "... not involved in a story or with characters really worthy of a full theatrical treatment" was the verdict of A.H. Weiler *(New York Times)*. "Silly ending in which the pair turn into James Bonds to wipe out the entire opposition against unlikely odds.... Nevertheless, *Hickey and Boggs* remains an extremely likeable film" (Tom Milne, British *Monthly Film Bulletin*).

Perhaps what was commercially wrong with this PG-rated production, which finished filming by October 1, 1971, but was not released until a year later, was that its story of greed and violence focused on two such untypical detective leads. They were closer (but not close enough) to Paul Newman's *Harper* (1966) than to Clint Eastwood's *Dirty Harry* (1971) or, more importantly, to such hip, swinging black investigators as Richard Roundtree's *Shaft* (1971) (q.v.). "Breaking archetypes, these men are not handsome, romanticized loners but are weary, displaced persons. Hickey's arrival home at night scares and angers his wife, who complains that she is not running a boarding house. Boggs is an alcoholic who spends most of his spare time in bars watching television commercials and brooding about his ex-wife. His singular enjoyment is watching her striptease act in a seedy nightclub, where she psychologically castrates him" (Elizabeth Ward in *Film Noir: An Encyclopedic Reference to the American Style,* 1979).

Bill Cosby later starred in "The Bill Cosby Show" (1969–71), "The New Bill Cosby Show" (host – 1972–73), "Cos" (host – 1975), and "The Cosby Show" (1984–   ). His 1969 prime-time TV special "Hey, Hey, Hey, It's Fat Albert" led to the Saturday morning cartoon show, "Fat Albert and the Cosby Kids" (a.k.a. "The New Fat Albert Show"). Not only one of TV's busiest spokespersons, he has authored best-selling books (*Fatherhood,* 1986; *Time Flies,* 1987) and has appeared in such non-genre films as *Mother, Jugs, and Speed* (1976), *California Suite* (1978), *The Devil and Max Devlin* (1981) and a concert film, *Bill Cosby Himself* (1983).

112. Hit! (Paramount, 1973). Color, 134 minutes.

Executive producer Gary Frederickson; *producer* Harry Korshak; *director* Sidney J. Furie; *screenplay* Alan R. Trustman, David M. Wolf; *art director* George Petitot; *set decorator* Leonard Maizola; *music* Lalo Schifrin; *assistant directors* Robin Clark, Louis Pitzele; *special effects* Joe Lombardi; *sound* David Ronne; *camera* John A. Alonzo; *editor* Argyle Nelson.

Cast: Billy Dee Williams (Nick Allen); Richard Pryor (Mike Wilmer); Paul Hampton (Barry Strong); Gwen Welles (Sherry Nielson); Warren Kemmerling (Dutch Schiller); Janet Brandt (Ida); Sid Melton (Herman); David Hall (Carlin); Todd Martin (Crosby); Norman Burton (The Director); Jenny Astruc (Mme. Frelou); Yves Barsacq (Romain); Jean-Claude Bercy (Jean-Baptiste); Henri Cogan (Bornou); Pierre Collet (Zero); Robert Lombard (Mr. Frelou); Paul Nercey (Jyras); Malka Ribovska (Mme. Orissa); Richard Saint-Bris (Monteca); Tina Andrews (Jeannie Allen); Frank Christi (Judge); Mwako Cumbuka (Boyfriend); Don McGovern (Roger); Glenn Stensel (Martin); Noble Willingham (Warden Springer); Lee Duncan (Pusher); Janear Hines (Esther); Jerry Jones (The Weasel).

"[*Hit!*] is a caper movie that was apparently designed as escapist entertainment, though by the time it enters its third hour you may well think you've been

Top: **Bill Cosby gets ready to silence the opposition in** *Hickey and Boggs* **(1972).**
Bottom: **Billy Dee Williams in** *Hit!* **(1973).**

trapped. It isn't easy to leave a movie after you've invested that much time and money in it, no matter how foolish it is. You have a right to know how it turns out" (Vincent Canby, *New York Times*).

Handsome black leading man Billy Dee Williams had already scored heavily in *Lady Sings the Blues* (1972) opposite Diana Ross, and *Hit!* reunited him with that film's director, Sidney J. Furie, as well as with one of the other featured players, Richard Pryor. "Critics may find *Hit!* implausible, incoherent and even immoral, but audiences should love it.... One selling problem is how to convince white filmgoers that *Hit!* is not just another urban blaxploitationer. Its drug-dealer plot handle and the presence of solo-starred Billy Dee Williams might seem to relegate the pic to the *Super Fly* pigeonhole" (Lee Beaupre, *Variety*).

When his teenaged daughter dies from a drug overdose, federal agent Nick Allen (Billy Dee Williams) plots retribution against the Marseilles-based dope ring which supplied the heroin. Despite his department's discouragement, Allen recruits his own commando team: Dutch Schiller (Warren Kemmerling), an overly violent narcotics agent not appreciated by his department; black engineer Mike Wilmer (Richard Pryor), whose wife was raped and killed by a junkie; Sherry Nielsen (Gwen Welles), a drug-addicted prostitute whom Allen buys with the promise of a huge heroin supply; Barry Strong (Paul Hampton), a Vietnam War veteran who got rich on the drug trade overseas and whom Allen threatens to expose; and Herman (Sid Melton) and Ida (Janet Brandt), an elderly Jewish ex-con couple whose boy was killed by drugs. Using a fishing boat that Wilmer overhauls, Allen and his commandos head to a deserted village in British Columbia, where the unique squad is trained for their mission: to kill the nine members of the French syndicate. The group then splits up, and they travel separately to Marseilles. In a barrage of controlled violence the enemy is routed, including assorted bodyguards. Each of the task squad makes his or her escape individually, and Allen, detained momentarily at the French border, is given the stamp of approval by his superiors.

To show just how manipulative Nick Allen can be, he takes the distraught Mike Wilmer to see the incarcerated man who was responsible for his wife's death. He even lets the poor soul beat up the jailed killer. As he pulls Wilmer off the man he says, "You want to kill somebody? I'll give you the right people to kill." Of Richard Pryor's appearance, Maurice Peterson (*Essence* magazine) applauded, "[He] gives his best performance yet ... he displays his highly polished wit and incredible intensity in a supporting role.... He is one of the few character actors who could not only carry a whole feature, he could fly with it."

Hit! is the male counterpart to the several Pam Grier films which used the same basic theme of personal revenge (*Coffy* [1973]; *Foxy Brown* [1974]; *Sheba, Baby,* [1975] [qq.v.]). Although *Hit!* has much higher production values and moves its setting out of the Los Angeles ghetto, it did not score the same box-office points. It was not what audiences expected.

When *Hit!* was released in Great Britain in early 1974 it was trimmed by 31 minutes.

113. Hit Man (Metro-Goldwyn-Mayer, 1972). Color, 90 minutes.

Producer Gene Corman; *director* George Armitage; *based on the novel* "Jack's Return Home" *by* Ted Lewis; *screenplay* Armitage; *art director* Lynn Griffin; *music* H.B. Barnum; *assistant director* George Van Noy; *sound* Alex Vanderkar; *camera* Andrew Davis; *editor* Morton Tubor.

Cast: Bernie Casey (Tyrone Tackett); Pamela [Pam] Grier (Gozeldo); Lisa Moore (Laural); Bhetty Waldron (Irvelle); Sam Laws (Sherwood); Candy All (Rochelle Tackett); Don Diamond (Theotis); Edmund Cambridge (Zito); Bob Harris (Shag); Rudy Challenger (Julius); Tracy Ann King (Nita); Christopher Joy (Leon); Roger E. Mosley (Baby Huey).

Having updated its 1950 crime melodrama *The Asphalt Jungle* into a black contemporary story, *Cool Breeze* (1972) (q.v.), Metro-Goldwyn-Mayer tried this gambit again with another one of its properties. It took *Get Carter* (1971), an underworld thriller set in Newcastle, England, and starring Michael Caine and Britt Eckland, and made it over as the black audience feature film *Hit Man*. Rising screen and television actor Bernie Casey gives a solid characterization in the title role, avoiding the cliches so entrenched already in the black movie genre.

The locale in *Hit Man* is black Los Angeles. "Its interest is life style rather than literary style, and as it turns out, that is interest enough" (Roger Greenspun, *New York Times*). The *Times* reviewer added, "There have been very few recent movies quite so pleasantly involved with their locations . . . and very few movies so aware of the kinds of unpretentious entertainment that merely being on location can offer. The dialogue, equally divided between innuendo and insult . . . is a kind of personality play of great resourcefulness and skill."

Small-time criminal Tyrone Tackett (Bernie Casey) comes from Oakland, California, to Los Angeles to attend his brother's funeral. But when he learns his brother was murdered he remains in town to solve the case and punish the culprits. He is a tough stud who prefers to work alone as he scurries through the maze of sleaze in the underworld of Los Angeles. He learns his niece (Candy All) had been involved in pornographic filmmaking for Theotis (Don Diamond), and that high-living crime lord Zito (Edmund Cambridge) and his henchman Shag (Bob Harris) had been part of the dirty dealing. Then there is porno film lead Julius (Rudy Challenger), who also happens to be an animal trainer. Involved in this journey through trash and scum are used car dealer and TV spokesman Sherwood (Sam Laws), loyal motel clerk Laural (Lisa Moore), Gozelda (Pamela [Pam] Grier), a busy sinister number fixated on becoming a porno superstar, and tough hooker Irvelle (Bhetty Waldron).

The action ranges from high-rises to seedy college campuses to tacky motels and on to the Watts Towers and a game preserve (where abused and bruised Pam Grier is left to her own devices with a rampaging tiger). Never does urban punk Tackett let down his defenses. In his way he is as corrupt and oblivious to others as those he hunts. He has no more morals than the scum around him. The one who sees best through his outer shell is Laural, the one person who really cares about him:

Bernie Casey and Candy All in *Hit Man* (1972).

TACKETT: I know how you like your men. Proud and erect.
LAURAL: You ain't the only one who fits the description.
TACKETT: I'm the only one here.
LAURAL: Give me a dime for a phone call. I'll fill the room.

Variety, which rated *Hit Man* "an okay black-audience programmer, cut well but thin from the formula cloth" gave the production a few back-handed compliments: "Though the gore is explicit (ditto the few erotic interludes), the story unfolds in a less frantic manner than usual; that is, everybody isn't running all the time, and the ... music, while lively, avoids except where appropriate the super-frenzy sound."

114.   The Hitter (Peppercorn-Wormser, 1979). Color, 85 minutes.
Executive producer Ronald K. Goldman; *producer* Gary Herman, Christopher Leitch; *associate producer* Ken Fink, Robert Reitanno; *director*

Leitch; *screenplay* Leitch, Ben Harris; *art director* George Corrin; *set decorator* Vincent Peranio; *makeup* Sirlord Donel; *costume co-ordinator* Bonnie Leitch; *music editor* Don La Fontaine; *assistant director* Fink; *special effects consultant* Tony Pamalee; *fight co-ordinator* Harry Madsen; *sound* Ron Harris; *sound editor* David Yewdall; *camera* Jacques Haitkin; *editor* Reitanno.

Cast: Ron O'Neal (Otis); Sheila Frazier (Lola); Adolph Caesar (Nathan); Bill Cobbs (Louisiana Slam); Dorothie Fox (Mabel); Alfice Brown (Sadie); Percy Thomas (Bootblack); Ed Heath (Bartender); Joe Pinckney, Tony Scott (Thugs); Gorham Scott, Joseph Evans (Card Players); Dana Terrell (Charlotte); Dee Porter (Gretchen); Gidget Pascale (Lucille); Carla Ness (Esther); Lisa Venables (Bridgette); Phillip Davis, William Bailey, Ira Martin (Boxers); Harry Madsen (Dirty Fighter); Joe Palazno (Kung Fu Fighter); Buddy Pulugi (First Fight Manager); Sam Katz (The Ringer); Rodney Lee (Intermediary); Norman Ross (Doctor); Dwight Smith (Shoeshine Boy).

The Hitter, shot on location in Baltimore, deals with country boy Otis (Ron O'Neal) who comes to the big city where he quickly learns, "This is the big league, big women, and big men." Otis is many different things to many people. Some know him as the Bayou Kid who plays pool as good as Minnesota Fats. Others call him Otis the Hick, and there are some who believe his moniker is Abraham Lincoln. He teams with Nathan (Adolph Caesar), a worn-out pimp, and finds himself engineered into returning to the fight game. He admits about his involvement with the profession, "I paid my dues, but I was in it for the wrong reason." It develops that once, while fighting in Philadelphia, he had spotted his father in the audience. It brought back such vivid, countless memories of his dad beating up his mother that he had gone crazy and killed his opponent. He had quit after that. But now with the prompting of Nathan and the encouragement of his lady love, Lola (Sheila Frazier), he is ready to tackle the sport again. His arch enemy proves to be crooked Louisiana Slam (Bill Cobbs), who sets up a final match in which Otis is shot and his girl is knifed to death. Those events lead Otis to seek revenge on Louisiana Slam.

It was quite a switch for the magnetic star of *Super Fly* (1972) and *Super Fly T.N.T.* (1973) (q.v.), to be in such lowly projects. But the energy of Ron O'Neal, his trademark, is still intact, and he proved as credible in the ring as at the pool table. His scenes with veteran actor Adolph Caesar have a ring of authentic camaraderie, and nothing could be finer than watching the two studs (of different generations) competing to see who can survive more quantity at the local whorehouse.

115. Honeybaby, Honeybaby (Kelly-Jordan, 1974). Color, 89 minutes.

Executive producer Quentin Kelly; *producer* Jack Jordan; *associate producer* Saladin Jammal; *director* Michael Schultz; *story* Leonard Kantor; *screenplay* Brian Phelan; *costumes* Yvonne Stoney; *makeup* Kjell Gustayson; *music/music director* Michael Tschudin; *music editor* Don La Fontaine; *assistant director* Kurt Baker; *sound* Lee Bost; *camera* Andreas Bellis; *editor* Hortense Beveridge.

Cast: Diana Sands (Laura Lewis); Calvin Lockhart (Liv); Seth Allen

(Sam); J. Eric Bell ("Skiggy" Arthur Lewis); Brian Phelan (Harry); Bricktop (Harry's Mother); Thomas Baptiste (General Christian Awani); Gay Suilin (Mme. Chan); Nabih Abdoul Hoson (Herb); Mr. Sunshine (Real Makuba).

Gifted black actress Diana Sands died of cancer on September 21, 1973, at the age of thirty-nine. She had appeared onstage in such productions as *Raisin in the Sun* (also the 1961 film version), several adaptations of Shaw and Shakespeare, and opposite Alan Alda in the hit Broadway comedy *The Owl and the Pussycat*. Onscreen she played in such films as *Executive Suite* (1954), *An Affair of the Skin* (1963), *The Landlord* (1970), and *Georgia, Georgia*. A year after her passing, *Honeybaby, Honeybaby* was released. This travesty of entertainment is "banal, not funny, and tedious" *(Variety)*. There is no sense to the scattered plot nor any rhythm to individual scenes. As for the production values, "Color quality is washed out, giving pic a home-movie quality. The musical score is of poor quality, and for some reason, is allowed to intrude on virtually every scene. Editing is chaotic giving film no real sense of place or time..." *(Variety)*.

Shot on location largely in Beirut, Lebanon, and New York City, the mishmash attempts to be a comic spy spoof filled with romance on the high seas. The film is framed by an (afterthought?) opening scene in which jive-talking, marijuana-smoking, sixteen-year-old Skiggy Lewis (J. Eric Bell) sits in a projection screening room recalling how his United Nations interpreter cousin Laura (Diana Sands) won a trip abroad on a TV quiz show. Before long, Laura encounters super-smooth soldier-of-fortune Liv (Calvin Lockhart) from Harlem's 127th Street. He is the type of man who "...moves things; I don't ask content — just size, shape, weight ... and price." They are caught up in a political tug-of-war between two Third World political factions over the method of best preserving the body of a beloved but deceased African premier. Little does Laura (the "Honeybaby" of the film) know that a microdot crammed full of vital data has been secreted in her passport and...

With little to work from, it appears the filmmakers attempted to salvage their material via heavy re-editing. It did not help. Diana Sands looks puzzled (ironically her onscreen character says, "Under stress I'm one of the calmest.... I know myself very well") and Calvin Lockhart seems detached (with good reason). Director Michael Schultz would fare much better with *Car Wash* (1976), *Cooley High* (1976) (q.v.), *Greased Lightning* (1977) (q.v.), and others. There is a brief cameo by pre–World War II European cabaret legend Bricktop.

Another Sands film posthumously released was *Willie Dynamite* (1974) (q.v.).

116. Honky (Jack H. Harris, 1971). Color, 92 minutes.

Producers Will Chaney, Ron Roth; *director* William A. Graham; *based on the novel* "Sheila" *by* Gunard Selberg; *screenplay* Chaney; *art director* Frank Sylos; *set decorator* Morris Hoffman; *wardrobe supervisor* Ray Phelps; *makeup* Rod Wilson; *music* Quincy Jones; *song* Jones and Bradford Craig; *music editor* Stanley Witt; *assistant director* Edward Teets; *special effects* Ben Smith; *sound* Barry Thomas; *camera* Ralph Woolsey; *editor* Jim Benson.

Cast: Brenda Sykes (Sheila Smith); John Nielson (Wayne "Honky" Divine); Maia Danziger (Sharon); John Lasell (Archie Divine); William Marshall (Dr. Craig Smith); Amentha Dymally (Mrs. Smith); Marion Ross (Mrs. Divine); John Fiedler (High School Guidance Counselor); Lincoln Kilpatrick (The Drug Pusher); John Hillerman (Bus Station Ticket Seller); *and:* Ed Anderson, Jerry Buitsche, Matt Clark, Ephtallia Davis, Debbie Duff, William Echinger, Ivor Francis, Richard Laurence, Bellyeio Miller, Joe Spaulding, Elliott Street, Tawny Tann.

The Civil Rights movement of the 1960s and early 1970s found vocal expression not only in the ghetto streets but also on school campuses. Interracial romances were still considered a hot, exploitable item, which was all the grist film distributor Jack H. Harris required to distribute this harmless potboiler. Filled with token outbursts of racism on both sides, what emerges is a highly romantic study of two teenagers who want to be left alone to enjoy one another's company. The prettified film was considered "daring" (within limits) for its time, but now seems tame. The engaging performances of the two leads are a definite plus.

White Wayne Divine (John Nielsen) is a typical high school youth living in suburban comfort in a Midwestern town. He works after classes at Ziegler's Market for $1 an hour and has plenty of friends at school. Black Sheila Smith (Brenda Sykes), who is academically at the top of her class, has an upscale lifestyle provided by her physician father (William Marshall), and she associates with her own group at school. At first Sheila is hesitant about the advances of this "honky." (She tells a friend, "Hell man, I don't underrate him, I ignore him.") When Divine and Sheila start falling in love, they each learn more about bigotry and discover how wide the generation gap is between each of them and their parents. Divine's parents (John Lasell, Marion Ross) are racist, and as for Sheila's affluent father, she confides to a friend, "Once a year he goes South to see his family.... [He's] the most hung up spade in the country." Sheila takes her new boyfriend to a black club, and he is confused by the smart talk, the ethnic jokes and everything else about the place. Before long the two withdraw money from Divine's father's bank account to buy a stash of marijuana from a pusher (Lincoln Kilpatrick), which they hope will finance their leaving town. They are helped along the way by Sheila's girlfriend (Maia Danziger), who has far more than a platonic interest in her black friend. When their money runs out in Omaha, they start hitchhiking to California. On the road Divine is beaten up by two white thugs and Sheila is raped.

The seduction scene between the two leads has a near-lyrical quality, bolstered by Quincy Jones's score and Billy Preston singing "Hey Girl." The film makes every effort to be hip about racial equality and to "reveal" that these teenagers are typical potheads of the early seventies. The cast is filled with performers on the rise. Brenda Sykes had appeared in such films as *The Liberation of L.B. Jones* (1970) (q.v.) and would go on to such features as *Black Gunn* (1972) and *Cleopatra Jones* (1973) (qq.v.) and to co-star in such teleseries as "Ozzie's Girls" (1973) and "Executive Suite" (1976–77). Urbane William Marshall would become the screen's *Blacula* (1972) (q.v.); Marion Ross (definitely not the apple-pie Mom here) would co-star as Marian Cunningham in the television sitcom classic "Happy Days" (1974–84); John Hillerman would be Jonathan Quale Higgins III of "Magnum, P.I." (1980–88); Lincoln Kilpatrick performed in several black action features and would be Detective Lieutenant Michael Hoyt on "Matt Houston" (1983–85); and veteran character actor John Fiedler, of the high-pitched voice, would be Mr. Peterson on "The Bob Newhart Show" (1973–78) and Woody on "Buffalo Bill" (1983–84).

Honky was filmed on location in Kansas City and in several southern California settings.

117. The House on Skull Mountain (Twentieth Century-Fox, 1974). Color, 89 minutes.

Executive producer Joe R. Hartsfield; *producer* Ray Storey; *co-producer* Tom Boutross; *associate producers* Monroe Askins, Albert Shepard; *director* Ron Honthaner; *screenplay* Midred Pares; *art director* James Newport; *set decorator* Dorothy Growe; *music* Jerrold Immel; *songs* Ruth Talmadge, Art Freeman, John Susan Welsh, Jaime Mendoza-Nava; *assistant director* Stephen P. Dunn; *sound* Bill Oliver; *camera* Askins; *editor* Gerard Wilson.

Cast: Victor French (Andrew Cunningham); Janee Michelle (Lorena Christophe); Jean Durand (Thomas); Mike Evans (Phillippe); Xernona Clayton (Harriet Johnson); Lloyd Nelson (Sheriff); Ella Woods (Louette); Mary J. Todd McKenzie (Pauline); Don Devendorf (Priest); Jo Marie (Doctor); Senator Leroy Johnson (Lawyer LeDoux).

"A black disaster epic ought to be the next project for rip-off entrepreneurs, now that we've had black carbon copies of almost every other kind of formula pic. This one ... is an anthology of horror film cliches" *(Variety)*.

On a dark rainy night with the lightning crackling, trouble is afoot at the hilltop manse. Pauline (Mary J. Todd McKenzie) lies dying and a quartet of relatives have come from afar to learn the contents of her will. Thomas (Jean Durand) the butler is a menacing presence who practices voodoo on the side. By the time Lorena Christophe (Janee Michelle) is left as the only beneficiary to survive, she and Andrew Cunningham (Victor French), who has learned there is black blood in his heritage, have fallen in love.

The House on Skull Mountain was filmed on location in Georgia at a cost of $350,000 (with financing by a group of black Atlanta businessmen). Georgia State Senator Leroy Johnson has a brief cameo role as LeDoux, the attorney who reads the will. This slack film was the directing debut of Ron Honthaner, the former associate producer of the "Gunsmoke" teleseries. The film's executive producer, Joe R. Hartsfield, had been a publicist on that same TV Western. Mike Evans would gain far more recognition as Lionel Jefferson of "All in the Family" and "The Jeffersons" and would be the co-creator of the spinoff series "Good Times" (1974–79).

118. The Human Tornado (Dimension, 1976). Color, 87 minutes.

Executive producer Rudy Ray Moore; *co-producer* Theodore Toney; *director* Cliff Roquemore; *screenplay* Jerry Jones; *set designers* Moore, Jimmy Lunch; *makeup* Marie Carter; *music* Arthur Wright; *assistant director* Cassius

Weathersby; *special effects* Harry Woolman; *camera* Bob Wilson, Gene Conde.

Cast: Rudy Ray Moore (The Dolemite); Lady Reed (Queen Bee); Jimmy Lynch (Mr. Motion); Howard Jackson (Himself); Gloria de Lani (Hurricane Annie); Jerry Jones (Pete); Java (Java); J.D. Baron (Sheriff); Jack Kelly (Captain Ryan); Herb Graham (Vince Cavalerri); Barbara Geri (Mrs. Cavalerri); James Cromartie (Jimmy); Louis Hudson (Bo); Ed Montgomery (Dough); Peachs Jones (T.C.); Freddie De Fox, Li'ly Nighten Gale (Maitre 'ds); Kathryn Hayes (Madam); *and:* John Alda, Xavier Chatman Dancers, Crey Colebrook, James Fouratt, Iola Henry, Rubert Huereta, Cesar January, Ray Johnson, Bob Rosenbaum, Fred Saunders, Doug Senior, Billy Watkins, Laurence Welcome, Gwendolyn Westbrook, O.C. Wilson.

A.K.A. *Dolemite II.*

"Nerve-Shattering. Brain-Battering. Mind-Splattering. A One Man Disaster!" So boasted the ad copy for this follow-up to 1975's *The Dolemite,* which had grossed a surprising $1,100,000 in domestic film rentals. The sequel also starred ex-boxer-turned-bawdy-nightclub-comedian Rudy Ray Moore and was as casually constructed as the original.

For the original *Dolemite,* Rudy Ray Moore served as co-producer, leading man, and even set decorator. The series opener was directed by co-star D'Urville Martin. The poorly constructed actioner focuses on the Dolemite (Rudy Ray Moore), a combination club owner/pimp/entertainer, who after release from prison (on a frame-up) decides to clean up his community of outside criminal influences. Helping him is his madame friend (Lady Reed). *Variety* noted that this film may be "...the first one to make use of massage parlors as a front for crime. The promise of something new in sending hookers to karate school never really pans out as the gals fail to perform to any impressive degree." Of this 91-minute feature, Linda Gross *(Los Angeles Times)* panned, "The film is shoddily made.... Jerry Jones' script lacks cohesion, logic and authenticity. D'Urville Martin directs without vigor or authority and the actors walk through their parts without conviction or ability."

The further adventures of the jive-talking super stud, *Human Tornado* opens with a long cinema verite monologue as the Dolemite spews forth one of his bathroom humor nightclub routines ("You and that man getting into bed to do your thing is mission impossible"). Then the real action begins. He is caught in bed with the voluptuous wife of the white hillbilly sheriff in Citronella, Alabama. She is shot dead by the deputy and the Dolemite makes his bare-assed escape. He an his pals commandeer a car and head for California, where they are soon embroiled in gangland warfare. It seems the white hoodlums, led by a Godfather type (Herb Graham), want to shut down the too-popular black nightclub run by Queen Bee (Lady Reed), one of the Dolemite's good friends. Later the Dolemite and his kung-fu-kicking pals rescue a pair of kidnap victims (including Lady Java). The streets of the ghetto are safe once again. An epilogue finds the Dolemite being gunned down, but then after his assailants leave, he revives, unbuttons his bullet-proof vest, and says into the camera's eye, "This mother-fucker thinks I'm dead. He don't know I'm the Human Tornado." Finis.

This crudely constructed outing unravels like a self-endorsement for the humor and sexual prowess of its star. His opening monologue is a succession of dirty jokes aimed at a blue collar audience, and thereafter the hotshot human tornado provides a visual endorsement of his way with women. "Ooh, Dolemite," moans the sheriff's pliant wife, "you're worth evey cent I pay for you." Obviously having heard all this before, the stud mumbles, "Let's get this shit over with. I don't have all day." When he combats the law enforcers in a gun battle, there is no contest. He is too smart and swift to be caught by the honkies and easily escapes. And so it goes as he and his cohorts strut into Los Angeles ready to tackle anyone or anything.

If inner city urban audiences found these basic and raw escapades amusing, critics did not. "A crude tasteless film like *The Human Tornado* doesn't happen all by itself. Somebody put a lot of effort into creating something so revolting" (Damielle Spencer, *Los Angeles Free Press*). "In the fight and chase sequences, shots are randomly paced, and often linger on characters frozen in motion awaiting the arrival of a punch or car crash. Continuity is virtually nonexistent . . . characters change clothing faster than a chameleon changes color" (Barry J. Prebula, *The Hollywood Reporter*).

For the uninitiated, the sexy Lady Java in the film is played by female impersonator Lord Java. The film's screenwriter, Jerry Jones, appears as a detective.

119. I Escaped from Devil's Island (United Artists, 1973).
Color, 87 minutes.

Producers Roger Corman, Gene Corman; *director* William Witney; *screenplay* Richard L. Adams; *art director* Roberto Silva; *set decorator* Jose Gonzalez; *music* Les Baxter; *assistant directors* Jaime Contreras, Cliff Bush; *sound* Jose Carles; *camera* Rosalio Solano; *editors* Alan Collins, Tom Walls, Barbara Pokras.

Cast: Jim Brown (Le Bras); Christopher George (Davert); Rick Ely (Jo-Jo); Richard Rust (Zamorra).

Sometimes black action pictures — or at least films starring black actors — broke away from ghetto dramas to other more exotic locales for their drama. *I Escaped from Devil's Island* (the film's title is the most imaginative element of this sour production) is an example. Set in 1918 at the notorious French penal colony, it exploits Jim Brown's sagging box-office status in a cheap story of two convicts (rebellious Brown and pacifistic Christopher George) who revolt against the inhumanities of prison compound life and make a break through the jungle with the guards pursuing.

Shot in the Philippines, *Variety* rated it ". . . a slovenly, gamy potboiler."

120. If He Hollers, Let Him Go (Cinerama, 1968). Color, 111 minutes.
Producer Charles Martin; *associate producers* John W. Rogers, Harry Kaye; *director/screenplay* Martin; *art director* James W. Sullivan; *set decorator* Dick Pefferie; *wardrobe* Forrest T. Butler, Sharon E. Swenson; *music/music director* Harry Sukman; *songs* Sammy Fain and Charles Martin; Coleridge-Taylor Perkinson; *choreography* James Hibbard; *assistant directors*

Raymond St. Jacques and Barbara McNair in *If He Hollers, Let Him Go* **(1968).**

Victor Vallejo, Michael Schoenbrun; *sound* Al Cuesta; *special effects* Justus Gibbs; *camera* William W. Spencer; *editor* Richard Brockway.

Cast: Dana Wynter (Ellen Whitlock); Raymond St. Jacques (James Lake); Kevin McCarthy (Leslie Whitlock); Barbara McNair (Lily Lake); Arthur O'Connell (Prosecutor); John Russell (Sheriff); Ann Prentiss (Thelma); Royal Dano (Carl Blair); Susan Seaforth (Sally Blair); Steve Sandor (Harry); James Craig (Police Chief); Don Newsome (William Lake); Gregg Palmer (Special Officer); James McEachin (Defense Counsel); Don Megowan (Officer); Chet Stratton (Jackson the Pilot); Edward Schaaf (Henry Wilson); Dort Falkenberg (Gas Station Attendant); Jason Johnson (Truck Driver); James H. Drake (Deputy); Pepper Martin (Prison Guard); Frank Gerstle (Sergeant); E.A. Sirianni (Doctor); Todd Martin (Officer); Harold J. Kennedy (Judge); Jon Lormer (Chaplain); Ed Cook (Officer); Mimi Gibson (Marion).

Black convict James Lake (Raymond St. Jacques), falsely sentenced for rape and murder, escapes from prison and meets wealthy Leslie Whitlock (Kevin McCarthy). The latter wants to use him to murder his wife, Ellen (Dana Wynter), but Lake instead tries to warn the heiress and then bolts. Later he returns and makes the Whitlocks drive him to their mountain lodge, where he tricks the husband into revealing his homicidal plot. He and Ellen flee to his brother's house, where he discovers his one-time girlfriend, nightclub singer Lily (Barbara McNair), is now his sister-in-law. With Lily's assistance Lake proves that the victim he was once accused of murdering was actually killed by her stepfather (Royal Dano). In a final scuffle when Whitlock arrives with the police, the wealthy man is killed. Ellen agrees to help clear Lake's criminal record.

If He Hollers, Let Him Go! (which has nothing to do with the Chester Himes detective novel of the same title) is a very confusingly scripted potboiler. It is elevated only by the steady characterizations of Raymond St. Jacques, Barbara McNair (in her screen debut), and Dana Wynter. Its hack plotline weaves back and forth with too many flashbacks, and its narrative proves to be at cross-purposes with itself continuously. Many of the supporting performers chew the scenery unmercifully. But what gave the film its topicality and box-office relevance was its black co-leads functioning and fumbling in a white-controlled society. As *Variety* assessed, "Plot derailment and meller climax relegate the Cinerama release to programmer status, but racial and sexual issues make for some strong selling values...." Raymond St. Jacques stated it more succinctly when he was asked about this film in an *Ebony* magazine interview in October 1969: "...artistically it was a fake, but the 'brothers' loved it because I kicked hell out of a white man." (Raymond St. Jacques was born in 1930 and began his acting career with the American Shakespeare Festival in Stratford, Connecticut. After his screen debut in *Black Like Me* [1964] he became a frequent screen performer.)

To be noted is Barbara McNair's fine singing of "Can't Make It with the Same Man Twice," "A Man Has to Love," and "So Tired."

121. In the Heat of the Night (United Artists, 1967).
Color, 109 minutes.

Producer Walter Mirisch; *director* Norman Jewison; *based on the novel by* John Dudley Ball; *screenplay* Stirling Silliphant; *art director* Paul Groesse; *set decorator* Robert Priestley; *makeup* Del Armstrong; *costumes* Alan Levine; *music* Quincy Jones; *song* Jones, Marilyn Bergman, and Alan Bergman; *assistant directors* Terry Morse, Jr., Newt Arnold; *sound* Walter Goss, Clem Portman, Charles Cooper, Kevin Cleary; *camera* Haskell Wexler; *editor* Hal Ashby.

Cast: Sidney Poitier (Virgil Tibbs); Rod Steiger (Sheriff Bill Gillespie); Warren Oates (Sam Wood); Quentin Dean (Delores Purdy); James Patterson (Purdy); William Schallert (Webb Schubert); Jack Teter (Philip Colbert); Lee Grant (Mrs. Leslie Colbert); Scott Wilson (Harvey Oberst); Matt Clark (Packy Harrison); Anthony James (Ralph Henshaw); Larry Gates (Eric Endicott); Kermit Murdock (H.E. Henderson); Khalil Bezaleel (Jess); Beah Richards (Mrs. Bellamy [Mama Caleba]); Peter Whitney (George Courtney); William Watson (Harold Courtney); Timothy Scott (Shagbag Martin); Michael LeGlaire (Dennis); Larry D. Mann (Watkins); Stewart Nisbet (Shuie); Eldon Quick (Charlie Hawthorn); Fred Stewart (Dr. Stuart); Arthur Malet (Ted Ulam); Peter Masterson (Arnold Fryer); Alan Oppenheimer (Ted Appleton); Philip Garris (Mark Crowell); Jester Hairston (Henry); Clegg Hoyt (Deputy); Phil Adams, Nikita Knatz (Young Toughs); David Stinehart (Baggage Master); Buzz Barton (Conductor).

See summary under *In the Heat of the Night* (NBC-TV, 3/6/88).

122. In the Heat of the Night (NBC-TV, 3/6/88). Color, 100 minutes.
Executive producers Juanita Bartlett, Fred Silverman; *producer* Hugh Benson; *director* David Hemmings; *suggested by the novel by* John Dudley

Ball *and the original screenplay by* Stirling Silliphant; *teleplay* James Lee Barrett; *production designer* Bill Hiney; *music* Dick DeBenedictis; *sound* Glenn Anderson; *camera* Brianne Murphy; *editor* Jack Harnish.

Cast: Carroll O'Connor (Chief Bill Gillespie); Howard E. Rollins, Jr. (Virgil Tibbs); Alan Autry (Bubba Skinner); Anne-Marie Johnson (Althea Tibbs); Christian Le Blanc (Junior Abernathy); David Hart (Parker Williams); Hugh O'Connor (Jamison); Peter Gabb (Horace Goode); Dennis Lipscomb (Mayor Findley); Doug Savant (Scott LaPeer); Kevin McCarthy (Harold LaPeer); Mills Watson (Dr. Bridges); David Harris (Willie Jones); Jill Carroll (Barbara); Maggie Blye (Dee); *and:* Robert Adams, J. Kevin Brune, Chuck Hicks, Dave Petitjean, Carol Sutton, John Wilmot.

> SHERIFF GILLESPIE: Got a name boy?
> VIRGIL TIBBS: Virgil Tibbs.
> GILLESPIE: Virgil . . . well. *(Chews gum meditatively)* I don't think we're goin' to have any trouble, are we, Virgil?
> TIBBS: *(Quietly burning inside)* No trouble at all.
> GILLESPIE: What's a northern boy doin' down here?

It is a hot September night in Sparta, Mississippi, a small cotton town "owned" by aristocratic local cotton plantation owner Eric Endicott (Larry Gates). Policeman Sam Wood (Warren Oates) has discovered the body of wealthy northern industrialist Leslie Colbert (Jack Teter), who was constructing a factory in town. It is clear the victim had been beaten to death and then robbed. At the train station Wood notices a solitary black man and arrests him — on nothing more substantial than he is a black stranger in town.

Down at the station house, middle-aged white Sheriff Bill Gillespie (Rod Steiger) insists, "I try to run a nice, clean safe town here." The newly appointed sheriff is as redneck as they come, full of misconceptions and overblown self-esteem. It confounds him to realize that not only is the arrested black man Virgil Tibbs (Sidney Poitier), an experienced police officer from Philadelphia's homicide division, but he earns $200 more a month than Gillespie (who had thought life was pretty good on $162.39 per week). Because the arrogant Gillespie is a complex man, another side of him is impressed by Tibbs's credentials, an almost unspeakable concept given Gillespie's general frame of reference in the Deep South. "No sir, I'm not prejudiced," Gillespie insists when he calls the Philadelphia police to confirm Tibbs's background. But he obviously is, or at least a part of him is. Before long Gillespie lets down some of his defenses (but never in front of his subordinates) to admit that homicide is *not* his specialty and that (in a backhanded way) he would be grateful for whatever assistance Tibbs can supply. He tricks the prideful black man into accepting the case. "You're so damn smart . . . smarter than any white man. . . . I don't think you could let an opportunity like that pass by." (It occurs to Gillespie that if the more quick-witted Tibbs fails in his special assignment, Gillespie can place the blame conveniently on the out-of-towner.)

With Tibbs (un)officially on the case, the northerner confronts the wealthy Endicott in the man's greenhouse. When tempers run rampant, the leading citizen is aghast at being questioned by a black man, and he slaps Tibbs for his

Sidney Poitier and Rod Steiger in *In the Heat of the Night* (1967).

impertinent interrogation. Tibbs returns the gesture in kind. Later several white youths come after Tibbs in a deserted warehouse. "Okay, black boy. We came here to teach you some manners." He barely escapes harm. (The town's blacks are agog at the newcomer's audaciousness and generally ignore him.) The investigation quickly teaches Tibbs a great deal about his own set of prejudices against rich whites as he proceeds methodically with the hunt for the murderer, always with nagging, intuitively observant Gillespie trailing at his heels. The clues lead to a randy teenager, Delores Purdy (Quentin Dean), who claims to be pregnant and blames policeman Wood. Tibbs finds the local abortionist, Mama Caleba (Beah Richards), and while he is talking with her, Delores and her hot-headed boyfriend, Ralph Henshaw (Anthony James), arrive. In a confrontation, Henshaw admits he is the killer. The case over, Gillespie kindly goes with Tibbs to the train station, even carrying his bag.

> GILLESPIE: Bye, bye. Virgil, you take care, you hear.
> TIBBS: *(Shyly)* Yeah.

The two men's lives will never be the same. Each has grown tremendously from knowing the other.

John Dudley Ball's 1965 novel served as the basis for this motion picture, which won five Oscars: Best Picture, Best Actor (Rod Steiger — Sidney Poitier was not even nominated), Best Screenplay, Best Sound, Best Editing. In addition it was nominated for Academy Awards for Best Direction and Best Sound Effects. The feature grossed a staggering $10,910,000 in domestic film rentals, consolidating Sidney Poitier's tremendous box-office appeal. It also led to two further, somewhat diluted big screen adventures of Virgil Tibbs with Sidney

Poitier: *They Call Me Mister Tibbs!* (1970) and *The Organization* (1971) (qq.v.), and a telefeature/series (1988) (see below).

In its day *In the Heat of the Night* was considered a landmark movie of integration. Although its depiction of police detective investigation was unexceptional, its characterizations were outstanding. Rod Steiger has never been better in a role and, for a change, Sidney Poitier's character was not entirely super-noble (he was bigoted in his fashion about whites). There was kinetic Mrs. Leslie Colbert (Lee Grant) in a cameo as the distraught widow of the murder victim who senses the intelligence and expertise of the black policeman's character; the old guard southerner Eric Endicott (Larry Gates); the pedestrian, not-so-bright deputy Sam Wood (Warren Oates); the frenetic, bumbling wrongdoer Harvey Oberst (Scott Wilson); and several others. They and the underlying racial tensions are what keep the film alive and worth watching more than two decades later.

The critics were duly impressed. "*In the Heat of the Night* is an American movie of great distinction.... Sidney Poitier adds a new dimension to the Noble Negro he has been portraying recently, providing a streak of bigotry and tension that gives superb complement to Steiger. Theirs is a remarkable duet" (Judith Crist, NBC-TV "Today Show"). "A film that is as fresh as this one deserves to be seen by fresh eyes and savored by fresh minds" (Joseph Morgenstern, *Newsweek* magazine). "Poitier is by no means cinema's only Negro star, but because of his many films and fine performances, he is certainly the pace setter.... The great advantage of *In the Heat of the Night,* not only for Sidney Poitier but everyone else connected with the project, is that it is a good movie" (Philip T. Hartung, *Commonweal* magazine).

With Sidney Poitier having made this cross-over movie in yet another genre, the path was clear for the black action cycle to take the next steps and reproduce the black law enforcer dealing in a white man's world for many other (usually lesser effort) films, telefilms, and TV series.

It was 21 years after the original motion picture that NBC-TV debuted a two hour movie-for-television adaptation, starring small-screen star Carroll O'Connor (the arch-bigot of "All in the Family") and Howard E. Rollins, Jr. (who had made a hit in *Ragtime* [1981] and *A Soldier's Story* [1984] and had appeared on television in such offerings as *Roots: The Next Generation* [1979] and the short-lived western series "Wildside" [1985]). The television feature was shot on location in Hammond, Louisiana.

In the telefeature Virgil Tibbs (Howard E. Rollins, Jr.) returns to Sparta, Mississippi, for his mother's funeral. He is accompanied by his wife (Anne-Marie Johnson). "Well Virgil. It's been a few years," says Chief Bill Gillespie (Carroll O'Connor) when he spots the Tibbses leaving church. Before long the town's mayor (Dennis Lipscomb) appoints Tibbs Chief of Detectives, and Tibbs and the chagrined Gillespie are squared off to solve together or separately the murder of a local high school girl, with a suspect being a black youth. In the midst of their investigation they must deal with the murder of a black prisoner (David Harris) and the interference of an opinionated old-time southerner (Kevin McCarthy) and his feckless son Scott (Doug Savant).

"Leaving well enough alone has never been one of television's admirable traits," complained Miles Beller *(The Hollywood Reporter)*. He added, ". . . one can only marvel about TV's tendency to reinvent the wheel as a square whenever it 'redoes' erstwhile movies and previously presented programming." As the two leads, ". . . O'Connor and Rollins play the push-pull relationship adequately enough, stereotypes with facets."

Daily Variety concluded: "Gillespie has softened considerably in the hands of O'Connor, whose Archie Bunker occasionally appears spectre-like but then vanishes. . . . Rollins' study of Tibbs, less commanding than Poitier's, has his strengths, but that element of rage lurking inside has been all but doused. It's a thoughtful, consistent interp, and fits the smaller screen."

The new *In the Heat of the Night* was the pilot excursion for the weekly hour series starring O'Connor and Rollins, which debuted shortly thereafter to middling audience response.

123. Iron Eagle (Tri-Star, 1986). Color, 119 minutes.

Executive producer Kevin Elders; *producers* Ron Samuels, Joe Wizan; *associate producer* Lou Lenart; *director* Sidney J. Furie; *screenplay* Elders, Furie; *production designer* Robb Wilson King; *art department supervisor* Ariel Roshko; *set decorators* Nancy Nye, David Varod; *costume designer* Rochelle Zaltman; *makeup* Karen Kubeck, Claudia Thompson, Zivit Yakir; *music* Basil Poledouris; *music co-ordinator* Leslie Morris; *orchestrator* Steven Scott Smalley; *music editor* Ken Johnson; *second unit director* James W. Gavin; *assistant directors* Alan C. Blomquist, Elie Cohn, Richard Graves, Sharon Shamir, Baruch Abulof, Larry Powell, Stan Zabka; *supervising sound editor* Keith Stafford; *sound editor* G.W. Davis, Don Isaac, Dick LeGrand, Anthony Ippolito, Leon Selditz; *sound* Dan Wallin, Bill Nelson, Eli Yarkony; *sound re-recording* Don MacDougall, John Mack, Richard Tyler; *technical adviser* M. Hodd; *stunt co-ordinators* Mike Rynyard, Chris Howell; *special aerial stunts* Art Scholl; *crowd marshal* Zeev Zigler; *special effects* Ken Pepiot, Varod; *camera* Adam Greenberg; *aerial camera* Frank Holgate; *editor* George Grenville.

Cast: Louis Gossett, Jr. (Colonel "Chappy" Sinclair); Jason Gedrick (Doug Masterson); David Suchet (Minister of Defense); Tim Thomerson (Ted Masterson); Larry B. Scott (Reggie); Caroline Lagerfelt (Elizabeth); Jerry Levine (Tony); Robbie Rist (Milo); Michael Bowen (Knotcher); Bobby Jacoby (Matthew); Melora Hardin (Katie); David Greelee (Kingsley); Michael Alldredge (Colonel Blackburn); Tom Fridley (Brillo); Rob Garrison (Packer); Chino "Fats" Williams (Slappy); Jay Footlik (Thatcher); Jacque Lynn Colton (Hazel); Shawnee Smith (Joanie); Heather De Vore Haase (Tally); Kathy Wagner (Amy); Kevin King (Farnsworth); Will Jeffries (Smithey); David Ward (Lieutenant Colonel Kerns); Terry Wills (Tally's Father); F. William Parker (Kingsley's Father); Albert R. Schara (Principal); Christopher Bradley (Airman); Michael Kehoe (Flight Control Officer); Steve Rabin (Air Policeman); Kevin Elders (Pilot); Tony Becker (Guard at Intelligence Center); Paul O'Brien Richards (Guard at Gate); Lance LeGault (General); Max Thayer (Intelligence Officer); Debbie Bloch (Family Friend); Roger Nolan (TV Reporter); Jerry Hyman (Marty); Uri Gabriel (Bilyad Guard); David Menachem (Bilyad Officer);

Yossi Shiloah (Tower Official); Itzik Saydof (Tower Worker); Arnon Zadok (Il Kharem Soldier).

For Louis [Lou] Gossett, Jr., it was a far cry, professionally, from the days of *The Skin Game* (1971) and its TV remake, *Sidekicks* (1974) (qq.v.), to *Iron Eagle* in 1986. In the interim, the Broadway actor (*Take a Giant Step, Lost in the Stars, A Raisin in the Sun, Carry Me Back to Morningside Heights,* others) had been featured in TV series ("The Young Rebels," "The Lazarus Syndrome," "The Powers of Matthew Star"), won an Emmy for Best Actor in a Drama Series for *Roots* (1977), and starred as Anwar Sadat in the 1983 miniseries *Sadat.* He had been cast in such features as *The Landlord* (1970), *White Dawn* (1974), *The Laughing Policeman* (1974), *Jaws 3-D* (1983), and the underrated science fiction extravaganza *Enemy Mine* (1985). Most importantly he had won an Academy Award as hardened Marine drill officer Sergeant Foley in *An Officer and a Gentleman* (1982) opposite Richard Gere. At the age of 46 he was finally a bankable box-office figure.

Iron Eagle represents how far black action films had traveled since their heyday in the early 1970s. No longer was having a black lead considered a big deal that must be explained away in the script or even self-consciously ignored. It was just there. Sometimes the fact would silently provide texture to the ensemble, adding dimension to the characterization of the (co)star, and the player's interaction with others on camera.

Such was the case with *Iron Eagle,* a right-wing escapist fantasy yarn in the *Rambo* tradition that garnered $10,000,000 in domestic film rentals. There was absolutely no logic to this derivative, flag-waving adventure, but audiences apparently did not mind at all. "It's certainly a change to see a kid determined to rescue his captive father instead of sitting around with the gang and moaning about how the old man mistreated him" *(Variety).*

In flight near a small Arab state, United States Air Force pilot Ted Masterson (Tim Thomerson) is shot down for supposedly infringing on their air space. He is captured and sentenced to hang in three days. The United States State Department is engulfed in bureaucratic red tape, which persuades Masterson's teenage son, Doug (Jason Gedrick), back at Beeker Air Force base to take decisive action. (He has just been told that his bid for the pilot training program has been rejected because of poor grades, although he is a crackerjack at simulation flight.) When he can persuade no government or military official to help save his father, he organizes his friends into stealing necessary reconnaissance information about the fortress where his father is being held. He persuades retired Colonel "Chappy" Sinclair (Louis [Lou] Gossett, Jr.), who has had twenty-two years in the service, to team with him on a two-man rescue mission. Thanks again to Doug's ingenious friends, the team "borrows" two F-16 fighter jets to use on the mission. Before they depart on their dangerous trek, Sinclair hands Doug a cassette tape, telling him to play it only if anything happens to Sinclair. The two attack the Arab air base successfully, but Sinclair is shot down. Doug plays the tape, which "talks" him through the remainder of the mission. After downing some of the enemy aircraft he lands on the runway to pick up his father. American fighter jets appear on the scene to hold off the pursuing craft, allowing Doug and his father to reach safety. They learn

Sinclair was picked up in Egyptian waters when he bailed out. The top brass United States government officials trade the team's silence for gaining Doug admission into the United States Air Force Academy.

"The rescue attempt is hardly believable, but the aerial scenes (shot over Israel using Israeli Air Force planes) have to be some of the flashiest ever filmed. And it's a treat to hear Gossett reel off such teeth-clenched lines as 'There's somethin' about maniacs messing with good men that always pisses me off.' . . . When director Sidney *(The Entity)* Furie yelled 'action' on this one, he meant it. This is a fast-moving, chauvinist's delight, corny enough in its macho posturing to be a real crowd pleaser" *(People* magazine).

The success of *Iron Eagle* naturally led filmmakers to do *Iron Eagle II* (1988).

124. J.D.'s Revenge (American International, 1976).
Color, 95 minutes.

Producer/director Arthur Marks; *screenplay* Jason Starkes; *music* Robert Prince; *song* Prince and Joseph A. Greene; *assistant director* Lee Rafner; *camera* Harry May; *editor* George Folsey, Jr.

Cast: Glynn Turman (Ike); Joan Pringle (Christella); Lou [Louis] Gossett, Jr. (Reverend Bliss); Carl Crudup (Tony); James Louis Watkins (Carl); Alice Jubert (Roberta/Betty Jo); Stephanie Faulkner (Phyllis); Fred Pinkard (Theotis); Fuddle Bagley (Enoch); Jo Anne Meredith (Sarah); David McKnight (J.D. Walker).

Life is difficult enough as it is without being possessed by the spirit of a dead gangster. Such is the fate of the lead character in *J.D.'s Revenge,* yet another distillation of the evil spirit possession theme of *The Exorcist* (1973), this time slanted to black audiences.

In a 1942 New Orleans slaughterhouse, J.D. Walker (David McKnight) indulges in murdering two victims in a family feud. The action jumps forward to the present, where dedicated law student Ike (Glynn Turman) finds himself being absorbed into the spirit and personality of the deceased J.D. Walker. The Jekyll-and-Hyde changes affect not only how he thinks, but how he dresses (zoot suits, a handy razor, etc.), where he hangs out (now the sleazy dives of skid row), and how he reacts to others. Ike/J.D. Walker wants revenge on revivalist minister Bliss (Lou [Louis] Gossett, Jr.), who had a part in the 1942 fatal events, and not even Ike's wife, Christella (Joan Pringle), nor the passengers of the taxi he drives are safe from his bizarre, violent behavior. Others caught up in the nightmarish web are Bliss's crooked brother Theotis (Fred Pinkard) and Theotis's sensual niece (Alice Jubert).

"Has enough offbeat elements to make it stand on it own," weighed *Variety,* who added, "This film is marred by too many cutaways to bloody doings in the slaughter-house and some corny trick shots of the dead gangster haunting Turman, but it has a supple camera." The *New York Times'*s Lawrence Van Gelder was not impressed: ". . . an excessive reliance on repetitive scenes of gore and a proclivity for mistaking repulsive effects for frightening ones."

But audiences responded to the fine acting (especially by Glynn Turman and Lou Gossett), the brooding New Orleans locations with its southern Gothic

Top: **Jason Gedrick** *(left)* **and Louis Gossett, Jr., in** *Iron Eagle* **(1985).** *Bottom:* **Joan Pringle and Glynn Turman in** *J.D.'s Revenge* **(1976).**

atmosphere, the intriguing (if unoriginal) plot gimmick, and of course the center focus of blood and guts. J.D.'s *Revenge* grossed a substantial $2,400,000 in domestic film rentals.

Glynn Turman and Joan Pringle had appeared together the same year in *Cooley High* (1976) (q.v.), and director Arthur Marx was no stranger to turning out noteworthy black action dramas such as *Detroit 9000* (1973), *Bucktown* (1975), *Friday Foster* (1975), and *The Monkey Hustle* (1976) (qq.v.).

125. Jimmy the Kid (New World, 1982). Color, 85 minutes.

Executive producers Harry Evans Sloan, Lawrence L. Kuppin; *producer* Ronald Jacobs; *director* Gary Nelson; *based on the novel by* Donald E. Westlake; *screenplay* Sam Bobrick; *music* John Cameron; *assistant director* Donald Robert.

Cast: Gary Coleman (Jimmy Lovejoy); Paul LeMat (John); Dee Wallace [Stone] (May); Don Adams (Harry Walker); Walter Olkewicz (Andrew Kelp); Ruth Gordon (Bernice Kelp); Cleavon Little (Herb Lovejoy); Fay Hauser (Nina Lovejoy); Avery Schreiber (Dr. Stevens); Pat Morita (Maurice).

The pint-sized (a result of a defective kidney at birth) but super-achieving black actor Gary Coleman (born February 8, 1968, in Zion, Illinois) not only starred in the sitcom television series "Diff'rent Strokes" (1978–86) as the irrepressible Arnold Jackson, but made frequent excursions into telefeatures and motion pictures. He did this often with the hope of expanding his acting range and audience. *Jimmy the Kid* was such an effort, borrowing heavily from the O. Henry short story "The Ransom of Red Chief."

Jimmy Lovejoy (Gary Coleman) is the precocious offspring of Herb (Cleavon Little) and Nina (Fay Hauser), a riding-high country music act. Lame-brained punk John (Paul LeMat), fat Andrew Kelp (Walter Olkewicz), John's testy mama (Ruth Gordon), and flakey May (Dee Wallace [Stone]) team together to kidnap Jimmy for a large ransom. With fumbling detective Harry Walker (Don "Get Smart" Adams) brought in to solve the caper, the slapstick action is very broad and juvenile. Before the film fades, the crooks have reevaluated their career paths, Jimmy's parents learn to appreciate their child, and Jimmy, who has had a ball outwitting and outmaneuvering everyone, takes stock of his pampered, too-adult self and decides being a kid is what he is and should be doing.

"Usually, kidnapping isn't too funny, and neither is New World's pickup vehicle, *Jimmy the Kid,* usually.... There's enough going on to intrigue and tickle the younger viewing segment, despite questionable subject matter and smatterings of anatomy language" *(Variety).* Thanks to Gary Coleman's popularity with younger filmgoers, this PG rated film earned $2,600,000 in domestic film rentals.

126. Joe's Bed-Stuy Barbershop: We Cut Heads
(First Run Features, 1983). Color, 60 minutes.

Producer Zimmie Shelton, Spike Lee; *director/screenplay* Spike Lee; *art director* Felix Deroy; *music* Bill Lee; *sound* Mark Quinlan; *camera* Ernest Dickerson; *editor* Spike Lee.

Cast: Monty Ross (Zachariah Homer); Donna Bailey (Ruth Homer); Stuart Smith (Teapot); Tommie Hicks (Nicholas Lovejoy); Horace Long (Joe Ballard); LeVerne Summer (Esquire); Africanus Rocius (Spinks); Robert Delbert (Fletcher); Alphonzo Lewis (Deacon); Christine Campbell (Hanna); William Badgett (Silas); Herbert Burks (True God); Vanita Taylor, Lynn Dummett (Jehovah's Witnesses); Loretta Craggett (Model); Curtis Brown (Photographer); Ahmad Carson (Squeeze); Carolyn Laws (Ms. Maxwell); Eric Wilkins (Man by Elevator).

Spike Lee rose to mainstream film prominence with *She's Got to Have It* (1986) and *School Daze* (1987), both of which impressed critics and audiences for their zany but thoughtful depiction of black culture. Lee made his professional motion picture debut as a filmmaker with *Joe's Bed-Stuy Barbershop: We Cut Heads* (1983), a 16mm production created to fulfill his master's thesis at New York University. Like Shirley Clarke's earlier *The Cool World* (1964), (q.v.), it provides a telling if flawed reflection of life and times on the ghetto streets.

When his partner dies, brooding Zack Homer (Monty Ross) is left in charge of their barbershop in Bedford-Stuyvesant, a black lower-middle-class section of Brooklyn, New York. Zack has old fashioned ideals; hates the new "faggoty" hair styles (so he does not get the younger customers his failing shop needs) and refuses to partake in the numbers racket ("the black man's Wall Street"), which could help keep the business open. The old-timers who hang out in the barbershop—their substitute for a neighborhood saloon—applaud Zack's uneconomical decisions, unlike the new breed of slick but vicious underworld figures inhabiting the community. Zack's college-bred, social worker wife Ruth (Donna Bailey) is convinced her husband should go with the new times (no matter what the ramifications), but a part of her admires his virtues, and she suggests they could move to Georgia to a farmhouse she inherited near Atlanta.

"There's certainly a small, resonant movie inside *Joe's Bed-Stuy Barbershop: We Cut Heads,* but it gets lost amid too plentiful and awkwardly executed ambitions" (Diane Jacobs, *Village Voice*). "Lee's secure comic sense is evident in the playful lulls when the characters jive each other or trade quips or dreams or their preferences in sneakers. Thanks to such moments, *We Cut Heads* is intermittently delightful" (Joseph Gelmis, *Newsday*).

The film's jazz score is by Spike Lee's father, bassist Bill Lee.

127. Johnnie Mae Gibson: FBI (CBS-TV, 10/21/86).

Color, 100 minutes.

Executive producers James S. Henderson, James G. Hirsch; *supervising producer* Deborah Ellis Leoni; *producer* Jim Begg; *associate producer* Vahan Moosekian; *director* Bill Duke; *teleplay* Hirsch; *art director* Gregory Melton; *set decorator* Michael Parker; *costumes* Giovanna Ottobre Melton; *music* Billy Goldenberg; *music editor* Jim Weidman; *assistant director* Charles Ziarko; *stunt co-ordinator* Robert Stephens; *sound* Dan Gleich; *supervising sound editor* Cathy Shorr; *camera* Hal Trussell; *editor* Jack Harnish.

Cast: Howard E. Rollins, Jr. (T.C. Russell); Richard Lawson (Adam

Prentice); William Allen Young (Marvin Gibson); John Lehne (Billy Whelan); Marta DuBois (Ginny Talbot); Lynn Whitfield (Johnnie Mae Gibson); Hugh Gillin (Phil Barnes); Henry G. Sanders (Al Melden); Veronica Redd (Momma Melden); Ed Lottimer (Neal Visser); Brian Degan Scott (Randy Abel); Johnny Weissmuller, Jr. (Agent Ed King); Robert Ford (Ed Brukoff); Abigail Van Alyn (Paulette Branzlik); Mia Simon (Tiffany Gibson); Frank Papia (Detective Wayne); Ajuana Harrison (Johnnie at Age Sixteen); Sandy Colton (Johnnie at Age Nine); Edward Faulkner (Tom Higgins); Cindy Herron (Gloria Powell); Karen Raff (Sherry); Eva Gholson (Brenda); Edward Blair (Wally Hubbard); James Brewster Thompson (Jackson); Peter Fitzsimmons (Larry Wansley); Frank Sheppard (Danny Arrilla); Jamila Jones (Clara Melden); Zorana Edun (Ruth Melden); Johnny Tidwell (Hotel Clerk); Adilah Barnes (Woman at Door); Robert Callahan (Edna Coglin); Vahan Moosekian (Waiter); James S. Henderson (Mr. Davis); Tiffany Gibson (T.C.'s Daughter); Badmi Bhanji (Voodoo Priestess); Pamela Goodwin, Delores Palmer, Karesia D. Thomas (Voodoo Dancers).

Johnnie Mae Gibson was the FBI's first black female agent. This is supposed to be her fact-filled story, but the opening credits advise "...due to the confidential nature of FBI operations ... actual cases are not portrayed."

The narrative opens in 1956 and traces the life and times of a young black girl named Johnnie Mae (Lynn Whitfield), who leaves her poor backwoods kinfolk, including her quick-tempered dad (Henry G. Sanders), to head out on her own. In Albany, Georgia, she meets and marries Marvin Gibson (William Allen Young). A few years later, without alerting her spouse, she joins the local police force, and thereafter signs on with the F.B.I. Before long she has left her family to fulfill her own goals. Married F.B.I. agent T.C. Russell (Howard E. Rollins) and Johnnie Mae both try to avoid becoming more than working partners when they go undercover to grab Miami gun-runners. Exhausted by the dangers and pressures of undercover work, Johnnie Mae later (1981) transfers to administrative work at the F.B.I. headquarters in Washington, D.C.

There are two central themes running throughout this small screen biography: 1) Can a woman be an F.B.I. operative and still retain her femininity with herself and others? 2) Can a black woman succeed in a white person's world? *Johnnie Mae Gibson: FBI* focuses a great deal of attention on the second question, but in very soft-pedaled terms. When Johnnie Mae announces she is to become a law enforcer, her bewildered insurance man husband is aghast, not only because she wants to wear the pants in the family, but because she intends to be a cop (still an unpleasant authority figure to blacks). "What kind of planet are you livin' on, black woman?" he asks. Later when she is on squad car patrol assignment she attempts to comfort a white woman victim, but the latter shrieks, "Do you think that just because you're wearing a blue suit, that gives you the right to lay your hands on white folk." The scenario lightly piles on such situations as Johnnie Mae survives the fourteen-week training course at the F.B.I. Academy in Quantico, Virginia. Her first real F.B.I. agent assignment is to trick a black woman into revealing the whereabouts of her black boyfriend wanted by the government agency. In a potentially telling sequence passed over too lightly by the hedging script, John-nie Mae relates how badly she felt arresting the man in a bar full of brothers and sisters who regarded her as the betrayer and the enemy. The am-I-still-a-desirable-female aspect comes into focus as Johnnie Mae loses her husband, who will not abide their too-frequent separations (when she is on assignment); when she reaches out to her black undercover partner (Howard E. Rollins) only to find he is married; and when she almost falls deeply in love with a handsome, caring black gun-runner (Richard Lawson), stepping back just in time to realize their two worlds can never mesh.

Johnnie Mae Gibson: FBI benefits from a strong supporting cast, especially Henry G. Sanders as her frustrated papa, Marta DuBois as her worldly F.B.I. Academy classmate, and especially Richard Lawson as the charismatic under-world figure she must arrest. The shame of the production is that it could have been so much more than just another gunplay narrative. "The Keystone Kops join the FBI in a 1930s-like telefilm," insisted *Daily Variety*. The trade paper's displeased reporter added, "The quick dash through the real Johnnie Mae Gib-son's life makes most of the men either weak or domineering, Johnnie Mae herself self-serving and probably unable to pass psychological requirements for the bureau." On the other hand, a more tolerant TV *Guide* magazine acknowledged that the direction is "deftly handled" and that Lynn Whitfield "gives a strong performance."

128. Joshua (Lone Star, 1976). Color, 80 minutes.

Producer/director Larry Spangler; *story/screenplay* Fred Williamson.

With: Fred Williamson, Isela Vega, Calvin Bartlett, Brenda Venus.

Fred Williamson's bouncy *Adios Amigo* (1976) (q.v.) obtained far greater notice than this rambling Western, also produced for the star's Po' Boy Pro-ductions. However, this time he allowed Larry Spangler, who had produced, directed, and conceived the stories for Williamson's *The Legend of Nigger Charley* (1972) and *The Soul of Nigger Charley* (1973) (qq.v.), to handle the producing and directing chores. It was not a wise decision.

Variety carped, "Plot is thin rendition of standard revenge scheme set in post–Civil War Period.... Williamson works hard ... to attain a 'presence,' complete with sparse, telegraphic dialog and ever-present cigar stub in mouth.... Despite R rating, item is relatively tame in the blood-and-guts and sex areas. Williamson fails to address so many questions in his script...."

When his mother, Martha, is shot by five desperadoes who also kill her employer and take off with the dead man's young wife, Joshua (Fred William-son)—fresh out of serving in the Union Army—pursues. One by one he kills his adversaries: one with a rattlesnake dropped from above, another with a knife, another by hanging, one by gunshot, and the final culprit by blowing up the cave in which he is hiding.

The production imitates Clint Eastwood's spaghetti westerns for Serge Leone in everything except the artistic and entertainment values. Fred William-son is the mysterious lone stranger out on a mission of revenge, cloaked in black and chewing on a cigar. He gives in to no one, although he does romance a Mexican woman along the way. But there is so much that is aimless in the film; and so many loopholes in the plot (why doesn't he finish off all the targeted men at one crack when he has multiple opportunities?) that every time one gets caught up in the story, interest wanes. And some of the dialogue is beyond trite: "You gotta have killing to have peace."

One noteworthy aspect of *Joshua,* besides its decent cinematography, is its unrelenting depiction of the loneliness, hostilities, and dangers a black man faced in the Old West. Wherever Joshua rides, because he is black he is regarded as a potentially troublesome character, one not to be trusted — one always to be an outsider.

129. Jumpin' Jack Flash (Twentieth Century–Fox, 1986). Color, 100 minutes.

Producers Lawrence Gordon, Joel Silver; *assistant producers* Richard Marks, George Owers, Elaine K. Thompson; *director* Penny Marshall; *story* David H. Franzoni; *screenplay* Franzoni, Patricia Irving, Christopher Thompson; *production designer* Robert Boyle; *art director* Frank Richwood; *set decorator* Donald Remacle; *costumes* Susan Becker; *makeup* Michael Germain; *music* Thomas Newman; *orchestrators* James Campbell, Armin Steiner; *stunts* Bennie E. Dobbins; *assistant directors* Beau E.L. Marks, K.C. Colwell, Michael Katleman; *computer effects* Steve Brumette; *special effects* Thomas Ryba; *camera* Matthew F. Leonetti; *editor* Mark Goldblatt.

Cast: Whoopi Goldberg (Terry Doolittle); Stephen Collins (Marty Phillips [Peter Kane]); John Wood (Jeremy Talbot); Carol Kane (Cynthia); Annie Potts (Liz Carlson); Peter Michael Goetz (Mr. Page); Roscoe Lee Browne (Archer Lincoln); Sara Botsford (Lady Sarah Billings); Jeroen Krabbe (Mark Van Meter); Vyto Ruginis (Carl); Jonathan Pryce (Jack); Tony Hendra (Hunter); John Lovitz (Doug); Phil E. Hartmann (Fred); Lynne Marie Stewart (Karen); Ken Woods (Jackie); Tracey Reiner (Page's Secretary); Chino "Fats" Williams (Larry the Heavyset Guard); Jim Belushi (Sperry Repairman); Paxton Whitehead (Lord Malcolm Billings); June Chadwick (Gilliam); Tracey Ullman (Fiona); Jeffrey Joseph (African Embassy Guest); Caroline Ducroca (French Embassy Guest); Julie Payne (Receptionist at Elizabeth Arden); Deanna Oliver (Karen at Elizabeth Arden); Carl LaBove (Earl the Guard); Donna Ponterotto (Pedicurist at Elizabeth Arden); Matt Landers (Night Guard at Bank); Jamey Sheridan, Charles Dumas (New York Officers); James Edgcomb, Gerry Connell (Lincoln's Aides); Miguel A. Nunez, Jr., Jose Santan, Bob Ernst (Street Toughs); Benji Gregory (Harry Carlson, Jr.); Kellie Martin (Kristi Carlson); Kim Chan (Dorean Flower Vendor); Anthony Hamilton (Man in Restaurant); Heide Lund (Woman in Restaurant); Kenneth Danziger, Eric Harrison (Embassy Computer Men); Edouardo DeSoto (Superintendent); Garry K. Marshall (Detective); Teagan Clive (Russian Exercise Woman); Tom McDermott (Minister); Mark Rowen (Blond Cab Driver); J. Christopher Ross (Hairdresser); Hilary Stern (Customer); George Jenesky (Man with Umbrella).

Born Caryn Johnson in New York in 1950, the self-named Whoopi Goldberg began her show business career with small assignments in Broadway musicals *(Hair, Jesus Christ Superstar,* and *Pippin)* and then relocated to California in 1974 with her daughter. She settled in San Diego and for the next six years worked with the San Diego Repertory Theater and the Spontaneous Combustion (improvisational troupe). Later in Berkeley, California, she developed her satirical characterizations for her one-woman performances, leading to her one hour *The Spook Show* (featuring four of her stage personalities), which she toured across the United States and in Europe and later, under the auspices of Mike Nichols, presented on Broadway in the fall of 1984. Then came *The Color Purple* (1985), for which she was Oscar-nominated as Best Actress for her telling performances as the touching Celie. In a complete turnabout she next starred in *Jumpin' Jack Flash,* a slapdash spy spoof.

Kooky computer operator Terry Doolittle (Whoopi Goldberg) works in the international money transfer department of a major New York City bank. Not content with just doing her boring job, she enlivens the daily routine by personal correspondence with her computer contacts. One day she receives a puzzling plea for help signed "Jumping Jack Flash." All she can fathom is that it originates from somewhere behind the Iron Curtain. Exhilarated by this challenge, she makes further contact with the mystery man and is directed to Department C at the British embassy. Pompous embassy official Jeremy Talbot (John Wood) insists no such departmet exists. Later Terry learns her man-in-trouble is a stranded British intelligence agent. She is directed to Jack's bachelor pad and a frying pan with four contacts scratched on it. She meets with one (Jeroen Krabbe) of the quartet, and he is killed while they talk; another does not answer his phone calls; a third, according to his wife, Liz Carlson (Annie Potts), is on the same dangerous trek as Jack; and detached Archer Lincoln (Roscoe Lee Browne) refuses to be pinned down to a conversation. By now eccentric Terry is determined to bring Jack home, no matter what the dangers. She gate-crashes a fancy ball at the British embassy, where she signs onto the computer and tampers with it as ordered. Later, she convinces Jack's ex-mistress (Sara Botsford) to persuade her influential husband to help Jack. Only after Terry is kidnapped by Talbot and his Soviet cohorts does she understand she has been a foil to set up Jack and that Talbot is the Russian mole. Fellow worker Marty Phillips (Stephen Collins), really special government agent Peter Kane, comes to Terry's rescue in the showdown. Not only is Terry given a departmental promotion, but her dream comes true; a dinner with Jack (Jonathan Pryce), who is now back in the Big Apple.

"Whoopi Goldberg has massive amounts of personality, every ounce of which she has to call upon to make this picture what it is: a pleasantly diverting affable adventure comedy. Eyes rolling, body flouncing, dander rising, she is onscreen almost constantly.... Even for those long stretches when she is just sitting at her terminal trading messages with the spy, she keeps a ferocious hold on the audience's attention, and their affection" (*People* magazine). Tom Milne (British *Monthly Film Bulletin*) recognized, "Since 'Jack' remains *in absentia* until the very end, Terry is provided with Peter Kane as a substitute partner; but too cautious to come down on one side of the racial divide by casting a black actor as Kane, or on the other by letting the black/white couple fall in love, the action fades out on a much vaguer hint of romance to come. Which is a dismal way of trying to have your cake and eat it."

Jumpin' Jack Flash has its own set of firsts. It was one of Hollywood's first major comedy productions to star a black woman. It was the first feature film directing assignment for Penny "Laverne and Shirley" Marshall (who went on to direct the huge box-office winner, *Big,* 1988). It was the first of Whoopi Goldberg's big screen action-comedies in which she plays a lovable eccentric. She lives in a cluttered Manhattan apartment, adores watching old movies on TV, and at the staid, robotic office brings warmth and excitement to the humdrum worklife of her co-workers (who are generally very bizarre themselves). If her work station is a jumble of knick-knacks, she is a whiz at the terminal keyboard. She may mutter to herself, wear a kookie hairdo and uncoordinated outfits, but she is a with-it gal always ready to reach out to help another.

Jumpin' Jack Flash makes its own points about a black woman intermingling in a still predominantly white world. When the innocent Terry is hustled down to the police station, she is hassled by a bigoted detective (Garry K. Marshall—brother of director Penny) and Terry zings back at the insensitive pencil pusher, "Every time you see a black woman, there has to be pimps and johns." When she maneuvers her way into the fancy-dress embassy ball, she arrives in the guise of a flashy party entertainer (not a guest), complete with gaudy blue sequinned dress and a blonde wig. To prove she has a right to be there, even as paid help, she starts singing (lip synching) a rockin' rendition of "How Many Heartaches" (till the tape gets stuck).

Throughout the film, Whoopi Goldberg's Terry Doolittle is many things at many times. She can be high tech (at the office), she can be accommodating (helping the British espionage agent at the embassy), she can be wistful and vulnerable (when Jack fails to show up for their arranged dinner at Orlando's Restaurant) and she can be madly slapstick. The buffoonery reaches its peak when she is in a telephone booth which the crooks lift up with a crane hook and drag along midtown streets with nonplussed Terry caught inside. Then there is her frenetic bout of escaping the hoods at the embassy as she scrambles along the roof, or her revelation walk down the city streets after being injected with truth serum.

Jumpin' Jack Flash cost an estimated $15,000,000 to mount, but only grossed $11,000,000 in domestic film rentals. It did not prevent the irresistible Whoopi Goldberg from starring in several others features in the mode of this artistic misfire.

130. A Killing Affair (CBS-TV, 9/21/77). Color, 100 minutes.

Executive producer David Gerber; *producer* James H. Brown; *associate producer* Audrey Blasdel-Goddard; *director* Richard C. Sarafian; *teleplay* E. Arthur Kean; *art directors* Ross Bellah, Robert Peterson; *music* Richard Shores; *camera* Al Francis; *editor* Ken Zemke.

Cast: Elizabeth Montgomery (Viki Eaton); O.J. Simpson (Woodrow York); Rosalind Cash (Beverly York); John Mahon (Shoup); Priscilla Pointer (Judge Cudahy); Allan Rich (Captain Bullis); Charlie Robinson (Buck Fryman); John P. Ryan (Flagler); Dean Stockwell (Kenneth Switzer); Dolph Sweet (Scotty Neilson); Todd Bridges (Todd York); Fred Stuthman (Lukens Switzer); John Steadman (Cooks); Michael Durrell (Cabrillo); Stephen Parr (Sergeant Boyle); Ed Knight (Kagel); Michael J. London (Sergeant Gould);

Morgan Farley (Mr. Macy); Georgia Schmidt (Mrs. Macy); Natalie Core (Mrs. Harrow); Eleanor Zee (Miss Slauson); Karmin Murcelo (Sergeant Bandini); Tony Perez (Jose Temple); Jay Ingram (Dyer); Jo Ann Lehmann (Virginia Colorado); Sari Price (Mrs. May); Robert Phalen (Sergeant Holt); Gil Stuart (Vincent); Cheryl Carter (Feeney); Mary Maldonado (Carmencita); Daniel Torppe (Buesuit); Yolanda Marquez (Mrs. Nogales); Timothy Wead (Tetley); Jim Veres (Saticoy); Fil Formicola (M.D.); Billy Jackson (Black Dude); Frank Doubleday (Driver); Bill J. Stevens (Man).

A.K.A. *Behind the Badge.*

"Daring implications of interracial love are hedged with a welter of subplots that turn the attention-holding two hour drama into an affair of overkill" *(Daily Variety).*

Police detective Viki Eaton (Elizabeth Montgomery) is white, snobbish and very chauvinistic abour her peers. Black co-worker Woodrow York (O.J. Simpson) is college-bred, married (with a child), and a maverick policeman who shoots to kill in the course of action and as such has been penalized. Viki and York make an unlikely working team, but they are assigned to the case of psychotic killer Kenneth Switzer (Dean Stockwell), who has been released from police custody on a technicality. Off duty, the two engage in a hesitant romance, which causes a lot of friction down at the squad room. The white law enforcers have it in for York because: 1) he is black, 2) he is an adulterer, 3) he is making it with a white cop who has ignored the other whites at the precinct, and 4) he's a cowboy–hotdog cop. Even his fellow black officers want to know if ". . . black chicks aren't good enough for you." By the time the slippery criminal has been dispatched, Viki and York have gone their separate paths, back to their own ethnic worlds. But (as the weak-minded teleplay allows) the reason for their separation is that York feels too much guilt about leaving his loyal wife (Rosalind Cash) and son (Todd Bridges).

131. Killpoint (Crown International, 1984). Color, 89 minutes.

Executive producers Roger Jacobson, Dana Welch; *producers* Frank Harris, Diane Stevenett; *associate producers* Leo Fong, Hope Holiday, Charles Goldman; *director/screenplay* Harris; *art director* Larry Westover; *set decorator* Jennifer Chung; *music* Herman Jeffreys, Daryl Stevenett; *songs* Jeffreys, Stevenett; *choreography* Fong; *stunts* Rick Avery, Gene Lehfeldt; *technical advisor/special effects* Ronald J. Adams; *camera/editor* Harris.

Cast: Leo Fong (Lieutenant James Long); Richard Roundtree (F.B.I. Agent Bill Bryant); Cameron Mitchell (Joe Marks); Stack Pierce (Nighthawk); Hope Holiday (Anita); Diana Leigh (Candy); Bernie Nelson (Pawnbroker); Danene Pyant (Chauffeurette); Marlene McCormick (Cafe Waitress); James P. Parker (Dan the Bartender); James Lew, Steve "Nasty" Anderson, Ray Dalke, Ed Otis (Nighthawk's Gunmen); Wardell Campbell (Sylvester); Richard L. Johnson (R.J.); Lee Wagner (Lee); Anthony Rivera (Sanchez); Ronnie A. Lopez, Larry Garcia, Anthony Moreno (Sanchez' Gang); Michael Farrrell (Captain Skidmore); Larry Lunsford (Agent Crawford); William Ryle (Watch Commander); Ed Michelotti (Leo De Julio); Alvin Cunningham (Snake); Carl Smith (Coroner); Joey Greenwood (Brad); Jesse Lee Hunter (Jess); Laverne

Lucille Brown (Bar Hooker); Jacquelyn Sawyer (Grocery Shopper); Troy Zuc-colotto (Muscleman); Ronn Kipp, Mike Smith, Gary Barnes (Police Officers); Steve Adams (Truck Driver).

Munitions dealer Nighthawk (Stack Pierce) and his cohort Joe Marks (Cameron Mitchell) steal a large supply of weapons from the National Guard Armory, planning to sell them to local street gangs. Soon thereafter a com-peting arms dealer is gunned down in a restaurant along with several innocent bystanders. As a result, Lieutenant James Long (Leo Fong) and F.B.I. agent Bill Bryant (Richard Roundtree) are assigned to the case, making the discovery that a supermarket robbery was committed with weapons supplied by Nighthawk and Marks. When psychotic Marks tortures and kills a prostitute named Candy (Diana Leigh), the police team note the similarity of the grisly murder to several previous homicides attributed to Marks. The trail leads to Candy's boss, Anita (Hope Holiday), who is later eliminated by the brutally expedient Nighthawk. Bryant is benched temporarily when he is wounded in a bar by Nighthawk. Long poses as an arms buyer to trap the culprits. In the final gunfight, Nighthawk is shot by Long and the wounded Marks.

"*Killpoint* . . . is an angry, violent and mean exploitation film . . . at times raw and amateurish. . . . The acting caliber of Pierce and Roundtree dominates the film. (Their presence also reminds us of how infrequently we see these talented and intense black actors on screen.) . . . There are too many horrible and gory sequences showing innocent people being murdered in the ensuing gang wars" (Linda Gross, *Los Angeles Times*).

Although the black exploitation and the kung fu film cycles rose and fell in the early to mid-1970s, martial arts gymnastics would repeatedly be brought back as a gimmick to bolster a conventional storyline. Since Lieutenant Long is a martial arts expert there are many exhibits of his karate and kung fu pro-ficiency, which forces the Bill Bryant character into the action background too frequently (a sad comedown for the once invincible Richard "Shaft" Round-tree). As *People* magazine assessed, "The ads said Richard Roundtree gave his 'toughest and roughest performance since Shaft.' The audience is never really sure, though, as he only appears in about a quarter of the film. . . . And none of it seems the same without that Isaac Hayes *Shaft* sound track."

Killpoint was shot on location in Riverside, California, by first-time feature filmmaker Frank Harris, who had previously been a TV news reporter and cameraman. Many members of the local police department and the cor-oner's office were corralled into the grainy proceedings, along with unsuspect-ing pedestrians on the street. Although *Variety* was of the opinion that "*Kill-point* delivers none of the fun that once made B-features so enjoyable," it grossed an impressive $1,600,000 in domestic film rentals.

132. The Klansman (Paramount, 1974). Color, 112 minutes.

Executive producers Bill Shiffrin, Howard Ephram; *producer* William Alexander; *associate producers* Joe Ingher, Michael Marcovsky, Rosemary Christenson, Peter A. Rodis, Alvin Bojar, Jery Levy, Daniel K. Sobel; *director* Terence Young; *based on the novel by* William Bradford Huie; *screenplay* Millard Kaufman, Samuel Fuller; *production designer* John S. Poplin; *set decorator* Raymond Molyneaux; *music* The Stax Organization; *song* Betty Crutcher and Mack Rice; *assistant directors* Ridgeway Callow, Joseph Nayfack, Gene Anderson; *second unit director* Nico Hartos; *stunt coordinator* Roger Creed; *special effects* Thol O. Simonson; *sound* Norman Lee Webster; *camera* Lloyd Ahern, Aldo Tonti; *editor* Gene Milford.

Cast: Lee Marvin (Sheriff "Big Track" Bascomb); Richard Burton (Breck Stancill); Cameron Mitchell (Deputy "Butt Cut" Cates); O.J. Simpson (Garth); Lola Falana (Loretta Sykes); David Huddleston (Mayor Hardy Riddle); Luciana Paluzzi (Trixie Cunningham); Linda Evans (Nancy Poteet); Ed Call (Sy Shaneyelt); John Alderson (Vernon Hodo); John Pearce (Tag Taggart); David Ladd (Flack); Vic Perrin (Hector); Spence Will Dee (Willie Washington); Wendell Wellman (Alan Bascomb); Hoke Howell (Bobby Poteet); Virgil Frye (Johnson); Robert Porter (Reverend Josh Franklin); Lee De Broux (Reverend Alverson); Charles Briggs (Associated Press Reporter); Morgan Upton (*New York Times* Reporter); Eve Christopher (Mrs. Shaneyfelt); Susan Brown (Maybelle Bascomb); Gary Catus (Charley Peck); Jeanne Bell (Rape Victim); Jo Ann Cowell (Annie); Scott E. Lane (Jim Hodo); Bert Williams (Doctor); Larry Williams (Lightning Rod).

Ellenton, Alabama, is a powder-keg as the black population and the right-wing white contingent (with its Ku Klux Klan faction) square off, with only placating Sheriff "Big Track" Bascomb (Lee Marvin) attempting to maintain a compromise of peace. When civil rights agitators appear, pursued by northern press and TV cameramen, the small town is ready to ignite. After a white woman, Nancy Poteet (Linda Evans), is raped, allegedly by black Willie Washington (Spence Will Dee), only the last-minute intervention of Bascomb—who takes the young man into custody—prevents the lynching party (including the town's deputy sheriff "Butt Cut" Cates [Cameron Mitchell]) from carrying out the hanging. The Klan wants blood, and they pursue two innocent blacks. They kill one and hunt the other (Garth [O.J. Simpson]), who takes his own revenge by eliminating his oppressors one by one. Meanwhile Nancy is banished by the townfolk for supposedly being with a black but is protected by reclusive Breck Stancill (Richard Burton), the reclusive aristocratic owner of Stancill's Mountain, where he permits blacks to live on the estate in shacks. Loretta Sykes (Lola Falana) returns to Ellenton to visit her dying relation, and the Klan assumes this educated visitor is another pesty demonstrator. Cates rapes her, and she is rescued by Bascomb, who orders her not to reveal what has happened. Later it is learned that the jailed Willie Washington has a solid alibi: he was with the wife of one of the Klan members the night of his "crime." As the civil rights demonstrations and Klan meetings continue, Stancill wallops Cates in a confrontation, then insures that Nancy leaves town safely. The Klan sets fire to the mountain, with Stancill being killed and Bascomb wounded, while the Klan is greatly reduced in numbers. Garth the black militarist remains alive to continue the fight.

"*The Klansman* is a perfect example of screen trash that almost invites derision.... There's not a shred of quality, dignity, relevance or impact in this yahoo-oriented bunk.... Bookers are hereby alerted to the possibility of racially-integrated displays of unanimous disapproval" *(Variety)*.

O.J. Simpson *(left)* **and Lee Marvin in** *The Klansman* **(1974).**

At the time this film gained notoriety because actor-turned-playboy Richard Burton was further diminishing his once lofty professional reputation by appearing in such claptrap, and much was made of the fact that his then (very briefly)-current girlfriend was black British model Jeanne Bell (given a tiny role in the film as a rape victim), which upset romanticists who felt he should be back with his former wife, Elizabeth Taylor. Watching his somnambulistic appearance as the drunken landowner with a conscience is embarrassing. The others overact (Cameron Mitchell), overreact (Lee Marvin), or merely look baffled (O.J. Simpson), embarrassed (Linda Evans), chagrined (Lola Falana), or coy (Luciana Paluzzi). It is hard to believe that Samuel Fuller co-authored the tawdry script.

When the film reached England in mid-1975, twenty-two minutes of this trashy feature were trimmed.

133. Knights of the City (Entertainment, 1985). Color, 89 minutes.

Executive producers Michael Franzese, Robert E. Schultz; *producers* Leon Isaac Kennedy, John C. Strong III; *director* Dominic Orlando; *story* Kennedy, David Wilder; *screenplay* Kennedy; *art director* Barbara Shelton; *set decorator* Regina McLarney; *costume designers* Celia Bryant, Beverly Safier; *makeup* Laurie Cocheo, Emily La Rosa; *music* Misha Segal; *additional music* Paul Gilreath; *music co-ordinators* John Lombardo, Roy Rifkind, Jules Rifkind; *music editors* Dan Carlin, Michael Linn; *additional music programming* Craig Cooper; *choreography* Jeff Kutash; *dance production co-ordinator* Gregory Schultz; *assistant director* Allan Herman; *stunt co-ordinators* Steve Boyun, Jeff Moldovan; *sound* Joe Foglia; *supervising sound editor* Tony Magro; *camera* Rolf Kesterman; *editors* John O'Connor, Nicholas Smith, Paul La Mori.

Cast: Leon Isaac Kennedy (Troy); Nicholas Campbell (Joey); John Mengatti (Mookie); Stoney Jackson (Eddie); Janine Turner (Brooke Delamo); Jeff Kutash (Flash); Michael Ansara (John Delamo); Dino Henderson (Dino); Curtis Lema (Ramrod); Marc Lemberger (Mr. Freeze); Jeff Moldovan (Carlos); Sonny Anthony (Sonny); Jay Armor (Redcap); Eddie Guy (Eddie); Peter Nicholas (Hairboy); Stan Ward (Buddha); James Reese (Alien); John Franzese (Pharaoh); Antone Corona (Eyepatch); Floyd Levine (McGruder); Dario Carnevale (Dario); Wendy Barry (Jasmine); Olga Rutz (Joey's Girl); Katie Lauren (Baby Jane); Leslie Wanger (Girl in Disco); Darren Robinson, Damon Wimbley, and Mark Morales (The Fat Boys); Smokey Robinson (Himself); Jessie Daiaz (Jessie); T.K. (Gustavo Rodriguez); Kurtis Blow (Himself); Jerry Silverman (Jailor); Lou Ann Carou (Receptionist); Michael Safier (Man in Waiting Room); Cammy Garcia (Beverly); Heather Lazlo (Brooke's Girlfriend); Michelle Garcia (Juliette); Joanna Tea (Older Sister); Dedric Fulton (Little Boy in Red); K.C. (Himself); Denny Tarrio (Himself); Joe Foglia (Studio Engineer); Nancy Raffa (Mrs. Delamo); Christina Wilfong (Delamo's Daughter).

Another of those street-gang-cum-music-videos that have peppered the 1980s cinema, filled with ethnic stereotypes and racial (in)tolerance. There are guest cameo appearances by such performers as Smokey Robinson, the Fat Boys, Kurtis Blow, and even the one-time host of TV's "Dance Fever," Denny Tarrio. "With overtones of everything from *West Side Story* to *Street of Fire,* this offers no surprises and, in its fight scenes as in its musical numbers, little excitement" (Kim Newman, British *Monthly Film Bulletin*).

Troy (Leon Isaac Kennedy) and his pals Mookie (John Mengatti) and Joey (Nicholas Campbell) are the leaders of a street gang that fights off the criminal elements that the police, including corrupt cop McGruder (Floyd Levine), are unwilling to combat. Mookie encourages Troy to focus his energy on the Royal Rockers, the rap band they have formed. A chance meeting in jail between the Royal Rockers and recording company executive John Delamo (Michael Ansara) gives the group an entree into the music business. Because of a misunderstanding with Delamo's daughter Brooke (Janine Turner), the Rockers disappears from Twilight Records, leaving a demo tape behind. Brooke hears the tape and realizes she has let a good thing disappear. She organizes a music talent contest for the street people, hoping Troy and his group will enter. They do, competing against Troy's former girl, Jasmine (Wendy Barry), who is now being sponsored by Troy's arch rival Carlos (Jeff Moldovan). The Royal Rockers win the big contest. When Carlos kills Jasmine, Troy confronts him, and they fight to the death. Thereafter Troy and his gang are reunited.

Location filming was accomplished in South Florida for this independent production. It was a sharp change of pace for Leon Isaac Kennedy, best known for his *Penitentiary* film series (q.v.). Although a good fifteen years too old for the role, he handles himself well both on the musical stage and in the building-top fight scene.

(Note: One of the similar style films was *Krush Groove* [Warner Bros., 1985]. It was also a rap musical and features a guest spot by the Fat Boys. It starred Blair Underwood, who would gain prominence as the upwardly mobile young black attorney on TV's "LA Law" [1987–   ]. Directed by Michael Schultz [*Car Wash,* others], *Krush Groove* grossed $5,100,000 in domestic film rentals, based on an estimated $3,000,000 production cost—which was far more than *Knights of the City* earned.)

134. Lady Cocoa (Moonstone, 1975). Color, 93 minutes.

Producer Matt Cimber; *associate producer* James A. Watson, Jr.; *director* Cimber; *screenplay* George Theakos; *wardrobe* Don Mulderick; *music/music conductor* Luchi De Jesus; *song* De Jesus and Lola Falana; *assistant director* Jef Richard; *stunt co-ordinator* Speed Stun; *special effects* Russell McElhannon; *sound* Dick Damon; *sound effects* Colin Waddy; *camera* Ken Gibb; *editor* Bud Warner.

Cast: Lola Falana (Cocoa DeLange [Alfansa King]); "Mean" Joe Greene (Big Joe); Alex Dreier (Lieutenant Ramsey); Gene Washington (Doug); Gary Harper (Arthur); James R. Sweeney (Desk Sergeant); Richard Kennedy (Waiter); Buck Flower (Drunk Gambler); John Goff (The "Sicilian"); La Verne Watson (Eddie's Girl); James A. Watson, Jr. (Eddie); Millie Perkins (The Contact).

Cocoa DeLange (Lola Falana), born as Alfansa King but now known as uppity Lady Cocoa to some, has been in Nevada State prison for more than a year for refusing to testify against her Harlem gangster lover, Eddie (James A. Watson, Jr.). She agrees—or so it seems—to turn state's evidence against him in exchange for twenty-four hours of freedom at Lake Tahoe's gambling resort, King's Castle. She is under the protective custody of two detectives: young and idealistic black police officer Doug (Gene Washington)—who falls in love with his ward—and older, jaded white cop Ramsey (Alex Dreier), who is not above double-dealing. Before long Eddie and his henchmen, including Big Joe ("Mean" Joe Greene) are out to silence Cocoa and her two protectors, even if it means driving a car onto the crowded main floor of the gambling casino, or using a cross-dressing hit man/lady (Millie Perkins). The final shootout is aboard a cabin cruiser on Lake Tahoe, with the gangsters taking the big fall.

Only thanks to lively songstress-turned-actress Lola Falana does *Lady Cocoa* come alive. She lives up to her reputation as the "first cat in the slammer." She is a tough-talking, kind-hearted moll who knows art, speaks French and quotes philosophy. Gene Washington and "Mean" Joe Greene had also co-starred that year in producer-director Matt Cimber's *The Black Six* (q.v.). Location work for *Lady Cocoa* was at King's Castle Hotel and Casino at North Lake Tahoe and at Nevada State Prison at Carson City. The *Los Angeles Times* was being more than generous when it reported, "Director Matt Cimber has created an ambiance of suspense and captured the claustrophobic, compulsive world of Nevada's mobsters and gamblers. The film is well photographed.... Acting ... is credible."

135. The Last Dragon (Tri-Star, 1985). Color, 109 minutes.

Executive producer Berry Gordy; *producer* Rupert Hitzig; *associate producer* Joseph Caracciolo; *director* Michael Schultz; *screenplay* Louis Venosta;

production designer Peter Larkin; *art director* William Barclay; *set decorator* Thomas Tonery; *costumes* Robert de Mora; *makeup* Allen Weisinger; *music* Misha Sega; *additional music* Willie Hutch, Norman Whitefield; *choreography* Lester Wilson; *assistant director* Thomas Reilly; *stunt co-ordinator* Frank Ferrara; *special effects* Gary Zeller; *special visual effects* Rob Blalack, Praxis Filmworks; *sound* Dennis Maitland; *camera* James A. Contner; *editor* Christopher Holmes.

Cast: Taimak (Leroy); Vanity (Laura); Christopher Murney (Eddie Arkadian); Julius J. Carry III (Sho'Nuff); Faith Prince (Angela); Leo O'Brien (Richie); Mike Starr (Rock); Jim Moody (Daddy Green); Glen Eaton (Johnny Yu); Ernie Reyes, Jr. (Tai); Roger Campbell (Announcer); Esther Marrow (Mama Green); Keshia Knight [Pullam] (Sophia); Jamal Mason (Roy); B.J. Barie (Jackie); Sarita Allen, Jacqui Lee Smith, Jodi Moccia (Angela's Singers); Sal Russo, Chazz Palminteri, Frank Renzulli, Torrance Mathis (Hoods); Andre Brown (Beast); David Claudio (Cyclone); Kirk Taylor (Crunch); Shonte, Janet Bloem, Lis Loving (Sho's Women); Henry Yuk (Hu Y); Michael R. Chin (Lu Yi); Fredric Mao (Du Yi); Thomas Ikeda (Master); W.H. Macy (J.J.); Trulie MacLeod (Margo); Gary Aprahamian (Jason); Lou David (Headline Killer); Verne Williams (Cujo); Captain Haggerty (Mr. Z.); Ernie Reyes Sr. (Martial Arts Fighter); Robert Silver (Cab Driver); Clayton Prince (Voice in Theater); Brandon Schultz (Tiny Kid); Carl Payne (Kid in Pizza Shop); Jeffrey Ward (Leroy's Stunt Double); William Taylor (Sho's Stunt Double); Anthony Cortino (Hairstylist); Sebastian Hitzig (Handsome Boy); Kim Chang (Girl Student); Derek Schultz (Boy Student); Rhonda Siberstein (7th Heaven Dancer); Peter Traina (Radio Smasher); Freddie Stroble (Transvestite); Jack Meeks, Joe Dabenigno (Policemen); Scott Coker, Soo Gin Lee, Julian Villanueva (Demo Team).

Berry Gordy, the founder and in 1985 still head of Motown Records, conceived this engaging blend of kung fu, street gang action, and music videos, which drew some of its premise from the mega hit *The Karate Kid* (1984). "No great work of art, pic does have its moments and is enough fun to find a following among the young" *(Variety)*. The prognosis was correct, for this shrewdly calculated yet charming excursion into nonsense earned an overall gross of $30,000,000 on an estimated cost of $10,000,000. It was directed by Michael Schultz, who that year had helmed the equally commercial *Krush Groove,* a rap musical (see under *Knights of the City*).

Black teenager Leroy (Taimak) lives in Harlem with his family and nobly dreams of becoming a martial arts master. Because he is so totally absorbed in "being" an Oriental kung fu and karate champ (even to wearing Chinese garb and eating popcorn with chopsticks), the neighborhood teasingly calls him "Bruce Leroy." This potential usurper irritates the local black bully, Sho'Nuff (Julius J. Carry III), who calls himself the Shogun of Harlem and wants no rivals to usurp his "throne." Leroy refuses to be tricked into fighting Sho'Nuff. Meanwhile white gangster Eddie Arkadian (Christopher Murney) from downtown wants to please his untalented girlfriend, Angela (Faith Prince), so he attempts to kidnap Laura (Vanity), the disc jockey hostess of a popular music video TV show. He intends to force her into showing Angela's videos on

Vanity and Taimak in *The Last Dragon* (1985).

the air. At the crucial moment Leroy witnesses the abduction and saves La
but being shy he disappears. Their paths cross again when, to save Laura'
disco club from the threatening Sho'Nuff and his men who are financed by
Arkadian, Leroy again comes to the rescue. He has now reached his dream goal
of being kung fu champ and has also won Laura's love.

Obviously expense was no obstacle in assembling this glitzy musical fantasy filled with martial arts, harmless street jive from assorted ethnic groups, and many, many musical interludes. Leroy's young sister is played by Keshia Knight Pullam, the Rudy of television's "The Cosby Show." Ex-Prince group star Vanity revealed yet again how beautiful she is.

136. The Last Fight (Movie and Pictures International, 1983). Color, 89 minutes.

Producer Jerry Masucci; *associate producer* Patricia Bennett; *director* Fred Williamson; *story* Masucci; *screenplay* Williamson; *costumes* Antoine Tony Greene; *music* Jay Chattaway; *songs* Gary W. King, Ruben Blades, Tito Perento, Chattaway; *special effects* Peter Kunz, Max Vogel; *camera* James Lemma; *editor* Daniel Loewenthal.

Cast: Willie Colon (Joaquin Vargas); Ruben Blades (Andy "Kid Clave" Perez); Fred Williamson (Jesse Crowder); Joe Spinell (Angelo the Boss); Darlanne Fluegel (Sally); Nereida Mercado (Nancy); Anthony Sirico (Frankie); Vinny Argiro (Detective Pantana); Jose "Chegui" Torres (Ex-Champ); Nick Corello (Pedro); Sal Corolio (Papa); Izzy Sanabria (Slim); Andy Gerado (Frank); Ally Stevens (Sal); Kurt Andon (Doctor); Marta Vianna (Mama); Darlene Masucci (Pretty Girl at Party); Adrienne Sachs (Jesse's Girlfriend); Stan Goldstein (Car Window Washer); Frankie Moia (Casino Pit Boss); Manuel Sebastian (Maitre d'); Tony Page (Casino Manager); Kevin Mahon, John Turner, John Lumis, Jenaro Diaz (Fighters); James Lovelett (Nightclub Fighter); Marvin Goldberg (Fighter Announcer); Jeff McBride (Casino Dealer); Jerry Masucci (Record Producer); Jon Fausty (Recording Engineer); Larry Silvestri, Michael Telesco, Steve Peluca (Cops); Frank Ferarra, Sandy Alexander, Dan Dod (Joaquin's Men); James Bymum (Kid in Pool Hall); Milton Cadona, Luis Kahn, Leopoldo Pineda, Luis Lopez, Jose Torres, Jose Mangual, Jr., Eddie Resto, Johnny Andrews, Jimmy Delgado (Members of Andy's Band); *and:* Don Dunphy, Don King, Salvador Sanchez, Bert Sugarman, Don James.

"*The Last Fight* is a lackluster little boxing melodrama that might have made it had actor-writer-director Fred Williamson put some more polish on his script (based on a story by his producer, Jerry Masucci)" (Kevin Thomas, *Los Angeles Times*).

Using a *Golden Boy* and *Body and Soul* (q.v.) premise, Andy "Kid Clave" Perez (Ruben Blades) is a fighter from the barrio of Panama City who has a good chance to become junior lightweight champion. But not only is he distracted by his budding recording career (as a primo salsa star), he has a penchant for gambling. The mob is not happy with these activities, and Mafia crime figure and nightclub owner Joaquin Vargas (Willie Colon) forces Perez to box under his auspices. He even throws in curvaceous Sally (Darlanne Fluegel) as part of the deal, much to the consternation of Perez's girlfriend,

cado). Later, Vargas orders the boxer's outspoken dad
~~worked~~ orked over. In the process the elder Perez dies. Ex-cop-
~~tective~~ ive and family friend Jesse Crowder (Fred Williamson)
~~dispatches~~ lispatches the gangsters after much gunplay. Meanwhile,
~~Perez~~ z has a blood clot on the brain, and he dies in the ring when
~~hit to~~ he head.

~~It~~ ıt swings wildly between moments of deluxe teatro ab-
surdo/ʙ ~~movies with~~ ~~ h trash and longer C-grade stretches of trash period. It is
sometimes primo street Latin cinema goof but more often it reeks of cheap production values, naked plot, and groaning dialogue. Schizoid, hilarious,
fascinating, violent, macho, phony, dumb, and fun — *The Last Fight* will
generate a buzz in the barrio and be a neglected low-camp item outside" (Pablo
Guzman, *The Village Voice*). "Biggest disappointment of *The Last Fight* is the
absence of a positive role model for the Hispanic audiences" *(Variety)*.

There is scant connection between the confident Jesse Crowder character
of *No Way Back* (1976) and *Death Journey* (1976) (qq.v.), and his awkward appearance in the R-rated *The Last Fight* beyond the fact that both are played
by filmmaker-actor Fred Williamson. There is a guest appearance by
featherweight champion Salvador Sanchez, who died in a car accident shortly
after the filming was finished in early 1982 and to whom this film is dedicated.
Fight commentator Don Dunphy, fight promoter Don King, and ex–light/
heavyweight star Jose "Chegui" Torres make brief cameo walk-ons herein.
Others paraded before the cameras are Bert Sugarman (editor of *Ring*
magazine), Don James (head of *Cable* magazine), and Izzy Sanabria *(Latin NY*
publisher). The film's producer and story originator, Jerry Masucci, owns
Fania Records. Recording star–actor Ruben Blades, who holds a law degreee
from the University of Panama and a masters in international law from Harvard University, would star in the comedy caper *Waiting for Salazar* (1988).
Salsa star Willie Colon had been partnered in the music industry with Ruben
Blades for six years before they split up.

137. The Legend of Nigger Charley (Paramount, 1972).
Color, 98 minutes.

Producer Larry G. Spangler; *associate producer* Steve Bono; *director*
Martin Goldman; *story* James Warner Bellah; *screenplay* Spangler, Goldman;
art director Merrill Sindler; *costumes* Joseph Garibaldi Aulisi; *makeup* Enrico
Cortese; *music/songs* John Bennings; *stunts* Jerry Gatlin; *assistant director*
John E. Quill; *sound* Jeffrey Haas; *special effects* Joe Day; *camera* Peter Eco;
editor Howard Kuperman.

Cast: Fred Williamson (Nigger Charley); D'Urville Martin (Toby); Don
Pedro Colley (Joshua); Gertrude Jeanette (Theo); Marcia McBroom (Julia);
Alan Gifford (Hill Carter); John Ryan (Houston); Will Hussung (Dr.
Saunders); Milt Moor (Walker); Thomas Anderson (Shadow); Jerry Gatlin
(Sheriff Rhinehart); Tricia O'Neil (Sarah Lyons); Doug Rowe (Dewey
Loynons); Keith Prentice (Nils Fowler); Tom Pemberton (Willie); Joe Santos
(Reverend); Fred Lerner (Ollokot).

Only a month after the black Western *Buck and the Preacher* (q.v.) was released came *The Legend of Nigger Charley*. But unlike the Sidney Poitier–Harry Belafonte feature, which invested its six-gun tale with humanity, *The Legend of Nigger Charley* is exploitive to the hilt. The teaser ad copy read, "Somebody warn the West. Nigger Charley ain't running no more."

In the Deep South of the 1850s, Charley (Fred Williamson) is given his freedom by his dying plantation owner (Alan Gifford). However, sadistic overseer Houston (John Ryan) intends taking over the plantation, and that includes the fates of the slaves. After killing Houston in a brawl, Charley escapes with two other slaves, Toby (D'Urville Martin) and Joshua (Don Pedro Colley). They head westward, always pursued by bounty hunter Nils Fowler (Keith Prentice). The slave catcher tracks the trio to a frontier town, where Fowler and his underlings are killed in the saloon shootout with the black men. The three ex-slaves are offered work by homesteader Dewey Lyons (Doug Rowe) and his half-breed Indian wife, Sarah (Tricia O'Neil), but Charley has promised himself never again to work for a white man. Later Charley realizes how much he cares for Sarah and returns to the ranch with his men, which now include an elderly half-breed called Shadow (Thomas Anderson) and a black stable boy named Willie (Tom Pemberton). Together they defeat the bogus Reverend and his squad of killers. When the smoke clears, the Reverend and his men are all dead, as are Shadow, Willie, and Joshua. Charley and Toby ride off together.

"For all the feverish activity, there has yet to be a film of rounded merit — one of skill, imagination and impact — about the black man and the Old West. Sadly *The Legend of Nigger Charley* is fair. Fair only. . ." (Howard Thompson, *New York Times*). But within its context of exploitation, violence, and adventure, *The Legend of Nigger Charley* achieves some of its creative goals. The opening plantation segment plays like a bad version of *Uncle Tom's Cabin,* but once the black fugitives head westward, the film becomes a full-bodied Western. It does seem a bit much to ask its viewers to accept that in the rough-tough Old West full of its own prejudices against minorities, three black men (no matter how rugged) could ride into town as bold as can be and survive the day. Thereafter, the film plays like any Western, with good triumphing over evil and the surviving heroes riding off into the sunset. And for its heroes it has a trio of strong, silent men: the muscular, handsome Charley; the brooding and powerful Joshua; and the lighthearted, resilient Toby.

Obviously, just like the similarly structured urban crime movies in which the blacks whip the evil white hoodlums, *The Legend of Nigger Charley* is structured to appeal to the black community, providing onscreen role models (of sorts) in a fantasy tale they can empathize with or just plain enjoy. The film never pushes the segregation issue too far. Charley has a romantic interlude at the plantation with a pretty slave (Marcia McBroom), but when he goes westward, the one woman attracted to him (and to whom he is attracted) is an outcast, a married half-breed (Tricia O'Neil), and they do not consummate their attraction.

At the finale of *The Legend of Nigger Charley,* Toby asks his saddlemate, "Which way we goin', Charley?" Charley replies, "Don't make no difference." But with this film grossing a sizeable $3,000,000 in domestic film rentals (on an estimated production cost of $400,000), it was clear the trail would lead to a celluloid sequel — *The Soul of Nigger Charley* (1973) (q.v.).

D'Urville Martin *(left)* **and Don Pedro Colley in** *The Legend of Nigger Charley* (1972).

With such films as *The Legend of Nigger Charley* and *Hammer* (q.v.), Fred Williamson was establishing himself as the premier black action star, superseding the earlier Jim Brown. Born in 1937 in Gary, Indiana, Williamson graduated from Northwestern University. He played professional football — in which he was known as "the Hammer" — for ten years with the Oakland Raiders and the Kansas City Chiefs and then turned to show business. He had a recurring role on Diahann Carroll's TV comedy series "Julia" (1970–71) as one of the star's boyfriends and made early feature film appearances in *M*A*S*H* (1970) and *Tell Me That You Love Me Junie Moon* (1970).

138. Leonard: Part 6 (Columbia, 1987). Color, 85 minutes.

Producer Bill Cosby; *director* Paul Weiland; *story* Cosby; *screenplay* Jonathan Reynolds; *production designer* Geoffrey Kirkland; *art director* Blake

Bill Cosby in *Leonard: Part 6* (1987).

Russell; *set decorators* Bill Beck, Paul Kraus; *costumes* Aggie Guerard Rodgers; *music* Elmer Bernstein; *choreography* Louis Falco; *special effects* Richard Edlund; *camera* Jan DeBont; *editor* Gerry Hambling, Peter Boita.

Cast: Bill Cosby (Leonard); Tom Courtenay (Frayn the Butler/Narrator); Joe Don Baker (Snyderburn); Moses Gunn (Giorgio); Pat Colbert (Allison); Gloria Foster (Medusa); Victoria Rowell (Joan); Anna Levine (Nurse Carvalho); David Maier (Man Ray); Grace Zabriskie (Jefferson); Hal Bokar (Andy); George Maguire (Madison); John Hostetter (Adams); William Hall (Monroe); George Kirby (Duchamp); Jane Fonda (Herself).

If anything could disprove the Hollywood maxim that entertainer Bill Cosby can do no wrong, it is *Leonard: Part 6*. Produced at an estimated cost of $27,000,000 it grossed only $3,000,000 in domestic film rentals, helping to topple the executive regime at Columbia Pictures. So abysmal was this movie that even Cosby himself denounced it to the press before the film opened in December 1987.

This alleged spy spoof opens with Frayn (Tom Courtenay) the butler announcing that because of national security the first five adventures of Leonard (Bill Cosby) cannot be revealed. Leonard is now a successful restaurateur, having abandoned his C.I.A. agent career. Living next door to the affluent Leonard is his ex-spouse, Allison (Pat Colbert), who years before became tired of Leonard's indiscretions. She is too preoccupied to do anything about dabbling actress daughter Joan (Victoria Rowell), who intends marrying a much older theater director named Giorgio (Moses Gunn). Meanwhile, bizarre Medusa (Gloria Foster) is plotting to take over the world by helping animals to rebel against their masters, all with the help of a magical sphere and liquid. C.I.A. man Snyderburn (Jon Don Baker) convinces Leonard to save humanity and combat Medusa. The mystical Nurse Carvalho (Anna Levine) provides Leonard with an assortment of helpful gadgets and tricks to survive this caper. Before the case is closed, Snyderburn has gone power-hungry, Allison has been captured by Medusa's minions, and an attack force of deadly lobsters have been sidetracked with drawn butter. Leonard escapes on an ostrich, and he and Allison resolve their domestic differences.

139. Let's Do It Again (Warner Bros., 1975). Color, 112 minutes.

Producer Melville Tucker; *director* Sidney Poitier; *story* Timothy March; *screenplay* Richard Wesley; *production designer* Alfred Sweeney; *set decorator* Ruby R. Levitt; *music* Curtis Mayfield; *stunt co-ordinator* Henry Kingi; *assistant directors* Reuben L. Watt, Richard A. Wells; *sound* Willie D. Burton, Harry W. Tetrick; *camera* Donald M. Morgan; *editor* Pembroke J. Herring.

Cast: Sidney Poitier (Clyde Williams); Bill Cosby (Billy Foster); Calvin Lockhart (Biggie Smalls); John Amos (Kansas City Mack); Denise Nicholas (Beth Foster); Lee Chamberlin (Dee Dee Williams); Mel Stewart (Ellison); Julius W. Harris (Bubbletop Woodson); Paul E. Harris (Jody Tipps); Val Avery (Lieutenant Bottomley); Jimmie Walker (Bootney Farnsworth); Ossie Davis (Elder Johnson); Doug Johnson, Cedric Scott, Richard Young (Biggie's Gang); Morgan Roberts (Fish 'n' Chips Freddie); Billy Eckstine (Zack); George Foreman (Factory Worker); Talya Ferro (Biggie's Girl); Mel Flory (Hotel Detective); Rodolfus Lee Hayden (Fortieth Street Black); Jayne Kennedy (Factory Secretary); Hilda Haynes (Telephone Operator).

With the hit comedy *Uptown Saturday Night* (1974) (q.v.) grossing $7,400,000 in domestic film rentals, it was natural to produce a slapstick sequel. *Let's Do It Again* used much of the same creative team as before. It would earn $11,800,000 in United States and Canadian film rentals, and its Curtis Mayfield soundtrack album (along with the title song sung by the Staples) became top sellers. Filled with wide-eyed double takes, madcap chases over rooftops and escapes out of window via sheets tied together, *Let's Do It Again* is a broad comedy filled with basic visual slapstick rather than clever verbal wit.

Atlanta milkman Clyde Williams (Sidney Poitier) and factory worker Billy Foster (Billy Cosby) belong to the Sons and Daughters of Shaka. Their lodge has lost its lease and needs $50,000 to create a new home for its members. Williams and Foster decide to solve the dilemma. Along with their wives, Dee Dee (Lee Chamberlin) and Beth (Denise Nicholas), they go to New Orleans, where they become involved in placing bets with rival bookies—oldtimer Kansas City Mack (John Amos) and dapper Biggie Smalls (Calvin Lockhart), who is attempting to take over Mack's turf. Thanks to Williams's ability to hypnotize skinny fighter Bootney Farnsworth (Jimmie Walker), their unlikely Great Black Hope becomes a surprise winner in the ring, and Williams and Foster make a killing with their bets. They and their wives hastily leave New Orleans before the gangsters realize what has happened. Six months later Mack appears at the lodge dedication ceremony with his thugs and forces Williams and Foster to "do it again." They must hypnotize Farnsworth again so he will win his rematch with Fortieth Street Black (Rodolfus Lee Hayden). Meanwhile, slippery Foster comes up with a three-part scheme to pull yet another sting on the underworld figures: Dee Dee and Beth pose as hookers and bet large amounts on the seemingly impossible proposition that both fighters will knock each other out in the ring (which is what happens when Williams spellbinds both boxers). The gangsters give chase to the out-of-towners, and the bookies are tricked into the police station, where they are made to contribute to the policemen's fund a goodly portion of the take. The quartet return to Atlanta richer, happier, and much wiser.

"It is apparent why Sidney Poitier set this project in motion and directed it; his making films for black audiences that aren't exploitation films. Poitier is trying to make it possible for ordinary, lower middle class black people to see themselves on the screen and have a good time. The only thing that makes the film remarkable is that Poitier gives an embarrassed, inhibited performance. As casual, lighthearted straightman to Bill Cosby, he is trying to be something alien to his nature. He has too much pride, and too much reserve, for low comedy..." (Pauline Kael, *New Yorker* magazine). Stephen Klain *(Independent Film Journal)* noted, "As he did in the previous film, Poitier has given himself relatively little to do as an actor, preferring to let the camera linger on Cosby, who lets all stops out." And Richard Eder *(New York Times)* confirmed, "The movie's main strength is Bill Cosby, who looks like a starved sheep in wolf's clothing, and is shifty and woebegone at the same time."

140. The Liberation of L.B. Jones (Columbia, 1970).
Color, 102 minutes.

Producer Ronald Lubin; *director* William Wyler; *based on the novel* "The Liberation of Lord Byron Jones" *by* Jesse Hill Ford; *screenplay* Stirling Silliphant, Ford; *production designer* Kenneth A. Reid; *set decorator* Frank Tuttle; *costumes* Seth Banks, Gene Ashman, Vi Alford; *makeup* Ben Lane; *music* Elmer Bernstein; *assistant directors* Anthony Ray, Mike Frankovich, Jr., Robert M. Jones; *second unit director* Robert Swink; *sound* Jack Solomon, Arthur Piantadosi; *camera* Robert Surtees; *second unit camera* Jordan Cronenweth; *editors* Swink, Carl Kress.

Cast: Lee J. Cobb (Oman Hedgepath); Anthony Zerbe (Willie Joe Worth); Roscoe Lee Browne (L.B. Jones); Lola Falana (Emma Jones); Lee Majors (Steve Mundine); Barbara Hershey (Nella Mundine); Yaphet Kotto (Sonny Boy Mosby); Arch Johnson (Stanley Bumpas); Chill Wills (Mr. Ike); Zara Cully (Mama Lavorn); Fayard Nicholas (Benny); Joseph Attles (Henry); Lauren Jones (Eileen); Dub Taylor (Mayor); Brenda Sykes (Jelly); Larry D. Mann (Grocer); Ray Teal (Police Chief); Eve McVeagh (Miss Griggs the Secretary); Sonora McKeller (Miss Ponsella); Robert Van Meter (Blind Man); Jack Grinnage (Driver); John S. Jackson (Suspect).

"Rather late in the racism-sex-violence genre of civil-wrongs films comes *The Liberation of L.B. Jones....* There is a pervading commercial patness to the fleshed-out script and the overall production. However true-to-life the characters and situations are, many another film already has made the ground covered almost stereotyped and cliche herein" *(Variety).*

Steve and Nella Mundine (Lee Majors, Barbara Hershey) come to Somerton, Tennessee, where he joins the law firm of his uncle, Oman Hedgepath (Lee J. Cobb). On the same train is black Sonny Boy Mosby (Yaphet Kotto), who has returned home for revenge against bigoted white policeman Stanley Bumpas (Arch Johnson) for having beat him as a child. Mundine persuades Hedgepath to handle the divorce case of urbane Lord Bryon Jones (Roscoe Lee Browne), a rich local black funeral director. Jones claims his wife, Emma (Lola Falana), had an affair with white policeman Willie Joe Worth (Anthony Zerbe); she in turn fights the claim, hoping a settlement will pay the costs for the baby she is expecting by Worth. When Worth learns of the suit, he beats up Emma, and when Jones will not see "reason," Worth and Bumpas arrest the undertaker. Jones escapes, but in a junkyard confrontation he refuses to run any more, and he is shot and castrated. Later the cops confess, but are not prosecuted. Meanwhile Mosby, not knowing of the policeman's newest racist crime, shoves Bumpas into a harvester. Disillusioned by local "law and order," the Mundines leave town—on the same train as Mosby.

Based on the 1965 novel *The Liberation of Lord Byron Jones,* this film was the final feature for three-time Academy Award–winning director William Wyler. It was shot on location in Humboldt, Tennessee. Columbia Pictures, like other major Hollywood studios, was turning out occasional social conscience pictures dealing with the plight of blacks. Yet no matter how sincere the effort, these pictures (especially those *not* starring Sidney Poitier) usually turned out as steamy and trashy soap opera rather than sturdy drama. Beyond the spectrum of small-minded whites and blacks stand two opposing black forces: the intellectual, mannerly black who tries to assimilate to the whites' standards (represented by always-polished Roscoe Lee Browne) versus the new breed of militant black (the energetic, quietly resourceful Yaphet Kotto) who uses brutal action rather than words to right wrongs.

141. The Lost Man (Universal, 1969). Color, 122 minutes.

Producers Edward Muhl, Melville Tucker; *associate producer* Ernest B. Wehmeyer; *director* Robert Alan Aurthur; *based on the novel* "Odd Man Out" *by* Frederick Laurence Green; *screenplay* Aurthur; *art directors* Alexander Golitzen, George C. Webb; *set decorators* John McCarthy, John Austin; *costumes* Edith Head; *music* Quincy Jones; *songs* Jones, Ernie Shelby, Willie Cooper; *assistant director* Joseph Kenny; *sound* Waldon O. Watson, William Russell; *camera* Jerry Finnerman; *editor* Edward Mann.

Cast: Sidney Poitier (Jason Higgs); Joanna Shimkus (Cathy Ellis); Al Freeman, Jr. (Dennis Laurence); Michael Tolan (Hamilton); Leon Bibb (Eddie Moxy); Richard Dysart (Barnes); David Steinberg (Photographer); Beverly Todd (Sally); Paul Winfield (Orville); Bernie Hamilton (Reggie Page); Richard Anthony Williams (Ronald); Dolph Sweet (Police Captain); Arnold Williams (Terry); Maxine Stuart (Miss Harrison); George Tyne (Plainclothesman); Paulene Myers (Grandma); Lee Weaver (Willie); Morris Erby (Miller); Doug Johnson (Teddy); Lincoln Kilpatrick (Minister); John Daheim (Officer Parsons); Sonny Garrison (Miller's Assistant); Virginia Capers (Theresa); Vonetta McGee (Diane); Frank Marth (Warren).

Top, left–right: **Fayard Nicholas, Roscoe Lee Browne and Yaphet Kotto in** *The Liberation of L.B. Jones* **(1970).** *Bottom:* **Joanna Shimkus and Sidney Poitier in** *The Lost Man* **(1969).**

Jules Dassin had transformed *The Informer* (1936), the John Ford milestone film about the I.R.A., into a contemporary story of black militants in *Uptight* (1968) (q.v.). Director Robert Alan Aurthur did the same with Carol Reed's classic *Odd Man Out* (1947), another highly regarded study of Irish freedom fighters that featured James Mason as the hunted Irish rebel leader. Starring in the title role of *The Lost Man* was a vast departure for Sidney Poitier. "The first time we see Sidney Poitier in *The Lost Man* we understand that this is going to be a different Poitier role, perhaps a key role in the development of the Poitier image. And it is. Poitier is not precisely a bad guy, but he is a long way from the milksop (if engaging) hero of *Lilies of the Field* or even of *In the Heat of the Night*" (Roger Ebert, *Chicago Sun-Times*).

Jason Higgs (Sidney Poitier), Reggie Page (Bernie Hamilton), and Eddie Moxy (Leon Bibb) quietly observe the police breaking up a peaceful demonstration by blacks outside a Philadelphia factory. Later Higgs contacts Dennis Laurence (Al Freeman, Jr.), the head of the protest, asking him to stage another demonstration the following day to divert attention from the payroll robbery he is planning. Laurence reluctantly agrees. Meanwhile Higgs meets white social worker Cathy Ellis (Joanna Shimkus), who falls in love with this puzzling man. The robbery goes off as planned with Higgs, Page, Moxy, and Orville (Paul Winfield) stealing the payroll and kidnapping plant supervisor Warren (Frank Marth) and his secretary (Maxine Stuart) as hostages. When they reach the getaway car, Warren makes a break for freedom. In the ensuing scuffle, Page is killed and Higgs is wounded. He flees on foot and while hiding out in a movie theater meets a manicurist (Beverly Todd) who helps him. Page phones Laurence, who arranges his escape by ship. Meanwhile Moxy and Orville are killed in a police ambush. Cathy hides Page and Laurence at her home, unmindful of her antagonistic lawyer father Dan Barnes (Richard Dysert). When she drives Page to the dock, Barnes calls the police, who wound Page in a later gunfight on the wharf. When Cathy returns to the scene she sees her love is dying. She draws police fire onto them. Laurence arrives to find his two friends dead.

"Sidney Poitier does not makes movies, he makes milestones. It is not necessarily his fault, but rather it is the result of an accident of timing combined with his affinity for working with second-rate directors. Because he is black, as well as a major movie star, his movies require social interpretations that have nothing to do with cinema.... He is a good actor, but it is his career that's important.... *The Lost Man* is Poitier's attempt to recognize the existence and root causes of black militancy without making anyone—black or white—feel too guilty or hopeless..." (Vincent Canby, *New York Times*). More aggravation at the commercialism of *The Lost Man* was exhibited by Charles Champlin *(Los Angeles Times):* "...*The Lost Man* is a notably offensive work, demeaning and damaging to the causes of social justice and social understanding.... The realities of ghetto misery and the earnest sacrifices of genuine leaders are cheaply made to serve the ends of what in its own terms is a trivial and derivative little charade. Violence would seem to have been repudiated in the blood-soaked finale, but the organization got away with the loot and Poitier's death looks not like irony but noble sacrifice."

The Lost Man was filmed on location in Philadelphia. It was not a sizeable money-earner, and thereafter Sidney Poitier returned to his more acceptable role of the supercool and supermoral hero. He and co-star Joanna Shimkus would marry in January 1976.

When *The Lost Man* opened in England in the spring of 1970 it was cut to 110 minutes.

142. The Mack (Cinerama, 1973). Color, 110 minutes.

Producer Harvey Bernhard; *associate producer* R. Hansel Brown; *director* Michael Campus; *screenplay* Robert J. Poole; *costumes* Mr. Marcus and June; *music/music director/songs* Willie Hutch; *technical advisors* Ward Brothers, Roosevelt Taylor, Jan Payton, Don Barksdale; *special effects* Neeman Tilla; *sound* Bud Alper; *camera* Ralph Woolsey; *editor* Frank C. Decot; *additional editor* Brown.

Cast: Max Julien (John "Goldie" Mickens); Don Gordon (Hank); Richard Pryor (Slim); Carol Speed (Lulu); Roger E. Mosley (Olinga); Dick Williams (Pretty Tony); William C. Watson, Jr. (Jed); George Murdock (Fatman); Juanita Moore (Mother); Paul Harris (Blind Man); Kai Hernandez (Chico); Annazette Chase (China Doll); Junero Jennings (Baltimore Bob); Lee Duncan (Sergeant Duncan); Stu Gilliam (Announcer); Sandra Brown (Diane); Christopher Brooks (Jesus Christ); Fritz Ford (Desk Sergeant); John Vick (Hotel Trick); Norna McClure (Big Woman); David Mauro (Laughing David); *and:* Bill Barnes, Jack Hunter, Jay Payton, Willie Redman, Roosevelt Taylor, Terrible Tom, Allen Van, Andrew Ward, Frank D. Ward, Ted Ward, Willie Ward.

"Remember a pimp is only as good as his product and his product is women — now you gotta go out there and get the best ones you can find and you gotta work them broads like nobody's ever worked them before. And never forget anybody can control a woman's body, but, see, the thing is to control her mind. You see, pimping is big business and it's been going since the beginning of time and it's goin' to continue straight ahead until somebody up there turns outs the light on this small planet. Can you dig it?"

Such is the nature of *The Mack,* a rough-and-tumble feature film education on how to become a first class flamboyant mack (the American variation of the French slang word for pimp — "maguereau"). It opens with John "Goldie" Mickens (Max Julien) released after five years in jail. He returns to Oakland, California, where he promises his religious mother (Juanita Moore), "I'm gonna make a lot of money. I'm gonna buy you all the things I used to promise you. I've got to go out and fight the man anyway I know how.... I'm gonna take care of you, Mama." And that way for Goldie is becoming a pimp. "I'm gonna be the meanest mack that ever lived," he insists. "I'm gonna be king.... I'm gonna be so cool they're goin' to have to change the name of the game and I'm gonna get the hottest bitches I can find.... I'm gonna have a whole boatload of money and then I'm gonna get myself some fine lookin' vines and a great lookin' ride and then I'm goin' to stir it all up."

In a montage of money, fancy clothes and flashy cars, Goldie moves up in the competitive world of prostitution. But things go wrong. He meets a well-to-do white prostitute named Diane (Sandra Brown), who changes his values and makes him forget Lulu (Carol Speed), an old sweetheart and now one of his girls. His militarist brother, Olinga (Roger E. Mosley), wants to clean up the neighborhood—and that includes Goldie's operations. Two harassing, bigoted, corrupt cops (Don Gordon, William C. Watson, Jr.) make life tough on Goldie. The big-time white hoodlum Fatman (George Murdock) wants to squeeze him in line, his mother gets beaten up and dies, and competitor Pretty Tony (Dick Williams) intends to take over the territory and even the score as his former hooker China Doll (Annazette Chase) has gone over to Goldie's side. Eventually Goldie and Olinga avenge their mother's death and kill the two homicidal cops, and, as the film ends, penniless Goldie is on a bus heading out of town, ready to rediscover his roots back in Alabama.

In some ways, *The Mack* reflects a variation on the American (capitalistic) ambition—pursuing the dream of prosperity. And success to impoverished, put-upon ex-convict Goldie is money. He tells a friend, "Ever since I was thirteen my biggest problem has been just to find the right road to get to that rainbow everybody talks about. Whereas most people get close enough to count the stripes they don't have the guts to reach out and take that pot of gold. I'm gonna walk off with the whole pot!" His ambition is to have "... a bankroll so big that when you walk down the street it's gonna look like your pockets has the mumps." As he realizes, "Being rich and black means something."

Throughout the film there is an oblique moralization which justifies the black pimps' and prostitutes' way of life. As one black hooker says to Goldie, "I just don't have to tell you how hard it is for a nigger to earn a living." It says it all. The film uses this thesis to glorify the pimp, considered a folk hero and enviable professional to some elements in the black community.

Variety noted that baby-faced Max Julien "Underplays his character convincingly." It was a long haul from the black militant of the low calibre *The Black Klansman* (1966) (q.v.). to *The Mack*. Along the way he had been featured in *Psych-Out* (1968), *The Savage Seven* (1968), *Uptight* (1968) (q.v.), and *Getting Straight* (1970), and had written the very successful *Cleopatra Jones* (1973) (q.v.). One of the strong elements in *The Mack* is the appearance of Richard Pryor as Goldie's long-time friend Slim. Slim has a telling scene where he breaks into sobs, begging his friend to help him get revenge on the punks who pulled a gun on him. Later in the story Slim is killed by the two villainous policemen.

The Mack was filmed on location in Oakland, California, and features scenes of the Players Ball (a fancy duds party for Bay area pimps and their women, in which the character Goldie is named Player of the Year) and a score by top Motown recording artist Willie Hatch. The film may be shoddy, manipulative, and low down (Vincent Canby of the *New York Times* insisted, "Even as action melodrama of a *Shaft* sort, the film is inept, so confused that occasionally it seems unreal. Plot elements bump into one another like air bubbles in a mostly empty stomach"), but it registered a strong audience appeal. It grossed $3,000,000 in domestic film rentals. The film was "Dedicated to a man, Frank D. Ward." who had appeared briefly in *The Mack*. A week after filming was completed, this leader of Oakland's black community had been found in the trunk of a car with his brains blown out. The movie's script was by Robert J. Poole, who had served a five-year prison term for having pimped for twelve years.

143. The McMasters (Chevron, 1970). Color, 98 minutes.

Executive producer Dimitri De Grunwald; *producer* Monroe Sachson; *director* Alf Kjellin; *screenplay* Harold Jacob Smith; *production designer/art director* Joel Schiller; *set decorator* George R. Nelson; *music/music director* Coleridge-Taylor Perkinson; *assistant director* Ray De Camp; *technical adviser* Rodd Redwing; *sound* John V. Speak; *special effects* Herman Townsley, Ted Alires; *camera* Lester Shorr; *editor* Melvin Shapiro.

Cast: Brock Peters (Benjie); Burl Ives (Neal McMasters); David Carradine (White Feather); Nancy Kwan (Robin); Jack Palance (Kolby); Dane Clark (Spencer); John Carradine (Preacher); L.Q. Jones (Russell); R.G. Armstrong (Watson); Frank Raiter (Grant); Alan Vint (Hank); Marion Brash (Mrs. Watson); Neil Davis (Sylvester); Paul Eichenberg (Jud); Richard Alden (Lester); Lonnie Samuel (Bull); Albert Hockmeister (Sheriff); Reverend David Strong (Otis); Duman Slade (Cullen); Joan Howard (Mrs. Spencer); William Kiernan (Bartender); Jose Maranio (Indian Joe); Leo Dillenschneider (Watson's Son); Richard Martinez (Black Fox); Joseph Duran (Black Cloud); Bill Alexander (Barber); Frank Nanoia (Rancher); David Welty (Kolby's Son).

A.K.A. *The Blood Crowd.* Released in England as *The McMasters... Tougher Than the West Itself.*

At the end of the Civil War, Benjie (Brock Peters) returns to the South, having fought for the North. His "wrong" loyalties have made him the enemy of bigoted, one-armed rancher Kolby (Jack Palance) and his ranch helper Russell (L.Q. Jones). The benevolent Neal McMasters (Burl Ives), who raised Benjie from childhood, offers him co-ownership in his ranch spread. Because Benjie is black no one will work for him, until members of the tribe of White Feather (David Carradine)—who owe Benjie a favor for having befriended the Indian chief—arrive to help with the roundup. White Feather offers his sister Robin (Nancy Kwan) as a wife to Benjie. When Kolby heads an attack on McMasters and Benjie, Robin is raped. Benjie begs the Indians to help, but they want no part in the white and black men's feud. The liberal Spencer (Dane Clark) tries to forestall trouble, but Kolby attacks the ranch again, and this time McMasters is murdered and the house burned. In a counterattack the Indians save Benjie from hanging and Kolby is killed. Benjie returns to the ranch and Robin.

There were many unusual facets to *The McMasters.* It was produced by an English company (Dimitri De Grunwald's London Screenplays); it was directed by Swedish actor Alf Kjellin; it was filmed fully on location at the New Mexico Film Center (Santa Fe) and elsewhere in the state. Most unusual of all, it was released simultaneously in New York City in two versions: one at 98 minutes, which had the approval of the producer, scenarist, and leading man, and a 90-minute edition favored by the distributor. The latter variation removed some of the violence, toned down the interracial angles, and made the ending less liberal.

Nancy Kwan and Brock Peters in *The McMasters* (1970).

Regardless of the controversy over the subject matter, the film was too stark and progressive to win its proper audience. "*The McMasters* strains for a degree of high seriousness appropriate perhaps to its themes but certainly not to its utterly brutal action; all the dialogue is deep and all the gestures are meant to be exemplary" (Roger Greenspun, *New York Times).* *Variety* reported, "Whether the complete absence of colorful backgrounds and highly photogenic scenery are necessary requisites of a western will be put to the test by this unusual drama...."

144. Man and Boy (Levitt-Pickman, 1972). Color, 98 minutes.

Executive producer William H. Cosby, Jr. [Bill Cosby]; *producer* Marvin Miller; *associate producer* R. Robert Rosenbaum; *director* E.W. Swackhamer; *screenplay* Harry Essex, Oscar Saul; *art director* Rolland Brooks; *set decorator* Anthony Mondello; *costumes* Glenn Wright; *makeup* Fred Williams; *music* J.J. Johnson; *song* Johnson; *music editor* Harry King; *assistant director* R. Robert Rosenbaum; *special effects* Geza Caspar; *stunt co-ordinator* Carl Brown; *sound* James Z. Flaster; *sound effects editors* Kay Rose, Chet Slomika; *camera* Arnold Rich; *editorial supervisor* Anthony Ippotito; *editor* John A. Martinelli.

Cast: Bill Cosby (Caleb Revers); Gloria Foster (Ivy Revers); Leif Erickson (Sheriff Mossman); George Spell (Billy Revers); Douglas Turner Ward (Lee Christmas); John Anderson (Stretch); Henry Silva (Caine); Dub Taylor (Atkins); Shelley Morrison (Rosita); Yaphet Kotto (Nate Hodges); Richard Bull (Thornhill); Robert Lawson (Lawson); Jason Clark (Red); Fred Graham (Joe Samsil); Jack Owens (Mark Atwell); Buster Shavers (Ted Richards); Sam Patridge (Steve Atwell); Horace Owen (Ralph Orteca).

"Low-key westerns for the whole family aren't grist for the grinds anymore, tending to languish on TV these days. But Bill Cosby and friends have revived the genre for the presumed purpose of letting the young generation know that there were some tough black folks in the Old West, who didn't take any guff from anybody" *(Variety)*.

When ex–Union soldier Caleb Revers (Bill Cosby) has a horse stolen from him, he and his twelve-year-old son, Billy (George Spell), set out in pursuit on foot, leaving the farm in the hands of Mrs. Revers (Gloria Foster), who is expecting a second child. Not only does Revers seek the purloined animal, he has another goal: "I brought the boy with me so he could see what's on the other side of the mountain." He is hopeful that en route he and moody Billy will come to terms and he can provide his son with a better perspective on the black man and his role in the West. Their odyssey through the southwest leads them into contact with burly Nate Hodges (Yaphet Kotto), who has never forgiven Revers for winning away the woman he wanted. Eventually the two men come to blows, and after a lengthy fist fight, Revers emerges the winner (demonstrating his masculinity to his gaping son). They encounter Rosita (Shelley Morrison), a sad Mexican widow, who offers herself to Revers in any way he will have her, all of which puzzles the teenager. They also meet vile black killer Lee Christmas (Douglas Turner Ward), who kidnaps Billy to draw Revers out into the open, and nasty Sheriff Mossman (Leif Erickson) and Caine (Henry Silva), who are no help. Through it all Revers and his son persevere and, before the finale, the two have found peace with one another.

Whatever its good intentions, *Man and Boy* is a syrupy sagebrush tale that meanders dreadfully, has sloppy editing, and overstates its message badly. "Pulled together taut and hard, along with some good, cutting dialogue, the film might have scored a neat homerun. But at least it puts Mr. Cosby on first base in screen drama" (Howard Thompson, *New York Times*). George Spell is excellent as the adolescent; he appeared previously as Sidney Poitier's son in *They Call Me Mister Tibbs!* (1970) and *The Organization* (1971) (qq.v.).

145. Mean Johnny Barrows (Dimension, 1975). Color, 90 minutes.

Executive producer Lee B. Winkler; *producer/director* Fred Williamson; *screenplay* Charles Walker, Jolevett Cato; *wardrobe co-ordinator* Emmett Cash; *wardrobe* Howard Stanley, Jeri Gray; *makeup* Marie Carter; *music* Paul Riser, Coleridge-Taylor Perkins; *music co-ordinator* Ms. Ray Singleton; *special effects* Jack DeBron; *camera* Bob Caramico.

Cast: Fred Williamson (Johnny Barrows); Roddy McDowall (Tony Da Vinci); Stuart Whitman (Mario Racconi); Luther Adler (Don Racconi); Jenny Sherman (Nancy); Aaron Banks (Captain O'Malley); Anthony Caruso (Don Da Vinci); Mike Henry (Carlo Da Vinci); Elliot Gould (Theodore Rasputin Waterhouse, the Professor); R.G. Armstrong (Richard); Vic Rogers (Tom); Gregory Bach (Bodyguard); Frank Bello (Joe); Louis Ojena (Louie); Al Hansen, Russ McGann, Phillip Roye, Emile Farcus (Cops); Hank Rolike (Charlie); Jan J. Madrid (Chef); Steve Wollenberg (Deliveryman); James E. Brodhead (Foreman); Charlotte Macik, Signe Johnson (Nurses); Leon Isaac [Kennedy] (Private Pickens); Leonard D. John (Thug); *and:* James Brown, Bob Phillips.

"Brutal! Blasting! Blazing! For Hire, a one-man death squad. Don't nobody fool with *Mean Johnny Barrows.*" So insisted the catchy ad copy for this latest Fred Williamson action film.

Former high school and college football player Johnny Barrows (Fred Williamson) is dishonorably discharged from the army during the Vietnam War for having (justifiably) hit a commanding officer. Although he had won a Silver Star, he returns home to Los Angeles to find he is a forgotten man and cannot get honest work because he is black and has no career training. Soon he meets gangster Mario Racconi (Stuart Whitman), who owns a restaurant, and is asked to become a hit man to remove the competition from the rival Da Vinci family. But Barrows refuses even after the senior Mr. Racconi (Luther Adler) is gunned down. Later Mario has provocative Nancy (Jenny Sherman) from the restaurant convince Barrows that Tony Da Vinci (Roddy McDowall) kidnapped and raped her, and Barrows snaps into action. In the retaliatory mob action, the flower shop of Don Da Vinci (Anthony Caruso) is burned and many of both gangs lie dead. At the finale Barrows is shot on a hillside by the duplistic Nancy.

The postscript to *Mean Johnny Barrows* dedicates the film "...to the veteran who traded his place on the front lines for a place on the unemployment line. Peace is hell." This provocative and timely subject was but one of the themes in this action entry. A great deal of the motion picture is focused on the special plight of the black man who, no matter what his sacrifices for his country, cannot find justice back home. "I ain't lookin' for no charity," Johnny Barrows insists as he wanders the streets seeking employment and a place to be. But wherever he looks potential employers discriminate against blacks or "warmongers" who served in Vietnam. Finally he comes across a menial position at a gas station and dares to ask what the salary is. "You colored boys are all the same. Always wanting to know when you get paid." Later when the owner tries to cheat him out of his minimal pay, Barrows beats him up and lands in jail. From then on, Barrows is an alienated, lost man, and his lowly job at the Mafia-owned restaurant is one step deeper into his private hell.

Another focus of *Mean Johnny Barrows* is a derivative one brought in the onslaught of movies imitating *The Godfather* (1972) and *The Godfather II* (1974)—that of the camaraderie of gangland life among the organization. Don Ricconi philosophizes to Barrows about the family and how it goes on even after an individual's death. Ironically it is precisely the immoral hoodlums Barrows abhors who treat him with respect (for his brawn and bravery), munificence, and brotherly love.

Linda Gross *(Los Angeles Times)* labeled this gangster study a "...claustrophobic downer that tries to tackle the problems of a Vietnam veteran for whom 'peace is hell.'" But there is a definite texture (albeit campy, with the phony Italian accents from the very Anglo-Saxon Roddy McDowall *et al.*), that pervades *Mean Johnny Barrows.* In its simplistic, determined approach there is an underlying integrity that unfortunately gets lost in its Mafia trappings and its too-frequent, too-heavy preaching. By far the strangest casting is the special guest appearance by Elliott Gould as the dropout Theodore Rasputin Waterhouse, known simply as "The Professor." Garbed in an eccentric array of castoffs, he provides Barrows with a crash course on street survival in the alleyways and at the soup kitchens. "If you want to be a bum, you've got to stay healthy," he insists.

Mean Johnny Barrows was made by Fred Williamson's Po' Boy Productions in conjunction with Brut Films under the working title *Bad Johnny Barrows*. It was released initially by Dimension Pictures in the fall of 1975 and grossed $300,000 in its first three weeks of distribution in the South. Then it was picked up by Atlas for distribution, as part of a multi-picture deal which included *Adios Amigo* (1976) (q.v.) and three other projects to be made by Williamson.

146. Melinda (Metro-Goldwyn-Mayer, 1972). Color, 109 minutes.

Producer Pervis Atkins; *director* Hugh A. Robertson; *story* Raymond Cistheri; *screenplay* Lonne Elder III; *art director* Edward C. Carfagno; *set decorator* Sal Blydenburgh; *makeup* Ray Brooks; *music* Jerry Butler, Jerry Peters; *stunt co-ordinator* George Fisher; *assistant directors* Charles Washburn, Ron Satlof; *sound* Jerry Jost; *camera* Wilmer C. Butler; *editor* Paul L. Evans.

Cast: Calvin Lockhart (Frankie J. Parker); Rosalind Cash (Terry Davis); Vonetta McGee (Melinda); Paul Stevens (Mitch); Rockne Tarkington (Tank); Ross Hagen (Gregg Van); Renny Roker (Dennis Smith); Judyann Elder (Gloria); Jim Kelly (Charlie Atkins); Jan Tice (Marcia); Lonne Elder III (Lieutenant Daniels); Edmund Cambridge (Detective); George Fisher (Young Man); Allen Pinson (Rome); Joe Hooker (Rome's Servant); Jack Manning (Bank Man); Gene LeBell (Hodd); Gary Pagett (Sergeant Adams); Khalil Bezaleel (Washington); Nina Roman (Bank Woman); Jeanne Bell (Jean); Evelyne Cuffee, Dort Dixon, Peaches Jones, Douglas C. Lawrence, Earl Maynard (Karate Group).

Although almost forgotten today, *Melinda* is a resilient motion picture which Howard Thompson *(New York Times)* weighed "...an engrossing tingler ... may miss the bullseye but it does rattle the target." James P. Murray (*Encore* magazine) endorsed, "...what gives it [*Melinda*] a measure of distinction are not the resemblances to other recent slick sex-and-violence films but the differences [there is no actual gunplay; the love relationship is three-dimensional; there are positive anti-drugs and pro-community messages within].... You can enjoy *Melinda* simply as diversion, but you'll also be impressed by its heavier aspects."

Melinda has an interesting genesis. It was produced by black former football star (Los Angeles Rams) Pervis Atkins, who had become a talent agent and was here making his film producing debut. It was directed by Hugh A. Robertson, the black film editor who was Oscar-nominated for his editing of *Midnight Cowboy* (1969). When he signed to edit *Shaft* (1971) (q.v.), his deal with Metro-Goldwyn-Mayer provided he next be allowed to direct a film. The script for *Melinda* is by Lonne Elder III, who authored the play *Ceremonies in Dark Old Men* and wrote the Oscar-nominated screenplay for *Sounder* (1972).

Narcissistic and hip disc jockey Frankie J. Parker (Calvin Lockhart) has a swinging pad, is loved by everyone (including himself), and has thrown over reliable publishing executive Terry Davis (Rosalind Cash) for the alluring,

Rosalind Cash and Calvin Lockhart in *Melinda* **(1972).**

mysterious Melinda (Vonetta McGee). When Melinda is murdered in his apartment, he becomes the target of both the police and the underworld (headed by
mobster Mitch [Paul Stevens] and his chief henchmen, ex-football player Tank
[Rockne Tarkington] and Gregg [Ross Hagen]). It develops that Melinda's
fatal problem was that she had taped Mitch's confession that he had murdered
a union official. Thankfully, ultra-contemporary Parker had enrolled in the
karate class run by businessman Atkins (Jim Kelly), which gives him the martial art edge in battling the crooks at the showdown.

With its toned-down violence (save for the pummeling the black Parker
gives the white Mitch character at the end) and deeper seriousness about life's
morality, *Melinda* represented a new wave in the black film cycle that attempted to respond to the backlash from the black community against the blaxploitation syndrome. The film grossed a sturdy $1,560,000 in domestic film
rentals.

Melinda should have done far more for the movie careers of its lead players, especially Calvin Lockhart and Rosalind Cash. The extremely handsome, cosmopolitan Lockhart provides a spellbinding performance as the biggest, baddest, and blackest deejee. Every time he passes a mirror he stops to study the perfection and appraises, "You are a pretty moth-uh." The thirty-eight-year-old performer, born in Nassau, was indeed a riveting presence in early 1970s Hollywood, appearing in a wide diversity of roles — from Genevive Waite's interracial lover in *Joanna* (1968), to the con artist in *Cotton Comes to Harlem* (1970) (q.v.), to the dedicated if frustrated vice-principal in *Halls of Anger* (1970) (q.v.), and on to the swish acting student of Mae West's *Myra Breckinridge* (1970). But the combination of his bad press relations and problems on the set, along with the downcycle of the black film cycle, militated against him. By the time of *Uptown Saturday Night* (1974) (q.v.), he was supporting Sidney Poitier and Harry Belafonte, and by the 1980s he was reduced to a few recurring episodes opposite Diahann Carroll in the teleseries "Dynasty" and to being almost invisible in Eddie Murphy's *Coming to America* (1988).

New Jersey–born Rosalind Cash was four years Lockhart's junior and had appeared with him on the New York stage in *Dark of the Moon* (1968) and in Lonne Elder III's *Ceremonies in Dark Old Men* (1968). After co-starring with Charlton Heston in *The Omega Man* (1971), she appeared in *Hickey and Boggs* (1972), *Uptown Saturday Night* (1974), *Cornbread, Earl and Me* (1974), *Dr. Black, Mr. Hyde* (1976), *Monkey Hustle* (1976) (qq.v.), and many others, including television's *Sophisticated Gents* (1981) (q.v.) and *Sister, Sister* (1982). Her role as the business executive who is human enough to love Flash (Frankie J. Parker) and to want racial equality in everyday life is a telling performance. In *Blacks in American Films and Television* (1988), Donald Bogle enthuses about her bank account withdrawal scene in which she meets overt discrimination with outrage. "Here in her best role of this period as a woman on the edge, holding on for dear life, struggling to keep a relationship with a man who hardly seemed her equal, Cash's tenacity and endurance, despite personal pain, made her a heroine for many black coeds of that era.... Cash's character won respect for plowing through life nonetheless and for displaying, when pushed, a resilient don't-mess-or-play-with-me toughness."

Also in the cast are Lonne Elder III (as the pressured police detective) and martial arts champion Jim Kelly, who would make his genre mark with *Enter the Dragon* (1973) and *Black Belt Jones* (1974) (qq.v.).

147. The Messenger (Snizzlefritz, 1986). Color, 95 minutes.

Producers Fred Williamson, Pier Luigi Ciraci; *director/story* Williamson; *screenplay* Brian Johnson, Conchita Lee, Anthony Wisdom; *music* William Stuckey; *camera* Giancarlo Ferrando, Craig Green, Andy Costikkan, Brice Kinney; *editor* Fiorenzo Mueller.

Cast: Fred Williamson (Jake Sebastian Turner); Sandy Cummings (Sabrina); Val Avery (Clark); Michael Dante (Emerson); Chris Connelly (F.B.I. Agent Parker); Cameron Mitchell (Police Captain Carter); Peter Turner (Harris); Joe Spinell (Rico); Sandy Cummings (Sabrina); Michael Dante (Emerson); *and:* Riccardo Parisio, Umberto Ramo, Susan Von Schaack.

Yet another of Fred Williamson's Po' Boy Productions made with Italian financing and shot on the international scene to maximize whatever audience allure that might provide. It is one of the least of the filmmaker's recent self-directed ventures.

After three years in an Italian prison, Jake Sebastian Turner (Fred Williamson) spends one night in Rome reunited with his wife Sabrina (Sandy Cummings). The following day she is shot dead, and he learns she was not only hooked on cocaine but involved in drug trafficking as well. He swears revenge on the drug ring. Meanwhile he is hired by a supposed do-gooder to return to the United States to eliminate a covey of drug bosses. His path leads to Chicago and a showdown in Las Vegas, where he discovers his benefactor had set him up merely to get rid of the competition.

Among those cornered in this incoherent gun caper are Christopher Connelly as a dedicated government narcotics agent and Cameron Mitchell as a puffy, crooked cop. There is much synthetic tough talk ("I'll grind your ass up and sell it for chittlin'," warns one arch gangster); lots of cynical talk (Turner talking about his dead wife: "Once a month for three years she dragged her butt up to prison to see me and that means more to me than whose fly she unzipped or whose tits she sucked"); and endless and amateurish shootouts.

148. Mister Mean (Lone Star/Po' Boy, 1977). Color 84 minutes.

Executive producer Jeff Williamson; *producer* Fred Williamson; *associate producer* Lee Thornberg; *director* Fred Williamson; *screenplay* Jeff Williamson; *music* Ohio Players; *sound* Roberto Alberghini; *camera* Maurizio Magi.

Cast: Fred Williamson (Mr. Mean); Lou Castel (Huberto); Raimind Harmstorf (Rommell); Crippy Yocard (Rene); Anthony Maimone (Don Rico); Rita Silva (Carla); Pat Brocato (Tony); David Mills (Lieutenant Rigoli); Stelio Candelli (Ranati); Tawfiq Said (Driver); Angela Doria (Farm Girl); Richard Oneto (Man); Satch (Satch); Charles Borromel (Johnny).

So many of Fred Williamson's caper movies seem to be products of a filmmaker in search of a good characterization and *the* proper showcase to present it. Often the only distinction and dimension his screen personae have are their unique surnames. Here he is Mr. Mean. "They used to call you the one man mean machine" says one person about him. He tells another, "Mean is a personality trait, not necessarily my character." Regardless, he is a strong-arm man and courier whose motto is "If the price is right, the job is right."

After a long-running battle at the Los Angeles freight yard (which really has nothing to do with the storyline beyond showing off the star's athletic abilities), the action switches to Rome, where Mr. Mean, who cannot speak Italian, meets with Don Rico (Anthony Maimone), who claims he is hiring the hit man on behalf of the Family. The target is Huberto (Lou Castel), a conniving ex-member who has established a profitable con game scamming contributions to a Help the Underprivileged Foundation. (Much is made of the fact that Mr. Mean was chosen for the task because he is black and an outsider, and that would prove definitely the killing is not an inter-family reprisal done by one of their own.) Meanwhile Huberto learns of his potential demise and hires his own hit man (Stelio Candelli) to eliminate Mr. Mean. Before Mr. Mean returns to

California, he has bedded an assortment of women, all the aggressive hoodlums have been dispatched, and Mr. Mean has even survived a rifle blast (thanks to a lucky medallion on his gold neck chain stopping the bullet) from a curvaceous hit lady, who returns to the States with her new lover.

As with so many of Fred Williamson's self-produced, low-budgeted features, much of this film's profits come from international co-financing and distribution to the action marketplaces of Europe and the Far East.

149. Monkey Hustle (American International, 1976). Color, 90 minutes.

Producer Arthur Marks; *associate producer* Robert E. Schultz; *director* Marks; *story* Odie Hawkins; *screenplay* Charles Johnson; *wardrobe* Llandys Williams; *music* Jack Conrad; *sound* William Pellak; *camera* Jack L. Richards; *editor* Art Seid.

Cast: Yaphet Kotto (Daddy Foxx); Rudy Ray Moore (Goldie); Rosalind Cash (Mama); Randy Brooks (Win); Debbi Morgan (Vi); Thomas Carter (Player); Donn Harper (Tiny); Lynn Caridine (Jan-Jan); Patricia McCaskill (Shirl); Lynn Harris (Sweet Potato); Fuddle Bagley (Mr. Molet); Frank Rice (Black Night); Carl Crudup (Joe); Duchyll Smith (Beatrice); Kirk Calloway (Baby D).

The huge success of Paul Newman and Robert Redford's *The Sting* (1973) certainly helped to inspire the likes of *Trick Baby* (1973) (q.v.) and such Sidney Poitier pell-mell comedies as *Uptown Saturday Night* (1974) and its sequel, *Let's Do It Again* (1975) (qq.v.). Another in the genre was *Monkey Hustle* (1976), which Lawrence Van Gelder *(New York Times)* described as a "...movie of jellied brains and idiot eyes." *Variety* was even more to the point: "...director Arthur Marx' failure to focus story and cast probably relegates pic to ghetto houses, where pic lacks enough action or sex to succeed. Cross-over possibilities are nil, since white audiences won't relate to any of it and probably can't understand most of the lingo spoken."

When an announced freeway project threatens to cause a black ghetto in Chicago to be torn down, the locals unite to oppose it via a big block party. Among the flavorful neighborhood characters involved are assorted hustlers, pimps, street kids, hookers, crooked cops, corrupt businessmen, and conniving politicians—all of whom cannot resist conning and stealing from one another. In particular there is racketeer boss Goldie (Rudy Ray Moore), fumbling thief Mr. Molet (Fuddie Bagley), kingpin scam artist (Daddy Foxx [Yaphet Kotto]), Daddy's young apprentice Baby D (Kirk Calloway), and Mama (Rosalind Cash), who has a weakness for the irrepressible Daddy Foxx.

This film emerged at the tail end of the 1970s black film period and reflected threadbare production values.

150. Mr. Ricco (Metro-Goldwyn-Mayer, 1975). Color, 98 minutes.

Producer Douglas Netter; *director* Paul Bogart; *story* Ed Harvey, Francis Kierman; *screenplay* Robert Hoban; *art director* Herman A. Blumenthal; *set decorator* Don Sullivan; *music* Chico Hamilton; *action co-ordinator* George Fisher; *assistant director* Daniel J. McCauley; *sound* Jerry Jost, Harry W. Tetrick; *camera* Frank Stanley; *editor* Michael McLean.

Advertisement for *Monkey Hustle* (1976).

Cast: Dean Martin (Joe Ricco); Eugene Roche (Detective Cronyn); Thalmus Rasulala (Frankie Steele); Denise Nicholas (Irene Mapes); Cindy Williams (Jamison); Geraldine Brooks (Katherine Fremont); Philip [Michael] Thomas (Purvis Mapes); George Tyne (Detectie Barrett); Robert Sampson (Justin); Michael Gregory (Detective Tanner); Joseph Hacker (Markham); Jay Fletcher (Detective Jackson); Oliver Givins (Calvin Mapes); Frank Puglia (Uncle Enzo); Ella Edwards (Sally); H.B. Barnum III (Luther).

Without his celluloid teammate Jerry Lewis or his later "Matt Helm" movie characterization, singer Dean Martin's screen career was a very mixed bag. *Mr. Ricco* was bottom of the barrel. "It's such a clumsy movie it makes all the actors look dreadful..." (Vincent Canby, *New York Times*). "The film is a tedious and corny hodgepodge..." *(Variety)*.

What gives this tiresome detective outing any uplift is its San Francisco locales and its black militarist subplot. San Francisco criminal attorney Joe Ricco (Dean Martin) is hired to defend a black client (Thalmus Rasulala) charged with homicide. Ricco saves the defendant, but later comes to believe that the black man may really be the one responsible for the death of several local policemen. Involved in the case are black activist Purvis Mapes (Philip [Michael] Thomas) and his sister Irene (Denise Nicholas), confused police detective Cronyn (Eugene Roche), dumb police investigator Barrett (George Tyne), as well as bigoted and very crooked law enforcer Tanner (Michael Gregory). Also on tap are Katherine Fremont (Geraldine Brooks) as Ricco's girlfriend and Jamison (Cindy "Laverne and Shirley" Williams) as the efficient law office secretary.

151. The Muthers (Dimension, 1976). Color, 88 minutes.

Presenter Larry Woolner;; *producer* Cirio H. Santiago; *associate producers* Annabelle Santiago, Forentino Sentos, Jr.; *director* Cirio H. Santiago; *story* Leonard Hermes; *screenplay* Cyril St. James; *music* Edd Villanueva; *special effects* Rolly Studoningo; *sound* Willie Arce, Willie De Santos; *camera* Richard Remias; *editor* Gervacio Santos.

Cast: Jeanne Bell (Kelly); Rosanne Katon (Anggie); Trina Parks (Marcie); Jayne Kennedy (Serena); J. Antonio Carrion (Montiero); John Montgomery (Turko); Sam Sharruff (Sancho); Dick Piper (Murphy); Ken Metcalfe (Barrows); Rock Monte (Rocc); Bill Baldridge (Captain Montes); Bert Oliver (Navarro); Claudine Santiago (Child).

This film is another of those hastily and poorly assembled action features produced in the Philippines and filled with poor acting, inferior dubbing, a confusing plotline, and minimal production values. Its best assets are its grabby title and the assemblage of attractive lead actresses.

Americans Kelly (Jeanne Bell) and Anggie (Rosanne Katon) head a pirate crew named "the Muthers," who are fighting to maintain their share of the profitable high seas. Kelly's sister Marcie (Trina Parks) is captured and sent to the plantation prison camp controlled by Montiero (J. Antonio Carrion). Kelly and Anggie slip into the compound, and once inside they learn what it is like to really fight for survival. They encounter Serena (Jayne Kennedy), the double-dealing mistress of the sadistic Montiero. At the end, Serena has a change of heart and sacrifices herself on the rope bridge so the others can escape. Once more on the high seas, the distaff pirates exclaim, "At last we are free—but never to go home." "But we are home," insists another joyously as they sail off into the sunset.

Taking its commercial cue from the Pam Grier mini-epics of the early 1970s, *The Big Doll House* (1971) and *The Big Bird Cage* (1972) (qq.v.), *The Muthers* is full of voyeuristic delights: scantily clad, incarcerated women being strung up and beaten; one comely victim being bitten on the breast by a snake and another girl bending over to suck out the poison; etc.

By the time this cheap flick reached videocassette, Jayne Kennedy was more of a TV and film name, and she was promoted heavily in the ad copy.

152. No Way Back (Atlas, 1976). Color, 91 minutes.

Executive producer Jeff Williamson; *producer/director/screenplay* Fred Williamson; *wardrobe co-ordinator* Emmett Cash III; *songs* Michael Terry, Walter Morse, Robert Brooks; *makeup* Zoltan Elek; *assistant director* Phillip Browning; *sound* Oliver Moss; *camera* Robert Hopkins; *editor* James E. Nownes.

Cast: Fred Williamson (Jesse Crowder); Charles Woolf (Pickens); Tracy Reed (Candy); Virginia Gregg (Mrs. Pickens); Stack Pierce (Bernie); Argy Allen (James Pickens); Paula Sills (Crowder's Secretary); Bobby Wood (Pete); Mary Mary (Prostitute); Nick Dimitri, Gene LeBell, Mike Henry, Peter Horak (Thugs); Louise Horowitz (Bank President); Leonard D'John (Amando); Mel Carter (Harold); Horace Jones, Chuck Duncan (Cops); Kitty Carl (Girl in Park); *and:* Don Cornelius.

"In the most blatant display of sexism on screen since the rape scene in *Bring Me the Head of Alfredo Garcia,* Fred Williamson brutalizes women and makes them beg for more in *No Way Back.*... [It] is a macho fantasy for urban black males, and is competently done on a sock-bam level. Whites and women should stay away, because the film revels in contempt for both categories" *(Variety).*

Tough Los Angeles private investigator Jesse Crowder (Fred Williamson) jaunts to San Francisco, where he meets his newest client in Ghiradelhi Square. James Pickens (Argy Allen) wants Crowder to find his missing brother (Charles Woolf), who embezzled a large sum of money from the bank where he works. His wife (Virginia Gregg) in Mill Valley can't imagine what happened to him. For a $3,000 retainer Crowder takes the case, and before long he has traced the missing Pickens to San Diego. The latter has the attractive black Candy (Tracy Reed) in tow. It turns out that she really works for gangster Bernie (Stack Pierce), who wants the money or else. Meanwhile, Mrs. Pickens, who had been using her husband all along, shows up with her brother-in-law to claim the cash for themselves and the hell with Pickens (who is disposed of by Bernie). The chase proceeds to the arid countryside, where Mrs. Pickens kills James Pickens and almost does in Candy. But Crowder, never far behind, arrives on horseback (!) and saves the day.

In a film filled with oversized performances and underdeveloped characterizations, Virginia Gregg's shrewish villainess stands out. The film's slick and macho hero enjoys several romps in bed with his obliging secretary (Paula Sills) and Candy, which does not stop the "good" guy from doing what is right at the close — sending Candy to jail (à la *The Maltese Falcon*).

CANDY: You really are a genuine bastard.
CROWDER: *(Smirking)* Just my nature baby.

Crowder's character never seems happier than when smashing a hood's head against a door or window, or landing a right cross to a thug's chin. He could just as easily have been working for the bad guys. He is always intimidating his contacts: "Be hard to play pool with a broken arm, brother." "If your correction ain't correct, I'll be back and I'll burn the place down."

The highlight of this film is an effervescent scene reminiscent of a similar one with young Tierre Turner in *Bucktown* (1975) (q.v.). Here the young white boy pimp named Pete (Bobby Wood), who packs a pistol, leads Crowder through the maze of tawdry life in the tenderloin, assuring the amused investigator he can show him where *all* the action is — and he does, including some willing prostitutes.

153. No Way Out (Twentieth Century-Fox, 1950). 106 minutes.

Producer Darryl F. Zanuck; *director* Joseph L. Mankiewicz; *screenplay* Mankiewicz, Lester Samuels; *art directors* Lyle Wheeler, George W. Davis; *costumes* William Travilla; *music/music director* Alfred Newman; *assistant director* William Eckhardt; *camera* Milton Krasner; *editor* Barbara McLean.

Cast: Richard Widmark (Ray Biddle); Linda Darnell (Edie); Stephen McNally (Dr. Wharton); Sidney Poitier (Dr. Luther Brooks); Mildred Joanne

Smith (Cora Brooks); Harry Bellaver (George Biddle); Stanley Ridges (Dr. Moreland); Dots Johnson (Lefty); Amanda Randolph (Gladys); Bill Walker (Mathew Tompkins); Ruby Dee (Connie); Ken Christy (Kowalski); Ossie Davis (John); Frank Richards (Mac); George Tyne (Whitey); Robert Adler (Assistant Deputy); Bert Freed (Rocky); Jim Toney (Deputy Sheriff); Maude Simmons (Luther's Mother); Ray Teal (Day Deputy); Will Wright (Dr. Cheney); Jack Kruschen (Man); Eileen Boyer, Johnnie Jallings, Marie Lampe, Gertrude Tighe (Telephone Operators); Frank Jaquet (Reilly); John Whitney (Assistant); Howard Mitchell (Bailiff); Charles J. Flynn (Deputy); Kitty O'Neil (Landlady); Emmett Smith (Joe); Ralph Hodges (Terry); Thomas Ingersoll (Priest); Wade Duman (Jonah); Fred Graham (Ambulance Driver); William Pullen (Ambulance Doctor); Jasper Weldon (Henry); Ruben Wendorf (Polish Husband); Laeola Wendorf (Polish Wife); Dick Paxton (Johnny Biddle); Stan Johnson, Frank Overton (Interns); Ralph Hodges (Terry); Harry Lauter, Harry Carter, Don Kohler, Ray Huke (Orderlies); Ann Tyrrell, Ann Morrison, Eda Reis Merin (Nurses); Kathryn Sheldon (Mother); *and:* Ernest Anderson, Eleanor Audley, Robert Davis, Ralph Dunn, J. Louis Johnson, Doris Kemper, Victor Kilian, Sr., Phil Tully, Ruth Warren, Mack Williams, Ian Wolfe.

Born in Miami in 1927, Sidney Poitier moved to New York in his late teens and by 1945 was appearing in productions of the American Negro Theatre and then on Broadway in *Lysistrata* (1946). He later acted with Ruby Dee and others at the Apollo Theatre in Harlem. In the fall of 1949 he was in his first film, an Army Signal Corps documentary titled *From Whence Cometh My Help. No Way Out* is the motion picture which launched Poitier's screen career.

No Way Out also set the path for future on-camera social conscience studies about the black man. It was directed and co-scripted by the articulate Joseph L. Mankiewicz, who the same year would win Oscars for his *All About Eve.*

Young black intern Luther Brooks (Sidney Poitier) works at a large county hospital under the tutelage of chief resident Dr. Daniel Wharton (Stephen McNally), the latter his only champion on the staff. When the gunshot-wounded Biddle brothers—Ray (Richard Widmark) and Johnny (Don Hicks)—are brought in for treatment, Brooks examines their condition. He determines that Johnny, who has lapsed into a coma, has a brain tumor. Johnny soon dies. The paranoid and bigoted Ray blames Brooks for his brother's death. He is so set in his judgment that he refuses an autopsy which could prove Brooks was right. Brooks begins to lose faith in himself, despite the encouragement from his wife (Mildred Joanne Smith), his mother (Maude Simmons), and the always-sympathetic Dr. Wharton. Wharton asks Ray's ex-wife, Edie Johnson (Linda Darnell), to reason with her ex-husband, but Ray later convinces her that it is all a trick. She is ordered to pass the word to his white pals in the slums to lash out at the blacks. Before the whites can attack, the black gangs surprise Biddle's cronies at a warehouse and the riot breaks out. Succumbing to the pressure of racism at the hospital, Brooks surrenders to the police and forces an autopsy by issuing a trumped-up murder confession. The coroner's verdict in court substantiates Brooks's diagnosis. Meanwhile Ray, with the help of his mute brother George (Harry Bellaver), escapes from the prison ward and forces Edie to set up an ambush for Brooks and his wife at Dr. Wharton's house. She later has a change of heart, calls the police and shows up at Wharton's to distract Ray from his scheme. Brooks is wounded, and Ray collapses from his previously crippled leg. Brooks saves the criminal from bleeding to death, soothing the sobbing man with, "Don't cry, white boy. You're gonna live!"

"Although its aim is not always as good as its intentions, *No Way Out* is a harsh, outspoken picture with implications that will keep you thinking about it long after leaving the theatre. That makes *No Way Out* an important picture." (Thomas M. Pryor, *New York Times*). *Variety,* who judged Poitier's performance "splendid," alerted, "For the general market, however ... *[No Way Out]* is a long, wordy, film with spotty prospects."

Among the others signed for *No Way Out* were several fellow players from Sidney Poitier's Harlem theatre days: Ruby Dee, Ossie Davis, Frederic O'Neal, and Hilda Simms.

154. Odds Against Tomorrow (United Artists, 1959). 95 minutes.

Producer Robert Wise; *associate producer* Phil Stein; *director* Wise; *based on the novel by* William P. McGivern; *screenplay* John O. Killens, Nelson Giddings; *art director* Leo Kerz; *set decorator* Fred Ballmeyer; *costumes* Anna Hill Johnstone; *makeup* Robert Jiras; *music* John Lewis; *assistant director* Charles Maguire; *sound* Edward Johnstone, Richard Vorisek; *camera* Joseph Brun; *editor* Dede Allen.

Cast: Harry Belafonte (Johnny Ingram); Robert Ryan (Earl Slater); Shelley Winters (Lorry); Ed Begley (Dave Burke); Gloria Grahame (Helen); Will Kuluva (Bacco) Richard Bright (Coco); Lou Gallo (Moriarity); Fred U. Scollay (Cannoy); Carmen de Lavallade (Kitty); Mae Barnes (Annie); Kim Hamilton (Ruth); Lois Thorne (Eadie); Wayne Rogers (Soldier); Zohra Lampert (Girl in Bar); William Zuckert (Bartender); Burt Harris (George); Clint Young (Policeman); Ed Preble (Hotel Clerk); Mel Stewart (Elevator Operator); Ronnie Stewart (Fan with Dog); Marc May (Ambulance Attendant); Paul Offman (Garry); Cicely Tyson (Fran); Lou Martini (Captain of Waiters); Robert Jones (Guard); Floyd Ennis (Sally); William Adams (Bank Guard); Fred Herrick (Bank Manager); Mary Boylan (Bank Secretary); John Garden (Bus Station Clerk); Allen Nourse (Police Chief).

Ex-cop Dave Burke (Ed Begley), who was removed from the police force for corruption, asks hot-tempered Earl Slater (Robert Ryan), a racially bigoted ex-convict from the South, to join with him in robbing a small-town bank in upstate New York. The third member of their team is black singer Johnny Ingram (Harry Belafonte), who desperately needs money to repay a large gambling debt owed impatient gangster Bacco (Will Kuluva). If Ingram cannot pay up, Bacco intends taking out his anger on Ingram's ex-wife, Ruth (Kim Hamilton), and their little girl. Despite the robbers' preparation, everything goes wrong on the heist. A gas station attendant recognizes Slater, and Ingram is detained as an accident witness. That night, per their plan, Ingram substitutes himself as the restaurant clerk bringing snacks into the bank for the late shift. But then the real delivery man arrives and soon Burke, who is driving the getaway car, is wounded by a policemen. Rather than be arrested, Burke kills himself. As Ingram and Slater flee the police, their racial antagonisms increase. The chase leads to the top of oil storage tanks, where the two enemies hide from the police. The two belligerent robbers fire their guns at one another and the tanks ignite. The next day, one of the men sifting through the debris asks about the corpses, "Which is which?" An ambulance attendant answers, "Take your pick."

A very grim drama that explores (without much exploitation) racial bigotry as two opposing forces meet head-on. The title refers to the inevitable doom that lies ahead when people cannot live in harmony together. The fact that the black and white combatants here are each criminals — of different degrees — adds texture to the proceedings. The *New York Times* rated this a "sharp, hard and suspenseful melodrama." *Variety* praised the film for being "taut" and noted, "The script uses the word 'ofay' a derogatory Negro term for whites seldom heard in films.... The home life of Belafonte's estranged wife is a unique view (for films) of a normal, middle-class Negro home — with an integrated Parent-Teachers Assn. meeting going on."

To be noted are the sharp performances by Shelley Winters and Gloria Grahame as two of Robert Ryan's girlfriends, and in a near walk-on in a club sequence, Cicely Tyson.

155. **One Down Two to Go** (Almi, 1982). Color, 84 minutes.

Executive producer Robert Atwell; *producer* Fred Williamson; *associate producers* Randy Jurgensen, Stan Wakefield, David Moon; *screenplay* Jeff Williamson; *music* Joe Trunzo; *camera* James Lemmo; *editor* Daniel Loewenthal.

Cast: Fred Williamson (Cal); Jim Brown (J); Jim Kelly (Chuck); Richard Roundtree (Ralph); Paula Sills (Teri); Laura Loftus (Sally); Tom Signorelli (Mario); Joe Spinell (Joe Spangler); Louis Neglia (Armando); Peter Dane (Rossi); Victoria Hale (Maria Rossi); Richard Noyce (Hank); John Guitz (Bob); Warrington Winters (Sheriff Lucas); Arthur Haggerty (Mojo); Irwin Litvack (Banker); Addison Greene (Pete); Dennis Singletary (Boy); John Dorish (Deputy); Robert Pastner (Slim); Patty O'Brien (Nurse); Aaron Banks (Armando's Trainer).

In *Three the Hard Way* (1974), *Take a Hard Ride* (1975) (qq.v.), and other entries, Fred Williamson had united several black action stars for boisterous cinematic romps. *One Down Two to Go* is the least of these ventures. As *Variety* hastened to add of this low calibre project, "The photography, lighting, sound and even the musical score are abjectly inadequate. Even the gunfire sounds like repeated pops of cap pistols."

When Ralph (Richard Roundtree), the promoter of a martial arts tournament, is squeezed out of the event's proceeds by mobsters, his pals Cal (Fred Williamson) and Chuck (Jim Kelly) show up to even the score.

156. **100 Rifles** (Twentieth Century-Fox, 1969). Color, 110 minutes.

Producer Marvin Schwartz; *director* Tom Gries; *based on the novel* "The Californian" *by* Robert MacLeod; *screenplay* Gries, (uncredited) Clair

Huffaker; *art director* Carl Anderson; *makeup* Ramon de Diego; *wardrobe* Oscar Rodriguez; *music* Jerry Goldsmith; *orchestrator* David Tamkin; *assistant director* Tony Tarruella; *sound* Roy Charman, David Dockendorf; *special effects* L.B. Abbott, Art Cruickshank; *mechanical effects* Alex Weldon; *camera* Cecilio Paniagua; *editor* Robert Simpson.

Cast: Jim Brown (Lyedecker); Raquel Welch (Sarita); Burt Reynolds (Yaqui Joe); Fernando Lamas (Verdugo); Dan O'Herlihy (Grimes); Hans Gudegast [Eric Braeden] (Von Klemme); Michael Foret (Humara); Aldo Sambreill (Sergeant Palestes); Soledad Miranda (Girl in Hotel); Alberto Dalbes (Padre Francisco); Carlos Bravo (Lopez); Jose Manuel Martin (Sarita's Father).

When *100 Rifles* was first released there was a tremendous huff and puff about the behind-the-scenes feuding of co-stars Jim Brown and Raquel Welch and their daring (for the time) onscreen bedding. Basically a routine Western, the interracial angle helped the shot-in-Spain sagebrush tale earn $3,500,000 in domestic film rentals.

After robbing an Arizona bank, half-breed Yaqui Joe (Burt Reynolds) heads across the border to Nogales, Mexico, where General Verdugo (Fernando Lamas), aided by his German military consultant, Von Klemme (Hans Gudegast [Eric Braeden]), are wiping out the Yaqui Indians. Joe is captured, but black United States Sheriff Lyedecker (Jim Brown) arrives and saves Joe from being shot. The two escape and meet Indian revolutionary Sarita (Raquel Welch), who later rescues them again from Verdugo's clutches, and who has a grudge to settle with railraod tycoon Grimes (Dan O'Herlihy), who forced her people from their land. The angered Verdugo then kidnaps children from a Yaqui village, causing Lyedecker to rescue them. He is now bent on destroying the General. Lyedecker captures Verdugo's troop train, which he uses to divert the general, while he and the Yaquis attack the enemy from behind. Verdugo is killed and his men overcome. Sarita also dies in the skirmish. Lyedecker returns to the United States alone; Yaqui Joe is now head of the Indians.

The teaming of three such disparate personalities as Jim Brown, Raquel Welch, and Burt Reynolds worked extremely well, especially with Reynolds's humorous approach to the nonsense. The highly touted seduction scene where Brown beds Welch was interpreted as socially significant by some and audacious by others. Regardless, it did a great deal to consolidate Brown's screen image as the great black stud of the screen.

157. One More Time (United Artists, 1970). Color, 95 minutes.

Executive producers Peter Lawford, Sammy Davis, Jr.; *producer* Milton Ebbins; *director* Jerry Lewis; *screenplay* Michael Pertwee; *production designer* Jack Stevens; *set decorator* Dimity Collins; *makeup* George Frost; *wardrobe* Ken Lawton; *music/music director* Les Reed; *songs* Reed and Jackie Ray; Bobby Doyle; Reed and Geoff Stephens; *sound* Gerry Humphreys; *special effects* Terry Witherington; *camera* Ernest W. Steward; *editor* Bill Butler.

Cast: Sammy Davis, Jr. (Charlie Salt); Peter Lawford (Chris Pepper/Lord Sydney Pepper); Maggie Wright (Miss Tomkins); Leslie Sands (Inspector Crook); John Wood (Figg); Sydney Arnold (Tombs); Edward Evans

Peter Lawford and Sammy Davis, Jr., in *One More Time* **(1970).**

(Gordon); Percy Herbert (Mander); Bill Maynard (Jenson); Dudley Sutton (Wilson); Glyn Owen (Dennis); Lucille Soong (Kim Lee); Esther Anderson (Billie); Anthony Nicholls (Candler); Allan Cuthbertson (Belton); Cyril Luckham (Magistrate); Moultrie Kelsall (Priest); Julian D'Albie (General Turpington-Mellish); Gladys Spencer (Lady Turpington-Mellish); Joanna Wake (Clair Turpington-Mellish); Juliette Bora, Florence George, Lorraine Hall, Thelma Neal, Amber Dean Smith, Carmel Stratton (Salt & Pepper Nightclub Girls); *and:* Peter Cushing, Mischa De Le Motte, Richard Golden, Walter Hopsburgh, Christopher Lee, Norman Mitchell, George McGrath, Geoffrey Morris, John Nettles, Norman Pitt, Peter Reeves, David Trevena.

The further adventures of Charlie Salt (Sammy Davis, Jr.) and Chris Pepper (Peter Lawford), who had starred to good results as Soho nightclub owners in *Salt and Pepper* (1968) (q.v.). This time the proceedings became more slapstick (it was directed by Jerry Lewis, who does not appear in the film), and the results were far less engaging as well as less profitable.

After the police shut down their Salt and Pepper Club, Charlie Salt (Sammy Davis, Jr.) and Chris Pepper (Peter Lawford) asks Chris's twin brother, Lord Sydney Pepper (Peter Lawford), to pay their fine. He refuses, and later Lord Sydney is found murdered. The enterprising Chris switches identities and claims it is Chris who has died. Later Salt and Pepper learn the dead nobleman had been engaged in diamond smuggling, and the police join in the chase to round up the culprits.

Other than demonstrating that interracial friendships can exist and affording Sammy Davis Jr., an opportunity to sing "When the Feeling Hits You," *One More Time* was once more too often. It dissipated the initial pleasing premise into buffoonery.

158. The Organization (United Artists, 1971). Color, 107 minutes.

Producer Walter Mirisch; *director* Don Medford; *based on a character created by* John Dudley Ball; *screenplay* James R. Webb; *production designer* James F. McGuire; *art director* George B. Chan; *set decorator* Marvin March; *costumes* Angela Alexander, Wes Jeffries, John K. Lemons; *makeup* Del Armstrong; *music* Gil Melle; *assistant director* Jack Reddish; *special effects* Sass Bedig, Norman O. Skeete; *sound* Robert Martin; *camera* Joseph Biroc; *editor* Ferris Webster.

Cast: Sidney Poitier (Lieutenant Virgil Tibbs); Barbara McNair (Valerie Tibbs); Gerald S. O'Loughlin (Lieutenant Jack Pecora); Sheree North (Gloria Morgan); Fred Beir (Bob Alford); Allen Garfield [Goorwitz] (Benjy); Bernie Hamilton (Lieutenant Jessop); Raul Julia (Juan Mendoza); Ron O'Neal (Joe Peralez); James A. Watson, Jr. (Stacy Baker); Charles H. Gray (Night Watchman Morgan); Jarion Monroe (Larry French); Dan Travanty (Sergeant Chassman); Billy "Green" Bush (Dave Thomas); Maxwell Gail, Jr. (Rudy); Ross Hagen (Chet); Paul Jenkins (Tony); John Lasell (Zach Mills); Lani Miyazaki (Annie Sekido); Garry Walberg (Captain Stacy); Desmond Wilson (Charlie Blossom); George Spell (Andy Tibbs); Wanda Spell (Ginny Tibbs); Graham Jarvis (William Martin); Colin Adams (Dan); Johnny Haymer (John Bishop).

There had been many complaints that *They Call Me Mister Tibbs!* (1970), the middling followup to the stellar *In the Heat of the Night* (1967) (qq.v.) had focused far too much attention on lawman Virgil Tibbs' home life. The third entry in the series, *The Organization* (1971), remedied that error, while also restructuring police detective Tibbs into more of a rebel law enforcer. Here the San Franciscan helps a diverse group of Third World vigilantes bust a global drug ring. Obviously superstar Sidney Poitier was borrowing from the tried-and-true plotlines of the emerging blaxploitation pictures. If only his character were not so cool and efficient, but would occasionally explode directly at the obscenities around him.

A San Francisco furniture factory is robbed and its manager found murdered. Police investigator Virgil Tibbs (Sidney Poitier) discovers the thiefs are a group of radicals, led by Juan Mendoza (Raul Julia), who were after $5,000,000 in heroin hidden there. However, they insist they did not commit the homicide. Mendoza claims once the police find a way to stop the dope trafficking, they will turn over the drugs. Tibbs, not confiding to his superiors, agrees to help these unusual community do-gooders. Factory watchman Morgan (Charles H. Gray) dies en route to the precinct, and Tibbs and his partner, Jack Pecora (Gerald S. O'Loughlin), learn from the man's widow (Sheree North) that he owned stock in the furniture company (a front for underworld activities). One of the frightened vigilantes (Ron O'Neal) makes his own deal with the mob about the missing heroin, but the distrustful thugs kill him and Annie Sekido (Lani Miyazaki) anyway. Tibbs is suspended from the force when the higher-ups realize he has been withholding information, and he turns in his badge, sure the narcotics division is full of corruption. Now he intends to solve the case on his own. The trail leads back to Mrs. Morgan, who is a syndicate runner, and to small-time punk Benjy (Allen Garfield). Using Mendoza and his friends as backups, Tibbs pursues the local pushers through the subway tunnels under construction. Later the syndicate heads are captured by the police, but they are eliminated by hired hit men before they can talk.

"Evolves largely as surface action and reaction so dear to TV's cops and robbers," insisted A.H. Weiler *(New York Times)*. "As before, Sidney Poitier . . . is incorruptibility incarnate, bending the rules only when a higher purpose is involved, but at last we're spared all but a small dose of those soporific interludes from family life that punctuated *They Call Me Mister Tibbs!!*" (David Wilson, British *Monthly Film Bulletin*).

159. Pacific Inferno (VCL, 1985). Color, 89 minutes.

Executive producer Jim Brown; *producers* Spencer Jourdain, Cassius V. Weathersby; *associate producer* Rod Perry; *director* Rolf Bayer; *screenplay* Bayer, Roland S. Jefferson, Eric P. Jones; *set designer* Vincente Bonus; *makeup* Carmelita Sioson; *costume designer* Bill Witten; *music editor* Doug Lackey; *military adviser* Dennis Juran; *special effects* Kim Ramos; *sound* Donald Santos; *sound editors* Earl Watson, Richard Anderson, David Lee Fein; *camera* Mars Rasca; *underwater camera* Ramos; *second unit camera* Jun Hasca; *editors* Richard C. Meyer, Ann Mills.

Cast: Jim Brown (Clyde Preston); Richard Jaeckel (Dealer [Robert Fletcher]); Tim Brown (Dawson); Tad Horino (Yamada); Dino Fernando (Totoy); Wilma Reading (Tita); Rik von Nutter (Dennis); Jimmy Shaw (Leroy); Vic Silayan (Fukoshima); Vic Diaz (Kempei); Butz Aquino (Dubayashi); *and:* Dick Adair.

Filmed in the Philippines but not released theatrically until 1985 (and that briefly), *Pacific Inferno* demonstrates how far Jim Brown's screen image had deteriorated by the late 1970s. This combat film, which opens with the bombing of Pearl Harbor, relies on a tremendous amount of stock footage to set its mood and provide the special effects. The acting is half-baked, the sentiments expressed are stale, and the action (except for borrowed footage from other war films) is vegetarian (of the "let's chase through the jungle" variety).

When the Philippines are captured by the Japanese in World War II, the prisoners include United States Navy divers Clyde Preston (Jim Brown), Dealer (Richard Jaeckel), and racial bigot Dennis (Rik von Nutter). Their Japanese captors are out to recover $16,000,000 in silver coins thrown into Manila Bay by a departing General Douglas MacArthur. To foster his escape from the enemy, Preston offers to betray the local resistance group, including lusty Tita (Wilma Reading).

Much is made (by executive producer Brown) of tough guy Brown's macho traits—his seething antagonism over military segregation (in World War II) and his way with women. (At one point Clyde Preston mumbles to uncomprehending Tita, "You're a whole lot of woman. No use putting it into words." So much for even the most basic courtship techniques.)

160. Penitentiary (Jerry Gross, 1979). 99 minutes.

Producer Jamaa Fanaka; *co-producers* Alicia Dhanifu, Al Shepard; *associate producers* Irving Parham, Leon Isaac Kennedy, Lynette Stansell;

director/screenplay Fanaka; *art director* Adel Mazen; *set decorator* Beverly Green Etheredge; *costumes* Debra Bradford, Deirdre Naughton; *makeup* Gregory Lewis; *music* Frankie Gaye; *song* Mark Gaillard and the Slim and Trim Band; *stunt co-ordinator* John Sherrod; *boxing adviser* Charles Young; *second unit director* Sherrod; *assistant directors* Jovon Gilloham, Yance Hamlett, Sergio Mimms; *sound* Ed White; *sound editor* Jim Nownes; *camera* Marty Ollstein; *additional camera* Stephen Posey; *editor* Betsy Blankett.

Cast: Leon Isaac Kennedy (Martel "Too Sweet" Gordone); Thommy Pollard (Eugene T. Lawson); Hazel Spears (Linda); Donovan Womack (Jesse Amos); Floyd Chatman (Hezzikia "Seldom Seen" Jackson); Wilbur "Hi-Fi" White (Sweet Pea); Gloria Delaney (Peaches); Badja Djola ("Half Dead" Johnson); Chuck Mitchell (Lieutenant Arnsworth); Cepheus Jaxon (Poindexter); Dwaine Fobbs ("Lying" Latney Winborn); Ernest Wilson ("Cheese"); Will Richardson (Magilla Gorilla); Elijah Mitchell, Darrell Harris, Lonnie Kirtz (Nuts); Tony Andrea (Moon); Ray Wolfe ("A" Block Night Guard); Charles Young ("Tough Tony," Manager and Referee); Michael Melvin, Steve Eddy (Bikers); Bill Murry ("Rappin" Larry); Terri Hayden (Counter Lady); Herman Cole (Cook); Carl Erwin (Sam Cunningham); Irving Parham ("A" Block Day Guard); Warren Bryant (Gay Boxing Spectator); Lorri Gay (Second Girl in Restroom); Thomas Earl Stiratt ("Wolf"); Walter Gordon (Second Male in Restroom); Joaquin Leal (Rubin); David Carter, Hassan Abdul-Ali, Marcus Guttierrez (Guards); Zee Howard (Female Lieutenant); Cardella Demilo, Onia Fenee, Deloris Figueroa, Ann Hutcherson, Gwynn Pineda, Irene Stokes, Beverly Wallace (Female Guard); Renee Armanlin, Zeola Gaye, Brenda Joy Griffin, Shelli Hughes, Sarah Jaxon, Jackie Shaw, Irene Terrell, Barbara Torres, Lisa Visco (Female Inmates); William Bey, Robert Wayne Cornelius, Shawn Davis, Quitman Gates, Dominic Giusto, Johnny Jones, Casey J. Littlejohn, Sam Olden, Tony Rapisarda, Tyrone S.B. Thompson, Edgardo Williams, Roderic Williams (Male Inmates).

See summary under *Penitentiary III*.

161. Penitentiary II (Metro-Goldwyn-Mayer/United Artists, 1982). Color, 103 minutes.

Producer/director/screenplay Jamaa Fanaka; *music* Jack W. Wheaton; *camera* Steve Posey; *editor* James E. Nownes.

Cast: Leon Isaac Kennedy (Martel "Too Sweet" Gordone); Ernie Hudson ("Half Dead" Johnson); Mr. T (Himself); Glynn Turman (Charles); Peggy Blow (Ellen); Cepheus Jaxon (Do Dirty); Marvin Jones (Simp); Donovan Womack (Jesse "The Bull" Amos); Ebony Wright (Sugar); Eugenia Wright (Clarisse); Ren Woods (Nikki); Marci Thomas (Evelyn); Dennis Libscomb, Gerald Berns (Announcers); Joe Anthony Cox (Midget); Sephton Moody (Charles, Jr.); Malik Carter ("Seldom Seen" Jackson); Stan Kamber (Sam).

See summary under *Penitentiary III*.

162. Penitentiary III (Cannon, 1987). Color, 91 minutes.

Producers Jamaa Fanaka, Leon Isaac Kennedy; *director/screenplay* Fanaka; *production designer* Marshall Toomey; *art director* Craig Freitag; *set decorator* Beverly Etheredge; *makeup/special effects* Mike Spatola; *music* Garry Schyman; *music editor* John Elizalde; *second unit director* John Sherrod; *assistant directors* Brent Sellstrom, Pat Kirck; *stunt co-ordinator* John Sherrod; *martial arts advisers* Hugh Van Patton, Glen Eaton; *sound* Oliver Moss; *supervising sound/foley editor* John Post; *camera* Marty Ollstein; *second unit camera* Joseph W. Calloway; *editor* Ed Harker.

Cast: Leon Isaac Kennedy (Martel "Too Sweet" Gordone); Anthony Geary (Serenghetti); Steven Antin (Roscoe); Ric Mancini (Warden); Marie Burrell Fanaka (Chelsea Remington); Raymond "The Haiti Kid" Kessler (Midnight Thud Jessup); Rick Zumwalt (Joshua); Magic Schwarz (Hugo); Jim Bailey (Cleopatra); Big Bull Bates (Simp); Big Yank (Rock); Bert Williams (Tim Shoah); Mark Kemble (Rufus); Jack Rader (Fred); Madison Campudoni (El Cid); Mike Payne (Jess); Drew Bundini Brown (Sugg); Ty Randolph (Sugar); J.J. Johnson, Earl Garnes (Announcers); Jim Phillips (Suited Gentleman); Faith Minton, Marcella Ross, Ray Hollitt (Female Boxers); Danny Trejo (See Veer); Mary O'Conner, Cardella Demilo (Female Guards); "Dr. De" Ron Demps (Referee).

As in most Hollywood success stories, the odds were certainly against success. There had already been several ripoffs of the *Rocky* (1976) (q.v.) film phenomenon, and *Penitentiary* not only borrowed from that cliched boxing world premise but mixed in elements from two other threadbare genres: prison yarns and blaxploitation features. This production starred a then–relatively unknown black performer (Leon Isaac [Kennedy]) and was independently financed and distributed. Its one known ingredient was black director Jamaa Fanaka, the U.C.L.A. Film School graduate who had already turned out *Welcome Home Brother Charles* (1975) and *Emma Mae* (1976) (q.v.). The resultant film, *Penitentiary,* grossed $13,120,235 on an estimated cost of $250,000. It not only spawned two sequels but created an alter ego for Leon Isaac Kennedy, that of "Too Sweet" Gordone, which for better or worse he has yet to shake.

Young black hitchhiker Martel Gordone (Leon Isaac Kennedy) gets into a fight with two bikers over a prostitute (Hazel Spear), who later disappears. As one of the bikers is killed in the skirmish, Martel is sent to a state prison, where his love of candy (especially Mr. Goodbars) causes him to be nicknamed "Too Sweet." In his cell block, Jesse Amos (Donovan Womack) is boss, and his chief henchman is the ferocious "Half Dead" Johnson (Badja Djola). The latter needles Gordone into a fight, and to everyone's surprise, Gordone wins. Because he comes to the rescue of Jesse's sexually humiliated cellmate Eugene T. Lawson (Thommy Pollard), Gordone and Jesse battle it out, and both men find themselves in solitary confinement. Later they are offered an opportunity to box in the prison tournament if there is no further trouble. As a bonus, winners in the matches are guaranteed a connubial visit, and the top champion will be considered for handling by the warden's brother-in-law, a fight promoter. Too Sweet now bunks in a cell with the aging Hezzikia "Seldom Seen" Jackson (Floyd Chatman), a former boxing trainer. At the championship match Gordone wins his bout and enjoys time with Linda (one of the female prison inmates bussed in to watch the boxing match), whom he learns is now imprisoned for her part in the biker's death. The vengeful Amos and Half Dead attack Gordone, and when Lawson rushes to his assistance, he is killed. Too Sweet fights Amos in another match. His fresh victory earns him his freedom, and he persuades Seldom Seen to become his professional trainer.

If anything makes *Penitentiary* work it is the earnestness of Leon Isaac Kennedy's performance as "Too Sweet" Gordone, prisoner #T80079. His acting may not always be subtle, but, like his boxing, it packs a wallop.

Leon Isaac (Kennedy) began his show business career as "Leon the Lover," a radio disc jockey in Cleveland. He later married personality-performer Jayne Kennedy, and they moved to Los Angeles in 1977. There he began producing and writing a radio talk show, "90 Tonight," as well as operating several discos. He had minor roles in such black action films as Jim Brown's *Hammer* (1972) and Fred Williamson's *Mean Johnny Barrows* (1977) (qq.v.), and co-starred with his wife in *Death Force* (1978), directed by Cirio H. Santiago and co-starring James Iglehart.

The script carefully builds Gordone as the heroic sort of person who gets into difficulty defending his new woman, notwithstanding that she is morally loose. Moreover, because Gordone is both a stranger in town and black the police do not take kindly to him, and he ends up in the penitentiary. Far more than many mainstream films, *Penitentiary* (like its followups) deals with the chronic problems of incarceration: the overcrowding, the hardened inmates misguiding the more innocent, the racial bigotry, and the rampant homosexuality. The scenario presents Gordone as a hero in a walled hell. "Don't nobody have to be nobody's property," he advises a less sturdy soul, and to prove his point he is ready to punch out anybody who looks at him the least bit funny. Interestingly, the narrative forces the fight profession upon Gordone. "I'm no boxer. I fight to protect myself," he insists. But the chance to get even with his mortal enemies behind bars and also to gain his freedom combine to push him into professional boxing. And just as Gordone has the sensitivity to come to the physcial rescue of Eugene Lawson, so he comes to be the emotional salvation of eccentric "Seldom Seen" Jackson ("I joke, and I laugh but I don't touch") who has been in prison for fifty of his sixty-five years. Their scenes together play wonderfully, and nowhere finer than at the finale, when Seldom Seen admits to his protege-benefactor:

> I'm afraid of the streets.... It just scares me going out there and being a nobody. What can I do? Who wants me? Who even will pay attention to an old out-of-date fool like me. Here I am somebody. I got my own TV, my own stereo, my own home. I mean somethin' in here. I got respect.

Too Sweet answers, "There's only one thing wrong. You ain't got no hope." Then he adds, "We can make it out there.... We can at least try!"

It all works wonderfully well with both the script and the performers.

"Fanaka has made an amazing leap from the befuddled, dull social consciousness of *Emma Mae,* his previous movie. *Penitentiary* in its angled photography is one of the most expressive American movies of the year and much more accomplished in its visuals than its acting.... Even as Fanaka makes us squirm by drowning us in raw sex and violence, he transcends the primitivism" (Tom Allen, *Village Voice*). "Filled with vividly drawn larger-than-life characters and loaded with action, *Penitentiary* bursts with energy and emotion. It's operating in the best, bravura sense.... Fanaka creates a world of overwhelming sexual tension and constant danger.... Comparisons to *Rocky* are inevitable, but *Penitentiary* is too vital and personal to be a copy of anything" (Kevin Thomas, *Los Angeles Times*).

It was nearly unavoidable that such a huge hit would generate a successor, and this time Metro-Goldwyn-Mayer/United Artists lured the team of Jamaa Fanaka and Leon Isaac Kennedy into repeating their efforts for *Penitentiary II*. This time they had a $1,000,000 production budget and even a guest cameo by Mr. T. The scenario trick, of course, would be how to get "Too Sweet" Gordone behind bars again.

Penitentiary II opens with what has to be one of the longest title card prologues in film history: "Our story continues with our hero, Martell 'Too Sweet' Gordone, trying to resume a normal life after serving time for a murder he didn't commit...." After explaining in elaborate detail that Too Sweet now lives with his sister and her family and that he has become a skating messenger delivering documents for his brother-in-law's law firm, it adds that if the ex-convict does not complete his obligations to his fight promoter, his parole officer threatens to return him to jail. Moreover, Too Sweet is advised, his mortal enemy "Half Dead" has escaped from jail and vows to kill Too Sweet.

The rather illogical narrative thereafter traces Too Sweet's courtship of Clarisse (Eugenia Wright), who is killed by the knife-wielding Half Dead (Ernie Hudson); and his two moronic and sadistic pals, Do Dirty (Cepheus Jaxon) and Simp (Marvin Jones). Her death forces Too Sweet to wake up to his present life. "I was dead," he admits. But now, "I'm going to box. I'm goin' to be someone. I'm gonna get respect...." All of this leads Too Sweet back to prison to fight Jesse "The Bull" Amos (Donovan Womack) while his brother-in-law (Glynn Turman) rescues his kidnapped family from Simon and Do Dirty. They rush to the prison, where a knocked-down Too Sweet revives in time to knock out the champ.

The results of *Penitentiary II* were artistically disappointing, although the film reportedly grossed several million dollars in worldwide distribution. "The producers of the film ... have expanded the cast to include more whites than the original movie, presumably to attract a broader audience.... Some of the boxing scenes are dramatic, but the movie becomes dreary and predictable less than halfway through. There are also several irrelevant subplots that weave through the film without adding anything to it" (Bill Kaufman, *Newsday*). "Such nonsense can only please limited audiences who can whoop it up. Upper echelons, however, could be embarrassed," gauged Archer Winsten *(New York Post)*. *Variety* was even more precise, branding the production a "...shoddy sequel that will be lucky to do a fraction of the business [of the original].... Still wearing three hats ... Fanaka winds up with a cheap, exploitative, preposterously dumb mess. Life does have its reverses." Vincent Canby *(New York Times)* knocked out this sequel: "The boxing sequences are so lethargic that the movie keeps cutting away from the ring during crucial fights, as if

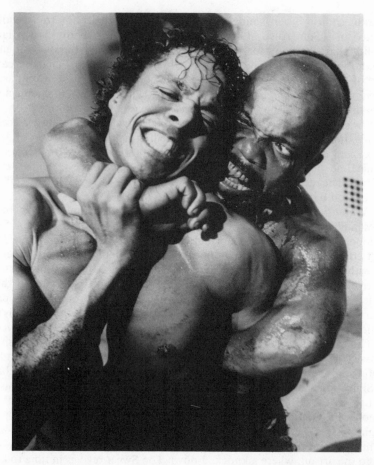

Leon Isaac Kennedy *(left)* **and Kessler Raymond in** *Penitentiary III* **(1987).**

embarrassed. The plot, pacing, action and especially, the violence are absurd."
But, discerned Canby, it has "...a self-assurance that is so brazen that it
almost persuades you that the film's ineptitude is its chosen style."

While Jamaa Fanaka struggled to break out of the *Penitentiary* rut, Leon
Isaac Kennedy had gone on to star in a remake of *Body and Soul* (1981) (q.v.)
and then appeared in such features as Chuck Norris' *Lone Wolf McQuade*
(1983), Mike Connor's *Too Scared to Scream* (1985), and Ronny Cox's *Hollywood Vice Squad* (1987), as well as headlining the street beat musical *Knights
of the City* (1985) (q.v.) and guest-starring on assorted teleseries. By 1987,
Fanaka and Kennedy bowed to the inevitable: *Penitentiary III,* manufactured by
Cannon Pictures for $2,000,000, eight times the cost of the original entry.

"Is *Penitentiary III* fun?" *Variety* asked rhetorically. "Are cartoons and
professional wrestling matches fun? If you answer yes to the second question
then this movie definitely is for you."

Thanks to epicene villain Serenghetti (Anthony Geary), the prison kingpin, Too Sweet is railroaded back into the penitentiary (he is slipped drugs and beats a ring opponent to death). Although he has again sworn off boxing ever again, he learns quickly there are two opposing prison boxing teams, one sponsored by the Warden (Ric Mancini), the other by his cellblock's monarch Serenghetti. To pressure Too Sweet into joining his squad, Serenghetti arranges to have Midnight Thud (Raymond "The Haiti Kid" Kessler), a homicidal midget boxer, attack the newcomer. But Too Sweet is victorious and, as punishment, he is given electro-shock treatment. Later, Midnight Thud becomes friends with Too Sweet. Meanwhile, seeing his prison friend Roscoe (Steve Antin) nearly killed in the ring, Too Sweet decides to fight again. Midnight Thud volunteers to be his trainer and teaches him assorted martial arts skills. In the climactic match Too Sweet is pitted against the oversized Hugo (Magic Schwarz), who has been given the drug enhancer. Nevertheless Gordon defeats his opponents. The victory signals the end of Serenghetti's reign.

"*Penitentiary III* ... is pure action fantasy, but Fanaka pushes its possibilities to the limit. Too Sweet, so well played by the wiry and talented Kennedy, is a mythical figure, the wronged, oppressed black man who overcomes injustice not merely by his fists but by strength of character, spirit and discipline" (Kevin Thomas, *Los Angeles Times*). "While *Pen III* is sensibly roped off into a tight strong ring—good guys vs. bad guy in the championship bout—there's a bevy of weird and bizarre between-story-round stuff that spruces up the formula.... Despite some expositional deliveries that clank against the action, *Penitentiary III* is a lean and mean entertainment" (Duayne Byrge, *The Hollywood Reporter*). Perhaps Jonathan Gold *(LA Weekly)* summed it up best: "Jamaa Fanaka brings us yet another poorly shot, abysmally lighted and thoroughly entertaining trip through his surrealistic pen, where S & M guards hang out in medieval dungeons and nasty mobmen run the joint from their plushy appointed cells. The picture isn't good, but it sure is fun."

Despite the highly favorable reviews for *Penitentiary III,* its distributor, Cannon Films, was undergoing financial woes, and its release pattern was sketchy and ineffective, leading to weak box-office results.

163. A Piece of the Action (Warner Bros., 1977). Color, 134 minutes.

Producer Melville Tucker; *associate producers* Pembroke J. Herring, Kris Keiser; *director* Sidney Poitier; *story* Timothy March; *screenplay* Charles Blackwell; *production designer* Alfred Sweeney; *set decorator* William J. McLaughlin; *costumes* David Rawley, Marie V. Brown; *music* Curtis Mayfield; *choreography* Arthur Mitchell; *stunt co-ordinator* Henry Kingi; *assistant directors* Dwight Williams, Craig Huston; *sound* Willie D. Burton, William McCaughey; *camera* Donald M. Morgan; *editor* Herring.

Cast: Sidney Poitier (Manny Durrell); Bill Cosby (Dave Anderson); James Earl Jones (Joshua Burke); Denise Nicholas (Lila French); Hope Clarke (Sarah Thomas); Tracy Reed (Nikki McLean); Titos Vandis (Bruno); Frances Foster (Bea Quitman); Jason Evers (Ty Shorter); Marc Lawrence (Louis); Ja'net DuBois (Nellie Bond).

"Take a dash of *Blackboard Jungle,* add a generous measure of *To Sir, With Love,* serve it up in the Chicago slums, and you have a pretty good idea of what's going on in this well meaning but rather silly film directed by Sidney Poitier. . . . Loads of action, a lively Curtis Mayfield score, and a few genuinely touching moments struggle to hold their own against soggy social commentary" (*People* magazine).

For the third screen teaming of Sidney Poitier and Bill Cosby, the formula did not vary from its predecessors (*Uptown Saturday Night* [1974] and *Let's Do It Again* [1975] [qq.v.]) — mostly wholesome slapstick conjectured to appeal to families, both black and white. The story opens in Chicago on August 9, 1975, as slick burglar Dave Anderson (Bill Cosby) breaks into a high-rise office building vault and makes his getaway with what proves to be Mafia funds. Meanwhile, in another part of town, Manny Durrell (Sidney Poitier) prepares to separate underworld figure Bruno (Tito Vandis) from $375,000.

Nearly a year later, police detective Joshua Burke (James Earl Jones) solves the two unrelated crimes himself. He brings Anderson and Durrell together (for the first time), and then begins anonymously blackmailing them into donating their services to a southside community improvement center run by Lila French (Denise Nicholas) and founded by Burke's late wife. Realizing they are stuck (till the statute of limitations runs out on their crimes), they are assigned to help thirty incorrigible ghetto youngsters become useful citizens with jobs — all in three weeks' time. When not assisting their exuberant charges in adjusting to everyday life, the two crooks attempt to locate their blackmailer's identity, all the while staying out of sight of Bruno and his hoods, who are on their trail. Later, Burke is unmasked, and he offers the men assistance in locating Durrell's live-in girlfriend, Nikki McLean (Tracy Reed), who has been kidnapped by Bruno. In a turnabout sting they gain the upper hand over Bruno and insure that their schoolroom charges have a future.

"[*A Piece of the Action*] allows director Poitier to touch just about every commercial base — action, comedy, romance, sentiment — while capping it all with an uplifting message on the virtues of self improvement. . . . Poitier has two things going for him: his own sincerity and the ingratiating spontaneity of its cast. Corny and hip, cynical and sentimental, formulaic and funky, *A Piece of the Action* may have a medicinal intent, but it goes down like ice cream soda" (David Ansen, *Newsweek* magazine).

A Piece of the Action grossed a very satisfactory $6,700,000 in domestic film rentals.

164. The Principal (Tri-Star, 1987). Color, 109 minutes.

Producer Thomas H. Brodek; *director* Christopher Cain; *screenplay* Frank Deese; *art director* Mark Billerman; *set decorator* Rick Brown; *costumes* Marianna Astrom-DeFina; *makeup* Steven D. Anderson; *songs* Jay Gruska, Bruce Roberts, Andy Goldmark, Jon Lind, Paul Gordon; *music director* Jellybean Benitez; *music editors* Ken Johnson, Steve Livingston; *stunt co-ordinator* Everett Creach; *special effects* David Pier; *supervising sound editor* Gilbert D.M. Archant; *foley editor* John Paul Jones; *camera* Arthur Albert; *additional camera* Phil Holahan; *editor* Jack Hofstra.

Cast: James Belushi (Rick Latimer); Louis Gossett, Jr. (Jake Phillips); Rae Dawn Cong (Hilary Orozco); Michael Wright (Victor Duncan); J.J. Cohen ("White Zac"); Esai Morales (Raymi Rojas); Troy Winbush ("Baby" Emile); Jacob Vargas (Arturo Diego); Thomas Ryan (Robert Darcy); Reggie Johnson (Jomo); Kelly Minter (Treena Lester); Ruth Beckford (Mrs. Jenkins); Julian Brooks (Kevin); Joan Valderrama (Secretary); Rick Hamilton (Mr. Harkley); Martin Pistone (Security Guard); Joe Flood (Terhune); Ann Armour (Mrs. Ripton); Tony Haney (Police Officer); Sharon Thomas (Kimberly); Daniel Royal (Will); Delores Mitchell (Mrs. Coswell); Zoltan Gray (Physical Education Teacher); John Allen Vick (Frank Valdis); Sean Allen Barnes (Rolf); Yuri Lane (Lance Woodbury); Steve W. Birger (Stevie B.); Gus Dimas (Gus); Leo Downey (George Pierce); Tom Winston (Principal O'Connor); Kathryn Knotts (Jan Buchanan); Marshall Jones (Gang Member); Josh Wood (Charles Lester); Mark Anger (Desk Officer); Frank Deese (Mr. Petersen); J.J. Johnson (Will); Doug White (Eric); Wat Takeshita (Maintenance Man); Elliott S. Valderrama (Drug Dealer); Joel Valentin (Kid); Tom Bryant (Shocked Teacher); Danny Kovacs (Substitute Teacher); Charmaine Anderson (Hilary's Student); Melanie G. Muters (Alley Girl); Linda Trowbridge (Nurse); Danny Williams (Dangerous Danny); Bill Yarbrough (Randall); Richard Duppell, Peter Fitzsimmons (Buddies); Jessica Wilson, Kaprice Wilson, Bridgette Rodriguez (Girls); Terry Coleman, Melissa Lee Holloman, Luis Zuno, Nemon Wade, Eural Wills (Students); James Edward Griffin, David Williams (Gang Students).

What to do with a dynamically talented and muscular Oscar-winning leading man who is over fifty, bald, and black? He can be the father figure fighter pilot in *Iron Eagle* (1985) (q.v.); he can co-star in jungle soldier-of-fortune fantasies with Chuck Norris (*Firewalker,* 1986); he can support new leading man James Belushi in *The Principal,* which grossed $9,000,000 in domestic film rentals.

Screwed-up teacher Rick Latimer (James Belushi) is ordered by the disgusted school board to take over as principal of the district's most trouble-plagued high school, Brandel High. This inner city school is a horror institution, with a black Victor Duncan (Michael Wright) and his gang of punks running the place instead of the teachers. Having a surge of enthusiasm for his post, Latimer decides on a regime of "No More" (...drugs, extortion, arson, etc.). His backup is the school's chief of security, Jake Phillips (Louis Gossett, Jr.), a former professional football player who is also a Brandel graduate. By risking his pride and well being, Latimer wins the respect of Phillips, attractive teacher Hilary Orozco (Rae Dawn Chong) and even of some of the pupils. But Latimer's wild side remains. When Hilary is raped in her classroom, he comes to her defense on his Honda motorcycle and charges up the stairs after the culprit (J.J. Cohen), the leader of the school's white faction. When Duncan and his goonies kill good-natured "Baby" Emile (Troy Winbush), Latimer tackles Duncan and his two chief henchmen. Phillips comes to the rescue to help even the score, and Latimer, who is shot by Duncan, is still able to pulverize his opponent.

With such physically exhausting but emotionally undemanding feature film assignments, little wonder that Lou Gossett, Jr., has turned to TV, and in the 1988–89 TV season starred (along with Peter Falk and Burt Reynolds) in NBC-TV's "Saturday Mystery Movie," a program of three revolving detective/action series.

The Principal was shot on location at Merritt College in Oakland, California. The "38th Avenue Locos," a Chicano gang, were used as extras in the film, and members of the Oakland branch of the Hell's Angels served as crowd controllers. Featured player Michael Wright had appeared to good effect in *Streamers* (1982), and Esai Morales gained prominence in the same year's *La Bamba* as singer Ritchie Valens's tormented brother.

165. Rappin' (Cannon, 1985). Color, 92 minutes.

Producers Menahem Golan, Yoram Globus; *associate producer* Jeffrey Silver; *director* Joel Silberg; *screenplay* Robert Litz, Adam Friedman; *production designer* Steve Miller; *set decorator* Bruce Miller; *costumes* Aude Bronson-Howard, Keven Faherty; *makeup* Bronson-Howard; *music* Michael Linn; *choreography* Edmond Kresley; *stunts* Edgar Mourino, Tom Wright; *assistant directors* Steven Felder, Tommy Burns; *camera* David Gurfinkel; *editors* Andy Horvitch, Bert Glatstein.

Cast: Mario Van Peebles (John Hood); Tasia Valenza (Dixie); Charles Flohe (Duane); Leo O'Brien (Allan); Eriq La Salle (Ice); Richie Abanes (Richie); Kadeem Hardison (Moon); Melvin Plowden (Fats); Harry Goz (Thorndike); Rony Clanton (Cedric); Edye Byrde (Grandma); Ruth Jaroslow (Mrs. Goldberg); Anthony Bishop (Mr. Fiorelo); Fredric Mao (Mrs. Chan); Michael Esihos (Stavros); Rutanya Alda (Cecilia); Brandi Freund (Rosalita); Debra Greenfield (Magnolia); David Butler (Bravman); Scott Peck (Oil Truck Driver); Clayton Hill (Kilroy); Joe Schad (Burton); Joe Marmo (Shortie Johnson); William Mort (Psycho); Tommy Ross (Duane's Gang Member); Harry Scanlon (Officer); Anthony Bradberry (Man in Bathroom); Don Brockett (Store Manager); Thomas Clint Clutter (Technician); Carl Fred Robinson (Bum); Angela De Filippo, Lyn Philistine (Girls); Dan Caliguire (Cecilia's Son); Warren Mills, Claudja Barry, Eugene Wilde, Joanna Gardner (Performers); Ice-T (Himself); Tracy Marrow, David Storrs, Eric Garcia, Henry Garcia, Ernest Cunningham (Ice-T Group); Christopher Johnson, Jack Reese, Stacey O'Neal, Rosie Steave, Arlinda Dickens (T-Force); Antoine Lundy, Steven Lundy, Trisco Pearson, Jessie Daniels, Charles Nelson (Force M.D.'s); Willie Cross, Salvador Irizarry, David Marshall, David Whitake, Troion Whitaker (Tuff, Inc.)

It was not until Clint Eastwood's *Heartbreak Ridge* (1986) that Mario Van Peebles became a really known quantity in the entertainment world. However, he had been in his father Melvin's *Sweet Sweetback's Baadasssss Song* (1971) and *Sophisticated Gents* (1981) (qq.v.), and they would appear together in *Jaws IV: The Revenge* (1987). Frequently Mario Van Peebles was cast as a punk (*The Cable Car Murder* [1971] [q.v.]), and often played in trash such as *Delivery Boys* and *Exterminator II* (both 1984). In 1985 he had the starring role in *Rappin'*, Cannon Pictures' minor bid to recreate the $15,733,000 which its earlier *Breakin'* (1984) had generated. It was followed by the same company's *Breakin' II: Electric Bugaloo* (1985).

However, *Rappin'* was not received joyously. "Billed as the craze sweeping the country, *Rappin'* is behind the times. . . . *Rappin'* is the kind of Hollywood production that makes street life look like Disneyland. The poor are pure, and the rich are scum with the thugs caught in the middle" *(Variety)*.

John Hood (Mario Van Peebles), known for his hot temper and his rap dancing abilities, is released from prison. He is determined to lead the good life, and that includes ridding his neighborhood of sinister land developers, led by Thorndike (Harry Goz), who are bent on tearing down the community. Then there is attractive Dixie (Tasia Valenza), whom he adores. To prove he is worthy of her he is determined to get a recording contract. Opposing him in his ambitions is Duane (Charles Flohe), the chief of the rival gang.

For the record there are seventeen songs in *Rappin'*, including the finale community sing-along, some of which were co-composed by the multi-talented Van Peebles (including "Two of a Kind," "Snack Attack," "Colors," "Lady Alcohol," and "The Courtroom"). The film was shot on the quick on location in Pittsburgh.

For Van Peebles, his big show business breakthrough would *not* be this retread of early 1970s blaxploitation motifs adorned with hip rap songs and dancing, but his 1988 television detective series, "Sonny Spoon."

166. Red Ball Express (Universal, 1952). 83 minutes.

Producer Aaron Rosenberg; *director* Budd Boetticher; *story* Marcel Klauber, Billy Grady, Jr.; *screenplay* John Michael Hayes; *art directors* Bernard Herzbrun, Richard H. Riedel; *music director* Joseph Gershenson; *camera* Maury Gertsman; *editor* Edward Curtiss.

Cast: Jeff Chandler (Lieutenant Chick Campbell); Alex Nicol (Sergeant Ernest Kalleck); Charles Drake (Private Ronald Partridge); Judith Braun (Joyce McClellan); Hugh O'Brian (Private Wilson); Jacqueline Duval (Antoinette DuBois); Jack Kelly (Private John Heyman); Cindy Garner (Kitty Walsh); Sidney Poitier (Corporal Andrew Robertson); Howard Petrie (General Gordon); Bubber Johnson (Private Taffy Smith); Robert Davis (Private Dave McCord); John Hudson (Sergeant Max); Frank Chase (Higgins); John Pickard (Major); Palmer Lee [Gregg Palmer] (Tank Lieutenant); *and:* Jack Warden, Richard Garland, Harry Lauter, Tommy Long, Arthur Space, Robert Karnes, Eugene Borden, Yola D'Arvil, Sid Clute, Emmett Smith, Nan Boardman.

During its four months of existence in the fall of 1944, the Red Ball Express was charged with moving 410,000 tons of supplies to the Allied army as it moved inland from Normandy into Germany during World War II.

Lieutenant Chick Campbell (Jeff Chandler) of the Red Ball Express must direct fuel to General George Patton for his tank command before the cut-off unit is destroyed in its French campaign. Making his non-stop task more difficult is disgruntled Sergeant Ernest Kalleck (Alex Nicol) and Corporal Andrew Robertson (Sidney Poitier). The latter feels he and the other blacks in the unit are subject to far too much racial discrimination.

This production-line movie is filled with lame cliches. It exploits a real-life situation (the black soldiers of the Red Ball Express who were commanded by white officers) by using rising film actor Sidney Poitier as a smoldering foil for Universal's contract leading man Jeff Chandler. The latter is so completely without artifice in his performance that he gives the tame film a badly needed shot of credibility.

Nonetheless, *Red Ball Express* played a part in the emerging racial consciousness that would sweep Hollywood nearly twenty years later: "...a unique film because it frankly discusses the question of color prejudice in the service. The Negro's attitudes and his treatment by certain of his fellow soldiers are brought into sharp focus here" (Joe Pihodna, *New York Herald-Tribune*).

In 1969, the made-for-television movie *Carter's Army* (q.v.) would tackle the subject of racial bigotry in the World War II army more directly and forcefully. During the 1973–74 TV season there appeared "Roll Out," featuring Stu Gilliam and Hilly Hicks, which dealt in comedic terms with the "Red Ball Express."

167. Riot (Paramount, 1969). Color, 97 minutes.

Producer William Castle; *associate producer* Dona Holloway; *director* Buzz Kulik; *based on the novel* "The Riot" *by* Frank Elli; *screenplay* James Poe; *production designer/art director* Paul Sylbert; *makeup* Charles Blackman; *assistant director* Danny McCauley; *music* Christopher Komeda; *songs* Komeda and Robert Wells; Johnnie Lee Willis, Deacon Anderson, and Blackman; *sound* John Wilkinson, Clem Portman; *camera* Robert Hauser; *editor* Edwin H. Bryant.

Cast: Jim Brown (Cully Briston); Gene Hackman (Red Fletcher); Ben Caruthers (Joe Surefoot); Mike Kellin (Bugsy); Gerald S. O'Loughlin (Grossman); Clifford David ("Big Mary" Sheldon); Bill Walker (Jake); Ricky Summers ("Gertie"); Michael Byron (Murray); Jerry Thompson (Deputy Warden Fisk); M. Gerri, John Neiderhauser (Homosexuals); Frank A. Eyman (The Warden).

"*Riot* is not a great movie, but it is a respectable one. It also confirms as fact Jim Brown's new status as a movie star. Although he really isn't much of an actor, that isn't a fatal handicap in the movies where—historically—a kind of physical presence and sense of personal style are often more important than a specific talent" (Vincent Canby, *New York Times*).

For decades, one of Hollywood's staples had been the prison picture. They were usually peopled with the likes of Wallace Beery (*The Big House,* 1930), Paul Muni (*I Was a Fugitive from a Chain Gang,* 1932), Edward G. Robinson (*Two Seconds,* 1932), Spencer Tracy (*Twenty Thousand Years in Sing Sing,* 1933), Humphrey Bogard (*San Quentin,* 1937), James Cagney (*Each Dawn I Die,* 1939), and Burt Lancaster (*Bird Man of Alcatraz,* 1962). Sometimes the focus was on women inmates, as in *Caged* (1949) and *Women's Prison* (1954). It was in *Riot* that the focus turned to the black convict as a force to be reckoned with both inside the big walls and out (if he escaped).

Black convict Cully Briston (Jim Brown), an intense man of few words, is sent to the isolation tank, where he becomes involved in a riot instigated by Red Fletcher (Gene Hackman). Having taken several guards hostage, the rioters control part of the 1200-convict prison. Fletcher pretends the uprising is due to grievances. Actually, he is stalling for time so he can escape through a tunnel shaft that goes beyond the prison walls. Because the media focuses on the prisoners' grievances, the prison officials negotiate with Fletcher and his cronies. During a party thrown by the rioters, the stool pigeon convicts who informed on their fellow inmates are judged guilty by a kangaroo court. Some of the rioters get drunk on homemade raisin jack brew, but crazed Joe Surefoot (Ben Carruthers) is stopped by Cully from killing the hostages. The warden returns from his vacation and announces drastic steps to regain order. Red and eleven others, including Briston, reach the tunnel shaft, but when they emerge outside, they are greeted by machine-gun fire and gas grenade explosions. Briston, Fletcher, and Surefoot have gas masks, and they reach the base of a guard tower. After Surefoot kills a guard he tries knifing Briston, but Fletcher stops him. Surefoot and Fletcher fight to the death, with Briston alone escaping.

The simplistic storyline of *Riot* may fade, as do the labored scenes of the transvestite homosexuals of Queens Row at the rioters' party. But remaining fixed in the mind are images of Jim Brown's Cully Briston jogging through the prison yard or walking down a cellblock corridor, always with tremendous presence and authority, as if he were back on the football field. Then there is the fantasy sequence where Briston dreams of a nice house and accommodating nubile women decorating the poolside. This is clearly Jim Brown at his Hollywood prime, both onscreen and off.

Riot was filmed entirely on location in Arizona State Penitentiary with prison warden Frank A. Eyman and several hundred inmates and personnel participating. The movie was based on the 1967 book by ex-convict Frank Elli. In the book, Cully Briston had been a white convict.

168. Rocky (United Artists, 1976). Color, 119 minutes.

Producers Irwin Winkler, Robert Chartoff; *director* John G. Avildsen; *screenplay* Sylvester Stallone; *production designer* Bill Cassidy; *art director* James H. Spencer; *set decorator* Raymond Molyneaux; *costumes* Robert Cambel; *makeup* Mike Westmore; *music* Bill Conti; *songs* Conti, Carol Connors, and Ayn Robbins; Frank Stallone, Jr.; *choreography* Stallone; *technical adviser* Jimmy Gambina; *stunts* Jim Nickerson; *assistant directors* Fred Gallo, Steve Perry; *special effects* Garrett Brown; *camera* James Crabe; *editors* Richard Halseyd, Scott Conrad.

Cast: Sylvester Stallone (Rocky Balboa); Talia Shire (Adrian); Burt Young (Paulie); Carl Weathers (Apollo Creed); Burgess Meredith (Mickey); Thayer David (Miles Jergens); Joe Spinell (Tom Gazzo); Jimmy Gambina (Mike); Bill Baldwin (Fight Announcer); Al Silvani (Cut Man); George Memmoli (Ice Rink Attendant); Jodi Letizia (Marie); Diana Lewis, George O'Hanlon (TV Commentators); Larry Carroll (TV Interviewer); Stan Shaw (Dipper); Don Sherman (Bartender); Billy Sands (Club Fight Announcer); Pedro Lovell (Spider Ricco); DeForest Covan (Apollo's Corner); Simmy (Club Cornerman); Tony Burton (Apollo's Trainer); Hank Rolike (Apollo Cornerman); Shirley O'Hara (Jergen's Secretary); Kathleen Parker (Paulie's Date); Frank Stallone (Time-

Top: Advertisement for *Riot* (1969). *Bottom: left–right:* **Carl Weathers, Frankie Van, and Sylvester Stallone in *Rocky* (1976).**

keeper); Lloyd Kaufman (Drunk); Jane Marla Robbins (Gloria the Pet Shop Owner); Jack Hollander (Fats); Joe Sorbello (Buddy the Bodyguard); Christopher Avildsen (Chiptooth); Frankie Van (Club Fight Referee); Lou Filippo (Championship Fight Announcer); Frank Stallone Jr., Robert L. Tangrea, Peter Glassberg, William E. Ring, Joseph C. Ciambelluca (Street Corner Singers); Butkus Stallone (Butkus the Dog); Joe Frazier (Paris Eagle). See summary under *Rocky IV*.

169. Rocky II (United Artists, 1979). Color, 119 minutes.

Producers Irwin Winkler, Robert Chartoff; *associate producer* Arthur Chobanian; *director/screenplay* Sylvester Stallone; *art director* Richard Berger; *set decorator* Ed Baer; *costumes* Thomas Bronson, Sandra Berke; *makeup* Michael Westmore; *music* Bill Conti; *songs* Frank Stallone [Jr.]; *choreography* Sylvester Stallone; *technical adviser* Al Silvani; *assistant directors* Jerry Zeismer, Elie Cohn; *camera* Bill Butler; *editors* Danford B. Greene, Stanford C. Allen, Janice Hampton, James Symons.

Cast: Sylvester Stallone (Rocky Balboa); Talia Shire (Adrian); Burt Young (Paulie); Carl Weathers (Apollo Creed); Burgess Meredith (Mickey); Tony Burton (Apollo's Trainer); Joe Spinell (Gazzo); Leonard Gaines (Agent); Sylvia Meals (Mary Anne Creed); Frank McRae (Meat Foreman); Al Silvani (Cutman); John Pleshette (Director); Stu Nahan (Announcer); Bill Baldwin (Commentator); Jerry Ziesmer (Salesman); Paul J. Micale (Father Carmine); *and:* Taurean Blacque, James Casino, Charles Coles, Samuel Davis, Doug Flor, Ruth Ann Flynn, Linda Grey, Robert Kondyra, Eddie Lopez, Earl Montgomery, Herb Nanas, Stuart Robinson, Frank Stallone [Jr.], James Zazzariono. See summary under *Rocky IV*.

170. Rocky III (Metro-Goldwyn-Mayer/United Artists, 1982). Color, 99 minutes.

Executive producer Herb Nanas; *producers* Irwin Winkler, Robert Chartoff; *director/screenplay* Sylvester Stallone; *production designer* William J. Cassidy; *art directors* Ronald Kent Foreman, Dennis Washington; *set decorator* Joe Mitchell; *costumes* Tom Bronson; *makeup* Michael Westmore; *music* Bill Conti; *songs:* Jim Peterlik and Frank Sullivan; Frank Stallone [Jr.]; Conti and Frank Stallone; *boxing choreography* Sylvester Stallone; *wrestling technical adviser* Tom Renesto; *stunt co-ordinator* Ron Stein; *assistant director* Cliff Coleman; *sound* Chuck Wilborn; *supervising sound editor* Frank Warner; *special effects* Howard Jensen; *camera* Bill Butler; *special camera* Neil Leifer; *editors* Don Zimmerman, Mark Warner.

Cast: Sylvester Stallone (Rocky Balboa); Carl Weathers (Apollo Creed); Mr. T (Clubber Lang); Talia Shire (Adrian Balboa); Burt Young (Paulie); Burgess Meredith (Mickey); Ian Fried (Rocky, Jr.); Hulk Hogan (Thunderlips); Al Silvani (Al); Wally Taylor (Clubber's Manager); Tony Burton (Duke); Jim Hill (Sportscaster); Don Sherman (Andy); Dennis James, Jim Healy (Wrestling Commentators); Ray Gedeon (Wrestling Referee); Gene Crane (Mayor); Stu Nahan, Bill Baldwin, Sr. (Title Fight/Rematch Commentators);

Jimmy Lennon (Title Fight Announcer); Marty Kenkin (Title Fight Referee); John David Morris (Doctor); Lou Filippo (Rematch Referee); Jeff Temkin (Rematch Ring Announcer); Marty Denkin (Title Fight Referee); John David Morris (Doctor); Lou Filippo (Rematch Referee); Jeff Temkin (Rematch Ring Announcer); Mario Machado (Interviewer); Tony Hernandez (Himself); Frank Stallone [Jr.] (Singer); Rabbi Philmore Berger (Rabbi); Big Yank (Sparring Partner); François Andre, Eddie Smith (Clubber's Cornermen); Chino "Fats" Williams (Derelict).
See summary under *Rocky IV*.

171. Rocky IV (Metro-Goldwyn-Mayer/United Artists, 1985).
Color, 91 minutes.

Executive producers James D. Brubaker, Arthur Chobanian; *producers* Irwin Winkler, Robert Chartoff; *director/screenplay* Sylvester Stallone; *production designer* Bill Kenney; *costumes* Tom Bronson; *music* Vince DiCola, Bill Conti; *choreography* Michael McKensie Pratt; *assistant directors* Duncan Henderson, Chris Ryan; *special effects* Howard Jensen; *sound* Chuck Wilborn; *camera* Bill Butler; *editors* Don Zimmerman, John W. Wheeler.

Cast: Sylvester Stallone (Rocky Balboa); Talia Shire (Adrian Balboa); Burt Young (Paulie); Carl Weathers (Apollo Creed); Brigitte Nielsen (Ludmilla); Tony Burton (Duke); Michael Pataki (Nicoli Koloff); Dolph Lundgren (Drago); R.J. Adams (Sports Announcer); Al Bandiero (American Commentator #2); Dominic Barto (Russian Government Official); Daniel Brown (Rocky Jr.'s Friend); James Brown (The Godfather of Soul); Rose Mary Campos (Maid); Jack Carpenter (KGB Driver); Mark Delessandro (Russian Cornerman); Marty Kenkin (Russian Referee); Lou Filippo (Las Vegas Referee); James "Cannonball" Green (Manuel Vega); Dean Hammond (Interviewer); Rocky Krakoff (Rocky, Jr.); Sergei Levin (Russian Ring Announcer); Anthony Maffatone (KGB Agent); Sylvia Meals (Mrs. Creed); Dwayne McGee (Limo Driver); Stu Nahan (Commentator #1), LeRoy Neiman (Ring Announcer); George Pipaski (Caretaker); George Rogan (Igor Rimsky); Barry Tomplins (American Commentator #1); Warner Wolf (Commentator #2 in Las Vegas); Robert Doornick (Voice of Sico the Robot); Jeff Austin, Richard Blum, Patrick Pankhurst, Craig Schaefer, Rolf Williams (Reporters).

Their domestic film rentals speak for themselves: *Rocky,* $56,521,647; *Rocky II,* $41,879,000; *Rocky III,* $66,235,909; *Rocky IV,* $75,974,593. The fact that *Rocky* cost $960,000 (on a twenty-eight-day shooting schedule) to produce while *Rocky IV* generated $30,000,000 in estimated production expenses says a great deal too. The legend of the rise and fall (and rise and fall, and rise and . . .) of Philadelphia's Rocky Balboa is firmly entrenched in cinema lore, as is the Academy Award *Rocky* won as Best Picture of 1976. Obviously, as the rentals substantiate, moviegoers have not tired of this softhearted underdog boxer who constantly renews his confidence an goes on to vicotry in the ring. A good deal of Rocky's resilience in the ring was due to his faithful trainer, Mickey (Burgess Meredith), and to Adrian (Talia Shire), who became his wife and the mother of their child, Rocky, Jr. Yet one of the strongest textures in this film series is the role of two black boxers, Apollo Creed (Carl

Weathers) in all four films and Clubber Lang (Mr. T.) in *Rocky III*. As foe or friend, they provide the challenge and competition that always lurks ahead. In its symbolic sense it was again black against white, and the latter did *not* always emerge the victor. Clearly the *Rocky* series owes a great deal to the black film cycle of the early 1970s, where ex-football star Carl Weathers had gotten his start (1975's *Bucktown* and *Friday Foster* [qq.v.]).

In *Rocky,* world heavyweight champ Apollo Creed decides to give an unknown boxer a chance to fight for the title, reasoning it would make an excellent public relations gimmick. In the Philadelphia boxing register he spots Rocky Balboa and decides, "That's the man!" In the big match, Creed dances around Balboa, but then Rocky comes forth with several well-placed punches and the slam match progresses. When the fight ends, both men can scarcely stand, and Creed has several cracked ribs. The judges' decision is two to one in favor of Creed, who insists he will not give Rocky a rematch. The latter mumbles that is fine because he only wanted to prove he could withstand the competition.

In *Rocky II,* Philadelphia's own is told further boxing could cost him vision in one eye, but he does not care, for he is too busy enjoying married life with Adrian. He tries a career as a television spokesman, but that doesn't work, nor does a job as a meat packer. Meanwhile, Apollo is frustated by the hate mail he is receiving claiming he had fixed the exhibition match with Balboa. So Creed challenges Rocky to a new contest to be held on Thanksgiving. Adrian gives birth to Rocky, Jr., and now encourages her husband to win. In the final round, Rocky reverts to being a southpaw and smashes repeatedly at the champion, who now, against his managers' orders, is trying to knock out the opponent. At the final count, Rocky is the winner.

For *Rocky III,* the hero of Philadelphia must step off his pedestal and back onto the canvas to silence the challenges of loudmouthed newcomer Clubber Lang (Mr. T). Apollo Creed appears on the scene to say he will train Rocky to help him get even with the crude Clubber, who had also insulted him if 1) Rocky will set up training headquarters in Los Angeles' black ghetto and train at the local gym against black fighters where Creed got his start; and 2) Rocky will grant him a special favor (which turns out to be a private rematch just to see, friend-to-friend, who is best). Under Apollo's grueling regimen, Rocky gains faith and soul and becomes a lean, mean machine able to recapture the title from Clubber.

In *Rocky IV* Apollo Creed is killed in an exhibition match with gigantic Russian Drago (Dolph Lundgren), and Rocky comes out of retirement (yet again!) to avenge his friend's death and to regain his country's honor against the Soviets. In the battle of freedom versus communism (i.e., red white and blue against red, rather than the white against black of the first three entries), Rocky wins (surprise!).

Everyone has his favorite quips about the staggeringly successful *Rocky* series; perhaps the best is from *People* magazine, prompted by *Rocky IV:* "Much, much further adventures of boxer Rocky Balboa settled one burning issue. Sylvester Stallone does better video workout routines than Jane Fonda. Let's face it, when you pay to see a *Rocky* film it's mainly for the privilege of watching Sly ripple as he totes that barge and lifts that bale in training to beat one more impossible foe."

In all four *Rocky* films critics and the public alike noted the classy performance by Carl Weathers as the intelligent, well-living black opponent who turns from deadly opponent to dedicated friend in the course of the entries. His controlled mixture of physical power and charisma make the characterization work. If anything the rapport between Apollo and Rocky is heightened by the appearance of the obnoxious braggart Clubber Lang (played in the mold of Muhammed Ali) in *Rocky III,* which provides a strong contrast between the two black boxers.

Post-*Rocky,* Carl Weathers went on to star in his own (short-lived) television series *Action Jackson* (1988) (q.v.), while Mr. T became a video fad in the teleseries "The A-Team" and in such feature films as *D.C. Cab* (1984) (q.v.). As for Sylvester Stallone, there is the upcoming *Rocky V* to look forward to.

172. Salt and Pepper (United Artists, 1968). Color, 102 minutes.

Executive producers Peter Lawford, Sammy Davis, Jr.; *producer* Milton Ebbins; *associate producer* Ted Wallis; *director* Richard D. Donner; *screenplay* Michael Pertwee; *production designers* Bill Constable; *art director* Don Mingaye; *set decorators* Scott Slimon, Andrew Low; *costumes* Cynthia Tingey, Charles Glenn; *makeup* Jimmy Evans; *music* John Dankworth; *songs* George Rhodes and Davis Jr; Leslie Bricusse; *choreography* Lionel Blair; *assistant director* Derek Parr; *sound* John Poyner; *special effects* Kit West; *camera* Ken Higgins; *editor* Jack Slade.

Cast: Sammy Davis, Jr. (Charles Salt); Peter Lawford (Christopher Pepper); Michael Bates (Inspector Crabbe); Ilona Rodgers (Marianne Renaud); John Le Mesurier (Colonel Woodstock); Graham Stark (Sergeant Walters); Ernest Clark (Colonel Balsom); Jeanne Roland (Mai Ling); Robert Dorning (Club Secretary); Robertson Hare (Dove); Geoffrey Lunsden (Foreign Secretary); William Mervyn (Prime Minister); Llewellyn Rees ("Fake" Prime Minister); Mark Singleton ("Fake" Home Secretary); Michael Trubshawe ("Fake" First Lord); Francisca Tu (Tsai Chan); Oliver MacGreevy (Rack); Peter Hutchins (Straw); Jeremy Lloyd (Lord Ponsonby); Sedan Lynch (Black Jack Player); Ivor Dean (Police Commissioner); Brian Harrison (Policeman); Harry Hutchinson (Manservant); Max Faulkner (Lieutenant); Beth Rogan (Greta); Rifat Shenel (Mario); Calvin Lockhart (Jones); Nicholas Smith (Constable); Susan Blair (Janice); Christine Pocket (Jill); Cassandra Mowan (Jean); Joe Wadham (Colonel Woodstock's Aide).

Two on-again, off-again members of Frank Sinatra's Rat Pack united as producers and stars for this congenial but tepid spy spoof which had the *then*-novelty (used successfully on the teleseries "I Spy," 1965–68) of a black and white lead team and the pseudo-hip ambiance of swinging Soho, mod Barnaby Street, and all that....

Charles Salt (Sammy Davis, Jr.) and Christopher Pepper (Peter Lawford), who own a Soho gaming club, find themselves being questioned by Scotland Yard Inspector Crabbe (Michael Bates) for two murders which occurred at their establishment. No sooner are they released than Colonel Balsom (Ernest Clark) of the British Secret Service has them kidnapped. They later uncover the diary of one of the victims (who was actually a British secret agent) and decide to track down the four important people listed therein. Three more killings occur, with the amateurs sleuths taken prisoner by the mad Colonel Woodstock (John Le Mesurier), who intends overthrowing the British government. They escape but cannot prove Woodstock's existence to Balsom. Later, Salt saves Pepper from being shot by Marianne Renaud (Ilona Rodgers). Eventually the two club men locate the conspirator's headquarters and save the day, leading to their being knighted by the Queen of England.

The British were not amused by this travesty. "Both the pseudo–Bond action and the slapstick comedy are excruciatingly ill-timed; any even tolerably witty joke is repeated several times over; and the studio-built Soho looks studio-built" (British *Monthly Film Bulletin*).

The multi-talented Sammy Davis, Jr., besides his several film excursions with Frank Sinatra and company (*Ocean's Eleven,* 1960; *Sergeants Three,* 1962; *Robin and the Seven Hoods,* 1964) had made several other forays into films. He co-starred in musicals such as *Porgy and Bess* (1959) and *Sweet Charity* (1968) and appeared in moody dramas such as *Anna Lucasta* (1958) and *A Man Called Adam* (1966) and in gangster melodramas such as *Convicts Four* (1962) and *Johnny Cool* (1963). He was an early television black detective in *The Pigeon* (1969), a telefeature pilot for a series that did not materialize, and at one point was "considered" for the Fred Williamson role in *Black Caesar* (1973).

For the record, Sammy Davis, Jr., sang "I Like the Way You Look," and the film did sufficient business to warrant a sequel, *One More Time* (1970) (q.v.). To be noted in *Salt and Pepper* is rising black performer Calvin Lockhart in a small role as Jones.

173. Savage! (New World, 1973). Color, 81 minutes.

Producer/director Cirio H. Santiago; *screenplay* Ed Medard; *music* Don Julian; *songs* Julian; Arthur G. Wright; Julian and Wright; *camera* Philip Sacdalan; *editor* Richard Patterson.

Cast: James Iglehardt (Jim Haygood, the Savage); Carol Speed (Amanda); Lada Edmun (Vicky); *and:* Aura Aurea, Vic Diaz, Eddie Gutierrez, Sally Jordan, Ken Metcalfe, Rossano Ortiz, Harley Paton, Marie Saunders.

Ex–Pittsburgh Pirate baseball player James Iglehardt had had tiny parts in such films as *Beyond the Valley of the Dolls* (1970), *Angels Hard as They Come* (1971), and *Seven Minutes* (1971) before he appeared in this grainy action quickie shot sloppily in the Philippines.

Jim Haygood (Jim Iglehardt) is responsible for the beach ambush and capture of a rebel army leader in an unnamed Latin American country. He celebrates at the local nightclub, where he meets Amanda (Carol Speed) and Vicky (Lada Edmund). Later, he is placed under arrest for the cold-blooded killing of the rebel chief, but he escapes. Leaving Vicky behind (after she is caught by the troops), he and Amanda flee, but they are imprisoned by the rebels, whom he then tricks by having their own planes attack them. Thereafter he teams with the rebels against his authoritarian superiors and rescues Vicky. He is supported by a task force of female commandoes as they fight against the government army. Vicky and her rebel lover are killed, but Haygood escapes, ready to lead yet another campaign against the enemy.

James Iglehardt would appear later in such unmemorable feature films as *Bamboo Gods and Iron Men* (1974) and *Death Force* (1979), the latter also directed by Cirio Santiago.

174. Scream, Blacula, Scream (American International, 1973). Color, 95 minutes.

Presenter Samuel Z. Arkoff; *producer* Joseph T. Naar; *director* Bob Kelljan; *story* Raymond Koenig, Joan Torres; *screenplay* Torres, Koenig, Maurice Jules; *art director* Alfeo Bocchicchio; *set decorator* Chuck Pierce; *makeup* Alan Snider; *music* Bill Marx; *music editor* Ving Hershon; *assistant directors* Reuben Watt, John Poer; *sound* Donald Johnson; *camera* Isidore Mankofsky; *editors* Fabian Tordjmann, Bruce Shoengarth.

Cast: William Marshall (Mamuwalde); Don Mitchell (Justin Carter); Pam Grier (Lisa); Michael Conrad (Sheriff Dunlop); Richard Lawson (Willis); Lynne Moody (Denny); Janee Michelle (Gloria); Barbara Rhoades (Elaine); Bernie Hamilton (Ragman); Arnold Williams (Louis); Van Kirksey (Professor Walston); Bob Minor, Al Jones (Pimps); Eric Mason (Milt); Sybil Scotford (Librarian); Beverly Gill (Maggie); Don Blackman (Doll Man); Judith Elliotte (Prostitute); Dan Roth (Cop); Nicholas Worth (Dennis); Kenneth O'Brien (Joe); Craig T. Nelson (Sarge); James Payne (Attendant); Richard Washington, Bob Hoy (Cops); James Kingsley (Sergeant Williams); Arnita Bell (Woman).

Grossing $1,000,000 in domestic film rentals (in the early 1970s) is a fact not to be taken lightly. However, artistically, *Scream, Blacula, Scream* is a poor successor to the stylish *Blacula* (1972) (q.v.): "...fails for lack of incident, weakness of invention, insufficient story" (Roger Greenspun, *New York Times*). There is too much exposition and ornate atmosphere and not enough action (okay, blood sucking).

The elaborate storyline opens as a voodoo high priestess dies. Among her followers is her son, Willis (Richard Lawson), who insists he is to be her successor. But Lisa (Pam Grier) and the others advise him this is not so. He leaves swearing to have revenge. A mysterious man gives him a bag of human bones and instructs him on the proper incantation to use. As Willis performs the ceremony, Blacula (William Marshall) is reincarnated. His first act is to turn Willis into a victim and slave. Using his African name of Mamuwalde, Blacula joins the voodoo cult. All this cultured gentleman will admit is that he is from the Saigo River region of Africa and that "I'm retired. I'm considerably older than I appear." Mamuwalde is extremely attracted by the lovely Lisa but put off by her special powers. ("When it comes to voodoo, Lisa has more natural power than anyone in the last ten years," one of her confederates insists.) When Blacula and Willis claim a growing list of victims, Sheriff Dunlop (Michael Conrad) and the police investigate. This leads to a bloody encounter between

Top, left–right: **Carol Speed, player, and James Iglehardt in** *Savage!* **(1973).** *Bottom:* **Pam Grier and William Marshall in** *Scream, Blacula, Scream* **(1973).**

of vampires. At the last moment, Lisa punctures a voodoo
which destroys Blacula.

conceits of this film is that Willis is extremely narcissistic.
e has no reflection, he complains, "I don't mind being a
t hip. A man gotta see his face...."

Scream was directed by Bob Kelljan, who had helmed
re (1970) and *The Return of Count Yorga* (1971). Pam
character was rather passive; the self-possessed rising black star was far
better represented in 1973 by her box-office hit *Coffy* (q.v.). As for William
Marshall, he would go on to play Judge Black in the teleseries "Rosetti and
Ryan" (1977) and emerge in the latter 1980s as one of the many strange denizens
of Pee Wee Herman's Saturday morning teleshow.

175. Shaft (Metro-Goldwyn-Mayer, 1971). Color, 98 minutes.

Producer Joel Freeman; *associate producer* David Golden; *director* Gordon Parks, Sr.; *based on the novel by* Ernest Tidyman; *screenplay* John D.F. Black, Tidyman; *art director* Emanuel Gerard; *set decorator* Robert Drumheller; *costume designer* Joe Aulisi; *makeup* Martin Bell; *music* Isaac Hayes; *song* Hayes; *assistant director* Ted Zachary; *sound* Lee Bost, Hal Watkins; *camera* Urs Furrer; *editor* Hugh A. Robertson.

Cast: Richard Roundtree (John Shaft); Moses Gunn (Bumpy Jonas); Charles Cioffi (Lieutenant Vic Androzzy); Christopher St. John (Ben Buford); Gwenn Mitchell (Ellie Moore); Lawrence Pressman (Sergeant Tom Hannon); Victor Arnold (Charlie); Sherri Brewer (Marcy Jonas); Rex Robbins (Rollie); Camille Yarbrough (Dina Greene); Margaret Warncke (Linda); Joseph Leon (Byron Leibowitz); Arnold Johnson (Cul); Dominic Barto (Patsy); George Strus (Carmen); Edmund Hashim (Lee); Drew Bundini Brown (Willy); Tommy Lane (Leroy); Al Kirk (Sims); Shimen Ruskin (Dr. Sam); Antonio Fargas (Bunky); Gertrude Jeannette (Old Lady); Lee Steele (Blind Vendor); Damu King (Mal); Donny Burks (Remmy); Tony King (Davies); Benjamin R. Rixson (Bey Newfield); Ricardo Brown (Tully); Alan Weeks (Gus); Glenn Johnson (Char); Dennis Tade (Dotts); Adam Wade, James Hainesworth (Brothers); Clee Burtonya (Sonny); Ed Bernard (Peerce); Ed Barth (Tony); Joe Pronto (Dom); Robin Nolan (Waitress); Ron Tannas (Billy); Betty Bresler (Mrs. Androzzi); John Richards (Elevator Starter); Paul Nevens (Elevator Man).

See summary under *Shaft's Big Score!*

176. Shaft in Africa (Metro-Goldwyn-Mayer, 1973).
Color, 112 minutes.

Producer Roger Lewis; *associate producer* Rene Dupont; *director* John Guillermin; *based on characters created by* Ernest Tidyman; *screenplay* Stirling Silliphant; *production designer* John Stoll; *art director* Jose Maria Tapiador; *music/music director* Johnny Pate; *song* Dennis Lambert and Brian Potter; *second unit director* David Tomblin; *assistant director* Miguel Angel Gil, Jr.; *stick fight arranger* Takahuki Kubota; *action co-ordinator* Miguel Pedregosa; *special effects* Antonio Molena; *sound* Peter Sutton, Hal Walker; *camera* Marcel Grignon; *editor* Max Benedict.

Cast: Richard Roundtree (John Shaft); Frank Finlay (Amafi the Slave Dealer) Vonetta McGee (Aleme); Neda Arneric (Jazar); Debebe Eshetu (Wassa); Spiros Focas (Sassari); Jacques Herlin (Perreau); Jho Jhenkins (Ziba); Willie Jonah (Oyo); Adolfo Lastretti (Piro); Marne Maitland (Colonel Gondar); Frank McRae (Osiat); Zenebech Tadesse (Prostitute); A.V. Falana (Ramila's Son); James E. Myers (Detective Williams); Nadim Sawalha (Zubair); Thomas Baptiste (Kopo); Jon Chevron (Shimba); Glynn Edwards (Vanden); Cy Grant (Emir Ramila); Jacques Marin (Inspector Cusset); Nick Zaran (Sadi); Aldo Sambreill (Angelo).

See summary under *Shaft's Big Score!*

177. Shaft's Big Score! (Metro-Goldwyn-Mayer, 1972).
Color, 105 minutes

Producers Roger Lewis, Ernest Tidyman; *associate producer* David Golden; *director* Gordon Parks, Sr.; *based on characters created by* Tidyman; *screenplay* Tidyman; *art director* Emanuel Gerard; *set decorator* Robert Drumheller; *costumes* Joe Aulisi; *makeup* Martin Bell; *music/songs* Parks; *orchestrators* Dick Hazard, Tom McIntosh, Jimmy Jones, Dale Oehler; *assistant director* William C. Gerrity; *stunts* Alex Stevens, Marvin Walters; *special effects* Tony Parmalee; *sound* Lee Bost, Hal Watkins; *camera* Urs Furrer; *editor* Harry Howard.

Cast: Richard Roundtree (John Shaft); Moses Gunn (Bumpy Jonas); Drew Bundini Brown (Willy); Joseph Mascola (Gus Mascola); Kathy Imrie (Rita); Wally Taylor (Kelly); Julius W. Harris (Captain Bollin); Rosalind Miles (Arna Ashby); Joe Santos (Pascal); Angelo Nazzo (Al); Don Blakely (Johnson); Melvin Green, Jr. (Junior Gillis); Thomas Anderson (Preacher); Evelyn Davis (Old Lady); Richard Pittmann (Kelly's Hood); Robert Kya-Hill (Cal Ashby); Thomas Brann (Mascola's Hood); Bob Jefferson (Harrison); Dan P. Hannafin (Cooper); Jimmy Hayeson (Caretaker); Henry Ferrentino (Detective Salmi); Frank Scioscia (Rip); Kitty Jones (Cabaret Dancer); Gregory Reese (Foglio); Marilyn Hamlin (Mascola's Girl); John Foster (Jerry); Joyce Walker (Cigarette Girl); Gordon Parks, Sr. (Croupier).

Meet rugged black stud John Shaft (Richard Roundtree), the enormously successful private detective of *Shaft*. This crossover film along with *Sweet Sweetback's Baadasssss Song* (1971), launched the explosion of blaxploitation pictures.

Critics and viewers alike have dissected this MGM feature (and its two followups) looking for telltale clues and hidden inner meanings that combined to make this *the* black action film experience of the 1970s. The answer is a combination of several key factors; a sturdy Ernest Tidyman novel, the sure hand of black director Gordon Parks, Sr., the screen presence of Richard Roundtree as the muscular gumshoe, and that most elusive of all ingredients—a well-timed release.

Born in New Rochelle, New York in 1937, Richard Roundtree was a fashion model before joining the Negro Ensemble Company's workshop in 1967. When he learned about the *Shaft* film project, he auditioned for Gordon Parks, Sr. (the first black director to helm a major studio film—*The Learning*

Tree [1969], based on his autobiographical novel of growing up in Kansas). Roundtree was hired. He became a nationally known performer with the mega-success of *Shaft*. (Ironically Roundtree was paid only $13,000 for the first *Shaft,* only $50,000 for making the second entry, and a little better thereafter.) But just as the three films (and brief teleseries) caused his fame, it was his professional undoing. He was stereotyped by the pathfinding black detective role and could never break from that characterization. He appeared in such feature films as the Western *Charley One Eye* (1973) (q.v.), *Earthquake* (1974), *Diamonds* (1975), and in a variation of *Robinson Crusoe* with Peter O'Toole called *Man Friday* (1976). He was among the many in television's *Roots* (1977) and by the 1980s was gracing such lower-end black action films as *The Big Score* (1983) and *One Down, Two to Go* (1983) (qq.v.), both turned out by filmmaker Fred Williamson, and in *Killpoint* (1984) (q.v.), where he played second fiddle to martial arts. His appearance in Clint Eastwood and Burt Reynolds's *City Heat* (1984) was negligible, and he was seen thereafter in the short-lived Western teleseries "Outlaws" (1987).

Warned that two armed black men from Harlem are waiting for him in his Times Square office (Room #410), black private investigator John Shaft (Richard Roundtree) hurls one through the window and strongarms the other into admitting he has been sent by wealthy uptown racketeer Bumpy Jonas (Moses Gunn). Police lieutenant Vic Androzzi (Charles Cioffi) of the 38th Precinct advises his friend and nemesis Shaft that unless he cooperates in helping to investigate the hoodlum's gangland activities, he will suspend his detective's license. Meanwhile, on his own, Jonas comes to Shaft's office and informs him his daughter Marcy (Sherri Brewer) has been kidnapped. Jonas is sure it was done by Ben Buford (Christopher St. John) and his black militants. Shaft finds this interesting, since he and Buford were childhood friends. Shaft tracks Buford to a Harlem slum tenement on Amsterdam Avenue, where he is conducting a meeting with six squad members. A machine-gun attack wipes out several of the underlings, but Shaft and Buford escape. Shaft convinces Buford he did not set up his friend but rather was seeking help to find Marcy. He then storms into Bumpas's office wanting to know if he was responsible. Bumpas says no, and now the likely suspects are the downtown Mafia, who want to pressure him out of trying to control all the uptown rackets. Shaft, Ben and some helpers track the Mafia goons to a Greenwhich Village hotel room where they are holding Marcy. Marcy is freed, and Jonas willingly pays Buford his fee of $10,000 per head, the funds being used by the black militants to release political prisoners.

"It's just a Saturday night fun picture which people go to see because they want to see the black guy winning," insisted director Gordon Parks, Sr. The viewer knows he is in for some fast action (the thumping Isaac Hayes score says so); some wise remarks (the blind newsstand dealer says to Shaft, "Everyone looks the same to me"), and a zingy plot premise where black is beautiful and white ain't so hot. (This was indeed trend-setting, making the good and bad blacks the good guys and most of the whites the scumbags.) But some of the white characters do not regard the emerging black citizen respectfully. As one prejudiced police underling tells Lieutenant Androzzi regarding Shaft, "You gotta lean on *that* kind." But cool, cool Shaft does not allow his black brothers to be disparaged by the cops: "My Negro friends don't walk around with rabbit feet no more," he insists to the police in general, and later says to Androzzi in mock seriousness, "You're a very wise Caucasian, Vic." At the film's finale there is a sly reversal of the black man always being left to clean up the white man's mess. Having solved this caper (at a neat $25,000 fee), Shaft calls Androzzi and casually sallies, "The case is busted wide open. Looks like you're goin' to have to close it, baby."

There *are* times when Shaft is not sure which side of the racial fence he is on. When lordly Bumpy Jonas hires Shaft he explains, "I want you because you're a black spade detective. I want you cause you got your other foot in whitey's trough and she [Marcy] could be anywhere." Yet later when Shaft is hailing a cab and the taxi driver zooms on by without bothering to stop, he screams, "You white muther!" In short, Shaft is in neither world, but a special planet unto himself.

Shaft is always his own man, all of which is in the tough tradition of Sam Spade and Philip Marlowe. Shaft would just as soon slam a man's head into a brick wall as spit at him, and if a client should dare call him about a case at the wrong hour (as Bumpy Jonas does when Shaft is bedding his woman), his response is likely to be, "Tell that bastard to kiss my black ass." The slickly dressed Shaft (in his trademark brown leather coat and his virile mustache) is the bane of the police, Mafia, and the Harlem gangs. He does not respect any authority figures of any fashion, being always distrustful of their postures, codes of ethics, and reliability. And, for their part, they either fear or need or can't kill him. As for Shaft's unorthodox life style (remember this was 1971), Shaft is depicted living a *Playboy* magazine fantasy with a trendy Greenwich Village pad and girlfriends (of all shapes and colors) hankering for his body (with the underlying texture that Shaft, being black, is super-endowed, always horny, and packs a mean wallop in bed). One scene finds him at one of his girls' apartments, lying in bed naked and waiting impatiently for her to get home. "I got to feelin' like a machine and that's no way to feel," he explains. (Being the post–Civil Rights Movement and pre–Women's Liberation heyday, Shaft's women are all machines, ready to service him.) And to show that this film has topical relevance and that Shaft is a complex character, at one point Shaft admits to his chick that he has a couple of problems: "I was born black and I was born poor."

Roger Greenspun *(New York Times)* noted, "...it has a kind of self-generated good will that makes you want to like it even when for scenes on end you know it is doing everything wrong.... Tin-eared and occasionally glass-eyed, he [director Parks] shows a grace in putting the horror of the city to the purposes of entertainment that seems especially welcome considering the options." Vincent Canby *(New York Times)* in a follow-up essay on *Shaft* enthusiastically tagged the film "a good Sataurday night movie" and in fact "the first good Saturday night movie I've seen in years." He admired the movie for its energy. "...the vitality is so freshly vulgar, so without solemnity except for its observance of private-eye conventions ... that the movie becomes the kind of entertainment to which any audience — black, white or you-name-it — can respond." Canby saw Shaft as a man who "...moves through Whitey's world with perfect ease and aplomb, but never loses his independence, or his awareness of where his life is really at." Equally enthusiastic was Maurice Peterson (*Essence* magazine), who applauded this film: "Never have we [the black people] been allowed to go to the movies just to enjoy ourselves—that is, not until the release of *Shaft.... Shaft* is the first picture to show a black man who leads a life free of racial torment. He is black and proud of it, but not obsessed with it.... Shaft keeps his blackness in perspective."

On the other hand, black critic Clayton Riley (writing as a guest reviewer for the *New York Times*) was not amused by *Shaft.* "To be blunt about it, *Shaft* is a disaster. Technically mediocre and, for the most part, poorly acted, it is a film that lacks both style and substance. Nothing is really examined...."

Made at a cost of $1,543,000, *Shaft* grossed $7,080,000 in domestic film rentals. The Isaac Hayes soundtrack proved a phenomenon all its own, helping to snowball the word-of-mouth about the breakthrough film. The soundtrack album became #1 on the charts for two weeks, remaining on the best-seller charts for 60 weeks. It was #1 on the rhythm-and-blues and jazz charts as an album and tape, and won a Grammy Award for Best Original Score written for a Motion Picture/TV Special. Three weeks after its release it had generated $1,000,000 in record sales; by October of 1971 (the film opened 7/1/71) it had earned $2,000,000 in sales and by November 1971 the double-album record set had sold over 1,000,000 units, and the single ("Theme from Shaft") had reached 1,350,000 units sold. The original theme song for *Shaft* won an Academy Award as well.

With such a box-office record, Metro-Goldwyn-Mayer could not resist a successor to *Shaft,* and a year later *Shaft's Big Score!* appeared.

Up in Harlem, Cal Asby (Robert Kys-Hill) is killed by his duplistic partner, Kelly (Wally Taylor), having stashed a racket-stolen $250,000 in a coffin. White mobster Gus Mascola (Joseph Mascola) wants the missing money and control of the numbers game throughout New York City, which displeases Harlem hoodlum Bumpy Jonas (Moses Gunn). John Shaft (Richard Round-tree), at the urging of black police Captain Bollin (Julius W. Harris), is brought in to solve the matter. This puts the detective in contact with Arna Asby (Rosalind Miles), the deceased's sister, and Rita (Kathy Imrie), the dead man's mistress. The final (overlong) confrontation is set in New York harbor and then in the channels and marshlands with a helicopter, a power boat and pursuit cars involved.

"Something happened on the way to the sequel," insisted Roger Greenspun *(New York Times).* "The new Shaft follows a new and glossier and tidier image, an image that is much more James Bond than [Humphrey] Bogart.... *Shaft's Big Score* is far more ambitious and professional than the original *Shaft.* But it is also more mechanical and more exploitive of the material. And so it become less responsible, less detailed, less personal, less serious and less fun."

Shaft's Big Score! used many of the same talents (including several black technicians) from the original film, with Ernest Tidyman and director Gordon Parks, Sr., contributing an original screenplay. When artistic differences

Richard Roundtree in *Shaft's Big Score!* (1972).

between MGM and Isaac Hayes could not be resolved, Parks (who also has a cameo in the film as a croupier) composed the new score in two weeks, and O.C. Smith sang the film's vocals. Made at a cost of $1,978,000, *Shaft's Big Score!* grossed only $3,936,000 in domestic film rentals. The film suffered, not only from its own artificiality, but from the competition of the mass of black action pictures generated by the original *Shaft.*

By the time of *Shaft in Africa* (1973), MGM was stretching the gimmick to the breaking point. Both Gordon Parks, Sr., and Ernest Tidyman had dropped out, and director John Guillerman and scripter Stirling Silliphant (of *In the Heat of the Night* [1967] [q.v.]) took over. Anxious to distinguish the newest *Shaft* from its competition, the movie opted for an international setting, transplanting John Shaft from New York City to the dark continent and on to Paris. What emerged was part *Shaft,* part *King Solomon's Mines* (1950), and part James Bond. (At one point, the still-snappy Shaft insists, "I'm not

Vonetta McGee and Richard Roundtree in *Shaft in Africa* **(1973).**

James Bond, simply Sam Spade.") When Emir Ramilla's (Cy Grant) son is killed in Paris, he hires Shaft for $25,000 to fly to Africa to learn who is behind the black slave trade (where blacks are exploited as cheap manual labor in Paris) and who killed his son. To persuade Shaft to take the bizarre, deadly assignment, there is the forceful Colonel Gondar (Marne Laitland) and the seductive Aleme (Vonetta McGee), daughter of the Ethiopian Emir, who indoctrinates him in the way of the Mantila tribe. Using the alias of Jawi, Shaft joins the caravan of black men at Addis Ababa being herded by camel caravan and ship to Paris. Along the way he is stymied by the double-dealing Wassa (Debebe Eshetu), helped by the native Kopo (Thomas Baptiste), and seduced by the mysterious and extremely randy Jaza (Neda Arneric), all of whom are killed. In Paris he finds it is Benson Amafi (Frank Finlay) who is the slave dealer. At the crazed man's chateau headquarters outside the city, Shaft helps several imprisoned blacks escape (they in turn drown Amafi) and blows up the manse/torture chamber.

With its exotic plot (including kick stick fighting) and locales (riding camelback over desert wastes), the visually colorful *Shaft in Africa* was indeed a long way from home. And having gone back to his roots, John Shaft was just not the same. (The title song even dared to ask "Are You Man Enough?) "It is less daring, less ethnically sophisticated, more antiseptic, more comfortably middle-class" decided Roger Greenspun *(New York Times)*. The R-rated film cost $2,142,000 to produce, but grossed only $1,458,000 in domestic film rentals. It was the end of *Shaft* in theatrical film format.

A few months after the final segment of the *Shaft* trilogy played the theatres, *Shaft* debuted as a 90-minute teleseries on CBS-TV on October 9, 1973, rotating with the "New CBS Tuesday Night Movies" and Jimmy Stewart's "Hawkins" detective series. It starred Richard Roundtree as the hip black private eye, with Ed Barth as Lieutenant Al Rossi of the New York Police Department. The Isaac Hayes theme song was intact, but because this was television, much of the violence, sex, and ethnic flavor had to be curtailed; and the flamboyantly brutal and rugged detective was a small-screen pussycat. What emerged was bland compared to the original. The show lasted only eight episodes before disappearing.

178. Sheba, Baby (American International, 1975). Color, 90 minutes.

Executive producer Mike Henry; *producer* David Sheldon; *director* William Girdler; *story* Sheldon, Girdler; *screenplay* Girdler; *production designer* J. Patrick Kelly III; *music director/arranger* Higgins; *music consultant* Larry Maxwell; *stunt co-ordinator* Richard Washington; *special effects* Gene Griggs; *sound* John Asman, James Mason; *sound effects* Tony Di Marco-Nesco; *camera* William Asman; *editors* Henry Asman, Jack Davies.

Cast: Pam Grier (Sheba Shayne); Austin Stoker (Brick Williams); D'Urville Martin (Pilot); Rudy Challenger (Andy Shayne); Dick Merrifield (Shark); Christopher Joy (Walker); Charles Kissinger (Lieutenant Phil Jackson); Charles Broaddus (Hammerhead); Maurice Downes (Killer); Ernest Cooley (Whale); Edward Reece, Jr. (Racker); William Foster, Jr. (Walda); Bobby Cooley (Tank); Sylvia Jacobson (Tail); Paul Grayber (Fin); Leroy Clark, Jr. (Customer); Mike Clifford (Policeman); Rose Ann Deel (Policewoman); Clayton Rose (Bum); Frank Groi, Bobby Evans, Bobby Stewart, James Durston (Hoods); Robert Drane (Officer); Melvin Jones, Herman Thompson, Bill Wilson (Railroad Men); Mary Minor, Henriette Brands, Joyce Jones (Pilot's Girls); Bobby Davis (Hit Man); Walter Evans (Customer); Charles North, Bill Embry, Dennis Williams, Mike Abrams (Bodyguards); Phil Kelley, Lloyd Poore (Dock Guards); Mary Perries, Jackie Patterson (Shayne's Clerks); Richard Taylor (Bartender); Joan Ray (Nurse); Toni Gorman, Tara Lang, Jeanie Care (Party Girls).

"Hotter 'n Coffy . . . Meaner 'n Foxy Brown" announced the ad campaign for *Sheba, Baby. "Pam Grier Is Queen of the Private Eyes,"* the promotional teasers read. This was a new type of screen role for sultry Pam Grier, but even if her on-camera part had altered, she was still the same fierce, action-ready woman ready to defend her friends, if not her honor, at a moment's notice.

Sheba Shayne (Pam Grier), one of Chicago's leading private investigators is called home to Louisville, Kentucky, to deal with racketeers intent on acquiring the loan company belonging to her father (Rudy Challenger), whether he wishes to sell or not. Hardly has she settled in when a bomb explodes in her father's car, almost killing her. White police Lieutenant Phil Jackson (Charles Kissinger) warns her not to interfere, and her dad is shot by the gangsters. She teams with her late father's partner, Brick Williams (Austin Stoker), who also becomes her lover. They learn the underworld leader causing all the problems is Shark (Dick Merrifield), a wealthy insurance businessman and yachtsman. (Shark's motto is, "Anything worth having, is worth stealing.") Sheba crashes a wild party aboard Shark's fancy boat, but is discovered and dives into the

Pam Grier and D'Urville Martin in *Sheba, Baby* **(1975).**

water. Meanwhile, the police have been called in (by Williams), leading to the final chase in which Sheba pursues the escaping Shark and kills him with a spear gun. Sheba informs Williams she must return to Chicago, but insists she will visit him often, since she is now also a partner in her father's business. She is not so congenial to Phil Jackson of the local police: "You can have you town back again, Lieutenant."

Acknowledging the growing backlash from the black community about black films that were violent for the sake of violence only, *Sheba, Baby* tries to justify (some of) the heroine's violent actions by 1) making her officially on the side of the law—in fact, she used to be a policewoman in her hometown before changing professions; 2) having her father be a very righteous member of the community; and 3) having the nasty mobsters wanting to do dirt to their brothers and sisters by taking over the loan business and raising the interest rates and tightening the collection methods. As usual, Grier's character is very liberated, insisting, "I'm not going to sit on the sidelines because I'm a woman." But, argued *Variety*, "...she is never allowed to show any detective smarts, only a penchant for violence—she loves to strongarm heavies while wielding a silver."

Compared to the gory and fast-paced *Coffy* and *Foxy Brown* (both 1974) (qq.v.), *Sheba, Baby* was slow going, with amateurish, shoddy action scenes. And, insisted Scott Meek (British *Monthly Film Bulletin*), "The characters are stereotyped in a way which would be offensive if they were token Negroes in a 'white' film: from Sheba's father, all dignity and concern for the community—and obviously a total convert to the whitest of American dreams—to the jivin' villains." As for Pam Grier, "Although she is no great shakes as an actress, she gives the impression of being as intelligent as she is beautiful" (Vincent Canby, *New York Times*). *Variety* summed it up: "Once you get past Grier's dazzling looks—and with coiffed hair, she looks better here than ever before—this is a flat suspenser kept unexciting by plodding pacing. . . ."

Sheba, Baby was shot on location in and around Louisville, Kentucky, by William Girdler, who had directed *Abby* (1974). Audiences, satiated with the formula blaxploitation screen violence and baffled by the tentativeness of this new entry, were not enthusiastic about *Sheba, Baby*. The grosses were down to $1,000,000 in domestic film rentals.

This was Pam Grier's final film under her AIP contract. While she announced her intentions of moving on to bigger and less stereotyping film projects—and was certainly deserving in talents and looks (she was often called the black Raquel Welch) to meet the challenge—her career took a nosedive. She would not be back on camera until 1977, and then in an abbreviated role as Richard Pryor's wife in *Greased Lightning* (q.v.). After that it was an uphill battle all the way. She would work in films, television, and on stage, but the momentum was gone. The black Queen of the B Movies was dethroned.

179. The Sheriff (ABC-TV, 3/30/71). Color, 78 minutes.

Executive producer Marvin Worth; *producer* Jon Epstein; *director* David Lowell Rich; *teleplay* Arnold Perl; *art directors* Ross Bellah, Cary Odell; *music* Dominic Frontiere; *camera* Emil Oster; *editor* Howard Kunin.

Cast: Ossie Davis (Sheriff James Lucas); Kaz Garas (Harve Gregory); Ruby Dee (Sue-Anne Lucas); Kyle Johnson (Vance Lucas); John Marley (Kinsella); Ross Martin (Larry Walters); Lynda Day [George] (Almy Gregory); Edward Binns (Paulsen); Moses Gunn (Cliff Wilder); Brenda Sykes (Janet Wilder); Joel Fluellen (Charley Dobey); Austin Willis (Judge); Parley Baer (Braden); Bill Quinn (Doctor); David Moses (Sopes); Lynette Piernas (Wilma).

"Jumped out of the chute as if it had firecrackers tied to its tail but except for a brief spurt of energy afterward, that's as far as it got with excitement or interest" (John Graf, *The Hollywood Reporter*). As in so many of these television cops-and-crooks dramas, the filmmakers think that screeching tires and slamming car doors are a substitute for good plotting and characterization.

Joining the bandwagon of showcasing (exploiting) black talent in major roles, this telefeature put forward a very believable Ossie Davis as the first black sheriff in a small California town, with his real-life wife (Ruby Dee) cast as his onscreen wife. When black coed Janet Wilder (Brenda Sykes) is beaten and raped, Sheriff James Lucas and his white deputy Harve Gregory (Kaz Garas) must solve the case, which leads to the arrest of violent insurance salesman Larry Walters (Ross Martin). Lynda Day [George] plays the deputy's racially bigoted wife.

180. Shoot It: Black, Shoot It: Blue (Levitt-Pickman, 1984). Color, 93 minutes.

Director Dennis McGuire; *based on the novel* "Shoot It" *by* Paul Tyner; *screenplay* McGuire; *music* Terry Stockdale; *sound* Wray Brevens; *camera* Bob Bailin; *editor* Bob Brady.

Cast: Michael Moriarty (Herbert G. Rucker); Eric Laneuville (Lamont); Paul Sorvino (Ring); Earl Hindman (Garrity); Linda Scruggs (Stacy); Bruce Kornbluth (Buddy); Anthony Charnota (Sal); Fred Burrell (Teacher); Lynda Wescott (Hattie); Val Pringle (Wardell); Buck Buchanan (Mark S. Johnson); George DiCenzo (George); Molly McGreevy (Salesgirl); Michael Shannon (Purcell); Joella Deffenbaugh (Brenda); John Quastler (Karl); Art Ellison (Leon); Gilbert Milton (Pops); Bob Phillips (Dougie); Cecil Burton (Old Woman); Linda McGuire (Victim in Park); Irene Ballinger (Bernice); LeRoy Vaughn (Coach); Don Peterson (Sniper); Tom Turner (Hot Camera Dealer); Ronnie Sellers (Black Cop).

A little-seen independent production that had sat on the shelf for many months before having limited release by Levitt-Pickman. "Contains the seed of an exciting thriller about police corruption and black vengeance, but ... fails to tackle its subject head on" *(Variety).*

Not-so-bright policeman Herbert G. Rucker (Michael Moriarty) has defects—he is violent and bigoted. When he arrests a black street thief, he coldly kills the captured man. The deceased's widow brings suit, but Rucker is convinced he has nothing to worry about, for who would convict a white cop of killing a black mugger? Then he learns that black cinema enthusiast Lamont (Eric Laneuville) had caught the homicide on film and is now trailing the policeman and filming the man's shoddy life. Later Rucker dies in a car crash when a black militant takes revenge and shoots out one of his tires.

Shoot It: Black, Shoot It: Blue was filmed in Kansas City. Eric Laneuville starred on "Room 222" (1971–73) and on "St. Elsewhere" (1982–88).

181. Shoot to Kill (Buena Vista, 1988). Color, 110 minutes.

Executive producer Philip Rogers; *producers* Ron Silverman, Daniel Petrie, Jr.; *associate producer* Fredda Weiss; *director* Roger Spottiswoode; *screenplay* Harv Zimmel, Michael Burton, Petrie, Jr.; *production designer* Richard Sylbert; *art director* John Willett; *set decorator* Jim Erickson; *costume designer* Richard Bruno; *music* John Scott; *second unit director/stunt co-ordinator* Fred Waugh; *assistant director* Michael Steele; *special effects supervisor* John Thomas; *sound* Simon Kaye; *camera* Robert Stevens; *second unit camera* Curtis Peterson; *editors* Garth Craven, George Bowers.

Cast: Sidney Poitier (Warren Stantin); Tom Berenger (Jonathan Knox); Kirstie Alley (Sarah); Clancy Brown (Steve); Richard Masur (Norman); Andrew Robinson (Harvey); Kevin Scannell (Ben); Frederick Coffin (Ralph); Michael MacRae (Fournier); Robert Lesser (Minelli); Milton Selzer (Mr. Berger); Les Lannom (Sheriff Arnett); Walter Marsh (Sam Baker); Frank C. Turner (Crilly); Samuel Hiona (Inspector Hsu); Michael Chapman (Lawyer); Janet Rotblatt (Mrs. Berger); Ken Camroux (Denham); Howard Storey (Fisherman); Fred Henderson (Agent Owenby); Robin Masumi Gildemeester (Maid);

Jerry Wasserman, Gloria Lee (F.B.I. Agents); Freda Perry (Computer Operator); Kevin McNulty (San Francisco Policeman); William Taylor (Police Captain); Ric Reid (SWAT Sergeant); Claire Brown (Mildred); Blu Mankuma (Undercover Priest); Gary Hetherington (Inspector); Allan Lysall (Sergeant); Michele Goodger (Woman with Stroller); Beatrice Boepple, Darcelle Chan (Nuns); Maryanne Danguy, Craig Saunders (Couple); Carole Henshall (Woman with Purse); Andrew Rhodes (Purse Snatcher); Bill Croft (Washington State Patrolman).

British release title: *Deadly Pursuit.*

It had been eleven years since Sidney Poitier had acted onscreen (*A Piece of the Action* [1977] [q.v.])—during which time he wrote his best-selling autobiography *This Life* (1980). In 1988 he returned in two features, which even combined together did not make a strong box-office impact. *Little Nikki* (shot before but released after *Shoot to Kill*) featured Poitier as an F.B.I. agent who must tell a youngster (River Phoenix) that his small-town parents are really deep-cover Russian K.G.B. agents. The general consensus was that the film was "mush" (*People* magazine). It grossed less than $2,000,000 in its two weeks of national box-office ticket sales.

In the R-rated *Shoot to Kill,* Poitier is again an F.B.I. agent, this time Warren Stantin, a smart-dressing San Franciscan who trails a homicidal jewel thief to Bishop's Fall in the Pacific Northwest. Determined to stop the villain from slipping over the border into Canada, he asks burly backwoodsman Jonathan Knox (Tom Berenger) to be his guide. The latter refuses. He is a loner (almost a hermit) who has no use for city people in general or this overachieving veteran law enforcer in particular. What finally persuades him to accept is that the crazed killer has kidnapped his trail guide girlfriend, Sarah (Kirstie Alley). So off they go over the rugged wintry mountain terrain in pursuit of the mountain-climbing party which is being diminished one by one by the crafty undercover murderer. The showdown occurs aboard a Vancouver ferryboat, with all the right people surviving and Steve (Clancy Brown), the killer, being shot underwater by Stantin.

There are several amazing aspects to this production lensed on location in British Columbia and San Francisco. The scenery is gorgeous, Tom Berenger is very credible as the irascible macho maverick, and Sidney Poitier at age 63-plus is amazingly fit and agile in this very athletically demanding role. It certainly was no accident that this film's premise of big-city Poitier helping out the know-it-all small-towner was so reminiscent of *In the Heat of the Night* (1967) (q.v.). But being the late 1980s, much of the racial conflict is either nonexistent or barely noticeable (in fact it is Poitier's character who brings the matter up finally in a joking manner, which causes even the taciturn recluse to smile).

While Janet Maslin *(New York Times)* argued this film "...has enormous momentum and a story full of twists and turns," more on mark was Sheila Benson *(Los Angeles Times):* "The movie is grisly, illogical, contradictory, borderline tasteless, riddled with plot holes.... All in all, the waste it represents—of talent, of intelligence of fine craftsmen and of the audience's good will—is enough to make one howl like a dog.... Poitier and Berenger roles are perfunctorily sketched, their exchanges sometimes excruciatingly embarrassing." *Variety* added that ". . . climactic action rests upon some coincidences that strain credulity, and goes on at undue length." *L.A. Weekly* insisted, "This is the kind of movie that'll look better when it's broken up by beer commercials."

Shoot to Kill had gross ticket sales of $28,898,804 after its nine weeks of release at the United States national box-office. All in all, it was not a promising return to the screen for one of contemporary Hollywood's most enduring leading men.

182. Sidekicks (CBS-TV, 3/21/74). Color, 78 minutes.

Producer/director Burt Kennedy; *based on characters created by* Richard Alan Simmons; *teleplay* William Bowers; *art director* Bill Maley; *set decorator* Ed Baer; *makeup* Layne Brittin; *music* David Shire; *assistant director* Paul A. Hemlick; *stunts* Jerry Gatlin; *camera* Robert B. Hauser; *editor* Michael Pozen.

Cast: Larry Hagman (Quince Drew); Lou [Louis] Gossett [Jr.] (Jason O'Rourke); Blythe Danner (Prudy Jenkins); Jack Elam (Boss); Harry Morgan (Sheriff Jenkins); Gene Evans (Sam); Noah Beery (Tom); Hal Williams (Max); Dick Peabody (Ed); Denver Pyle (Drunk); John Beck (Luke); Dick Haynes (Man); Tyler McVey (Jones); Billy Shannon (Carl).

Three years after the theatrical Western feature *Skin Game* (1971) (q.v.), this remake arrived for television audiences. Lou Gossett again co-starred, but now with Larry Hagman as his con artist saddle pal in the good Old West. Once again the premise (much dissipated here) finds a rascally white man named Quince Drew (Larry Hagman) and a quick-thinking New Jerseyite named Jason O'Rourke (Lou [Louis] Gossett [Jr.]) always one step ahead of the law and victims who have been stung by their scams. One of their frequent ruses is for Drew to sell O'Rourke as a slave for $1,000, and then they each disappear real quick. Above and beyond its physical dangers, this routine has little appeal for the bright and prideful O'Rourke. As his colleague admits, "I suppose it's understandable you should feel bitter about slavery."

The bulk of this too-episodic comedy focuses on the two men's encounters with the rambunctious Prudy Jenkins (Blythe Danner), the tomboy daughter of a hot-headed sheriff (Harry Morgan). When a cantankerous bank robber (Jack Elam) breaks out of jail and flees with his gang, O'Rourke and Drew are mistaken for part of his motley crew.

Sue Cameron *(The Hollywood Reporter)* was being overly generous when she assessed, "A very entertaining show and would probably do well as an hour series."

183. Silver Streak (Twentieth Century-Fox, 1976). Color, 113 minutes.

Executive producers Frank Yablans, Martin Ransohoff; *producers* Thomas L. Miller, Edward K. Milkis; *director* Arthur Hiller; *screenplay* Colin Higgins; *production designer* Alfred Sweeney; *set decorator* Marvin March; *costumes* Phyllis Garr, Michael Harte; *makeup* William Tuttle; *music* Henry Mancini; *stunt co-ordinator* Mickey Gilbert; *sound* Hal Etherington; *sound editors* William Hartman, Edward Rossi; *special effects* Fred Cramer; *camera*

Top: **Sidney Poitier and Tom Berenger in** *Shoot to Kill* **(1988).** *Bottom, left–right:* **Louis Gossett, Jr., Larry Hagman, and Jack Elam in** *Sidekicks* **(1974).**

David M. Walsh, Ralph Woolsey; *process consultant* Bill Hansard; *editor* David Bretherton.

Cast: Gene Wilder (George Caldwell); Jill Clayburgh (Hilly Burns); Richard Pryor (Grover Muldoon); Patrick McGoohan (Roger Devereau); Ned Beatty (Sweet [F.B.I. Agent Stevens]); Clifton James (Sheriff Oliver Chauncey); Ray Walston (Edgar Whiney); Stefan Gierasch (Johnson/Professor Schreiner); Len Birman (Chief); Valerie Curtin (Plain Jane); Richard Kiel (Reace/Goldtooth); Lucille Benson (Rita Babtree); Scatman Crothers (Ralston the Porter); Fred Willard (Jerry Jarvis); Delos V. Smith (Burt); Matilda Calnan (Blue-Haired Lady); Nick Stewart (Shoe Shiner); Margarita Garcia (Mexican Mama San); Jack Mather (Conductor); Lloyd White (Porter); Ed McNamara (Benny); Raymond Guth (Night Watchman); John Day (Engineer); Tom Erhart (Cab Driver); Gordon Hurst (Moose); Jack O'Leary, Lee McLaughlin (Fat Men); Henry Beckman, Steve Weston, Harvey Atkin (Conventioneers).

"It ain't gonna be too exciting, but we'll get you there on time," insists Ralston (Scatman Crothers) the porter as publisher George Caldwell (Gene Wilder) boards the Silver Streak luxury train heading from Los Angeles to Chicago. This is okay by Caldwell, who is making his first train trip and looking forward to a little peace and quiet: "I just want to be bored," he says. But the porter's warning is only half-right; *Silver Streak* is (sometimes) exciting and fun, and (occasionally) fast-paced.

Caldwell is heading eastward for his sister's wedding, and he soons meets attractive Hilly Burns (Jill Clayburgh), the private secretary to a mysteriously secluded art historian named Professor Schreiner. He and Jill spend the night together, and later he insists that he witnessed Schreiner being dropped from the train's roof. His investigations lead to his being thrown off the train, and zany farmer Rita Babtree (Lucille Benson) flies him in her biplane to the junction to meet the express train. Still pursuing his theory, Caldwell is introduced to the "real" professor by jet-setter Roger Devereau (Patrick McGoohan), chairman of the board of the Chicago Art Institute. He also meets vitamin salesman Sweet (Ned Beatty), who claims he is riding the train for the action aboard: "It's a cat house on wheels.... It's something about the movement of the train that does it ... all that motion makes a girl horny." (One of the annoying contrivances of this film, incidentally, is the time each character spends establishing his reasons for taking the train instead of flying.) But later Sweet reveals himself to be an F.B.I. agent and says Devereau is a wanted criminal who would be ruined by Schreiner's investigation of fake Rembrandt canvases. When Sweet is killed by Devereau's thugs, it is innocent Caldwell whom the porter finds holding the gun. He escapes to the roof and after killing pursuing henchman Reace (Richard Kiel) he is again knocked off the train. In a nearby small town he steals a police car from Sheriff Oliver Chauncey (Clifton James), not knowing that a handcuffed black city slicker named Grover Muldoon (Richard Pryor) is in the back seat. At Kansas City the two men board the train again and force a confession from Devereau. Later they jump off again to avoid F.B.I. agents. The train is stopped to search for Caldwell and there is a violent shootout. Devereau forces the train's engineer to push full throttle ahead, but soon he and the driver are dead. When the detached locomotive crashes into the Chicago railroad station, Caldwell, Grover Muldoon, Hilly, and Raston are still aboard — they miraculously survive. The ever-resourceful Muldoon drives off in a car from a station lobby display, leaving Caldwell and Hilly to pursue their courtship.

If the critical consensus was that *Silver Streak* borrowed too much from 1930s thrillers (such as *The Lady Vanishes,* 1938) without the requisite charm, there was no doubt that Richard Pryor was *the* hit of the film. He is only in the last third of what *Variety* labeled a "train comedy often derailed." But he makes every moment count! As Pauline Kael describes (*New Yorker* magazine): "For about fifteen minutes Pryor gives the picture some of his craziness. His comedy isn't based on suspiciousness about whites, or on anger, either; he's gone way past that. Whites are *unbelievable* to him. He's stupified at the ignorance of the hero (Wilder), and he can't believe the way this white man moves. . . . When Pryor is required to show pure-hearted affection for Wilder you have never seen such a bad actor."

Grover Muldoon is a savvy small-time crook who has just been caught by the law when pop-eyed George Caldwell appears out of nowhere onto the scene. This Muldoon dude may be down (he is handcuffed and on his way to jail), but he is not out. He has his priorities (comfortable survival) and knows his criminal limits: "I don't mess with the Big M." (The "M" refers to murder; if this had been a few years earlier in Hollywood the "M" would have referred to "the Man.") When the two flee the law and stop at an auto lot to get new wheels the easy way, an attendant pointing a rifle in his direction confronts reluctant car thief Muldoon: "Hold it right there nigger." Then, proving to the audience and himself that nothing fazes him and he can handle any situation, he toys with his would-be assailant, mocking him. "Ain't nobody gonna mess with you. . . . I mean it, man. You a pretty bad old dude." And before long he and Caldwell are driving off in their new car.

Glib, mocking Muldoon is at his best when in Kansas City he helps Caldwell disguise himself so they can board the train once again. Caldwell wipes black shoe polish over his face, buys some hip clothing from passersby and with a newly acquired radio held to his ear (and hiding his face) ludicrously sways back and forth as a jivin' black man. Having tried to teach Caldwell how to act black, Muldoon is taken aback by his cohort's exaggerated performance and sarcastically remarks, "We'll make it by the cops. I hope we don't see no Muslims."

Back on the train Muldoon disguises himself as a porter (a send-up, but at the same time a reflection of the stereotypes black man's roles in movies of the pre–1970s) and in a change of character bursts out angrily when Devereau makes a disparaging remark. "Who are you calling nigger, huh? You don't know me well enough to call me no nigger. I'll slap the taste out of your mouth. You don't know my name. I'll whup your ass . . . beat the white off your ass." By now he is wildly waving a gun at the amazed villain.

The jive-talkin' scene to get the two men past the police became a cinema classic, even though there were those who thought the sequence was demeaning to blacks (which may explain the abrupt and volatile explosion in the porter

Gene Wilder takes instruction on how to pass for black from Richard Pryor in
Silver Streak **(1976).**

versus the killer scene). Director Arthur Hiller reshot the lavatory disguise
scene twice to appease any qualms co-star Richard Pryor had regarding the
delicate scene. Later the director admitted there was very little noticeable
difference between either take.

To everyone's amazement, *Silver Streak,* with location filming in Calgary,
grossed $30,018,000 in domestic film rentals. Gene Wilder and Richard Pryor
would next reteam for *Stir Crazy* (1980) (q.v.), directed by Sidney Poitier.

184. Skin Game (Warner Bros., 1971). Color, 102 minutes.
Executive producer Meta Rosenberg; *producer* Harry Keller; *director*
Paul Bogart; *story* Richard Alan Simmons; *screenplay* Pierre Marton [Peter
Stone], (uncredited) David Giller; *art director* Herman Blumental; *set
decorator* James Payne; *makeup* Gordon Bau; *music* David Shire; *assistant
director* Cliff Coleman; *sound* Fred Faust; *camera* Fred Koenekamp; *editor*
Walter Thompson.
Cast: James Garner (Quincy Drew); Lou [Louis] Gossett [Jr.] (Jason
O'Rourke); Susan Clark (Ginger); Brenda Sykes (Naomi); Edward Asner
(Plunkett); Andrew Duggan (Calloway); Henry Jones (Sam); Neva Patterson
(Mrs. Claggart); Parley Baer (Mr. Claggart); George Tyne (Bonner); Royal
Dano (John Brown); Pat O'Malley (William); Joel Fluellen (Abram);
Napoleon Whiting (Ned); Juanita Moore (Viney); Dort Clark (Pennypacker);
Robert Foulk (Sheriff); Athena Lourde (Margaret); George Wallace (Auc-
tioneer); James McCallion (Stanfil); Tracy Bogart (Lizabeth); Mary Rings
(Emaline); Don Haggerty, Jason Wingreen (Speakers); Sam Chew (Courtney);

Al Checco (Room Clerk); Jim Boles (Auction Clerk); Paris Nathan Earl, Edward Lee McClain, Eugene Smith, Bill Terrell (the Songhais); *and:* Forrest Lewis.

"*Skin Game* is the title of one of the most pleasantly outrageous films you're likely to see in a family theatre. It's not a sexploitation film, it's the first film to intelligently satirize the subject of slavery. Your eyes do not deceive you, the film really does make a mockery of 200 years of terror and agony—but not without scoring many serious points along the way" (Maurice Peterson, *Essence* magazine).

In the pre–Civil War West, con man Quincy Drew (James Garner) and well educated Jason O'Rourke (Lous Gossett), a black man from New Jersey, have a thriving business. In the smaller hamlets of Kansas and Missouri, Drew puts O'Rourke up for sale as his slave and then rescues him *after* the payment. When he meets attractive pickpocket Ginger (Susan Clark) he realizes he has found his match and tells her about his and O'Rourke's con game. Meanwhile O'Rourke has met the slave Naomi (Brenda Sykes) and has Drew buy her for him. No sooner has the sale happened than John Brown (Royal Dano) and his followers tear into town and take off with all the blacks, including O'Rourke and Naomi. Drew rescues his friends, and they plan one more scam (to make up for the money Ginger has stolen from them) and then retire. But they have not counted on crossing paths again with the sadistic slave dealer Plunkett (Edward Asner), whom they had tricked previously. Ginger reappears to free Drew from jail. Together they head to the Calloway spread, where enslaved O'Rourke and Naomi have joined with the Songhais (African slaves working on the spread) and plan to ride on to Mexico. Drew heads off to a new life with Ginger.

This was definitely a new Hollywood where such a film could be made and be widely distributed and not badly upset either race. At the time it was considered a congenial comedy spoof of sagebrush tales, sting-like movies, and a continuation of the interracial buddy picture started with *The Defiant Ones* (1958) (q.v.). There were some who questioned why Lou Gosset had a subordinate role to James Garner in the wisecracking proceedings, and this led Peterson of *Essence* to suggest, "...white writer, Pierre Marton, may not have been able to overcome some racist attitudes of his own.... The author may have portrayed the slaves more thoroughly had he more insight in the black experience—certainly Brenda Sykes's part, as Jason's black lover, could have been expanded—but his understanding of whites is complete. If you can laugh at the slaves, you'll scream at the bigots."

Skin Game would be remade three years later as a movie-for-television entitled *Sidekicks* (q.v.).

185. The Slams (Metro-Goldwyn-Mayer, 1973). Color, 91 minutes.

Producer Gene Korman; *director* Jonathan Kaplan; *screenplay* Richard L. Adams; *art director* Jack Fisk; *wardrobe* Jodie Tillen; *music* Luther Henderson; *assistant directors* Thalmus Rasulala, Nate Long; *sound* Bill Kaplan; *camera* Andrew Davis; *editor* Morton Tubor.

Cast: Jim Brown (Curtis Hook); Judy Pace (Iris Daniels); Roland "Bob" Harris (Captain Stambell); Paul E. Harris (Jackson Barney); Frank De Kova

(Campiello); Ted Cassidy (Glover); Frenchie Guizon (Macey); John Dennis (Sergeant Flood); Jac Emil (Zack); Quinn Redecker (Warden); Betty Cole (Mother); Robert Phillips (Cobalt); Jan Merlin (Saddler); Dick Miller (Cab Driver); *and:* Carmen Argenziano, Rudy Challenger, John Lipton.

Jim Brown had revived his failing film career with *Slaughter* (1972) and *Slaughter's Big Rip Off* (1973) (qq.v.), which may have been the reason for titling this prison yarn with an "SL" word.

Tough Curtis Hook (Jim Brown) hides $1,500,000 in mob money and throws away a suitcase full of heroin. Both were stolen from the syndicate that preys on the ghetto. Hook is wounded by his double-crossing confederates and, when his van crashes, he is hospitalized and transferred to "the Slams"—the California Penal Institution. Although he learns the syndicate has ordered a contract on his life, Hooks will not cooperate with the F.B.I., which wants information on the Mafia. Inside the prison, loner Hook also refuses to join with white hoodlum Campiello (Frank De Kova) and his faction or with the rival black gang headed by Macey (Frenchie Guizon). Hooks has no one to turn to, not even the head guard, for Captain Stambell (Roland "Bob" Harris) also wants to use him to get to the stolen cash. The only alternative is escape. Hooks turns to his girlfriend, Iris Daniels (Judy Pace), and old friend Jackson Barney (Paul E. Harris) to help carry out his ingenious plan. When Stambell discovers Hooks about to make a break, the inmate kills his captor, puts his clothes and ID bracelet on the dead man, and drops him into a cement mixer. Hooks makes good his escape and is soon on the high seas with Iris.

Not in the same caliber as Jim Brown's earlier *Riot* (1969) (q.v.), this was still several layers above *I Escaped from Devil's Island* (1973) (q.v.). Evidently sensing that audiences were tiring of the overplayed black action film formula, this movie focused more on the prison film genre for its inspiration. But without a doubt, it is very vicious and savage going, with lots of bloodshed, sadism, and tough hombres running the corridors of prison. There are many macabre touches (Stambell's remains oozing out in front of prison officials) and an impish sense of the ridiculous (the prison guard who frets about his job ruining his new manicure).

The Slams, which *Variety* slammed as a "racial prison meller for people who hate people," did not break the $1,000,000 mark in domestic film rentals, and Jim Brown's career, along with the black film cycle, continued to skid downward. Jonathan Kaplan, besides directing *The Student Teachers* (1973) and *Night Call Nurses* (1974), would guide Isaac Hayes in the genre piece *Truck Turner* (1974) (q.v.).

186. Slaughter (American International, 1972). Color, 92 minutes.

Executive producer Samuel Z. Arkoff; *producer* Monroe Sachson; *associate producer* Don Williams; *director* Jack Starrett; *screenplay* Mark Hanna, Williams; *set decorator* Carlos Gardner; *makeup* Sara Mateos; *music/music director* Luchi De Jesus; *songs* Billy Preston; De Jesus and Ric Marlow; *stunt co-ordinator* Paul Knuckles; *camera* Rosalio Solano; *editor* Clarence C. "Renn" Reynolds.

Cast: Jim Brown (Slaughter); Stella Stevens (Ann Cooper); Rip Torn

(Dominick Hoffo); Don Gordon (Harry Bastoli); Cameron Mitchell (Inspector A.W. Price); Marlene Clark (Kim Walker); Robert Phillips (Frank Morelli); Marion Brash (Jenny); Norman Alfe (Mario Felice); Eddie LoRusso (Little Al); Buddy Garion (Eddie); Ronald C. Ross, Ricardo Adalid, B. Gerardo Zepeda (Hoods); Roger Cudney (Gio); Lance Winston (Interne); Juan Jose de Laboriel (Uncle); Francisca Lopes de Laboriel (Aunt).

See summary under *Slaughter's Big Rip Off*.

187. Slaughter's Big Rip Off (American International, 1973). Color, 93 minutes.

Executive producer Samuel Z. Arkoff; *producer* Monroe Sachson; *associate producer* Don Williams; *director* Gordon Douglas; *based on the character created by* Williams; *screenplay* Charles Johnson; *art director* Alfeo Bocchicchio; *set decorator* Tony Montenaro; *makeup* Bob Westmoreland; *music* James Brown, Fred Wesley; *music supervisor* Barry De Vorzon; *assistant directors* Ray Taylor, Robert Della Santina; *stunt co-ordinator* Blake Wilcox; *special effects* Logan Frazee; *sound* John V. Speak; *camera* Charles Wheeler; *editor* Christopher Holmes.

Cast: Jim Brown (Slaughter); Ed McMahon (Duncan); Brock Peters (Reynolds); Don Stroud (Kirk); Gloria Hendry (Marcia); Richard Williams (Joe Creole); Art Metrano (Burtoli); Judy Brown (Norja); Eddie LoRusso (Arnie); Jackie Giroux (Mrs. Duncan); Russ Marin (Chief of Detectives Crowder); Tony Brubaker (Ed Pratt); Gene LeBell (Leo); Fuji (Chin); Russ McGinn (Harvey); Scatman Crothers (Cleveland); J.J. Saunders (Fry Cook); George Gaynes (Warren); Piper Alvez (Creole's Girl); Lisa Farringer (White Chick); Frank Talman (Pilot); Bill Cameron (Bartender); Pamela Miller (Burton's Girl); Marianna Case (Warren's Date); Lillian Gray (Waitress); Chuck G. Niles, Reg Parton (Announcers); Junero Jennings (Parking Attendant); Lisa Moore (Prostitute); Sable Sperling, Gayle Lynn Davis (Girls); Shanon Lanne (The Redhead).

There was *Shaft* ("Shaft's his name; Shaft's his game") (q.v.) in 1971, and now came *Slaughter* ("It's not only his name, it's his business and sometimes — his *pleasure!*"). It was a partially successful attempt to revive Jim Brown's film career, which had ground to a halt. He had three releases each in 1968, 1969, and 1970, but *none* in 1971.

Why the downslide in his career? "I was blackballed from the business," he told *Chicago Daily News* reporter David Elliott in August 1972. "In fact, I actually saw the letter that was circulated among the producers in Hollywood, telling them why I ought to be kept out of pictures." (The unstated reason was attributed to his bad temper both on and off sets, which led to bad press and court appearances.) Regarding his new action film series, "I guess you could say *Slaughter* was influenced by *Shaft,* but only because *Shaft* was so big it influenced all black movies. I liked it a lot. I liked that guy's number, just walkin' down the street to that fine music." It was a mellower, more perspicacious star who reflected, "And I still think black movies can talk to whites, too. You can start with a specialized market, that's fine, but the big money is still in the general market and black films will have to face that fact or we'll never have a real back movie business."

When his gangster father and his mother are murdered in Cleveland, Ohio, by underworld connections, ex–Green Beret Slaughter (Jim Brown) starts a one-man massacre of the culprits. Inspector A.W. Price (Cameron Mitchell) of the United States Treasury Department advises Slaughter that his rampage has killed many, but he let the man who hit his parents get away at the airport. Price blackmails Slaughter into helping him nab the kingpins of the operation, including Dominick Hoffo (Rip Torn).

The action shifts to Mexico, where brutish casino owner Hoffo controls the criminal activity, including that of slinky Ann Cooper (Stella Stevens), who is on everyone's menu as a tasty dish. While Slaughter and his helper, Harry Bastoli (Don Gordon), are building their revenge dossier, Hoffo is rebelling against aging mobster chieftan Mario Felice (Norman Alfe). After telling him "You're obsolete, Mario," he kills the godfather figure on the racquetball court. The payoff comes when Slaughter, using Green Beret tactics, launches the offensive against Hoffo. By now Ann, who has been slapped silly by Hoffo for sleeping with Slaughter, has come over into the anti–Hoffo camp. The other strong-arm men are slaughtered, but Hoffo escapes and Slaughter pursues him. After a wild car chase through the city and countryside, Hoffo's car crashes, and he is pinned inside. Cool Slaughter shoots two rounds from his gun into the overturned vehicle, which incinerates the screaming mobster.

As was standard practice for such blatant action films, *Slaughter* is filled with racial slurs tossed back and forth between the Italian gangsters and their black adversaries. Someone is always stupidly saying to Slaughter, "Who do you think you are, nigger?" and he promptly shows them with well-placed jabs to the jaw. (Insanely idiotic Hoffo makes the same deadly mistake when he is trapped at the finale in his car; this time the insult leads to his demise.) When Slaughter thinks he hears strange sounds in his bathroom, he promptly fires off several rounds, shooting up the room. And because Slaughter gets frustrated chasing the elusive villains at the airport, he slams his car into their plane. As David Elliott *(Chicago Daily News)* summed it up, ". . . Brown is playing what he was meant to play and can play better than anyone else: the black superman with a discernible link to the brother in the ghetto, plus enough mean, cool style to give him a patina of James Bond. . . . Compared with a male model like Richard 'Shaft' Roundtree, Brown is the real 'bad thing'. . . ."

It is difficult to call Slaughter heroic, since he is seeking revenge for the death of a gangster and constantly employs unnecessarily brutal tactics. But Brown's saving grace in all this celluloid mayhem are his brawn and his taciturn nature. He is the cool, silent leading man who enjoys his macho romps in bed with every willing lady, but who occasionally can toss out a *bon mot,* as in the symbolic card game at the casino between him and Felice where a smirking Slaughter comes up with "blackjack." Not so with Rip Torn as the mugging Italian Mafioso or Norman Alfe as the Godfather, the latter of whom moans in his Italian accent, "It makes me sad. There's no respect anymore."

Slaughter was shot in Mexico City for approximately $750,000, and it grossed $1,200,000 in domestic threatrical revenue. It paved the way for Jim Brown to make *Black Gunn* (1972) (q.v.) at Columbia Pictures and the sequel, *Slaughter's Big Rip-Off,* the following year.

Jim Brown and Ed McMahon in *Slaughter's Big Rip Off* (1973).

"*The Mob Put the Finger on Slaughter* . . . so he gave them the finger right back — curled around a trigger! . . . . The *Baddest Cat* that ever walked the earth." This was *Slaughter's Big Rip Off,* in which Jim Brown continued to strut cockily down the street kicking ass (and teeth) wherever he went.

Having survived his encounter in Mexico with the crime syndicate, Slaughter is still being pursued by the gangsters. When his good friend Ed Pratt (Tony Brubaker) is killed in Los Angeles from the air by mob men, Slaughter wants revenge. Reynolds (Brock Peters), a black detective, offers assistance, telling the renegade, "You've got a reputation Slaughter," and, "The citizens are real uptight these days. A lot of gunshots and screams could cause nervous breakdowns." But Slaughter prefers to work alone, and he finds clues at the criminal-infested Tempo Club, where he encounters sleepy pimp Joe Creole (Richard Williams), who has his hands into several rackets. Girlfriend Norja (Judy Brown) leads Slaughter to drug addict Burtoli (Art Metrano), who points the way to the killer plane's pilot. But Slaughter arrives to find the man dead and Reynolds already on the scene. The latter now persuades the ex–Green Beret to break into the safe of crime leader Duncan (Ed McMahon) and steal the names of syndicate members. (He is convinced his precinct boss, Chief of Detectives Crowder [Russ Marin], is on the payoff list.) Using multi-talented Creole for support, Slaughter accomplishes his task. It turns out Crowder is one of Duncan's confederates, and the corrupt policeman hires two martial arts experts, Leo (Gene LeBell) and Chin (Fuji), to dispose of Slaughter. They fail, and Duncan's assistant, Kirk (Don Stroud), captures Marcia (Gloria Hendry), another of Slaughter's girlfriends. She dies in a car crash, but Slaughter (also captured) survives and with a machine gun raids Duncan's headquarters. He retrieves the telltale list from Duncan and kills Kirk. Slaughter flies to Paris and relaxation.

Slaughter's Big Rip Off, wrote Lawrence Van Gelder in the *New York Times,* is the type of movie one judges "in terms of body count, quarts of gore expended, variety of weaponry, number of panes of glass shattered, excellence in portrayal of death throes and destruction of automobiles. It tempts the viewer to subtract points for a flaccid thigh on a bikinied extra in the background or a bald tread on the tire of a car sinking underwater after hurtling off a cliff with the hero and his girl inside."

Even thought *Slaughter's Big Rip Off* boasted the direction of veteran Gordon Douglas, a higher budget than its original, the dubious casting of Johnny Carson "Tonight Show" sidekick Ed McMahon as an arch criminal, and a middling score by James Brown, the Godfather of Soul, the movie grossed only $1,000,000 in domestic film rentals. The bloom was off this property.

188. Some Kind of Hero (Paramount, 1982). Color, 97 minutes.

Producer Howard W. Koch; *co-producer* James Kirkwood; *associate producer* Robert Boris; *director* Michael Pressman; *based on the novel by* Kirkwood; *screenplay* Kirkwood, Boris; *art director* James L. Schoppe; *set decorator* John Anderson; *makeup* Monty Westmore; *music* Patrick Williams; *song* Williams and Will Jennings; *music editor* Roberta Doheny; *technical adviser* Lieutenant Colonel Dennis Foley; *stunt co-ordinator* Richard Washington; *sound* Gerald G. Jost; *supervising sound editor* Elizabeth Bergeron; *camera* King Baggott; *editor* Christopher Greenbury.

Cast: Richard Pryor (Eddie Keller); Margot Kidder (Toni Donovan); Ray Sharkey (Vinnie DiAngelo); Ronny Cox (Colonel Powers); Lynne Moody (Lisa Keller); Olivia Cole (Jessie Keller); Paul Benjamin (Leon); David Adams (The Kid); Martin Azarow (Tank); Shelly Batt (Olivia); Susan Berlin (Jeanette); Tim Thomerson (Cal); Mary Betten (Teller); Herb Braha, Peter Jason (Honchos); Anthony R. Charnota (Commander); Matt Clark (Mickey); Jude Farese (Bandit); Elizabeth Farley (Secretary); John Fujioka (Captain); Raymond Guth (Motel Clerk); Anne Haney (Monica); Mary Jackson (Frances); Caren Kaye (Sheila); Enid Kent (Reporter); Nan Martin (Hilda); Bill Morey (Major); Warren Munson (Bank President); Kenneth O'Brien (Bartender); Antony Ponzini (Sal); Kario Salem (Young Soldier); Pearl Shear (Customer); Sara Simmons (Nurse); John Van Ness (Aide); Sandy Ward (Colonel); Danny Wong (Guards); David Banks (Disc Jockey); David Byrd (Doorman); Kenneth S. Eiland, Alberto Isaac, Leigh Kim (V.C. Guards); Stephen Kuramada (Dentist); Richard McKenzie (Psychiatrist); Nicholas Mele (Officer); Harvey Parry (Old Drunk); Bill M. Ryusaki (Basketball Player); William Schoeneberger (EKG Technician); Hayward Soo Hoo (Soldier).

Richard Pryor was intrigued with making *Some King of Hero,* based on James Kirkwood's well-regarded 1975 novel, because it provided him ". . . the opportunity to do some work that doesn't depend on my being zany. I'm a character and not a carcicature." Shot in May and June of 1981, *Some Kind of Hero* was a return of comedian Pryor to the dramatic timbre of *Blue Collar*

(1978) (q.v.). It offered him a solid starring role in a tale of bitter ironies and absurdities.

American soldier Eddie Keller (Richard Pryor) was a prisoner-of-war of the Viet Cong for six years. When he returns to Los Angeles in 1975 he finds he has a six-year-old daughter; his wife, Lisa (Lynne Moody) is living with another man; his bookstore business has gone bust; and his mother has suffered a paralyzing stroke and is in an expensive nursing home. Furthermore, the Army is withholding his extensive back pay because he signed a confession of complicity in Vietnam to obtain medical attention for his dangerously ill cellmate, Vinnie DiAngelo (Ray Sharkey). While filling out a loan form at a bank (which refuses his application for lack of collateral), Keller observes how easily three robbers succeed in their holdup bid. Meanwhile he meets aristocratic hooker Toni Donovan (Margot Kidder) from Beverly Hills, who offers to help him financially, but the ex-soldier instead buys a water pistol to start his own criminal life. He bungles his first attempts but, eventually, he robs two bank customers with briefcases full of United States Treasury bonds. He arranges to sell the bonds to gangsters. Certain that he will be double-crossed by the underworld, he asks Toni to wait for him in her car and, meanwhile, eliminates the advance guard of hoods. He calls the police, whose arrival creates a diversion and he and Toni make their getaway, having both the bonds and the cash. He sends cash to take care of his mother and returns the bonds to the bank.

The critical reaction was very mixed to this project. "Why is it that our most audacious comic actor continually saddles himself with mediocre projects and hack directors...?" asked David Ansen (*Newsweek* magazine). He added, "...since Pryor gives one of his subtlest, most sustained performances, *Some Kind of Hero* always remains watchable (no thanks to the photography, which appears to have been processed in a mud bath). But it's high time Pryor stopped redeeming badly made movies and surrounded himself with talents equal to his own." "Overall, however, *Hero* cutes up distinctly acute situations because it wants to be all things to all people, and it almost succeeds, because it trades on its advantage that no chameleon is more charming than Pryor. Its divided tone ends up self-parodying, a fatigued exercise in mock heroics" (Carrie Rickey, *Village Voice*). "He [Richard Pryor] is very fine indeed, whether he is responding with wary reason to the idiotic demands of the television cameras [to kiss the ground as he returns to the United States as, albeit, a second class hero], or his tumultuous arrival home, or is attempting his first, unsuccessful bank heist.... Mr. Pryor displays a dramatic intelligence, wit and method that are completely new, though they are very much the extensions of the personality he reveals in *Live on the Sunset Strip*" (Vincent Canby, *New York Times*). In reassessing the film and Pryor's performance when *Some Kind of Hero* turned up on television, Kevin Thomas *(Los Angeles Times)* noted, "Unfortunately, this 1982 film is a highly even and underdeveloped movie that falls apart at the finish. Still, if you watch it for Pryor alone you won't be shortchanged. He is by turns tender, hilarious, thoughtful, sexy, scared and deadly efficient."

Despite its up-and-down reviews and its anemic ethnic stance (in the book the "hero" was white), *Hero* grossed $11,000,000 in domestic film rentals.

189. The Sophisticated Gents (NBC-TV, 9/29–30, 10/1/81).
Color, 200 minutes.

Executive producer Daniel Wilson; *producer* Fran Sears; *associate producers* Melvin Van Peebles, Linda Feitelson; *director* Harry Falk; *based on the novel* "The Junior Bachelor Society" *by* John A. Williams; *teleplay* Van Peebles; *art director* Tom Rasmussen; *music* Benny Golson; *song* Von Peebles; *camera* Terry K. Meade; *editor* Betsy Blankett.

Cast: Sonny Jim Gaines (Chappie Davis); Paul Winfield (Richard "Bubbles" Wiggins); Bernie Casey (Shurley Walker); Rosey Grier (Cudjo Evers); Thalmus Rasulala (Kenneth "Snake" Dobson); Robert Hooks (Ezzard "Chops" Jackson); Raymond St. Jacques (Dartagnan Parks); Ron O'Neal (Clarence Henderson); Melvin Van Peebles (Walter Moon [Silky Porter]); Dick Anthony Williams (Ralph Jopkin); Rosalind Cash (Christine Jackson); Ja'net DuBois (Onetha Wiggins); Alfe Woodard (Evelyn Evers); Joanna Miles (Sandra Dobson); Janet MacLachlan (Diane); Bibi Besch (Simone Parks); Denise Nicholas (Pat Henderson); Marlene Warfield (Lil Joplin); Beah Richards (Miz Porter); Albert Hall (Swoop Ferguson); Harry Guardino (Collins); Robert Earl Jones (Big Ralph); Lynn Benesch (Rene Marcus); Al Fann (Sugar); John Zaremba (Mayor Farrington); Charles Blackwell (Heflin); Dennis Patrick (Wilbur Marcus); Davis Roberts (Perkins); Lee Hamilton (Gail); Stymie Beard (Mickey Mouse); Wayne Stone (Stash Qualek); Wally Taylor (Griggs); Candace McKendree (Stewardess); Randy Lindsay (Caged Man); Gene Whittington (Worker).

Just on the basis of its assemblage of fine black performers, *The Sophisticated Gents* is a noteworthy project. *Daily Variety* judged it "...a telefilm of depth and compassion, of richness and complexity. Rough edges may show through, but it's still a moving experience." John O'Connor *(New York Times)* found it "...one of the more fascinating television movies of the year."

Nine athletes from a black group who have known each other for twenty-five years and have remained loyal get together to celebrate the approaching seventieth birthday of Chappie Davis (Sonny Jim Gaines). He was the perceptive coach who spotted the greatness within each of the men and encouraged them all in their athletic endeavors. Among those showing up at the reunion (and for the Black Arts Festival) are Dartagnan Parks (Raymond St. Jacques), a singer who has had a career of sorts of Europe, along with his protective, loyal wife (Bibi Besch), who helps him to cover over the fact that he is homosexual; chic magazine editor Ezzard "Chops" Jackson (Robert Hooks) and his roving wife (Rosalind Cash); Ralph Jopkin (Dick Anthony Williams), a successful playwright, and his wife (Marlene Warfield); Clarence Henderson (Ron O'Neal), a California college professor who has a snobbish wife (Denise Nicholas); city commissioner Kenneth "Snake" Dobson (Thalmus Rasulala) and his equally power-hungry white wife (Joanna Miles); and Walter Moon (Melvin Van Peebles), a.k.a. Silky Porter, a pimp in deep trouble for having committed a murder. Others in the group are stocky Cudjo Evers (Rosey Grier), Shurley Walker (Bernie Casey), and the group's president, Richard "Bubbles" Wiggins (Paul Winfield).

Left–right: **Dick Anthony Williams, Bernie Casey, and Rosey Grier in** *The Sophisticated Gents* **(1981).**

Problems arise when Swoop Ferguson (Albert Hall), a black cop who was not allowed into the group because he was five years younger than the rest and who holds a grudge against the "Gents," seeks his revenge and some dollars besides. Then there is Collins (Harry Guardino), a white Los Angeles cop, who is bad through and through.

Regarding this drama, Donald Bogle perceived in *Blacks in American Films and Television* (1988), "...this is a sophisticated race movie: fiercely determined to tell a story to a black audience, the drama operates at its own speed, unconcerned with the fact that whites might not understand what's going on or might be scared by it. What makes it all work, of course, are the actors, who are comfortable with their dialogue and their attitudes and are invigorated by the jazzy, sexy style of the script.... These are not the formula performances of formula TV."

As for the script by Melvin Van Peebles (who had conceived that groundbreaking *Sweet Sweetback's Baadasssss Song* [1971] [q.v.]), *Daily Variety* reported, "...he knows humanity, whatever the color, and he suggests life and all its goods and bads; Van Peebles is a genuine artist."

The Sophisticated Gents had been conceived and filmed in 1979, but it was not until 1981 that it made its hesitant television debut, and then its power was diminished by being broken into three segments for successive night viewing.

190. The Soul of Nigger Charley (Paramount, 1973).

Color, 110 minutes.

Producer/director/story Larry Spangler; *screenplay* Harold Stone; *art director* Gene Rudolph; *music* Don Costa; *assistant director* Angelo Laiacona; *sound* Leland M. Haas; *camera* Richard C. Glouner; *editor* Howard Kuperman.

Cast: Fred Williamson (Charley); D'Urville Martin (Toby); Denise Nicholas (Elena); Pedro Armendariz, Jr. (Sandaval); Kirk Calloway (Marcellus); George Allen (Ode); Keven Hagen (Colonel Blanchard); Michael Cameron (Sergeant Foss); Johnny Greenwood (Roy); James Garbo (Collins); Nai Bonet (Anita); Robert [Bob] Minor (Fred); Joe Henderson (Lee); Dick [Richard] Farnsworth (Walker); Tony Brubaker (Aben); Boyd "Red" Morgan (Donovan); Al Hassan (Vet); Ed Hice, Henry Wills (Mexicans); Phil Avenetti (Pedro); Fred Lerner (Woods).

A year after *The Legend of Nigger Charley* (1972) (q.v.) came its successor, with film producer and scripter Larry Spangler directing the follow-up.

In the post–Civil War period seventy-one former slaves are being held down Mexico way by vicious Colonel Blanchard (Kevin Hagen) and other ex-Confederates who still insist blacks should serve whites. Under General Hook, they have set up a compound to make use of this "free" manual labor, and replenish their manpower by constant raids up North on unprotected blacks. Free-lancing cowboys Charley (Fred Williamson) and his indestructible sidekick Toby (D'Urville Martin) come to the rescue, receiving much-needed assistance from money-loving Mexican bandido (Pedro Armendariz, Jr.) and his mean hombres to defeat these culprits. On tap are Elena (Denise Nicholas) as Charley's romantic interest and Marcellus (Kirk Calloway—in a very effective characterization) as a youngster whose parents died at the hands of Blanchard and his marauders.

The financial rewards for this successor vehicle were diminished: the market was being oversaturated with such products, *Soul of...* was too episodic and too long (110 minutes), and worst of all, the violence and gore were not up to the original. Nevertheless, admitted *Variety,* "[Fred] Williamson delivers strongly, perhaps exposing the soul of the title, and in an authoritative performance fulfils all demands of his role."

191. Soul Soldiers (Hirschman-Northern, 1970). Color, 103 minutes.

Producers James M. Northern, Stuart Z. Hirschman; *director* John Cardos; *screenplay* Marlene Weed; *art director/set decorator* Phedon Papmichael; *costumes* Frances Dennis; *makeup* Barry Noble; *music* Stu Phillips; *song* Phillips, Bob Stone; *special effects* Harry Woolman; *camera* Lewis J. Guinn; *editors* Guinn, Mort Tubor, Russ Mannarelli, Dick Dixon.

Cast: Robert DoQui (Trooper Eli Brown); Janee Michelle (Julie); Lincoln Kilpatrick (Sergeant Hatch); Isaac Fields (First Sergeant Robertson); Rafer Johnson (Private Armstrong); Cesar Romero (Colonel Grierson); Barbara Hale (Mrs. Grierson); Isabel Sanford (Isabel); Steve Drexel (Captain Carpenter); Russ Nannarello, Jr. (Lieutenant Bitelow); Robert Dix (Walking Horse); Otis Taylor (Private Adams); Bill Collins (Private Washington); John Fox (the Sigifier); Byrd Holland (the Stuler); Bobby Clark (Kayitah); Bernard Brown, Clarence Comas, Donald Diggs, Jeff Everett, Cal Fields, Perry Fluker,

Rafer Johnson in *Soul Soldier* **(a.k.a.** *Soul Soldiers***), 1970.**

Noah Hobson, Earl Humphrey, De Vaughn LaBon, Rod Law, Jim Pace, John Nettles, Eric Richmond (Troopers of the 10th Cavalry); *and:* Barbara Brown, Edith Hazley, Stuart Z. Hirschman, Lee James, Jon Jon, Hank Lowery, Rava Malmuth, Barry Noble, Steve Paullada, John Ramsey, Wanda Roberts, Marchita Stanton, Mollie Stevenson, Leah Weed, Charles Wells, George Wells, Paul Wheaton, David White.

    A.K.A. *Men of the Tenth; Soul Soldier.*

    This was *the* movie that started the craze of violent black westerns. Actually, when it was made, the working (and early release) title was *The Red, White and Black,* and the "names" in the cast were Cesar Romero, Barbara Hale, and Robert Dix (son of silent/early talkie star Richard Dix).

    White Colonel Grierson (Cesar Romero), along with his wife (Barbara Hale), heads a western outpost at Fort Davis, Texas, which happens to be the headquarters for the all-black Tenth Cavalry. Among the black troopers are Eli Brown (Robert DoQui) and Hatch (Lincoln Kilpatrick), who in typical Army tradition fight over a woman (Janee Michelle). Nevertheless, they work as a team, along with the other troopers (Rafer Johnson, Isaac Fields) to combat the rampaging Indians (the "red" of the title).

    At the time of its first screenings, no one, including the distributors, realized what trendsetting material they had in hand. "The tone of the humor is perilously close to 'minstrel.' It is truly embarrassing to watch this slapdash, sloppy and utterly superficial movie," snapped Howard Thompson *(New York*

Times). Even the usually perceptive *Variety* was caught off-guard, judging it "an okay general audience period film" but at least noting, "The staging and editing of some action scenes is often exciting." The film's recurring theme of the black man feeling empathy for another trounced-upon minority, the Indians, made little impact initially on viewers, but it would turn up in such later films as Sidney Poitier's *Buck and the Preacher* (1972) and Fred Williamson's *The Legend of Nigger Charley* (1972) (qq.v.).

By early 1971 this film was reissued as *Soul Soldiers* and not so quietly made a great deal of box-office action. This was the first film directed by actor John Cardos.

192. South Bronx Heroes (Zebra/Continental, 1985). Color, 85 minutes.

Producer William Szarka; *associate producers* Jon Kurtis, Don Schiffrin; *director* Szarka; *screenplay* Szarka, Schiffrin; *additional dialogue* Marc Shmuger, Mario Van Peebles; *music* Al Zima, Mitch Herzog; *associate director* Sean Ward; *sound* Michael Trujillo; *camera* Eric Schmitz; *editors* Jim Rivera, Eli Haviv, Szarka.

Cast: Brendan Ward (Paul); Mario Van Peebles (Tony); Megan Van Peebles (Chrissie); Melissa Esposito (Michelle); Martin Zurla (Bennett); Jordan Abeles (Scott); *and:* Barry Lynch, Dan Lauria, Bo Rucker, Sean Ward.

A.K.A. *Revenge of the Innocents; The Runaways.*

One of the scads of independent productions of the 1980s that first saw major distribution through the video cassette market. It is noticeable for another (over)-enthusiastic performance by Mario Van Peebles, this time joined by his real-life sister, Megan.

An interweaving story of blacks and whites. Black Tony (Mario Van Peebles), fresh out of a Mexican jail, returns to the South Bronx and moves in with his teacher sister, Chrissie (Megan Van Peebles). Meanwhile white Paul (Brendan Ward) and his eleven-year-old sister, Michelle (Melissa Esposito), have run away from their offensive foster father, Bennett (Martin Zurla), and find refuge in a South Bronx apartment building. Paul and Tony meet when Paul and Michelle break into the latter's apartment (to take a shower), and before long Tony decides to "help" his new friend blackmail Bennett, who not only has a kiddie porn business going, but has killed one of his young subjects. Eventually Bennett is caught and given over to the F.B.I.

Variety judged that it "lacks the oomph and tough approach to make waves.... Hoary use of fadeouts between scenes and generally sluggish pacing hurt as well."

193. Speeding Up Time (Cougman, 1975). Color, 90 minutes.

Producer/director/screenplay John Evans; *production designer/costumes* Heidemarie Rosendahl; *music* David T. Walker; *camera* Villis Lapeniecks, Bob Maxwell, Mike Margulies.

Cast: Winston Thrash (Marcus); *and:* Pamela Donegan, Ellen Brown, Ojenke, Harry Dolan, Paris Earl, Jay Jones, Henri White, Louise Springs.

John Evans, who turned out such genre pieces as *The Black Godfather*

(1974) (q.v.) and *Blackjack* (1978), was responsible for this big-themed but low-budgeted effort. Marcus (Winston Thrash) has dreams about black preparedness and retaliation for all the injustices endured by his race. As he tells his mama, "A man should be able to pick the way he wants to live and die." When his mother dies in a fire, the enraged Marcus goes on a rampage which leads him from the back alleys and byways of Los Angeles' Watts to ghetto gang meetings, determined to find those responsible for her death. There is a lot of pontificating about black militancy, too much jerky action in the chases on foot and by car, and throughout grainy photography and stilted, shrill performances.

194. The Split (Metro-Goldwyn-Mayer, 1968). Color, 91 minutes.

Producers Irwin Winkler, Robert Chartoff; *director* Gordon Flemyng; *based on the novel* "The Seventh" *by* Richard Stark [Donald Westlake]; *screenplay* Robert Sabaroff; *art directors* Urie McCleary, George W. Davis; *set decorators* Keogh Gleason, Henry Grace; *makeup* William Tuttle; *music* Quincy Jones; *songs:* Jones and Sheb Wooley; Jones and Ernie Shelby; *assistant director* Al Jennings; *sound* Larry Jost; *special effects* Virgil Beck; *camera* Burnett Guffney; *editor* Rita Roland.

Cast: Jim Brown (McClain); Diahann Carroll (Ellie); Julie Harris (Gladys); Ernest Borgnine (Bert Clinger); Gene Hackman (Lieutenant Walter Brill); Jack Klugman (Harry Kifka); Warren Oates (Marty Gough); James Whitmore (Herb Sutro); Donald Sutherland (Dave Negli); Jackie Joseph (Jackie); Harry Hickox (Detective); Joyce Jameson (Jennifer); Warren Vanders (Mason); George Cisar (Doorman); Karen Norris (Proprietress); Duane Grey, Reg Parton, Cal Brown, Jon Kowal, John Orchard (Guards); Barry Russo (Maccione the Top Guard); Ron Stokes (Detective); Anne Randall (Negli's Girl); Beverly Hills (Receptionist); Robert Foulk (Sergeant); Bill Couch, Howard Curtis, Chuck Kicks, Gene LeBell, George Robotham, Carl Saxe (Physical Instructors); Thordia Brandt, Fabian Dean (Clerks); Dee Carroll, Edith Evanson (Women); Lou Whitehill, Ron McCavour (Policemen); Orriel Smith, Cherie Lamour (Teenagers); Chance Gentry (Policeman); Jose Gallegos (Father); Tina Menard (Mother); Priscilla Ann (Daughter); Anthony Carbone (Man); Vanessa Lee (Little Girl); Jonathan Hale (Ticket Seller); Geneva Pacheco (Concessionaire).

Professional football player (Cleveland Browns) Jim Brown was born (1935) on St. Simons Island, Georgia, and educated at Syracuse University. In 1964 he appeared in an episode of the television spy series "I Spy" and played a cavalry sergeant in the post–Civil War Western *Rio Conchos,* co-starring with Richard Boone, Stuart Whitman and Edmond O'Brien. That same year he received the Hickok Belt, given to the athlete of the year. He returned to show business in 1967 for *The Dirty Dozen* and by that time had decided to retire from sports and concentrate on a film career. Part of Brown's charisma and flash—in contrast to the screen's then-reigning black superstar, Sidney Poitier—was being a lean, rough machine who only talks when he has something tough to say. His attitude towards the film establishment appeared to be no different from his approach to the annoying opposition on the gridiron. ". . . [T]hese film people were used to dealing with cats that let them get away with anything. But they don't mean a damn to me. I let 'em know right off that I didn't come into the movies with my hat in my hand asking somebody to do me a favor." In 1968 he made three motion pictures: *Dark of the Sun* with Rod Taylor and set in Africa; *Ice Station Zebra,* an expensive espionage adventure yarn with Rock Hudson and Ernest Borgnine; and MGM's *The Split.* The last is an adaptation of a 1966 novel by Richard Stark (Donald Westlake) and was originally planned as a starring vehicle for Lee Marvin, Brown's co-star in *The Dirty Dozen.*

Experienced thief McClain (Jim Brown) returns to Los Angeles after two years away and persuades his ex-wife, Ellie (Diahann Carroll) to put him up at her apartment. With his criminal friend Gladys (Julie Harris) he devises a scheme to rob the receipts from the Los Angeles Coliseum during a championship football game. To carry out his plan he recruits a gang, subjecting likely candidates to a brutal and full-of-surprises qualifications test. His chosen squad consists of gym instructor Bert Clinger (Ernest Borgnine), hired killer Dave Negli (Donald Sutherland), safe cracker Marty Gough (Warren Oates), and driver Harry Kifka (Jack Klugman). The heist is successful, and he hides the $50,000 at Ellie's place. Later she is attacked by her psychopathic landlord, Herb Sutro (James Whitmore), who kills her and takes the gang's money, which he has found. The others think McClain has taken the cash, and they try to torture its whereabouts from him. When they start quarreling, McClain escapes, with Gladys and Kifka killed in the melee. After Sutro is shot by crooked police Lieutenant Walter Brill (Gene Hackman), McClain knows it must be Brill who has the money. McClain makes a deal with him, and together they eliminate the surviving team members. It is Brill's plan to give McClain his one-sixth, keep his share, and return the rest to the authorities, thus earning a promotion. As McClain boards a plane for Mexico, he is troubled by his memories of Ellie and his promises to her to go straight.

Commercially *The Split* was right on target with filmgoers' changing interests in the late 1960s. It combined a daring robbery caper with lots of violent action and had as its virile lead a handsome and macho black. (Those filmgoers who harped on the plot contrivances or the poorly defined characterizations were considered bad sports.) Not only is Jim Brown's McClain a forceful, virile personality, but he torments and tortures his white confederates into submission, always seeming to come out on top against the opposition. His only weaknesses are his conscience and his enduring affection for his ex-wife. The critics continued to call Brown's onscreen capering stiff and flat, but a growing audience (especially black males) rallied to this new screen hero who, in such films as *The Split,* could be mean and unbeatable, have a white girl pal (Julie Harris) and continue to attract a sophisticated lady like Diahann Carroll.

Beyond the then-novelty of having two black performers in leading roles in a major motion picture from a top Hollywood studio, *The Split* gave audiences its kicks with the lengthy training montage in which bad Jim Brown outflanks his applicants at every turn. Also noted was the music. "Quincy Jones' score is in the contemporary groove, and three songs have a pleasant modern sound" *(Variety).*

Diahann Carroll and Jim Brown in *The Split* (1968).

For the next few years Jim Brown would be the ranking black personality in Hollywood, although he never broke into the top ten box-office earners of the year as did Sidney Poitier with consistency. After his disenchantment with the studio system, he would be off the screen all of 1971 and return in 1972 with *Slaughter* (q.v.), and several other low-budget entries, all in the post–*Shaft*-violence and black-is-beautiful modes.

195. The Spook Who Sat by the Door (United Artists, 1973).
Color, 102 minutes.

Producers Ivan Dixon, Sam Greenlee; *associate producer* Thomas G. Neusom; *director* Dixon; *based on the novel by* Greenlee; *screenplay* Greenlee, Melvin Clay; *art director* Leslie Thomas; *set decorator* Sheryl Kearney; *costumes* Henry Salley; *makeup* Bernardine Anderson; *music* Herbie Hancock; *sound* Jake Speak; *special effects* Roger Frezee; *camera* Michel Hugo; *editor* Michael Kahn.

Cast: Lawrence Cook (Dan Freeman); Paula Kelly (Dahomey Queen); Janet League (Joy); J.A. Preston (Reuben Dawson); Paul Butler (Do-Daddy Dean); Don Blakely (Stud Davis); David Lemieux (Pretty Willie); Byron Morrow (General); Jack Aaron (Carstairs); Joseph Mascolo (Senator); Beverly Gill (Willa); Bob Hill (Calhoun); Martin Golar (Perkins); Jeff Hamilton (Policeman); Margaret Kromgols (Old Woman); Tom Alderman (Security Officer); Stephen Ferry (Colonel); Kathy Berks (Doris); Stephen Ferry II (Boy Guardsman); Frank Lesley (Commentator); Harold Johnson (Jackson); Anthony Ray (Shorty Duncan); Audrey Stevenson (Mrs. Duncan); John Charles

(Stew); Ponicano Olayta, Jr. (Soo); Sidney Eden (Inspector); Colostine Boatwright (Dancer); Johnny Williams (Waiter); Frank E. Ford, Doug Johnson, Virgie Johnson, Robert Franklia, Don Greenlee, Harold Harris, Jim Heard, Johnnie Johnson, Larry Lawrence, Ramon Livingston, Tyrone Livingston, Walter Loew, Rodney McGrader, Clinton Malcome, James Mitchell, Leonard Norris, Kenneth Lee Orme, Ernie Robinson, Orlanders Thomas, Perry Thomas, Maurice Wicks, Bobbie Gene Williams, Cora Williams, Mark Williams.

By 1973 black action films had reached their peak and were beginning to fade as sure-fire box-office. It was also in that year that two of the most violent black militant motion pictures debuted: Twentieth Century–Fox's *Gordon's War* (q.v.), and United Artists' *The Spook Who Sat by the Door,* each created by a black director. The latter lacks the professional slickness of the former, but it is by far more inflammatory, furious, and bloody than its compatriot.

Dan Freeman (Lawrence Cook) has done everything the right way. He studied hard, earned good grades, served in Korea, and has been very patient. But he is black and is stuck in a career rut. Then, in a token bid to avoid charges of discrimination, the Central Intelligence Agency announces it will finally allow blacks to join the C.I.A., convinced that none will meet the extra-grueling weeding-out process planned for them. But mild-mannered, bespectacled Freeman fools them both academically and physically and passes all the requirements. The agency is forced to accept him as one of their own. Still hopeful for his day in the sun, Freeman, the model worker, looks forward to going into the field for the agency. Instead he is relegated to being the very visible (but non-functioning) black C.I.A. agent, escorting sightseeing parties through unclassified sections of the home office. After five years of continued discrimination and frustration, he quits and returns to Chicago to join a social service foundation. Slowly it dawns on the do-gooder that pacification is not the way. Militancy *must* be the new order. "You really want to mess with whitey. I can show you how," he tells his brothers. He recruits a task force from the city's black ghetto and, using all he knows from his C.I.A. days of guerilla warfare (including martial arts) and weaponry, he trains a cadre of black belligerents (including the Cobras). Soon his men are robbing banks, stealing equipments from national armories, and fighting the authorities as race riots break out in the ghetto. The metropolis becomes a raging battle zone. Through all of this Freeman insists, "This is not about hating white folks. This is about loving freedom enough to fight and die for it." But in his struggle, there is no place for friendship. When Reuben Dawson (J.A. Preston), his one-time-friend-turned cop, interferes once too often with the revolution, Freeman stabs him, reasoning, "Anybody who gets between us and freedom has got to go." Before dying, Dawson shoots Freeman. The film concludes with a postscript, stating that after word of martyred Freeman's death spread, eight major American cities are in "condition Red"—a state of uproar. The war of liberation continues.

Vincent Canby *(New York Times)* acknowledged that *The Spook Who Sat by the Door* is "...a difficult work to judge coherently. It is such a mixture of passion, humor, hindsight, prophecy, prejudice, and reaction." Walter Burrell

(*Soul* magazine) offered that it was "...one of the most intellectually revolutionary, socially pertinent, meaningful motion pictures of our lifetime. If white America will only listen to it and study it, they can carry away a wealth of information...." There *is* a great deal going on in this film. The full spectrum of black society is presented, from the professional upper classes down to the skid row bums, and all angles of political thought from the "Uncle Toms" to the ardent black activists and revolutionaries. There is a revealing restaurant sequence between Freeman and a neighborhood figure named Mrs. Duncan (Audrey Stephenson). In its wry way it states so much about one type of person who refuses to see a situation as it is, but instead interprets everything with a chip on his shoulder (without which, of course, many of these black action films would have no premise).

MRS. DUNCAN: He's [her son Shorty] got a job now, makin' good money! He just bought me a color TV set!

FREEMAN: I hear he's running numbers, pushing drugs. I hear he's hooked.

MRS. DUNCAN: He ain't no real junkie. Sure he shoots up now and then. I don't think he got no more than a $20 or $30 habit and that ain't no habit.

FREEMAN: Did you ever think he could end up in jail?

MRS. DUNCAN: Not unless someone turns the heat on in the precinct and then I can't hardly see why they'd be after Shorty, because he ain't into it that much.

FREEMAN: Did Shorty ever think about finishing at least school?

MRS. DUNCAN: No. He don't want no part of the school. You know how them teachers are.

FREEMAN: Without an education what's he going to do?

MRS. DUNCAN: Mr. Freeman, you know there ain't nothing out there for us. *(She resumes eating.)*

The Spook Who Sat by the Door is full of massive riot assaults, with cars overturned and burned, apartment buildings ablaze, clubbings and shootings, police and National Guard advancing with billy clubs, tear gas guns and pistols. Bruised bodies and corpses are everywhere, along with mass hysteria as the turmoil and destruction mounts. Not only is it white against black, but there are black law enforcers pushing back, with merciless force, the black rioters. (And this is paralleled by the uppity segment of the ghetto, who look down on the tactics of their more basic, angered brethren.) One grisly sequence has the street gangs capturing the brutally nasty head of the National Guard, painting him black, and feeding him with acid. While on his drug trip, he runs amok and is shot by one of his Guard snipers.

Three black women play a prominent part in the film. There is the memory of Freeman's grandmother. When he was a boy he had taught her to read, and that joyous experience gave him the incentive to excel. There is Joy (Janet League), who had been Freeman's social worker girlfriend in Chicago, but who decides to play it safe and marry a doctor. She keeps returning to his life throughout the film, amazed by the transformation in her first love. Then there is the Dahomey Queen (Paula Kelly), a prostitute on U Street in D.C. whom Freeman sees a great deal. She is a perceptive gal who realizes that this client is "...one of those quiet kind of cats you don't mess with..." She is later recruited by the government to spy on Freeman when he becomes a militant leader in Chicago.

There was a great deal of uproar when this violent film received only a Parental Guidance (PG) rating from the Motion Picture Association of America. According to *Variety,* "...because this ... production shows no nudity nor explicit sex, and muffles most of the violent action in a jangled series of crowd shots, MPAA deemed it worthy of a PG.... Many viewers of whatever complexion may find this pic far more offensive than the celebrated X-rated UA release, *Last Tango in Paris.*" Many reviewers sympathetic by birth or philosophy to the black cause endorsed this film as did Emerson Batdorff of *The* (Cleveland) *Plain Dealer:* "In an extremely bitter movie, we are given sensible reasons why blacks hate whites. The reasons have been given before; nothing is new here except that killing movies ... usually are too simplistic to bother to explain.... It's not a cheerful picture at all. Unfortunately it seems realistic because it holds out no hope."

The film's title has a double meaning: "Spook" refers to a C.I.A. agent and is an epithet for a black as well.

196. Stir Crazy (Columbia, 1980). Color, 111 minutes.

Executive producer Melville Tucker; *producer* Hannah Weinstein; *associate producer* François deMenil; *director* Sidney Poitier; *screenplay* Bruce Jay Friedman; *production designer* Alfred Sweeney; *costumes* Patricia Edwards; *makeup* Richard Cobos; *music* Tom Scott; *songs* Michael Masser and Randy Goodrum; Scott and Rob Preston; *choreography* Scott Salmon; *assistant directors* Daniel J. McCauley, Joseph Moore, Don Wilkerson; *stunt coordinator* Mickey Gilbert; *sound* Glenn Anderson; *sound effects* Jeff Bushelman, Pat Somerset; *camera* Fred Schuler; *editor* Harry Keller.

Cast: Gene Wilder (Skip Donahue); Richard Pryor (Harry Monroe); Georg Stanford Brown (Rory Schultebrand); JoBeth Williams (Meredith); Miguel Angel Suarez (Jesus Ramirez); Craig T. Nelson (Deputy Ward Wilson); Barry Corbin (Warden Walter Beatty); Charles Weldon (Blade); Nicholas Coster (Warden Henry Sampson); Joel Brooks (Len Garber); Jonathan Banks (Jack Graham); Erland Van Lidth De Jeude (Grossberger); Lee Purcell (Susan); Karmin Murcelo (Theresa Ramirez); Franklyn Ajaye (Young Man in Hospital); Estelle Omens (Mrs. R.H. Broache); Cedrick Hardman (Big Mean); Henry Kingi (Ramon); Pamela Poitier (Cook's Helper); Alvin Ing (Korean Doctor); Joseph Massengale (Ceasar Geronimo); Herman Poppe (Alex); Luis Avalos (Chico); Esther Sutherland (Sissie); James Oscar Lee (Kicker); Rod McCary (Minister); Claudia Cron (Joy); Bill Bailey (Announcer); Donna Benz (Nancy); Grand Bush (Big Mean's Sidekick); Thomas Moore (Judge); Danna Hansen (Mrs. Sampson); Gwen Van Dam (Mrs. Beatty); Herb Armstrong (County Jail Guard); Herbert Hirschman (Man at Dinner Party); Don Circle (Bank Teller); Kenneth Menard (Repairman); Billy Beck (Flycatching Prisoner).

With domestic film rentals of $58,364,420, *Stir Crazy* must have done something right. The public obviously approved of this Gene Wilder–Richard Pryor reteaming (after *Silver Streak* [1977] [q.v.]) directed by Sidney Poitier, even if the critics had serious reservations. "Writer Bruce Jay Friedman has obviously tailored the roles to his stars, but he's left the plot hanging by the threads" (David Ansen, *Newsweek* magazine). "It's a slovenly, loose-jointed movie, with anecdotes that lead nowhere and minor performances that don't come off; but none of that would matter if Pryor and Wilder had been allowed to work up a performing rhythm suited to their talents" (David Denby, *New York* magazine). Richard Corliss (*Time* magazine) apparently couldn't decide how he felt about this screen farce: "Viewers ... must stand around as *Stir Crazy* makes wrong turns, slogs across Saharas of unnecessary plotting, and unravel at its denouement. But that may simply make the triumph of Wilder and Pryor all the more savory."

When store detective/would-be playwright Skip Donahue (Gene Wilder) and waiter/would-be actor Harry Monroe (Richard Pryor) both lose their jobs in New York City, they head to California. Along the way in the Southwest, in the hick town of Glenboro, they become involved inadvertently in a bank robbery and find themselves sentenced to 125 years in prison. At Glenboro State Prison they must cope with the hardened inmates, including cellblock dictator Jack Graham (Jonathan Banks), mass murderer Grossberger (Erland Van Lidth de Jeude), Mexican Jesus Ramirez (Miguel Angel Saurez), and homosexual Rory Schultebrand (Georg Stanford Brown). Warden Walter Beatty (Barry Corbin) discovers Donahue has a talent for bronco riding (he survives on the administrator's mechanical bucking bull) and enters him in the Top Hand competition with the men of Warden Henry Sampson's (Nicolas Coster) rival prison. Because Donahue is in a power position he insists on having a special training crew, consisting of Monroe, Schulterbrand, Ramirez, and Grossberger. They execute a complex escape during the rodeo while Donahue throws the competition to his rival (Joseph Massengale) and even persuades the latter to not hand over the prize money to the wardens but instead give it to the prisoners. In the midst of their escape, Donahue and Monroe learn the real bank robbers have been caught, and Donahue announces his love for Meredith (JoBeth Williams), the assistant attorney helping on their case.

With each new movie Gene Wilder has become more hysterical and shrill, and Richard Pryor must look on in amazement, scorn, and half-hearted acceptance. The highlight of this improbable slapstick comedy is when the two stars enter the cellblock and confront the menacing greeting committee, comprised of mostly mean black dudes. In a scene reminiscent (imitative) of the jivin' dude bit from *Silver Streak*, Pryor — fearful of sexual assault — tells his pal, "Gotta get bad," and he struts away in macho tough guy fashion. Wilder mimics his friend's walk in exaggerated fashion — "We bad, we very bad" — hoping to stay out of trouble by acting black in this black man's domain — prison.

There was a postscript to *Stir Crazy* when it was turned into a brief-running teleseries on CBS-TV from April to December 1985. It featured Larry Riley (Harry Fletcher) and Joseph Guzaldo (Skip Harrington) as two victims falsely accused of murder and pursued (weekly) from city to city by unrelenting police Captain Betty (Jeannie Wilson).

In the fall of 1988 Gene Wilder and Richard Pryor re-teamed again for the theatrical feature *See No Evil, Hear No Evil* (1989) set in New York City with Pryor cast as a blind man, Wilder as a deaf man, and Kirsten Childs as Pryor's sister.

197. Street Smart (Cannon, 1987). Color, 95 minutes.

Producers Menahem Golan, Yoram Globus; *director* Jerry Schaltzberg; *screenplay* David Freeman; *production designer* Dan Leigh; *art director* Serge Jacques; *set decorators* Raymond Larose, Katherine Mathewson; *costumes* Yo Ynocenio; *music* Robert Irving III, Miles Davis; *camera* Adam Holender; *editor* Priscilla Nedd.

Cast: Christopher Reeve (Jonathan Fisher); Morgan Freeman (Fast Black); Kathy Baker (Punch); Mimi Rogers (Alison Parker); Jay Patterson (Leonard Pike); Andre Gregory (Ted Avery); Anna Maria Horsford (Harriet); Frederick Rolf (Joel Davis); Erik King (Reggie); Michael J. Reynolds (Art Sheffield); Shari Hilton (Darlene); Donna Bailey (Yvonne); Ed Van Nuys (Judge); Daniel Nalrach (Singer); Rick Aviles (Solo); Les Carlson (Marty); Bill Torre (Hotel Clerk); Richard Mullaly (Suburban John); Marie Barrientos (Hispanic Prostitute); Eddie Earl Hatch (Flashy Man); Joe Dorian Clark (Transvestite); Grace Garland (Black Prostitute); Wally Martin (Lowlife); Robert Morelli (Undercover Cop); Shawn Laurence (Bartender); Kelly Ricard (Woman Magistrate); David Glen (Jay); Ulla Moreland (Ted's Wife); Francisco Gonzales (Pablo); Lynne Adams, Claudette Roach, Rudi Adler, Melba Archer, Ian Beaton, Victor Bowen, Lois Dellar, Chui-Lin Mark, Manon Vallee, Carole Zelles (Reporters); Danny Brainin (TV Cameraman); Ernest Devereaux (Kid); Walter Allen Bennet, Jr. (Ball Player); Steve Michaels (Taxi Inspector); Margarita Stocker (Intellectual Woman); Eve Napier (Trish); Ruth Dahan (Mrs. Silverbeard); Vera Miller, Nadia Rona (Party Guests); Terry Haig (Marshall); Donald Lamoureux (Prison Reporter); Carol Ann Francis (Susan); Ann Pearl Gary, Emmanuelle LaSalle (Waitresses).

This was another artistic/commercial fiasco from trouble-plagued Cannon Pictures. "A dubious title for a dumb movie," *People* magazine insisted. The review goes on to explain, "Assuming a know-it-all attitude about how the underworld and the media operate in the Big Apple, the plot actually is naive." But this trashy feature starring Christopher "Superman" Reeve does have one redeeming aspect: Morgan Freeman as Fast Black, the brutal black murderer who is mistaken as the media-hyped pimp-of-the-hour. Tennessee-born (1937) Freeman had attended Los Angeles City College and had appeared in such feature films as *Who Says I Can't Ride a Rainbow* (1971), *Brubaker* (1980), *Eyewitness* (1981), *Harry and Son* (1984), *Teachers* (1984), *Marie* (1985), and *That Was Then ... This Is Now* (1985). He was Oscar-nomincated as Best Supporting Actor for *Street Smart,* but lost to Sean Connery of *The Untouchables.*

Pretentious, lazy journalist Jonathan Fisher (Christopher Reeve) is assigned by his frenetic editor, Ted Avery (Andre Gregory), at their slick weekly New York magazine to write a lead article on the lifestyle of a colorful pimp. Too unimaginative to do his job, Fisher makes up the article, and when it is published both it and he become a media sensation. Assistant district

Christopher Reeve held at gunpoint by Morgan Freeman in *Street Smart* (1987).

attorney Leonard Pike (Jay Patterson) is convinced that Fisher's fictitious anti-hero is really murderous Fast Black (Morgan Freeman), who is in the process of being prosecuted. The law demands Fisher's notes—but he has none. Fast Black, who faces a life sentence, insists he make up documents to clear his name or he will kill the glib writer. Fast Black introduces the prim writer to the grittiness and violence of urban street life. Using his newfound street smarts, Fisher maneuvers Fast Black into being liquidated by a competitor. Meanwhile, Fisher returns to his uptown girlfriend, Alison Parker (Mimi Rogers), passing off his romance with hooker Punch (Kathy Baker) with the assertion, "It didn't mean anything. It just kind of happened."

In his *Movie Home Companion 1988* (1987) Roger Ebert enthuses over "...two wonderful performances ... by Morgan Freeman, as a Times Square pimp, and by Kathy Baker, as one of the hookers he controls. They play their characters as well as I imagine them being played. Freeman has the flashier role, as a smart, very tough man who can be charming or intimidating—whatever's needed.... Freeman's dialogue is particularly good, as he analyzes Reeve's motives, talks about people who condescend to him, and terrorizes Baker for becoming Reeve's friend. There is one powerful, frightening scene where he threatens her with scissors...." And Ebert adds as a postscript,

"When an actor like Freeman goes to the trouble of creating a great character, the film should go to the trouble of providing him with a final scene."

Most of *Street Smart* was shot in Canada, with Montreal substituting for New York City.

198. Sugar Hill (American International, 1974). Color, 90 minutes.

Executive producer Samuel Z. Arkoff; *producer* Elliott Schick; *director* Paul Maslansky; *screenplay* Tim Kelly; *makeup* George Edds; *music* Nick Zesses, Dino Fekarais; *assistant director* Xavier Reyes; *sound* Darin Knight; *special effects* Roy L. Downey; *camera* Bob Jessup; *editor* Carl Kress.

Cast: Marki Bey (Diana "Sugar" Hill); Robert Quarry (Morgan); Don Pedro Colley (Baron Samedi); Richard Lawson (Valentine); Betty Anne Rees (Celeste); Zara Cully (Mama Maitresse); Larry D. Johnson (Langston); Charles Robinson (Fabulous); Rich Hagood (Tank Watson); Ed Geldhart (O'Brien); Thomas C. Carroll (Baker); Albert J. Baker (George); Raymond E. Simpson (King); Charles Krohn (Captain Merrill); Jack Bell (Parkhurst); Peter Harrell III (Police Photographer); Walter Price (Preacher); Judy Hanson (Masseuse); Tony Brubaker (Head Zombie).

A.K.A. *The Voodoo Girl; Zombies of Sugar Hill.*

Because Langston (Larry D. Johnson), the black owner of the popular Club Haiti, will not sell out to white racketeer Morgan (Robert Quarry), he is pummeled to death by Morgan's gang. Langston's very attractive girlfriend, Diana "Sugar" Hill (Marki Bey) vows revenge. She visits voodoo mamaloi Mama Maitresse (Zara Cully), who lives in a deserted mansion near the swamps. The old woman calls up the force of Baron Samedi (Don Pedro Colley) and his fellow zombies from the netherworld to help Diana achieve her goal. The Baron and his squad brutally murder each of Morgan's men. Valentine (Richard Lawson), Diana's former boyfriend and a detective, investigates the rash of murders and with the help of white researcher Parkhurst (Jack Bell) uncovers the fact that in the seventeenth century, boatloads of chained slaves were brought from Guinea and later buried near the swamp. Diana asks the Baron to stop Valentine's investigation and to harm him. Meanwhile the Baron helps Diana get her final revenge on Morgan and his racist girlfriend, Celeste (Anne Reeves). Morgan is led into quicksand, and Diana is carried off screaming into the world beyond by Morgan and his fellow cadavers.

This supernatural film (the ad copy read, "Her Voodoo Powers Raised the Dead, She's *Super*-Natural!") was directed with atmospheric style by Paul Maslansky. It has its wry moments, as when it becomes clear the mock-comic black Baron would rather have Diana's earthly body rather than her ethereal soul. Then there is the death of Fabulous (Charles Robinson), the one black member of Morgan's gang, who is killed by female zombies in a massage parlor. A great deal of violence is depicted graphically as the murderous gang is decimated, each in grisly fashion: one is fed to voracious pigs; another is locked in a coffin full of poisonous snakes; another is led by voodoo to stab himself; a fourth is destroyed on the docks. (There is even a final viewing of the assembled corpses when Morgan is tricked into the gloomy mansion.)

Variety noted simply, "*Sugar Hill* carries enough novelty and offbeat

Left–right: **Zara Cully, zombies, and Marki Bey in** *Sugar Hill* **(1974).**

action as an exploitation subject to rate good response in its intended market."
Other critics looked for deeper meaning. "... [This film] has a bit of an edge
over many contenders by virtue of the fact that its vengeance is given a certain
historical-political dimension. Morgan's gang, represented throughout as the
arm of white exploitation and racism, is obliterated by the corpses of black
slaves in a dream of apocalypse out of Nat Turner, which lends a certain
resonance to an otherwise mechanical plot."

Zara Cully would gain greater prominence as George Jefferson's demanding mother on television's "The Jeffersons."

199. Super Fly (Warner Bros., 1972). Color, 96 minutes.

Producer Sig Shore; *associate producer* Irving Stimler; *director* Gordon
Parks, Jr.; *screenplay* Phillip Fenty; *costumes* Nate Adams; *makeup* James
Farabee; *music/songs* Curtis Mayfield; *music director* Marvin Start; *assistant
director* Kurt Baker; *sound* Harry Lapham; *camera* Jmaes Signorelli; *editor*
Bob Brady.

Cast: Ron O'Neal (Youngblood Priest); Carl Lee (Eddie); Sheila Frazier
(Georgia); Julius W. Harris (Scatter); Charles McGregor (Fat Freddie); Henry
Shapiro (Robbery Victim); K.C. (Pimp); Jim Richardson (Junkie); Sig Shore
(Deputy Commissioner Reardon); the Curtis Mayfield Experience
(Themselves); Nick Sands, Bob Richards (Contract Men); Chris Arnett (Coke
Buyer); Mike Richards (Deputy Commissioner); Cecil Alonzo, Gene
Chambers, John Williams (Militants); Jim Richardson, Mike Bray (Junkies);

Bob Bonds, Al Kiggin, Floyd Levine, Harry Manson, Fred Rolof, Alex Stevens (Cops).

See summary under *Super Fly T.N.T.*

200. Super Fly T.N.T. (Paramount, 1973). Color, 87 minutes.

Producer Sig Shore; *director* Ron O'Neal; *story* Shore, O'Neal; *screenplay* Alex Haley; *production designer* Giuseppe Bassan; *makeup* Marcello de Paalo; *music* Osibisa; *production supervisor* Alfredo Cooms; *sound* Jack Cooley; *sound editing* Ray Bevans; *special effects* Celeste Battistelli; *camera* Robert Gaffney; *supervising editor* Luis San Andres; *editor* Bob Brady.

Cast: Ron O'Neal (Youngblood Priest); Roscoe Lee Browne (Dr. Lamine Sonko); Sheila Frazier (Georgia); Robert Guillaume (Jordan Gaines); Jacques Sernas (Matty Smith); William Berger (Lefevre); Roy Bosler (Customs Man); Silvio Nardo (General); Jeannie McNeill (Riding Instructress); Dan Davis (Pilot); Luigi Orso (Crew Chief); Ennio Catalfamo (Photographer); Francesco Rachini (Warehouse Custodian); Ferrucio Brusarosco, Fernando Piazza, George Wang (Poker Player); Rik Boyd (Rik).

A year before *The Mack* (1973) (q.v.) glamorized the life of the black pimp, the "fast, flashy and funky" *Super Fly* did the same over-romanticizing of a crafty black drug dealer. It was released by Warner Bros., who the same year promoted the exploits of a female black super-character, *Cleopatra Jones* (q.v.). Youngblood Priest is a light-skinned Harlem super-entrepreneur of dope. He's a fancy dresser (wide-brim hats, calf-length, sweeping coats, and a gold cross around his neck) with long hair, mustache, and a mean strut, as well as a tough dude whose insolent smile belies his sensitive, articulate inner self. And, of course, his crowning possessions are his mammoth flashy car (an $18,000 Cadillac) and his hip downtown apartment. To the producers' joy, this celluloid figment became a box-office sensation; to the black community's perturbation, this mythical "hero" of the bad streets became a role model for impressionable young filmgoers, who thought it cool the way he punched and outmaneuvered honkies and snorted coke while hot-tubbing or fornicating; and to film critics' horror, it unleased a host of genre imitations, all featuring drugs, sex and violence.

Youngblood Priest (Ron O'Neal) has fifty men out on the New York City street all pushing dope (mostly to white people). His partner is Eddie (Carl Lee) and his career inspiration is Scatter (Julius W. Harris). This "Super Fly" is a fearless, no-nonsense business man who conducts his own strong-arm operation when any of his stooges or clients act up. He lives and dresses well, has an adoring beautiful black woman named Georgia (Sheila Frazier) and an equally impressed white doll (Polly Niles). He has it all. As one friend says, "Eight-track stereo, color TV in every room and you can snort half a piece of dope ever' day. That's the American dream.... Well, ain't it?" But Priest is tired of this high-pressured existence. He wants to make one final score (which incidentally will "stick it to the Man") by buying 30 keys of coke for $300,000 and distributing it for $1,000,000. He is tired of seeing his friends wasted in the three-way warfare between corrupt cops, the white racketeers, and the Harlem underworld. He wants to go straight, get his head clean. Buying a contract on

Left–right: **Nate Adams, Ron O'Neal and Julius W. Harris in** *Super Fly* **(1972).**

the corrupt Deputy Commissioner Reardon (Sig Shore—the film's producer), he turns the sting on his white confederates and gets his cache of money.

Like most such black action films there was something said about the white establishment being at fault for the path of life chosen by the black "hero" and his pals. For example, Eddie (Carl Lee) rationalizes his criminal life by explaining, "I know it's a rotten game, but it's the only one the Man left us to play." That is this film's extent of moralizing or preaching; it makes no other justifications for Priest's high-steppin', criminal way of life.

There was critical endorsement for this stylish, atmospheric film. "*Super Fly* is almost exclusively an action movie, but with the distinction that all the action means something, and is not simply a lot of running or driving or flying around for the mechanical titillation of the customers. The film's gut pleasures are real and there are a lot of them. But, they always connect with one or another in a world so precisely, cruelly, excitingly balanced...." (Roger Greenspun, *New York Times*.) In retrospect, it is hard to imagine anyone else in the sexy lead role but magnetic Ron O'Neal, whose super identification with the part became a mixed career blessing. (Born in Utica, New York, in 1937, Ron O'Neal performed with the Karamu Playhouse in Cleveland and later was in several Negro Ensemble Company productions in New York City. He would later return to the New York stage in such fare as *Macbeth, All Over Town,* and *Agamemmon.* He was in such motion pictures as *Move* [1970] and Sidney Poitier's *The Organization* [1971] [q.v.]. After the *Super Fly* entries he drifted in and out of screen acting assignments such as *Master Gunfighter* [1975], *Brothers* [1977] [q.v.], *When a Stranger Calls* [1979], *A Force of One* [1979], *The Final Countdown* [1980], *St. Helena* [1981], and *Red Dawn* [1984]. He was in such telefeatures as *Freedom Road* [1979], *Brave New World* [1980], *Sophisticated Gents* [1981] [q.v.], *Shannon* [1982], and *Playing With Fire* [1985]. He was the Sultan of Johore on the television series "Bring 'Em Back Alive [1982–83] and has a recurring role as Lieutenant Isadore Smalls on "The Equalizer" [1986–   ].)

The mood-evoking romantic soundtrack score by Curtis Mayfield rose to the top of the album charts and remained number one for five weeks, staying on the charts for 46 weeks in all. It won Gold Disc standing and by June of 1973 (a year after the film's release) it had sold over 2,000,000 copies. Two singles from the album, the "Super Fly" theme and "Reddie's Dead," sold a million copies each.

This Gordon Parks, Jr., film (his directing debut) grossed a whopping $6,400,000, and led to the inevitable sequel. But this moneymaker suffered the same film industry syndrome as so many other unique productions: the follow-up was not as good as the original. And this one was even worse because it was shot on the cheap in Europe and allowed Ron O'Neal to be star, director, and co-originator of the story. The screenplay for *Super Fly T.N.T.* was by Alex Haley, who later wrote the acclaimed book *Roots*. Warner Bros. backed off from distributing this film, made for $750,000, and it was picked up by Paramount Pictures.

None of the pizazz that made *Super Fly* so striking was evident in the over-indulgent sequel. The music was blah, the pacing sluggish, the photography and editing crude, and Youngblood Priest (Ron O'Neal), the black prince of the streets who seems so at ease snaking on down Fifth Avenue or bashing chins in a dark alley, seems lost in Rome while attempting to live *la dolce vita*. His ever-lovin' girl Georgia (Sheila Frazier) asks, "What are we going to do now?" The poor, confused, spiritless, ex-drug dealer rambles on in a circuitous answer:

> I don't know. All I can come up is what I don't want to do. I know I don't want to hustle any more. Don't need no money. Funny thing is the money don't seem to be getting it anyhow. I can't stay on my ass either. Ain't my nature to sit on my ass. I just gotta get the pieces together, baby . . . who I am or what I'm supposed to be or something.

This cynical expatriate is not the likely subject for a cracking good action movie. Nor is the meandering pace helped by long interludes of the leaden character playing poker, riding by famous Italian landmarks, or being lured to Africa on a gun-running mission by urbane Dr. Lamine Sonko (Roscoe Lee Browne) to help a small oppressed country combat French imperialists. When the regenerated Priest returns to the patiently waiting Georgie, the viewer's feeling is, "So what?"

Lee Beaupre *(Variety)* assessed correctly, "As with many actors, however, he [Ron O'Neal] needs strong directorial guidance to curb his less attractive excesses. Here he permits himself to indulge in unbecomingly effete mannerism. . . . While his wardrobe descends from *Super Fly*'s high style to high camp."

This mediocre film soon disappeared from the marketplace. Critics such as Howard Thompson *(New York Times)* dismissed it as "a wet firecracker." Others noted that, like the fast-fading *Shaft* series (which coincidentally also went to the dark continent for its finale, *Shaft in Africa* [1973] [q.v.]), *Super Fly* lost its punch when it left the streets of Harlem.

201. Super Spook (Levitt-Pickman, 1975). Color, 103 minutes.

Producer Ed Dessisso; *director/story* Anthony Major; *screenplay* Dessisso, Leonard Jackson, Bill Jay, Tony King, Major; *music* Rheet Taylor; *camera* Jim Walker; *editor* Sandy Tung.

Cast: Leonard Jackson (Super Spook); Bill Jay (Hi Yo); Tony King (Sergeant Sandwich); Bob Reed (Reverend Ignatius Dooley Tile); Virginia Fields (Bag Woman); Marcella Lowery (Bag Woman's Daughter); Sam McKnight (Big D).

Shaft (1971) (q.v.) and its imitators were fantasies restructuring life; *Super Spook* is a satirical approach to *Shaft*. Unfortunately it is without sufficient production values or comic invention to work. Super Spook (Leonard Jackson) and his sidekick Hi Yo (Bill Jay) fight the good fight to rid Harlem of corrupt influences, but they bumble and stumble and can't succeed. A.H. Weiler *(New York Times)* acknowledged that this film is "A good deal less than persuasive as comedy...."

202. Superman III (Warner Bros., 1983). Color, 123 minutes.

Executive producer Ilya Salkind; *producer* Pierre Spengler; *associate producer* Robert Simmonds; *director* Richard Lester; *based on comic strip characters created by* Jerry Siegel, Joe Shuster; *screenplay* David Newman, Leslie Newman; *music* Ken Thorne; *from original material composed by* John Williams; *songs* Giorgio Moroder; *assistant directors* David Lane, Dusty Symonds; *production designer* Peter Murton; *art directors* Brian Ackland-Snow, Charles Bishop, Terry Ackland-Snow; *set decorator* Peter Young; *costumes* Vangie Harrison; *director of special effects/miniatures* Collin Chilvers; *flying/second unit director* David Lane; *stunt co-ordinator* Paul Weston; *makeup* Paul Engelen, Stuart Freeborn; *sound* Roy Charman, John Richards; *sound editors* Don Sharpe, Archie Ludski, Paul Smith, Rocky Phelan; *supervisor of optical/visual effects* Roy Field; *model unit camera* Harry Oakes; *process camera* John Harris; *Zoptic front projection supervisor* David Wynn Jones; *traveling matte supervisor* Dennis Bartlett; *aerial Wesscam camera* Ronald Goodman; *background camera* Bob Bailin; *optical/matte camera* Peter Harman, Martin Body; *camera* Robert Paynter; *editor* John Victor Smith.

Cast: Christopher Reeve (Superman/Clark Kent); Richard Pryor (Gus Gorman); Jackie Cooper (Perry White); Margot Kidder (Lois Lane); Annette O'Toole (Lana Lang); Marc McClure (Jimmy Olsen); Annie Ross (Vera Webster); Pamela Stephenson (Lorelei Ambrosia); Robert Vaughn (Ross Webster); Gavan O'Herlihy (Brad); Graham Stark (Blind Man); Henry Woolf (Penguin Man); Gordon Rollings (Man in Cap); Peter Wear (Bank Robber); Justin Case (Mime); Bob Todd (Dignified Gent); Terry Camilleri (Delivery Man); Stefan Kalipha (Data School Instructor); Helen Horton (Miss Henderson); Lou Hirsch (Fred); Bill Reinbold (Wages Man); Shane Rimmer (State Policeman); Al Matthews (Fire Chief); Barry Dennen (Dr. McClean); Enid Saunders (Minnie Bannister); Kevin Harrison Cork (D.J.); Robert G. Henderson (Mr. Simpson); Paul Kaethler (Ricky); R.J. Bell (Mr. Stokis); Pamela Mandell (Mrs. Stokis); Peter Whitman (Man at Cash Point); Ronnie Brody (Husband); Sandra Dickinson (Wife); Philip Gilbert (Newsreader); Pat Starr (White Coated Scientist); Gordon Signer (Mayor); John Bluthal (Pisa Vendor); George Chisholm (Street Sweeper); David Fielder (Olympic Runner); Robert Beatty (Tanker Captain); Chris Malcolm, Larry Lamb (Miners).

Superman III was a further dissipation of a spectacular movie series begun in 1978, but at least was better than the much-maligned *Superman IV* (1985). But, warned *People* magazine, "The film [#3] loses most of its sparkle three-fourths of the way through, bogging down in an endless, metaphysical junkyard battle between Superman's good and evil sides and finishing with the requisite scene of mass destruction." Sheila Benson *(Los Angeles Times)* carped, "*Superman III* has about half the invention, the sparkle and the originality you might hope for." Rex Reed *(New York Post)* aptly summed it, "Is it a bird? Is it a plane? No, it's Supertrash."

There were those who thanked God for Richard Pryor's appearance in this feature, and others who wanted to know why Pryor had so demeaned himself in such an unrealized role. The interesting aspect is that the filmmakers here, as in the *Rocky* (q.v.) series, chose a black actor to represent the (symbolic) foe of the white hero.

Clark Kent (Christopher Reeve) returns to Smallville for a high school reunion, and he renews his acquaintance with Lana Lang (Annette O'Toole), a classmate now divorced. Meanwhile back in Metropolis evil tycoon Ross Webster (Robert Vaughn) blackmails ex-restaurant worker and befuddled computer wizard Gus Gorman (Richard Pryor) into helping control the world's coffee market. Superman (Christopher Reeve) combats their sinister machinations. Webster taunts Superman with vampish Lorelei Ambrosia (Pamela Stephenson) and weakens the Man of Steel by confronting him with artificial kryptonite. The latter is temporarily sidetracked from being the super-helpful person he usually is and even becomes a temporary ally of Webster. But thanks to Lana's son Ricky (Paul Kaethler), who spurs Superman onto being his true self, Superman reverts back to form. Gus helps in their battle to squash Webster.

203. Sweet Jesus, Preacher Man (Metro-Goldwyn-Mayer, 1973). Color, 103 minutes.

Executive producer Ronald Goldman; *producer* Daniel B. Cady; *director* Henning Schellerup; *screenplay* John Cerullo, M. Stuart Madden, Abbey Leitch; *set decorator* Ernest Williams III; *sound* Clark Will; *special effects* Harry Woolman, Rick Helmer; *camera* Paul E. Hipp; *second unit camera* Ray Icely; *editor* Warren Hamilton, Jr.

Cast: Roger E. Mosley (Holmes/Lee); William Smith (Martelli); Michael Pataki (State Senator Sills); Tom Johnigarn (Eddie Stoner); Joe Tornatore (Joey); Damu King (Sweetstick); Marla Gibbs (Beverly Soloman); Sam

Laws (Deacon Greene); Phil Hoover (George Orr); Paul Silliman (Roy); Chuck Lyles (Detroit Charlie); Norman Fields (Police Captain); Della Thomas (Foxey); Amentha Dymally (Mrs. Greene); Patricia Edwards (Marian Hicks); Chuck Douglas, Jr. (Lenny Soloman); Vincent LaBauve (Bobby Thompson); Chuck Wells (Eli Stoner); Betty Coleman (Maxine Gibbs); Lillian Tarry (Mother Gibbs); Lou Jackson (Randy Gibbs); T.C. Ellis (Earl Saunders); Lee Frost (Policeman); JoAnn Bruno (Widow Foster); Reverend K.D. Friend (Funeral Minister); Billy Quinn (Sweetstick's Bodyguard); Bob Angelle, Dan Black, Bruce Hall, Curtiss Price, Don Senette, John Washington (Militants).

On orders from his white Mafia bosses including Martelli (William Smith), a black hit man (Roger E. Mosley) goes deep undercover posing as a Baptist preacher at a Los Angeles ghetto church. Before long, he decides he wants the local action (prostitution and drugs) for himself. In the midst of his dual existence he finds time for sweet-talking assorted women (Marla Gibbs, Amentha Dymally, Betty Coleman, and Jo Anne Bruno).

Variety, by now as satiated as the public with such cliched offerings, noted, "Surprisingly, both sex and violence portions, pic's major lures, are presented in a curiously desultory fashion...."

204. Sweet Sweetback's Baadasssss Song (Cinemation, 1971). 97 minutes.

Producer/director/screenplay/music Melvin Van Peebles; *makeup* Nora Maxwell; *assistant director* Clyde Houston; *second unit director* Jose Garcia; *dubbing* Art Piantadosi; *sound editors* John Newman, Luke Wofram; *special effects* Cliff Wenger; *camera* Bob Maxwell, Garcia; *editor* Van Peebles.

Cast: Melvin Van Peebles (Sweetback); Simon Chuchster (Beetle); Hubert Scales (Mu-Mu); John Dullaghan (Commissioner); Rhetta Hughes (Old Girl Friend); *and:* Bruce Adams, Michael Agustus, John Allen, Johnny Amp, Mike Angel, Vincent Barbi, Steve Cole, the Copeland family, Jerry Days, Sonya Duncan, Maria Evonee, Nick Ferrari, Norman Fields, Jeff Goodman, Ted Hayden, Jon Jacobs, Bill Kirschner, Curt Matson, Chet Norris, Ron Prince, Lavelle Roby, Ed Rue, Jon Peter Russell, Jo Tornatore, Mario Van Peebles, Megan Van Peebles, Joni Watkins.

Because the creator of a trailblazing film is so absorbed with his thematic innovation, often his pathfinding venture is inferior technically. Typically he has no budget (his concept is not proven box-office), nor extra energy to devote to production values. Because ground-breaking films are imitated *ad nauseum,* frequently in retrospect the trend-setting motion picture appears unoriginal and intellectually unsophisticated. Such is the case with Melvin Van Peebles's outrageous *Sweet Sweetback's Baadasssss Song.* It, along with *Shaft* (1971) (q.v.), set the pathway for the blaxploitation features of the 1970s. It solidified a concept that Hollywood had been toying with gingerly in previous years. This development paralleled the Civil Rights movement as focused on the leadership of Dr. Martin Luther King and the tremendous ramifications of his 1968 assassination. *Sweet Sweetback* had the audacity to depict in raw cinema a situation where a black man could stand up to "the [white] Man" and get away with it. Equally as important, it demonstrated that there was a filmgoing audience (both in the black community and outside) ready to pay box-office dollars to watch and experience such a newly defined concept.

Sweet Sweetback's Baadasssss Song opens with the title card, "This film is dedicated to all the Brothers and Sisters who have had enough of The Man." It starts with Sweet Sweetback at the age of twelve enjoying the pleasures of a woman and being commended for his sexual prowess. It jumps to his adulthood, where he is a ghetto pimp in Southern California exploiting his women for cash and using them for pleasure, and always enhancing his (legendary) reputation as a great stud. One day he agrees to go along with two white vice squad cops for an interrogation at the precinct so they will appear to be on the job to their superiors. On the way downtown, the racist cops brutalize a brother (deafening him with gunshots fired next to his ears). Sweetback explodes in anger (surprising even to himself) and beats the cops to death. (At one point he screams out, "You bled my momma. You bled my poppa. But you won't bleed me!") Now he is a fugitive, always one step ahead of the law. He finds refuge among his street cohorts and previous lovers, all of them on the wrong side of the law themselves. Every time the police catch up with him and Sweet Sweetback seems overwhelmed he manages to escape. Finally he crosses over the border into Mexico, still his own man against "the Man." The final title card warns, "Watch Out. A baad asssss nigger is coming back to collect some dues."

Sweet Sweetback's Baadasssss Song is very episodic, with musical bridges (the debut album of Earth, Wind and Fire) tying together this odyssey through the black underground. The lead character says little, almost a silent observer of the hell around him. The grainy photography and jerky sequences make this film a cinema verité look at oppressive ghetto life and provide, as one character in the picture says, "an overdose of black misery." The film is full of crude sex scenes (e.g., Sweet Sweetback copulating with a white girl as a group of bikers gather to watch) and ironic scenes of strong bigotry (e.g. white aggressors thinking they have found the fugitive Sweet Sweetback, beat up an innocent black man caught in bed with a white gal. "It's not him," one cop says. "So what," spit back the others, who have enjoyed the attack).

Melvin Van Peebles was born in Chicago in 1932, the son of a tailor. A graduate of Ohio Wesleyan Univeristy, he spent over three years in the United States Air Force as a navigator. By the late 1950s he had become interested in filmmaking and was shooting experimental short subjects. But as with flying, he could not break through racial discrimination and get a job of his choice in the motion picture industry. He and his family went to Holland in 1959, where he took graduate classes at the University of Amsterdam and acted at the Dutch National Theater. Knowing that if he published a viable novel, the French film industry would have to allow him to direct his own story, he wrote several books, including *La Permission*. He directed and wrote the screenplay for the low-budget film version, which as *The Story of a Three-Day Pass* was shown at the San Francisco International Film Festival (1967) as the French entry. It became a cult hit. The controversial and publicity-conscious black filmmaker soon became a much-discussed creative force. Van Peebles directed *Watermelon Man* (1970) with Godfrey Cambridge for Columbia Pictures (not a box-office winner).

So Van Peebles was already a known film industry entity when he shot this film for under $500,000 in nineteen days. He used largely non-union black personnel. As he would explain to *Newsweek* magazine in 1971, "All the films about black people up to now have been told through the eyes of the Anglo-Saxon majority—in their rhythms and speech and pace. They've been diluted to suit the white majority, just like Chinese restaurants tone down the spices to suit American tastes. I want white people to approach *Sweetback* the way they do an Italian or Japanese film. They have to understand *our* culture. In my film, the black audience finally gets a chance to see some of their own fantasies acted out—about rising out of the mud and kicking ass."

If it had been difficult to finance and shoot *Sweet Sweetback,* it was almost impossible to find distribution, especially after it was X-rated by the Motion Picture Association of America. (Van Peebles made much of it being rated X by an all-white jury.) At first, according to Van Peebles, only two theaters in the United States agreed to show it: a triple-bill movie house in Detroit and one in Atlanta, Georgia. Per the filmmaker, "Well, after the first showing [in Atlanta] people filed out of the theater very quietly. But by the next showing of *Sweetback* the lines were all around the block. By the third show it was just like Detroit. People were screaming, walking out with their pride."

When the daring film finally opened in New York in April 1971—thanks to Van Peebles' talent at promoting his project in any and every sector—the *New York Times*'s Roger Greenspun had mixed feelings about the film and its creator. He reported that Van Peebles ". . . has the talent, the intelligence and even the instincts of a good filmmaker. . . ." Then he added, "But in this movie the failure is so very nearly total that the ideas all turn into cliches and positively collaborate in taking things down." Later in his review he admits, ". . . the moments [in] which I really sense Van Peebles as a valuable presence are few and fleeting. But there are such moments, mostly in the brothel near the beginning . . . that show the director at work in the kind of moviemaking I hope he'll some day complete."

As the artistic and economic impact of this film became apparent, the critics used *Sweet Sweetback* as a platform for arguing their aesthetic theories. In a Sunday *New York Times* essay, reviewer Vincent Canby judged, "If Van Peebles' intent was to make a contemporary folk parable about a black saint, he has, I think, failed, not because his film vision is too grand, but because it's too simple. The movie looks exceedingly busy, but it isn't. . . . Behind this busy technique is a slight pale, escape drama, about a black man. . . . Nothing except camera technique is turned inside out in *Sweet Sweetback's Baadasssss Song.* It may be—as some of its supporters claim—the Black Experience in America, distilled to its essence. My feeling, distilled to its essence, is that that experience deserves a better film." In the same day's *New York Times,* black guest reviewer and commentator Clayton Riley acknowledged, "The film is an outrage. Designed to blow minds. A disgraceful and blasphemous parade of brilliantly precise stereotyping [of] Blacks and Whites, all drawn extravagantly and with impossible dimensions, all haunting our memory of what is true." But he also perceived, "With a nonprofessional cast, he charts a course through cinematic waters no one else has even put a toe in, makes visual revolutionaries of us all, lets us see a sector of ourselves we wish, perhaps, he had left alone.... I don't know if Van Peebles will be immortalized on a wall or put against one." Kevin Thomas *(Los Angeles Times)* praised, "...Van Peebles emerges with an emphatic style, one that captures the restless tempo of ghetto life in a jagged flood of vivid, often surreal images." In *Essence* magazine, Maurice Peterson decided, "Melvin Van Peebles is a general among filmmakers, strategically breaking open the film industry for himself and all black filmmakers to follow. His third and latest movie ... is not a great film, and it is not his best. Yet, it is an important film because it genuinely reflects the ghetto experience."

Sweet Sweetback's Baadasssss Song would gross $4,100,000 in domestic film rentals, an amazing box-office receipt for such an independent production. With the pattern set from this film and *Shaft,* Hollywood capitalized quickly on the emerging trend and then cast it aside in the mid-1970s when it found it no longer profitable.

After he personally turned *Sweet Sweetback* into a box-office success and himself into a media sweetheart as the multi-talented black expatriate who made good, Van Peebles turned to Broadway with *Ain't Supposed to Die a Natural Death* (1971) and *Don't Play Us Cheap* (1972), the latter of which he turned into a film. He moved into television and wrote the surprisingly sentimental *Just an Old Sweet Song* (1976), a CBS-TV telefeature starring Cicely Tyson and Robert Hooks. He was replaced as director of Richard Pryor's film *Greased Lightning* (1977), and his telefeature *The Sophisticated Gents* (q.v.), was begun in 1979 but did not get telecast until 1981. He was off–Broadway in 1981 directing *Bodybags* (1981) and handling multiple functions (directing, writing, music, lyrics) in *Waltz of the Stork* (1982), in which he appeared along with his son Mario. With his son he was co-featured in *Jaws IV: The Revenge* (1987). Also in the 1980s, Van Peebles gained recognition as being the first black trader on the American Stock Exchange.

205. T.N.T. Jackson (New World, 1975). Color, 70 minutes.

Producer/director Cirio H. Santiago; *screenplay* Dick Miller, Ken Metcalf; *art director* Ben Otico; *music* Tito Sotto; *assistant director* John Amazon; *sound* William Arkush, Demetrio de Santos; *camera* Felipe J. Sacdalan; *editors* Gervasio Santos, Barbara Pokras.

Cast: Jeanne Bell (T.N.T. Jackson); Stan Shaw (Charlie); Pat Anderson (Elaine); Ken Metcalfe (Sid); *and:* Chiquito, Chris Cruz, June Gamble, Percy Gordon, Leo Martin.

Rough-talking T.N.T. Jackson (Jeanne Bell) of Harlem, U.S.A., arrives in Hong Kong searching for her brother, Stack. The trail leads to a black brother named Charlie (Stan Shaw), who is involved in the heroin trade with his boss, Sid (Ken Metcalf). Charlie has already killed her brother, but T.N.T. does not know this when she seek information from the man. He pushes her into an affair, insisting, "Baby, I don't do favors and when I give, I get." By the finale, Sid and his white mistress, Elaine (Pat Anderson), are dead, and martial arts whiz T.N.T. has disposed of the dastardly Charlie.

"She's a one mama massacre squad," proclaimed the ads for this undistinguished action film, which was a poor imitation of that superior male

fantasy flick, *Cleopatra Jones* (1973) (q.v.). However, the few joys in this entry
are not the attractive but impassive Jeanne Bell karate-chopping and hapkido-
kicking her way through the hackneyed storyline, but in the scenery and the occasional offbeat dialogue interchanges. Right at the beginning T.N.T. is
depicted as a hot-tempered, no-sass-taking gal. No sooner has she landed in
Hong Kong and "accidentally" met white gal Elaine, who volunteers her help,
than T.N.T. is calling her "bitch." But then smart-mouthed Elaine (who is actually a police contact) has just advised the newcomer, "this isn't a safe place
for a bimbo." Later the two cross further verbal barbs:

> T.N.T. Honey. Get off my back.
> ELAINE: How amusing. I've never tried it that way.

When Charlie asks T.N.T., "What's your line?" she zings back, "You name it,
I do it." If only more of this film could have had that kind of double-entendre
smartness.
   T.N.T. Jackson was made in the Philippines and on location in Hong
Kong. *Variety* dismissed this pastiche with, "...the cartoon-level screenplay
... puts them [the kung fu sequences] into a laughable, often offensively
callous, context which producer-director Cirio Santiago fails to overcome with
his routine direction." Kevin Thomas *(Los Angeles Times)* was also perturbed
by the "...humorless bitter characters who related by fighting and killing. The
script is excessively racist."
   Actor Stan Shaw choreographed the martial arts scenes.
   T.N.T. Jackson grossed $1,300,000 in domestic film rentals.

206. The Take (Columbia, 1974). Color, 91 minutes.

   Executive producer Stanley Rubin; *producer* Howard Brandy; *director*
Robert Hartford-Davis; *based on the novel* "Sir, You Bastard" *by* G.F.
Newman; *screenplay* Del Reisman, Franklin Coen; *art director* Kirk Axtel;
music Fred Karlin; *assistant director* Robin Clark; *sound* Harold Etherington;
camera Duke Callaghan; *editor* Aaron Stell.
   Cast: Billy Dee Williams (Sneed); Eddie Albert (Chief Berrigan); Frankie
Avalon (Danny James); Sorrell Booke (Oscar); Tracy Reed (Nancy); Albert
Salmi (Dolek); Vic Morrow (Manso); A. Martinez (Tallbear); James Luisi
(Benedetto).
   By 1974 Hollywood was turning out so many blaxploitation features that
it had reached the point where a black performer could be in a film with no *real*
social conscience references to his color other than what the filmgoer brought
to the picture. In a continuation of the cross-over image he had established in
Hit! (1973) (q.v.), handsome and charming leading man Billy Dee Williams
starred as ranking cop named Sneed who is "on the take," as is fellow police
officer Dolek (Albert Salmi). They work for badgered Berrigan (Eddie Albert),
their harassed police chief. Sneed takes his ill-gotten proceeds from the underworld, controlled by Manso (Vic Morrow), and has his financial advisor, Oscar
(Sorrell Booke), invest it. Attractive Nancy (Tracy Reed) shares the good life
with self-absorbed Sneed. Once again it is shown that crime does *not* pay.

The hackneyed cops-and-robbers film was shot on location in New Mexico and was most notable for featuring ex–Beach Party singing star Frankie Avalon as a stool pigeon. *Variety* branded this a "routine police meller." Such films as *The Take* did nothing to enhance the screen career of Billy Dee Williams.

207. Take a Hard Ride (Twentieth Century–Fox, 1975). Color, 103 minutes.

Producers Harry Bernsen, Leon Chooluck; *director* Anthony M. Dawson [Antonio Margheriti]; *screenplay* Eric Bercovici, Jerry Ludwig; *art director* Julio Molina; *makeup* Carmen Martin; *music* Jerry Goldsmith; *stunts* Hal Needham, Juan Majo; *special effects* Luciano D'Achille, Antonio Molina; *camera* Riccardo Pallotini; *editor* Stanford C. Allen.

Cast: Jim Brown (Pike); Lee Van Cleef (Kiefer); Fred Williamson (Tyree); Catherine Spaak (Catherine); Jim Kelly (Kashtoh); Barry Sullivan (Sheriff Kane); Dana Andrews (Morgan); Harry Carey, Jr. (Duper); Robert Donner (Skave); Charles McGregor (Cloyd); Leonard Smith (Cagney); Ronald Howard (Halsey); Ricardo Palacios (Calvera); Robin Levitt (Chico); Buddy Joe Hooken (Angel).

Dying cattleman Morgan (Dana Andrews) asks helper Pike (Jim Brown) to deliver $86,000 from the sale of cattle in Abilene, Texas, to Morgan's widow at the spread in Sonora, Mexico. There Morgan is to become a partner in the new ranch cooperative. As Pike makes his way southward, the ride becomes harder. He is pursued by a bad lot including card sharp Tyree (Fred Williamson), heartless bounty hunter Kiefer (Lee Van Cleef), greedy sheriff Kane (Barry Sullivan), disreputable French gal Catherine (Catherine Spaak), and mute Indian Kashtoh (Jim Kelly).

Fred Williamson, Jim Brown, and Jim Kelly had teamed in *Three the Hard Way* (1974) (q.v.) to good results, but such was not the case in this spaghetti Western filmed on the cheap in the Canary Islands by Italian director Antonio Margheriti. In his 1½ star review, Jerry Oster *(New York Daily News)* scorned it as "spiceless," while Vicent Canby *(New York Times)* chided, "It goes on and on — it lurches, really — in little fits and starts of inspiration from dimly remembered earlier movies." Kevin Thomas *(Los Angeles Times)* branded it "a glum international western" which "compounds trite plotting and dialogue with unrelentingly tedious pacing in which pauses are held to the point of self-parody."

Of the three black male leads, Fred Williamson came off best with his good-bad cardplayer, a cheerful crook with a crafty sparkle in his eyes and a facetious remark always on his lips. As the honest cowpoke Pike, Jim Brown proved only that he could stay in the saddle while remaining emotionally immobile, and as the silent Indian, martial arts champ Jim Kelly had to reach beyond his acting acumen. *Take a Hard Ride* demonstrated two new factors in the Hollywood scene: violent black Westerns such as *The Legend of Nigger Charley* (1972) (q.v.) were now antique items, and always-busy film actor and director Fred Williamson had outdistanced top-billed Jim Brown as a popular and enduring black leading man.

Left–right: **Fred Williamson, Catherine Spaak, Jim Brown, and Jim Kelly in** *Take a Hard Ride* **(1975).**

208. The Tatoo Connection (World Northal, 1978). Color, 95 minutes.

Producer H. Wong; *director* Lee Tso-Nam; *screenplay* Luk Pak Sang; *music* Anders Nelsson, Perry Martin.

With: Jim Kelly, Chen Sing, Tan Tao Liang, Norman Wingrove, Bolo Yung.

Martial arts star Jim Kelly was reaching the end of his cinema popularity in this tattered, poorly dubbed mishmash which finds him as an American insurance agency representative in Hong Kong pursuing smugglers — led by underworld kingpin Bolo Yung — who have stolen an extremely precious diamond. Chen Sing, one of Yung's hoods, loves club singer Tan Tao Liang, but she is owned by the sadistic boss. Slam! Bang! Kick! Pow! Junk! Linda Gross *(Los Angeles Times)* rated it all "garish and violent" and judged of star Kelly that he ". . . exhibits less acting talent here than usual, but next to grass roots crew he is a polished pro."

209. Tenafly (NBC-TV, 2/12/73). Color, 100 minutes.

Executive producers Richard Levinson, William Link; *producer* Jon Epstein; *director* Richard Colla; *teleplay* Levinson, Link; *art director* George C. Webb; *music* Gil Melle; *camera* Emil Oster; *editor* Robert L. Kimble.

Cast: James McEachin (Harry Tenafly); Ed Nelson (Ted Harris); David Huddleston (Lieutenant Sam Church); John Ericson (Ken Shepherd); Mel Ferrer (Charlie Rush); Rosanna Huffman (Lorrie); Lillian Lehman (Ruth Tenafly); Lillian Randolph (Aunt Gertrude); Bill Walker (Uncle Walter); Paul M. Jackson, Jr. (Herbert Tenafly); Anne Seymour (Mrs. Castle); *with:* Don Beckley, Jack Denton, Bert Holland, Jackie Russell, Dwan Smith, Leonard Stone.

James McEachin and Lillian Lehman in *Tenafly* **(1973).**

Anxious to beat CBS-TV (who was preparing "Shaft" as a teleseries) into the marketplace with a black detective show, NBC-TV came up with "Tenafly," which it tested as a made-for-television feature in early 1973. "Distinct possibilities in sleuth division" was *Daily Variety*'s decision.

Instead of presenting the usual — a vicious black loner taking on the world with his fists and gun — *Tenafly* presented the unusual. (It was developed by the creator of "Columbo" and "Murder, She Wrote.") Harry Tenafly (James McEachin) is a happily married black Los Angeles detective who spends his weekends at home cutting the grass and enjoying suburban life with his understanding wife (Lillian Lehman) and their son (Paul Jackson). He may wear a floppy beach cap and leisure garb, but this police detective is a shrewd man with a meticulous mind. Tenafly is assigned to investigate the murder of the wife of talk show host Ted Harris (Ed Nelson). While the finger of guilt points at family friends and lawyer Charlie Rush (Mel Ferrer), the radio personality is the culprit (a fact made clear to viewers early on in the telefeature).

Equal on-camera time is devoted to police sleuthing and to Tenafly's congenial home life, as well as to Aunt Gertrude (Lillian Randolph), who wonders what happened to her vanishing husband (Bill Walker).

Convinced they had a viable entry for the new season, NBC-TV launched "Tenafly" on October 10, 1973 (one day after the TV "Shaft" debuted) as a 90-minute series, one of four rotating properties in the network's "Tuesday/ Wednesday Mystery Movie" show. But like "Shaft" on TV, this property was not what viewers expected or wanted. The violent action, the pulsating music, the slice of ghetto street life, were all missing. Like "Shaft," "Tenafly" the series disappeared after one season.

210. That Man Bolt (Universal, 1973). Color, 105 minutes.

Producer Bernard Schwartz; *associate producer* Philip Hazelton; *directors* Henry Levin, David Lowell Rich; *screenplay* Quentin Werty, Charles Johnson; *art director* Alexander Golitzen; *set decorator* Chester R. Bayhi; *music* Charles Bernstein; *assistant director* Phil Bowles; *stunt co-ordinator* Erik Cord; *martial arts adviser* Emil Farkas; *sound* Melvin M. Metcalfe, Sr.; *camera* Gerald Perry Finnerman; *special camera effects* Albert Whitlock; *editor* Carl Pingitore, Robert F. Shugrue.

Cast: Fred Williamson (Jefferson Bolt); Byron Webster (Griffiths); Miko Mayama (Dominique Kwan); Teresa Graves (Samantha Nightingale); Satoshi Nakamura (Kumada); John Orchard (Carter); Jack Ging (Connie Mellis); Ken Kazama (Spider); John Vassili Lambrinos (Raoul De Vargas); Paul Mantee (Mickey); David Chow (Chinese Thug).

A.K.A. *Thunderbolt; To Kill a Dragon.*

To his credit, as he plodded (and still does) through one grade-B action picture to another, Fred Williamson never lost his chosen screen presence. Lawrence Van Gelder *(New York Times)* analyzed the star's charisma as ". . . a ready smile, an unforced display of charm and a redeeming glint of mockery of the time-honored incredible foolishness in which he is enmeshed." Williamson required all the élan he could muster for the foolishness this time, which cast him as a dashing international courier and troubleshooter, a black James Bond of free enterprise. He has four residences (Hong Kong, Paris, London, and the United States) and a black belt in karate.

Jefferson Bolt (Fred Williamson) is hired to carry a million dollars from Hong Kong to Mexico City with a stopover in Los Angeles. Reaching Los Angeles, Raoul De Vargas (John Vassili Lambrinos) is told by the syndicate (which hired Bolt but is now uncertain of his skills or loyalties) to grab the money. Bolt escapes and heads to Las Vegas, where he has casino owner Connie Mellis (Jack Ging) check the money's origin. (It turns out the money is counterfeit.) Meanwhile, Bolt enjoys reacquainting himself with club singer Samantha Nightingale (Teresa Graves), but she is killed later in error by De Vargas. Bolt dispatches De Vargas and arrives in Hong Kong to avenge Samantha's death. Officious and offensive Britisher Griffiths (Byron Webster), who has been tracking Bolt all along, admits he is a government agent out to break the smuggling ring—headed by wealthy banker-businessman Kumada (Satoshi Nakamura)—that hired Bolt in the first place. After seducing Kumada's mistress, Dominique Kwan (Miko Mayama), Bolt joins with the government agents to destroy Kumada's fuel depot aboard two tankers and then goes to this enemy's island fortress. He eliminates a long-standing adversary, Spider (Ken Kazama). But before he can kill Kumada, Dominique kills him. Bolt ends up with the money, which everybody thought had been lost or destroyed.

There is not much that is right about this hack film. It boasts two directors (and all the conflicting style that brings) because Henry Levin, who handled the Hong Kong sequences, became ill and was replaced by David Lowell Rich for the American portions. If Williamson's character says "charming" once, the script has him say it two dozen times. It is the full range of his reaction to any situation, pleasant or otherwise. The scriptwriter makes him the type of man who says politely, "I always pay my debts in full," with the director(s) underlining in crude style the irony of the words. Characters mouth such platitudes as "You need friends, even bad ones like me." As with so many black action pictures of the mid-1970s, the black ghetto genre was spliced with the martial arts formula, and, here, with a strong dash of James Bond (a decade after that particular species had peaked). Actor Bryon Webster bears an uncanny resemblance to Robert Morley and milks that coincidence to a fare-thee-well. Neither the screeching car chases, the shooting fests, nor the Oriental defense arts are performed with much conviction.

Alan R. Howard of *The Hollywood Reporter* judged correctly when he wrote the story for *That Man Bolt:* ". . . lacks locomotion, character relationships and makes the lot almost incoherent. The movie has all the trimmings of an acceptable action film but none of the clarity or zest necessary to such entertainments."

211. They Call Me Mister Tibbs! (United Artists, 1970).
Color, 108 minutes.

Executive producer Walter Mirisch; *producer* Herbert Hirschman; *director* Gordon Douglas; *based on the character created by* John Dudley Ball; *story* Alan R. Trustman; *screenplay* Trustman, James R. Webb; *production designers* Clifford Yates, James F. McGuire; *art director* Addison F. Hehr; *set decorator* Edward G. Boyle; *makeup* Mark Reedall, Pat Fleming; *music* Quincy Jones; *assistant directors* Rusty Meek, Hal Washburn, Fred Brost; *technical adviser* Hal De Windt; *special effects* Justus Gibbs; *camera* Gerald Finnerman; *editor* Bud Molin.

Cast: Sidney Poitier (Lieutenant Virgil Tibbs); Martin Landau (Reverend Logan Sharpe); Barbara McNair (Valerie Tibbs); Anthony Zerbe (Rice Weedon); Jeff Corey (Captain Marden); David Sheiner (Herbert Kenner); Juano Hernandez (Mealie); Norma Crane (Marge Garfield); Edward Asner (Woody Garfield); Ted Gehring (Sergeant Deutsch); Beverly Todd (Puff); Linda Towne (Joy Sturges); George Spell (Andrew Tibbs); Wanda Spell (Ginger Tibbs); Garry Walberg (Medical Examiner).

Virgil Tibbs had exited from *In the Heat of the Night* (1967) (q.v.) on a wonderfully high note. The exemplary black detective returned to the screen on a far lesser plane (in every respect) in *They Call Me Mr. Tibbs!* (1970).

George Spell and Sidney Poitier in *They Call Me Mister Tibbs!* **(1970).**

According to Alvin H. Marill in *The Films of Sidney Poitier* (1978), "Poitier—now working out of San Francisco—is again up to here in a complex killing, but despite the militant tone of the title, and having gotten sainthood off his back, he does nothing more than methodically solve the murder of a hooker strangled in her flossy apartment, and demonstrate he's really just a plain cop with a wife, a mortgage, and two kids who fight and give mommy a headache."

Lieutenant Virgil Tibbs (Sidney Poitier) of the Homicide Division of the San Francisco Police Department is given an anonymous tip that a woman named Joy Sturges (Linda Towne) has been killed and that Reverend Logan Sharpe (Martin Landau) was seen leaving the lady's apartment (#3-A) at 110 St. James Street. It develops that the crusading minister, who heads the ghetto fight for community improvement and self-government, is a personal friend of Tibbs. When questioned, Sharpe admits that among his many calls that afternoon to congregation members he had visited Joy. The initial police investigation reveals there are several other key suspects: building janitor Mealie (Juano Hernandez) has his fingerprints all over the murder weapon, a blood-stained statue; Rice Weedon (Anthony Zerbe), a drug pusher and owner of the apartment house, has disappeared; realty company owner Woody Garfield (Edward Asner) is on record as having paid the victim's rent; and Garfield's hot-tempered wife, Marge (Norma Crane), may have known about her husband and Joy. The hunt focuses on Weedon; after he escapes again from Tibbs, prostitute Puff (Beverly Todd) alerts Tibbs that Mealie may have further information. Mealie's data redirects the trail to Sharpe, who confesses to killing Joy because she questioned his masculinity. When Tibbs refuses to postpone arresting the clergyman until after the voting is finished on a community issue he endorsed, Sharpe escapes and throws himself under a truck.

The critics were not pleased with this second installment of what would be the Virgil Tibbs trilogy. "With *They Call Me Mister Tibbs!*, Poitier establishes another inalienable right, that of the black movie star to make the sort of ordinary, ramshackly entertaining, very close to pointless movie that a white movie star like Frank Sinatra has been allowed to get away with for most of his career.... Tibbs is a type without being a person. He is the Good Black Cop, a role Poitier already played with fine artistic and financial results..." (Vincent Canby, *New York Times*). "The picture is an amiable and mildly idiotic one that would have done better, I should think, chopped up as soap opera on television..." (Penelope Gilliant, *The New Yorker*). Regarding Poitier, Jim Meyer *(The Miami Herald)* voted, "...I'd be less than honest if I said he's great in this film. If anything, this could be his weakest characterization ever."

What annoyed reviewers and filmgoers alike was the excessive amount of screen time devoted to Virgil Tibbs's home life as he romances and spars with his wife (Barbara McNair), encourages their young daughter (Wanda Spell), and chides their mischievous but basically bright and good-hearted son (George Spell). Rather than focus on the police action drama, director Gordon Douglas chooses to linger everlastingly on coy domestic scenes such as Tibbs punishing his son's cigarette-smoking by making the youth puff on a foul-tasting cigar. Right out of TV-land are such harangues by Tibbs's wife as, "You're never home. Why don't you stay home and control your son? You can't solve that murder and you're late for dinner as usual. You go in there and make him pick it up [the mess] if you can."

They Call Me Mister Tibbs! earned a respectable $2,350,000 in domestic film rentals, leading to the following year's *The Organization* (1971) (q.v.).

212. The Thing with Two Heads (American International, 1972). Color, 93 minutes.

Presenter Samuel Z. Arkoff; *executive producer* John Lawrence; *producer* Wes Bishop; *director* Lee Frost; *story* Frost, Bishop; *screenplay* Frost, Bishop, James Gordon White; *makeup* Rick Baker; *creative makeup designers* Dan Striepeke, Gail Brown, Tom Burman, Charles Schram, White, Peter Peterson; *music* Robert O. Ragland; *songs* David Angel, Porter Jordan; *stunts* Bud Elkins, Paul Nuckles; *camera* Jack Steely; *editor* Ed Forsyth.

Cast: Ray Milland (Dr. Maxwell Kirshner); Rosey Grier (Jack Moss); Don Marshall (Dr. Fred Williams); Roger Perry (Dr. Philip Desmond); Kathy Baumann (Nurse Patricia); Chelsea Brown (Lila); John Dullaghan (Thomas); John Bliss (Dr. Donald Smith); Rick Baker (Gorilla); Lee Frost (Sergeant Hacker); Dick Whittington (TV Newscaster); William Smith (Hysterical Condemned Man); Tommy Cook (Chaplain); Bruce Kimball (Police Lieutenant); Jane Kellem (Miss Mullen); Wes Bishop (Dr. Smith); Roger Gentry (Police Sergeant); Britt Nilsson (Nurse); Phil Hoover (Policeman); Rod Steele (Medical Salesman); Michael Viner (Prison Guard); Jerry Butler, George E. Carey, Albert Zugsmith (Guest Performers).

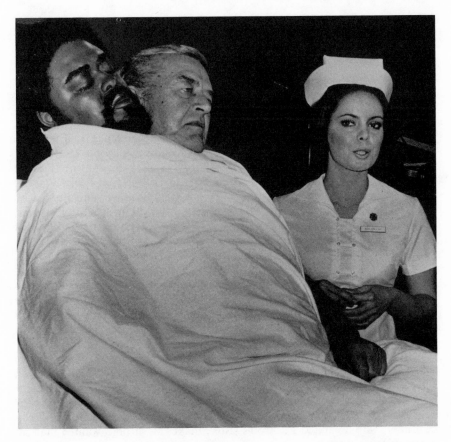

Rosey Grier and Ray Milland are *The Thing with Two Heads* (1972); Kathy Baumann is the nurse.

This is one of those absurd cheap exploitation pictures whose plot is as extravagantly silly as its title. This minor entry not only has the distinction of co-starring Academy Award winner Ray Milland and ex-pro football star Rosey Grier, but it throws in bigotry as well.

Scientist Dr. Maxwell Kirshner (Ray Milland) realizes he is dying of cancer and has his head transplanted onto the body of a condemned killer, intending, as with his previous gorilla experiments, to remove the unwanted head in later surgery. To his surprise the racist finds his head is now on the body of a black man, Jack Moss (Rosey Grier). Since Moss (equally surprised by the turn of events) controls his body, he escapes the operating theater before the next operational step occurs. Moss is intent on proving his innocence of the homicide, of which he is accused, and he must elude the police till he does. Kirshner is intent on gaining control of his body.

The inept car chases are equalled only by the amateurish special effects makeup.

213. Thomasine and Bushrod (Columbia, 1974). Color, 93 minutes.

Producers Harvey Bernhard, Max Julien; *director* Gordon Parks, Jr.; *screenplay* Julien; *production designer* Dale Beldin; *costumes* Andra Lilly; *music* Coleridge-Taylor Perkinson; *song* Arthur Lee; *assistant director* Robert Anderson; *sound* Tom Overton, Dennis Jones; *camera* Lucien Ballard; *editor* Frank C. Decot.

Cast: Max Julien (Bushrod); Vonetta McGee (Thomasine); George Murdock (Sheriff Bogardie); Glynn Turman (Jomo); Juanita Moore (Pecolia); Joel Fluellen (Nathaniel); Jackson D. Kane (Adolph); Bud Conlan (Mr. Tyler); Kip Allen (Jenkins); Ben Zeller (Scruggs); Herb Robins (Dodson); Harry Luck (Sheriff); Jason Bernard (Seldon); Paul Barby (Teller); Scott Britt (Frank); Geno Silva (Taffy); John Gill (Card Dealer); Dave Burleson (Card Player); James Sargeant (Farley); Leigh Potter, Tedi Altrice (Washerwomen); Charles Gaines (Bar Customer); Katy Martin (Mrs. Tyler); Patricia Milner (Mrs. Carter); Brad Woolley (Ricky); Lilybell Crawford (Lady in Bank); Max Cisneros (Kane); Neil Davis (Barber); Raleigh Gardenhire (Renegade).

Max Julien, the iconoclastic film personality who had starred in *The Mack* (1973) (q.v.), had originally written *Cleopatra Jones* (1973) (q.v.) for screen actress Vonetta McGee, with whom he shared his off-screen life. Finally the two highly publicized black lovers were united in this imitation *Bonnie and Clyde* (1967), set in the Southwest of 1911 to 1914. Their director was the well-regarded Gordon Parks, Jr., whose only previous feature film had been *Super Fly* (1972) (q.v.).

In 1911 Texas, ex–bounty huntress Thomasine (Vonetta McGee) is on the rough edge, and ends up in prison. There she learns her ex-lover, Bushrod (Max Julien), is still alive, but that he has given up being an outlaw and is now a horse breaker. When she gets out of prison she locates him, and together they embark on a fresh life. But a deadly encounter with Adolph Smith (Jackson D. Kane), who assaulted Bushrod's sister, makes Bushrod a wanted man all over again.

Thomasine and Bushrod become bank robbers. They become folk heroes as they move from town to town (usually in a fancy automobile) and always sharing their spoils with Indians, Mexicans and poor whites. Hot on their trail is vindictive white Sheriff Bogardie (George Murdock), who wants revenge on Bushrod for having humiliated him. Blind gypsy woman Pecolia (Juanita Moore) warns them of impending trouble, but they do not heed her. Later, when the duo get into trouble, it is their mysterious Jamaican friend, Jomo (Glynn Turman), who appears suddenly to save them. Bogardie guns down Jomo, and later the sheriff shoots Thomasine. Bushrod, also mortally wounded, kills Bogardie before he dies.

What gives the PG rated *Thomasine and Bushrod* is engaging flavor is not its period settings (for there are many anachronisms in language and props), nor its derivative outlaws-versus-the-law theme, and certainly not its pacing (for there are many torpid sequences), but the obvious chemistry between the co-leads. Thomasine is the type of sassy lady, who is self-sufficient, liberated, yet comfortable enough with herself to be feminine and playful. She is the holdup lady who wants equal billing on the wanted posters. In contrast (especially to the macho black action heroes of the 1970s), Bushrod may be manly and daring, but he craves the quiet, peaceful life. Clearly an intriguing twist on the historic roles of male and female, with only occasional reversions to macho supremacy, as when Bushrod becomes angered and slaps his lady love.

Nora Sayre *(New York Times)* judged this offbeat entry "a black Western of considerable freshness," and *Variety* praised, "Julien's story is straightforward for the most part, his dialog realistic and characters well developed." Unfortunately, targeted audiences of the day preferred their filmgoing more violent, and *Thomasine and Bushrod* was not a large success at the box-office.

It marked the virtual end of Max Julien's screen career, while Vonetta McGee would continue to expand as an actress both in genre films (*Brothers* [1977] [q.v.]), and in mainstream productions (Clint Eastwood's *The Eiger Sanction* [1975]). In the 1980s she continued her career mostly on television — even to being the nun Sister Indigo on Robert Blake's short-lived teleseries "Hell Town" (1985) and then opposite Jimmie Walker in "Bustin' Loose" (1987–88). As for Gordon Parks, Jr., he would return to more commercial form in *Three the Hard Way* (1974), *infra*.

Thomasine and Bushrod was shot on location in New Mexico in and around Santa Fe.

214. Three the Hard Way (Allied Artists, 1974). Color, 93 minutes.

Presenter Emanuel L. Wolf; *producer* Harry Bernsen; *associate producer* Leon Chooluck; *director* Gordon Parks, Jr.; *screenplay* Eric Bercovici, Jerry Ludwig; *costumes* William Platt; *makeup* Webster C. Phillips; *music/music director* Richard Tufo; *music supervisor* Carl Prager; *songs* Tufo and Lowell Simon; *assistant director* Eugene Anderson; *stunt co-ordinator* Hal Needham; *sound* Alan Bernard; *special effects* Joe Lombardi; *camera* Lucien Ballard; *editor* Robert Swink.

Cast: Jim Brown (Jimmy Lait); Fred Williamson (Jagger Daniels); Jim Kelly (Mr. Keyes); Sheila Frazier (Wendy Kane); Jay Robinson (Monroe Feather); Charles McGregor (Charley); Howard Platt (Keep); Richard Angarola (Dr. Fortrero); David Chow (Link); Marian Collier (Eva); Junero Jennings (House); Alex Rocco (Lieutenant DiNisco); Corbin Bernsen (Boy); Renie Radich (Girl); Janice Carroll (Nurse); Angelyn Chester (Chicago Girl); Norman Evans (New York Cop); Pamela Serpe (Countess); Marie O'Henry (Princess); Irene Tsu (Empress); Robert Cleaves (Doctor); Roberta Collins (Lait's Secretary); Lance Taylor (Pool Player); Jeanne Bell (Polly); Victor Brandt, Mario Roccuzzo, Don Gazzeniga (Guards); Fred Cash, Sam Gooden, Ralph Johnson, Reggie Torian (The Impressions).

If one black action star isn't enough to draw in lots of moviegoers, how about teaming three together? If the overplayed black action genre seemed stale by the mid-1970s, how about combining it with bits of the equally overplayed martial arts and James Bond species? And, for good measure, hire perceptive director Gordon Parks, Jr., best known for his premier feature film, *Super Fly* (1972) (q.v.). The resulting amalgam is *Three the Hard Way*.

Top: **Vonetta McGee and Max Julien in** *Thomasine and Bushrod* **(1974).** *Bottom, left–right:* **Fred Williamson, Jim Brown, and Jim Kelly in** *Three the Hard Way* **(1974).**

Los Angeles–based record promoter Jimmy Lait (Jim Brown) learns from seriously wounded House (Junero Jennings) that there is a growing conspiracy against the black race. Before House can reveal more facts, he is killed, and Lait's girlfriend, Wendy Kane (Sheila Frazier), is kidnapped. She is held prisoner by deranged financier Monroe Feather (Jay Robinson), a neo–Nazi who has had Dr. Fortrero (Richard Angarola) develop a serum which will kill only black people. It is Feather's plan to foster racial purification. Understanding the task ahead, Lait teams with his Chicago friend, Jagger Daniels (Fred Williamson), and their New York karate expert pal, Mr. Keyes (Jim Kelly), to combat Feather's death squad. Learning that Feather intends to contaminate Los Angeles, Detroit, and Washington, D.C., the trio separates for each to tackle one city. They succeed in overwhelming Feather's goons (who intend to feed the deadly serum into the cities' water supplies) and then rejoin to storm Feather's headquarters. Feather, Dr. Fortrero and their underlings are eliminated, and Wendy is rescued.

With such an outrageous plot, little wonder that crashing cars and exploding buildings are scenario highlights. As for the hero trio, "They all swagger too much and don't know what to do with their hands when they aren't massacring the enemy. Sometimes they play chess" (Vincent Canby, *New York Times*). Regarding the overall movie, "It's the kind of film that cues soundtrack lyrics about making the world more peaceful to scenes depicting principals blowing off the heads of opponents" *(Variety)*.

But the film's producers knew what they were doing when they concocted this synthetic actioner. Made on an estimated budget of $1,400,000, it grossed $3,000,000 in domestic film rentals. It led to further teaming of the dynamic threesome in tales of violence and mayhem.

Jay Robinson, who is featured herein as the white supremacist, made a screen speciality of such raving lunatics; he was the Emperor Caligula in *The Robe* (1953) and its sequel, *Demetrius and the Gladiators* (1954). In the small role of "the boy" is Corbin Bernsen, who would rise to TV prominence in "L.A. Law" (1986–).

215. Three Tough Guys (Paramount, 1974). Color, 92 minutes.

Producer Dino De Laurentiis; *director* Duccio Tessari; *screenplay* Luciano Vincenzoni, Nicola Badalucco; *art director* Francesco Bronzi; *music* Isaac Hayes; *assistant director* Gianni Cozzi; *sound* Paul Oddo; *camera* Aldo Tonti; *editors* Mario Morra, Richard Marks.

Cast: Lino Ventura (Father Charlie); Isaac Hayes (Lee Stevens); Fred Williamson (Joe Snake); Paula Kelly (Fay Collins); William Berger (Captain Ryan); Luciano Salce (Bishop); Vittorio Sanipoli (Mike Petralia); Jacques Herlin (Tequila); Jess Hahn (Bartender); Lorella De Luca (Anne Lombardo); Thurman E. Scott (Tony Red); Mario Erpichini (Gene); Guido Leontini (Sergeant Sam); Joel Cory (Truckdriver); Dutchell Smith (Streetwalker); Ira Rogers (Lou); Margot Novick (Prostitute); Tommy Brubaker (Hood); Buddy Stein (Cab Driver); Max Kleven (Huge Man); Walt Scott (Petralia's Man); Frank Grimaldi (Blinky); Emanuele Spatafora (Joe Bell); Hans Jung Bluth (Mechanic).

Isaac Hayes in *Three Tough Guys* **(1974).**

Dino De Laurentiis had great success with his rash of Mafioso gangster films in the 1970s. He had already used black action star Fred Williamson to flush out the rise and fall of underworld figure *Crazy Joe* (1974) (q.v.), and now Williamson was teamed with Oscar-winning song writer Isaac Hayes (making his screen debut) and Italian-born character lead Lino Ventura. It was an intriguing combination. "For a 'B' flick, it offers suspense and action without pandering to racism. As a plus, it has some very witty dialog and excellent photography; and, needless to say, Isaac Hayes' musical score is dynamite" (Maurice Peterson, *Essence* magazine).

In Chicago, Father Charlie (Lino Ventura) is a very unusual priest, for he is an ex-convict. And, most unusual, he is one who has not severed all his ties to the criminal world or ways. To set the record straight about a dead friend, Father Charlie goes on a rampage, but he knows he cannot do it alone. He teams with framed ex-cop Lee Stevens (Isaac Hayes) to hunt down multiple-killer Joe Snake (Fred Williamson), the clever criminal responsible for Stevens's now serving time as a defrocked cop and short order cook. Before the score is settled with Joe Snake, the ambitious hoodlum has permanently silenced prostitute Fay Collins (Paula Kelly), who had stashed away $1,000,000 in stolen bank money (the crux of the vendetta).

"International junk of no interest" was Vincent Canby's *(New York Times)* verdict of this mindless, violent powerplay, even with Isaac Hayes's fresh soundtrack score. (And it is Hayes who gets to beat up Williamson at the film's finale.)

Location filming for *Three Tough Guys* was accomplished in Chicago, with interiors shot in Rome. Most of the supporting cast's dialogue was (poorly) redubbed for United States distribution. "The few non-dubbed performers— Hayes, Williamson, Kelly—are nearly as unconvincing as the others," complained Lee Beaupre *(Variety),* but he noted, "Thurman E. Scott stands out in a small role by offering the first vocal parody of Mae West by a black male."

216. ...Tick ...Tick ...Tick (Metro-Goldwyn-Mayer, 1970.) Color, 96 minutes.

Producers Ralph Nelson, James Lee Barrett; *associate producer* William S. Gilmore, Jr.; *director* Nelson; *screenplay* Barrett; *art directors* George W. Davis, William Glasgow; *set decorators* Robert R. Benton, Don Greenwood, Jr.; *music* Jerry Styne; *songs* Glasner Brothers and Jimmy Payne; John Hartford; Jack Clement; Glasner Brothers; Arthur Owens; *music supervisor* Mike Curb; *assistant directors* Michael Glick, Newt Arnold; *recording supervisor* Franklin Milton; *sound* Bruce Wright; *camera* Loyal Griggs; *editor* Alex Barton.

Cast: Jim Brown (Sheriff Jimmy Price); George Kennedy (John Little); Fredric March (Mayor Jeff Parks); Lynn Carlin (Julia Little); Don Stroud (Bengy Springer); Janet MacLaughlin (Mary Price); Richard Elkins (Bradford Wilkes); Clifton James (D.J. Rankin); Bob Random (John Braddock); Mills Watson (Deputy Joe Warren); Bernie Casey (George Harley); Anthony James (H.C. Talbert); Dub Taylor (Junior); Ernest Anderson (Homer); Karl Swanson (Braddock, Sr.); Barry Cahill (Bob Braddock); Anne Whitefield (Mrs. Dawes); Bill Walker (John Sawyer); Dan Frazer (Ira Jackson); Leonard O. Smith (Fred Price); Renny Roker (Shoeshine Boy); Roy E. Glenn, Sr. (The Drunk); George Cisar (Barber); Paulene Myers (Mrs. Harley); Dino Washington (Randy Harley); Calvin Brown (Harrison Harley); Beverly Taylor (Sara Jean).

In 1970 Hollywood was still easing into racial integration themes with b-i-g message pictures packed with (they hoped) enough action to keep audiences awake. Who else could play the action lead but peripatetic Jim Brown, caught in a black-versus-white confrontation in the steamy Deep South. Seen today this film seems generated by a computer scenarist, and many of the performances, especially Fredric March's, are overblown. Brown is his usual stiff, awkward, but forceful self, with Janet MacLachlan impressively thoughtful in her abbreviated, reactive role as the sheriff's concerned wife. Howard Thompson

(New York Times) judged it a "conventionally rigged account" but noted that "Mr. Brown stands straight and tall." Thompson went on to amplify, "It is the sight and sound of Mr. Brown that makes and saves the picture. Still a tenative actor, this big, fine-looking giant of a man has a rock-ribbed sincerity and natural dignity that rivet attention as he handles his first trouble."

Jimmy Price (Jim Brown) is the first black sheriff in Colusa County, Mississippi, elected with the help of Northern organizers (who have flown back home) and against the votes of the local Ku Klux Klan. Elderly Mayor Jeff Parks (Fredric March) advises Price on his first day in office to arrest wealthy young white John Braddock (Bob Random) for vehicular manslaughter. That evening bigoted Bengy Springer (Don Stroud), ex-sheriff John Little's (George Kennedy) former deputy, beats up Price's black deputy (Richard Elkins)—a Vietnam veteran—and mean Springer insists he will kill Price. Meanwhile Price, unmindful that it may cost him black support, arrests black militant George Harley (Bernie Casey), who has raped a young girl. When Braddock's father (Karl Swenson) threatens Price that he will bring friends to get his snobbish son released from jail, Spunky John Little comes to Price's rescue by accepting a deputy's badge. Price asks the mayor to call in federal troops to prevent a riot, but the distraught mayor delays. Price and Little prepare to stand off the mob. At the last minute they are joined by recruits from Jimmy's, a whites-only local bar.

For Jim Brown, who had played a lawman in the Old West in *100 Rifles* (1969) (q.v.), this was an extension of his "good black man" image which, by the time of his movie comeback in *Slaughter* and *Black Gunn* (both 1972) (qq.v.), would alter drastically.

217. To Kill a Cop (NBC-TV, 4/10–11/78). Color, 200 minutes.

Executive producer David Gerber; *producer* James H. Brown; *director* Gary Nelson; *based on the novel by* Robert Daley; *teleplay* Ernest Tidyman; *art directors* Ross Bellah, Ward Preston; *costume designer* Grady Hunt; *music* Lee Holdridge; *technical adviser* Sonny Grosso; *sound* Mike Traynor, George Roncone; *special effects* Ed Drohan, Marcel Vercoutere; *camera* Gayne Rescher; *editors* Donald R. Rode, Harry Kaye.

Cast: Joe Don Baker (Chief Earl Eischied); Louis Gossett, Jr. (Everett Walker); Patrick O'Neal (Police Commissioner); Desi Arnaz, Jr. (Martin Delahanty); Christine Belford (Agnes Cusack); Eartha Kitt (Paula); George Di Cenzo (Captain Cornworth); Julius W. Harris (Detective Baker); Joyce Van Patten (Betty Eischied); Ken Swofford (Lieutenant Fitzgerald); Alan Fudge (Ralph O'Connor); Rosey Grier (Albert Hoyt); Diana Muldaur (Florence Kowski); Alan Oppenheimer (Captain Finnerty); Eddie Egan (Chief Ed Palmer); Gene Woodbury (Mark D.); Kim Delgado (Butch); Robert Hooks (Captain Pete Rolfe); Scott Brady (Inspector James Gleason); Nathan George (Charles); Milton Selzer (Myron Klopfman); Ric Mancini (Mike Cusack); Rosalind Miles (Ida); Allen Price (Richie); Joe Maross (District Attorney); David Toma (Louis); Sonny Grosso (Malfitano); *and:* Chip McAllister, Heshimu Cumbuka, Bill Deiz, Terrence McNally, Al White.

This project proved to be one of those big two-part telefeatures that looks much better in the promotional ad campaign than in the gritty actuality.

Black militant Everett Walker (Louis Gossett, Jr.) has been out of the country and out of touch for over a decade. He returns to New York bent on stirring up a revolution and recruits a new radical squad, including killers Mark D. (Gene Woodbury) and Charles (Nathan George), and the unwilling Paula (Eartha Kitt). His plan involves a police massacre. Squashing the situation is New York City's finest, Chief of Detective Earl Eischied (Joe Don Baker), who must administer his staff, solve and prevent crimes, juggle politics with the likes of the police commissioner (Patrick O'Neal), and stave off his ex-wife (Joyce Van Patten) while pacifying his girlfriend (Diana Muldaur). Weaving in and out of the action are such black law enforcers as Captain Pete Rolfe (Robert Hooks) and Detective Baker (Julius W. Harris). For the obligatory young-romantic interludes there are Martin Delahanty (Desi Arnaz, Jr.) and Agnes Cusack (Christine Belford), two members of the patrol team. *Daily Variety* endorsed the production as being "directed imaginatively" and acknowledged that "[Ernest] Tidyman supplies strong narrative and solid characters."

The telefeature boasted three real-life (ex) New York policemen: on-camera were Eddie Egan and David Toma and Sonny Grosso (who also served as technical adviser). Joe Don Baker reprised his role as the maverick cop in the NBC-TV "Eischied" series (1979–80).

218. Together Brothers (Twentieth Century–Fox, 1974).
Color, 94 minutes.

Executive producer Sanford Howard; *producer* Robert L. Rosen; *director* William A. Graham; *story* Jack De Witt; *screenplay* De Witt, Joe Green; *costumes* Raymond H. Summers; *music* Barry White; *songs/music arrangers* White and Gene Page; *music director* Page; *creative/technical consultant* Dr. Arthur Thomas; *assistant directors* James H. Brown, Jay Daniel; *sound* Bud Alper, Richard Portman; *camera* Philip Lanthrop, Charles Rosher; *editor* Stanley E. Johnson.

Cast: Ahmad Nurradin (H.J.); Anthony Wilson (Tommy); Nelson Sims (A.P.); Kenneth Bell (Mau Mau); Owen Page (Monk); Kim Dorsey (Gri Gri); Ed Bernard (Mr. Kool); Lincoln Kilpatrick (Billy Most); Glynn Turman (Dr. Johnson); Richard Yniguez (Vega); Mwako Cumbuka (Strokes McGee); Frances Williams (Mama Wes); Craig Campfield (Maria); Bessie Griffin (Reverend Brown); Lynne Holmes (Sugar); Danny Big Black (Armstrong); Gloria Calomee (Alice Martin); Charles Lemons (Matthews); Joe Zapata (Chicano); Leah Ward (Clutie); William Dagg (Desk Officer); Roberta Ester (Nurse); Ernest Boyde (Harry); John Jennings (Policeman); Lane Mitchell (Dude); Angela Gibbs (Francine); Howard Picard (Police Detective).

This variation of the "Boy Who Cried Wolf" theme was made over into the black idiom. With its uncompromising study of life on the rough side of the ghetto (in Galveston, Texas), *Together Brothers* is a far cry from the typical blood and guts of let's-get-whitey pictures of this period. "Laced with all the elements required for this type of attraction, word-of-mouth should help its chances in general market where very often good black films have more appeal than many mediocre white features" *(Variety)*.

When "Mr. Kool" (Ed Bernard), a black cop beloved in the neighborhood,

Lincoln Kilpatrick and Anthony Wilson in *Together Brothers* **(1974).**

is gunned down everyone wants to know the reason. "Why him?" says one cop.
"Because he was a black cop in the jungle," responds another. Everyone is sure
the senseless crime will never be solved. But this is not good enough for fifteen-
year-old H.J. (Ahmad Nurradin), who intends to avenge the death of his
friend. Helping him is young Tommy (Anthony Wilson), who was traumatized
by witnessing the homicide, along with the rowdy members of H.J.'s gang. As
their home-brewed investigation pushes onward, H.J. breaks into the local
police station to gain a list of suspects in the killing. He begins tracking the
clues up and down the streets of the ghetto, leading him to whores, crooks,
plain folks, and the bizarre. The path turns to blondized drag queen Maria
(Craig Campfield) who, it develops, has been harboring Mr. Kool's killer, the
deranged Billy Most (Lincoln Kilpatrick). Before the chase is over, innocent
Francine (Angela Gibbs) has been stabbed to death, Maria has been strung up
by Billy Most, and the police capture the psychotic killer.

Even with its inferior cinematography and low production values, *Together Brothers* presents a striking microcosm of street life, from the black and Chicano gangs, to the pimps, prostitutes, storekeepers, barroom and poolhall dwellers, and everyday folk of the ghetto—all with their hopes, frustrations and resentments against the Man. The pacing is extremely slow, with character vignettes frequently impeding the forward thrust of the plot. But holding the motion picture together is an energetic performance by Ahmad Nurradin (in his film debut) and, especially, that of winsome Anthony Wilson as the little boy left speechless by the friendly cop's death. Without saying a word throughout most of the picture, he registers very credible reactions ranging from fear to puzzlement to boredom to engrossment. By the end of the thriller, with the crazed Billy Most jail-bound, his voice returns. "I want to go home, I'm hungry," he says and the film ends on this upbeat note of normalcy.

The soundtrack music for *Together Brothers* is by Barry White and his group, Love Unlimited.

219. Top of the Heap (Fanfare, 1972). Color, 83 minutes.

Producer Christopher St. John; *associate producer* Richard Kobritz; *director* St. John; *story* Bradford Cray; *screenplay* St. John; *art director* Norman Houle; *set decorator* Robert Signorelli; *costumes* Eddie Marks; *makeup* Maurice Stein; *music* J.J. Johnson; *sound effects* Gene Elliot; *special effects* Tim Smyth; *camera* Richard Kelley; *editor* Mike Pozen.

Cast: Christopher St. John (George Lattimer); Paula Kelly (Black Chick the Singer); Florence St. Peter (Viola Lattimer); Leonard Kuras (Bobby Gelman); Patrick McVey (Tim Cassidy); John Alderson (Captain Walsh); Ingeborg Sorenson (Nurse Swenson); Allen Garfield [Goorwitz] (Taxi Driver); Ron Douglas (Hip Passenger); Almeria Quinn (Valerie Lattimer); Beatrice Webster (George's Mother); Essie McSwine (African Dancer); Jerry Jones (Club Owner); Willie Harris (Bouncer); Tiger Joe Marsh (Man with Knife); John McMurtry (Dope Dealer); Raymond O'Keefe (Bus Driver); Brian Cutler (Rookie Policeman); Hedgemon Lewis, Kenneth Norton (Men in Bar); Oamu King, Ji-Tu Cumbuka (Drug Peddlers); Marilyn Wirt (Nurse); Angela Seymour (Young Hooker); Joe Tornatore (Policeman); Ann Mason (Walsh's Secretary); Maria Lennard, Mayrtia Varna, Dan Roth, Arnold Dover (Reporters); June Fairchild (Balloon Thrower); Cliff Emmich (Hard Hat); Pamela Whorf (Girl Rioter); Richard M. Dixon (The President).

"All you care about is puttin' on that damn uniform and gun and playin' the big nigger cop," yells George's mother (Beatrice Webster). But George Latimer (Christopher St. John) has other problems. He is sick of being a Washington, D.C., cop. "I'm tired of having to look at all the shit I see everytime I go out there on the street with that gun strapped to my hip.... I've been living that way for twelve long-assed years. I used to really think I was going to make it. Yeah, had me some plans. Twelve years as a flat-footed cop for what? I ain't goin' out there anymore to fight the Man's war no more."

George is having problems with his wife (Florence St. Peter) and can't seem to satisfy his struggling club singer–mistress (Paula Kelly). His thirteen-year-old daughter (Almeria Quinn) is on the verge of being drug-addicted. He is passed over for a promotion at the precinct, and he is short of money. Patronized by the white police bureaucracy, he is scoffed at by his brothers and sisters for being part of the white establishment police force. Little wonder that the distraught man screams, "I can do anything I goddam want," and takes to dreaming and fantasizing of a different way of life, whether it be as a jungle lord, a heroic astronaut on the moon, or having a rampant affair with a voluptuous blonde nurse at the hospital. But his dreams (nightmares?) end, and after a halfhearted attempt at breaking free of his chains, he settles back into "normalcy." He adjusts to his mother's death in Alabama, he gives up his mercenary mistress, and he returns to his family and to his job as a cop. Back on night patrol in a quiet residential part of town, he is killed by an assassin's bullet.

Christopher St. John had gained popularity as the black militant Ben Buford in *Shaft* (1971) (q.v.), and in this self-controlled production he ambitiously attempts to present multi-levels of thought and frustration regarding a black in a black-and-white world. "Occasionally manages to develop a measure of genuine interest as a movie, to break out of the already deadly stereotypes of black-white confrontations films to become ironic, sometimes fantatic, and even comic" (Roger Greenspun, *New York Times*). *Variety* noted, "Script proceeds on theory that an over-abudance of four-letter words and salty language creates realism."

220. Top Secret (NBC-TV, 6/4/78). Color, 100 minutes.

Executive producer Sheldon Leonard; *producer* David Levinson; *associate producers* Michael Economou, Leon Chooluck; *director* Paul Leaf; *teleplay* Levinson; *art director* Pier-Luigi Basile; *music* Tea Macero, Stu Gardner; *camera* Gabor Pogany; *editor* Economou.

Cast: Bill Cosby (Aaron Strickland); Tracy Reed (McGee); Sheldon Leonard (Carl Vitale); Gloria Foster (Judith); George Brenlin (Murphy); Paolo Turco (Gino); Luicano Bartoli (Pietro); Marisa Merlini (Rosa Tattaglia); Francesca DeSapio (Brigitte); Leonard Traviglio (Tomas); Byrna Rostran (Christian); Craig Hill (Zeeger); Walter Williams (Macaferri); Nat Bush (Sergeant); Paul Leaf (Painter).

It had been a decade since Bill Cosby played glib Alexander Scott in "I Spy" (1965–68). He returned to the espionage game in this mild telefeature produced by (and co-starring) Sheldon Leonard, the executive producer of "I Spy." Artists' agent Aaron Strickland (Bill Cosby)—who is working for the United States government—must recover a cache of plutonium before terrorists explode it. Strickland leaves his cozy, cool pad and his mate, Judith (Gloria Foster), to team with co-agent McGee (Tracy Reed), a very self sufficient, attractive operative. The film is mild diversion at best, but several degrees more entertaining than the international intrigue of Cosby's later *Leonard: Part 6* (1987) (q.v.).

221. Trading Places (Paramount), 1983). Color, 106 minutes.

Executive producer George Folsey, Jr.; *producer* Aaron Russo; *associate producers* Sam Williams, Irwin Russo; *director* John Landis; *screenplay*

Timothy Harris, Herschel Weingrod; *production designer* Gene Rudolf; *set decorators* George De'Titta, Sr., George De'Titta, Jr.; *costumes* Deborah Nadoolman; *makeup* Jack Engel; *music* Elmer Bernsten; *orchestrator* Peter Bernstein; *music editors* Jeff Carson, Kathy Durning; *sound* Frank J. Graziadei, Dan Wallin; *supervising sound editor* Charles L. Campbell; *camera* Robert Paynter; *editor* Malcolm Campbell.

   Cast: Dan Aykroyd (Louis Winthorpe III); Eddie Murphy (Billy Ray Valentine); Ralph Bellamy (Randolph Duke); Don Ameche (Mortimer Duke); Denholm Elliott (Coleman); Kristin Holby (Penelope Witherspoon); Paul Gleason (Clarence Beeks); Jamie Lee Curtis (Ophelia); Alfred Drake (President of Exchange); Bo Diddley (Pawnbroker); Frank Oz (Corrupt Cop); James Belushi (Harvey); Pat Franken, Tom Davis (Baggage Handlers); Jim Gallagher, Bonnie Behrend, Jim Newell, Richard D. Fisher, Jr., Anthony DiSabantino, Sunnie Merrill, Mary St. John, David Schwartz, Maurice Woods, Bonnie Tremenal (D & D Employees); Tom Degidon, Alan Dellay, Ray D'Amore, Herb Peterson, Walt Gorney, William Magerman, Florence Anglin, Bobra Suiter, Sue Dugan, B. Constance Barry (Duke Domestics); P. Jay Sidney (Heritage Club Doorman); Avon Long (Ezra); Tom Mardirosian (Officer Pantuzzi); Charles Brown (Officer Reynolds); Robert Curtis-Brown (Todd); Nicholas Guest (Harry); John Bedford-Lloyd (Andrew); Tony Sherer (Philip); Robert Earl Jones (Attendant); Robert E. Lee, Eddie Jones, John McCurry, Peter Hock (Cops); Clint Smith (Doo Rag Lenny); Ron Taylor (Big Black Guy); James D. Turner (Even Bigger Black Guy); Giancarlo Esposito, Steve Hofvendahl (Cellmates); James Eckhouse (Guard); Gwyllum Evans (President of Heritage Club); Michele Mais, Barra Kahn (Hookers); Bill Cobbs (Bartender); Joshua Daniels (Party Goer); Jacques Sandulescu (Creepy Man); W.B. Brydon (Bank Manager); Margaret H. Flynn (D & D Receptionist); Kelly Curtis (Muffy); Tracy K. Shaffer (Constance); Susan Fallender (Bunny); Lucianna Burchanan (President's Mistress); Paul Garcia, Jed Gillin (Junior Executives); Jimmy Raitt (Ophelia's Client); Kate Taylor (Duke's Secretary); Philip Boxco (Doctor); Bill Boggs (Newscaster); Deborah Reagan (Harvey's Girl Friend); Donn McLeod (Gorilla); Stephan Stucker (Station Master); Richard Hunt (Wilson); Paul Austin, John Randolph Jones, Jack Davidson, Bernie McInerney (Traders); Maurice D. Copeland (Secretary of Agriculture); Ralph Clanton, Bryan Clark (Officials); Gary Klar, Afemo Omilami (Longshoremen); Shelly Chee Chee Hall (Monica); Donna Palmer (Gladys); Barry Dennen (Demitri).

   More for what it does not say than for what it does say, *Trading Places* represents an early 1980s vision of mixing two opposing types (a white blue-blooded wimp and a black resourceful con man) and revealing how each will react if his lifestyle is drastically reversed. "It's all outrageously contrived and only surprising restraint by director John ... Landis makes it work" (*People* magazine). The fact that this production was a hip retelling of Mark Twain's oft-filmed *The Prince and the Pauper* novel bothered hardly anyone, and because it was the 1980s and not the 1970s, the tale is told with comic satire, not bitter dramatics.

   When con artist Billy Ray Valentine (Eddie Murphy) is wrongly arrested for mugging a member of the Main Line at Philadelphia's Heritage Club, the elderly Duke brothers (Don Ameche, Ralph Bellamy) make a $1.00 bet to test their long-argued theory of heredity versus environment. The wealthy men have Valentine released from jail and established in the home of commodity broker Louis Winthorpe III (Dan Aykroyd). Meanwhile, they arrange for Winthorpe to be arrested as a petty thief. Before long Winthrope has lost his position, his credit, his fiancee, and his reputation. The only "good" thing to jump into his life is Ophelia (Jamie Lee Curtis), a hooker with a fondness for drugs and him. On the other hand, Valentine, ensconced in his new life, does well on the stock exchange and develops a new set of values (which includes dropping his old street pals). After overhearing his benefactors discussing their lifestyle manipulations he rushes to save Winthorpe from suicide. Along with Ophelia and the butler Coleman (Denholm Elliott), the two new friends turn the tide on the meddling Duke brothers by bankrupting them.

The public heartily endorsed *Trading Places,* which grossed $40,600,000 domestically. For his second theatrical feature film (following *48 Hours* [q.v.]), Eddie Murphy was teamed with his "Saturday Night Live" TV comedy mate, Dan Aykroyd. Murphy brought a vibrancy to his scam-artist-with-a-heart-of gold and a vitality to his delivery of sassy punch lines. It confirmed him as the hottest emerging screen superstar. Yet there were those who wondered why his character did not end up with a romantic partner, as did Aykroyd, or why the script showed him first shunning his ghetto pals and then (inadvertently) embarrassing them when he invites them to a party at his splendiferous, stuffy manse, where they prove to be desperately out of place.

In *Cineaste* magazine, Ron Edelman observed, "*Trading Places* is the epitome of product. There is Eddie Murphy for the black moviegoer; Murphy and Dan Aykroyd for the *Saturday Night Live* crowd; Ralph Bellamy and Don Ameche for those over fifty...; and Jamie Lee Curtis, baring her breasts, for dirty old men from eighteen to eighty-five.... It is the creation of a computer, a movie made by dealmakers and not filmmakers."

222. Trick Baby (Universal, 1973). Color, 89 minutes.

Executive producer James Levitt; *producer* Marshal Backlar; *director* Larry Yust; *based on the novel by* Iceberg Slim [Robert Beck]; *screenplay* Yust, T. Raewyn, A. Neuberg; *music* James Bond; *music supervisor* Ed Michael; *sound* John Brasher; *camera* Isidore Mankofsky; *editor* Peter Parasheles.

Cast: Kiel Martin (White Folks [Johnny O'Brien]), Mel Stewart (Blue Howard); Dallas Edward Hayes (Dot Murray); Jan Leighton (Carlson); Byron Sanders (Parkview Clerk); Dick Boccelli (Vincent); Jim Mapp (Doc); Bob Brooker (DuSable Clerk); Ronald Carter (Bartender); Celeste Creech, Delores Brown-Harper (Hookers); Jacqueline Weiss (Aunt Rose); Father James Kelly (Priest); Charles Weldon (Tough); Charles Clarke (Cab Driver); Beverly Ballard (Susan); Vernee Watson (Cleo Howard); Donald Symington (Morrison); Don Fellows (Phillips); Tom Anderson (Felix the Fixer); Clebert Ford (Josephus); Fuddle Bagley (Percy); Ted Lange (Melvin the Pimp); Tony Mazzadra (Nino Parelli); David Thomas (Frascatti); Jim King (Duke); Anthony Charnota (Bobby); John Aquino (Frank).

Mel Stewart and Vernee Watson in *Trick Baby* **(1973).**

A.K.A. *The Double Con.*

One of those intriguing film ventures that got overlooked in the rash of black exploitation features, this film is a black version of *The Sting* (1969) with a flavor and seriousness all its own. "Much of the spoken rationalization is nonsense, but the physical action is often very true, not especially violent, but exciting" (Roger Greenspun, *New York Times*). The film is based on a novel by Iceberg Slim [Robert Beck], a Chicago-born operator who knew all the street games firsthand and thought up this novel while in prison.

Youngish "White Folks" (Kiel Martin) is a light-skinned black man who operates confidence games in Philadelphia with his older partner, Blue Howard (Mel Stewart). One of their scams is on Mr. Frascatti (David Thomas), whom they shake out of $10,000. When the elderly man has a heart attack over the matter, his nephew, Nino Parelli (Tony Mazzadra), a Mafia boss, orders dishonest black police detective Dot Murray (Dallas Edward Hayes) to find those responsible. Murray is quickly convinced that White Folks and Howard are the men in question, and he demands hush money from them. They put him off with countless promises and excuses. Meanwhile they practice their art on three white land developers, but the scheme goes afoul. Murray catches up with the duo, and White Folks is wounded. Later, in a gun battle, the cop is killed, and Howard dies in White Folks's arms.

There are several engaging sequences in this spicy study of the life and times (and death) of con men, as the film follows the adventures of the crooks while they unspool their elaborate schemes for exploiting their victims. The side plot of the two men avoiding the corrupt black cop does nothing but drag down the movie to the blood-and-guts level. Mel Stewart is especially effective as the elder crook, who has a telling death scene where he rattles off the do's and don't's of the con game (including avoiding marks who stutter, are cross-eyed or are on their way home from funerals). Of Mel Stewart's performance, *Cue* magazine weighed it "pure gold."

For the record the film's title refers to the younger con man, the son of a black hooker and a white "score." His real name is Johnny O'Brien, his friends call him "White Folks," and his enemy labels him "Trick Baby."

223. Trouble Man (Twentieth Century–Fox, 1972). Color, 99 minutes.

Executive producer John D.F. Black; *producer* Joel D. Freeman; *director* Ivan Dixon; *screenplay* Black; *art director* Albert Brenner; *set decorator* Morris Hoffman; *makeup* Bernardine Anderson; *music/song* Marvin Gaye; *assistant directors* Reuben Watt, Albert Shepard; *sound* Richard Overton, Theodore Soderberg; *special effects* Logan R. Frazee; *camera* Michael Hugo; *editor* Michael Kahn.

Cast: Robert Hooks (Mr. "T"); Paul Winfield (Chalky Price); Ralph Waite (Pete Cockrell); William Smithers (Captain Joe Marks); Paula Kelly (Cleo); Julius W. Harris (Mr. Big); Bill Henderson (Jimmy); Vince Howard (Preston); Larry Cook (Buddy); Akili Jones (Chi); Rick Ferrell (Pindar); Stack Pierce (Collie); Edmund Cambridge (Sam); Felton Perry (Bobby); Wayne Storm (Frank); Virginia Capers (Macy); James Earl "Texas Blood" Brown (Pool Shark); Jita Hadi (Leroy); Tracy Reed (Policewoman); John Crawford (Sergeant Koeppler); Howie Steindler (Howie); Danny Lopez (Young Boxer).

Black director Ivan Dixon, who would later turn out the impressively violent *Gordon's War* (1973) (q.v.)—which would also star Paul Winfield and also be released by Twentieth Century–Fox—was responsible for *Trouble Man,* his first theatrical feature film behind the camera. "Like indistinguishable tin soldiers, the pseudo–Black movies continue to march on and *Trouble Man,* true to its predecessors, parades its share of stereotype, cardboard characters caught up in a condescendingly hypothetical situation comprising an hour and a half of banal escapist fare" (Walter Burrell, *Soul* magazine). The film's producer (Joel Freedman) and scripter (John D.F. Black) had served similar capacities on *Shaft* (1971) (q.v.).

When rival Los Angeles gaming syndicates explode into bloodshed over their roving crap games which continually get held up, super-tough and super-cool Mr. T. (Robert Hooks) steps in wearing an expensive three-piece suit and carrying an automatic gun to settle the score. (*"One Cat ... Who Plays Like an Army!"* announced the ads; he prefers to think of himself as a black Robin Hood.) On one side there is Chalky Price (Paul Winfield) and his white partner, Pete Cockrell (Ralph Waite); and on the other, their rough adversary, Mr. Big (Julius W. Harris). Scattered in the plot also are bewildered police detective Captain Joe Marks (William Smithers), who thinks Mr. T. is behind all the trouble; luscious Cleo (Paula Kelly), Mr. T's main squeeze; and Jimmy (Bill Henderson), who owns the pool hall where snazzy Mr. T. has his headquarters. The final shootout occurs in Century City (former backlot of adjacent Twentieth Century–Fox) at the Century Plaza Hotel.

Ralph Waite and Robert Hooks (and Robert Hooks and Robert Hooks and Robert Hooks and...) in *Trouble Man* **(1972).**

When Vincent Canby *(New York Times)* picked the ten worst films of 1972, *Trouble Man* was in the select company of such entries as *Young Winston, Savage Messiah, Portnoy's Complaint* and *The Public Eye.* In making his selections, Canby explained, *"Trouble Man* ... stands out as one of the worst black rip-off films of the year because so many good people were involved in it."

On the plus side there is Marvin Gaye's score (and theme song, which he sings), which made a dent on the album and singles charts. Professional billiard player James Earl "Texas Blood" Brown made his film debut in *Trouble Man.*

224. Truck Turner (Amiercan International, 1974). Color, 91 minutes.

Producers Fred Weintraub, Paul M. Heller; *associate producer* Marty Hornstein; *director* Jonathan Kaplan; *story* Jerry Wilkes; *screenplay* Leigh Chapman, Oscar Williams, Michael Allin; *costumes* Ann McCarthy; *music/songs* Isaac Hayes; *assistant director* Hornstein; *stunt co-ordinator* Eddie Smith; *consultant* Williams; *sound* Darin Knight; *sound effects* Marvin Kerner; *camera* Charles F. Wheeler; *editor* Michael Kahn.

Cast: Isaac Hayes (Matt "Truck" Turner); Yaphet Kotto (Harvard Blue); Alan Weeks (Jerry); Annazette Chase (Annie); Nichelle Nichols (Dorinda); Sam Laws (Nate); Paul Harris (Gator [Richard Leroi Jones]), John Kramer (Desmond); Scatman Crothers (Duke); Chuck Cypher (Drunk); Dick Miller (Fogarty); Bob Harris (Snow); Jac Emil (Renop); Stan Shaw (Fontana); John Dennis (Desmond's Guard); John Evans (Police Lieutenant); Clarence Lockett (Preacher); Clarence Barnes (Toro); Don Watters (Val); Eddie Smith (Druggist);

Esther Sutherland (Black Mama); Earl Maynard (Panama); Henry Kingi (Candy Man); Larry Gabriel (Travis); Don Megowan (Garrity); Cheryl Samson (Taffy); Edna Richardson (Frenchie); Bernadette Gladden (Racquel); Tara Stronmeier (Turnpike); Lisa Farringer (Annette); Sharon Madigan (Nurse); Mel Novak (Doctor); Randy Gray (Kid in Hospital); Annik Borel (Stalingrad); Stymie Beard (Jail Guard); Johnny Ray McGhee (Hired Killer); Donnie Williams (Highway Department Man); Wendell Tucker (Wendell); Jac Emil (Reno).

"He's a skip tracer, the last of the bounty hunters. *If You Jump Bail... You're His Meat!"*

The idea of a bare-chested, muscular black dude packing mean firearms was a lot of people's fantasy trip in the early 1970s as black action pictures abounded. It must also have been the trip of Academy Award–winning songwriter, arranger, and singer Isaac Hayes, who starred in this unsubtle exploitation feature.

To some they are skip tracers; to others they are bounty hunters. But by any name they get their man. Matt "Truck" Turner (Isaac Hayes) and his partner Jerry (Alan Weeks) are hired to find a vicious pimp hood named Gator (Paul Harris). One lead is Dorinda (Nichelle Nichols), Gator's girlfriend and the madam of a ritzy whorehouse. Truck's friend Duke (Scatman Crothers) alerts them that bigshot gangster Harvard Blue (Yaphet Kotto) is also looking for Gator. In a shootout, Truck and Jerry kill their prey. At Gator's funeral, Dorinda urges her late lover's friends to avenge Gator's death. Harvard Blue takes on the challenge, anxious to get even with the men who interfered with his business. Jerry is killed in an ambush, which sends Truck into a shooting rampage at Dorinda's brothel and later at Harvard Blue's mansion. While visiting his friend Nate (Sam Laws) in the hospital, Harvard Blue and his underlings arrive, and Truck kills them one by one. His job accomplished, he returns to his shoplifting girlfriend, Annie (Annazette Chase).

The reviewers were unimpressed by the film's recurring displays of black machismo, tough lean characters, and salty language ("She's called Turnpike 'cause you gotta pay to get on and pay to get off"). Reported the jaded A.H. Weiler *(New York Times),* "...its constant barrage of chases, bloody fights and shoot-outs is as unusual as a local 4th of July fireworks display." As the lead character ("Tell 'em you were hit by a Truck!"), Isaac Hayes abandoned his trademark array of fancy jewelry and got down to basic artillery to back up his tough talk. There were some viewers who were appreciative of Hayes' fanciful screen personae. "He comes off quite convincing," reported William D. Ruffin in *Soul* magazine. "As the tough no-b.s.-taking guy who hunts down bail skippers for a bail bondsman, Hayes is very real and believable and the dialogue between him and his partner Alan Weeks is straight off the streets." Needless to say, Isaac Hayes contributed the score and song for this production.

Truck Turner grossed $2,230,000 in domestic film rentals. Earlier the same year Isaac Hayes appeared in the Italian/U.S. co-production, *Three Tough Guys* (q.v.). When *Truck Turner* was released in England in the spring of 1975, eight minutes were cut from the running time.

Pam Grier and victim in *The Twilight People* (1972).

225. The Twilight People (Demension, 1972). 84 minutes.

Producers Eddie Romero, John Ashley; *director* Romero; *screenplay* Romero, Jerome Small.

Cast: John Ashley (Matt Farrell); Pat Woodell (Neva Gordon); Jan Merlin (Steinman); Pam Grier (The Panther Woman); Eddie Garcia (Pereira); Charles Macaulay (Dr. Gordon); Ken Metcalfe (The Antelope Man); Tom Gosalve (The Bat Man); Kim Ramos (The Ape Man); Mona Morena (The Wolf Woman); *and:* Andres Centenera, Centon Gonzales, Johnny Long, Romeo Mabutol, Letty Mirasol, Roger Ocomapo, Max Rojmo, Angelo Ventura, Vic Unson.

This film proved to be just another variation of H.G. Wells's *The Island of Dr. Moreau,* shot in the Philippines in 1971 by prolific filmmaker Eddie Romero. Typically, it had inferior production values, post-dubbing for many of the performers, and yet, despite it all, it was entertaining on a minimal level.

While skin-diving in the South Pacific, soldier of fortune Matt Farrell (John Ashley) is pulled from the ocean and taken to the laboratory headquarters of the deranged Dr. Gordon (Charles Macauley), whose goal is transform mankind into supermen. His more rational daughter, Neva (Pat Woodell), wants Farrell to help her free the test-tube subjects, including the Panther Woman (Pam Grier). Farrell and Neva escape after finding that the doctor has been killed by one of his subjects, the Tree Woman.

Pam Grier's role of the Panther Woman would be the most exotic of her career to date, paving the way for her starring features during the height of the black action film craze.

226. Uptight (Paramount, 1968). Color, 104 minutes.

Producer Jules Dassin; *associate producer* Jim DiGangi; *director* Dassin; *based on the novel* "The Informer" *by* Liam O'Flaherty; *screenplay* Dassin, Ruby Dee, Julian Mayfield; *production designer* Alexandre Trauer; *art director* Phillip Bennett; *set decorator* Ray Moser; *costumes* Theoni V. Aldredge; *makeup* Bob Sidel, Bob Morley; *music/songs* Booker T. Jones; *assistant directors* Martin Hornstein, William McGarry, Reuben Wat; *dialogue coach* William Watts; *sound* Terry Kellum, David Forrest; *camera* Boris Kaufman; *editor* Robert Lawrence.

Cast: Raymond St. Jacques (B.G.); Ruby Dee (Laurie); Frank Silvera (Kyle); Roscoe Lee Browne (Clarence); Julian Mayfield (Tank Williams); Janet MacLachlan (Jeannie); Max Julien (Johnny Wells); Juanita Moore (Johnny's Mother); Richard Anthony Williams (Corbin); Michael Baseleon (Teddy); Ji-Tu Cumbuka (Rick); John Wesley [Rodgers] (Larry); Ketty Lester (Alma); Robert DoQui (Street Speaker); James McEachin (Melo); Vernett Allen (Ralph); Errol Jaye (Mr. Oakley); *and:* Mello Alexandria, Alice Childress, Isabelle Cooley, Kirk Kirsey, Van Kirsey, David Moody.

This was the first Hollywood feature to deal with contemporary black revolutionaries, those who demanded the use of violence to gain their rights after nonviolent leader Dr. Martin Luther King, Jr., was assassinated. Filmmaker Jules Dassin turned to Liam O'Flaherty's 1925 novel *The Informer* and John Ford's 1935 film for a plot on which to rest his topical 1960s subject. The fact that *The Informer* dealt with a very different time and a very different struggle (the Irish versus the English in their ongoing war) were problems Dassin and his screen collaborators (Ruby Dee, Julian Mansfield) could not overcome.

It is 1968 Cleveland, four days after the assassination of Dr. Martin Luther King, Jr. The overheated city is in turmoil, and riots are brewing everywhere. Johnny Wells (Max Julien), Rick (Ji-Tu Cumbuka), and Larry (John Wesley [Rodgers]) rob an ammunition arsenal. Their steelworker friend Tank Williams (Julian Mayfield) was supposed to be part of the operation, but he had gotten drunk (after twenty years at the mill he lost his job, and he became even more depressed after the death of Dr. King) and was of no use. Because Williams was not on the heist, everything did not go as planned, and Wells had to shoot a watchman in the getaway. Black militant leaders B.G. (Raymond St. Jacques) and Corbin (Richard Anthony Williams) expel Williams from their revolutionary organization. Police informer Clarence (Roscoe Lee Browne) tells Williams there is $1000 for information leading to Wells' capture and suggests that if he helps out, any incriminating photograph of Williams in the police files will be removed.

Williams finds himself increasingly isolated from his ghetto brothers and even from his girlfriend, Laurie (Ruby Dee), who has become a prostitute to support her children. When he gets drunk again, Williams (who among other motives wants money to keep Laurie off the streets) tells the police where Wells is hiding. The police barricade the area, and the fugitive is shot down in the midst of a riot. When Williams is seen spending an excessive amount of money the next day, the militants assume he (not Clarence) must be the one who betrayed Wells. Understanding his end is near, Williams returns to the steel mills, pursued by Larry and Rick. He makes his presence known to his one-time friends and is shot.

"*Uptight* is really a film, hammered out to capitalize upon, rather than explore the complex facets of racial problems," argued *Variety*. The reviewer explained, "Besides bestowing undue nobility to black militants, it also succeeds in displaying a series of all-black, modern-day character stereotypes.... The array of two-dimensional blacks herein constitutes a sugar-coated patronizing of the very minority group which the film seeks to depict in comprehensive fashion."

With on-location lensing in Cleveland, this was the first American-made film for director Jules Dassin in nearly two decades, who had left the United States during the height of the anti-communist witch-hunting. Much of *Uptight* reflects Dassin's stay in Greece, for this film has the feel of Greek tragedy, with the characters acting as chorus spokepersons for polemics tossed back and forth from tenement fire escape to fire escape. There is very little feeling in *Uptight* that the characters are real. As Pauline Kael (*New Yorker* magazine) expressed it, "Everybody tries hard, but the material doesn't transfer successfully, and the movie lacks spirit."

Uptight was an artistic and commercial misfire, but it gave hints of new trends in Hollywood filmmaking.

227. Uptown Saturday Night (Warner Bros., 1974).
Color, 104 minutes.

Producer Melville Tucker; *associate producer* Pembroke J. Herring; *director* Sidney Poitier; *screenplay* Richard Wesley; *production designer* Alfred Sweeney; *set decorator* Robert de Vestel; *makeup* Monty Westmore; *music* Tom Scott; *song* Scott and Morgan Ames; *assistant directors* Bruce Chevillat, Charles C. Washburn; *sound* George A. Maly, Frank C. Regula, Harry W. Tetrick; *camera* Fred J. Koenekamp; *editor* Herring.

Cast: Sidney Poitier (Steve Jackson); Bill Cosby (Wardell Franklin); Harry Belafonte (Geechie Dan Beauford); Flip Wilson (The Reverend); Richard Pryor (Sharp Eye Washington); Rosalind Cash (Sarah Jackson); Roscoe Lee Browne (Congressman Dudley Lincoln); Paula Kelly (Leggy Peggy); Lee Chamberlin (Mme. Zenobia); Johnny Sekka, Lincoln Kilpatrick, Don Marshall (Geechie's Henchmen); Calvin Lockhart (Silky Slim); Ketty Lester (Irma Franklin); Harold Nicholas (Little Seymour).

Fully understanding that film audiences (of any race) were oversatiated with black violence pictures, Sidney Poitier turned to manufacturing a slick slapstick comedy as his own anecdote to the trend of black action adventures. Exceedingly popular in its day (it grossed $7,400,000 in domestic film rentals, based on an estimated $2,500,000 production cost), *Uptown Saturday Night* is by no means a good film, but it is zany entertainment featuring several name black performers in madcap roles.

One Saturday night, factory worker Steve Jackson (Sidney Poitier) and cab driver pal, Buddy Wardell Franklin (Bill Cosby), sneak out for some drinks, gambling, and broads up at the exclusive club of Madame Zenobia (Lee

Left–right in foreground: **Sidney Poitier, Harry Belafonte, and Bill Cosby in** *Uptown Saturday Night* **(1974).**

Chamberlin. In the midst of their enjoyment, the club is raided by Silky Slim's men. Later Jackson realizes his $50,000 winning lottery ticket was in his wallet which was stolen in the heist. Jackson and Franklin decide to track the culprits themselves. They hire a faltering private investigator, Sharp Eye Washington (Richard Pryor), who takes a $200 fee and then zooms off. They seek help from pompous Congressman Lincoln (Roscoe Lee Browne). He is not cooperative, but they learn his flashy wife is Leggy Peggy (Paula Kelly), one of the frequenters of Madame Zenobia's. This good-time gal touts them to Little Seymour (Harold Nicholas), a punk who has the two meddlers beaten up. Their next stop is Geechie Dan Beauford (Harry Belafonte), a ghetto crime lord who is ready to take on his rival, Silky Slim (Calvin Lockhart). The latter makes a call on Beauford while Jackson and Franklin are there, and Silky is recognized as the leader of the heist. Jackson and Franklin next concoct a scam which brings both Slim and Geechie Dan to the church's charity picnic, where the police are on hand to arrest the assorted crooks. Slim makes a short-lived getaway with the suitcase containing the prize ticket. During the struggle, the suitcase is thrown over a high bridge. The boys jump into the river to retrieve it.

"*Uptown Saturday Night* is essentially a put-on, but it's so full of good humor and, when the humor goes flat, of such high spirits that it reduces movie criticism to the status of a most nonessential craft" (Vincent Canby, *New York Times*). Penelope Gilliat (*New Yorker* magazine) acknowledged it "...is a larky story that nobody but blacks could have pulled off." Less enthusiastic was Paul D. Zimmermann (*Newsweek* magazine): "Poitier is not an inventive comic talent—he is erratic behind the camera and amiable but not funny in front of it. When the funny set pieces stop, the film sputters—but not before delivering a carnival of fine comic characters." *Variety* added, "Actor Poitier also dampens the proceedings with a bland, comically mistimed performance that suffers greatly in comparison to Cosby's fast-living rendition of his carefree buddy." Walter Burrell (*Essence* magazine) chided, "...one walks away a bit dissatisfied.... One is left with the feeling these great talents could have used a vehicle more suited to their abilities."

Besides Bill Cosby's spirited appearance and the fumbling antics of Richard Pryor (in what amounted to a walk-on role), the highlights of *Uptown Saturday Night* are Paula Kelly as the fast-living lady who knows how to enjoy herself and Harry Belafonte doing a wonderful send-up of Marlon Brando in *The Godfather* (1972), complete with puffed cheeks, pencil mustache, and gruff voice. (Belafonte also has a drag scene in the frantic picnic finale.)

Uptown Saturday Night was produced as Poitier's contribution to the First Artists Production Company, Ltd., which he had formed in mid-1969 with Paul Newman and Barbra Streisand. (Steve McQueen and still later Dustin Hoffman joined the unit.) So successful was *Uptown Saturday Night* that a sequel, *Let's Do It Again* (q.v.), appeared the following year.

228. Velvet Smooth (Howard Mahler; 1976). Color, 80 minutes.

Producers Marion Schild, Michael Fink, Joel Schmid; *associate producer* Janice Fink; *director* Michael Fink; *screenplay* Leonard Michaels, Jan Weber; *music* Media Counterpoint; *martial arts choreography* Owen Wat-son; *assistant director* Hal Hutkoff; *camera* Jay Dubin; *editors* Schild, Schmid.

Cast: Johnnie Hill (Velvet Smooth); Owen Wat-son (King Lathrop); Emerson Boozer (Mat); Rene Van Clief (Frankie); Elsie Roman (Ria); Moses Illuya (Sergeant Barnes); Frank Ruiz (Lieutenant Ramos); James Durran (Calvin Christopher); Thomas Ageio (Snake); Wildrew Roldan (Rodriquez); Michael Scorpio (Martinez); Allen Ayers, Jr. (Johnson); Hector Quinones (Player); Sidney Filson (Dealer); Sam Schwartz (Captain O'Reilly); Gary Catus (Digger); Tanka Ramos (Thug with Snake); Teddy Wilson, Chino Diaz, James Martin, Butch Oglesby (Masked Men); Jack Levy (Dry Cleaning Store Owner); Greer Smith (Hooker).

This economy feature was yet another effort to create a super-cool black heroine, but with such reduced production values that the entertainment possibilities proved to be minimal.

Velvet Smooth (Johnnie Hill) is a private detective with a support staff of women. She is hired by King Lathrop (Owen Wat-son), ghetto ganglord, to find out who is behind the rash of outside action that is crowding his turf. Velvet is the type of wise lady who tells her helpers, "Money and power do strange things to people. Don't trust anyone." Especially not Calvin Christopher (James Durran), who is Lathrop's chief accountant and the most likely suspect. But even when her theory is proven correct ("I had a gut feeling," she admits), that is not the end of the case nor the finale of this protracted adventure. There are, believe it or not, corrupt white cops involved, and that leads to Lieutenant Ramos (Frank Ruiz) and Sergeant Barnes (Moses Illuya) and a final shootout, and then a twist on the denouement.

Velvet is one of those sassy chicks who says such hip things as, "You make the rules, baby. It's your turf." When confronted with a thug, her interrogation consists of, "Don't jive me, man. Who set me up?" punctuated with a swift karate chop to a pressure point.

Bringing down the enjoyment level still further is an obnoxious composite score.

229. A View to a Kill (Metro-Goldwyn-Mayer/United Artists, 1985). Color, 131 minutes.

Producers Albert Broccoli, Michael G. Wilson; *associate producer* Thomas Pevsner; *director* John Glen; *based on characters created by* Ian Fleming; *screenplay* Richard Maibaum, Wilson; *production designer* Peter Lamont; *art director* John Fenner; *set decorator* Crispian Salles; *costumes* Emma Porteous; *music* John Berry; *song* Duran Duran and Barry; *second unit director* Arthur Wooster; *sound* Derek Ball; *special effects supervisor* John Richardson; *camera* Alan Hume; *editor* Peter Davies.

Cast: Roger Moore (James Bond); Christopher Walken (Max Zorin); Tanya Roberts (Stacey Sutton); Grace Jones (May Day); Patrick Macnee (Tibbett); Patrick Bauchau (Scarpine); David Yip (Chuck Lee); Fiona Fullerton (Pola Ivanova); Lois Maxwell (Miss Moneypenny); Desmond Llewelyn (Q); Geoffrey Keen (Minister of Defense); Manning Redwood (Bob Conley); Alison Doody (Jenny Flex); Willoughby Grazy (Dr. Carl Mortner); Robert Brown (M); Walter Gotell (General Gogol); Jean Rougerie (Aubergine); Daniel Benzali (Howe); Bogdan Kominowski (Klotkoff); Papillon Soo Soo (Pan Ho); Mary Stavi (Kimberley Jones); Dominique Risbourg (Butterfly Act Compere); Carole Ashby (Whistling Girl); Anthony Chin (Taiwanese Tycoon); Lucien Jerome (Paris Taxi Driver); Albert Simono (Paris Police Sergeant); Joe Flood (U.S. Police Captain); Gerard Buhr (Auctioneer); Dolph Lundgren (Venz); Tony Sibblad (Mine Foreman); Bill Ackridge (O'Rourke); Ron Tarr, Taylor McAuley (Guards); Peter Ensor (Tycoon); Seva Novgorodtsev (Helicopter Pilot); Sian Adey-Jones, Samina Afzal, Celine Cawley, Nike Clarki, Helen Clitherow, Maggie Defreitas, Gloria Douse, Caroline Hallett, Deborah Hanna, Josanne Haydon-Pearce, Ann Jackson, Terri Johns, Karen Loughlin, Angela Lyn, Patricia Martinez, Kim Ashfield Norton, Elke Ritschel, Lou-Anne Ronchi, Helen Smith, Jane Spencer, Paula Thomas, Mayako Torigai, Tony White (Girls).

A View to a Kill was Roger Moore's seventh and final appearance as Ian Fleming's super secret agent James Bond in the long-running film series. The spy thriller was much maligned for its unsubtly contrived plot, its unimaginative unfolding, and the general tiredness of the John Glen–directed proceedings. At an estimated production cost of $30,000,000, it grossed only $25,000,000 in domestic film rentals, having to rely on overseas, television, and cassette fees to make a profit.

In the midst of the critical pannings the film suffered (especially for Christopher Walken as the drearily depraved Max Zorin), one performer stood out (literally) above the rest: "... singer Grace Jones, who, with her panther's look, makes an ideal villain—in a class with Gert Frobe as Goldfinger or Richard Kiel as Jaws" (*People* magazine). "Grace Jones is a successful

Roger Moore and Grace Jones in *A View to a Kill* **(1985).**

updating of the Jaws-type villain. Jones just oozes '80s style and gets to parade in a number of sensational outfits (designed by Emma Porteous) giving a hard but alluring edge to her character" *(Variety)*.

British secret agent 007 James Bond (Roger Moore) is assigned to investigate global industrialist Max Zorin (Christopher Walken). In Paris his contact is murdered by May Day (Grace Jones), Zorin's black mistress. It develops that Zorin and May Day are offshoots of genetic experiments by ex–Nazi Dr. Carl Mortner (Willoughby Grazy). The case leads to San Francisco and to Zorin's mining operations, which are geared to cause earthquakes and destroy the computer chip industry in Silicon Valley, thus allowing Zorin world control of the microchip market. Bond infiltrates the mines and forestalls the explosion, helped by May Day, who sacrifices her own life in the process. In the final pursuit, Zorin falls from his dirigible.

It was a crafty piece of casting that brought the tall, very slender Grace Jones to *A View to a Kill*. The filmmakers were hoping to gain new young audiences for the series by hiring an exotic personality from the world of music. (In a similar ploy, Tina Turner had co-starred with Mel Gibson in *Mad Max Beyond Thunderdome* [1985].) Jones proved an excellent choice for the nefarious hit lady. As May Day, Jones has a look that can kill, and if that doesn't work, her martial arts skills will do the trick. Jones had performed similar chores in Arnold Schwarzenegger's *Conan the Destroyer* (1984) and would be a most provocative and deadly vampire in the satirical yet gory *Vamp* (1986). Today Grace Jones remains an exciting and unusual film presence in search of a full-dimensional role.

230. Vigilante (Film Ventures, 1983). Color, 90 minutes.

Executive producers John Packard, Jerry Masucci, Kenneth Pavia; *producers* Andrew Garroni, William Lustig; *director* Lustig; *screenplay* Richard Vetere; *production designer* Mischa Petrow; *special makeup effects* Cecilia Verandi; *music* Jay Chattaway; *assistant director* Randy Jurgensen; *sound* Gary Rich, Arthur Sokainer; *special effects co-ordinator* Gary Zeller; *camera* James Lemmo; *additional camera* Michael Spera; *editor* Lorenzo Marinelli.

Cast: Robert Forster (Eddie Merino); Fred Williamson (Nick); Richard Bright (Burke); Rutanya Alda (Vickie Merino); Don Blakely (Prago); Joseph Carberry (Ramon); Willie Colon (Rico); Joe Spinell (Eisenberg); Carol Lynley (District Attorney Fletcher); Woody Strode (Rake); Vincent Beck (Judge Sinclair); Bo Rucker (Horace); Peter Savage (Mr. "T").

A.K.A. *Street Cop.*

In the 1980s there was a rash of feature films focusing on community action to clean up the streets, including *Fighting Back* (1982) starring Tom Skerritt, Michael Sarrazin and Yaphet Kotto. Black performers were now part of the ethnic mix and in such films could be found on either side of the morality fence.

In a poor neighborhood area of New York City, factory worker Eddie Merino (Robert Forster) is unconvinced of the theory of co-worker Nick (Fred Williamson) that the community's criminal element (including dope pushers and pimps) should be removed by force. However, when his child is killed and his wife (Rutanya Alda) is knifed, he changes his mind. Gang leader Rico (Willie Colon) is put on trial for the crimes but is given only a two-year suspended sentence. The infuriated Merino attacks the judge and is thrown into prison for contempt of court. Meanwhile Nick and his friends are eliminating the drug pushers and their bosses any way they can. When Merino is released from jail he joins their effort à la *Death Wish.*

Variety judged, "Even without the ultra-violence, *Vigilante* is simply too grim and nihilistic to justify its existence as entertainment." But the trade paper noted, "Film's best moments are provided by Woody Strode, who projects a quiet authority as a fellow prisoner who creates a show-stopping scene when he beats up two monstrous young thugs terrorizing Forster in prison."

Vigilante was made in early 1982 but was not released in the United States until the spring of 1983. Also in 1983 Fred Williamson would direct and co-star with salsa star Willie Colon in *The Last Fight* (q.v.).

231. Warrior of the Lost World (American National Enterprises, 1983). Color, 86 minutes.

Producers Roberto Bessi, Frank E. Hildebrand; *director/screenplay* David Worth; *production designer* Antonello Geleng; *makeup effects* Otello Fava; *costume designers* Fabrizio Caracciolo, Maurizio Paiola; *music* Daniele Patucchi; *song* Mike Fraser, Douglas Meaker, Patucchi; *choreography* Pino Pennesi; *assistant director* Tony Brandt; *stunt co-ordinator* Remo De Angelis; *special effects* Roberto Arcangeli; *camera* Giancarlo Ferrando; *editor* Cesare D'Amico.

Cast: Robert Ginty (Warrior); Persis Khambatta (Natasia); Donald

Pleasence (Prosser); Fred Williamson (Henchman); Harrison Muller (McWayne); Laura Nucci, Philip Dallas, Vincio Recchi (Elders); Janna Ryan, Consuelo Marcaccini (Amazons); Dan Stephens, Stefano Mior (Martial Artists); Urs Athaus, Lucien Bruchon, Harrison Muller, Jr.; Norvyen Antonelli (Mercenaries); Ennio Antonelli (Trucker); Russell Case, Hernani Morevia (Outsiders).

Another ripoff of the *Mad Max* series that had done so much for the Australian film industry and star Mel Gibson.

The opening title card of *Warrior of the Lost World* informs, "The nuclear war has been forgotten. The earth is in ruins.... An evil despot names Prosser has organized a deadly militia to rule, called the Omega. In the wasteland survive a small group called the Outsiders, they struggle against Prosser and his Omegas. Into the conflict rides one man, on his speedcycle. He is destined to become the Warrior of the Lost World."

With his interactive motorcyle (much like the car in the teleseries "Knightrider") the Warrior (Robert Ginty) sets out on his mission to help Professor McWayne (Harrison Muller) and his daughter Natasia (Persis Khambatta) carry out their rebellion against the sinister Prosser (Donald Pleasence). Helping Prosser in his evil machinations is the Henchman (Fred Williamson), who does his best to lead the Outsiders astray.

With his name still a draw on the international marketplace, Fred Williamson made several guest appearances in nihilistic adventure yarns in the 1980s, including this one and *Warriors of the Wasteland* (q.v.). *Warrior of the Lost World* was made in Italy in 1983 but received its United States release on video cassette in 1985.

232. Warriors of the Wasteland (New Line, 1984). Color, 91 minutes.

Producer Fabrizio De Angelis; *director* Enzo Girolami Castellari; *story* Tito Carpi; *screenplay* Carpi, Castellari; *production designer* Antonio Visone; *makeup* Gianni Morosi, Alberto Travaglini; *wardrobe* Mirella Pedetti; *music* Claudio Simonetti; *music director* Claude King; *stunt co-ordinator* Riccardo Pitrazzi; *sound* Masimo Loffredi; *special sound effects* Tullio Arangeli, Claudio Gramighna; *special effects* Germano Natali; *camera* Fausto Zuccoli; *editor* Gianfranco Amicucci.

Cast: Timothy Brent [Giancarlo Prete] (Skorpion); Fred Williamson (Nadir); Anna Kanakis (Alms); Venatino Venantini (Moses); *and:* Enzo Girolami Castellari, Andrea Coppola, George Eastman, Mark Gregory, Zora Kerowa, Patsy May McLachlan, Luigi Montefiori, Thomas Moore, Ivano Silveri, Massimo Vanni.

A.K.A. I Nuovi Barbari; 2019: I Nuovi Barbari.

People magazine insisted, "This ghastly little number is a must for the next Fred Williamson film festival.... Williamson, Timothy *(Great White)* Brent and George Eastman tool around a nuclear-war devastated landscape in what seem to be used-car-lot rejects remodeled with help from the James Bond Special Effects Handbook."

It is the year 2019 and a group of survivors of the nuclear holocaust are in search of the source of distant radio signals. They are easy victims for the

Templars, whose chief enemy is Skorpion (Timothy Brent). Skorpion agrees to rescue Alma (Anna Kanakis), and he is helped by the bowman Nadir (Fred Williamson), who is armed with explosive arrows. Skorpion is captured and defiled by the homosexual Templars and later rescued by Nadir.

"This is the minestrone version of *Mad Max 2,* shamelessly watered-down, warmed-over, and spiced with odd lumps of both *Damnation Alley* and, incongruously [George A.] Romero's *Knightriders.* It would be totally indigestible, of course, were it not for the inevitable absurdities that mark the gulf between inspiration and arrogantly inadequate execution" (Paul Taylor, British *Monthly Film Bulletin*).

As always, Fred Williamson breezes through the tripe with an élan that is remarkable, even uttering such absurd bits of dialogue as, "It is easy to take something serious that is true."

233. White Fire (Trans World Entertainment, 1985).
Color, 91 minutes.

Executive producers Tony Edwards, John L. Coletta; *in association with* Chris Davis; *producers* Jean-Marie Pallardy, Alan G. Rainer; *in association with* Sedat Akdemir, Ugur Terzioglu; *director/screenplay* Pallardy; *music director* Jon Lord; *songs* Limelight and Vicky Browne; *assistant director* Sabine Marand; *stunt director* Benito Stefanelli; *camera* Roger Felous; *editor* Bruno Zincone.

Cast: Robert Ginty (Beau Donnelly); Fred Williamson (Noah); Belinda Mayne (Ingrid); Jess Hahn (Sam); Mirella Banti (Sophia); Gordon Mitchell (Yilmaz).

In early 1980s Istanbul, Beau Donnelly (Robert Ginty) and his sister, Ingrid (Belinda Mayne), are diamond smugglers who team with unscrupulous mines security official Yilmaz (Gordon Mitchell) and their longtime friend Sam (Jess Hahn) to steal a 2,000-karat diamond. When Ingrid is killed, the distraught Donnelly finds a look-alike named Olga and has her converted into a replica of his sister via plastic surgery. While carrying out the plan to infiltrate the mine, Donnelly falls in love with the girl. But they have not counted on cultured hit man Noah (Fred Williamson) entering the scene and pursuing the diamond.

"Even guest star Fred Williamson, cast as a villain but predictably turning into Mr. Nice Guy in the final reel, fails to save this one" *(Variety).* As the sophisticated crook, Williamson's Noah tosses off French words at a moment's notice, engages in a few nasty deeds, is forced occasionally to mouth pretentious dialogue ("You would not like the doctor degraded because of you") and, after the diamond has been lost in a mine cave-in, is made to ignore all past motivation and becomes Mr. Joviality. The trouble shooter smilingly advises Donnelly, the new Ingrid, and Sam to scram before he changes his mind: "As the sheriff always said [in Western movies], 'You all get out of my town before dark.'"

Made in Turkey in the summer of 1983, *White Fire* was first distributed in the United States in 1985 on video cassette.

234. Willie Dynamite (Universal, 1973). Color, 102 minutes.

Producers Richard D. Zanuck, David Brown; *director* Gilbert Moses III; *story* Ron Cutler, Joe Keyes, Jr.; *screenplay* Cutler; *art director* John T. McCormack; *set decorator* Claire P. Brown; *costumes* Bernard Johnson; *music* J.J. Johnson; *songs* Johnson and Moses III; *assistant directors* James Hogan, William Holbrook; *sound* Waldon O. Watson Henry Wilkinson, Ronald Pierce; *camera* Frank Stanley; *editor* Aaron Stell.

Cast: Roscoe Orman (Willie Dynamite); Diana Sands (Cora); Thalmus Rasulala (Robert Daniels); Joyce Walker (Pashen); Roger Robinson (Bell); George Murdock (Celli); Albert Hall (Pointer); Norma Donaldson (Honey); Juanita Brown (Sola); Royce Wallace (Willie's Mother); Judy Brown (Georgia); Marilyn Coleman (Connie); Mary Wilcox (Scatback); Marcia McBroom (Pearl); Jack Bernardi (Willie's Lawyer); Ted Gehring (Sergeant); Ron Henriquez (Cyrus); Wynn Irwin (Bailiff); Richard Lawson (Sugar); Ken Lynch, Davis Roberts (Judges).

The ads may have read like a typical slice-of-rough-life actioner: "Ain't no one crosses *Willie 'D.'* He's tight, together, and mean. Chicks, Chumps, he uses 'em all. He's got to be Number-One." However, *Willie Dynamite* is a partially successful effort to unexploitively tell the saga of the fall of a pimp. "Unlike its precursor, *The Mack* [1973, q.v.] *Willie Dynamite* does not serve up one-dimensional characters, exploiting the mystique, grandeur and violence of their lifestyles without beginning to examine their conscience. Ron Cutler and Jay Keyes have written an excellently constructed screenplay that does not sacrifice glamor, humor or action for the sake of intelligence and purpose" (Maurice Peterson, *Essence* magazine).

Super-pimp Willie Dynamite (Roscoe Orman) has a new girl in his New York City stable named Pashen (Joyce Walker). But she is still so new to the game that she is salvageable, and social worker Cora (Diana Sands), an ex-hooker, intends to rehabilitate her. Others involved in the moral tug-of-war are Bell (Roger Robinson), Willie's chief competitor; Pointer (Albert Hall) and Celli (George Murdock), two determined vice officers; Daniels (Thalmus Rasulala), who is Cora's lover and an assistant district attorney; and Willie's mother (Royce Wallace), who does not approve of her flashy son's lifestyle. After Pashen gets busted twice and beaten up in jail, she agrees to go to one of Cora's relatives to think about changing her lifestyle. Meanwhile Mr. Dynamite buckles under the pressure of his rivals, and when his mother dies, he is haunted into (one hopes) reform by her disgust at his illicit trade.

Coming as it did so late in the onslaught of such genre films, *Willie Dynamite* suffered because it was neither here nor there. *Variety* labeled it "an okay morality play," but the *New York Times* carped, "The costumes, language, melodrama, performances and even the soundtrack music are so outrageously broad it seems as if the film were putting itself on, parodying such earlier live-action black carbons as *The Mack* and *Cleopatra Jones*. Not at all. It wants a piece of the same action." Even more upset by this production was Ed Eckstine (*Soul* magazine): "It is demeaning to me as a Black man to see such a statement on life and manhood as is projected in the film *Willie Dynamite*. . . . There has been so much adverse reaction to the films that white directors have

Top: **Roscoe Orman** *(left)* **and player in** *Willie Dynamite* **(1973).** *Bottom:* **Bernie Weissman** *(left)* **and Lawrence Hilton-Jacobs in** *Youngblood* **(1978).**

been trying out that the directors of this film have found a switch so they can still deal with a pimp but at the same time project a moral."

One of the most publicized elements of this motion picture was the appearance of Diana Sands, who died of cancer three months before its release. *Variety* memorialized, "She is among a group of other fine performers, such as James Edwards, who were in retrospect just a few years too early to realize before untimely death their full potential on the screen. Fate robbed them of an assured eventual widespread public recognition, but a lot of fine stage work and some sporadic film credits at least show what talent was there."

The prolific J.J. Johnson provides the score while Martha Reeves (without the Vandellas but with the Sweet Things) sang the background songs. The far-out wardrobe for the pimps was by black designer Bernard Johnson.

235. Youngblood (American International, 1978). Color, 90 minutes.

Producers Nick Grillo, Alan Richie; *associate producer* Hal DeWindt; *director* Noel Nosseck; *screenplay* Paul Carter Harrison; *art director* James Dultz; *wardrobe* Adrianne Levasque; *music/songs* War; *assistant director* Bill Kerr; *stunt co-ordinator* Eddie Smith; *sound* Jan Schulti; *camera* Robbie Greenberg; *editor* Frank Morriss.

Cast: Lawrence-Hilton Jacobs (Rommel); Bryan O'Dell (Youngblood Gordon); Ren Woods (Sybil); Tony Allen (Hustler); Vince Cannon (Corelli); Art Evans (Junkie); Jeff Hollis (Pusher); Dave Pendleton (Reggie Gordon); Ron Trice (Bummie); Sheila Wills (Joan); Ralph Farquhar (Geronimo); Herbert Rice (Durango); Lionel Smith (Chaka); Maurice Sneed (Skeeter-Jeeter); Ann Weldon (Mrs. Gordon); Isabel Cooley (School Principal); Bernie Weissman (Bernie the Bodyguard).

Lawrence-Hilton Jacobs was best known for playing Freddie "Boom Boom" Washington on the TV sitcom series "Welcome Back, Kotter" (1975-79) and for his role of Noah in *Roots* (1977). One of his forays into theatrical motion pictures was *Youngblood,* the story of a returning Vietnam War G.I. who fights new wars on the ghetto streets of Los Angeles.

Rommel (Lawrence-Hilton Jacobs) has more than his share of adapting to civilian life after Vietnam. Before long he is ignoring his wife, Joan (Sheila Wills), and is back with his gang, the Kingsmen, causing severe gang problems in Los Angeles. When Youngblood Gordon (Bryan O'Dell) is suspended from school he has no one to turn to, especially not his wayward mother (Ann Weldon). Before long he and his pal Bummie (Ron Trice) have been initiated into the Kingsmen with Rommel as their hero. Complications set in when the Kingmen decide to rid the neighborhood of drugs, which means squeezing out white syndicate financier Corelli (Vince Cannon) and his black associate Reggie Gordon (Dave Pendleton), Youngblood's brother.

Rumbles comes and rumbles go, but this was no *West Side Story* (1961). "*Youngblood* is a C+/B− as movies go, a violent little film that initally pretends to some heavy moral statement yet ends up actually saying nothing. In fact, it manages to degenerate from a tacit putdown of needless violence into a guts and glory shootout and chase" (Leonard Pitts, Jr., *Soul* magazine).

The film's original score was written and performed by the group War.

Index

*References are to entry numbers, except **boldface** references, which are to pages and indicate photographs.*

A

"The A-Team" 75, 171
Aaron, Caroline 45
Aaron, Jack 195
Aaron Loves Angela 1
Abanes, Richie 165
Abbott, L.B. 156
Abby 2, 39; **p. 6**
Abdul-Ali, Hassan 160
Abdul-Jabbar, Kareem 15
Abelardo, Maria 15, 30
Abeles, Jordan 192
Abrams, Mike 178
The Absent-Minded Professor 83
Abubadika, Mwina Imiri 87
Abulof, Baruch 123
Achorn, John 11
Ackland-Snow, Brian 202
Ackridge, Bill 229
Across 110th Street 3; **p. 8**
Action Jackson 4, 171; **p. 10**
Adair, Alice 12
Adair, Dick 159
Adalid, Ricardo 186
Adams, Arthur 106
Adams, Bruce 204
Adams, Christopher 12
Adams, Colin 158
Adams, David 188
Adams, Don 125
Adams, Lynne 197
Adams, Nate 199
Adams, Phil 49, 121
Adams, Quincy 109
Adams, R.J. 171
Adams, Richard L. 119, 185
Adams, Robert 122
Adams, Ronald J. 131
Adams, Steve 131
Adams, William 154
Adamson, Al 22, 32, 84, 108
Adamson, Chuck 11
Adamson, Gina 32
Adeolu, Funso 72
Adey-Jones, Sian 229

Adios Amigo 5, 128, 145
Adler, Gilbert 58
Adler, Luther 73, 145
Adler, Robert 153
Adler, Rudi 197
Adu, Frank 3
Adu, Jab 72
Afzal, Samina 229
Agamemnon 200
Ageio, Thomas 228
Agustus, Michael 204
Ahern, Lloyd 132
Ahlberg, Mac 59
Aiello, Danny 92
Ain't Supposed to Die a Natural Death 204
Ajaye, Franklyn 196
Akahoshi, Steve 90
Akdemir, Sedat 233
Akins, Claude 80, 85
Albaicin, Rafael 60
Alberghini, Roberto 148
Albert, Arthur 164
Albert, Eddie 206
Albertson, Eric 104
Alch, George 108
Alda, John 118
Alda, Rutanya 165, 230
Alden, Richard 143
Alderman, John 26, 31, 61
Alderman, Tom 195
Alderson, John 132, 219
Aldredge, Theoni V. 226
Aldredge, Tom 72
Aldrich, Frank 1, 3
Alegre, Alona 30
Alexander, Alphonso 54
Alexander, Angela 158
Alexander, Arlene 41
Alexander, Bill 143
Alexander, Jim 54, 103
Alexander, John, Jr. 74
Alexander, Sandy 136
Alexander, William 132
Alexandria, Mello 226
Alexis, Alvin 45
Alfasa, Joe 43
Alfe, Norman 186
Alford, Vi 140

Ali, Muhammad 41, 106; **p. 65**
Ali, Rahaman 106
Alice, Mary 87
Alires, Ted 143
All, Candy 98, 113; **p. 168**
All About Eve 153
"All in the Family" 117
All Over Town 200
Alldredge, Michael 123
Allen, Argy 152
Allen, Bambi 8
Allen, Bill 78
Allen, Debbie 85
Allen, Dede 154
Allen, Eddie 88
Allen, Gary 33
Allen, George 190
Allen, Georgia 105
Allen, John 204
Allen, Jonelle 65
Allen, Kip 43, 213
Allen, Raymond 76
Allen, Sarita 135
Allen, Seth 115
Allen, Stanford C. 169, 207
Allen, Ta-Ronce 55, 111
Allen, Todd 95
Allen, Tony 235
Allen, Vernett 226
Aller, Luis 60
Alley, Kirstie 181
Allin, Michael 89, 224
Alonzo, Cecil 19, 199
Alonzo, John A. 112
Alper, Bud 23, 27, 61, 82, 142, 218
Alpert, David 37
Altrice, Tedi 213
Alvez, Piper 187
Amazon, John 205
The Amazons 62
Ameche, Don 221
American Graffiti 68
American Pop 99
Ames, Morgan 227
Amicucci, Gianfranco 44, 232

339

P

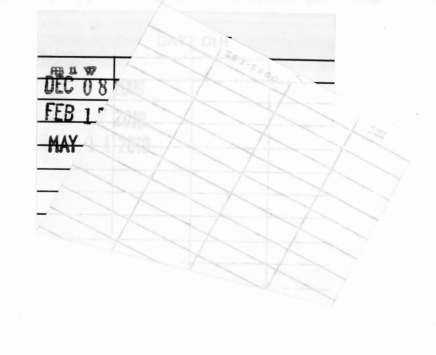